INVESTMENT
MANAGEMENT

INVESTMENT MANAGEMENT

Stephen Lofthouse

JOHN WILEY & SONS, LTD

Chichester · New York · Weinheim · Brisbane · Singapore · Toronto

Published in 2001 by John Wiley & Sons Ltd,
Baffins Lane, Chichester,
West Sussex PO19 1UD, England

National   01243 779777
International   (+44) 1243 779777
e-mail (for orders and customer service enquiries): cs-books@wiley.co.uk
Visit our Home Page on http://www.wiley.co.uk

Other Wiley Editorial Offices

John Wiley & Sons, Inc., 605 Third Avenue,
New York, NY 10158-0012, USA

Wiley-VCH GmbH, Pappelallee 3,
D-69469 Weinheim, Germany

John Wiley & Sons Australia, Ltd, 33 Park Road, Milton,
Queensland 4064, Australia

John Wiley & Sons (Asia) Pte Ltd, 2 Clementi Loop #02-01,
Jin Xing Distripark, Singapore 129809

John Wiley & Sons (Canada) Ltd, 22 Worcester Road,
Rexdale, Ontario M9W 1L1, Canada

Library of Congress Cataloging-in-Publication Data

Lofthouse, Stephen.
     Investment management / Stephen Lofthouse.
        p. cm.—(Wiley finance series)
     'This book is the second edition of Equity investment management [c1994]. Because
the coverage has been extended the title has been changed to more accurately reflect the
content'—T.p. verso.
     Includes bibliographical references and index.
     ISBN 0-471-49237-X
     1. Portfolio management.   2. Investment analysis.   I. Lofthouse, Stephen. Equity
investment management.   II. Title.   III. Series.
HG4529.5 .L63 2001
332.6—dc21

                                                                                 2001017658

British Library Cataloguing in Publication Data

A catalogue record for this book is available from the British Library

ISBN 0-471-49237-X

Typeset in 10½/12½ Times by Dorwyn Ltd, Rowlands Castle, Hants.
Printed and bound in Great Britain by Biddles Ltd, Guildford and Kings Lynn.
This book is printed on acid-free paper responsibly manufactured from sustainable forestation, for which
at least two trees are planted for each one used for paper production.

For Jill, with thanks.

Contents

Preface

This book is the second edition of *Equity Investment Management*. Because the coverage has been extended, the title has been changed to reflect the content more accurately, although there is still an equity bias. The book is written for investment professionals and students taking investment courses. The students may be seeking professional qualifications or taking university courses that have a professional orientation rather than a theoretical financial economics orientation.

Key features of the book include:

- emphasis is placed on constructing a portfolio rather than financial theory;
- complex theories are outlined in a simple and intuitive manner;
- statistical and mathematical notions are discussed in a way that will be accessible to readers with an arts background;
- the major UK and US empirical studies are discussed;
- practical implications of academic work are stressed;
- ample references are given to enable readers to pursue in greater depth topics that particularly interest them;
- stockbroking, consultant and trade, as well as academic, sources are drawn on.

Both investment practitioners and students will benefit from reading this book:

- Young fund managers and analysts will get a broad overview of the process of constructing a portfolio as well as detailed discussion of issues they face every day.
- Experienced professionals will be brought up to date on the latest theories and evidence.
- Students will find that this book is much easier to read than most investment textbooks.

Although written specifically for investment professionals and students, other groups, such as investment fund trustees and private investors, will find that this book will enable them to have a more informed discussion with their investment managers.

I am grateful to Jane Raybould for commenting on most of the equity chapters, to the British Library of Political and Economic Science and the Library of Congress for the use of their resources, and the authors and publishers who allowed me to use copyright material.

Stephen Lofthouse
lofthouse_s@hotmail.com
September 2000

Introduction

It is better to have a permanent income than to be fascinating.
Oscar Wilde

Investment management is the process of managing investment funds to achieve specific objectives. By investment funds, we mean funds of money with an investment horizon longer than, say, a year. Management of money with a short-term perspective, such as the working cash balances held by a bank or a currency trader, is outside the scope of this book. Investment managers are the people who manage investment funds. In the UK, they are usually called fund managers. In the US the terms portfolio manager and money manager are often used.

This book examines how investment managers do, or should, manage investment assets. Investors can be divided into private investors and institutional investors. Institutional investors include pension funds, charities (endowments), insurance companies, investment trusts (closed-end funds) and unit trusts (mutual funds). Private investors, often called private clients (individual investors or retail investors), may manage their own money or give it to managers specializing in private client accounts. Or they may manage their own money but invest through institutional investors by buying investment trust shares or unit trust units, buying insurance investment products, or topping up their occupational pension entitlements.

In this book, we are concerned with institutional investment management, although much of the analysis is also applicable to private clients. Private client money management is, however, complicated by more complex tax considerations than institutional management. Also, because private client funds are often small, there are constraints on what can be done.

At the start of the twentieth century, private clients were an important class of investors, but by the end of the century their significance had shrunk, and institutional investors dominated the financial markets. At the end of 1998, UK institutional investors accounted for 52.3% of UK ordinary shares, overseas investors (predominantly institutions) another 27.6%, and private investors 16.7% (Hill and Duffield, 2000). The rise of the institutional investor was the result of a variety of changes in the structure of society, the growth of occupational pension funds, tax policies that favoured investment via insurance companies and pension funds over direct investment, the advent of unit trusts, and so on.

Institutional investors should not be thought of as a homogeneous group. Different types of institutional investors face different tax regimes, different regulatory constraints (such as solvency ratios for insurance companies and minimum funding requirements for pension funds), and different investment horizons. The importance of nominal returns (actual money returns) versus real returns (nominal returns adjusted for inflation) also varies amongst institutional investors. And within each category there may be different objectives. For example, some charities are wealthy and can take a long-term view, while others live hand to mouth, and have an overwhelming need for immediate income.

PORTFOLIO CONSTRUCTION

The central task of investment management is to construct a portfolio. To do this, an institutional or private investor should address six broad issues:

1. The investment objectives.
2. The asset classes to include in the portfolio.
3. The strategic weights to assign to those classes over the long-term.
4. The short-term tactical weights to assign.
5. The selection strategies to use within each asset class.
6. Evaluate how well the decisions made in steps 2–5 have met the objectives.

In subsequent chapters we discuss all these issues.

The potential number of asset classes that could be included in a portfolio is large—cash, equities, bonds, property, gold, silver, art, etc. These asset categories can be subdivided further. Equities can be split into domestic and foreign; large and small stocks (including venture capital); actual stocks and derivatives (e.g. futures and options), and so on. Table 1.1 shows the average asset allocation at a broad level of aggregation for more than 1500 UK occupational pension funds.

It is clear from Table 1.1 that equities, and to a lesser extent bonds, dominate pension fund portfolios. If we look at other countries, equities and bonds tend to dominate their pension fund portfolios, although most countries are less pro-equity than the UK. Our discussion of asset categories in this book will be limited to those shown in Table 1.1, although we will also exclude property.

MAJOR ASSET CATEGORIES

We will briefly outline here each of the asset categories shown in Table 1.1. More complete discussions appear later in the book.

TABLE 1.1 Asset allocation of UK pension funds at end of 1999

Asset	% of fund
UK equities	51.2
Overseas equities	24.5
North America	4.8
Europe	9.6
Japan	4.9
Pacific (excl. Japan)	3.0
Other international	2.2
UK conventional bonds	8.4
UK index-linked bonds	4.1
Overseas bonds	3.9
Cash/other	3.7
Property	4.1
Total	100

Source: The WM Company, **www.wmcompany.com.**

Cash

The term cash usually covers cash and near-cash, i.e. assets that do not put the initial value at risk and can quickly (within 24 hours) be turned into cash. Money market instruments, such as Treasury bills and commercial paper, fall into this category. Treasury bills are often mentioned in this book and are government IOUs of three or six months' duration. UK Treasury bills pay no interest but are issued at a discount to par value. For example, if a bill was for three months, then it might have a stated value in three months (the par value) of £100, but be issued at £99. This is approximately equivalent to a 4% yield.

Cash has two roles in a portfolio—as a lubricant and as an investment. Cash flows in and out of portfolios. There may be payments out (say to pensioners), payments in (say from an employer making contributions), income from investments (dividends, interest, rents, etc.), precommitted outgoings (e.g. some bonds are bought by instalments), and so on. Since these movements don't all occur on the same day, most portfolios will have some cash to smooth things out. Some investments are also not continuously available, for example a particular property development, and cash may be held so that when such opportunities arise they may be taken up without having to sell other assets.

Cash may also be an attractive investment. It pays interest—providing it's not kept as pound notes in a drawer—and has a known value. When markets are crashing, cash may offer the best returns. Even when markets are not falling, the low-risk nature of cash may make it attractive.

In small portfolios, cash may simply be kept in a deposit account, much as the ordinary investor keeps cash. Or the bond managers may manage cash. Larger organizations may have a specialist money markets management team. We will not discuss the mechanics and tactics of investing cash in the money markets, but we will discuss the strategic role of cash.

Equities

Equities, also called ordinary shares or common stock, provide ownership and participation rights in companies (e.g. Bass plc). The shareholders of a company collectively own the company and can organize its affairs. Typically, the management of a company is delegated to professional managers, responsible to a board of directors. The directors, in theory, answer to the shareholders. There has been much debate in recent years as to whether these agents act in the interests of their principals (the shareholders) or themselves. These concerns are not new. Adam Smith (1776, p. 741) noted the problem more than 200 years ago:

> The trade of a joint stock company is always managed by a court of directors. The court, indeed, is frequently subject, in many respects, to the control of a general court of proprietors. But the greater part of those proprietors seldom pretend to understand any thing of the business of the company; and when the spirit of faction happens not to prevail among them, give themselves no trouble about it, but receive contentedly such half yearly or yearly dividend, as the directors think proper to make to them . . .. The directors of such companies, however, being the managers rather of other people's money than of their own, it cannot well be expected, that they should watch over it with the same anxious vigilance with which the partners in a private copartnery frequently watch over their own. Like the stewards of a rich man, they are apt to consider attention to small matters as not for their master's honour, and very easily give themselves a dispensation from having it. Negligence and profusion, therefore, must always prevail, more or less, in the management of the affairs of such a company.

Part of a company's profits are distributed to shareholders in the form of dividends. The shareholders are, however, residual claimants on a company's profits and assets. Creditors have to be paid before shareholders. In a period of poor trading, after the creditors have been paid there may be nothing left to distribute to the shareholders. If trading is so bad that a company becomes bankrupt, the creditors have the first claim on the value of any assets that exist. Only if anything remains will the shareholders get any payment. But in good times, the creditors get the same fixed amount and don't share in the growth of profits and increased asset values. This all belongs to the shareholders. Ordinary shares are therefore quite risky, but can be very profitable. While individual companies may suffer misfortunes, we might expect equities in general to share in the growth of the economy over a period of years. In any one year, or even a number of years, however, the whole equity market may perform poorly.

The shares of large companies are traded on stock exchanges. This makes buying and selling the shares easier, and aids the raising of new capital. Most shares are quoted on only one exchange, for example the London Stock Exchange, but some large companies, especially those with substantial international business, are quoted on a number of exchanges. The Anglo-Dutch company Shell, for example, is quoted on the London, Amsterdam and New York exchanges. To be quoted, or 'listed', on a stock exchange, a company will have to meet the exchange's listing requirements. These will include financial reporting standards, how long an historical record must be provided, how much stock must be freely tradable (e.g. if family trusts control 99% of a company, then there is little likelihood of a fair price being established), and so on. Some countries have secondary exchanges with less demanding listing requirements— for example, a more limited financial history might be acceptable—geared towards small and young companies. In the UK, the secondary exchange is the Alternative Investment Market (AIM).

Companies that are not quoted are usually, but not necessarily, small. Although there is no organized market in their shares, institutional investors may still buy into these companies, sometimes taking very large positions, with the expectation of eventually selling all or part of the holding to another institutional investor, or to a trade buyer (i.e. another company), or selling shares in the stockmarket if the company becomes quoted. Money invested in such companies is usually described as venture capital or private equity.

Institutional investors may have their own venture capital team or use some form of pooled vehicle, such as an investment trust (see p. 15). An example of a venture capital transaction is the £41.6 million purchase of 75% of the ordinary shares of Inchcape Shipping Services (ISS) in March 1999 by Electra Investment Trust. ISS was a £47.5 million buy-out from Inchcape. ISS is the world's largest independent shipping agency network. Venture capital is a very specialized activity and we will not discuss it further.

In the last two decades, many shares have been issued as a result of the British government denationalizing—or privatizing—many industries. This has substantially increased the size of the equity market, and changed its composition. Many nationalized industries were what economists term natural monopolies, and consequently many ingenious, and sometimes silly, regulatory frameworks have been established to try and ensure competition or to avoid abuse of dominant market positions. While the British privatization programme is ending, many European and developing world countries have substantial programmes in prospect.

Bonds

Bonds are debt instruments that do not have ownership or participation rights. Bondholders are creditors. Some types of issuer are listed below:

- companies, e.g. Land Securities plc
- governments
    national, e.g. France
    regional, e.g. Quebec
    local, e.g. Manchester
    government agencies, e.g. Tennessee Valley Authority
- supranational bodies, e.g. the World Bank

Traditionally, a bond is for a fixed period (maturity) during which time the bondholder receives interest payments at a fixed rate (the coupon) and at the end of the period (the redemption date) the amount borrowed (the principal) is repaid (redeemed). However, there are many variations of this 'plain vanilla' bond; these are discussed in Chapter 18. In the context of Table 1.1, one variation needs to be explained here. The UK government issues bonds, known as 'gilts', and these have usually been vanilla versions, or modest variations thereof. In particular, the coupon and principal were, until 1981, fixed in money terms. Thus, if you bought a £1000 bond and the coupon was 10%, you would get £100 every year for the life of the bond, and £1000 on redemption. In 1981, the government issued bonds whose coupon and principal were indexed to the retail price index (RPI). For example, assume, for simplicity, a £100 one-year indexed bond with a 3% coupon, with inflation at 6% over the relevant period. You would get £31.80 interest (£100 × 0.03 × 1.06) and a repayment of £106 (£100 × 1.06). (A proper calculation is given on p. 332). To distinguish between the two types of bonds, the original bonds are known as conventional and the new type as index-linked (or colloquially 'linkers').

Whereas the future capital value of an equity, and the income payments it will make, are both uncertain, providing a bond does not default, both its income stream and repayment value are known with certainty. In the case of a conventional bond, the money values of these two things are known, whereas in the case of an index-linked bond it is the real—inflation-adjusted—values that are known.

Finally, we should mention preference shares. These are shares, but have some bond characteristics. They receive fixed-income payments, and rank behind creditors for payments but ahead of ordinary shareholders.

Property

We shall use the terms 'property' and 'real estate' to cover land and buildings. Most investors who hold direct property investments will own buildings. And while homes are clearly buildings, these are usually excluded from UK institutional portfolios. UK property investment is mainly shops, offices and industrial buildings.

The value of a building depends on its prospective rental flow. This will benefit from strong economic growth and inflation, but will suffer from recession and from physical and economic obsolescence of the buildings. There is, in addition, the quality of the tenant to consider, i.e. is there a risk that the tenant will default on rent payments? Property is more akin to equities than bonds. There are prospects for growth of capital value and rental income, but there are also many uncertainties. Further, property is very illiquid, which is to say it takes time to arrange property deals. Also, there may be no market at all in some properties that are adversely affected as a result of, say, a new motorway diverting away all traffic, or a major local employer going bust and resulting in people moving away.

Institutional investors may buy existing property, but they may also enter partnerships with developers to build office blocks, shopping malls, etc.

Domestic Versus Foreign Assets

UK investors are not restricted to purchasing assets in the UK. Investing overseas changes the risks and rewards that investors face. The UK is a reasonably large country, but it is still only a small percentage of the entire world. The UK equity market is about 10% of the world equity market by value, and the UK bond market is about 3% of the world bond market. Yet most pension fund investments (and insurance company and charity investments) are made in UK assets. In most countries, institutional investors invest primarily at home.

Equities have been classified historically by their domicile, whereas bonds have been classified by their currency of issue. For example, shares in Glaxo Wellcome are classified as UK shares because the company is based in the UK, even though it trades internationally and its shares are quoted on the New York Stock Exchange as well as the London Stock Exchange. But a bond issued by that company in the Eurobond market, denominated in dollars, with interest and principal repayment in dollars, would be classified as a dollar bond. With the adoption of a single currency in much of Europe, it remains to be seen whether a Belgian investor, say, will classify the shares of the Dutch-domiciled ABN Amro as foreign (domicile) or domestic (currency).

STRATEGY AND TACTICS

Having decided on the asset categories to be included in the portfolio, a decision must be made on asset allocation, and in particular the strategic asset weights. These weights can be viewed as those that would be applicable if the manager had no views about likely short-term market performance. They can also be viewed as the weights that the fund will actually have, on average, over a five- to ten-year period, assuming there is no reason to change them during that period. We discuss how these weights might be set in Chapter 22.

The strategic asset class weights should be set with a central value and a range around that to set the bounds for short-term tactical deviations. Depending on the manager's view of short-term market prospects, the manager will position the fund at the high or low end of the tactical ranges. Tactical asset allocation is discussed in Chapters 22–24. Table 1.2 shows a sample asset allocation guideline that an investment manager might work with. This guideline might be for the manager of a young pension fund that had no short-term liabilities and whose trustees were not risk-averse. The fund has decided it will invest only in the assets shown and that the appropriate strategic stance is to be entirely invested in equities with a 70/30 split between domestic and foreign equities. No weights have been set for individual foreign markets. The tactical range shows that if cash or fixed-interest securities seem more attractive than equities on a short-term basis, then up to 15% and 20%, respectively, can be invested in those assets. The current position shows how the fund is actually invested now.

TABLE 1.2 Sample asset allocation guidelines

Asset	Strategic weight (%)	Tactical range (%)	Current position (%)	
Fixed interest	0	0–20	0	
UK, conventional				
UK, index-linked				
International				
UK equities	70	50–80	75	
Overseas equities	30	10–40	20	
US				7
Europe				5
Japan				5
Other				3
Cash	0	0–15	5	

The next step in managing a portfolio is to select an investment style for constructing equity and fixed-income subportfolios. Equity share and sector selection techniques are discussed in Chapters 6–17. Fixed-interest portfolios are discussed in Chapters 18 and 19. The share and bond selection evidence presented in these chapters is drawn primarily from the UK and the US. Some investors and clients have decided that fund managers can't consistently beat markets' returns, i.e. equity managers can't beat the return on the entire equity market and similarly bond managers can't beat the bond market. The solution is to buy a fund that holds shares or bonds that aims to track the appropriate market. These funds are called index funds and are discussed in a number of chapters. Trying to match the return from a benchmark is called passive investment management, whereas trying to find mispriced securities and asset classes is called active investment management.

Much of what is discussed in the chapters already mentioned is equally applicable to international markets. However, international markets do raise some special issues and these are discussed in Chapter 20.

Derivative securities—securities that derive their value from the value of other securities—are not listed separately in Table 1.1, but can be important. They can be used to increase a portfolio's risk exposure, or decrease it, or change the nature of the risks borne. Derivatives are discussed in Chapter 21.

In Chapter 25, we examine some of the issues involved in reviewing and evaluating portfolio performance.

The six broad issues listed on p. 2 are probably listed in their order of importance in determining returns. However, we tackle them out of order—for pedagogical reasons—and devote a disproportionate amount of space to share selection, because most fund managers spend most of their time on share selection.

Before we do this, we will round off this chapter with a discussion of the major institutional investors.

THE MAJOR INVESTORS

The major institutional managers in the long-term asset market are:

- pension funds
- charities
- insurance companies
- investment trusts
- unit trusts and open-ended investment companies (OEICs).

While not investors, consultants are also important.

Pension Funds

Pension funds are entities established to invest funds to meet pension liabilities. They are normally established on a company basis, although before the Thatcher privatization programme, many 'companies' were an entire industry (e.g. the Post Office, the Coal Board, British Railways, etc.).

The state pension scheme (the 'old-age pension') is a pay-as-you-go scheme. Essentially, payments are made out of current income. While the state can do this because it can always meet its liabilities by raising taxation or simply printing money, schemes in the private sector are fully funded to avoid the bankruptcy of an employer resulting in an inability to pay pensions. Fully funded means that funds are built up by payments made by employers, and usually employees as well, in advance of the pension liabilities having to be met. The funds are invested with the expectation that they will be sufficient to pay pension entitlements when these are due.

The funds of a pension scheme are kept separate from those of the employer by placing them in a trust. A trust is a legal relationship, created by a trust document, whereby assets are placed under the control of trustees for the benefit of beneficiaries. The trustees have to ensure that the assets are managed in accordance with the terms of the trust deed. The beneficiaries are those who can benefit from the trust, which, in the case of a pension fund, are the employees and specified kin (e.g. the widow of an employee). The benefits of a pension fund are normally underwritten by the employer rather than the fund. In other words, if it looked as though the fund would be unable to meet its liabilities, the employer would make good the deficiency by topping up the fund.

For a young growing company such as an Internet company, the contribution inflow and the income produced by the investments will exceed any pension payment outflows. Over the years, the inflows may well move more in line with outflows. In a declining industry, where the workforce is old and falling in numbers, outflows may exceed inflows. The Pensions Act 1995 requires a minimum funding requirement (MFR) to be met, with assets and liabilities defined in a particular way. If assets are less than 90% of liabilities, then the shortfall must be made up within one year, or by 2003 if later (this is a transitional provision). If assets are less than 100% of liabilities, then the shortfall must be made up within five years (or by 2007, if later). If assets are not well above liabilities, the MFR will encourage funds to make more use of assets whose values are unlikely to crash than has been the case to date.

Historically, there were two main ways in which pension funds were administered. Self-administered funds invested directly in the various markets, whereas insured schemes had the funds managed by a life assurance company, with the actuarial risk borne by that company. These terms remain in use, but nowadays the insured schemes do not usually offer a guarantee.

Self-administered is an awkward term, not meaning exactly what it appears to. It refers to the administration of the fund rather than the investment management. In some cases, self-administered funds do have their own in-house staff who carry out investment management, but in many cases self-administered funds are managed by external managers. These are managers unrelated to the fund that are capable of managing investment funds. They may be independent fund management firms, but are more likely to be a division of a clearing bank, merchant bank, stockbroker, unit trust company, investment trust company or insurance company.

Most of the nationalized industries had in-house teams, and following privatization some still do. Some nationalized industries, for example British Rail, switched to external managers while still nationalized. Some companies used to have in-house teams but have switched to external managers, for example Unilever, while other companies continue with in-house managers, for example BP in the UK. Usually, in-house managers are not looking to manage other organizations' funds, while external managers are keen to win new accounts.

There are two main types of employer pension scheme: final salary (or defined benefits) schemes, and money purchase (or defined contributions) schemes.

Final Salary

The vast majority of members in occupational pension schemes are in final-salary schemes. What this means is that employees' pensions are based on their salary near to retirement. Because of inflation, most people will earn a higher salary in the final years of their working life than in the early years. Some will hope to get a higher salary because of promotion. Clearly, it is desirable (for employees) to have a pension based on their earnings at the end of their working life rather than at some other stage. Final-salary schemes do this, although the details vary. Some use the average of the last three working years, some use the best three consecutive years in the last 13 years, and there are other formulas. These formulas determine employees' pensions in the year of retirement. If they were still working, they would expect to get pay rises every year. The average pay increase is about 2% above inflation. Pensioners are not so lucky. The best they can reasonably hope for is to have their pension fully indexed to the inflation rate, perhaps with some additional increases.

Money Purchase

There are a large number of money-purchase employers' schemes, although there are fewer members of these schemes than of final-salary schemes. In money-purchase employers' schemes, the combined employer/employee contributions are invested. When an employee retires, the value of the investments is used to buy an annuity to pay a pension. Insurance companies usually manage money-purchase schemes. An annuity is like a reverse insurance policy. Instead of paying money each year to an insurance company to get a lump sum at the end of the period, a lump sum is paid to an insurance company for the right to an income for as long as the employee lives.

In a money-purchase scheme, what the pension is worth will depend on how much was invested, how well the investments performed, and what the interest rates were when the annuity was bought. With a final-salary scheme, the employer will be investing the contributions to provide a pension. If the investments perform poorly, the employer will have to top up the pension pot. In a final-salary scheme, the employer bears the risk of bad investment performance. In a money-purchase scheme, the employee bears that risk. But if investment performance is good, the employee gets the reward in a money-purchase scheme. Currently there is a shift by employers to money-purchase schemes.

Personal pension plans are available to employees who do not have an occupational pension (and in certain other situations). Personal pension plans are always money-purchase, or defined-contribution, schemes. The vast bulk of personal pension plans are with life insurance companies, although this may change because of increased competition from investment trust and unit trust companies.

The size of the various types of funded pension schemes is shown in Table 1.3.

TABLE 1.3   Size of various types of funded pensions, 1998

Type	£ billion
Self-administered pensions	748
Insurance-administered occupational pensions	140
Insurance-administered personal pensions	276
Total	1164

Source: Insurance Trends (2000, p. 24).

Because wages have historically risen at about 2% above the inflation rate, i.e. there has been a steady growth in real incomes, final-salary schemes have to invest predominantly in assets likely to show similar growth if they are to be able to meet their liabilities. Money-purchase schemes are not under similar pressure to meet liabilities (which will always match the assets), but clearly they will be unattractive to employees unless they do aim to achieve real growth. Firms selling such products are under competitive pressure to strive for real growth.

Because pension funds are largely exempt from income tax and capital gains tax (but see p. 154), asset allocation is not greatly constrained by tax consider- ations. We have already seen in Table 1.1 the average asset allocation of a sample of pension funds. We can explain the broad pattern in general terms. Equities offer a share in the growth of the economy and seem a natural core asset for pension funds. Index-linked gilts also offer real growth of income and capital, but being less risky may be expected to offer lower returns. Foreign equities also offer real growth prospects and provide diversification from UK equities. But they are mismatched with UK pension liabilities because they are not denominated in sterling. This sets a limit to how much it is prudent to invest overseas. Over the years, property has offered protection against inflation, but property is illiquid and the market is prone to large cyclical swings. The asset allocation shown in Table 1.1 seems broadly what one might expect given the various assets' characteristics, and the nature of pension funds.

Charities

Most charity funds are tiny and may consist of only a bank account, or perhaps a small holding in one of the unit trusts that are specifically for charities. On the other hand, large charities, for example those related to some of the colleges of Oxford University, or the £13 billion Wellcome Trust, will have portfolios that are similar to a typical pension fund. Exactly what assets a charity can hold will depend on whether it is subject to the Trustee Investments Act 1962, whether the trustees set constraints of their own (e.g. a health-related charity may pro- hibit holding tobacco companies' shares, or a religious charity may prohibit holding shares of arms manufacturers), and the charity's resources in relation to its objectives. Charity funds are largely exempt from tax (but see p. 154). Exter- nal managers usually manage large charity funds.

Insurance Companies

Insurance activities are often divided into two categories: general insurance and long-term insurance. Most large companies carry out both activities, but the funds have to be kept separate. We will look at each activity in turn.

General Insurance

General insurance covers business such as fire and accident, motor, and marine, aviation and transport insurance. The insurer incurs liabilities to meet claims from policyholders for losses incurred during a specified period, typically one year. For example, when you have paid your annual car insurance premium, the insurer faces potential claims on your policy for one year. Against this, the insurer holds assets. About half the value of the assets might represent provisions to meet expected claims with the other half held on prudential and statutory grounds (UK general insurers must hold free reserves of between 16% and 18% of net premiums) in case actual claims are higher than expected, or the value of the assets fall.

Insurers collect their premiums before they meet claims. Consequently there are two potential sources of profit: the difference between revenue and costs, and the returns achieved on investing the premiums until claims have to be met. While profitability considerations may suggest investing in assets such as shares, prudence demands that the short-term nature of the business be reflected in large cash holdings. But this latter point must not be overstated. It is unlikely that a company's general business will fall dramatically from one year to the next, and this means that new business will automatically provide liquidity. Also, continually rolling over short-term investments is expensive. Both these points suggest some longer-term investments.

Long-Term Insurance

Long-term insurance can be divided into two categories: life insurance and group pensions business. *Life insurance* is a contract between an individual—you—and an insurance company, that covers a specified period (the term), during which you pay so much per month or year (premiums) to the company; when you die, it pays out a lump sum (the sum assured). There are three main types of life insurance:

- *Term insurance:* a temporary insurance policy—you pay premiums for a specified term and the sum insured (or 'assured') is paid only if you die during that term.
- *Whole-life (or whole-of-life):* you pay premiums until your death or a specified age, and the sum assured is paid on your death, whenever that is.
- *Endowment:* premiums are paid for a specified term and the sum assured is paid at the end of the term or on earlier death.

Additionally, there are *annuity policies*: in return for (usually) a lump sum, the insurance company pays a regular income for a specified term.

There are significant differences between these forms of life insurance. Term insurance is pure protection, whole-life insurance is both protection and investment, and endowment insurance is mainly investment.

Term insurance is a bit like contents insurance. When you insure your home contents you don't know if you will be burgled. You might not, so you might never get a payout. Term insurance is much the same. If you die during the term, there is a payout, but if you don't, there isn't.

With whole-life insurance, there will be a payout because you will die. You are therefore buying both protection and an investment. (Term and whole-life insurance do have something in common: *you* won't get the sum assured, because you will be dead when it's paid.)

Endowment insurance will pay out regardless of whether you live or die, so you might collect the payout. The investment element is at its highest with endowment insurance. You can buy an endowment policy as a free-standing protection plus investment package, but most people who have an endowment policy have it in conjunction with a mortgage.

Each of these types of policy comes in a variety of forms. For example, whole-life and endowment policies may be 'with-profits' or unit-linked. *With-profits policies* offer both a guaranteed sum and a share of the investment returns of the insurance company's life fund. The objective of the fund is to be able to pay the guaranteed benefits and to be able to pay good bonuses or profits—hence the name 'with-profits'. Because of the guaranteed benefits, although the fund will be invested in a number of asset types to try and achieve a good return, there will be a heavy weighting in bonds because of their guaranteed returns on specific dates. Actuaries value these funds to make sure they can meet their obligations, and tend to err on the side of caution. Sums are set aside to reserves, but the annual valuations still produce surpluses and these form the basis of bonuses. There are two important bonuses, the annual reversionary bonuses and the terminal bonus.

Once a *reversionary bonus* is declared, it cannot be lost. Consequently, these bonuses tend to be somewhat lower than fund performance justifies. Moreover, the full declared value of reversionary bonuses is available only at the time of payout. At the end of the plan, a *terminal bonus* will reflect overall investment performance. The terminal bonus may be up to half the total bonus. Both terminal and reversionary bonus rates may be reduced in some years (compared with previous year's levels). In particular, many companies have been cutting these rates in the last few years.

An example may be useful. In return for agreeing to pay a certain premium per month, you may be guaranteed £10 000 at the end of 25 years. Assume that at the end of year one, you get a reversionary bonus of 5%. This will raise your guaranteed sum to £10 500, i.e. an increase of 5%. If you get another reversionary bonus of 5% in year two, the sum will be £11 025. If this happens for 25 years, then the guaranteed sum will rise to nearly £34 000. At the end of the 25 years, you will get a terminal bonus, which is usually quite large, so you might get a total of, say, £60 000.

In a *unit-linked plan*, the insurance company maintains a fund that is divided for accounting purposes into units. Unit-linked does not necessarily imply that the investments are being made in units of a unit trust (unit trusts are discussed on p. 17). There is a guaranteed sum assured, but the death benefit will be the higher of that sum and the value of the units at the time of death. You can usually invest in cash, fixed-interest stocks, equities, property and a managed fund (which will invest in all of these asset types). The return you get will be a function of the funds you select. Their performance will depend on the performance of the underlying markets and the manager's performance. Most unit-linked policies are flexible and allow a choice as to the amount of insurance cover. The lower the cover, the higher the investment content of the policy.

Unit-linked policies are riskier for the policyholder than with-profits policies. Reversionary bonuses can't be withdrawn, even if the stockmarket collapses in the last year of your policy, whereas the value of units will collapse with the market—you will, however, get the sum assured if this is more than the value of your units.

The second major activity of a long-term insurance company is *pension business*. We have already discussed pension funds. To recap, an insurance company may administer and manage a company's entire pension scheme, usually investing in its with-profits or unit-linked funds, may manage a personal pension plan, or may manage a company's pension fund that the company self-administers. In the latter case, the fund is likely to be segregated rather than pooled, i.e. the pension fund's assets will be managed as a distinct portfolio and not put into a fund that pools various clients' contributions.

Insurance company fund taxation is complex but, broadly speaking, life insurance funds are taxed at a rate of 20% on income and capital gains. This taxation affects asset allocation somewhat because UK bonds are free from capital gains tax.

Given the long-term nature of life insurance business, we might expect a heavier weighting in equities than in the case of general funds. But we noted various guarantees that suggest a reasonable weighting in bonds. However, this should be put into context. First, as long as the insurance company keeps selling its products, it has an ongoing source of liquidity. Second, many investment products are not one-off transactions, but involve continuing payments, so even with no new business, cash would be automatically generated. Third, with-profit guarantees are so limited that they are not a substantial constraint on decision making. Fourth, in most circumstances, capital gains from bonds held to maturity are unlikely to be significant, so the presence or absence of capital gains tax is not of great significance, while the higher income from a bond is subject to income tax. Fifth, with-profit funds are under competitive pressure to provide high returns, and this points away from bonds.

In sum, we might expect general insurance business to have some equity exposure, but to have more short-term assets than long-term insurance funds. This is the broad picture shown in Table 1.4. We might also expect both types of insurance fund to be more cash/bonds oriented and less equity oriented than self-administered pension funds. Comparison of Tables 1.1 and 1.4, show that this is the case.

Investment Trusts

Investment trusts are not trusts in the legal sense, but joint stock companies incorporated with limited liability under the Companies Acts. They are just like other companies in terms of having a capital structure with shareholders and perhaps some borrowings, having a board of directors, issuing an annual report and accounts, and so on. They are quoted on the stock exchange, and their

TABLE 1.4   Asset distribution of general and long-term insurance funds (end-1998)

Assets	General funds (%)		Long-term funds (%)	
Current assets	18		8	
UK public sector bonds (mainly gilts)	21		16	
of which: gilts up to 5 years		12		3
Company securities (mainly equities)	34		66	
Overseas government, etc. securities	13		2	
Property	2		6	
Other investments	5		2	
Agents' balances, including outstanding premiums	9		0	
Reinsurance balances, outstanding dividends, interest, etc.	5		1	
Total assets	106		101	
Borrowings	−6		−1	
Total net assets	100		100	

Source: Calculated from ONS data.

shares are bought and sold in the same way as other companies' shares. Investment trust companies differ from other companies only in their objectives—they don't make anything or provide any services, they just invest in other companies' shares or in other types of asset.

Investment trusts are described as closed-end investment funds because, as companies, they have the typical capital structure of UK companies. UK companies have traditionally had fixed, rather than variable, capital structures. Companies issue a fixed number of shares and, if they wish to change this, they have to get the approval of their shareholders. This can be obtained, but happens infrequently. Shareholders can't get their money back from the company, although they can sell their shares to other investors. All this means that the money being invested is not changed for long periods: the investment fund is 'closed'.

There are nearly 300 investment trusts quoted on the London Stock Exchange. They have a variety of objectives. Some invest anywhere in the world, while others are restricted to particular regions or types of asset. Some stress capital growth, while others stress a high or growing income. The Association of Investment Trusts, the industry's trade association, classifies trusts into categories such as international (general), international (capital growth), UK (income growth), North America, Far East (excluding Japan), property, continental Europe, commodity and energy, emerging markets, smaller companies, and venture and development capital.

Capital gains tax is not payable on transactions within the trust. Income is taxed, but income paid out to shareholders carries a tax credit. Shareholders pay capital gains tax in the normal way when they sell a trust's shares based on the change in the price of those shares. There is a tax disadvantage if the fund holds a substantial number of bonds. Not surprisingly, investment trust's assets are predominately equities. With this exception, the investment managers can treat the fund as though it is tax exempt when planning their investment strategy.

Investment trusts may be 'self-managed' or the investment management may be given to external managers. Self-managed investment trusts have an in-house team of investment managers who are employees of the trust. Self-management is uncommon, although some of the biggest trusts, for example Alliance Trust (£1.7 billion) and Scottish Investment Trust (£1.3 billion), are self-managed. In most cases, external managers manage the investments and are, theoretically, controlled by the directors. In reality, the directors are often involved in some way with the managers who launched the trust (e.g. as an employee or director of the manager), or have some commercial interest in not rocking the boat (e.g. as a manager of another investment trust), and often appear to be acting on behalf of the managers (Lofthouse, 1999).

Unit Trusts and Open-Ended Investment Companies

Unlike investment trusts, unit trusts really are trusts in the legal sense. The assets are placed under the control of trustees (typically large banks) for the benefit of beneficiaries. The trustees have to ensure that the assets are managed in accordance with the terms of the trust deed. Arguably, they also have a duty to fire poorly performing managers, but they never do this (Pennington, 1990; Lofthouse, 1997). The beneficiaries are the unit holders, i.e. individual and institutional investors. Many of the best-known unit trust managers also manage investment trusts and pension funds. Some are insurance companies. The managers are responsible for the day-to-day investment management. The managers are also the promoters of a trust, and will take the initiative in launching new trusts.

The pool of investments that makes up the unit trust is divided into equal portions, or units. Unit trusts are open ended in the sense that anyone can buy units from the managers who will create new units for them, or sell back their units for cancellation or liquidation by the managers. The managers make corresponding purchases or sales of investments. Purchasers and sellers of units do not have to deal directly with the manager; they can get an agent, such as a stockbroker or independent financial adviser, to act for them.

As with investment trusts, unit trusts have a wide range of objectives, and portfolios vary according to the objectives. Broadly speaking, unit trusts offer the same range of objectives as investment trusts. However, because of a slight difference in taxation treatment, there are unit trusts that invest solely in cash or in bonds. As with investment trusts, the managers may act as though they are managing a tax-exempt fund.

While OEICs have long existed in Europe, they were only recently permitted to be formed in the UK. Technically, an OEIC is a company with variable share capital—an open-ended company. The corporate code governing OEICs is a special free-standing code, outside of the Companies Acts. An OEIC is thus like an investment trust in as much as it is a company, but like a unit trust in as much as it is open ended. As far as most investors are concerned, the major difference between an investment trust and a unit trust is that the former is open ended and the latter is closed ended. This difference carries over between investment trusts and OEICs. For most investors, OEICs are just revamped unit trusts.

OIECs have been introduced because although the UK has a well-developed fund-management industry, unit trusts do not appeal to most continental Europeans. They are not familiar with the legal concept of a trust and prefer a company structure. It remains to be seen how many unit trusts will be converted to OIECs and whether Europeans who distrust British beef will trust British firms with their life savings.

Consultants

Insurance companies typically manage their own investment funds. Individual firms of managers launch investment trusts and unit trusts and, in general, may expect to retain the investment management task. It is questionable how informed many of the private client buyers of these products are about judging investment performance. Indeed, we have seen from the personal pension misselling scandal, and from the Office of Fair Trading's comments on endowment mortgages, that many investors actually have no idea what the product is that they are buying. Again, various surveys by the financial and trade press have shown huge differences in the cost of various products. For example, personal pension providers in one survey had costs that reduced an assumed precharge investment return of 9% to anywhere from 8.3% to 6.5%. In competitive industries, we would expect firms with cost/charge structures up to three and a half times (2.5%/0.7%) another firm's to go bust. Insurance companies do strive for good investment performance to use as a marketing weapon, but it is doubtful that performance is the factor that dominates consumers' decisions when dealing with insurance companies.

Investment managers of pension funds face a different situation. The performance of a pension fund matters to an employer, and the employer has the financial resources to be well informed. The trustees of the fund have various legal duties, and usually there is not an in-house manager. All this has made it possible for a service industry to develop selling information and advice to pension fund trustees. (The situation is somewhat similar for charity funds.) Well-known performance measurement firms include the WM Company and Combined Actuarial Performance Services (CAPS). Some firms of consulting actuaries have specialist departments or subsidiaries offering advice on manager selection. Among the more prominent are Watson Wyatt, Bacon and Woodrow, William M. Mercer, Hymans Robertson, and Aon Consulting. We will follow US terminology and refer to these advisors as consultants.

Pension funds readily switch managers when they experience poor performance. The trustees of such funds will usually turn to a consultant to provide lists of potential managers, organize the collection of information about managers by means of questionnaires and interviews, ensure performance data are put on a consistent basis, and, for a short list chosen by a fund's trustees, organize a 'beauty parade'. At the beauty parade, the managers explain their method of management and the trustees have a chance to question the managers. While the outcome is often unsatisfactory, as we shall discuss in Chapter 26, there is little doubt that pension fund and charity managers feel under intense competitive pressure to generate high returns. Some observers think that the result has been to encourage managers to pay more attention to what other managers are doing than to the liability structure of funds.

READ BEFORE YOU PROCEED

This concludes our introduction. The reader is not required to have any mathematical ability—beyond being able to do 'sums'—to understand this book: the few equations that are included are always repeated in words. A one-semester or half-year course in statistics for social scientists would be useful, but is not essential. Readers without any statistical training, however, should read the short appendix at the end of the book before proceeding further as we assume familiarity with the terms discussed there.

2

Portfolio Theory

To be in the game, you have to endure the pain.
George Soros

Chapters 2–4, covering portfolio theory and asset-pricing models, are the hardest chapters in the book for readers who are not used to diagrams or equations. But the diagrams are easy to understand, and all the important equations are stated in words. Many books shuffle the material of these chapters to the back of the book, perhaps hoping to get the reader's interest before presenting the difficult stuff. But the concepts in these chapters infuse all financial theory and analysis, so we shall begin with portfolio and asset-pricing theory. To reassure you that this apparently abstract material is worth studying, it's useful to begin with a short history of the concepts to be discussed. (All the unusual terms used are discussed fully later on.)

Everybody knows the proverb, 'Don't put all your eggs in one basket.' If you bet on one thing and it goes wrong, the results are dire. With financial assets, the same principle applies. The obvious solution is to diversify, i.e. hold several assets. Investors have probably always understood this. Certainly, if we look back to investment trust portfolios in the nineteenth century, we find diversified portfolios. But the diversification was 'naive': a bit of this, a bit of that. Markowitz (1952, 1959) set out a way of diversifying so that for any degree of risk, the investor got the best return possible, or alternatively, for any return bore the lowest risk. Portfolios that achieve this are said to be efficient, and all of them together form the efficient frontier. The trick, it turns out, is to concentrate not on individual asset's risks, but on whether assets' risks are correlated.

Calculating efficient frontiers for different asset classes—cash, bonds, UK equities, US equities, French equities, property, etc.—is now commonplace. Not every investor does this, but all institutional investors involved in investment strategy will at least know about the technique.

It is perhaps hard for younger readers to appreciate how feeble computing power was in the 1950s. Perfectly sound ideas might be impractical if they required many calculations. Unfortunately, Markowitz's analysis required masses of calculations and some unusual inputs. Sharpe (1963) proposed a 'single-index model' as a means of reducing the computations. This model used the concept of a stock's beta. This was followed quickly by what is now called the capital asset pricing model, developed by Sharpe (1964), Lintner (1965) and Mossin (1966), which states that an asset's equilibrium return is a linear function of its systematic risk. The validity of the theory has been challenged, but betas are readily available from commercial suppliers and stockbrokers. Contrary to what most textbooks say, beta is probably not widely used for selecting shares, at least not in the UK. However, some firms use it in their capital budgeting decisions. Alternative asset-pricing models exist, in particular the arbitrage pricing theory.

What these models have done is make everyone more aware of the trade-off between risk and return. If you pick share A rather than share B, and A returns more than B, this is only impressive if they have similar risk. Otherwise, a risk-adjusted return should be calculated. These notions have affected how academics conduct studies, and how fund managers' performances are assessed.

Part and parcel of modern portfolio theory is the idea of an efficient market. Information is analysed so quickly that public information is unlikely to be helpful in picking high-performing shares. If the market reflects all that is known, only randomly occurring news should cause share prices to move. In that case, looking at past prices won't be helpful. The evidence for this theory was good at first, but recently the evidence has been more mixed. But it's one thing for the market to be modestly inefficient, and another for fund managers to use this to outperform. Generally, managers seem unable to beat the market. The combination of the theory of efficient markets and unimpressive fund manager performance has been enough to lead some clients to have their assets invested to simply match the performance of an index. These 'index funds' account for between one quarter and one third of institutional investments.

So, does the theory we are going to discuss have any relevance in the real world? Yes. We begin with a discussion of risks and returns.

CALCULATING RETURNS

We will look separately at returns and risk before bringing them together. Obviously, investors are interested in knowing their returns. Here we show how to calculate them.

Money Returns

The money return on an investment over a particular period is the gain or loss in the capital value of that investment plus any payments received, i.e.

Money return = (income + change in capital value) × number of units.

For example, if 1000 shares of company X are bought at a price of £1, and these are valued at £1.20 at the end of the period, and the shares paid a dividend of 10p, then the money return is:

$$\text{Money return} = [(\pounds1.20 - \pounds1) + 10p] \times 1000 = \pounds300.$$

To make it clear that the return includes income and not just capital gains, the word 'total' is sometimes inserted before 'return'.

Percentage Return

How worthwhile is a return of £300? It depends on how much was invested. To allow for the sum invested, we calculate the percentage return, or the money return divided by the initial investment, i.e.

$$\text{Percentage return} = \frac{\text{money return}}{\text{initial investment}} \times 100\%.$$

For our example:

$$\frac{\pounds300}{\pounds1000} \times 100\% = 30\%.$$

We could have arrived at this number by a different route. We could have calculated the percentage capital return or capital gain, (£200/£1000) × 100% = 20%, and the percentage income return or dividend yield, (£100/£1000) × 100% = 10%. Adding the two together gives 30%.

Annualized Percentage Return

A return of 30% seems attractive, but whether it is will depend on the holding period. If the holding period was four years, then the return would seem less attractive. To compare investments with different holding periods, it is usual to calculate an annualized percentage return. This is done using a scientific calculator as it involves taking the nth root of the money return divided by the initial investment, where n is the number of years. From this, 1 is subtracted. For our example:

$$\text{Annualized percentage return} = \left(\frac{\pounds1300}{\pounds1000}\right)^{1/4} - 1 = 6.78\%.$$

Why wasn't the return 30%/4, or 7.5%? Because of the effect of compounding, i.e. earning a return on the previous year's return—getting interest on your interest, in everyday language. For example:

$$\text{Year 1: } \pounds1000 \times 1.0678 = \pounds1068$$
$$\text{Year 2: } \pounds1068 \times 1.0678 = \pounds1140$$
$$\text{Year 3: } \pounds1140 \times 1.0678 = \pounds1218$$
$$\text{Year 4: } \pounds1218 \times 1.0678 = \pounds1300$$

Average Returns

Investors often want to know what the average return from an asset has been over some period, for example the average return from equities over the last five years. We can calculate this as either an arithmetic average or geometric average (see Appendix). Assume that the returns have been +10%, +30%, –25%, +15% and –9%. The arithmetic average is:

$$\frac{10\% + 30\% - 25\% + 15\% - 9\%}{5} = 4.2\%.$$

The geometric average is:

$$(1.1 \times 1.3 \times 0.75 \times 1.15 \times 0.91)^{1/5} - 1 = 2.3\%.$$

Notice that in calculating the geometric average, each percentage return has been rewritten as a decimal and added to 1. Even negative percentages become positive numbers written this way. As you can see, the geometric average is lower than the arithmetic average. Whenever the returns are not constant, the geometric return will be lower than the arithmetic.

Real Returns

We mentioned in Chapter 1 the difference between nominal (money) returns and real (inflation-adjusted) returns. Investors often simply add or subtract to switch from real to nominal. For example, if inflation is 2% and nominal returns are 5%, then real returns are 3% (i.e. 5% – 2%). Strictly speaking, the real and nominal rates are connected as follows:

$$1 + \text{nominal rate} = (1 + \text{real rate}) \times (1 + \text{inflation rate})$$

where each rate is a percentage expressed in decimal terms. For our example:

$$1 + 0.05 = (1 + \text{real rate}) \times (1 + 0.02).$$

Rearranging terms:

$$\text{Real rate} = \frac{1.05}{1.02} - 1 = 0.0294, \text{ or } 2.94\%.$$

RETURNS FROM SOME MAJOR UK ASSET CLASSES

In Figures 2.1 and 2.2, we show graphs of annual total returns since the Second World War for UK cash (as measured by Treasury bills), UK conventional gilts and UK equities. In Figure 2.3, we show annual returns from UK conventional gilts, UK equities and UK index-linked gilts.

Simply by looking at Figure 2.1, it is hard to tell whether cash or gilts have the higher average return. What is clear is that the return from cash hasn't varied much in comparison to that from gilts. If the future is like the past, then the average return from each asset may be our best guess of what the future return

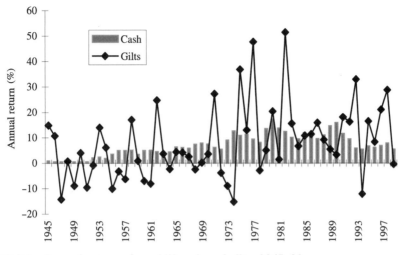

FIGURE 2.1 Annual returns from UK cash and gilts, 1945–99
Source: Drawn from data in CSFB (2000, p. 101).

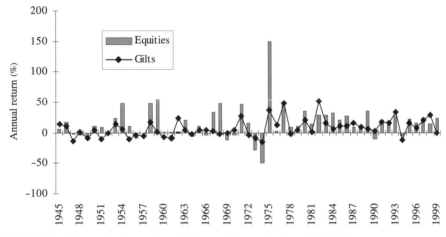
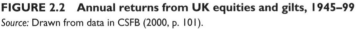

FIGURE 2.2 Annual returns from UK equities and gilts, 1945–99
Source: Drawn from data in CSFB (2000, p. 101).

will be. But in any year, it won't necessarily be a good guide for gilts, because the returns have been so variable.

In Figure 2.2, we again show the returns from gilts, but this time the comparison is with equities. It is clear that the average return from equities is higher than that from gilts, but the returns are even more variable than those from gilts. Finally, in Figure 2.3, equities again are the most profitable asset and the most variable, while index-linked and conventional gilts have roughly similar variability.

The returns shown in Figures 2.1–2.3 are nominal returns. These returns will reflect the historical rate of inflation. When we say that past returns may be a guide to future returns, this should be qualified. It is more likely that past real returns will be a guide to the future than past nominal returns. For example,

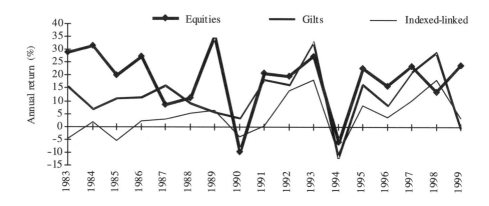

FIGURE 2.3   Annual returns from UK equities, gilts and index-linked, 1983–99
Source: Drawn from data in CSFB (2000, pp. 101 and 106).

inflation was above 20% at one stage in the 1970s; now it is about 2%. It is implausible that cash would offer the same nominal return then and now. So, if we want to use past returns as a forecast of future nominal returns, we should use historical real returns and then add the expected inflation rate.

Dimson et al. (2000) have produced new indexes for returns from the start of the last century. In Table 2.1, the average annual nominal returns for equities cash and gilts are shown for the entire century and two subperiods. In Table 2.2, the nominal and real returns are shown for the century.

TABLE 2.1   Annualized nominal returns (%) of UK asset categories, 1900–99

	1955–99		1900–54		1900–99	
	Arithmetic mean	*Geometric mean*	*Arithmetic mean*	*Geometric mean*	*Arithmetic mean*	*Geometric mean*
Equities	18.3	15.4	7.0	6.2	12.1	10.2
Bonds	9.4	8.5	3.3	2.9	6.1	5.4
Bills	8.3	8.3	2.5	2.5	5.1	5.1
Inflation	6.4	6.3	2.6	2.3	4.3	4.1

Source: Dimson et al. (2000, p. 9). Copyright © Dimson, Marsh and Staunton—ABN AMRO/LBS, 2000.

TABLE 2.2   Annualized returns (%) of main UK asset categories, 1900–99

Asset category	Nominal return	Real return
Equities	10.2	5.9
Bonds	5.4	1.3
Bills	5.1	1.0
Inflation	4.1	NA

Source: Dimson et al. (2000, p. 15). Copyright © Dimson, Marsh and Staunton—ABN AMRO/LBS, 2000.

RISK

Risk is a complex concept, and quite tricky to measure. We will approach it by a couple of examples. Imagine a friend says that she is going to open several coffee shops and become the next Starbucks. You might feel that it would be great if she did achieve this, but also note that most small businesses go bust. You might conclude that what she is planning is risky. Now imagine a friend has decided to retire early and doesn't have much in the way of pension entitlements. She plans to put her assets into a building society account because the 6% she can get will meet her income requirements. You might point out that while she probably won't lose her cash, interest rates might fall. A return of 6% with inflation around 2% is quite a high real return. It's conceivable that rates could fall to 3% or 4%, especially if inflation falls further. Her income would fall dramatically. So, while she won't lose her money, she may not achieve her expected return. Cash is risky in this case.

Risk, then, is the possibility that we won't achieve our expectations: this may involve actual loss, but it doesn't have to. If we form our expectation of future returns by some kind of average of past returns, we can form our notion of risk by the extent past expectations would have been dashed. Clearly, the greater the variability of past returns, the more frequently we would have been disappointed. We can measure the variability of past returns by calculating their standard deviation or variance (the standard deviation squared).

The returns and standard deviations for UK equities, gilts and cash are shown in Table 2.3 in both real and nominal terms. The table confirms what Figures 2.1–2.3 suggested. Equity returns are much more variable than those from gilts and cash, i.e. equities are riskier than gilts, which are, in turn, riskier than cash. The return statistics show that the riskier the asset, the higher its return.

TABLE 2.3 Annual mean real returns and standard deviations (%) for the UK, 1900–99

Asset category	Arithmetic mean return	Standard deviation
Equities	7.8	20.1
Bonds	2.2	14.6
Bills	1.2	6.6
Inflation	4.3	6.9

Source: Dimson et al. (2000, p. 21). Copyright © Dimson, Marsh and Staunton—ABN AMRO/LBS, 2000.

Using the standard deviation to measure risk has, in this case, given us results that are intuitively correct. But there is an odd feature of the use of the standard deviation. The statistic is calculated using all dispersions from the mean. But do investors really think returns that are above the expected return constitute risk?

When Markowitz was developing his analysis, he tried to avoid this problem and considered using a measure of downside risk, or returns below the expected return. The measure is called semivariance. However, the computational problems involved in using this were too demanding at the time and he instead used standard deviation. Look at Table 2.3 again. If we assume that the distribution of returns for the three asset classes are distributed normally, we can estimate that there is a 68% chance of equities in any one year of returning (in real terms) between –12.3% and +27.9%, and gilts returning between –12.4% and +16.8%. You might feel that gilts are actually riskier than equities.

While there may be more realistic measures of risk, there is a trade-off between realism and analytical complexity, and the standard deviation is not that bad a measure. If returns are approximately normally distributed, then the returns above the expected return will mirror the returns below it. In that case, including above-average returns is unproblematic. Stock returns cannot be completely symmetrical because losses can never exceed 100% (we are excluding options and short positions), while gains can be many times the sum invested. The distribution will be a bit lopsided or skewed to the right. But in many situations this will not be a problem, and often a skewed distribution can be transformed mathematically (by using natural logarithms) into a distribution that is normal. For most cases, standard deviation is an adequate measure of risk, but it is an imperfect measure.

INVESTOR UTILITY

We saw in Table 2.3 that for the major asset classes, higher returns have been achieved only at the cost of bearing higher risk. Investors will have to make a trade-off between risk and return. Each investor will have his or her own idea of the appropriate trade-off, just as each consumer has his or her own idea of the appropriate trade-off between, say, quality branded goods and cheaper own-label value goods. What assumptions can we make about how investors will make the risk/return trade-off?

It seems likely that with risk held constant, investors will always prefer more return. People just don't get fed up with money! It also seems likely that investors will prefer less risk for any given return, i.e. investors will be risk-averse. What this means is that they will refuse a fair bet. Offered a bet with a 50/50 chance of either winning £10 000 or losing £10 000, most investors would turn down the offer. The reason is that money, like most goods, has declining marginal utility. The benefit, or utility, you get from each addition of a good gets smaller and smaller. Say you have £50 000 in savings. If you take the bet, you will end up with either £40 000 or £60 000. Diminishing marginal utility suggests that the pain from your savings falling to £40 000 would exceed the pleasure of them rising to £60 000. Diminishing marginal utility implies that most investors will be risk-averse. Just how risk-averse will vary from person to person.

THE RISK REDUCTION EFFECTS OF DIVERSIFICATION

We have looked at risk and return for broad asset classes, such as equities in general. Now let's look at risk and return for individual shares and portfolios.

The same approach to measuring returns and risks adopted for all equities can be used for individual shares. Portfolios, however, typically consist of several asset categories and a number of shares and bonds. Does the picture on risk and return change when assets are combined and portfolios are constructed? Indeed it does.

To understand this, imagine two companies, one an accountancy partnership specializing in insolvency and the other an advertising agency. The insolvency partnership will do well in recessions and, let us assume, will do badly in good times. And vice versa for the advertising agency. Let us assume that good and bad times occur with equal frequency. If we assume some profit and loss figures, we might have the situation shown in Table 2.4.

TABLE 2.4 Profits and losses for two companies

Economic cycle	Advertising agency	Insolvency practice	50% advertising and 50% insolvency
Growth	+100	−50	+25
Recession	−50	+100	+25

Although both companies deliver profits of 50 units over an entire economic cycle, profits are very variable. Each company is risky. An investor owning either company would have variable profits, but if both companies were owned in equal amounts, profits would be stable. Diversification would eliminate risk because the returns from the two companies are related negatively. When one goes up, the other goes down. Diversification achieved by combining an advertising agency and a luxury car distributor would not be so effective—both companies are likely to do well and badly at the same time.

Constructing a plausible example of perfect diversification is quite difficult—when the economy does badly, most companies and their stocks do badly. And vice versa when the economy does well. However, companies' share prices do not move exactly in tandem, so selecting a basket of stocks at random will reduce risk.

In our simple two-company example, we chose companies whose returns were perfectly negatively correlated. When one did well, the other did badly. By holding both assets in a 50/50 ratio, the portfolio risk was totally eliminated. Because most assets move together to some extent, i.e. their returns are weakly positively correlated, diversification will only reduce risk, not eliminate it. Of course, if asset returns are perfectly positively correlated, diversification will not achieve risk reduction. In short, the risk of a portfolio is a function not only of the risk of each of the assets comprising the portfolio but also the degree of correlation between the returns of the assets. With anything less than perfect correlation of returns, diversification will reduce risk.

Having discussed the effect of diversification in a general way, we will now examine how you calculate a portfolio's expected return and risk.

Portfolio Expected Return

A portfolio's expected return is simply the weighted sum of its components' expected returns. For example, assume a two-share portfolio with expected returns and planned weights as shown below:

Share	Expected return (%)	Weight (%)
A	16	70
B	12	30

Expected portfolio return = (expected return for share A × weight)
+ (expected return for share B × weight)

i.e. $(16\% \times 0.7) + (12\% \times 0.3) = 14.8\%$.

Some investors sell shares they don't own: they 'short' the share. For example, imagine in the above example that the investor is investing £10 000, and decides to short share B. Instead of spending £3000 on B, the investor receives £3000. Imagine he puts the £3000 he didn't spend on B into A, and also the £3000 sale proceeds (i.e. £13 000 in total). The expected return would be $(16\% \times 1.3) + (12\% \times -0.3) = 17.2\%$.

Portfolio Risk

Portfolio risk is a much more tedious calculation than portfolio expected return. We need to know the weights of the assets included in the portfolio, their standard deviations (or variances) and, recalling Table 2.4, their correlation with each other. For a two-asset portfolio consisting of shares A and B:

Portfolio variance = [(portfolio weight of A)^2 × variance of A] +
[(portfolio weight of B)^2 × variance of B]+ (2 × weight
of A × weight of B × correlation coefficient of A and B
× standard deviation of A × standard deviation of B).

The last three items of the equation (correlation coefficient of A and B × standard deviation of A × standard deviation of B) are often replaced with the term the covariance of A and B. Written as words, the equation is long enough to make even inumerate readers yearn for mathematical symbols. But it is easy enough to use. Imagine our two shares, A and B, have variances of 625 (standard deviation of 25) and 100 (standard deviation of 10), respectively, and are perfectly negatively correlated so their correlation coefficient is −1. If we weight them equally to form a portfolio, the portfolio variance will be:

$$(0.5^2 \times 625) + (0.5^2 \times 100) + (2 \times 0.5 \times 0.5 \times -1 \times 25 \times 10) = 56.25.$$

So, the variance is 56.25 and the standard deviation is 7.5. The portfolio has a lower standard deviation than either asset. This is a consequence of their negative correlation. To see the effect of correlation, we rework the above calculation with different correlations given in Table 2.5. Clearly, diversification works best with assets that have negatively correlated returns. But we can see that even for assets that are to some extent positively correlated, there is a reduction in portfolio standard deviation. With a correlation of 1, the portfolio standard deviation is just the weighted sum of the components' standard deviations. For our equally weighted two-share portfolio, this is $(25 + 10)/2 = 17.5$. In Table 2.5, we see that even with a positive correlation of 0.5, the portfolio standard deviation is less than the simple weighted average.

TABLE 2.5   Variance and standard deviation with various share correlations

Correlation	−1.0	−0.5	0.0	0.5	1.0
Variance	56.25	118.75	181.25	243.75	306.25
Standard deviation	7.5	10.9	13.46	15.61	17.5

What happens if, for a given correlation, we vary the weights of shares A and B in our portfolio? The returns and standard deviations for various portfolios of A and B and for three different correlations are shown in Table 2.6. We construct our portfolios by mixing different amounts of A and B. For example, in the first portfolio we only have A. In the next, 80% of the investment is put in A and 20% in B. And so on, down the list. Irrespective of the correlation of A and B, the return will just depend on the returns from A and B and the amount invested in each share. The standard deviation of the portfolios will vary with the correlation between A and B.

For each correlation, we will look in more detail at the effect of varying the asset mix. In Figure 2.4 we have plotted the first three columns of Table 2.6

TABLE 2.6   Returns and standard deviations for portfolios with various component correlations

Portfolio (%A/%B)	Return (%)	Standard deviation (%)		
		Correlation −1	Correlation +1	Correlation −0.5
100/0	16.0	25.0	25.00	25.00
80/20	15.2	18.0	22.00	19.08
60/40	14.4	11.0	19.00	13.45
40/60	13.6	4.0	16.00	8.72
29/71	13.2	0.0	14.35	7.18
20/80	12.8	3.0	13.00	7.00
0/100	12.0	10.0	10.00	10.00

(including all the intermediate combinations of A and B not shown in the table). If you start at the top right of the long line in Figure 2.4, you can read off from the axes the return and standard deviation. This is the portfolio consisting solely of A. As we move down the line, more of B is being added to the portfolio at the expense of A. Inevitably, the return falls, because B has a lower return than A. The standard deviation also falls, partly because B has a lower standard deviation than A, but also because of the negative correlation. That is why the portfolio composed of 29/71 (actually 28.57/71.43) has zero standard deviation despite share B having a standard deviation of 10. Whenever two assets have perfect negative correlation, it is possible to construct a portfolio with no risk. As the amount of B in the portfolio continues to rise, the standard deviation rises because the smaller and smaller amounts of A have less and less diversifying effect. Eventually, at the right end of the short line, we are 100% in B, as a glance at the return and standard deviation will confirm.

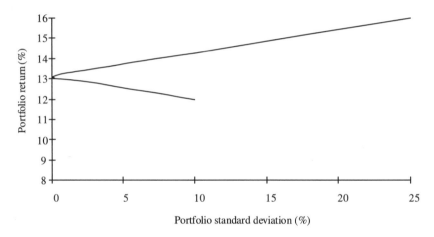

FIGURE 2.4 Portfolios formed by varying amounts of A and B that are perfectly negatively correlated

Columns 1, 2 and 4 of Table 2.4, or Figure 2.5, show the effect of perfect positive correlation. In this case, a portfolio's expected return and its standard deviation are simply the weighted sum of its components' expected returns and standard deviations. A straight line is traced out between 100% in share A and 100% in share B.

If we superimposed Figure 2.5 on Figure 2.4, we would get an upside-down triangle. Since the two graphs are for the extreme correlation values, all other correlations will plot return/standard deviation trade-offs somewhere between these two possibilities. For example, columns 1, 2 and 5 of Table 2.4, or Figure 2.6, show the return and standard deviation from a portfolio formed from assets that have a correlation of –0.5.

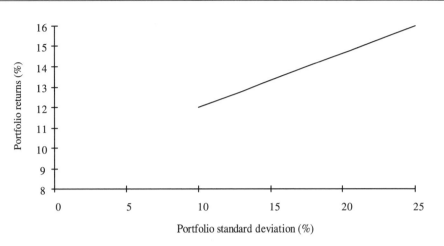

FIGURE 2.5 Portfolios formed by varying amounts of A and B that are perfectly positively correlated

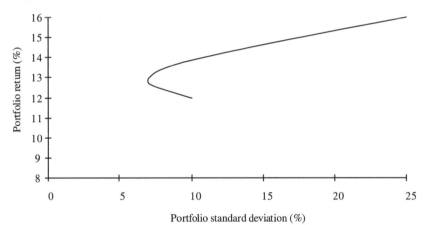

FIGURE 2.6 Portfolios formed by varying amounts of A and B that have a negative correlation of –0.5

THE EFFICIENT FRONTIER

Let's now abandon this simple world of two-share portfolios. In the real world, we find that it is possible to construct innumerable portfolios. A portfolio could consist of a single share, or two shares, or 100 shares, or one share and one bond, and so on. Calculating the return and risk for each portfolio would be hard work. Nonetheless, we shall assume all the calculations are made for all possible portfolios comprised of risky assets and we can plot the risk and return for each portfolio. Some of the portfolios are represented by the dots in Figure 2.7.

The dots (and all those that we omitted) represent the attainable set of portfolios. Consider portfolios A and B. Both have the same risk in terms of portfolio standard deviation. To read off the risk, just cast your eye down the dotted

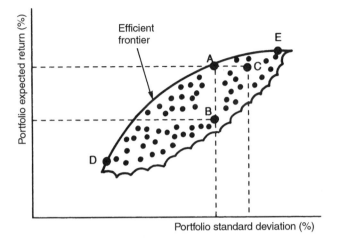

FIGURE 2.7   The attainable set and efficient frontier

vertical line that passes through the two portfolios. Now look across to the left along the dotted horizontal lines to read off the returns. Portfolio A has a higher return than portfolio B and is said to dominate it. Portfolio A offers the same risk and a better return. Now compare portfolios A and C. Both offer the same return, but if we look down to the risk axis we see that C is much riskier. Portfolio A has the same return as C, but less risk. Portfolio A dominates C and all other portfolios with the same return. Portfolio A can be described as efficient: no other portfolio offers as much return as A with as little risk, or as little risk with as high a return. By a series of similar arguments, we could establish all the efficient portfolios and thence the efficient frontier, which is shown as the curved line. We could have applied similar arguments to Figures 2.4 and 2.6. Nobody would invest in portfolios on the lower segments of the risk/return line because for each portfolio there is another directly above it offering the same risk but a higher return.

The efficient frontier traces out the efficient portfolios that dominate other portfolios. Portfolios around A in Figure 2.7 will usually contain more assets than those around portfolios E and D. Which portfolio amongst the efficient frontier portfolios is optimal? The answer will vary with an investor's risk preference. Very risk-averse or conservative investors will tend to choose portfolios near portfolio D, i.e. low risk and low return, while more aggressive investors will tend to choose portfolios near portfolio E, i.e. high risk and high return.[1]

Because we have selected our optimal portfolio on the basis of its expected, or average (mean), return and its standard deviation ($\sqrt{\text{variance}}$), this approach is sometimes described as mean-variance optimization.

---

[1] It is usual in textbooks to derive the optimal portfolio by drawing a series of risk/return indifference curves for the investor, and finding the point of tangency between an indifference curve and the efficient frontier. But this takes us no further than saying the investor picks the portfolio that he prefers, while baffling readers who are diagram-averse.

Elegant, But How Practical?

The above approach, due to Markowitz, is undoubtedly an elegant piece of work. But how practical is it? When we made calculations, we used only two assets, and the arithmetic was simple enough. The problems begin when we move to a realistic number of assets. When we calculate the portfolio standard deviation, we have to allow for the correlations between assets. For A and B, there is one correlation. For A, B and C there is the correlation of A and B, A and C, and B and C. For A, B, C and D, there is A and B, A and C, A and D, B and C, B and D, and C and D. As you can see, the number is beginning to soar. The number of correlations for n assets is given by $n(n-1)/2$. So, for 500 shares, the number of correlations would be $500 \times 499/2 = 124\,750$. This is usually described as 'computationally burdensome'! Does this mean the analysis is irrelevant? No, because in some situations, for example deciding weights for broad asset allocation between bonds, equities, property, etc., both domestically and internationally, the number of inputs required is small. But for selecting a share portfolio, the Markowitz model looks a non-starter. We discuss this in further detail later.

Earlier, we mentioned briefly why it is hard to get complete diversification of risks. We noted that while different companies will be affected by different factors, broad movements of the economy will also affect them. In fact, we expect most of a stock's return to be determined by the return on the market. When we hear that the market is up 20 points, we expect that any diversified portfolio of stocks will have gone up by some similar amount, and vice versa for falls. This suggests another way of obtaining an efficient frontier.

THE MARKET MODEL

In Figure 2.8, an individual share's returns have been plotted relative to the market's return. The latter is measured by a broad index such as the FTSE All-Share Index or the S&P 500. A line that best fits the observations shown in Figure 2.8 can be calculated using regression analysis. It is called the characteristic line. The equation of the line shown in Figure 2.8 can be written:

Security's expected return = alpha + (beta × market return) + unexplained residual

where alpha (α) is the intercept term, beta (β) is the slope of the line, and the residual (ε) is a random error term. The equation shown above is often called the market model. The market model expresses the relationship of a share's return to the market's return.

There are three parts to the market model equation. The intercept term gives a return for a share that is independent of the market. The slope term, beta, indicates how the share's returns vary with the market's returns. The market has a beta of 1, and if a share has a beta equal to 1 (and, necessarily, an intercept of zero), the share's returns will go up and down with the market's. If beta is greater than 1, the share exaggerates market moves and returns more than the

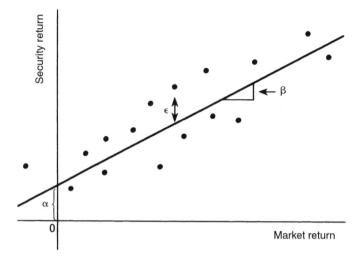

FIGURE 2.8   Relation between share and market return

market when market returns are positive, and less when market returns are negative. If beta is less than 1 but greater than zero, the share's returns are less than the market's when market returns are positive and greater than the market's when the market returns are negative. If the beta is negative, share and market returns move in opposite directions.

The third part of the equation is the residual error. As you can see in Figure 2.8, the observations don't fall neatly along the line. The regression line relates the share return to the market's return. But if there is news that relates just to the share—perhaps Lord Archer is appointed to the board—the share's price movement will reflect more than just the market's move. Some assumptions are made about the residual error:

- The error is assumed to be random and on average zero—the errors above the line are offset by errors below the line.
- The error is assumed to be uncorrelated with the market, e.g. if the market moves a lot, we don't expect the error to be larger.
- The error terms of assets are assumed to be uncorrelated—this means, possibly implausibly, that if the error term on one day is very high for BP Amoco, it won't be high for Shell.

Diversification and Systematic and Unsystematic Risk

We have seen that diversification reduces, but does not usually eliminate, risk. The reason is that shares are affected by both broad market factors and factors unique to the share. When we diversify, these unique risks will tend to cancel out. So risk has two components: company risks that can be eliminated by diversification, and market risk that cannot be escaped. The market risk is often called systematic risk, and the specific risk is often called unsystematic or idio-syncratic risk. In Figure 2.9, the risk-reduction effect of diversification is shown for UK and US stocks. Increasing the number of stocks held reduces risk, but only up to a point. After a while, investors cannot escape from general market fluctuations. Figure 2.9(b) also shows the benefits of diversification if foreign stocks are included. Because the world's stockmarkets are not perfectly syn-chronized, some of the risk inherent in the fluctuations of one market can be diversified away by adding foreign stocks that, at least partially, march to the beat of a different drummer. Notice that you don't need many stocks—around 20, selected randomly—to achieve most of the benefits of diversification.

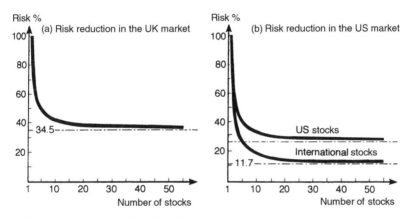

FIGURE 2.9   Risk reduction by diversification
Source: Solnik (1974, pp. 50–1). Copyright © 1974. Association for Investment Management and Research. Reproduced and republished from the *Financial Analysts Journal* with permission from the Association for Investment Management and Research. All rights reserved.

We can redraw Figure 2.9 to show the risk-reduction effect of diversification in terms of total, systematic and unsystematic risk. This is done in Figure 2.10. With a well-diversified portfolio, investors bear mainly systematic risk.

Market Model Implications

In the previous section, we saw that total risk (measured by the standard devia-tion of returns) was made up of systematic risk and unsystematic risk. We can think of return in the same way, i.e.

Security return = systematic return + unsystematic return.

The systematic return is perfectly correlated with the market return, and is given by beta times the market return. The unsystematic return is not correlated with the market. As we saw earlier, the expected return of a share will be its alpha, or intercept—which represents the average value of the unsystematic returns over time—plus its beta times the market's return. The error term drops out on the

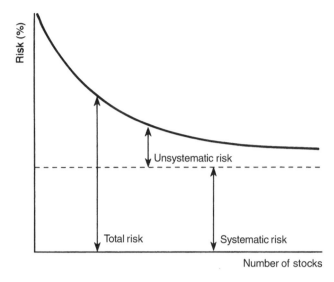

FIGURE 2.10   Types of risk and diversification

assumption that it is zero. If we assume for share A an intercept of 2% and a beta of 1.2, and the market return is 4%, then A's expected return will be:

$$\text{Expected return for share A} = 2\% + (1.2 \times 4\%) = 6.8\%.$$

The expected return of a portfolio will be the weighted average of the component alphas, plus the weighted average of the component betas times the market's return. The error term will be the weighted average of the component errors but will drop out on the assumption it is zero. If we assume a portfolio equally weighted between share A, as described above, and share B, with an intercept of 0.5, and a beta of 0.9, then the expected portfolio return will be:

$$(2\% \times 0.5) + (0.5\% \times 0.5) + [(1.2 \times 0.5) + (0.9 \times 0.5)] \times 4\% = 5.45\%.$$

Turning to risk, the risk of a security is simply the standard deviation of the two return components:

$$\text{Security risk} = \text{systematic risk} + \text{unsystematic risk}.$$

Or, security standard deviation = (security beta × market standard deviation) + standard deviation of unsystematic risk.

The portfolio risk is made of the same two types of risk as security risk, but the portfolio beta factor in the systematic risk is now the weighted average of the security betas. The unsystematic risk of a portfolio is trickier to calculate. But recall that as a portfolio is diversified, unsystematic risk tends to zero. Accordingly, for a diversified portfolio:

$$\text{Portfolio standard deviation} = \text{portfolio beta} \times \text{market standard deviation}.$$

The point is this. The risk of a security on its own is one thing, but when held in a portfolio another. Its unique risk doesn't matter. All that matters is its systematic or market risk, which means how sensitive it is to market movements. This sensitivity is measured by beta. In the context of a portfolio, a security's risk is given by its beta. A well-diversified portfolio, say 100 shares, selected randomly, will look pretty much like the market. Unique risk will be diversified away, and the portfolio beta will be 1. But say we selected 100 shares at random from all those shares with betas of 1.5 (if there are 100 such shares). We would again eliminate unique risk, but the portfolio would be highly sensitive to the market. If the market rose by 10%, then our portfolio would rise 15%. And if the market fell 10%, then we would lose 15%.

MARKOWITZ VERSUS THE SINGLE-INDEX MODEL

What we have shown is how to obtain risk and return figures for a portfolio using a different approach to that described earlier. The approach to constructing a portfolio that we have just described is based on relating returns and risks to a single factor—the market. The market may be defined as an index such as the S&P 500 or the FTSE All-Share. Accordingly, the approach is often described as a single-factor model or single-index model. Instead of the complex equation for variance used in the Markowitz analysis, we can now calculate portfolio variance simply by knowing the variance of the market and the betas of the portfolio constituents.

Which is the better way to construct a portfolio, the Markowitz model or the single-index model? As so often, the answer is that it all depends . . ..

On sheer number crunching, the Markowitz model loses. The required inputs for a 500 security model are shown in Table 2.7. For the Markowitz model, we need the return and risk of each security, and the correlation (covariance) of the return of each security with every other. For the single-index model, we need the return and risk of every security plus that of the entire market, and the covariance (i.e. beta) of each security with the market. However, with current computing power, number crunching is not decisive, especially when the asset universe is small, such as selecting between different asset classes.

TABLE 2.7   Data inputs for portfolio selection, 500 security universe

	Return	Variance	Covariance	Total
Markowitz	500	500	124 750	125 750
Single-index	501	501	500	1502

Nonetheless, there is a problem with the numbers required for the Markowitz model. Where do the covariances come from? One answer is history, but do we really expect the relationships between securities to be fixed? Another answer is to estimate them. But how? The oil analyst knows about oil shares—a request to provide the expected covariance of BP Amoco with Vodaphone, Unilever, Bank of Scotland, etc. would not be received well! The single-index model is much more operational in this regard. But while it is operational, are the results worthwhile?

There are two issues here. First, the single-index model only provides an estimate of true portfolio variance. If the assumption that residuals are uncorrelated is wrong, then the portfolio variance will be wrong. If the residuals are mainly positively correlated, then the estimated risk will be too low. Second, although betas are easier to estimate than correlations between shares in different sectors, can betas in practice be estimated accurately? We take each issue in turn.

Imagine that the government makes a surprise announcement that it will charge all car owners within the M25 a £3000 p.a. pollution tax. We would expect car sales to fall, and this to affect all UK-based car manufacturers. All car distributors inside the M25 are likely to be affected too, as well as garages, petrol suppliers, etc. In short, there is an industry effect that is likely to cause all of these groups' shares to suffer a negative residual. King (1966) investigated the industry effect in the US and found it to be significant, accounting for about 10% of total security variance. Nonetheless, while residuals are correlated, the effect may not be great. Cohen and Pogue (1967) compared the solutions to the portfolio selection problem given by the Markowitz model, the single-index model and multi-index models. The latter are models that include both a market index and industry indexes. They found that the *ex post* performance of the index models was not dominated by the Markowitz model, and the multi-index models were not superior to the single-index model.

Turning to betas, analysts could be asked to forecast betas for the stocks they follow. How good they would be at this is not known. Given this, the obvious thing to do is calculate historical betas and see if they are good predictors of future betas. The first problem is how to calculate historical betas. The principle is clear enough: we wish to calculate the slope of the line that best fits a scatter plot of a share's return against the market's return. But do we use daily data, weekly, monthly, annual, or what? You get different results with different data frequency. And for how long a period do we collect the data? A typical approach is to use monthly data collected over five years. Five years is thought to be long enough to catch a complete economic cycle (although the 1990s cycle exceeded that) and not so long for a company to have completely changed its business.

In a study using stocks on the New York Stock Exchange, Blume (1971) found that historical betas were poor predictors of future betas. For example, he calculated betas using data for the period July 1954–June 1961, and then again for the period July 1961–June 1968. If historical betas predict future betas, then there should be a high correlation between betas in the two periods. Blume found a correlation of 0.6, or a coefficient of determination of 0.36. This means that about two-thirds of the variation of a future beta was unexplained by the historical beta. However, when he formed portfolios of shares, the portfolio historical beta was a good predictor of the future portfolio beta. For example, a 10-share portfolio had a correlation coefficient of 0.92, and a 50-share portfolio had a correlation coefficient of 0.98.

So, while beta is stable for portfolios, it is not for individual securities. Can individual betas be improved? One way of thinking about this is to ask why individual betas are unstable. One answer is that they are measured with estimation error. Would we expect a very high beta to have been over- or underestimated? The error is likely to have been an overestimate, and vice versa for low betas. This suggests that betas might regress to the mean, i.e. betas above 1 will tend to decline and betas below 1 will tend to rise. And they do. Blume (1975) suggested a correction to allow for this, specifically:

$$\beta_{forecast} = 0.343 + 0.677\beta_{historical}.$$

Imagine the historical beta was 1.5, then our best guess of the future beta would be:

$$\beta = 0.343 + (0.677 \times 1.5) = 1.36.$$

Bloomberg, a firm that provides investment data, offers adjusted betas using a similar equation. There are other statistical methods of adjusting betas but we will move on to an entirely different approach.

The above adjustment procedure is a one-size-fits-all approach. But perhaps we should be regressing not to the market mean but to an industry mean. Or perhaps small firms suffer greater estimation errors so should have a greater adjustment factor than large firms. More generally, perhaps betas can be better estimated by looking at a range of fundamental accounting and market factors. A number of studies (e.g. Beaver et al., 1970; and Rosenberg and McKibben, 1973) have reported that these factors do improve beta forecasts. Fundamental betas are sold by a number of information providers, the best known being BARRA, formed by Barr Rosenberg, author of many studies in this area.

A VOLATILITY UPDATE

Earlier, we said that 20 stocks were sufficient to remove most idiosyncratic risk in the UK or US equity market. This is the number most frequently reported in textbooks, but it may no longer be true. Consider first market volatility. Investors often say that the market has become more volatile in recent years. Certainly, market volatility changes from time to time, with occasional spikes, but over the last 40 years the average level of volatility hasn't changed much. Why do investors think it has? One reason may simply be that, for example, you often hear that the FTSE 100 index has moved 100 points in a day. That didn't happen in the past. The problem with this argument, of course, is that when the index was at 1000, 100 points was a large percentage change. Now, with the index over 6000, 100 points isn't a large percentage change. Some investors, therefore, probably think the market is more volatile than it is because they confuse absolute numbers with percentage changes. But some probably feel that the market is more volatile because individual stocks seem to be more volatile. At least in the US, individual stocks are more volatile.

Campbell et al. (2000), using daily stock price movements of 9000 US firms over the period 1962–97, decomposed the risk of individual stocks into market-wide, industry-wide and firm-specific volatility. While they didn't find much change in volatility at the market or industry level, they did find the variance of the individual stocks had increased significantly, more than doubling between 1962 and 1997. How can individual stocks become more volatile while the market as a whole hasn't? The answer is that there has been a huge decrease in the correlations among individual stock returns.

The lower correlation between stocks means that the benefits of portfolio diversification have increased. Despite the lower correlations, the increased volatility of individual stocks means that a larger number of stocks, selected randomly, must be held to achieve the same amount of risk reduction as in the past. In Figure 2.8, we saw that about 20 stocks were sufficient to achieve most of the benefits of diversification. During the 1986–97 period, this number rose to 50.

Why has individual stock volatility increased? Campbell et al. (2000) suggest three reasons. First, conglomerates have gone out of style and companies are more focused. This makes them riskier. Second, a greater proportion of the US market is now controlled by financial institutions who may tend to behave in much the same way at much the same time. (In another study, Malkiel and Xu (1997) find that stocks are more volatile when the proportion of institutional investor ownership is high.) Third, at the end of the 1990s, the growth of day trading by individual investors will have boosted the volatility of some stocks.

So, if you want to be well diversified, how many stock should you hold? It depends on what you think will happen to individual stock volatility.

CONCLUDING COMMENTS

In this chapter, we argued that investors are concerned with both risk and return, and that uncertainty and nasty surprises constitute risk. Investors are assumed to be risk-averse and they will bear more risk only for the prospect of extra returns. We argued that risk could be measured by the variability of returns. The statistical measure of variability commonly used is the standard deviation, which is related to the variance. Combining securities into a portfolio reduces risk providing the securities' returns are not perfectly correlated.

Once securities are combined in a portfolio, the portfolio expected return will be the weighted average of the returns of the securities, and the portfolio standard deviation will depend on the standard deviations and proportions of each of the component securities as well as their covariance. From any group of securities, many portfolios can be formed but some portfolios will dominate other portfolios, i.e. they will offer more return for the same amount of risk or less risk for a given return. The combination of these dominant or efficient portfolios traces out an efficient frontier of portfolios. The portfolio on the efficient frontier that investors choose will depend on their degree of risk aversion.

Implementation of the above analysis is relatively easy for limited numbers of assets, but is difficult when there are many securities. An alternative analysis uses the single-index model. This model does not require the correlation of returns between every asset; instead, it relates each asset's return to that of the market via the asset's beta. It measures risk by relating the portfolio beta to the market's standard deviation. The benefits of diversification accrue through additional securities reducing unique risk. One of the key assumptions of the model is violated in the real world, but in practice this does not matter. There are problems in using historical betas as an estimate of future betas, but there are a number of ways of improving the situation. It is possible to use the single-index model to construct an efficient frontier when a large number of securities are involved.

3

The Capital Asset Pricing Model

Read Ben Graham and Phil Fisher, read annual reports, but don't do equations with Greek letters in them.

Warren Buffett

The previous chapter looked at portfolio selection. The Markowitz model had a number of assumptions hidden away. We assumed an initial amount of wealth and a single investment holding period, and assumed that all assets were risky. Moreover, if we assume there is no pair of perfectly negatively correlated assets, then it is not possible to construct a riskless portfolio. Now we will consider the implications of a risk-free asset and the possibility of borrowing. Before we do this it is worth stating the key assumptions of the Markowitz model and also the capital asset pricing model (CAPM, pronounced 'cap-m') that we will discuss in this chapter.

The Markowitz assumptions are:

- investors are risk-averse utility maximizers;
- investors judge investments solely by their expected return and standard deviation of returns;
- taxes and transaction costs are irrelevant.

CAPM assumptions are all of the above plus:

- investors all have the same one-period investment horizon;
- unrestricted borrowing and lending at the risk-free rate is possible;
- all investors have identical expectations with regard to return, standard deviations and covariances.

We need not go through the reasons that all these unrealistic assumptions are necessary. More to the point is whether they make the analysis useless. Economists would argue that no model is an exact description of reality and we can test the model's predictions in the real world to see whether it offers useful analysis. We will look at some tests later in the chapter. Another response is to change the assumptions one by one, making them increasingly more realistic, and see what happens. We'll do that for one of the assumptions.

COMBINING RISKY AND RISK-FREE ASSETS

We now extend the last chapter's discussion of the efficient frontier by introducing a risk-free asset, one that has a known return for a period equal to the investor's holding period. This is usually assumed to be a Treasury bill. Such an asset will be risk free—in the sense of having a certain return—and its life is the same as the investment horizon so it will have a standard deviation of zero. If you refer back to the formula for portfolio variance on p. 30 and insert zero for the variance and standard deviation of the risk-free asset, you will see that all that remains is the risky asset's variance. Therefore when a risky and a risk-free asset are combined, the expected return and standard deviation of the new portfolio will simply be the weighted average of each asset's return and standard deviation. For example, if a risk-free asset has an expected return of 5% and a zero standard deviation, and a risky asset has a return of 10% and a standard deviation of 10%, then the returns and standard deviations of various portfolio mixes of the assets will be as shown in Table 3.1. If the expected return and standard deviation data in Table 3.1 are plotted, a straight line will be traced out.

TABLE 3.1   Combining a risk-free and risky asset

Risk-free/risky asset	Expected return (%)	Standard deviation (%)
100/0	5.00	0.00
75/25	6.25	2.50
50/50	7.50	5.00
25/75	8.75	7.50
0/100	10.00	10.00

What happens in terms of the efficient frontier when we combine a risky portfolio with a risk-free asset? In Figure 3.1, three possible risky portfolios lying on the efficient frontier are combined with a risk-free asset. Portfolio R is a portfolio consisting of a risk-free asset. Portfolio A is a portfolio on the efficient frontier. The line connecting them represents various possible portfolios consisting of combinations of the risk-free asset and the risky portfolio. This set of portfolios dominates all the risky portfolios on the efficient frontier below portfolio A. Why? Because for every portfolio on the efficient frontier there is one on the line RA that has the same risk but a higher return, or has the same return and a lower risk. If we now look at the line connecting portfolios R and B, we see that it dominates all the portfolios on line RA. We can keep drawing new lines that dominate the others until we get to the line that is a tangent to the efficient

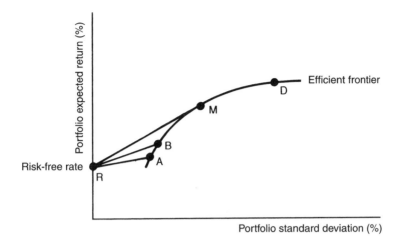

FIGURE 3.1   Feasible and efficient portfolios with a risk-free asset

frontier. This line produces a set of portfolios that dominates all portfolios below point M. Since no possible set of portfolios can be drawn to the north-west of line RM, once a risk-free asset is introduced, the new efficient frontier will be the straight line RM and then the curve MD.

In ordinary language, investing in a risk-free asset might be called lending (to the government). In effect, line RM traces out different combinations of lending and a risky portfolio (M). What happens if investors can borrow, and can do so at the same rate as they can lend? If we go back to Table 3.1 and extend the table by entering a new line with –25% of the risk-free asset and 125% of the risky asset, we can calculate a return and standard deviation of 11.25% and 12.5%, respectively. What we are doing is continuing to extend the straight-line relationship we have established. This means that Figure 3.1 can be redrawn as shown in Figure 3.2. The new straight-line efficient frontier is called the capital market line. It shows the risk/return relationship for efficient portfolios when borrowing and lending are possible at the same rate of interest. The proportion of risky assets to the risk-free asset an investor holds will vary depending on the investor's risk aversion. For example, a nervous investor might hold 75% risk-free and 25% risky, while a bolder type might hold 0% risk-free and 100% risky.

Figure 3.2 has a peculiar implication. All investors will want to invest in a portfolio on the efficient frontier, and where they invest on the frontier will depend on their attitude to risk. But notice that every point on our straight-line efficient frontier involves the same risky portfolio. Every investor will hold the same risky portfolio but have a different amount of risk-free lending or borrowing depending on their risk aversion. This result is known as the separation theorem, i.e. the selection of the optimal portfolio of risky assets is separate from an investor's attitude to risk and return. Can everyone invest in the same risky portfolio? Only if that portfolio is the market portfolio, i.e. all investors hold all securities in proportion to their market capitalization.

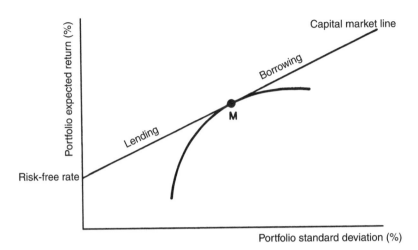

FIGURE 3.2   Efficient frontier with borrowing and lending

Imagine a security, say HSBC shares, is not included in the market portfolio. If nobody holds it, its price should move towards zero. But as that happens, its expected return will become increasingly attractive. Presumably at some point it will be bought and held in the portfolio. This argument is perfectly general: not only does it apply to other shares, it must apply to bonds, property, etc. Thus, the market portfolio includes all assets, although in practice many investors just relate the argument to ordinary shares.

In Figure 3.3, we again draw the capital market line and show the market portfolio, but omit the curved efficient frontier. We have also indicated the return for the market and the market standard deviation. The capital market line shows the risk and return relationship for efficient portfolios. Because it is a straight line, we can easily calculate its equation: we need to find the intercept and the slope of the line. The intercept is simply the risk-free rate. Slope is given by rise divided by run, i.e. how much the return changes (rise) for a change in risk (run). If we move from the risk-free portfolio to the market portfolio, the 'rise' is the market return less the risk-free return. The 'run' is the change from zero to the market's standard deviation. Therefore the expected return is:

$$\text{Risk-free rate} + \left[\frac{(\text{market return} - \text{risk-free return})}{\text{market standard deviation}} \times \text{portfolio standard deviation} \right].$$

A risk-free asset receives a return, but since it bears no risk, it cannot be a reward for risk bearing. Presumably, the return is a reward for postponing consumption. The first term therefore is the price of time. The second term, the slope of the capital market line, is the reward per unit of risk borne. Thus the expected return of an efficient portfolio is:

Expected return = price of time + (price of risk × amount of risk).

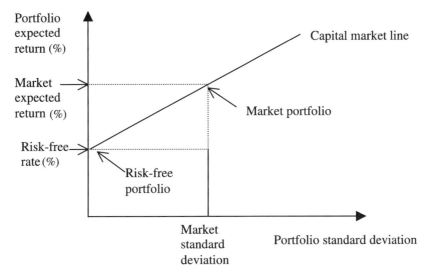

FIGURE 3.3   The capital market line

THE SECURITY MARKET LINE

The capital market line relates only to efficient portfolios. The risk/return relationship for individual securities or inefficient portfolios requires further analysis.

Diversification eliminates unsystematic risk. If investors do not like risk, they can eliminate unsystematic risk by diversification. Should they be rewarded for bearing unsystematic risk? Presumably not, since they can eliminate it easily by diversifying. On first consideration, it appears implausible that stocks with significant unsystematic risk do not get a reward for that risk. Consider, however, the matter from a different angle. Assume unsystematic risk is rewarded. Investors would search for stocks with high unsystematic risk. Once a portfolio of 20–50 stocks was formed, most of the unsystematic risk would have been diversified away. Yet, investors would be getting a reward for bearing the now nonexistent unsystematic risk. Presumably, there would be a scramble for these wonderful stocks and their price would be bid up until any portfolio constructed from them achieved no extra return. From that point on, unsystematic risk would go unrewarded.

What this implies is that if investors expect a return for suffering risk, then it must be the amount of systematic or market risk that a stock bears that is important in pricing the stock. As we argued in the last chapter, in the context of a portfolio, beta is the correct measure of a security's risk.

If we assume that assets with the same risk will have the same return, investors who hold a share that has the same risk as the market portfolio, i.e. it has a beta of 1, will expect to get the market return. If investors hold a share with a beta of zero, they will expect to earn the riskless rate of return, the return from Treasury bills.

Portfolios that are formed by a mixture of these two shares will have a return and risk that are the weighted averages of the return and risk of the two shares. In short, the returns and risks will trace out a straight line as shown in Figure 3.4.

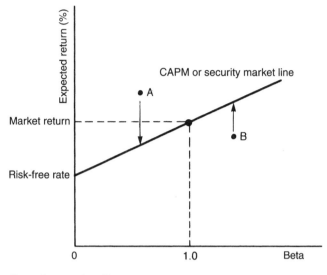

FIGURE 3.4   Security market line

We calculated the equation of the capital market line by finding the intercept and slope. We can do the same for the security market line:

Security expected return =

$$\text{risk-free rate} + \left[\frac{(\text{market return} - \text{risk-free return})}{1 - 0} \times \text{security beta} \right]$$

which simplifes to:

Security expected return =

$$\text{risk-free rate} + \left[(\text{market return} - \text{risk-free rate}) \times \text{security beta} \right].$$

This equation is known as the Capital Asset Pricing Model.

Notice that the risk-free rate and the market return appear in this equation and are not functions of the asset being priced. The only asset-specific measure is beta. The difference in return between any two assets will be solely related to the difference in their betas. All stocks will be priced on the security market line. Will risky assets always offer higher returns? The answer must be no, because if they did they could not be said to be risky. The *expected* return will be higher, but the *realized* return may turn out to be lower.

In Figure 3.4, we have shown two securities, A and B. Neither falls on the security market line. Can such assets exist? Yes, but not for long. Security A offers an exceptional return for the amount of risk it bears. Investors will rush to buy such a security and their demand will push up its price. As this happens, the prospective return will drop. The buying will carry on until the asset is priced on the security market line. Security B, on the other hand, will suffer a falling price until it too is priced on the line.

Let's look at a simple arithmetical application of the security market line equation given above. Imagine that the risk-free rate is 10%, the return from the market is 15%, and a share has a beta of 1.2. If we substitute these numbers into the equation we get:

$$\text{Expected rate of return } (\%) = 10 + [(15 - 10) \times 1.2] = 16.$$

Is this share cheap because it is expected to return more than the market? No: the share has a higher return than the market consistent with its higher risk. A share with an expected return of, say, 18% and a beta of 1.2 would be cheap. We would expect buyers to rush in and buy that share until its price had risen by enough to bring the expected return down to 16%.

The Capital Market Line and the Security Market Line

If you refer back to Figure 3.3 and compare it with Figure 3.4, you will see that the diagrams are similar but not identical. The capital market line is drawn using the standard deviation as the measure of risk, whereas the security market line uses beta. The capital market line is drawn to reflect total risk, whereas security market line is drawn to reflect only systematic risk. In equilibrium, only fully-diversified portfolios lie on the capital market line. Individual securities will plot beneath it. For the security market line, all securities and portfolios will plot along the line. The capital market line tells us whether a portfolio is efficient, whereas the security market line tells us whether a stock or portfolio is properly priced.

THE ZERO-BETA CAPITAL ASSET PRICING MODEL

We began this chapter with a number of assumptions. We will look at one of them before moving on to discuss how the CAPM might be used and what empirical tests of it have discovered.

In the real world, investors do not face the same rate for borrowing and lending. Accordingly, Figure 3.2 can be redrawn with a line for borrowing and another for lending. The line for borrowing will be a tangent line from a return that is higher than that from the risk-free asset to the original curved efficient frontier. This is shown in Figure 3.5. The efficient frontier will consist of the straight line that involves lending up to its tangency point with the original curved efficient frontier, a section of the original frontier, and then the straight-line efficient frontier that involves borrowing from its tangency point with the curved efficient frontier. The dotted parts of the lines are not available to the investor. (The investor cannot borrow at the lending rate, so the part of the line

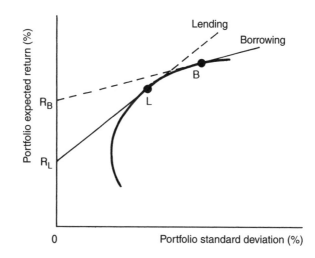

FIGURE 3.5 Efficient frontier with borrowing and lending at different interest rates

from the risk-free lending rate to the right of point L can be ignored. Similarly, the investor cannot lend at the borrowing rate so that part of the line from the risk-free borrowing rate to the left of point B can be ignored.) Any portfolio on the curved segment will be an efficient portfolio.

If the market portfolio does not lie on the curved segment, then the CAPM does not hold. If the market portfolio lies on the curved section, then we can draw a straight line that is a tangent to it. This will intersect the vertical return axis somewhere between the risk-free rate and the market return—this is just a matter of geometry. What exactly is this intercept? If we mapped this capital market line onto a security market line, the market portfolio would plot at the intersection of the market return and a beta of 1, while the intercept would be the return associated with a beta of zero. This is shown in Figure 3.6, along with the security market line for the standard CAPM. The zero-beta CAPM shows the returns associated with risky assets if investors can borrow and lend at the rates associated with a zero-beta asset. Note that the zero-beta version of CAPM has a flatter line than the standard version.

TESTING THE CAPITAL ASSET PRICING MODEL

We have given an outline of the CAPM. The next question is, is it true? The CAPM implies that:

- there is a linear relationship between systematic risk (beta) and expected return;
- the slope of this relationship is the market return less the risk-free rate;
- unsystematic risk is not rewarded;

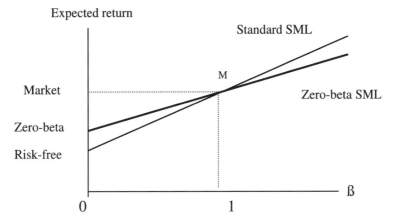

FIGURE 3.6 **Zero-beta security market line and standard security market line**
(SML, security market line)

- on average, over long periods, securities with high betas produce higher returns;
- the market portfolio is mean-variance efficient.

If we knew expected returns and betas, all we would have to do to test the theory would be to plot the two against each other. Unfortunately, neither is known, and we have to estimate them. As we saw in the previous chapter, measuring individual betas is subject to a lot of error, and we get better results by using portfolios of betas.

The Case For the Capital Asset Pricing Model: I

Three early major US studies were by Black et al. (1972), Fama and MacBeth (1973) and Sharpe and Cooper (1972). They used different analytical methods but essentially used the same data for US equities. We will summarize the results of the first two studies and outline the third.

Black et al. (1972) found over the period 1931–65 that higher beta risk and higher reward go together, but the security market line cut the intercept above the risk-free rate—the zero-beta model (Figure 3.6) seemed to be better supported than the standard CAPM. They split their data into four subperiods. For the period July 1948–March 1957, the line was very flat indeed—there was very little reward for bearing risk. For the period April 1957–December 1965, the security market line had a negative slope, i.e. low beta shares returned more than high beta shares. Fama and MacBeth (1973) studied the period 1935–68. They found beta and returns were positively related for the entire period and for eight of nine subperiods. They found the relationship to be linear, and unsystematic risk did not affect returns. Again, the zero-beta model seemed better supported than the standard model.

Fund managers may be more interested in a test that took the form of simulated portfolio strategies. Sharpe and Cooper (1972) looked at a strategy of buying portfolios of stocks with different betas. They looked at all New York Stock Exchange stocks for the period 1931–67. For every year, they calculated betas for stocks by using the previous 60 months of data. They then ranked stocks by their betas, and split the stocks into deciles, i.e. the highest beta stocks were grouped into one portfolio, the next highest in another, and so on. For every year, they constructed new portfolios in the same manner. They then looked at a strategy of buying the highest beta portfolio every year (strategy 10), the next highest beta portfolio (strategy 9), through to the lowest beta portfolio (strategy 1). Finally, they looked at the return from each strategy and the actual betas for each strategy. (Remember, they forecast each year's beta using past data, so what they thought would be the highest beta portfolio didn't necessarily turn out to be.) Their results are shown in Table 3.2. The results show a strong relationship between betas and arithmetic returns and a weaker relationship between betas and geometric returns. Past betas appear useful in constructing portfolios that have specified beta levels, i.e. the portfolio betas are not ranked perfectly in order but the ranking is broadly correct.

TABLE 3.2   Returns to beta strategy, 1931–67

Strategy	Average annual returns (%)		Portfolio betas
	Arithmetic	Geometric	
10	22.67	14.52	1.42
9	20.45	14.21	1.18
8	20.26	14.79	1.14
7	21.77	15.84	1.24
6	18.49	13.00	1.06
5	19.13	15.00	0.98
4	18.88	14.69	1.00
3	14.99	12.14	0.76
2	14.63	12.40	0.65
1	11.58	9.89	0.58

The Case Against the Capital Asset Pricing Model: I

All in all, the evidence for the CAPM appeared fairly strong, at least by the standards of most social science. However, a number of later studies showed that variables such as low price-earnings ratios (e.g. Basu, 1977) and size (e.g. Banz, 1981) explained returns even after controlling for systematic risk. Portfolios of small stocks with the same beta as portfolios of large stocks earned higher returns during the period 1936–75 in the US. The CAPM appeared to be missing a factor. Subsequently, a number of factors were found that appeared to be related to returns. Many are discussed elsewhere in this book.

Next, a number of studies found no relationship between beta and returns in a number of markets. For example, Corhay et al. (1987) found no relationship between beta and returns for the US, UK and Belgium for the period 1971–83. In France, investors were penalized for bearing risk. Other studies appeared to show no relationship between beta and returns in the UK.

Some studies found that unsystematic risk and other forms of risk were rewarded in the US, for example Friend et al. (1978), Lakonishok and Shapiro (1984), and Fuller and Wong (1988). For the UK, Corhay et al. (1988), found a significant positive relationship between risk and return when risk was measured by either total risk (variance), unsystematic risk or skewness. When fund managers are asked what they conceive risk to be, they usually give a multidimensional response. For example, Gooding (1978) found that US institutional fund managers' concepts of risk included company risk, beta and standard deviation of return. All this suggests that, contrary to the theory, systematic risk is not the only risk that is rewarded.

The Case Against the Evidence

All studies have problems matching real evidence to theories. But the CAPM is especially hard to test. First, the theory deals with expectations, but what we measure are outcomes. While some form of estimate of future betas is usually made, returns are usually measured as average realized holding period returns, but this isn't necessarily what investors expected the return to be. For example, investors might price UK water utilities in accordance with CAPM given their expectations, but if the water regulator unexpectedly changes the rules of the game, the measured relationship between risk and return may be poor. Sharpe (cited in Burton, 1998) argues:

> 'Is beta dead?' is really focused on whether or not individual stocks have higher expected returns if they have higher betas relative to the market. It would be irresponsible to assume that is not true. That doesn't mean we can confirm the data. We don't see expected returns; we see realized returns. We don't see ex-ante measures of beta; we see realized beta. What makes investments interesting and exciting is that you have lots of noise in the data. So it's hard to definitely answer these questions.

Second, the CAPM assumes everybody has the same investment horizon but doesn't specify what that is. If we test the theory over holding period x, but really it should be y, then we may reject the theory based on period x even though it holds for period y, and vice versa.

The third reason the theory is hard to test is that it is actually untestable (Roll, 1977; Roll, 1978; Roll and Ross, 1994). The CAPM involves the market portfolio, but the sorts of tests we have described do not. The point is this: it can be shown that for a population of securities, there will be a linear relationship between the betas of the securities and their expected returns if, and only if, the betas are computed using a portfolio on the efficient frontier. Say we choose an index that is, *ex post*, on the efficient frontier, then linearity between the security betas and returns is automatic. But this tells us that this portfolio is mean-variance efficient; it doesn't tell us whether the market portfolio, *ex ante*, is. If we choose a portfolio that is not on the efficient frontier, there will not be a linear risk/return relationship. But this simply tells us something about that portfolio and nothing about the market portfolio. Accordingly, using a portfolio such as the S&P 500 as a benchmark for testing the CAPM renders the results meaningless. The only valid test of the CAPM must be whether the market portfolio is mean-variance efficient. As the market portfolio cannot be measured, this test is impossible. This argument is generally known as Roll's critique.

Despite Roll's critique, studies relating beta and returns are still reported. Roll's arguments are not in dispute. What is disputed is their empirical relevance, i.e. whether in practice tests are highly dependent on the index being used (see Stambaugh, 1982). Another approach is to ask what correlation there has to be between the proxy and the true market portfolio for rejection of the CAPM by the proxy to imply rejection of the CAPM with the market portfolio (see Kandel and Stambaugh, 1987; Shanken, 1987; and Kandel and Stambaugh, 1995).

There is a more pragmatic response to Roll's critique. Nobody ever thought that everybody held the same market portfolio, consisting of all world assets. That is just a consequence of an implication of CAPM. Nonetheless, the implication that risk and return are related, that the relationship is linear, that systematic risk is the relevant risk, and so on is all quite plausible. Why not just ignore how these results were arrived at and test them for shares against a very broad market index, or all shares on the New York Stock Exchange, etc.? Investors will be interested in the results irrespective of the theoretical basis. In that spirit, let's continue.

The Case Against the Capital Asset Pricing Model: II

The most important recent paper rejecting the CAPM is by Fama and French (1992), who report finding no relationship in the US between beta and returns over the period 1963–90 and only a weak relationship over the 1941–90 period. They find that small market capitalization firms, and those whose book value (i.e. net asset value; see Chapter 13) is high in relation to their price, earn higher returns. Since for long periods there is no relationship between betas and returns, and since other factors do explain returns, they reject the CAPM.

The Case For the Capital Asset Pricing Model (and Beta): II

There have been two types of response to Fama and French (1992). One has been to attack their study; the other has been to show that beta is relevant notwithstanding their study.

Anti-Fama and French

Fama and French report various tests of significance, i.e. for a particular finding, what is the probability that it is just a chance observation? The problem is that the risk premium (return – risk-free rate) is highly variable. For example, for the period 1941–90, the expected return compensation is 0.24% per month, or about 3% p.a., i.e. for an increase in beta of 1, return increases 0.24% per month. The standard error of this estimate is, however, 0.23%. Roughly speaking this gives a t statistic of 1, which means we can't say with any confidence that the true expected return compensation isn't really zero. This is how Fama and French read the evidence. But it also means that we can't say with confidence that it isn't 6% p.a. either.

Most studies, including Fama and French's, use monthly returns for calculating betas, i.e. a stock's beta is usually measured by calculating the regression equation of its monthly stock returns against the corresponding returns of the S&P 500. Kothari et al. (1995) use annual returns for calculating betas. When they apply this approach to US stocks for the period 1927–90, they find a strong relationship between beta and returns. Broadly speaking, if we constructed two portfolios whose betas differed by 1 (say 0.5 v. 1.5), the higher beta portfolio would have earned about 9% p.a. more than the lower beta portfolio.

With regard to the two factors that Fama and French thought explained returns, Kothari et al. found much weaker effects. Black (1993) has argued that the size effect may simply be a result of data mining, and may be sample specific. We discuss this in Chapter 13. With regard to the book value finding, Kothari et al. argue that this could be a result of a looking backward bias. Compustat provided the data used by Fama and French. There may be a bias created by Compustat back-filling data, which means in 1990, say, we add data for earlier years. But if many firms with high book-to-price go bust before 1990, they may not be included and therefore are not included in the sample. Those that survive will be included and their historical data added. This will mean that returns to high book-to-price firms will be overstated. Using a sample free of this bias, they found the effect of book-to-price much reduced. Inevitably, Fama and French (1996b) dispute these findings.

Finally, a number of attempts have been made to include human capital in the benchmark portfolio, and also to allow the value of betas to vary over time. This work is beyond the scope of this book.

Beta is Informative

Imagine that we decide that there really is no relationship between beta and returns: that the CAPM is wrong. That doesn't mean beta would be of no interest, providing that we think beta measures risk, or at least a portion of risk. If there is no reward for risk, you should buy low beta stocks and reduce risk without having to sacrifice return. Black (1993, p. 9) explains: 'Beta is a valuable investment tool if the line [relating average return and risk] is as steep as the CAPM predicts. It is even more valuable if the line is flat. No matter how steep the line is, beta is alive and well.'

Chan and Lakonishok (1993) argue that what really concerns fund managers is downside risk. Does beta help here? To find out, they look at the 10 largest down-market months in the US between 1926 and 1991. They form 10 beta-sorted portfolios for each occasion. What they find is a near monotonic relationship between beta and return in each of these months. For example, in October 1987, which was the second worst month in their universe, the market fell by more than 22%. The lowest beta portfolio fell by about 17%, whereas the highest beta portfolio fell by nearly 34%. And in the biggest up-market months? High beta portfolios win. This doesn't mean, however, that beta risk will earn a higher reward over a market cycle: Fama and French's evidence implies that the pluses and minuses wash out, leaving risk unrewarded.

Grundy and Malkiel (1996) conduct a somewhat similar analysis. They study the years 1968–92 for the US market. They examine bear markets, which they define as at least a 10% fall, peak to trough, in the S&P 500 and a broader market index. They find 13 such episodes, ranging in length from 31 days to 458 days, and with falls ranging from 13% to 47% as measured by the S&P 500. They found that high beta stocks fell much more than low beta stocks. The aggregate data for all 13 episodes were strictly monotonic for beta deciles, i.e. if the lowest beta portfolio is labelled 1 and the highest beta portfolio is 10, portfolio 10 fell more than 9, which fell more than 8, which fell more than 7, etc.

UK Evidence

A number of papers look at the UK evidence. We shall mention just four; as you will see, they cover similar and short periods. The first three are essentially replications of Fama and French (1992). Strong and Xu (1997) mainly study the period 1971–92, but also present some results from 1960. They find some evidence of a positive premium for beta, but not when size or accounting variables are added to their regression equation. Size (i.e. small-capitalization—'small-cap'—firms earn more) dominates beta in explaining returns over the period 1960–92. However, size becomes insignificant when they add book-to-market equity or leverage variables for the period for which they have accounting data, 1973–92. Chan and Chui (1996) studied the period 1971–90. Not surprisingly, their results are similar to those of Strong and Xu. Broadly speaking, these studies support Fama and French in finding no role for beta in explaining returns; they also do find a role for book-to-market. But size drops out, and leverage is important. Miles and Timmermann (1996) studied the period May 1979–April 1991. Beta had no explanatory power, book-to-market did, and to a lesser extent company size and liquidity did.

Clare et al. (1998) employ a different estimation technique than that used in most of the literature. They claim a number of advantages for their approach

(p. 1214), but the points are somewhat technical. The most important thing to know is that they could estimate beta on the assumption that nonsystematic returns were not correlated, and then allowing the nonsystematic correlations to be whatever they were. On the first assumption, for the period 1980–93, beta had a trivial effect on return and was statistically insignificant. But in the second case, the estimate of beta risk was about 3.4% p.a. and statistically significant. They then included the Fama and French variables (size, book-to-market, etc.) but found them all to lack statistical significance. In short, their findings are quite different from Fama and French's. There is a role for beta and no role for Fama and French variables, but residual risks are correlated.

What Does it all Mean?

We can summarize the evidence:

- For some periods, in some countries, the CAPM is supported. However, it is the zero-beta form, rather than the standard CAPM, that is supported.
- For many countries, over long periods there is no relationship between beta and returns.
- Contrary to the CAPM, unsystematic risk appears to be rewarded.
- Contrary to the CAPM, variables other than beta are related to return. These variables are not necessarily the same in all countries.
- Even if the CAPM is false, the finding that there is no return for beta risk is a useful finding for investors.
- For major market moves, there has been a strong relationship between beta and returns.

The evidence tilts towards rejecting the CAPM. If the CAPM is rejected, then at least one of the following must be true:

- There is no relationship between risk and return.
- Beta is the wrong measure of risk.
- Average realized returns are useless as estimates of expected returns.
- As the theory has not been tested against the market portfolio, the tests are irrelevant.

Economists would be reluctant to accept the first point. Beta may well be an inadequate measure of risk. The third point is surely right, and more work in this area may be expected. The last point is technically right, but most academics probably wouldn't see that as the source of the problem.

In the next chapter, we discuss a different approach to risk and return; in Chapter 13, we have another stab at the problem. There are more twists in this story than anything written by Patricia Cornwell.

USING THE CAPITAL ASSET PRICING MODEL

Whether you want to use the CAPM or beta depends on how you read the evidence. If you think there might be some merit in the CAPM or betas, there are four main applications.

One use of the CAPM is in share selection, which was discussed implicitly with regard to Figure 3.4. If we calculate a security market line, then all stocks should lie along it. Stocks off the line are mispriced: stock A in Figure 3.4 should be bought, and stock B should be sold. The general case is shown in Figure 3.7. The expected return for the stocks might have been calculated by techniques such as the dividend discount model or the appropriate price-earnings ratio (both of which are discussed in Chapter 10).

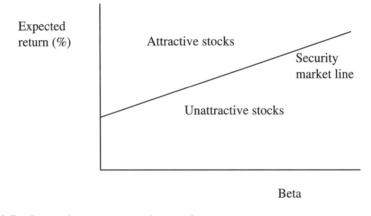

FIGURE 3.7   Attractive v. unattractive stocks

Betas might be used in overall market strategy. An investor who thought that the market was going to rise might wish to hold high beta stocks to earn an above-market return (Figure 3.8). Note that this strategy relies on the investor having both the ability to call the market and sufficient skill to overcome the transaction costs of adjusting the portfolio. If an investor has no market timing skill and always holds high beta stocks, he might achieve a high return, but this would be purely a return for bearing risk.

Another use of the CAPM is to determine 'the price of risk' (see Fouse, 1976). A security market line for the equity market may be relatively flat or it may rise steeply. In the first case, the market is giving little extra reward for taking on risk, whereas in the second it is offering a larger reward. Investors who calculate empirical security market lines at various times will see whether the market is offering a low or high degree of return for bearing risk. If the line is relatively flat, then there is less attraction in having a high-risk equity portfolio (Figure 3.9). If the line is high or low relative to cash or gilts, then equities are over-weighted or underweighted accordingly (Figure 3.10).

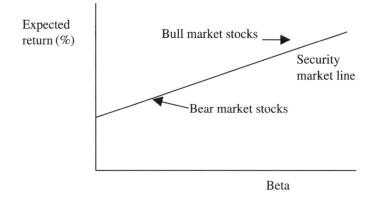

FIGURE 3.8   Betas of stocks for bull and bear markets

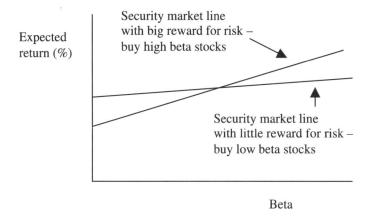

FIGURE 3.9   Appropiate betas for high and low rewards for risk

Finally, betas might be used in evaluating portfolio performance or a share-selection scheme. A share-selection scheme that earns an above-market return is not necessarily a successful scheme if all it has done is to pick risky shares. Some adjustment for risk must be made. Recall our earlier example of a share with a beta of 1.2 being expected to earn 16% when the market was returning 15% and a risk-free asset was returning 10%. If a share-selection scheme picked shares with an average beta of 1.2, it could only be said to be successful if the shares returned more than 16%. We can see whether we have made an abnormal return by using betas to tell us what a normal return is. Notice the implication of this statement. Testing a share-selection scheme always involves a test of a joint hypothesis: both the asset pricing model that is being used and the selection process are being tested simultaneously. When a share-selection process, for example, is rejected as having no value, it could be that the selection process is valid but the asset pricing model is false.

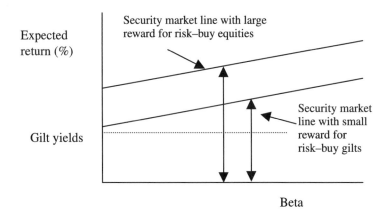

FIGURE 3.10   **Attractive v. unattractive asset classes**

CONCLUDING COMMENTS

In this chapter we introduced a risk-free asset and found that all investors should hold the same portfolio of risky assets—the market portfolio—and achieve their desired risk/return position by lending or borrowing. The total risk that a stock bears can be divided into market-related, or systematic, risk and stock-specific, or unsystematic, risk. A well-diversified portfolio will bear little unsystematic risk. Since unsystematic risk can be eliminated, it seems unlikely that it will be rewarded. Total risk is not the relevant concept for pricing securities: systematic risk is. Beta measures a security's systematic risk relative to that of the market. The CAPM states that:

Security expected return = risk-free rate + [beta × (market return − risk-free rate)].

Recent research shows that the evidence supporting the CAPM is weak, but betas seem to have a place in the professional's toolkit irrespective of the validity of the CAPM.

4

Arbitrage Pricing Theory

The APT [arbitrage pricing theory] is based on the notion that the market prices risk by looking at central systematic risks such as inflation and the business cycle. That is about as close to common sense as economics gets.

Stephen Ross

INTRODUCTION

Some years ago, the author was told by a fund manager that modern portfolio theory was nonsense—a common view. A week later, the same manager was overheard explaining to a young fund manager why it wasn't wise to buy certain stocks: 'They are bull market stocks. They are OK while the market is going up, but you'll get killed when the market turns down.' This sounds suspiciously like an explanation that high beta stocks are risky. While many investors resist the abstract formulation of CAPM, they often think unknowingly in CAPM terms. But few think solely about risk in CAPM terms. If we had asked the same fund manager why mining stocks were performing so well in 1999, we might have been told that in late 1998 there were fears that the world economy was slowing down, but in 1999 it became apparent that this was wrong. Mining stocks are heavily exposed to recession risks, and therefore do well when prospects look good. Again, if asked why house builders were doing badly at the end of 1999, despite apparently cheap ratings, we might have been told that the continuing strong growth might cause interest rates to rise, and that house builders are heavily exposed to interest rate risk. In short, many investors seem to see risk in terms of broad economic factors. So does one asset-pricing theory.

The CAPM has only a single systematic risk factor—the market—but it seems that a multifactor theory might be helpful. In fact, there are some multifactor theories that are extensions of the CAPM. Some are rather formal, some rather ad hoc. We discuss an ad hoc model in Chapter 17. Here we will focus on the most general multifactor theory, the arbitrage pricing theory (APT). The notions behind APT are simple, but the maths and statistics are not. We will concentrate on the notions and applications.

APT was propounded by Ross (1976), and has been described as a mixture of common sense and algebra. APT is an equilibrium theory, like the CAPM. Both seek to explain how investors will behave and, as a result, how asset prices will be set, and the relationship between risk and return that will prevail in the market. APT asserts that a few systematic factors affect the long-term average returns of assets. It accepts that daily price movements of individual assets are affected by many factors, but it focuses on the major, systematic factors. The unsystematic factors, or idiosyncratic influences, that affect individual stocks or sectors can be diversified away, and it is unlikely that they will be rewarded or, in the jargon, priced. The major factors will affect all securities and it is unlikely that they can be diversified away. Accordingly, they will affect the expected return from a security.

APT has nothing to say about what exactly the systematic risks are or how many there are. On purely empirical grounds, Burmeister et al. (1997) suggest five factors:

- inflation
- business cycle
- investor confidence
- time horizon
- market timing.

Even well-diversified portfolios will have different exposures to the systematic factors. Since risk exposure will determine returns, the risk-exposure profile will determine the returns and volatility of a portfolio. Systematic risks explain only about one-quarter of the price fluctuations of a share, but about 97–99% of the fluctuations of a large diversified portfolio, which Roll and Ross define as one with more than 40 stocks, and with no heavy concentration in any one of them.

The returns on a security will depend on anticipated and unanticipated changes in the economy. Anticipated events will be incorporated into asset prices. We know that industrial production, for example, fluctuates, and we can measure the sensitivity of asset returns to industrial production. What happens if industrial production is unexpectedly low? Companies with a high sensitivity to changes in industrial production will probably do poorly, and this will affect the return earned on their shares. The CAPM views risk in terms of an asset's sensitivity to market returns. The APT views risk in terms of sensitivity to unanticipated changes in major factors.

Systematic and Unsystematic Risk

Let's go through the analysis in more detail, using a stock as an example. We will use X-traordinary.com, a new Internet stock (we apologize if there is such a company). On the basis of fundamental analysis, we can come up with a return expectation for X-traordinary.com shares in the next month, year, or whatever. The actual return will hopefully reflect our expectations, but probably not exactly. That's because the actual return will contain a risky component that reflects information we didn't expect. For example, the chancellor may put a special tax on telephone calls, gross national product (GNP) figures may be unexpectedly bad, inflation prospects may worsen, and the tabloids may report that the company chairman formerly owned, and appeared on, a pornographic website. The actual return for X-traordinary.com in the next month can be expressed as:

Actual return = expected return + unexpected return

or:

Actual return = expected return + surprise.

The unexpected part of the return, the surprise, is the risk of the investment. If we got what we expected, there would be no risk. If we view risk in this way, we can divide it into two parts, systematic and unsystematic (or idiosyncratic). Systematic risk is risk that affects nearly all assets (e.g. poor GNP figures), whereas unsystematic risk affects only one or a few assets (e.g. our newspaper exposé). We can rewrite X-traordinary.com's return as:

Actual return = expected return + systematic risk + unsystematic risk.

The unsystematic risk should not be correlated with the unsystematic risk of another, unrelated share. It might be weakly correlated for shares in the same industry. Systematic risks are likely to be correlated, and therefore total returns are likely to be correlated. A surprise in GNP is likely to affect nearly all firms. The sensitivity of a share to a systematic risk factor can be measured by using a beta coefficient. This coefficient may be large or small, positive or negative. For example, better-than-expected GNP may have a positive effect on an upmarket department store chain, but a negative effect on a chain of thrift shops.

Let's assume that the five factors listed earlier are the true systematic risk factors (we will discuss whether they are later). Then the actual return for X-traordinary.com will be:

Actual return = expected return + β_1(unexpected inflation) + β_2(unexpected business cycle) + β_3(unexpected investor confidence) + β_4(unexpected time horizon) + β_5(unexpected market timing) + unsystematic risk

where the first and last terms on the right-hand side are as before, and the other five terms are the systematic risks. β_1 is the inflation beta, β_2 the business cycle beta, etc. This equation is a five-factor model. The nature and importance or otherwise of the systematic factors is determined by the structure of the economy. The betas tell us how sensitive a particular asset is to these factors.

How would we use this? Imagine we were looking at the one-year return, and we knew the betas to have the following values: $\beta_1 = 2$, $\beta_2 = 1$, $\beta_3 = -1$, $\beta_4 = 1.5$, and $\beta_5 = 2$. Say we expected 5% inflation but it turned out to be 3%. The surprise would be 2%. Surprises can be calculated for the other factors in the same way: we will assume the surprises for the other factors were 1%, 2%, 3% and –4%, respectivevly. From this information, we can calculate the systematic risk portion of return:

$$= (2 \times 2\%) + (1 \times 1\%) + (-1 \times 2\%) + (1.5 \times 3\%) + (2 \times -4\%) = -0.5\%.$$

If we assume we had expected a return of 10%, and we had a favourable unsystematic contribution of 2%, then the return from all components will be made up as follows:

$$\text{Return} = 10\% + (-0.5\%) + 2\% = 11.5\%.$$

The analysis so far has been for a single security. Let's now look at a portfolio. The return on a portfolio is the weighted average of the returns of the individual assets. In the factor model, we have seen that an asset's return is subject to systematic and unsystematic risk. However, if the unsystematic risks of different assets are not correlated, when we construct a widely diversified portfolio, the negative unsystematic risks should offset the positive. In other words, the unsystematic risk should be diversified away. Accordingly:

Portfolio return = expected return + β_1(unexpected inflation) +
β_2(unexpected business cycle) + β_3(unexpected investor confidence) + β_4(unexpected time horizon) + β_5(unexpected market timing).

If we continue to believe (from Chapter 2) that investors are risk-averse, they will seek to avoid unnecessary risk and will want to hold well-diversified portfolios. An investor planning to add an asset to a portfolio will consider that asset's contribution to the portfolio's risk and return. Only systematic risk need be considered when assessing the risk of a well-diversified portfolio. Accordingly, only systematic risk will affect return.

The Role of Arbitrage

In Figure 4.1, we have plotted expected return for an asset or portfolio against its beta for one of the factors. The line cuts the vertical axis where beta is zero. A zero beta means the asset has no exposure to risk factor x, i.e. it is risk free. In

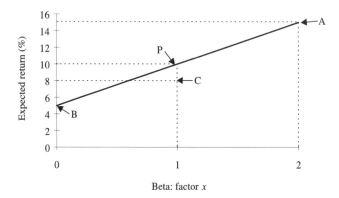

FIGURE 4.1   Expected return and factor exposure

this chart, then, the risk-free rate of return is 5%. How steep the line is will show how much influence the factor has on return—the steeper the line, the greater the influence. Asset A has an expected return of 15%, and B has an expected return of 5%. We'll come back to C and P shortly.

How can we be sure that returns and risks really will be related in the manner shown? The theory makes no assumptions about investors making mean-variance decisions. The theory does, however, assume arbitrage is possible and this will ensure a linear relationship between factor risks and rewards. The theory assumes that two securities with the same sensitivity to economic factors will offer the same return in the same way that two shares of the same company sell at the same price. If this were not the case, an investor could earn a risk-free profit.

We saw in Chapter 3 that the CAPM made a number of assumptions. APT also makes a number of assumptions, including:

- short selling (i.e. selling securities you don't own) is unrestricted and the cash proceeds are available;
- there are no transaction costs;
- there are numerous securities so that idiosyncratic risk can be diversified away.

Given these assumptions, we can examine the role of arbitrage. Because there are a number of factors, and securities can have a different sensitivity to each, it is easy to get lost in the algebra, or multidimensional geometry, of arbitrage. We will assume a simpler situation. Imagine three assets that have different betas for factor x and zero betas on all other factors. We will work with Figure 4.1; in Table 4.1, we show the data underlying the diagram.

TABLE 4.1 Asset factors and factor betas

	Asset A	Asset B	Asset C
Expected return (%)	15	5	8
Factor beta	2	0	1

If we construct a portfolio (P) divided evenly between assets A and B, then our portfolio beta will be the weighted average of the two betas:

$$(0.5 \times 0) + (0.5 \times 2) = 1$$

while the expected return will be the weighted average of the two returns:

$$(0.5 \times 5\%) + (0.5 \times 15\%) = 10\%.$$

In other words, we have constructed an asset P with the same beta as asset C but a higher return. If we assume that two assets with the same risk characteristics must offer the same return, arbitrage will take place, with C being sold and P being bought. No net investment is being made and there is no change in risk, but there is a better return. This is the proverbial free lunch. If we assume that the transactions don't affect the risk-free rate, then the price of A is forced up and that of C down. This will continue until P has the same return as share C. This will happen if, for example, C is priced to offer a return of 9% and A to offer 13%, because P's return is now:

$$(0.5 \times 5\%) + (0.5 \times 13\%) = 9\% = C's\ return.$$

The beta/returns of the assets now plot as a straight line, and no profitable arbitrage opportunities exist. Strictly speaking, then, the theory assumes not that arbitrage is possible but that in equilibrium there are no arbitrage possibilities.

In the above example, we ended with the risk-free rate at 5%, and an asset with a beta of 1, returning 9%. The market price of risk for the factor being discussed is 4% (9% – 5%)—it's the extra return you get for bearing one unit of the factor risk. If an asset has a beta of 2 for this factor, its expected return will be 5% + (4% × 2) = 13%.

We can generalize the above argument. The expected return on any asset depends on the asset's sensitivity to unanticipated movements in major economic factors. Specifically:

APT expected return = risk-free rate + β_1(market price of risk for factor 1)
+ β_2(market price of risk for factor 2) + . . . +
β_n(market price of risk for factor n).

To provide an example, we will return to the five factors mentioned earlier, explain how they are defined, and then compute an expected return. The following definitions are taken from Burmeister et al. (1997). Remember that this is not the formal theory of APT that is being discussed but one group's application of it.

An Arbitrage Pricing Theory Expected Return Example

We begin with the five factors and how they are measured.

Inflation Risk

Inflation rates are estimated at the start of a month from historical inflation rates, interest rates, etc. Unanticipated inflation is the difference between the start-of-month forecast rate and the end-of-month actual. Most shares have a negative exposure to inflation risk, so a positive surprise (higher inflation) has a negative contribution to return. Industries selling 'necessities' are least sensitive to inflation risk, and industries selling 'luxuries' most sensitive to the squeeze on real income produced by higher inflation. Asset-based industries, such as real estate, may benefit from higher inflation.

Business Cycle Risk

Business cycle risk is the risk of unanticipated changes in the level of real business activity. As with inflation above, a start-of-month and end-of-month comparison is made. If activity is better than expected, then shares positively exposed to business cycle risk will outperform. For example, retailers would be expected to outperform utilities.

Confidence Risk

Corporate bonds offer higher yields to redemption than do government bonds, reflecting their greater risk. (Bonds are discussed in Chapter 18.) Corporate bonds in turn range from relatively secure bonds (e.g. those of blue-chip companies) to relatively risky bonds (e.g. those of leveraged buy-outs). The spread between risky bonds and government bonds varies; it is narrower when investors are confident, and wider when they are not. Confidence risk is defined by Burmeister et al. (1997) as the unanticipated changes in investors' willingness to undertake risky investments, and measured by whether 20-year maturity risky bonds yield more or less than their average spread over government bonds. If the spread is narrower, then investors are confident and securities positively exposed to this risk will rise in value. Most shares are positively exposed, with small shares having the greatest exposure.

Time Horizon

Short and long interest rates are used to measure time-horizon risk, the risk of unanticipated changes in investors' desired time to payout. The current spread between the return on 30-day government bills and 20-year bonds is compared with the historical spread. If the spread is narrower, then 20-year bonds return less than usual over short rates, which means investors are prepared to wait longer for their returns. Shares positively exposed to time-horizon risk will rise in price (decreasing their future returns). In this situation, growth stocks will benefit more than income stocks.

Market Timing Risk

This is calculated as that part of the S&P 500 return that is not explained by the above four factors and the intercept. Almost all stocks have a positive exposure to this factor.

Expected Return

The econometrics of estimating the APT equation are beyond the scope of this book. We can assume away the problem by suggesting use of a software package, such as BIRR® Risks and Returns Analyzer® (http://www.birr.com). Imagine we have estimated the data shown in Table 4.2. If we assume a 6% risk-free rate (e.g. the rate on 30-day government bills), we can calculate the expected return for the market using the APT equation above. Expected return is:

$$6\% + (0.3 \times 2.5\%) + (0.5 \times -0.5\%) + (-0.5 \times -4\%) + (2 \times 1.5\%) + (1 \times 3.5\%) = 15\%.$$

Imagine we construct a portfolio that has the same exposure to risk factors as the market with one exception, we have an inflation exposure of 1. We can replace the term $(0.3 \times 2.5\%)$ in the previous calculation with $(1 \times 2.5\%)$. The difference between the two—$(0.7 \times 2.5\%) = 1.75\%$—is the amount we expect to earn above the index for bearing more inflation risk than the index.

TABLE 4.2 Risk exposure and price of risk for a market index

Risk factor	Index exposure (betas)	Price of risk (%/year)
Inflation	0.3	2.5
Business cycle	0.5	−0.5
Investor confidence	−0.5	−4.0
Time horizon	2.0	1.5
Market timing	1.0	3.5

MAKING THE THEORY OPERATIONAL

APT does not specify the systematic factors that are priced, thus to make the theory operational we need to determine the factors. We have seen one group's empirical factors. But, in general, how do we determine the factors? There have been two approaches. One is purely empirical; the other uses explicitly defined factors. We can call these 'unspecified factor tests' and 'specified factor tests', respectively.

Unspecified Factor Tests

Unspecified factor tests use two groups of statistical techniques, known as factor analysis and principal components analysis. These techniques have been used a lot in psychology and market research, but less often in economics. There are many versions of these techniques, but all are complex. (A simple introduction is given by Kritzman, 1993). The basic procedure is to take many observations of returns for many securities and then find groups of stocks whose returns are highly correlated with each other but not with stocks outside the group. This procedure should identify a few underlying factors that explain returns. Once a set of factors has been obtained, regression analysis is used to determine how returns are related to the factors. Those factors with statistically significant coefficients are 'priced', i.e. they affect returns.

Roll and Ross (1980), in an early study using factor analysis, examined the US equity market for the period 1962–72. Factor analysis is computationally demanding, so they split their sample into 42 subsamples of 30 stocks each. The number of factors varied with each subsample, but they concluded that there were at least three, but no more than four, common factors affecting returns. Subsequent US studies using factor analysis found different numbers of priced factors: anywhere from one to six factors have been reported.

There are many problems with the above approach. One is that the number of factors discovered may be dependent on the sample size. That would not really be surprising—presumably there are industry- and firm-specific factors and, as the sample size increases, more of these will be included. But that is not the same as saying these factors are priced. The number of factors that actually affect returns may not depend on sample size (e.g. see Dhrymes et al., 1985; Roll and Ross, 1984; and Ross, 1985.)

Principal components analysis has been used by a number of researchers, and up to five factors have been found, although one factor often dominates the returns.

Both factor analysis and principal components analysis produce factors that are simply statistical groupings—they are not identified as real economic variables, although the pattern of correlations may suggest which economic variables the factors represent. A way of avoiding this problem is to use the second approach to identifying factors: pre-specify economic factors that are likely to be relevant and see if they are rewarded.

Pre-specified Factor Tests

How might one pre-specify likely common factors? One approach would be to deduce some factors from economic and financial theory. Taking this tack, an obvious starting point is the dividend discount model (discussed in Chapter 10). Chen et al. (1986) specified a number of variables that would appear relevant on this basis, i.e. factors that could affect the discount rate or expected cash flows. For the period 1958–84, they found for the US, that the following variables were priced:

- changes in industrial production;
- changes in the risk premium (the difference between long-term government bond yields and corporate bonds rated Baa and under);
- changes in the term structure (i.e. the difference between long-term and short-term government bond yields);
- measures of unanticipated inflation and changes in expected inflation.

Chen et al. (1986) specifically tested for whether the market portfolio was priced: it wasn't.

A number of other researchers have used pre-specified variables, and while the US results vary a bit in each study, the general stability of the results appears to suggest that this is the better approach.

TESTING THE ARBITRAGE PRICING THEORY

A major problem with APT is that it has few hypotheses that can be rejected. The theory does not specify factors, neither the number nor their identities. When APT is made operational, the researcher is testing simultaneously that the statistical techniques used are appropriate, that the true factors have been found, that the unanticipated factor change is measured correctly, and that the factors are priced as the theory asserts. There are two ways of testing the theory. First, one can estimate the return relationship and consider the appropriateness of the factors, but this does not seem very scientific. Alternatively, one can see if APT can account for features of the financial markets that cannot be explained by the CAPM. A short summing-up of the US results of such tests is that APT shows promise of being able to help explain small-firm, January and other apparently anomalous effects that we shall discuss in this book. In the UK, the position is a little less promising.

Diacogiannis (1986), for the period 1956–81, found that the number of factors he identified varied as the size of the group changed, and that for the same groups examined at different periods, the number of factors again changed. He felt that APT could not be used for making predictions. Abeysekera and Mahajan (1987) found that over the period 1971–82 the risk premia for the factors they identified were not significantly different from zero. Beenstock and Chan (1986; 1988) measured UK common factors by both the unspecified and pre-specified approaches. In their factor analysis, they found 20 factors. In their pre-specified analysis, they used 11 variables and found that the data (for October 1977–December 1983) suggested a four-factor model. The risk factors were an interest rate, fuel and materials costs, the money supply and inflation. Poon and Taylor (1991) attempted to test the applicability of the Chen et al. (1986) study to the UK. For the period 1965–84, Poon and Taylor concluded that the macroeconomic factors that Chen et al. claimed affected returns in the US did not affect UK returns in the same way.

Before discussing some more recent UK studies, we need to return to the theory. Ross assumes that unsystematic risks are not correlated. But we know some must be. An announcement by the health minister on tobacco advertising will affect all tobacco companies, but it is not a systematic risk for the whole economy. If we assume an exact factor structure (i.e. no correlation between unsystematic risks), then we are forced to treat this industry-specific risk as pervasive. If we assume an approximate factor structure, then we can recognize that the unsystematic risks may be modestly correlated, but still accept that only systematic risks are priced.

Clare et al. (1997) used UK data for the period 1978–90. They used an estimation technique that assumed an exact factor structure, and found that no risk factors were priced. When they used an estimation procedure that allowed an approximate factor structure, they found five macroeconomic variables to be priced: a proxy for default risk (the difference between debenture yields and a long gilt), the RPI, the yield on debentures and loan stock, bank lending, and the return on the market portfolio. Clearly, the estimation method affects the results obtained. The results in the study that best support the APT are derived from assumptions that are at odds with the APT. Note too, that Baron et al. (1995) had reported eight priced factors for the UK.

Garrett and Priestly (1997) produced evidence of correlation of unsystematic risk amongst UK shares and again found that with an exact factor structure no factors were priced, and with an approximate structure a number of factors were priced—four were priced at the usual 5% level of significance and a further two at 10%. There was an overlap in the factors priced by Clare et al. (1997), but also some differences.

Antoniou et al. (1998) find stability of the UK return-generating process from one sample to another. In the first sample (69 shares), they find six factors that are priced. They pre-specify these in the second sample, and find five are significant. Two of these, however, have a change in sign. They explain that two outlier shares (i.e. shares that have extreme values compared with other shares) cause this. If the effects of the outliers are removed, then the three factors that are common to both samples explain a high percentage of variation in security returns. This, the authors suggest, shows stability in the return-generating process. It does if you can throw out results you don't like after inspecting the results: but how would you know what to discard in advance? Second, the two samples are taken from the same time period—the stability most investors would be interested in is whether results obtained in this time period apply to the next time period.

Where does that leave us? It is hard to say. There is something inherently unsatisfactory about factor analysis. And while pre-specified factors may seem more appealing, the results have unrealistic levels of significance because of the data mining that has gone on and is unreported. For the UK, different researchers find different factors, the factors appear unstable, and between zero and 20 factors have been reported. APT may be true, but there is scant evidence in the UK that the systematic risk factors can be identified. If APT has a role in fund management, the risk factors would have to be calculated continuously (e.g. monthly) and it should be expected that the factors would change over time, or at least change in importance. With that less than ringing endorsement, let's briefly look at how the theory could be used.

APPLYING THE ARBITRAGE PRICING THEORY

There are a number of ways of applying APT. In the same way as an expected return for a stock can be calculated using CAPM's security market line and the stock's beta, so a return for a stock can be calculated based on its exposure to various factors. It's harder to draw a diagram because several factors are involved. But the basic idea is the same. If, based on a fund manager's estimates, perhaps obtained by a dividend discount model (see Chapter 10), the stock appears to offer more than the theory says it should, then it is a buy; if less, it is a sell.

The CAPM and the arbitrage pricing model can produce quite different expected returns. An example of this is shown in Table 4.3, based on estimates derived from an 815 US stock sample for the period 1970–79 that was then used to forecast returns for a 17-stock hold-out sample.

TABLE 4.3 CAPM and APT estimates of expected return

Company	CAPM (%)	APT (%)
American Broadcasting Company	21.5	14.3
American Hospital Supply	22.9	12.8
Baxter Travenol Laboratories	21.0	11.6
CBS	18.2	13.9
Chris Craft Industries	22.2	17.1
Cook International	16.7	20.2
Ipco Corporation	29.3	32.7
Matrix Corporation	24.7	25.3
Metromedia	22.9	19.2
Napco Industries	22.6	16.4
Parker Pen	21.7	22.6
Rollins	24.3	16.2
SBS Technologies	21.7	22.3
Storer Broadcasting	20.4	15.4
Taft Broadcasting	25.2	21.1
Teleprompter	36.0	28.4
Western Union	19.1	10.8
Average	23.0	18.8
Standard deviation	4.43	6.05

Source: Bower et al. (1984, p. 38).

APT would normally be used with the emphasis on factor weightings rather than individual stock selection. For example, a fund manager might have ranked stocks' expected performance in quintiles (1 = best, 5 = worst). If he buys the 'best of the best', he may select a portfolio that has a factor exposure quite different to that of the market index. He might use APT to select stocks from his quintiles 1 and 2 so that he maintains the same exposure to risk factors as the market index.

Another approach would be to take an active tactical bet. If investors thought they could forecast a surprise in a particular factor better than other investors, for example better than expected industrial production, they could construct a portfolio that had high exposure to that one factor and a market exposure to the other factors. In this use of the model, the investors are not buying mispriced stocks. The stocks should be properly priced for their exposure to a particular risk. What the investors are doing is attempting to be rewarded for their ability to forecast which risks are worth bearing.

A second tactical factor approach is based on the fact that the market index may not be an efficient portfolio with regard to factor risks and returns. The strategy would be to calculate the return per unit of risk for each factor and construct a portfolio that is loaded up relative to the index on higher return factors. It is debatable that this approach can be said to be genuinely producing superior performance. All that is happening is that bigger risks are being borne for bigger returns. The APT is an equilibrium theory—this means that investors get paid returns commensurate with the risks they bear—there are no free lunches. This strategy seems to be based on performance-measurement deficiencies.

A strategic way of using factor bets would be to ask whether the institution owning the portfolio is itself affected by any of the factor risks. If it is, it could be worth tilting the portfolio exposure to that factor to have an appropriate offsetting effect. For example, a pension fund may require its income to rise when inflation is high. It should hold a portfolio that has a high sensitivity to inflation. It may or may not earn more than the market, but if inflation soars, it will achieve its strategic objective.

APT can also be used to construct a passive portfolio (see Chapters 6 and 17) and in performance measurement (Chapter 25).

CONCLUDING COMMENTS

APT is an equilibrium theory of security prices. It makes different assumptions to the CAPM, and the market portfolio has no special status in the analysis. A distinction is made between systematic and unsystematic risk. The latter can be diversified away and should not be rewarded. Systematic risk factors have pervasive effects. These risk factors are left unspecified by the theory. If investors engage in arbitrage, the equilibrium expected return for a security will be a linear function of its sensitivities to the factors.

Attempts to determine the factors have been made using both unspecified factor techniques (using factor analysis and principal components analysis) and pre-specified factors. Results in the UK have been generally disappointing. The number of factors, and what they are, varies with each study. As many as 20 factors have been found, and as few as none. If APT estimates were reliable, then they could be used in fund management in a number of ways. APT has not set the fund-management industry alight. The best known practitioners of APT are Roll and Ross Asset Management, which began in 1986. They currently manage portfolios in Brazilian, Dutch, French, Japanese and US equities, as well as internationally diversified equities.

Most investors probably believe that risk has many sources. Ad hoc multifactor models are discussed in Chapter 17.

5

Behavioural Finance

> We are for deletion of the deductive method of Ricardo: that is to say of deduction
> from unverified assumptions . . . but we are not against deduction from verified gener-
> alizations and principles.
>
> T.E. Cliffe Leslie

Many readers will have been unhappy with the previous chapters. Some will not
have liked the theoretical nature of the discussions. Well, theories tend to be
abstract and theories are useful for organizing your thoughts. Other readers may
accept the need for theoretical discussion but argue that the particular theories
were poor theories, linked only tenuously to supporting evidence. We have some
sympathy for that view, but all we can do is set out what is currently available
and invite you to improve it. Some readers may respond to this by suggesting
that we start with some realistic assumptions. Real people don't optimize, maximize, and so on—we've been discussing how some abstract economic man might
invest, not how real investors do. Indeed, part of the analysis assumed that
investors make decisions consistent with the theories, and were doing so even
before the theories were set out. Given that two of the key figures won the Nobel
prize, and one published his theory in the *Journal of Economic Theory*, a journal
with a very unfavourable maths-to-jokes ratio, this all seems a bit improbable.

What we are encountering here is a long-standing dilemma in economic
theory—the trade-off between abstraction and realism. 'Unrealistic' assumptions are not always inferior to realistic assumptions in terms of predictive
usefulness. For example, sociologists and psychologists can tell us a great deal
about crime and criminals, but they are not necessarily better at offering advice
on how to control crime than an economist who simply believes that people
always act in a way to ensure that their benefits exceed their costs. The economists would calculate the benefit and costs in terms of their expected value, i.e.
the actual values times the probability of them occurring.

Most of us are law breakers at one time or another: nearly everybody exceeds
the speed limit sometimes. The probability of being caught isn't great, the penalty
for breaking the law is not very high in financial terms, and the social stigma of
being caught for speeding is low. The expected cost is therefore low. However,
once speed cameras are installed, the equation changes. The probability of being

caught is 100% if the camera has film. Most apparently don't, but drivers still stick to the speed limit because the expected costs of not doing so now exceed the benefits. Even without cameras, many people will change their behaviour after they have been convicted for speeding. This is because the costs begin to soar as repeated offences lead to loss of your driving licence and insurance problems.

The above example is trivial, but it does illustrate how a simple assumption can make correct predictions. Defenders of the assumption of rational maximizing investors not only have common sense on their side—people like to have more money than less—but claim that arbitrage will ensure that the rational outcomes will prevail. Even if most people are irrational, rational investors can be relied on to engage in arbitrage to force the rational outcome. We need to look at this in more detail.

THE ROLE OF ARBITRAGE

You will recall from Chapter 4 that arbitrage is the process of making a risk-free return by selling (buying) an asset that is too dear (cheap) and buying (selling) another asset with similar relevant characteristics that is correctly priced or is cheap (dear). As long as there are some arbitrageurs, prices can be forced to their 'correct' level even if many investors are irrational. That is what supporters of abstract assumptions claim. But there are a number of problems with this argument (see Shleifer and Vishny, 1977; and Thaler, 1999).

First, arbitrageurs don't hold a portfolio in the way a pension fund manager would. They don't have a stock of assets to sell from. Therefore, if an asset looks expensive, there must be a mechanism by which it can be sold short. Second, for prices to be forced to the correct level, only arbitrageurs can short, otherwise irrational investors might short the stock that the arbitrageurs think is cheap, leading to no change in price. Third, the true value of assets must be known at some period. Fourth, the arbitrageur must have a long time horizon. Fifth, there must be a good substitute for any asset. Sixth, the arbitrageurs must have sufficient financial resources.

Obviously, not all these conditions are satisfied in the real world. We will comment on some of them. Imagine that the UK equity market is overpriced. The market can be shorted via the derivatives markets (see Chapter 21). But what is there to hold that is a risk-free substitute for UK equities? Put differently, there is a 'wrong price' asset to sell, but what is the 'right price' equivalent asset to buy so that one is only exposed to the difference? For asset classes there will often be no good substitute, although within the class there may be (e.g. BP Amoco for Shell). We might therefore expect that prices within classes of assets will be closer to 'true' values than the price level of the class will be.

Arbitrageurs are also likely to have both finite and short time horizons. In the short run, cheap stocks/markets often get cheaper, and dear stocks/markets dearer. Even if the arbitrageur engages in a self-financing pair of transactions, when the trade moves against him, he will have to put up cash to maintain the position. The arbitrageur will need to have sufficient funds or lines of credit. Since the idea is not to make medium-term investments, the arbitrageur is unlikely to want to have an open or even a net investment for long, and banks will watch losing positions carefully. There is a danger that arbitrageurs will be forced to liquidate their positions at the worst possible time.

Imagine that 'value' stocks are currently cheap and 'growth' stocks dear. (These terms are discussed in Chapters 12 and 13.) Imagine that over the long term, value stocks outperform. An arbitrageur could put together a portfolio of value stocks and short a portfolio of growth stocks. The problem for an arbitrageur is that evidence of value stocks being cheap may take a long time to become clear, and sentiment may cause growth stocks to outperform for some years. Since there is no way to hedge against this sentiment, and since the time period for the arbitrage to work could be long, it is unlikely that arbitrageurs will become involved in this sort of trade.

Rarely will we know the true value of an equity. (On the assumption of no default, we can calculate the precise value of a bond.) But there are some stocks that are Siamese twins (see Froot and Dabora, 1999). The best known are the British/Dutch companies Shell/Royal Dutch and Unilever PLC/Unilever N.V. These companies resulted from mergers but both component companies continue in existence and are quoted. Profits and dividends are, however, merged and shared—in the case of the oil twins, there is a 60/40 ratio in favour of Royal Dutch—so that the British and Dutch quoted companies in each set of twins are nearly identical. They are not actually identical because of some minor points, because the British and Dutch tax the dividends differently, and because each company is subject to its national law. For example, when the UK had a prices and incomes policy, the British dividend payout was capped by legislation whereas the Dutch payout wasn't. (The unpaid portion was paid on the demise of the policy.) Nonetheless these shares are as close as one gets to perfect substitutes. The tax differential adversely affects UK companies and pension funds investing in Royal Dutch by 0.64% p.a. and 0.74% p.a., respectively, and favourably affects Dutch pension funds by 1.23% p.a.. There is no dividend tax effect on UK private investors, Dutch private investors and companies, or any class of US investor (until 1994 when pension funds got higher after-tax returns from Royal Dutch).

While the tax differentials may justify prices not being exactly in the ratio 60/40, it is hard to understand why the price has at times deviated by more than 30% from this ratio. Shell is one of the UK's biggest companies; Royal Dutch is one of the Netherlands's biggest companies, and it is also in the S&P 500. If arbitrage could be so ineffectual for several years on these companies, how much faith in arbitrage forcing rational prices should we have?

THE PSYCHOLOGY OF INVESTMENT

If we expect arbitrage to have a limited role, then it becomes an empirical issue as to whether having more realistic assumptions will improve financial theory. There are three branches of psychology that might be useful in suggesting how real people behave: cognitive psychology, social psychology and social-cognitive psychology. Cognitive psychology deals with issues such as how we acquire and remember information, how we process that information, and how we make judgements and decisions. Social psychology studies individual behaviour in a social context. Social-cognitive psychology puts cognitive psychology in a social context.

Cognitive Psychology

Cognitive psychology has a variety of implications for investors and academics. Some are fundamental to the investment management process, while some re-late more to clients and consultants.

Investment decisions are made in conditions in which we don't know what the outcomes will be. Because we have a history of asset returns, and experience of how various factors relate to different investments, we can 'play the odds'. Put this way, an obvious way to study how people make decisions in conditions of uncertainty is to offer samples of people a variety of gambles with known odds and known monetary outcomes. For ease of explanation, we can divide our discussion into three parts. First, do people specify the odds and outcomes correctly? Second, do people treat probabilities as decision weights? Third, does money equal value? We'll treat these questions in reverse order. We draw heavily on Kahneman and Tversky (1984) and Tversky and Kahneman (1974; 1981); see also Kahneman and Riepe (1998).

The Value Function

In Chapter 2 we said that people were risk-averse. This is the classic economic assumption that was set out in 1738 by Bernoulli. Bernoulli noted that if you offered someone a sure £8000, say, or an alternative of an 85% chance of winning £10 000 and a 15% chance of winning nothing, usually the sure thing was taken. However the expected value of the alternative is $(0.85 \times £10\,000) + (0.15 \times £0) = £8500$. Ber-noulli's explanation of why people select the lower sum is that monetary value is not the same as the subjective utility, or value, to a person. If we assume diminishing marginal utility, then the benefit we get from each extra pound (£) is less than from the previous one. Thus the extra utility of going from £1000 to £1100, is less than going from £100 to £200. Going back to the wager, we conclude that the subjective value of £8000 is worth more than 85% of £10 000, and we assume that although the higher expected monetary sum has been rejected, the higher expected utility or value has been accepted.

This analysis is usually conducted in terms of changes in total wealth. Kahne-man and Tversky believe that thinking in terms of gains and losses is more apt, and they suggest a value function such as is shown in Figure 5.1. In the bottom half of the diagram, the value curve is closer to the vertical axis than is the curve in the top half. What this means is that if you mark off on the utility axis equal

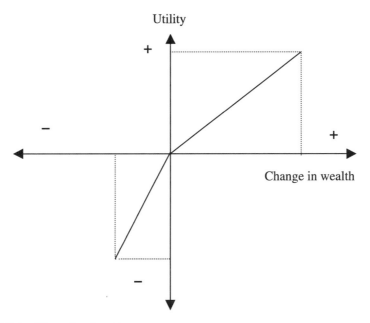

FIGURE 5.1   The value function

sums of utility on either side of the vertical axis, and then read off the corresponding changes in wealth figures, you see that it takes a much bigger gain in
wealth to offset the pain of a loss of wealth. We have used straight lines for the
value function, but Kahneman and Tversky provide a more complex shape, with
the top line bending down and the bottom line flaring out to the left. The effect
of this is that the value of a loss of £200 compared with a loss of £100 is greater
than the loss of £1100 compared with a loss of £1000.

The shape of the curve in the bottom half of Figure 5.1 has the implication that
when losses are involved, people will become risk-seeking. You don't believe it?
Would you rather lose a sure £8000 or take a gamble that involves an 85%
chance of a loss of £10 000 and a 15% chance of no loss? Most people take the
gamble, although the expected loss is £8500 versus the sure loss of £8000.

This analysis suggests we behave differently depending on whether we are in the
top or bottom half of the curve. Circumstances will dictate which half we are in. Or
will they? Consider the following problem. Imagine you are at the start of 2000,
when there is a flu mini-epidemic. Imagine 600 people are expected to die. Two
vaccines are available, but neither is 100% effective. If you administer vaccine ABC
to all vulnerable people, 200 will be saved. For vaccine EFG, on the other hand,
there is a one-in-three chance it might save all 600, but there is a two-in-three chance
that nobody will be saved. Before you read on, which vaccine would you use?

In France they also face a flu mini-epidemic. If they use their vaccine PQR,
400 people will die. If they use vaccine XYZ, there is a one-in-three chance
nobody will die, and a two-in-three chance that 600 will die. Which vaccine
should the French use?

Most readers will have opted for ABC and XYZ. But if you examine the options carefully, you will see that ABC and PQR are identical, as are EFG and XYZ. Most people make inconsistent choices. The reason is that the identical problems were framed differently. In the UK problem, everything is in terms of lives saved, i.e. gains. In the French problem everything is in terms of deaths, i.e. losses. This leads most people to answer the UK problem in terms of the top half of the diagram—risk-averse—and to answer the French problem in terms of the bottom half of the diagram—risk-seeking.

This analysis is empirically well founded. So how might we use it in investment analysis?

Investment Applications

First, the value function shown in Figure 5.1 is not symmetrical with regards to gains and losses. Losses really hurt. You might need a gain of £1000 to offset the hurt of a loss of £400. Accordingly, a standard deviation of returns does not really capture risk—losses are not simply gains with negative signs. Using standard deviation as a measure of risk is better than nothing, but there is probably a better measure.

Second, as we shall see in Chapter 24 many academics argue that the excess return that equities have historically offered over bonds seems too high. Equities are risky, but not as risky as the rewards seem to imply. Prospect theory suggests a solution to this equity risk premium problem. We discuss this solution in Chapter 24, but in essence, if we weight possible losses at 2.5 × possible gains, a much higher return is required from equities than would appear necessary at first sight.

For a third application, imagine two investors, A and B, who both bought the same share but at different times. A paid £1; B paid £2. Yesterday the price was £1.60, but today it falls to £1.50. Who is most upset? The economist's answer is that both are upset equally. Past costs are irrelevant—both had a £1.60 asset yesterday and both have a £1.50 asset today. Non-economists say B will be most upset. Both investors will think in terms of their purchase price. By this measure, A has given up a bit of his gain but is still in the top half of the value function, but B has suffered increased losses and is in the bottom half.

An implication of prospect theory is that if an investor holds an asset that has gone up and one that has gone down, and he has to raise cash, he will sell the winner. He will be risk-averse for his winner, and risk-seeking for the loser. This behaviour contradicts traditional market advice—run your winners, cut your losses.

Barber and Odean (1999) used data from 10 000 accounts at a US brokerage firm over the period 1987–93. They found that investors sold a higher percentage of their winning stocks compared with their losing stocks. They explained their results in terms of prospect theory. They looked at alternative explanations but rejected them. One rejected explanation was that losing stocks are held because they are expected to bounce back. While this couldn't be tested directly, an *ex post* test was made. The return from winners that were sold over the following year was 3.4% more than for losers not sold. In other words, if investors expected a bounce back, they were mistaken.

Probabilities as Decision Weights

In the traditional expected value model, probabilities act as decision weights and the expected value is a linear function of the probabilities. Thus if we imagine a value of £100 and odds of 0%, 30% and 95%, the expected values are £0, £30 and £95. If we now increase all these probabilities by 5% to 5%, 35% and 100%, the expected values are £5, £35 and £100. Unfortunately, this is not how people appear to treat decision weights. Moving from zero probability to a small probability, or from a high probability to certainty, are given higher weights than equivalent percentage changes in the middle range of probabilities. Low probabilities are overweighted, and high probabilities underweighted. The effect is that people are often risk-seeking when gains are unlikely, and risk-averse when losses are unlikely. If offered £10 or a 1% chance in a lottery with a prize of £1000, most people select the lottery—they overweight the low probability of winning. If offered a 99% chance of winning £1000, most people will pay more than £10 to change the odds to 100%—they are underweighting the high probability of winning.

Investment Applications

These findings might have implications for derivatives markets (Shiller, 1999). Relative to a rational pricing model, such as the Black–Scholes model (see Chapter 21), deep out-of-the-money and deep in-the-money options in the major markets appear to be overpriced. Near-the-money options appear to be priced correctly. These pricing errors appear consistent with the distortion of probabilities discussed. But other explanations are possible, including other behavioural theories; see, for example, Shefrin (1999).

Odds and Outcomes

In the previous section, we considered how known probabilities are treated. But are investors good at determining the true odds of the various outcomes they foresee? Tversky and Kahneman (1974) pull together some of the relevant literature. In assessing probabilities, people use a few heuristics, which are short-cut methods that simplify the judgement required. Three heuristics are representativeness, availability, and adjustment and anchoring. These heuristics are useful, but can mislead and produce consistent errors.

Representativeness

When faced with questions of the type 'What is the probability of A belonging to class B?', people often rely on the degree to which A resembles B. Is a short, slim person who likes to read more likely to be a professor or a van driver? The description (partially) resembles our image of professors. But there are many times more van drivers than professors, so it may well be the former. The obvious answer ignored the prior probability of each outcome.

Decision makers also make errors in terms of ignoring sample size (small samples are less reliable than large), overstating the predictive value of relationships, failing to allow for regression to the mean (the tendency for extreme outcomes to be followed by outcomes closer to the average), and so on. In general, people don't seem to understand chance. For example, most people expect a random pattern to be apparent in the total data and in every bit of it. Thus a coin sequence of H-T-H-T-H-T is seen as random, but H-H-H-T-T-T is not (H = heads, T = tails). A random pattern will include many short runs and a few long runs. What most people think of as random is not random, but involves negative serial correlation (negative correlation between succeeding observations).

Availability

Often people assess the frequency of an outcome by its availability, or how readily examples can be brought to mind. While frequently occurring events will be more available, so too will more familiar events, or very vivid events. For example, people who experienced the stockmarket crash of 1987 are more likely to think of market crashes than students who look at statistics on market movements.

Is superior investment management common? Well, unless you've been reading some dreary performance data, you probably can't name any poor managers. But we have all read endless articles on Peter Lynch, George Soros and Warren Buffett. We probably think superior management is more common than it is: ease of retrievability will bias judgements. So, too, will the method of search. For example, in words of three letters or more, is the letter k more commonly found as the first letter of a word, or as the third? We can easily list words beginning with k, but it is harder to think of words with k as the third letter. So although most people select the first letter, it is actually the third.

People often see two events as happening together more often than they really do. Even if they counted the number of common occurrences correctly, they would probably still draw the wrong conclusion. People often see correlations where none exist. To assess whether two variables are positively correlated, say share yield and performance, we need to look at four combinations: high score and good performance (+,+), low score and bad performance (–,–), high score and bad performance (+,–) and low score and good performance (–,+). The first two combinations support a positive correlation, the other two don't. Various studies (e.g. Smedslund, 1963) find that people tend to base their decision solely on the +,+ outcome, i.e. they look for confirmation.

Adjustment and Anchoring

Often an estimate is made by taking an initial value (e.g. last year's profits) and adjusting it. The estimate will thus depend on the initial value—the estimate is anchored to it—and adjustments are typically insufficient.

Anchoring is seen in many guises. Here is a test that you can take. Taking no longer than five seconds, estimate the value of the following:

$$8 \times 7 \times 6 \times 5 \times 4 \times 3 \times 2 \times 1$$

Would your answer have been different if the calculation was the following?

$$1 \times 2 \times 3 \times 4 \times 5 \times 6 \times 7 \times 8$$

One study found the median answer for the first was 2250 and 512 for the second. This demonstrates anchoring. Adjustment was also insufficient: the correct answer is actually 40 320.

Investment Applications

We noted that most people see a short run in data and assume that it can't be random. This shows up in various ways. Many investors see chart patterns and immediately assume the charts are saying something. Sometimes they might be, but if random numbers are plotted, patterns appear too, and these have no meaning. Again, if a manager outperforms for a couple of years in succession, and can tell a good story, many clients will be only too willing to believe they have found a good manager. This is partly because they don't understand that short runs are consistent with random outcomes and partly because, as we shall see, people don't like explanations that involve chance.

At the start of 2000, Internet stocks were hot. Everybody knew that: it was in the press constantly. Internet stocks represented the class of winning stocks. In January 2000, Blakes Clothing announced it was to receive a capital injection and become an Internet business. The price rose 1700% in a day and a firm with prospective assets of £3 million was valued at £220 million. Here the prior probability had gone out of the window. This was a small start-up: most fail. The management was unproven. Few businesses can transform every £1 of capital into assets worth about £75. Although the Internet may be a huge hit, most Internet stocks are likely to end up worthless. For example, in the US there were nearly 1000 car manufacturers in the 1920s. Nearly all went bust. And, finally, this wasn't even an Internet company, it just said it would be. Sell!

Social-Cognitive Psychology

We will look at two issues—overconfidence and faulty explanations.

Overconfidence

In a review of the social psychological perspective on mental health, Taylor and Brown (1988, p. 197) found that '. . . normal individuals possess unrealistically positive views of themselves, an exaggerated belief in their ability to control their environment, and a view of the future that maintains that their future will be far better than the average person's.' In general, people are affected by overconfidence.

We are overconfident in the accuracy of our judgments and abilities. For example, most car drivers see themselves as more skilful and less risky than the average driver (Svenson, 1981). One study of car drivers (Preston and Harris, 1965) found that a group of 50 drivers who had been involved in accidents that resulted in hospitalization still saw themselves as more skilful than the average driver. Police records indicated that 34 of the 50 had been responsible for the accident and the 50 had a higher frequency of prior traffic violations than average. In a different type of study, Oskamp (1965) asked psychologists to make personality judgements based on case study information. Their confidence in the correctness of their judgements soared as more data were given, but the confidence was out of proportion to the actual correctness of the decisions.

You might expect that events would soon show us that we were unduly confident in our abilities. However, we are protected by the attribution error (discussed in the next section) and the hindsight bias—the false belief held by people who know the outcome of an event that they would have predicted the outcome. In its simplest form, the hindsight bias can be demonstrated by giving outcome information to one group and not to another, and asking both groups to estimate the probability of various possible outcomes, without using knowledge of actual outcomes. The group with actual knowledge of the outcome will assign that outcome with a higher probability, despite claiming not to have used the information (Fischoff, 1975). In another study, Fischoff and Beyth (1975) had subjects estimate the probability of various outcomes occurring as a result of President Nixon's visits to Peking and Moscow in 1972. After the event took place, the subjects were asked to give the probabilities for the various outcomes that they had before the event occurred. The subjects made the actual outcome, or what they thought to be the actual outcome, more probable than they had before the event.

It would appear that when we add new information, we cannot go back to the old information. It's like adding ink to water: once done, the two are irretrievably mixed. The reason we can't avoid the hindsight effect is that knowing the outcome inhibits thinking about alternatives.

Investment Application

It would be odd if overconfidence and hindsight bias did not affect money managers and private investors. When we look at the turnover in financial markets, it is hard to believe that there is enough superior information to justify all the trading that takes place. It seems possible that overconfidence leads investors to trade too much relative to the value of their information. We might test this by computing the returns from stocks bought versus stocks sold. Barber and Odean (1999), for the sample discussed earlier, found that over horizons of four months, one year and two years, sells outperformed buys. Trading a lot is bad for your wealth. When investors were ranked by turnover by Barber and

Odean, the households in the top turnover quintile earned a net annualized geometric mean return of 11.4% while those in the bottom quintile earned 18.5%.

These findings don't directly connect confidence with turnover. To do this, the authors selected subsamples of male and female investors. Men in general are more confident than women, although this is highly task dependent. However, men feel more competent than women in financial matters, so we can assume men are likely to be more overconfident than women in share dealing. For the samples, the men traded 45% more actively than the women: they also underperformed the women by about 1% p.a.

Random is Unreasonable

According to attribution theory, we tend to attribute actions taken by people in terms of situational causes or dispositional causes, i.e. in terms of external or internal factors. In general, people strongly prefer to attribute outcomes to people rather than situations—this has been described as the fundamental attribution error (Ross, 1977). Of course, when things go wrong for us, we explain the outcome in terms of the situation.

People find it hard to accept that outcomes may be random. Langer (1975) distinguishes between chance events and skill events. In a skill event, there is a causal link between behaviour and the outcome, while in the case of chance events it's just luck that determines the outcome. Do people recognize the distinction? Langer thought they didn't. Most people have a concept of a 'just world' that requires outcomes to be related to causes. When faced with chance, people often act as though it's controllable. When asked to throw a low number on a die, many people throw the die softly.

In tasks involving skill, people tend to prepare for the task, familiarize themselves with the activity, practise, think of strategies, and so on. Langer set up a series of experiments involving purely chance events, but she encouraged or allowed the subjects to engage in skill behaviours. By doing so, Langer expected to induce a skill orientation, or an illusion of control. In one experiment, lottery tickets were sold in two offices. The tickets cost a dollar and the prize was to be the total sum raised, which participants were told would be about $50. Half the purchasers were simply given a ticket, whereas half selected their ticket (a 'skill' behaviour). The ticket seller then tried to buy tickets back on the grounds that somebody in the other office wanted into the lottery but there were no tickets left. The average price requested by those given a ticket was $1.96, but $8.67 by those who had selected their tickets.

Investment Applications

When investment managers get great results, they quickly tell you how good they are: it's me! But if the manager uses an investment style and gets poor results we hear, 'The poor results are to be expected as value stocks are out of favour by the market for the time being': it's the situation. But maybe it's chance. Managers are unlikely to see it that way; after all, they engage in skill behaviours. All the clients who use active managers presumably believe that active management can work. To prove it they can point to a firm that's hot. Moreover, when they select fund managers, they listen to presentations, interview managers, get briefings from consultants, and so on. They too engage in skill behaviours, so how could the outcome be random?

Social Psychology

One of the obvious features of social life is how much we conform. In fact we conform so often we usually don't have to think about it. At your first football match as a spectator you probably realized you should stand at the exciting bits, put your arms in the air for a goal, and go 'Ohhh!' at a missed goal. You can even do all this if you watch the game on TV in a pub. But if you watch a film in a cinema, you are not expected to stand up and cheer at the car chases.

Two types of conformity can be distinguished: 'informational social influence' and 'normative social influence' (Deutsch and Gerard, 1955). In the first, we accept a group's beliefs as providing true information. In the second, we don't have a change in beliefs, we just conform for the benefits of doing so.

One well-known study on conformity is by Sherif (1937). Subjects were seated alone in a dark room and told to stare at a pinpoint of light 15 feet away. They were then asked how far the light had been moved—it hadn't, but there is a perceptual illusion that the light moves. Three subjects gave estimates varying from about half an inch to seven and a half inches. The experiment was repeated, but this time the subjects were together and heard each other's responses. The estimates ranged from two inches to four inches. This was repeated twice more: the final estimates converged at a little over two inches. Was this convergence the result of normative or informational social influence? This was tested by conducting solo sessions instead of group sessions, but making the group norms available. The individual estimates continued to pull towards the group norms. Presumably the conformity was caused by what was perceived as information.

In another experiment, Asch (1951) sat seven men around a table and asked them to make various line comparisons. For example, a standard line was shown and then three comparison lines. Two of these might be shorter than the standard line and one the same length. The tests were constructed so that it was obvious which line matched the standard line. The subject sat in seat six, and the other six subjects were actually confederates of the experimenter. Each of the group gave his answer in turn. In the first two trials, all gave the correct answer. In 12 out of 16 subsequent trials, the confederates unanimously chose the wrong line. One-quarter of the subjects continued to give the correct answer, but about one-third gave the confederates' answer in half or more of the 12 trials.

It would seem from the experiment that normative influence is strong. Asch interviewed the subjects after the experiment. Some admitted they had not wanted to be different. Others claimed they had thought the others must be right, and their perception wrong. Of course, these subjects may not have told the truth, but if they did, it would appear that even in an unambiguous situation, people will perceive the views of others as carrying some information.

How does this relate to investment? We'll answer that after discussing cascades.

You may have experienced the following. You are on holiday in a strange town, and you are hungry. You set out to find a restaurant. You see one across the street that looks acceptable and head towards it. When you get to the restaurant you notice it is nearly empty. You stop, head down the street and find one that is full. You go in. Why? The answer is that you only get limited information from looking at a restaurant from the outside. One that is full, however, gives you information that a lot of people seem to like it. You conform to their behaviour because it has given you new information. The large difference in numbers in the restaurant is so conclusive that all rational followers will imitate their predecessors. They are in an informational cascade.

The cascade is based on little real information. Perhaps the busy restaurant got a head start by being half-full from one coach party. The outcome that has been reached is precarious. A change in coach party stops or a review in a tourist guide noting that the restaurant was the 'coach parties' favourite' might well end the restaurant's popularity. And note too that there is no deep logical reason for the restaurant's popularity—or at least no relevant reason: the owner could be the driver's brother-in-law.

Your choice of restaurant may well have been unwise. The non-coach-party people who went to the restaurant before you were in a cascade, and their actions were uninformative. Cascades can therefore lead to bad decisions, but new information can end them.

Cascade theorists (e.g. Hirshleifer, 1995; and Devenow and Welch, 1996) have applied this basic analysis (in a much more rigorous form) to a number of social trends and fads. They usually exclude the stockmarket from their analysis because the cost of conforming to other investors' behaviour, i.e. buying stocks, is not constant as prices rise as investors follow each other. But the cascade model can be modified to allow for this.

Investment Application

Where has all this led us? Rational economic man would always pay the right price for the equity market. But real people might not. If other people are buying the stockmarket, and we can detect this because the All-Share Index is rising, won't this make us adjust our view in a positive direction because we will perceive their actions as being informative? On Wall Street they say, 'Don't fight the [prices] tape,' and almost everywhere somebody will say, 'The trend is your friend.' Unlike Asch's subjects, some of whom were persuaded to change their view even when the answer was self-evident, investors deciding on the correct level of the market face an inherently complex problem. And some investors—professional fund managers—may follow the crowd because of normative social influence: it's better to be wrong with the crowd and keep your job. The cascades argument suggests market swings could be started on the basis of very little real information and suddenly end.

If one reasons in this way, then it becomes at least possible that the level of the equity market will vary too much relative to a rational model. And this is what Shiller (1981) found, as we discuss in Chapter 22.

CONCLUDING COMMENTS

If arbitrage is easy, a few rational investors might be able to force assets to the 'fair price'. But there are reasons to believe that arbitrage will often fail to do this. In that case, how individuals make decisions may affect how securities are priced. There is a large behavioural literature. Some of it relates to fundamental theoretical issues, some explains the behaviour of investors more than the behaviour of prices. Some of the literature is bad science. Academics pull a finding or concept out of a psychology text and then find some investment issue it seems to explain. But this is not much of a test: the procedure is known as 'exampling not sampling'. We think the literature is, nonetheless, worth following. Fama (1998) does not: indeed, it seems to confirm his belief in efficient markets, a concept discussed in the next chapter. This reminds us of another finding from a dip in the psychology texts. People find it hard to change their beliefs. This is because new evidence tends to be processed according to existing beliefs, or mental sets (e.g. see Russell and Jones, 1980). Indeed, when contradictory evidence exists, as occurs in the investment literature, original views may be reinforced. For example, Lord et al. (1979) set up an experiment in which people holding views for or against capital punishment were shown one study supporting their view and one that didn't. The experimenters found that the subjects believed the study supporting their view but not the other. The result was that both sides ended up feeling their views had been reinforced. Thus, where evidence is unlikely to be decisive, additional evidence may not narrow disagreement.

6

The Efficient Market

Clearly the price considered most likely by the market is the true current price; if the market judged otherwise, it would quote not this price but another price higher or lower.

Louis Bachelier

The efficient market theory (EMT) states that security prices fully reflect all available information. This theory has been subjected to much research and analysis, and has been a major source of disagreement between academics and practitioners. The practitioners have tended to resist the theory while the academics have forcefully promoted it. Before we see why the theory has been so divisive, we should make a link with Chapters 3–5.

For the CAPM or the multifactor APT to be true, markets must be efficient. Recall points A and B in Figure 3.4 that were not on the security market line. We assumed that buyers and sellers would quickly step in to force the stocks onto the line. If that did not happen, the line would not describe the market trade-off between risk and return. There would, in fact, be no consistent relationship between risk and return. Asset-pricing models need the EMT. However, the notion of an efficient market is not affected by whether any particular asset-pricing theory is true. If investors preferred stocks with high unsystematic risk, that would be fine: as long as all information was immediately reflected in prices, the EMT theory would be true.

EFFICIENT MARKET THEORY: A PROBLEM FOR SOMEONE

Although the EMT can be stated simply as in the first line of this chapter, academics debate the exact specification of the theory (e.g. Ball, 1989). Nonetheless, for the purposes of this book, we need not get involved in the debate. The above definition will suffice, or the more operational version that says that all prices reflect all information up to the point where the benefits of acting on the information equal the costs of collecting it. Prior to the 1950s, it was believed that traditional investment analysis could be used to outperform the stockmarket. In the 1950s studies began to appear (e.g. Kendall, 1953) that suggested that changes in security prices followed a random pattern. This generated theorizing and research that led to the efficient market notion. (There had been earlier empirical studies pointing in the same direction, e.g. Bachelier, 1900, but these studies had been ignored.)

How could price changes have no pattern? The answer is obvious—once we have been told. If we assume that people who play the market are keen to make money, we should expect them to grab every potentially profitable opportunity. The moment there is a chance to make money they will act, and prices will rise or fall in response to their purchases and sales, and stocks will then be priced so that there is no opportunity to make further profits. Stocks will be priced at their intrinsic value. This does not mean all stocks have to offer the same expected return—investors may well want additional returns for bearing extra risks—just that stocks will be priced at whatever seems the proper price allowing for risk.

For this model to work well, there will have to be an abundant flow of information, prices will have to respond quickly to changes in information, investors will have to make rational decisions, and it must be possible to deal easily, frequently and cheaply. Now we might argue as to exactly what 'rational' means, but in general all these conditions seem to be met by the typical modern stockmarket.

Because of our assumptions, it would seem that stock prices should fully reflect all available information. Of course, when new information comes along, prices may well change. For news to be news, it must be independent of earlier items. Thus, rational profit-maximizing investors will have driven all prices to a level that reflects available information, and they will react to all pieces of news. Since the new information will arrive randomly, the percentage price changes should be random. Stock prices thus might be expected to take a random walk. If the market is inefficient, there may be patterns to share prices. For example, at the time of writing Internet stocks are at very high valuations. Either they are correctly anticipating an extraordinary growth in earnings, or they have overreacted and soared past fair value. In that case, prices will eventually fall. The pattern then would have been a series of price increases followed by a series of price decreases. Now imagine a small, regional company that is not researched by major brokers. It may announce unexpectedly good profit figures and good prospects. The share price may take some time to reflect the company's results and prospects. In this case, the price will steadily increase until fair value is reached.

An interesting paradox in the concept of an efficient market was quickly noted. Analysts make the market efficient, but as a result there is no benefit from any piece of research because it is instantly reflected in market prices. It is not worth undertaking information gathering. Yet, if all the analysts left the profession, prices would become inefficient and there would be scope for research to add value. Slightly more formally, if markets are fully efficient, then prices will adjust instantaneously to new information. Therefore, no trades will take place and it will not be worth collecting information. Accordingly, a market can only be efficient if some people (often described as noise traders) believe that it is not efficient and trade on something other than new information. Moreover, the market must be sufficiently inefficient to allow informed traders to recover their costs of collecting information or none would be collected (see Grossman and Stiglitz, 1980).

In a famous review of the literature, Fama (1970) divided work on the efficient market into three increasingly wide categories depending on the information assumed to be impounded in prices. In the weak-form hypothesis, security prices reflect all security market information including all past prices, volumes, etc. In the semi-strong hypothesis, all publicly available information is reflected in security prices. In the strong-form hypothesis, all public and private information (i.e. information not generally available, such as that company executives might possess about their companies) is impounded in prices.

Version of theory	Information impounded in prices
Weak form	Past prices of securities
Semi-strong form	All publicly available information
Strong form	All public and private information

Most practitioners disputed the theory when it was first proposed. Chartists (see Chapter 15) look at past prices to deduce what will happen to future prices. This approach can have no value according to the weak-form EMT. Fundamental research (i.e. research on economic and financial factors) fares no better if the semi-strong hypothesis is correct. Now for the extremely well-paid security analysts, fund managers and brokers' salespeople, this is pretty threatening stuff. But it would be awkward for the academics if the EMT was shown to be false. After all, the EMT is little more than the spelling out of the consequences of the behaviour of a competitive market. As Marsh and Merton (1986, p. 484) have noted:

> To reject the Efficient Market Hypothesis for the whole stock market . . . implies broadly that production decisions based on stock prices will lead to inefficient capital allocations. More generally, if the application of rational expectations theory to the virtually 'ideal' conditions provided by the stock market fails, then what confidence can economists have in its application to other areas of economics where there is not a large central market with continuously quoted prices, where entry to its use is not free, and where shortsales are not feasible transactions?

STARTS WELL . . .

At an empirical level, the efficient market school seemed to win the argument at first, not so much because the evidence was overpowering but more because there was persuasive evidence that went against the then prevailing belief that charts and sound fundamental analysis were self-evidently useful. The general academic view appeared to be that the weak-form hypothesis was true, the semi-strong form was mainly true, and the strong form probably was not.

The evidence was never quite as strong as it appeared. Some of the early evidence suggested inefficiencies, but not once transaction costs were allowed for. One problem with this is that transactions' costs depend partly on the investor's circumstances. If investors have to buy equities simply because they have new cash flow or because they have sold bonds to go into equities, then they will suffer transaction costs. These are inescapable and would be involved if they bought the market as a whole. For such investors, pre-transaction cost outperformance is relevant. Of course, if the strategy involves endless turnover, then transaction costs will consume profits. For market makers, who have negligible dealing costs, even a strategy that required frequent transactions might be consistent with market inefficiency. Nonetheless, the economic value of the inefficiencies noted in early studies was usually modest.

With regard to the evidence relating to technical analysis, it is probably fair to say that technical analysis was not rejected by numerous specific tests. Rather, the argument took the form that academics could not find patterns in past prices and technical analysts used past prices, therefore technical analysis was wrong. Further, technical analysts did not present any evidence to support their approach. However, not all studies found random price patterns. For example, an early UK study by Kemp and Reid (1971) concluded that share price movements were 'conspicuously non-random' over the period they studied (28 October 1968–10 January 1969).

With regard to the semi-strong version, the evidence generally showed that a specific event was fully in the price and the market had anticipated this over a period of some months or years. For example, Fama et al. (1969) found that abnormal returns accrued to stocks that had a share split for a period of two years before the split, but returns were normal after the split. Stock splits probably follow good news and a rising share price, hence the rising returns before the split. By the time the split occurs, all the good news is in the price. But, one may ask, once the market latches onto something, why does it take a couple years to be fully impounded in the price? Is such evidence for or against the theory?

Even though questions could be raised about the meaning of some of the studies, any reasonable person would have to have conceded that the evidence was sufficiently strong that the onus was now on investors to prove any claim that they could outperform the market. It appeared that the market was reasonably efficient, information was quickly incorporated into prices, and there was little in the way of evidence that suggested that there were more fund managers with good records than chance alone might allow. Indeed, some academics gave the impression that about all that could be said for fund management was that it was an indoor job that paid well and involved no heavy lifting.

. . . SECOND THOUGHTS

From the late 1970s onwards, numerous studies have appeared that suggest that the market is less than perfectly efficient. Fama (1991) reviewed the literature again. He again discussed the literature in three categories but he replaced weak-form efficiency with tests for return predictability, the semi-strong form with event studies and the strong form with tests of private information. The biggest change over the 20-year period since his first review has been the research on return predictability. In particular, there is now a huge literature on time-varying returns (e.g. are years of good returns likely to be followed by poor returns?) and cross-sectional returns (e.g. are stocks with low price-earnings ratios associated with high returns?). These studies appear to show that the market is much less efficient than the academics previously thought, although there is a problem of interpretation here.

To give an example, one finding that has been noted many times is that small market capitalization stocks have outperformed large ones over long periods, even after allowance for risk differences as measured by beta. One could say the studies refute the EMT. However, the standard practice of scientists is not to let go of an old theory that has served well until a new theory is available to take its place. In the meantime, the refuting evidence is labelled as an anomaly and is encompassed in rather ad hoc modifications to the old theory. It is hoped that the anomalies may eventually be shown to be mistaken or that a new theory will emerge. The process of ad hoc modifications seems an inevitable course in the case of the EMT because all tests are tests of a joint hypothesis. They test an asset-pricing theory at the same time as the efficient market hypothesis. How do we know that small stocks return 'too much'? Only by knowing what the right return is, and we know this through the application of an asset-pricing theory. It might turn out that many of the anomalies are not anomalies of the EMT at all, but are a result of deficient asset-pricing theories. For example, small stocks are more illiquid than large stocks. Maybe investors require an extra return for suffering illiquidity as well as bearing risk. In that case, the EMT need not be wrong, but the simple one-factor CAPM would be.

We are not going to review the evidence for and against the EMT here. Subsequent chapters discuss many of the most important studies in the context of investment management. But we will comment briefly on the state of the EMT. The theory seems to have gone through three stages. There has been a swing from believing that the market was inefficient to a decade in which the academics believed that it was efficient, at least in the weak form and semi-strong form. In the last 20 years, there has been a steady stream of reported anomalies or exceptions to market efficiency. There has also been research suggesting that the entire market can be grossly mispriced as it overreacts to events or gets caught up in fads or speculative bubbles. Does all this mean we should abandon the efficient market notion? Probably not. If investors can make a quick profit, presumably they will—it still seems that the basic economic model of self-interest will force the market towards efficiency. There is still a lot of evidence of efficiency or near-efficiency. And the evidence of inefficiencies is tricky to interpret because of the joint hypothesis problem. Nonetheless, academics have become more aware of the circumstances under which the EMT might not hold. As we shall see later, it may not hold where arbitrage is difficult. The evidence overall probably warrants the view that it is possible to beat the market but it will require some effort and organization to do so: possible, but hard.

IMPLICATIONS OF EFFICIENT MARKET THEORY FOR FUND MANAGERS

We now relate some of the above discussion and that of the previous chapters to the task of fund management. We assume that investors try to price stocks in some rational way based on their intrinsic value (which we discuss in more detail in Chapter 10). How do asset-pricing models relate to that valuation? The CAPM, for example, asserts that investors demand a higher expected return for bearing risk. The relevant risk for pricing securities is systematic risk and this can be measured by beta. In the process of deriving a stock's intrinsic value, investors will allow for its level of risk. The EMT asserts that all relevant information is impounded in prices. Profit-oriented investors will ensure that stocks are priced at their intrinsic value, after due allowance for risk.

The implications of the EMT are that:

- investors can't use public information to earn abnormal returns;
- new information that implies a change in intrinsic value will be acted upon quickly.

How much faith investors have in the EMT should determine their approach to managing investments. Funds may be managed passively or actively. A passive manager simply aims to match the return on some appropriate index, whereas an active manager aims to purchase mispriced securities and assets and thereby earn a positive abnormal rate of return. Passive managers assume that:

- the market does not misprice securities or assets; *or*
- the market does misprice securities and assets, but managers are not able to take advantage of the mispricing.

Passive managers will adopt a strategy of determining the appropriate strategic asset class allocation and then broadly diversifying within each asset class. This might be achieved via index funds, which are discussed in Chapter 17.

Active managers assume that:

- the market misprices securities and/or assets; *and*
- managers are able to recognize the mispricing.

Active managers may attempt to outperform by either or both of:

- security selection
- asset class selection.

Active managers can make three kinds of bets:

- *Information bet:* the active managers assume they have knowledge that no-body else has, e.g. they have better company profit forecasts, or that they can respond faster to new information.
- *Valuation bet:* the active managers assume that a security or asset class is mispriced on the basis of generally known information.
- *Factor bet:* active managers (and passive managers) can make a factor bet if there is a priced factor that earns an abnormal return, and the risks associated with that factor are not risks that affect the investor.

This last point needs spelling out. Academics typically try to explain away anomalies as a problem with the CAPM: they say that risk is not being measured correctly or should be broadened to include other factors, such as liquidity. Perhaps so, but investors should ask whether these factors matter to them. Even with the CAPM, an investor can earn more than the market, providing more risk is borne. If you don't mind risk, then bear it, and have the prospect of a higher return. Similarly, if small stocks enjoy a premium because of poor liquidity, and poor liquidity is not of concern to an investor, then the poor liquidity should be borne and the extra return enjoyed. Whether the extra returns are worth having depends on what matters to an investor.

Ibbotson (1989) gives a useful analogy:

> In assessing value, car buyers look first at the chronological age of a car, secondly at its condition . . . .. Thus an owner of a two-year-old car with 5000 miles would have a very hard time selling it as a nearly new car; it would be priced as a two-year-old car. Because of its low mileage, it might be priced at the high end of the range for two-year-old cars of that make and model, but it would be very cheap for a car with only 5000 miles on it.
>
> A buyer might regard this offering as expensive (compared with other two-year-old cars) or cheap (compared with other 5000 mile cars). When most buyers emphasize the car's age, then the clever buyer who appraises the car according to mileage gets a bargain. This example shows vividly that, depending on the scaling (age or mileage), the same good can be seen as cheap or expensive. Like our mispriced car, a stock might be seen as cheap on one scale and expensive on another.

The assumption of this book is that the market is not perfectly efficient, and investors are interested in more than risk and return, and it is possible to earn an abnormal return. Accordingly, we look at various strategies based on information, valuation and factor bets. We concentrate on bets that have yielded abnormal returns, although some popular strategies that do not appear to work are also discussed.

Believing that there are exploitable inefficiencies does not mean that we think it is easy to outperform. The market is 'reasonably' efficient. This suggests that if we are to base investment strategies on research findings that imply market inefficiency, we should always ask ourselves why a 'sure thing' way of making money survives. Why have other investors not snapped up the opportunity? If we think we can satisfactorily explain the existence of the opportunity, we should be more confident about acting on it. For example, most investments are managed not by their owners but by agents (fund managers) who may be controlled by other agents (e.g. trustees) acting for the owners. It may be that these agents will act in a different way than the ultimate owners might because the agents are mainly concerned with keeping their jobs. Performing well is part of that, but they may believe that they are less likely to be fired if they act in a way that conventional wisdom suggests is prudent.

Again, it is generally assumed that investors process information efficiently and are risk-averse. But what if human decision making has some consistent biases, or people are not always risk-averse? We saw some examples of biases and risk-seeking in Chapter 5.

Of course, in some cases we may note that anomalies have generated abnormal returns in the past but we cannot explain why. Some would argue that the anomalies may not be true and we should ignore them. Beware of quasi-academics bearing anomalies, as someone once put it. There is, however, an argument for acting on them anyway. If the anomalies are true, then one should be trading on them. If the anomalies are false, then the market is efficient. If the market is efficient, then the anomaly strategies will yield the risk-adjusted market rate of return. They cannot yield more but they cannot yield less either. If they did, they would give a negative signal and a consistent signal is not possible in an efficient market. Thus, an anomaly-based strategy dominates a random one: 'Heads you win; tails you tie' (Joy and Jones, 1986, p. 53.) Against this, one can argue that if you concentrate on one type of stock, your diversification must be poor and you are bearing unnecessary risk.

MEASURING THE MARKET

So far we have talked about the 'market' as though it were self-evident what the market is. Of course, there are many different markets—equities, bonds, properties, foreign exchange, and so on. Some markets may be efficient while others may not be. For example, because of the 'lumpiness' of property (usually you can't buy 1% of a shop freehold, for example) and because each property is unique (no two properties have the identical location), we might be sceptical that the property market will be efficient.

Let's concentrate just on equities. What exactly is the equity market and how do we measure it? The answer is that we define what we are interested in, and then calculate an index. This will give us a snapshot statistic that tells us whether the market as a whole is up or down, and by how much. The index also provides a benchmark for measuring the performance of a portfolio against. There are a number of ways that an index can be constructed; we examine them in the remainder of this chapter.

Different market indexes give different answers to how a market has performed over a given period. This is a consequence of differences in:

- *objectives:* some indexes attempt to measure the performance of the entire market and some just a part of it. In the UK, the FTSE All-Share attempts to measure the entire quoted share market whereas the FTSE 100 covers the largest 100 companies;
- *sample size:* a small sample will give a less reliable guide than a large sample. Many of the oldest indexes use quite small samples. This was because of the computational burden of a large sample, especially if the index was updated throughout the trading day. Nowadays, this is not an important consideration;
- *weighting:* there are a number of methods of weighting the sample members. The principal methods are price-weighted, capitalization-weighted and equal-weighted;
- *computational method:* some indexes use a geometric average, while others use an arithmetic average.

We will organize our discussion of actual indexes in terms of the weighting method they use.

Price-Weighted Indexes

The Dow Jones Industrial Average (DJIA), probably the best known index in the world, is price-weighted. The average was introduced on 26 May 1896 with 12 stocks: currently it consists of 30 actively traded major stocks, primarily industrials, but also including American Express, J.P. Morgan, and American Telephone and Telegraph (AT&T). The constituents, which change from time to time, represent around 20% of the market value of New York Stock Exchange stocks. Only General Electric survives from the original index. The DJIA stocks at the start of April 2000 are shown in Table 6.1.

The DJIA is calculated by adding the closing prices of the component stocks and using a divisor that is adjusted for splits and stock dividends equal to 10% or

TABLE 6.1   Constituents of Dow Jones Industrial Average as at April 2000

Allied Signal	Intel
Aluminum Co. of America	IBM
American Express	International Paper
AT&T	J.P. Morgan
Boeing	Johnson & Johnson
Caterpillar	McDonald's
Citigroup	Merck
Coca-Cola	Microsoft
DuPont	Minnesota Mining & Manufacturing
Eastman Kodak	Philip Morris
Exxon	Proctor & Gamble
General Electric	SBC Communications
General Motors	United Technologies
Hewlett-Packard	Walt Disney
Home Depot	Wal-Mart Stores

more of the market value of an issue, and for constituent substitutions and mergers. An example will make this clearer. Assume, for simplicity, there are only three stocks, X, Y and Z, trading at 100, 50 and 20, respectively.

Step 1: Calculate the starting date (1/1/1999) arithmetic average of current prices:

Company	Share price ($)
X	100
Y	50
Z	20
Total	170
Arithmetic average	56.67

Step 2: Set starting value of index, say 1000.

Step 3: Calculate an index divisor that makes the starting arithmetic average price equal 1000, i.e.

$$\text{Index divisor} = \frac{\text{average price}}{\text{index value}} = \frac{56.67}{1000} = 0.05667.$$

Step 4: Calculate the end date (31/12/1999) arithmetic average:

Company	Share price ($)
X	120
Y	60
Z	24
Total	204
Arithmetic average	68

Step 5: Calculate the index value:

$$\text{Index} = \frac{\text{average price}}{\text{index divisor}} = \frac{68}{0.05667} = 12.00$$

i.e. the index has risen by 20%.

Step 6: To allow for a change to an index constituent, assume that stock Z is removed from the index and stock A, with a price of 50, replaces it. Unless the divisor is changed, then the index will rise from 1200 to 1353, i.e. [(120 + 60 + 50)/3 = 76.67]/0.05667 = 1352.92. This makes no sense: we don't want the index to change simply because of a new constituent. We want 76.67 divided by an adjusted divisor to equal 1200, i.e.

$$\text{Adjusted index divisor} = \frac{\text{average price}}{\text{index value}} = \frac{76.67}{1200} = 0.06389.$$

Despite its fame, the DJIA is not a very good index. Thirty stocks is a small sample of the market, and more stocks would give a better picture. Secondly, the index will change by a different amount for equal percentage price changes, depending on the original price of the stock whose price is changing. In our example, each stock rose by 20%, as did the index. But imagine that X rises 40%, Y rises 20%, and Z is unchanged, i.e. the stocks rise by 20% on average. The arithmetic average in Step 4 above would now be 73.33, so the index would be 1294 (73.33/0.05667), or up 29.4%. Thirdly, there is no recognition that stocks have different market values, i.e. that some stocks are more important than others: capitalization-weighted indexes do recognize this.

The DJIA is not the only price-weighted index; for example, the Nikkei-Dow Jones Average is an arithmetic average of prices for 225 stocks on the First Section of the Tokyo Stock Exchange.

CAPITALIZATION-WEIGHTED INDEXES

A capitalization-weighted index is based on the initial total value of a sample of stocks. The market capitalization ('market-cap') of a stock is the number of shares in issue multiplied by the price of a share. The market capitalization of a sample of shares is simply the sum of the market-caps of all the shares in the sample. The advantage of 'cap-weighting' is that each company's influence on index performance is directly proportional to its relative market value. It is this characteristic that makes cap-weighted indexes the standard benchmark for measuring the performance of actual portfolios.

In the UK, the major index for measuring the whole market's performance is the FTSE All-Share Index.[1] This is an arithmetic, capitalization-weighted index consisting of nearly 800 companies. The basis of construction is best explained by an example, which, for simplicity, has only three stocks:

---

[1] The FTSE All-Share Index was previously called the FT-A All-Share Index, and many studies discussed in this book refer to the earlier name.

Step 1: Calculate the starting date (say, 1/1/1999) market-cap:

Company	Share price (£)	Shares in issue (m)	Market value (£m)
X	1.00	40	40.00
Y	1.50	15	22.50
Z	4.80	18	86.40
Total market value			148.90

Step 2: Set starting value of index, say 1000.

Step 3: Calculate the index divisor that makes starting market-cap = 1000, i.e.

$$\text{Index divisor} = \frac{\text{total market value}}{\text{index value}} = \frac{148.90}{1000} = 0.1489.$$

Step 4: Calculate the end date (say, 31/12/1999) market-cap:

Company	Share price (£)	Shares in issue (m)	Market value (£m)
X	1.20	40	48.00
Y	1.80	15	27.00
Z	3.84	18	69.12
Total market value			144.12

Step 5: Calculate index value:

$$\text{Index} = \frac{\text{total market value}}{\text{index value}} = \frac{144.12}{0.1489} = 967.9$$

i.e. the index has fallen by:

$$\frac{967.9 - 1000}{1000} \times 100 = -3.21\%.$$

Step 6: To allow for a change to an index constituent, follow Step 6 in the price-weighted index discussion above.

In the above example, two stocks rose by 20% and one fell by 20%. The index is down, however, because the stock that fell has a market-cap greater than the other two stocks combined.

The FTSE All-Share Index is one of a series of indexes constructed by the Financial Times, Institute and Faculty of Actuaries, and the Stock Exchange. These include:

- *FTSE 100 (the 'Footsie'):* consists of 100 largest companies and represents over 70% of the All-Share by market capitalization. It is constantly updated during the trading day;
- *FTSE 250:* the 250 shares below the FTSE 100 by market capitalization;
- *FTSE 350:* FTSE 100 plus FTSE 250;
- *FTSE SmallCap:* FTSE All-Share stocks, excluding largest 350.

In the US, the major broad cap-weighted index is the S&P 500 Composite Stock Price Index (S&P 500). It comprises 500 stocks that are traded on the New York Stock Exchange, American Stock Exchange and Nasdaq National Market. The stocks in the index are not the largest 500, but are chosen on the basis of:

- being a leading company in a leading industry;
- being a US company (except for non-US companies that have been in the index for decades);
- maintaining a representative sector—consumer cyclicals, healthcare, technology, etc.—balance;
- being an easily tradable stock;
- being fundamentally sound, because minimizing index turnover is important.

A broader US index is the Russell 1000, consisting of the largest 1000 stocks. The Russell 2000 consists of the stocks ranked 1001 through to 3000 in terms of market capitalization. The broadest US index is the Wilshire 5000, which is cap-weighted and consists of all regularly traded shares on the New York Stock Exchange, American Stock Exchange and Nasdaq, in total about 7100 stocks.

Finally, all international markets have a local index, but the construction methods vary. The FT/SP Actuaries World Indexes and the Morgan Stanley Capital International Indexes are arithmetic capitalization-weighted indexes that cover all the major international markets in a consistent manner.

EQUAL-WEIGHTED INDEXES

In an equal-weighted index, both market capitalization and price are ignored, and an equal notional amount of money is invested in each stock. Although this sounds bizarre, it is the equivalent of selecting stocks randomly. If you don't know whether the stock you will select is large or small, you might make an equal investment in each selection. Geometric or arithmetic averaging may be used. An example using geometric averaging follows.

Step 1: Calculate an index of the price change for each stock for a period:

	Share price		
Stock	1/1/1999	31/12/1999	Index of change
X	100	120	1.2
Y	8	10	1.25
Z	50	45	0.90

Step 2: Calculate the geometric mean:

$$\text{Geometric mean} = (1.2 \times 1.25 \times 0.9)^{1/3} - 1 = 0.1052.$$

Step 3: To calculate the new index, assume the previous index was 1000. The new index is $1000 \times 1.1052 = 1105.2$.

In the US, the Value Line Composite Average is an index based on the 1700 stocks covered in the Value Line Investment Survey. The index is calculated by taking daily price changes and geometrically averaging them. In the UK, the FT Ordinary Share Index (FT30) is a geometric average equal-weighted index. For many years, this was the standard UK benchmark, although it is quite hopeless for performance measurement purposes. First, the sample size of 30 shares is too small. Second, if any company becomes bankrupt, its price will be zero, which will mean the index falls to zero. Consequently, sick companies have to be removed from the index before their demise. Third, if there is variability in a series, the geometric mean is always lower than the arithmetic mean. This makes it an easy benchmark to beat.

CONCLUDING COMMENTS

The EMT states that security prices fully reflect all available information. The early evidence supported the theory, but evidence collected in the last 20 years has raised a number of doubts. There would appear to be a number of inefficiencies in markets that can be exploited to increase returns. These are discussed in this book. It is probably fair to describe security markets as nearly efficient. However, one has to be careful when there appear to be market inefficiencies. There is a difficulty in assessing evidence because testing the efficient market theory always involves a joint test of an asset-pricing model. Often a seeming refutation of the efficient market theory may instead be a refutation of the asset-pricing model used in the analysis. A sensible precaution is to try and explain why an apparent inefficiency persists. Sometimes one will conclude that it is the asset-pricing model that is at fault, but that is not without interest. Perhaps the factor that appears to be generating the extra return is not one that concerns the investor and so exposure to that factor should be accepted.

It makes sense for investors to try to outperform the market if they believe that markets are inefficient and that they can exploit the inefficiency. Most of this book is geared to such investors, who will make information, valuation or factor bets. Investors who believe either that the markets are efficient, or that they are inefficient but that investors are incapable of exploiting the inefficiency, should adopt a passive investment style and use index funds.

Whether you are trying to beat the market, or match it, a definition of the 'market' is needed. We examined the various ways market indexes have been constructed.

7

Introduction to Share and Sector Selection

They told me to buy this stock for my old age. It worked wonderfully. Within a week I was an old man.

Eddie Cantor

In the next 10 chapters, we look at ways of selecting shares and sectors within a stockmarket. As we saw in the last chapter, there are two broad approaches: passive and active. These two approaches are shown schematically in Figure 7.1.

Passive managers aim to match the performance of an index, whereas active managers aim to outperform an index. Passive managers have to decide which index to track, and how they will do this. There are four main operational approaches: full replication, stratified sampling, optimization and use of derivatives. Passive investing is discussed in Chapter 17.

There are two main approaches to active management: technical analysis and fundamental analysis. Technical analysis uses a variety of techniques such as analysing past share price movements, watching what supposedly knowledgeable investors are doing, taking contrary opinions, and so on. Technical analysis is discussed in Chapter 15.

With passive investment and technical analysis, it is possible to know nothing about the company whose shares you are buying or selling. Fundamental analysis, however, requires considerable knowledge. One of the classic texts of fundamental analysis is Graham and Dodd's *Security Analysis*, first published in 1934. It has been updated over the years, and the most recent edition is by Cottle, Murray and Block (1988). They argue (p. 8) that to make valuation judgements, an analyst must use a process that achieves:

- a true picture of a company as a going concern over a representative time span
- a carefully prepared estimate of current normal earning power
- a projection of future profitability and growth with an informed judgment as to the reliability of such expectations
- a translation of these conclusions into a valuation of the company . . .

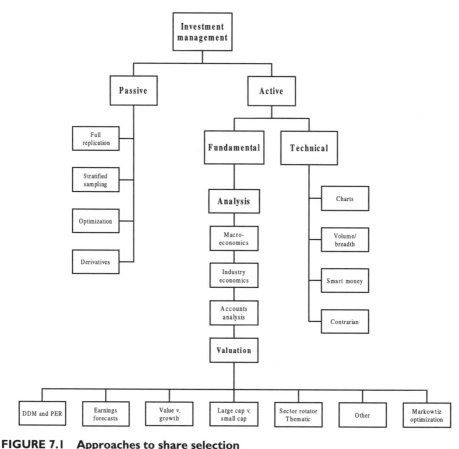

FIGURE 7.1 **Approaches to share selection**
(DDM, dividend discount model; PER, price-earnings ratio)

To achieve this an analyst will need to have economic forecasts for the economy and the industry the company is in, and detailed knowledge of the company's position within the industry. The analyst will also have to understand the financial statements of the company. The process is illustrated in Figure 7.1, and shown in greater detail in Figure 7.2. This approach is sometimes described as 'top-down'. Analysts who largely ignore the economy and focus on companies are sometimes said to have a 'bottom-up' approach. (Fund management houses that aren't quite sure what they do often say they use both approaches.)

Having acquired the necessary information, what does one do with it? How do we go from company information to valuing a share? The various approaches to selecting shares are usually described as investment styles. Some styles are shown in the bottom row of Figure 7.1. In reality, fund managers make much finer distinctions, for example:

- value;
- growth;

- small-cap;
- mid-cap;
- large-cap;
- small-cap value;
- mid-cap value;
- large-cap value;
- small-cap growth;
- mid-cap growth;
- large-cap growth;
- micro-cap (very small firms);
- income: seeks current income substantially above broad market yield;
- momentum: manager buys and sells on basis of rates of change of prices or earnings;
- earnings revisions: buying stocks for which analysts are revising their earnings forecasts upwards;
- core: manages fund to make only limited deviations (in terms of sectors, beta, PER, etc.) from a major market index, such as the FTSE All-Share or S&P 500;
- index;
- speciality: invests in narrow area, for example venture capital, biotechnology and technology;
- equity sector rotation: makes significant sector bets—shares could be selected by a variety of methods;
- thematic: overweight stocks that are beneficiaries from a theme, such as the 'greying population', the growth of the Internet, etc.;
- equity market timing: moves into or out of equities based on view of market direction. Equity exposure may be adjusted by transactions in stocks, futures or options;
- quantitative: uses formal quantitative model;
- eclectic: approach that doesn't fall into any of the above categories;
- style timing: changes selection approach systematically in belief that all selection approaches have predictable good and bad periods.

Most of these styles are discussed in Chapters 9–16, and Chapter 17 integrates some of the material in these chapters. Before we begin, it is useful to provide some general comments about the problems encountered in research on share selection techniques.

Although Figure 7.1 shows a clear distinction between technical and fundamental analysis, the distinction is actually somewhat blurred. Momentum share-selection approaches have been classified as technical analysis because they follow the technician's relative strength approach, and make no valuation judgement. But earnings-revision approaches have been classified as fundamental because analysis of earnings is at the heart of fundamental analysis, although earnings revisions do not involve valuation issues. Again, buying small-cap stocks is thought of as a fundamental approach to investing, but it does not

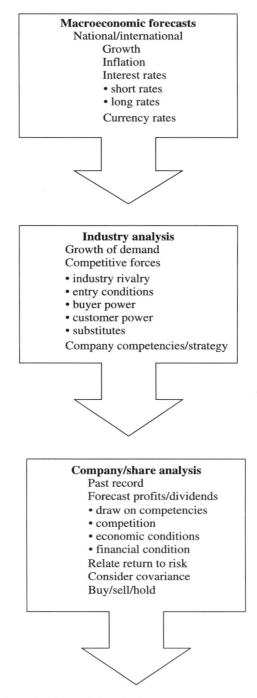

FIGURE 7.2   Top-down fundamental analysis

involve valuation. Nonetheless, we will discuss this approach as if it were fundamental analysis, mainly because the 'small-cap effect' is usually analysed in the
same way by academics as other fundamental factors are.

KEEPING SCORE

In the following chapters, we will look at some of the ways investors have tried
to beat the market. In assessing these attempts, there are a number of potential
pitfalls that should be avoided. These pitfalls are worth reviewing before we look
at any research. First, the pitfalls have not always been avoided in all published
studies and due allowance must be made. Second, they are seldom avoided in
the best-seller type of investment books, or in advertisements for financial products. Third, many investment managers play around with data on systems such
as Datastream and Bloomberg in the hope of spotting an investment system and
are often unaware of the methodological problems.

Omitting Dividends

Some studies simply compare stock price performance with a price index. With
this measure, any system that has a bias towards stocks with low yields, for
example one involving 'growth' stocks, will appear to be more successful than it is.

Transaction Costs

Many studies show good gross returns but neglect to consider transaction costs. This
may be noted and dismissed with a casual 'The profits indicated are so large that it is
clear that the system would be profitable after transaction costs.' Whether this is
true or not depends on how much trading is required and on the type of stocks being
traded. A few trades a year that cost 1–2% will soon consume abnormal profits, but
often the cost is much higher—some small UK stocks have bid–ask spreads of 10%.
With smaller companies, the true cost may well be in excess of some notional
calculation of commission, stamp duty and the usual spread. The stock may be so
illiquid that either the deal cannot be effected, or it can only be done over a period
or at a huge discount or premium to the apparent price.

Bid–Ask Bounce

US shares are quoted at the last traded price. This could be the bid price, the ask
price, or somewhere in between. If you measure the returns from thinly traded
shares with wide spreads over short periods, negative serial correlation may appear.
But this may simply be a result of a share bouncing between the bid and ask prices.

Time Period

Even relationships that have held up well over long periods don't necessarily hold true every year. Accordingly, studies that use very short time periods should be distrusted. For example, if you looked at the performance of UK small companies relative to large ones over the period 1986–88, you would find that small companies substantially outperformed. But if you took the period 1989–91, the following three years, you would find the opposite. Three years is too short a period to base a conclusion on.

Ex Post Selection Bias or Survivor Bias

If you have ever bought a stock that has gone bust, you may have dreaded the end-of-year newspapers that publish the 10 best- and worst-performing shares. Who needs reminding that they have bought one of the worst-performing shares in the market? But when you look at the list you find that the worst-performing share has lost 'only' 92% of its value, or some such number. What has happened is that the computer tape has removed stocks that have gone bust: they no longer exist and have no end-of-year price. This can pose a problem for researchers.

Consider a system of buying awful stocks, measured perhaps in terms of very high gearing, or three consecutive years of declining sales, or whatever. One could search a database and test this investment system. There is a good chance that it will seem to work. Bad firms are probably more likely to go bust or get turned around than other firms, i.e. they are likely to generate more extreme results, but the computer tape will have systematically excluded all the firms that have gone bust. There is a bias in the test in favour of the hypothesis.

Look-Ahead Bias

Many systems effectively require knowledge of the future. One form of look-ahead bias is involved if, say, one relates contemporaneous changes in variables when in fact one is not actually known at the time. For example, one might believe that the money supply affects the stockmarket. Thus, February's money supply might affect February's stockmarket levels. But the February money supply numbers are not known until March, so the model is only useful if one can forecast February money supply numbers.

Look-ahead bias affected some of the early studies of the low price-earnings effect. Computing price-earnings ratios with year-end prices and earnings assumes earnings information that is not available to investors for some months. This can create a bias. Banz and Breen (1986, p. 780) give an example:

> The annual COMPUSTAT file reports earnings of $1.24 per share for Zenith for year end 1978. The 12-month earnings per share actually observed by the investor as of

December 31, 1978 was $0.85 per share. At a December 31, 1978 price of $12.87, the earnings yield [i.e. (earnings per share/price) × 100] computed using the COMPUSTAT data file was 9.6%, whereas the earnings yield using observed data was 6.6%. As might be expected, the price of Zenith went from the year-end price of $12.87 to a March ending price (when the new earnings were known to investors) of $15.00.

Failure to Adjust for Risk

As we have discussed, it is generally thought that investors will only bear extra risk for extra reward, and risky assets are expected to produce higher returns than less risky assets. Accordingly, if an investment system selects risky assets it should only be considered a successful system if it produces returns greater than expected from a portfolio with an equivalent risk level. Recall that any test of an investment system that adjusts for risk is really a test of two things at once: the investment system, and the belief that risk is rewarded and the study is using the correct measure of risk. Academic studies have measured risk in a variety of ways, such as total risk, beta risk, and even unsystematic risk.

Misleading Graphs

Many a fund manager will show clients a graph of the close relationship between two variables of interest. And the client and fund manager will believe what they think they see. But the relationship may be poor, for most of us cannot read a graph correctly. The graph in Figure 7.3 shows two variables, bond yields and equity yields. There appears to be a relationship as both trend down together: when bond yields fall, so do equity yields, i.e. the equity market rises (assuming no dividend cuts). But could you make timing decisions based on this? Look closely. In four of the 10 years, the lines move in opposite directions: the relationship is less useful than it might have appeared. Anyway, this is the wrong

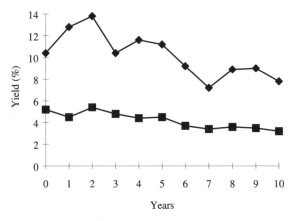

FIGURE 7.3 Bond and equity yields

comparison. The bond yield isn't available before the equity yield, so unless it is easier to forecast, it isn't very helpful. Of course, one could take last year's bond yield to forecast this year's equity yield. If this is done, the yields still move in the opposite direction in four periods. In general, it is changes that are of interest in forecasting returns, and many graphs of levels should be converted to graphs of changes to see the value of the relationship for timing or selection purposes.

Statistical and Practical Significance

Many academic investment studies report that their findings are statistically significant. What this means is that the finding is unlikely to be just a chance observation. For example, if we flip a coin 10 times, we may find that we observe six heads. That doesn't mean the coin has a bias. Even with a fair coin, there is a high probability that we will get six heads. In fact, the probability is so high that we would say that the finding was not statistically significant. It is usual to calculate the degree of statistical significance for research findings. Say we find two attributes of a stock are related to returns. The findings might be statistically significant at the 1% or 5% level. This means there is only a one in 100 or a one in 20 chance of the findings being the result of chance rather than being true findings. Our findings are statistically significant in the sense of probably being true, but they might not be of practical significance. For example, the finding might show us how to make an extra 0.25% a year. This is not of much practical significance. If, however, we could make 5% extra a year, that would be of practical significance. It is important to look to see that findings are of both statistical and practical significance.

Data-Mining

It is often not difficult to find a statistical relationship that fits a set of data reasonably well. But if one has no theoretical reason for the relationship, it may just be a chance finding. If you go to a party and study the other guests, you can probably find some odd feature about the group. Perhaps there is a large number of people whose names begin with B, or perhaps there is a disproportionate number of people with blue eyes. Because you've gone data-mining—you've mined the data until you struck a finding—you've probably found a statistical relationship that has no general validity. While the finding holds for this party, it won't necessarily hold for the next, even if the finding is statistically significant. The point is that if we check whether names beginning with, A, B, C, etc. are common, we are actually making 26 tests on the data. And if we also check for blue eyes, left-handedness, and so on, then the number of tests soars. Even if there is no relationship for any of these attributes, a 5% significance test means there is a one in 20 chance that an attribute will appear significant even if it isn't. If we randomly select enough attributes, some will falsely appear significant.

Academic researchers don't intend to go on data-mining expeditions but they almost certainly do. American researchers frequently use two databases, COMPUSTAT and that of the Center for Research in Security Prices (CRSP). If 100 researchers each test the same database for different investment hypotheses, a few will appear to be statistically significant based on chance. These findings may be published and the others will not. The problem is that we will never know how many other tested hypotheses failed. This is an important issue. For example, there is a large amount of literature on which part of the year produces the best returns. With no prior theoretical expectations, this is a topic ripe for data-mining and spurious relationships.

Out-of-Sample Data

A more subtle form of data mining is to take a well-accepted system and establish the decision rules for using it from one set of data and then calculate the returns from that system on the same data. It should work well—that's why the rule was chosen! One should always be sceptical of investment systems that are shown to work on the data that were used to construct the system. Accordingly, one should always look for an appraisal of a system made on data that were not used in the system's construction. This is usually called an out-of-sample or a hold-out test. Often researchers refuse to do this because they have only a small data set.

Misleading Predictive Power

A predictive relationship may be true, but weak: it may not explain much of the variation in returns. If, however, one is selecting a small number of stocks from a large universe, one may get good results even with a weak relationship. It may be possible to select a high-performance portfolio of 20 stocks from a universe of 1000. Quite a lot of studies use small portfolios. A fund manager who feels obliged to have a 50-stock portfolio and can only select from 400 blue-chip stocks may find the relationship to be of no value.

Hedge Studies

Sometimes studies are set up as hedge studies. You buy the best stocks and sell short the worst, so that you make no net investment. Often such studies show good returns. However, notice that this is really the previous problem made twice as bad. The researcher now gets to select twice from extreme observations. Most managers don't short stocks, so the returns from short positions are not especially interesting.

Equal Weighting Versus Capitalization Weighting

Many studies calculate returns on a equal-weighting basis, i.e. all stocks are treated equally in calculating returns. Say we select two samples of three stocks. The first sample's stocks return 12%, 13% and 29%. The second sample's stocks return 12%, 13% and 14%. On an equal-weighted basis, the first sample offers the highest return. But what if each stock has a market capitalization of £1 billion, except the one that returned 29%, which has a £5 million capitalization. Now which sample do you think has the higher return? Notice that an equal-weight strategy cannot be implemented by all investors. If we all put one-third of our portfolio into the smallest stock, it would no longer be the smallest stock.

Dating Events

The academic literature often makes heroic dating assumptions. Often large statistical studies simply assume that the event of interest took place on the last day of a month. If you are running tests on 50 years of data with 1000 stocks, you can imagine why it is done. The effect on the results is unclear.

Non-synchronous Trading

Imagine something happens that will clearly negatively affect the value of all shares. Perhaps the government decides to make a one-off tax charge of 20% on last year's company profits. Shares across the board should fall. However, not all shares will trade everyday. Therefore, while many shares will fall on the day of the announcement, some might not fall until the next day. What this means is that the fall on day one has an above-average chance of being repeated on day two, or, in jargon, prices are positively serially correlated. From this, one might deduce share trading decision rules. But the rules won't work, because the moment we try to trade, the price will change.

Unwarranted Generalization

Many academic studies exclude financial stocks from their sample because they claim, for example, that financial ratios of industrial and financial stocks are not comparable. The study then goes on to report that, say, stocks with low price-earnings ratios outperform those with high. But that only applies to the sample. Given that financials constitute over one-fifth of the UK market and about one-third of many European markets, it is a big step to generalize the study to the entire market.

Short-Term Clients

The UK firm Phillips and Drew Fund Management (PDFM) is one of the largest UK managers. PDFM is a value manager, and had very poor results for much of the 1990s when growth stocks performed well, and by some standards equity markets looked expensive. Before that, it had good results and won many accounts. In the second half of the 1990s, it lost accounts. What's this got to do with evaluating an investment system? The point is that many investment systems have good and bad periods. Over 20 years the system may work, but if it starts with five bad years, there may not be many clients sticking around to benefit from the next 15 years. Of course, if you are a client of 25 years standing, you may say, 'I've seen all this before, it will be OK.' But inevitably, firms with good records win clients after especially good periods, so a disproportionate number will begin with bad returns. Value investing may or may not be a good investment system, but theoretical returns will not necessarily be achieved by clients who don't stay the course. Investment systems need to be checked for their pattern of returns—for psychological reasons some systems may be hard to implement. Indeed this must be so. If it wasn't, everyone would invest in successful systems and they would cease to be successful.

CONCLUDING COMMENTS

In this chapter we have outlined the large number of methods that are used to select stocks. We classified the approaches as passive or active, and subdivided the latter into fundamental or technical. In the next 10 chapters we look at these approaches in more detail.

Do any of these approaches have value? We shall discuss this in subsequent chapters. Here we looked at a number of factors that should be taken into account when assessing claims of success for investment systems. It would be tedious to keep making these points every time we report a study so the reader should bear them in mind. We will, however, illustrate many of these problems in our discussion of some of the studies.

8

Economic Fundamentals

Economics is a subject that does not greatly respect one's wishes.

Nikita Khrushchev

In this chapter, we look at two different types of economics: macroeconomic forecasting and industrial economics. Macroeconomics is the economics of aggregates; it is concerned with the price level of the entire economy, the rate of growth of the economy, and so on.

It is beyond the scope of this book to teach economic forecasting. What we aim to do is provide some understanding of the basis of the numerous economic forecasts that investors will encounter. Macroeconomic forecasts are important for both company and industry studies, and therefore share selection, and also for decisions about which type of asset—for example, equities or bonds—to favour. Although this chapter falls in the share selection part of the book, it is also relevant for asset selection, and some of our comments relate to that.

Warren Buffett has argued that if you put managers with good reputations into industries with bad reputations it is the managers who lose their reputations. In forecasting the prospects for a firm, knowledge of its industry's dynamics is essential. Experienced analysts understand their industries, but often in a highly intuitive way. Inexperienced analysts may be aided by a formal industry model to structure their thoughts. The second half of this chapter summarizes some of the factors that industrial economists would consider when studying an industry.

FORECASTING THE ECONOMY

The stockmarket is intimately linked to the economy. Changes in GNP—the nation's income—impact firms' sales and prices, which in turn affect revenues, costs and profits. This feeds through to dividends and retained earnings. Changes in GNP affect the general price level and interest rates. Dividends, growth and interest rates are all factors in determining share prices. Understanding and forecasting changes in the economy might be expected to be important for anyone wishing to analyse the stockmarket, whether at the share level or the market as a whole.

Notice the qualifier 'might' in the previous sentence. There are two reasons for this. First, we would not expect an exact one-to-one correspondence between changes in the economy and changes in the level of the stockmarket or changes in the prices of individual shares, if only because investors try to anticipate the economy's moves. Thus, one has to forecast both the course of the economy and how much has been discounted by investors. Second, economic forecasting skills might be so poor that, in practice, and especially at the share level, there is no added value from forecasting.

Share analysts have to consider the state of the economy, asset allocators do not. For some investors, for example those whose liabilities lie far in the future and who are not worried by volatility, a policy of always being fully invested in an equity index fund would be an option that ignores economic conditions.

Despite these cautionary comments, a great deal of effort is made in the financial markets to forecast the economy. It therefore seems worth spending a few pages on the major forecasting methods.

There are five main forecasting methods:

- cyclical indicators
- survey data
- single-equation models
- structural econometric models
- vector autoregressive methods.

The poor record of forecasters a decade or so ago caused some heart searching and a shift in forecasting methods. Let's quickly run through the approaches.

Cyclical Indicators

Cyclical indicators, often called leading indicators, are used to forecast changes in GDP. They have been more popular in the US than the UK. The Office for National Statistics (ONS) published leading indicators for the UK until January 1997 when they were withdrawn and the resources used elsewhere in ONS. The idea of cyclical indicators is that as the economy passes through a business cycle—certain sequences are played out in roughly the same order as in previous cycles. Some events will lead the cycle, some will be coincident with the cycle, and some will lag it. The ONS cyclical indicators consisted of four composite indexes: longer leading, shorter leading, coincident and lagging. The theory of the indicators is set out in *Economic Trends*, numbers 257, 271 and 477.

The longer-leading composite index had the following component series:

- three-month rate of interest (inverted);
- financial surplus/deficit of industrial and commercial companies;

- dwelling starts;
- CBI quarterly survey: optimism balance;
- yield curve (inverted).

The shorting-leading index comprised:

- FTSE 500 index;
- change in consumer borrowing outstanding;
- new car registrations;
- EC/Gallup survey: consumer confidence index;
- CBI survey—new orders, past four months, balance.

The coincident composite index had the following component series:

- gross domestic produce (GDP) factor cost;
- output of production industries;
- index of volume of retail sales;
- CBI survey: below-capacity utilization (inverted);
- CBI survey: change in stocks of raw materials;
- M0 (a money supply measure) divided by GDP deflator.

The lagging index comprised the following component series:

- adult unemployment index (inverted);
- employment in manufacturing industries;
- investment in plant and machinery in manufacturing industries;
- level of stocks and work in progress, manufacturing industry;
- engineering orders on hand.

Notice the substantial use made of survey information. Notice also that a stock-market index is included in the leading indicators. We shall return to this later. Up until the time the indicators were dropped, the longer- and shorter-leading indicators led the economy by 10 and four months, respectively, and the lagging indicator lagged by 11 months. These numbers are median values; the range was very wide: the longer-leading indicator had lagged (sic) the cycle by two months and led by as much as 31 months.

We noted above that the shorter-leading indicator includes the stockmarket. There is obviously an element of circularity here—the indicators are used to forecast the economy to help forecast the stockmarket and yet the stockmarket is being used to forecast the economy. However, if use of the stockmarket index improved the cyclical indicators, then it would be pointless not to use this information. The stockmarket gives very noisy signals—prices jump around a lot—and using cyclical indicators provides additional information.

Since the indicators are no longer published, why mention them? There are three reasons. First, other countries publish leading indicators and they provide a painless forecasting aid for non-economists looking at overseas economic activity. Second, the notion of a leading indicator is a general one. The cyclical indicators are restricted to economic growth—for inflation, etc., one has to turn to other sources. In the US, there are some readily available leading indicators of inflation (e.g. see Cullity, 1987), and in both the UK and the US some stockbrokers have developed leading indicators for inflation. Third, many industry analysts use leading indicators specific to their industry to help them forecast.

Survey Data

As we have seen, survey data are included in the cyclical indicators. Survey data are important, if only because they are available sooner than other forms of data. There are many surveys available but the most useful is the CBI survey. Its data appear before more detailed government surveys, and it has a longer record than other surveys, which makes it easier to establish its statistical properties. The CBI's business optimism measure is particularly useful for forecasting changes in national income. A wide range of information relating to inflation, consumer behaviour and growth is provided. Non-economists will find press reports of the CBI surveys easy to assimilate. Other surveys covering exports, particular regions and other areas of special interest are reported in the press with varying degrees of coverage.

Probably the best of the US surveys is the National Association of Purchasing Management's *Report on Business*, which is widely followed. There is a UK sister organization that has been producing a comparable UK survey for a decade or so, the *Purchasing Managers' Report on Business*.

Structural Econometric Models

Most of the major UK stockbroking firms forecast the UK economy by means of a structural macroeconomic econometric model. A macroeconomic model is a simplified representation of the entire economy expressed in equation form; its goal is to forecast variables such as national output, inflation, and the balance of payments.

We can look at some of the issues involved in structural models by means of a simple example. If we view national income in terms of the nation's expenditures, we might define it as follows:

$$Y = C + G + I + X - M$$

i.e. national income (Y) is made up of consumer expenditure (C), plus government expenditure (G), plus business investment (I), plus exports (X), minus imports (M). To forecast Y, we need to know the value of all the other variables, which the econometrician will attempt to forecast by a series of equations. Consumption, for example, might be forecast by an equation that includes income and interest rates, i.e. we spend more when we have more income and interest rates are low. Most variables in a model will be endogenous, i.e. determined within the model, but some will be exogenous, i.e. determined outside the model. For example, in a model of the UK economy, the level of exports will be partly determined by the level of world trade, which will not be determined in the model but will be given a value assumed by the econometrician. Notice that in our example, income depends partly on consumption and consumption in turn depends partly on income. A model is much better at keeping track of these simultaneous interactions than a human forecaster. Econometric models vary as to the number of equations they contain, ranging from a handful to hundreds. These equations are all based on appropriate economic theory.

The structural econometric approach appears to be very scientific and disciplined, but is less so in practice. There are similarities with a Punch and Judy show. At first sight Mr Punch appears to act as he pleases, but one soon realizes that a guiding hand is involved. So too with econometricians and their models.

Although economic theory is used to guide the specification of the model, there are sometimes competing theories to choose from. Moreover, theory seldom specifies the exact form of the equation to be used or, if it is thought that some effects take place with a lag, the length of the lags. For example, will 1% off interest rates when they are 15% have the same effect on consumption as 1% off rates when they are 6%, and will you spend more immediately after a cut in rates has been made or will you wait a month or two? Usually the form of the equation and length of the lags is determined by playing with the data until the best fit is found. Behavioural equations (e.g. the consumption equation) will not provide an exact fit to the data, if only because not every relevant factor will be included in the equation. They will have a residual error term. Many theories involve expectations and it is unclear how these should be modelled. Usually expectations are assumed to be based on past and current values of a variable, e.g. expected inflation for 2002 will be low because it is now and has been in the recent past. But what would happen if there was a change in government? Would expectations be formed on past data then? After the problems discussed have been resolved, the next stage is to estimate the model. At this stage, some theoretically relevant variables may not appear to be statistically significant and may be dropped from the model. Lag structures may be altered. There is a back-and-forth process between theory and the data.

If the model has been completed to the econometrician's satisfaction, a forecast can be made. This will require some exogenous values to be inserted by the econometrician. When the econometrician makes a forecast, the result may turn out to be implausible. At that point, the econometrician may tamper with the model by changing the residuals to get a more plausible forecast. The published forecast of a model may well owe as much to the econometrician's interventions as to the model's structure.

Clearly, a great deal of work goes into building a structural econometric model. How good are the results? The general feeling is that they are not very good. Davies and Shah (1992) give a typical gloomy assessment (Davies was one of the UK chancellor's external advisers panel—the 'Seven Wise Men'). They argue that the models are fine when not much changes, but they cannot cope with big changes in the economic environment, such as oil price shocks and high inflation. They fail when they are most needed. This is because: (a) there is a large subjective element in model building, as we have seen; (b) the equation estimation is based on data that are frequently revised (i.e. the CSO publishes data that the econometrician uses, and a year or two later the CSO revises— changes—the data, so the econometrician has used the wrong data when estimating a forecasting relationship); and (c) many relationships are unstable, especially if economic policy changes. For example, UK consumption in the early 1990s was lower than most of the models forecast because of the effect of a new phenomenon, negative house equity. All this may make some investors agree with Ezra Solomon, who apparently said, 'The only function of economic forecasting is to make astrology respectable.'

Despite these gloomy comments, there are numerous econometric forecasts produced by the UK Treasury, UK stockbrokers, and various commercial organizations. Moreover, investors study these forecasts. Which forecaster is best? Evaluating econometric forecasts is not simple, but the general finding is that there is no consistently best buy amongst forecasters. Combining forecasts leads to increased accuracy and, somewhat surprisingly perhaps, simple averaging of forecasts is useful (Clemen, 1989).

There is good news and bad news for investors on structural economic models. The good news is that non-econometricians can relax. They do not have to understand the details of structural econometric forecasts. They can simply look at the forecasts of a large group of forecasts and average them. This sort of information is periodically available in the *Financial Times*, or on subscription from organizations such as Consensus Economics, or free from HM Treasury (http://www.hm-treasury.gov.uk/e_info/forc/comp/main.html). The bad news is that these average forecasts will not be very accurate.

Single-Equation Models

We have seen the complexity and the problems of structural econometric models, and we have seen that simpler methods, such as leading indicators or surveys, provide some useful information. In the US, there have been attempts to make econometric forecasts of single variables, such as GNP changes or inflation, from a single equation that uses traditional leading indicators, survey data and financial spread variables.

Financial spread variables include the term spread, the difference between three-month and 10-year bond yields (see Estrella and Hardouvelis, 1991, for a very favourable review of the merits of this indicator) and the quality spread, the difference in yields on corporate and government bonds. What is the rationale for using financial spread variables? Briefly, for the term spread, rising short rates relative to long suggests economic policy is being tightened and this signals a slow-down in GNP. For the quality spread, corporate bonds yield more than government bonds because corporate issues may default; when the spread widens, this signifies a belief that default is more likely, something associated with a slow-down in GNP.

Davies and Shah (1992) claimed good results for forecasting the annual change in the UK's GDP based on an equation that included the following variables:

- the 20-year gilt yield less the FT500 earnings yield;
- the 20-year gilt yield less the three-month interbank rate;
- the annual change in real oil prices;
- ONS longer-leading indicator.

There are two problems with this type of equation. First, we are back to forecasting GNP for the financial markets by using the financial markets themselves. However, this would not be a problem for an industry analyst. Second, many equations are tested and the one used is the one that worked historically. The dangers of data-mining are clear enough. This is a general problem for single-equation forecasts. They are likely to offer great promise because freed from the necessity of specifying a detailed and consistent theory, the forecaster is set loose to find a good historical fit. Such fits can be found, but will they apply in the future? Even good out-of-sample historical fits are no guarantee of future fits. What does seem likely is that UK forecasters will make more use of financial spread variables, which do have some theoretical justification and have worked for long periods in a number of countries.

Vector Autoregressive Models

We referred earlier to the macroeconometric models as structural. This means that the specific relationships between the variables are based on economic theory, although as we saw earlier, in practice there is a back-and-forth movement from theory to data. Econometricians switch from theory to imposing their own beliefs or seeing which equation fits the data best. One could argue that the data should completely determine the forecasting equation. Vector autoregressions (VARs) are a means of doing this. The forecaster specifies the variables that are believed to be relevant based on prior theory, and the largest number of lags required, and then lets the data speak. The model estimates how variables are related to lagged values of other variables and without restriction as to which variables affect which.

VAR models are attractive in being easy to construct (by people who like that kind of thing!), require little subjective input from the forecaster, and, because they can operate with few variables, are easy to update. There are, however, two major technical problems. First, macroeconomic series are highly correlated with their own past values and with other series, and this makes it hard to estimate parameters accurately and decide whether they are statistically significant. Second, if there are many lags, the number of estimates relative to the amount of data becomes large, and this makes the forecasts less reliable. One can overcome this by reducing the number of lags, but this undermines the approach of letting the data speak.

VAR models are a relatively recent development—interest in these models was sparked by Sims (1980). The models are becoming increasingly popular, and the academic journals carry an increasing number of articles on them. In the financial sector, the Bank of England has reported work on a VAR model of inflation (Henry and Pesaran, 1993) and stockbroker Goldman Sachs (Davies and Shah, 1992) has reported a VAR model of GDP.

Summing Up

There are many forecasting methods and none is foolproof. Combining forecasts, even by the simple procedure of averaging, is worthwhile. A workable strategy for non-economists would be to average the forecasts produced by econometric models and try to assess the likelihood of the forecasters being right and the direction in which they are likely to revise their forecasts by carefully following developments via survey data. Structural economic models have often failed when big changes in the economy have taken place. If a major economic change takes place, you may be well advised to treat the models with an extra degree of scepticism. Problems with structural economic models have led to more interest in single-equation models and VAR forecasts. It is too early to say whether these approaches will improve economic forecasts.

The problem of forecasting can lead investors in two distinct directions. One is to work hard at improving forecasting skills. The other is to take the view that forecasting the future is for astrologers and to devise investment strategies that minimize the use of forecasts. Unfortunately, this latter option is not available to a share analyst engaged in fundamental research.

INDUSTRY ECONOMICS

Some years ago, executives were told that they would produce better strategies if they remembered SWOT: strengths, weaknesses, opportunities and threats. This is now viewed as old-fashioned, but the SWOT framework is still useful because it is an easily remembered acronym that readily encompasses more recent approaches.

When deciding what strategy to employ, it would seem self-evident to ask—although many executives seem not to—what your firm is good or bad at doing. What are the firm's strengths and weaknesses? Or, put differently, what are the firm's resources that will give it a competitive advantage? This is nowadays described as the resource-based theory of the firm.

How well a firm does, whether measured by profits, growth or something else, will be affected not only by its competitive advantage, but also by the opportunities and threats generated in its markets. This will depend to a large extent on the structure of the market and the conduct of other firms, which will determine the profitability of the industry. This is the traditional subject matter of industrial economics.

Some writers have tried to establish which approach to strategy is better, the resource-based approach or the industrial economics approach. The SWOT framework pulls the two together and that seems the sensible approach. Both approaches are relevant, and the relative weighting of each probably varies from firm to firm, industry to industry, over time, and in any event is probably impossible to determine at any moment.

As well as the profitability of the firm's industry and the value the firm adds or subtracts relative to the average firm in its industry, a firm's profit or loss will depend on the state of the economy. Most firms make larger profits in a boom than in a recession. Some industries have more difficulty coping with high inflation than others do. Again, some industries are more affected by currency fluctuations than others. This is one reason why we looked at macroeconomic forecasting.

The Five Forces[1]

Historically, economists have been more interested in public policy than business decision-making. Porter (1979, 1980) has, however, repackaged the traditional public policy-oriented industrial economic analysis known as the structure/conduct/performance approach into a form that analysts will find useful. He talks of the 'five forces' that determine the degree of competition within an industry—the rivalry amongst existing firms, the threat of new entry, the threat of substitute products and services, the bargaining power of suppliers, and the bargaining power of buyers. These are shown in Figure 8.1.

Why would an analyst want to make an economic analysis of an industry? Porter (1980, pp. 3–4) explains:

> The intensity of competition in an industry is neither a matter of coincidence nor bad luck. Rather, competition in an industry is rooted in its underlying economic structure and goes well beyond the behavior of current competition. The state of competition in an industry depends on five basic competitive forces . . . the collective strength of these forces determines the ultimate profit potential in the industry . . . .. The goal of competitive strategy for a business unit in an industry is to find a position in the industry where the company can best defend itself against these competitive forces or can influence them in its favour.

---

[1] The remainder of this chapter is taken from Lofthouse (2001).

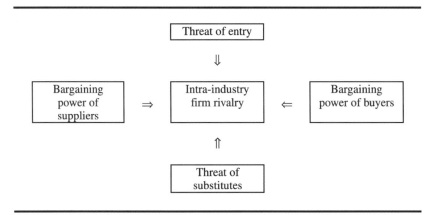

FIGURE 8.1   Porter's five forces

In short, if we want to forecast long-term prospects for a firm we should know something about the forces affecting competition in the industry it is in. We will discuss each of the forces.

Intra-Industry Rivalry

Rivalry amongst the firms within an industry may be intense or somewhat restrained. In some industries, firms are constantly varying their marketing mix (i.e. price, product attributes, promotional strategy and distribution strategy) to gain or protect market share. In other industries, rivalry is less intense; indeed, in some industries, firms will formally collude. Some of the factors that affect the intensity of rivalry are discussed below.

Degree of Concentration

When there are only a few firms in an industry, or, more accurately, a few firms with a large market share, the firms are likely to be aware of each other. This may make competition very intense. But a price cut, say, by one firm will take business from the others, and they may retaliate. As a result, unless the price cuts increase total industry sales substantially, all are likely to be worse off. There must therefore be a temptation to collude, formally or informally, to act in the collective interest. The nature of rivalry may also be affected. Promotion and product differentiation may be preferred to price cutting.

Slow Industry Growth

A firm seeking to grow in a growth industry does not necessarily take sales from another firm. In a slow-growth industry, market share gains must come at the expense of other firms.

High Fixed Costs

Where fixed costs (i.e. costs that don't vary with output) are high, there is pressure to produce at full capacity. When demand is weak, perhaps during a recession, there is likely to be aggressive price cutting as each firm tries to fill its plant.

Size of Capacity Increases

In some industries, the production technology is such that capacity increases can only be made in large increments. As a result, the industry will suffer from periodic excess capacity, and there is the likelihood of price wars.

Degree of Product Differentiation

For products lacking significant product differentiation, usually referred to as commodity products (whether or not they are commodities), competition will largely be based on price and service. Consequently, price competition will be intense. Demand for highly differentiated products will be less responsive to price changes, and price competition will be less intense.

Diversity of Competitors

The 'social structure' of an industry is hard to pin down, but is a relevant consideration. Some industries are highly localized, and the firms in it understand the rules of the game. In other industries, there is not only geographical dispersion (perhaps including foreign competitors), but the industry may contain firms that operate only in that industry, others that are vertically integrated, and some that are highly diversified. These firms may have different objectives, strategies and timescales. These differences may lead to periods of intense competition, or restrain the industry from raising its margins.

Exit Barriers

Exit barriers are barriers to a firm leaving an industry. They affect competition amongst firms within the industry, and may affect entry too—if you can't get out you might not want to go in. Exit barriers may be considered to be simultaneously an exit and entry barrier. The usual type of exit barrier is a large sunk cost—a cost that once incurred cannot be recovered. There are no exit barriers for a local 'light moves' furniture removal business. If things don't work out, you just sell your van and move on. But businesses with expensive specialized equipment are in a different position. If another sugar refiner won't buy your refinery, you will have to write the whole thing off (less scrap value). Sunk costs in this case are large. Once a firm has entered the industry, it can't change its mind cheaply. When exit costs are high, low profits do not induce firms to leave an industry. The result is excess capacity, intense competition and poor profitability.

Entry Conditions

In a competitive system, abnormally high profits in an industry will encourage firms outside the industry to enter it. Indeed, some firms within the industry may attempt to expand. This increase in supply will lead to a fall in price. A barrier to entry is something that gives incumbents a persistent advantage and stops entry occurring even when there is a profit incentive for entry. Clearly, if a firm has a monopoly position, but entry is easy, it is unlikely to have anything other than short-lived market power if it charges high prices. If entry is difficult, even firms in markets that are not monopolies may be able to charge more than the competitive price.

Barriers to entry are tricky to define. Most economists would probably settle for something along the lines that a barrier to entry exists when a potential entrant to an industry bears a cost that is not borne by the incumbent firms. Sometimes, impediments to entry are distinguished from barriers to entry; whereas barriers are effective for a long period, impediments merely slow down the speed of entry.

So, what might constitute a barrier to entry? Candidates include:

- capital requirements
- economies of scale
- absolute cost advantages
- product differentiation
- access to distribution channels
- legal and regulatory barriers
- retaliation
- exit barriers.

Capital Requirements

Many industries have large capital requirements, and this obviously restricts the number of potential entrants. For example, the cost of entry to the commercial jet passenger aeroplane manufacturing industry are such that Boeing and Airbus are probably not constantly looking over their shoulders for potential new competitors. But the number of industries that fall into this category is very small.

Economies of Scale

In some industries, the minimum efficient scale (MES) may be a large percentage of industry output. A firm that enters at less than the MES may suffer a substantial cost disadvantage. So why not enter at MES and take market share from the incumbents? This would mean that entry must be made at a larger scale, and some firms will not have the financial resources to enter. But as long as some firms can enter, then this isn't really a barrier. Yet entry may be a risky strategy even for a large firm. To get consumers to switch to another supplier may be a slow and costly business. This, however, is not a point about economies of scale but rather the marketing advantages of incumbent firms (discussed below).

A more complex argument relates to sunk costs. If economies of scale are important, entry will have to be on a larger scale than where there are no economies; this will involve larger fixed costs, some of which will be sunk costs. Larger sunk costs will have a significant effect on industry output. Existing firms may react by cutting prices. Once in the industry, their sunk costs are irrelevant for pricing decisions and they only have to cover variable costs. A firm planning to enter the industry will want to earn at least a normal return on all its costs, and may therefore be deterred from entry.

Absolute Cost Advantages

Incumbents may have cost advantages unrelated to scale economies. They may have access to low-cost inputs, the best sites (e.g. having landing slots at Heathrow), and will be some way down the learning curve. The learning curve is the notion that costs fall with cumulative output, as workers and managers learn with experience.

Product Differentiation

Product differentiation in itself is not a barrier to entry, but a number of factors related to product differentiation—advertising, goodwill, product proliferation and switching costs—may be barriers.

Advertising can be a barrier in at least three ways—through lagged effects, economies of scale and absolute costs. Let's look at each in turn. Advertising appears to have a lagged effect—ads made in previous years may affect sales this year. This may be because it takes a series of ads to persuade the consumer to act. Or it may be that the consumer is convinced by the earlier ads, but wasn't in the market then. Whatever the reason, the result is that an entrant will have to spend more to have the same effect as an incumbent. To see that, imagine an incumbent spends £10 million every year, which increases profit (before advertising costs) by £10 million in that year. Assume also that there is an annual decay effect of 50% for two years, that is to say the ad is 50% as effective in the following year (= £5 million profit) and 50% effective again the next year (= £2.5 million profit). To match the effectiveness of £10 million of advertising this year by an incumbent that has been advertising in previous years, an entrant would have to spend £17.5 million.

Consumers know existing products and they may have goodwill towards the brand and exhibit considerable brand loyalty. To get consumers to try a new brand may be a slow and expensive process. Even if there are no lagged effects from advertising, an entrant may have to spend more than an incumbent to achieve the same response. Given that we would expect the new brand to have a low initial market share, advertising costs per unit of sales will be extremely high.

To achieve any response to ads, it is likely that some minimum sum has to be spent. Thereafter, extra ads may draw a more than proportionate response, i.e. there are initially advertising economies of scale. Where the minimum sum is substantial, small-scale entry will suffer from high advertising/sales ratios.

Finally, if large-scale advertising is required, this will increase the absolute cost of entry.

Of course, none of these points is insurmountable, and incumbents will have borne similar costs in the past. But again, the sunk cost nature of advertising may affect a potential entrant's view. If the entry is not successful, then the advertising expenditure will be completely lost. Entry requiring high advertising expenditure is therefore especially risky.

Another product differentiation barrier to entry is product proliferation. Imagine an industry consisting of four firms, each with one product and a 25% market share. Imagine also that 25% of customers randomly switch products every year. If a new firm enters the industry, it may expect to achieve first-year sales of 5% (i.e. one-fifth of 25%). But if each firm produces six products, and the new entrant produces only one, it would expect to achieve a 1% market share (i.e. one-twenty-fifth of 25%), a much less attractive prospect.

There is nothing to stop the new entrant introducing six new products. While possible, this is unlikely to occur. Existing products are likely to have left few exploitable niches, but in any event the advertising burden is likely to be an even greater hurdle. Distribution might also prove a problem (see below).

The soap industry is one in which economies of scale are exhausted at low levels of output, but a few firms dominate the industry. This position appears to be maintained by created barriers to entry by product and brand proliferation and heavy advertising.

Some products involve switching costs and this can constitute a barrier to entry. The manuscript of this book was word-processed using Microsoft Word™. While it is not impossible to learn another word-processing program, it is clearly a chore. To change to another program will involve switching costs in terms of time and learning. To overcome this, a competitor's word-processing program will have to offer exceptional functionality and a competitive price.

Distribution Channels

In some cases, the distribution channel may welcome a new product, but often a manufacturer has a difficult time obtaining distribution. An obvious example is the UK food retailing industry. Here, a few chains control the bulk of the UK grocery distribution. A handful of people could therefore effectively kill a new product launch by refusing to stock the product. And, since their shelves are already full, to sell a new product requires giving less space to an existing product. Why, for example, stock another cola drink if it means displacing Coke, Pepsi or the chain's own brand? To obtain shelf space in this case would be both difficult and expensive. Distribution channels can be an important barrier to entry.

Government Policy

Some economists argue that the longest lasting barriers to entry are usually a result of government policy. The government, or another public body, can erect barriers by granting local or national monopolies, by licensing regulations (e.g. the need to pass 'the Knowledge' to drive a London black cab), by patent law, and so on.

Retaliation

The final barrier is the potential entrant's view of the likely response by the incumbents. They may cut prices, increase output, or make life difficult in other ways for an entrant.

Mobility Barriers

Although one can think of an industry as a single entity, in reality we observe that the firms in an industry often differ from each other along a variety of dimensions—breadth of product line, geographical markets served, nature of distribution channel, and so on. These differences arise because the firms within an industry do not all adopt the same competitive strategy. This is a consequence of different competencies, history and other factors. Therefore, some industries can be viewed as being composed of strategic groups—groups of firms following broadly similar strategies. Firms within a strategic group are likely to see the other members of the group as their primary competitors, rather than all the members of the industry.

Entry barriers are industry characteristics that inhibit new entry. If the concept of strategic groups is accepted, what may be an entry barrier protecting firms following one strategy may not protect other firms following a different strategy. For example, the barriers that may exist to protect a research-oriented pharmaceutical company, such as Glaxo Wellcome, may not protect a manufacturer of generic drugs. The heavy marketing and research expenditure of Glaxo Wellcome protects it not only from firms outside the industry but also from the generic drug manufacturers within the overall industry but outside its strategic group. Entry barriers may be generalized to mobility barriers, or barriers that stop firms within an industry shifting strategy, which provides one explanation why some firms in an industry persistently earn more profit than others.

Supplier Power

Suppliers that have power can squeeze the industries they serve, by raising prices or reducing quality, thereby capturing some of the value created in the buyer industries. Suppliers with power will probably fall into one or more of the following categories:

- The supplier industry is dominated by a few firms and sells to an industry in which there are many firms.
- The suppliers sell unique products or products with high switching costs, so that the suppliers can't easily be played off against each other.
- The suppliers sell a product for which there is no readily available substitute product from another industry.
- The suppliers have the ability to integrate forward and compete with their current customers.
- The buyers are not a large proportion of the suppliers' business, so the health of the buyer industry is not of great concern to the suppliers.

Buyer Power

Buyers with power can force down prices or demand higher quality without full recompense, and capture some of the value created by the suppliers. Buyers with power will likely fall into one of the following categories:

- A few large firms dominate the buyer industry, while the supplier industry has many small firms. Even if there are few suppliers, the buyers may have substantial power if the suppliers have high fixed costs and are therefore very volume oriented.
- The buyers are purchasing commodity-type products, with little differentiation and no switching costs.
- The product being bought is a component of the buyer industry's output and is a significant proportion of total cost, making the buyers highly value conscious.
- The buyer industry has low profitability, and is therefore highly value conscious.
- The product being bought does not affect the buyer's product quality, so substitution is easy.
- The buyer can integrate backwards and make the product itself.

Competition from Substitutes

The profit potential of an industry will be constrained if substitutes exist that perform the same functions as the industry's product. The Post Office has a monopoly in the UK on letter delivery below £1 per item, but it is subject to competition from a variety of substitutes. For example:

- telephones compete with letter mail for some types of communications;
- fax transmission competes with letter mail for sending documents and some types of communications;

- email competes with letter mail for sending some documents and some types of communication;
- company messengers may be used to deliver letters and small packages, e.g. in London, stockbrokers and law firms are located in small geographical areas and both industries use company messengers.

The significance of such substitutes will depend on the willingness of consumers to consider a substitute, the relative price/performance of the substitute, and any switching costs. For example, while it might be sensible to request literature from a company by email, most people would think it inappropriate to send out electronic wedding invitations. Where a switch can be considered, relative price/ performance is important: a substitute need not be cheaper if it offers better features. Finally, switching costs may constrain a substitute's growth. Many households in the UK do not have a computer link to an email service. To switch from letters to email may involve a cost of £500 plus a willingness to grapple with new technology. For many people, email is thereby rendered unattractive, although the cost per email sent would be much cheaper than the letter alternative. But switching costs can change. In January 2000, OnDigital announced that it was going to offer email on its digital TV service.

Substitutes may be more than a constraint on growth: they may eliminate firms or whole industries. The most famous statement of this view is by Joseph Schumpeter (1943, pp. 84–85). Schumpeter thought that models of competition, which focus on price, product competition and sales effort were limited:

> In capitalist reality as distinguished from its textbook picture, it is not that kind of competition which counts but the competition from the new commodity, the new technology, the new source of supply, the new type of organization (the largest-scale unit of control for instance)—competition which commands a decisive cost or quality advantage which strikes not at the margins of the profits and the outputs of the existing firms but at their foundations and their very lives. This kind of competition is as much more effective than the other as a bombardment is in comparison with forcing a door, and so much more important that it becomes a matter of comparative indifference whether competition in the ordinary sense functions more or less promptly . . . .. It is hardly necessary to point out that competition of the kind we now have in mind acts not only when in being but also when it is merely an ever-present threat. It disciplines before it attacks.

Of course, not all competition is as dramatic as that propounded by Schumpeter. But the notion of competition as rivalry coming both from within an industry and from without, affecting every aspect of a product's manufacture and how it is sold, is an important one. Schumpeter referred to the process as creative destruction.

If we view competition in the way Schumpeter did, we might argue that a monopoly will exist only when it is granted by the government or where there is some barrier to other firms acquiring the resources to compete. Even where there is a barrier to entry, the monopolist may still face competition from a new product that removes its market.

Resources

We have outlined Porter's five forces, a framework for assessing the state of competition in an industry. If it is accepted that the profitability of industries is not a matter of chance but depends at least partly on the state of competition, then the five forces analysis provides a way of thinking about the likely profitability of an industry and the factors that may change it.

Analysts will want to know the prospects of a firm relative to its industry. Is the firm positioned correctly relative to where the competitive forces are greatest or least for it? The answer will depend on the resources available to the firm. Resources are anything that provide a strength or weakness in attaining the firm's objectives. They may be conventional assets owned or controlled by the firm, or they may be more intangible, such as routines (the regular and predictable behavioural patterns that firms develop), learning by doing, brand names, and corporate reputation. An example of a conventional resource would be a restaurant's premises. A good location would be a strength, but a poor location would be a weakness. Resources may or may not be tradable, and in some cases it may not be clear exactly what the resource is, as may often be the case with routines.

A firm's resources determine what it can do, and the scope of its market opportunities. Resources will only offer sustained competitive advantage if they have a number of characteristics:

- *Demand relevance:* it probably doesn't need saying that a resource is valuable only if it is relevant to demand. IBM's reputation as a computer industry giant is of little relevance to consumers purchasing their second personal computer. They will be well enough informed not to need the security blanket of the IBM name.
- *Scarcity and imitability:* resources that are scarce and hard to copy are more valuable than those that are not. Unique resources, such as a patent, will be hard to copy. Resources that are difficult to discern (causal ambiguity in the jargon) are especially valuable. Why did UK stockbroker James Capel consistently get rated best for institutional research in the 1980s, when its research was easily obtainable by competitors to analyse, and it didn't train analysts but hired them from other firms where they were often not highly rated? Why did it slide down the rankings in the 1990s after its parent HSBC exercised managerial control in 1990?

  While a firm may have a scarce resource, it may not be the basis for building a business if competitors can use a different resource to overcome it. Apple had an excellent operating system, but Microsoft overwhelmed it.
- *Durability:* resources that are durable are a more attractive foundation for competitive advantage than those that aren't. Corporate and brand reputations are often long-lasting.
- *Appropriability:* even if a resource can generate higher returns, this is only valuable to a firm to the extent that the firm can obtain those returns. For

example, in mainly people-based industries, such as stockbroking, fund management, advertising and so on, if an identifiable individual or small group generates a large percentage of revenues, the individual or individuals may capture the revenues either by leaving the firm or by demanding higher remuneration. Revenues generated by a large team-based operation using complex routines are much more likely to be captured by the firm. Some resources, such as corporate reputation, are largely firm specific.

In short, firms are different. They have different resources. Some are good at one thing, some another, and some are not much good at anything (these might still earn superior returns if there are barriers to entry). Sensible business strategy will be based on matching a firm's superior resources that provide a competitive advantage to opportunities in the environment. In the general business literature, these superior resources are often described as core competencies.

Although the idea of building on resources or core competencies is simple enough, identifying such competencies in practice is another matter. One way of proceeding would be to split the firm into functional areas (e.g. organization, personnel, marketing, technical and finance), then subdivide each functional category (e.g. marketing might be split into sales force, knowledge of the customer's needs, breadth of the product line, product quality, etc.) and search for competencies in each area (e.g. see Buchele, 1962). Examples of core competencies might be speed of new product development, brand management, reputation for quality, strength of central financial control, capability in basic research, and so on.

In making judgements about competencies, one might draw on the historical experience of the company, direct competitors' experiences, consultants' opinions, judgements based on published material, and so on. Analysts can ask companies what their core competence is. The answer will depend on who is asked. Research suggests that what is seen as a core competence varies with organizational level and functional area (e.g. Stevenson, 1976; and Bowman and Daniels, 1995). Lower-level managers will put more emphasis on technical skills and less on financial than will top-level managers. It is a useful exercise for senior managers to discover what lower-level personnel think are the strong points of the organization. When judging competencies, it is not what a firm thinks it does well that matters, but what it does better than its competitors.

All of this may seem somewhat subjective. And it is. There is a clear danger that the resource-based theory is simply a tautology. Firms build on their resources—how could they do otherwise?—but we can't identify the resources in advance. Of course, the popular literature, including articles in the *Harvard Business Review*, appears persuasive. The success of firms that have built on competencies is shown. The problem is that the competencies are pulled out of the air after the event to explain the example. As Geroski (1998, p. 286) notes:

> Stimulating as it is, the competences literature has yet to progress much beyond tautology. It is much easier to invent competences which might explain what we observe than

it is to independently try to measure competences and then try to correlate them with observed performance differences between firms.

That said, it does seem that many a firm would benefit from asking what is necessary to succeed, and what it brings to the party. Perhaps highly sophistic-ated analysis isn't always necessary. Analysts should at least know what a firm's senior managers think are its core competencies.

Changing Scope

A firm's activities are not set in stone. It can change the scope of its activities by expanding or contracting. To expand, it can change its position in its existing industry (or industries) or move into new industries. And there are the options of internal growth or acquisition.

Table 8.1 shows some ways in which a firm might change its scope by changing its products or markets.

TABLE 8.1   Changing a firm's scope

	Current products	New products
Current markets	Market penetration increase market share: internal growth horizontal merger increase product usage	Product development product improvements product-line extension new products
New markets	Market development geographic expansion new segments	Diversification vertical integration related diversification unrelated diversification

Assuming for whatever reason that a firm wants to grow, it has two options: internal growth and external growth, i.e. growth by acquisition. Which is the better route will obviously depend on the circumstances, and firms may use both methods. Some general points are worth making.

Acquisitions may offer the following advantages:

- *Speed:* fully operational plant, personnel and market share are available quickly.
- *Management:* an acquirer may have insufficient management resources to develop a new area or oversee a bigger operation: an acquisition can provide those resources.
- *Competition:* a competitor or potential competitor may be removed.

Acquisitions may suffer from the following disadvantages:

- *Imperfect fit:* the acquired firm may not have the most up-to-date plant, the labour force may be difficult, and the firm may engage in businesses that are not required.
- *Integration difficulties:* there may be a widespread culture clash, or key executives might be unwilling to work together.
- *Wrong price:* why is the firm being sold? Does it have problems that a bidder can't detect and therefore it is mispriced, or is it excellent but still mispriced?

Mergers and takeovers are often a source of much market excitement. Nearly all of them are deemed by analysts to be a good thing. History suggests something different. Economists have used four ways to assess the effects of mergers.

- stockmarket reactions
- the effect on profitability
- post-acquisition divestment
- characteristics of acquirers.

The findings are easy to summarize. There is little evidence that mergers benefit the acquiring firm. If there are any benefits, they appear to be captured by the shareholders of the firm being bid for. Apart from the victim's shareholders, the main beneficiaries are the managers of the acquiring firm. Presiding over a larger firm, they are likely to enjoy higher salaries and be less prone to takeover themselves.

Whatever the evidence on mergers in general, there is obviously a wide range of outcomes. Some are spectacularly successful. Is it possible to detect any characteristics that differentiate between the good and bad merger? A recent US study (Healy et al., 1997) found three:

- friendly takeovers outperformed hostile takeovers;
- takeovers with payment in shares and debt outperformed cash transactions;
- takeovers of highly overlapping businesses outperformed those of unrelated businesses.

In general, unrelated diversification seems to be the worst merger strategy. But that does mean the optimal level of diversification for most firms is zero. Perhaps firms would improve their diversification if they asked the following questions (Markides, 1997):

- What are our core competencies?
- What core competencies are needed to succeed in the new market?
- If we don't have all the core competencies, can we buy, grow or innovate around the missing ones?

- Can other firms easily enter the new market by imitating or purchasing the necessary core competencies?
- Will entry into the new area provide a stepping stone into other attractive areas?

First-Mover Advantages

The preceding industry analysis covers broad issues. Now we will consider a quite narrow issue, that of first-mover advantage. In the last few years, many analysts and financial commentators have stressed the importance of first-mover advantage. The argument is that in many industries, but not all, in the mature phase of the product lifecycle, the one or two firms that emerge as industry leaders were among the first to enter the industry. It would appear that in many industries, launching your product before other firms gives you an advantage. This has been named first-mover advantage (for surveys of the literature, see Robinson et al., 1994 and Mueller, 1997). The source of this advantage may come from both demand and supply factors (see Mueller, 1997).

On the demand side we sometimes find:

- *Switching costs:* there may be money costs or learning costs to bear if a consumer switches to another supplier. As we noted earlier, if you have learned how to use one firm's piece of software, then you probably don't want to learn another firm's;
- *Network effects:* some goods have more value the more other customers use them. Credit cards are only useful if many suppliers accept them, which in turn will be related to the number of credit-card customers. Once a firm has a large network of customers, it will be hard for other firms to compete;
- *Quality concerns:* many existing purchasers may not switch to a new entrant because of concerns over quality. To take the remaining, less keen consumers, a new entrant may have to sell at a price well below the first-mover. In the drugs industry, brand-name drugs often retain large market shares even when equivalent generic drugs are sold at a fraction of the price of the brand-name drug;
- *Habit formation:* consumers may simply get used to a first-mover's product and not bother to evaluate new alternatives.

Supply-side advantages of being a first-mover include:

- *Economies of scale and of learning:* if there are scale and learning economies, the first-mover has more time to expand and achieve the scale economies and to be some way down the learning curve, thereby achieving lower-cost production than new entrants;

- *Pre-empting scarce resources:* a first-mover may be able to pre-empt scarce resources, such as skilled labour, distribution outlets, shelf space or raw materials.

Nonetheless, there may be advantages from being a later entrant, including:

- *Ability to benefit from first-mover mistakes:* the first-mover may make product-positioning and marketing mistakes. For example, the first-mover may produce a single product while the mass market is really segmented, and a later entrant may see this and offer several products. Or the first-mover may spend inadequate sums on advertising and distribution;
- *Ability to use the latest technology:* where technological progress is rapid, a later entrant may be able to use a superior, second-generation production process;
- *Superior resources:* a first-mover may prove that a market exists, but lack sufficient resources to maintain market leadership when larger competitors enter the industry.

Much of the academic literature, and almost all popular commentary, suggests that the advantages of being first dominate any disadvantages. Some studies claim to demonstrate this. But there are grounds for scepticism (e.g. see Vander-Werf and Mahon, 1997). Some studies identify as a pioneer not 'the pioneer' but 'one of the pioneers'. Clearly this confounds first-mover with early followers. Second, when the first-mover is determined by surveys, the firm identified is often the first successful firm rather than the first-mover, which may have been unsuccessful and is now forgotten. Third, some studies have been based on a survey of existing firms: firms that have gone bust are excluded, and this biases the results. Fourth, it is possible that the early entrants are those most likely to succeed because they have the relevant competencies, and so we are measuring the effect not of being first but of being competent.

Using an historical approach that avoids some of the above problems, one study found first-movers to be far less dominant in long-term market leadership than popularly believed (Tellis and Golder, 1996). One reason why the possible advantages of being a first-mover noted above are not decisive is that they are dependent on the size of the market. The market for new products is often small, and the advantages noted would accrue to the firm that takes the primitive innovation to the mass market. This may be an early follower rather than the first-mover.

Even if it could be shown that successful first-movers make high returns, this doesn't necessarily make product innovation a worthwhile strategy. For example, if 10 pharmaceutical firms try to be a product innovator and spend £100 000 each on research and development, but nine are unsuccessful and give up, and only one is successful (the first-mover) and earns £1 000 000, overall the 10 firms have made no profit at all. Clearly, attempting to be a first-mover only makes sense if there is some reason to believe that you have a better chance of success than other firms. So, is it worthwhile to adopt a strategy of being a product or quality innovator? Sometimes.

CONCLUDING COMMENTS

Fundamental analysis requires knowledge of the economy, industries and firms. In this chapter, we have provided some background information on economic forecasts, and some industrial economics useful in structuring analysis of an industry. In the next chapter, we look at financial statement analysis, another pillar of fundamental analysis.

9

Accounting Fundamentals

I think business is very simple. Profit. Loss. Take the sales, subtract the costs, you get this big positive number. The math is quite straightforward.

Bill Gates

Knowledge of accounting is essential for anybody following an active investment strategy. Unfortunately, accounting is somewhat difficult to discuss. The danger is that a 25-page discussion is long enough to bore the reader but short enough to be useless in practice. What we have opted to do is to briefly outline the key financial statements, and then go on to look at some of the ways they might be analysed, making no claim that the novice would be able to calculate all the numbers for a real firm. Then we move on to some new types of analysis and some controversial issues. Hopefully this latter material will encourage the novice accountant to read books such as Holmes and Sugden (1999) and Sutton (2000) (the former is UK oriented, the latter is pan-European.)

The form and content of accounts of quoted companies is determined by company law, stock exchange listing requirements, and the Financial Reporting Council. The latter is a body established by government to set and enforce accounting standards. Two bodies report to it: the Financial Reporting Review Panel, which is concerned with enforcement, and the Accounting Standards Board, which develops and issues accounting standards. The Accounting Standards Board may begin with a discussion paper, move on to a financial reporting exposure draft (FRED), and then a financial reporting standard (FRS). These standards are numbered and usually referred to as, for example, FRS 14 (which deals with earnings per share).

THE BASIC FINANCIAL STATEMENTS

The key financial document for a firm is its annual report and accounts (R&A). Within it are four important statements: a balance sheet, a profit and loss statement (P&L), a cash flow statement, and a statement of total recognized gains and losses.

The Balance Sheet

A real balance sheet has many entries and attached notes, but in essence there are three main components: assets, liabilities and shareholders' funds. Assets are resources that are expected to bring the company some benefit. They may be tangible or intangible. Liabilities are obligations of the company that may be expected to lead to resources being claimed from it. Shareholders' funds are the difference between the two. We can express the relationship between these three categories as an identity:

$$\text{Assets} - \text{liabilities} = \text{shareholders' funds}$$

or, alternatively:

$$\text{Assets} = \text{shareholders' funds} + \text{liabilities.}$$

The first identity looks at matters from the shareholders' point of view, while the second is from the company's point of view. A real balance sheet might look like that shown in Figure 9.1. We will comment on the entries.

Fixed assets are assets that are intended for continuing use in the business. Tangible fixed assets will include items such as plant and machinery, land and buildings, and so on. They are normally subject to depreciation (although freehold land isn't). Depreciation is a way of spreading the cost of an asset over its expected economic life. For example, plant costing £100 might be depreciated at 10% per annum. This will show up in two ways. In the P&L, a depreciation charge (i.e. cost) of £10 will appear—reducing profits—and the value in the balance sheet would be written down to £90. Depreciation is purely notional; the cost of plant is fully borne when it is purchased. Depreciation charges do not involve cash flows.

Intangible fixed assets are non-monetary fixed assets that have no physical substance but can be identified and controlled by a company. These take a number of forms, including copyright, patents and, perhaps more widely encountered, purchased goodwill. Goodwill is the difference between an entity's purchase consideration and its net asset value. For example, you might buy the corner newsagent for £50 000, but the value of the premises might be only £30 000. The difference is goodwill. This has to be amortized (i.e. depreciated) over the asset's useful economic life unless this exceeds 20 years, when the asset must be reviewed annually for any reduction in value.

Fixed-asset investments include investment in subsidiaries and investment in associated undertakings. Subsidiaries are companies whose board of directors is controlled by the company owning some or all of its shares. An associated undertaking is one that is not a subsidiary but where the investing company is effectively a partner or where it has at least 20% of the voting equity and a long-term interest.

Current assets are assets that are expected to be turned into cash within a year. Stock is a term that covers a variety of assets. For a manufacturer, stocks might be raw materials as purchased, or finished goods, or items somewhere in between ('work in progress'). For a retailer, stocks will usually consist entirely of

	£m
Fixed assets	
Tangible assets	300
Intangible assets	80
Investments	20
	400
Current assets	
Stocks	40
Debtors falling due within one year	200
Debtors falling due after one year	10
Cash at bank and short-term investments	50
	300
Creditors: amounts falling due within one year	
Borrowings	(50)
Others	(200)
	(250)
Net current assets	**50**
Total assets less current liabilities	**450**
Creditors: amounts falling due after one year	
Borrowings	**(150)**
Net assets	**300**
Capital and reserves	
Called-up share capital	60
Share premium account	80
Revaluation reserve	20
Profit and loss account	130
Shareholders' funds	**290**
Minority interests	**10**
Total capital employed	**300**

FIGURE 9.1   Balance sheet for XYZ, 31/12/99

finished goods purchased. There are various rules that have to be followed when valuing stocks, but nonetheless stock values should be approached with a degree of scepticism, especially during a recession.

Debtors are another current asset, representing amounts owed to the firm. Amounts due after more than a year are shown separately. Some businesses' turnover is mainly in cash, whereas for others it is mainly on credit. The significance of debtors will vary accordingly.

Cash as an asset is usually straightforward, unless held in a country that does not permit remittances. Also, cash may be held on deposit as security for loans to subsidiaries and is therefore not available.

Current asset investments are short-term investments not intended to be held on a continuing basis; usually they will be some form of money market instruments, such as commercial paper and certificates of deposit.

Turning now to liabilities, creditors are shown under two main headings: amounts falling due in under a year and amounts falling due after a year. In Figure 9.1, the short-term creditors have been divided into borrowings and others. Borrowings will include items such as bank overdrafts, loan notes and finance leases. Others will include trade creditors (the counterpart to debtors), corporation and other tax due, and the proposed dividend.

Creditors falling due after one year will usually consist of bank loans and perhaps capital market investments such as debentures. We can bring all of the above together:

	£m	£m
Fixed assets	400	400
Current assets	300	
Creditors (<1 year)	(250)	
Net current assets	50	50
Total assets less current liabilities		450
Creditors (> 1 year)	(150)	(150)
Net assets		300

Having discussed one side of the first identity shown earlier, we move to the other side, shareholders' funds. Shares are issued with a face, or par, value. For example, XYZ's ordinary shares may have a par value of 60p. However, this is not necessarily the price at which they are issued. Had 100 million shares been issued at £1.40 (i.e. a par value of 60p plus a premium of 80p), the sum received would be shown in the accounts as called-up share capital £60m and share premium account £80m. The share capital usually consists predominantly of ordinary shares, but some companies also have preference shares, deferred shares, and warrants, etc.

The revaluation reserve relates to changes in the valuation of assets. For example, if the company owns property, and a valuation shows that it has increased in value, then this unrealized gain will be credited to the revaluation reserve. Shortfalls are debited to the revaluation reserve.

The profit and loss account reserve comprises retained profits and losses. For example, the retained profit of £32m shown in Figure 9.2 will have been included in this reserve. This completes the capital and reserves of XYZ, although other types of reserve can be found in practice.

You will see in Figure 9.1 that shareholder's funds do not quite equal net asset value. The reason is that the balance sheet shown is a consolidated balance sheet. When a company owns subsidiaries, it produces a consolidated statement that incorporates their assets and liabilities. If it does not own 100% of the subsidiaries, then a minorities item must be entered. This shows the interest of the minority shareholders in the assets consolidated into XYZ.

Finally, note the date at the top of Figures 9.1 and 9.2. The balance sheet is struck on a specific date, while the P&L is for a period. Many companies have seasonal businesses. Their debtor/creditor position can vary substantially

	£m
Turnover	900
Cost of sales	(650)
Gross profit	250
Distribution costs	(60)
Administrative expenses	(100)
Operating profit	90
Share of operating profits of associated undertakings	10
Profit on ordinary activities before interest	100
Interest receivable (payable)	1
Profit on ordinary activities before taxation	101
Tax on profit on ordinary activities	(33)
Profit on ordinary activities after taxation	**68**
Minority interests	**(1)**
Profits for the financial year	67
Dividends	35
Retained profit for the financial year	32
Earnings per share	XXX

FIGURE 9.2   Profit and loss account for XYZ, year ended 31/12/1999

through the year. If we drew up a balance sheet for XYZ at a different date, the picture might be very different.

The Profit and Loss Account

The P&L account is drawn up from the shareholders' point of view. It covers activity through the financial accounting period. It begins with turnover, the value of sales to external customers. Cost of sales, i.e. raw materials and wages, is deducted to produce gross profit. Distribution costs and administrative expenses—costs that cannot be allocated to particular products—are then deducted to give operating profit or loss. Operating profit is also called trading profit. The notes to the accounts will carry information on the number of employees, their wages and other costs, and details of directors' emoluments. The depreciation charge is shown in the notes, as is the cost of hiring plant and machinery.

Next, we see the company's share of profits of associated undertakings. It is the share of the profits, not dividends, that is shown here. Adding share of associated undertakings' profits to operating profit produces profits on ordinary activities before interest.

Interest is usually shown as a single net figure of income paid and received. The notes will show a detailed breakdown in terms of interest paid on bank loans and overdrafts, on loans repayable within five years, and on other loans.

The amount of taxation suffered is the next item. This will be spelt out in the notes. Company taxation is too complex an issue to discuss here, although we will briefly discuss some issues when we discuss dividend yield (see p. 154).

As with the balance sheet, an adjustment must be made for minority shareholders. Their share of the profit after tax is deducted, leaving profits for the financial year. From this profit number, earnings per share (EPS) can be calculated; indeed, it must be shown on the P&L:

$$EPS = \frac{\text{profit attributable to ordinary shareholders}}{\text{weighted average number of issued ordinary shares}}.$$

Finally, deduction of the value of any dividends paid will produce the retained profit for the financial year.

Producing a P&L statement might not seem very controversial. You just follow the rules and that's that. If only things were so simple. Prior to FRS 3, there was considerable interest in (and abuse of) items that went above and below the line, which was a notional line falling under the profit figure for profits attributable to ordinary shareholders from which EPS was calculated. Two types of special accounting item were defined: exceptional items and extraordinary items. Exceptional items were items that fell within the normal activities of the firm but had to be disclosed separately, whereas extraordinary items fell outside the firm's normal activities and were not expected to recur frequently or regularly.

Many firms treated unusual positive items as exceptional, and unusual negative items as extraordinary. So a property sale would appear above the line, and redundancy costs in an industry suffering secular decline would appear below it. FRS 3 tightened the definition of extraordinary items and required both types of item to be included in the EPS calculation. The result is that profit figures, and EPS, can be volatile from year to year. To overcome this, analysts will calculate 'normalized' EPS. Many follow the Institute of Investment Management and Research (their professional body) recommendation on how to calculate 'headline' earnings. These are reported earnings adjusted for non-trading items such as profits or losses on the sale or termination of an operation, profits and losses on the disposal of fixed assets, and amortization of goodwill. The result is that accounts might show three EPSs: the FRS 3 version, the company's preferred version, and headline EPS. Most investors focus on headline EPS.

The Cash Flow Statement

The purpose of a cash flow statement is to show how a company raised and spent cash during the financial year. It provides information that can be used to assess a company's liquidity and solvency. Figure 9.3, shows a cash flow statement for XYZ. We have omitted specific numbers, and just show the main headings and some examples of entries for particular headings.

Net cash inflow (outflow) from operating activities

Dividends received from associated undertakings

Returns on investments and servicing of finance
Interest received
Interest paid
Dividends paid to minority interests
Net cash outflow (inflow) from returns on investment and servicing of finance

Taxation paid

Capital expenditure
Purchase of tangible fixed assets
Sale of tangible fixed assets
Net cash outflow (inflow) from capital expenditure

Acquisitions and disposals
Purchase of subsidiary
Net cash outflow (inflow) from acquisitions and disposals

Equity dividends paid

Cash outflow (inflow) before management of liquid resources and financing

Management of liquid resources
Decrease (increase) in short-term investments
Net cash inflow (outflow) from management of liquid resources

Financing
Increase in loans
Net cash inflow (outflow) from financing

Increase (decrease) in cash in the year

FIGURE 9.3   Cash flow statement for XYZ, year ended 31/12/1999

It is easier to understand the point of a cash flow statement by ignoring the details and looking at the big picture. Cash flow statements deal with three types of activity: operating, investing and financing. *Operating activities* comprise the sale of goods and their associated costs. Since the accounts don't usually show the cash receipts and payments, operating cash flow is derived indirectly by adjusting profits for non-cash items, such as depreciation and changes in operating working capital (e.g. the change in stocks over the year and the change in debtors). *Investing activities* cover purchases and sale of, for example, plant and machinery, property and financial assets. *Financing activities* show how a firm increases or reduces its capital by issuing or redeeming its shares or debt, and paying dividends. Each of these three activities can lead to inflows or outflows of cash. Adding them together, and then adding the value of cash at the start of the year, produces the year-end cash figure.

Looking at the operating activities, we can see whether the cash flow is positive or negative. If it is negative, this may be the result of making losses or of rapid expansion (costs preceding revenues). In either case, the question arises as to how the position will be financed. If a firm has positive operating cash flow, the next question is whether it is self-financing, i.e. covering its investing activities and dividend payments. If it is not, how is it financing the shortfall? It may be issuing debt or equity securities, selling investments, running down cash, etc. Each course of action has different implications. If the firm is self-financing (has positive free cash flow in the jargon), how is it using its cash? Is it investing, building up cash balances, etc.?

Statement of Total Recognized Gains and Losses

The statement of total recognized gains and losses brings together those gains and losses that have passed through the P&L and those that haven't. Important information often gets lost in the notes to the accounts. This statement—a financial reporting standard requirement for less than a decade—makes it harder for such information to be ignored. For example, in 1988 Polly Peck made an operating profit of £157 million. This appeared in the P&L. It also lost £170 million on adverse exchange rate movements (it borrowed in hard currencies and had deposits in the weak Turkish lira). The currency loss bypassed the P&L and appeared in the reserves. A statement of total recognized gains and losses would have brought the operating profit gain and the exchange rate loss together.

ANALYSING ACCOUNTS

There are a number of steps in analysing accounts. Three questions need answering:

- Is the company earning a satisfactory profit, and what are the prospects?
- Is the company going to have enough cash?
- How risky is the company?

Background

To understand a firm's accounts, it is useful to know as much as possible about the firm and the industry it is in. That will put the accounts in context. The first thing to do is work out what the company does. The R&A will tell you in broad terms, but you will want to know all you can. Which industries does the company operate in, and which segments of those industries? For an automotive company, you might be making distinctions such as cars versus vans/trucks, luxury cars versus mass market, sales to retail versus sales to fleets, and so on. And you will want to know which countries the products are made in and sold in.

Accounts usually contain a chairman's statement, and may contain an operational review and a financial review. All will help provide more understanding of the firm and industry. The chairman's statement will be the most general, and is likely to cover prospects and report on current trading. Reading the previous few years' statements and noting the subsequent profit outcomes will give a feel for what the chairman might mean by 'We expect a satisfactory outcome for the year' or 'While demand is strong for our products, margin pressure is relentless'.

You may not get all the information you want in the accounts, and you should look at any literature the company publishes, whether sales catalogues, reports to employees, or public relations literature. If the company has made capital issues, there will have been prospectuses issued at the time. The company or its industry may have been subject to a report by the Monopolies and Mergers Commission (now the Competition Commission). Searching sources such as McCarthys and FT Profile may throw up newspaper stories about the company. And market research organizations, such as Mintel, may have issued reports on the firm's industry. Most industries have some sort of trade magazine. Some have trade bodies that can be very helpful.

Having decided what segments of what industries the company is in, and where, you might search for relevant statistical series. The trade magazines may publish them and make life easy, or your may have to use an ONS series. The object is to relate industry analysis, or profits, or prices, or whatever, to series such as GNP changes, the level of interest rates, the strength of the pound, and so on.

The most volatile components of GDP are investment and stocks. For example, imagine ABC industry produces 100 units of widgets a year and has been investing in 10 units of replacement plant and machinery and a further 10 units for expansion. Say ABC's sales falls 5% from 100 to 95. It might decide that it should put its expansion investment on hold. The plant and machinery industry's output will fall 50% from 20 to 10. Similar magnification of effect occurs when stocks are cut. It is obviously important to know which factors drive industry demand and how responsive your firm is to changes in these factors. It is rare for an industry to be unaffected by macroeconomic forces. Published statistics are a guide to the past—to forecast future output there is a need for analysts to have some feel for macroeconomic forecasting (see Chapter 8).

The sorts of factors we have discussed affect all firms in an industry. But for a particular firm, sales will also depend on its share of the market. Is the firm winning/losing market share because of superior/inferior products? Is it opening new shops or building more plant? In short, an analysis of the industry is required (see Chapter 8). It is sensible to look at the accounts of the competitors, both for comparative purposes and to understand how they see prospects. Sometimes competitors' chairmen are more forthcoming about industry prospects.

Adjust the Data

Companies can set out their financial statements in a number of ways and still satisfy accounting standards. Some analysts will recalculate some of the entries either to make them more meaningful (in their view), or to make them more comparable with competitors' accounts. For example, any expenditure by a company must appear either in the P&L as an expense (expensed) or in the balance sheet as a capital asset (capitalized). If an expenditure passes through the P&L, profit will be reduced by the full sum spent in the year it is spent. If the expenditure appears in the balance sheet as an asset, profits are reduced over a number of years by a much smaller sum each year, depending on the rate of depreciation. Research and development (R&D) is normally expensed, but may be capitalized. An analyst that does not like R&D being capitalized might adjust the numbers in the accounts.

Summarize the Data

When satisfied with the numbers, they should be summarized. The data may be assessed either at a point in time—cross-sectional analysis—or over time—time-series analysis.

Cross-Sectional Analysis

Two standard techniques for cross-sectional analysis are *common-size statements* and *ratio analysis*. Common-size analysis makes it easier to compare firms in the same industry that are different sizes. Imagine that Sainsbury is being studied. It is difficult to judge Sainsbury in isolation, but data on Safeway, Tesco and ASDA might provide a useful basis for comparison. Unfortunately, the companies are different sizes. However, a common-size balance sheet can be calculated for each by expressing the components of each balance sheet as a percentage of the relevant net assets and total capital employed. A common-size P&L can be calculated by expressing the P&L components as a percentage of turnover. For example, let's take XYZ's P&L in Figure 9.2. Setting turnover at 100%, cost of sales is 72.2% of turnover, gross profit is 27.8%, distribution cost is 6.7%, and so on.

   A better-known approach is ratio analysis. Financial ratios (such as current assets divided by current liabilities) are computed for the company being studied and for comparison companies. Financial ratios are discussed below.

Time-Series Analysis

Time-series analysis uses the techniques of *trend statements*, *ratio analysis* and *variability analysis*. Trend statements are usually made for selected items in the P&L. A starting date is chosen and the item of interest is given a value of 100. Subsequent years' values are shown relative to the base date. Thus, if turnover is being examined and it rises 20% in the second year, the value shown is 120. Ratio analysis involves financial ratios being calculated for a company for a number of years and the results are then examined for any patterns or trends.

Variability analysis uses the value of a financial ratio, say operating profit divided by turnover, over time. For example, say this ratio has been as high as 20% and as low as 2%, and on average has been 9%. A variability ratio could be calculated by subtracting the lower figure from the higher, and dividing by the mean, which in this case gives a ratio of 2. The same ratio could be calculated for competitors.

A Cautionary Note

While all of the above techniques are sensible enough, in practice they may be less useful than hoped:

- Traditional accounts make no allowance for inflation, and this distorts the picture. Historical asset costs may bear little resemblance to current values, turnover should have increased automatically with inflation, and so on.
- Accounting practices may have changed over time so that particular types of cost may be charged to different areas of the firm. This may be a particular problem for firms with a number of divisions or overseas subsidiaries.
- Firms may have changed their accounting policies over the years. R&D may once have been expensed and now is capitalized. In this case, it may be possible to adjust the figures, but not in all cases.
- Accounting standards change over the years and this makes figures from different periods hard to compare.
- Accounting standards vary from one jurisdiction to another, so that even in the same time period it may be difficult to obtain comparative data for a firm whose major competitors are overseas.
- Companies change their composition of businesses over time, which makes comparison over time difficult.
- Companies that have the same core businesses may have different secondary businesses, and comparisons with other firms in the same period may be difficult.

All these difficulties also apply to ratio analysis, to which we now turn.

Ratio Analysis

There are many accounting ratios, and it is useful to group them into four categories:

- *Liquidity ratios:* measures of how easily a firm can meet its short-run obligations.
- *Gearing or leverage ratios:* measures of how heavily in debt a company is and, because debt gets the first call on resources, how geared shareholders' returns are.

- *Efficiency ratios:* measures of the efficiency of a firm.
- *Market ratios:* measures of how a company is rated in the stockmarket.

In Table 9.1, we show some of the ratios in each category that might be calculated.

Two things should be noted about Table 9.1. First, many accountants will compute the same ratios in slightly different ways. Second, many more ratios might have been listed. Those listed are well known, but not necessarily the most useful for every company.

The liquidity ratios provide information about the risk of the firm not being able to meet its short-term liabilities. The gearing ratios provide information about the long-term risks of insolvency. The first four shown are traditional financial ratios. But they relate to the past. What would happen if economic circumstances change? To answer that, it is useful to look at past sales variability. If sales have been very volatile, then the greater the risk from high financial gearing. As well as financial gearing, operational gearing has to be considered. Costs can be split into fixed (those that don't change with changes in output, e.g. the cost of security guards, rent) and variable (those that do change, e.g. raw materials). A firm with high fixed costs will experience sharp drops in profitability when demand falls, and strong gains when demand rises. It would have high operational gearing.

Performance ratios are usually examined by analysts, but what they show is debatable. They relate to the past, and are based on historical costs that have been subjected to depreciation charges that may bear little relation to any decline in economic value. Moreover, while a high return on capital is usually applauded, arguably the firm would be underinvesting, since it would be rational to keep investing until the return equalled the cost of capital.

We discuss market ratios elsewhere in this book, but it is worth mentioning the taxation of dividends. Until April 1999, companies were subject to advance corporation tax (ACT). The rules were complex, but from the viewpoint of the investor, what happened was that if a firm declared a net dividend of, say, 80p, it paid 80p to the investor and 20p to the Inland Revenue as ACT. The investor received a tax credit. The investor who was not liable to tax (pension funds, charities, etc.) reclaimed the 20p, and so got 100p. A lower-rate (20%) taxpayer had nothing further to pay, and a standard-rate (23%) taxpayer had, by concession, nothing further to pay, so they both got 80p. The higher-rate (40%) taxpayer had another 20% to pay (at a later date) and so ended up with 60p. Dividends were shown in the press grossed up, i.e. pre-tax, or 100p in this case. Dividend yields were calculated on gross dividends.

Under the present system there is no ACT, but a net dividend carries a 10% tax credit. So, for an 80p net dividend, the tax credit would be 8.89p (because 8.89p is 10% of 88.89p, or 80p plus 8.89p). Tax-exempt investors receive the 80p but cannot reclaim the 10% credit. Lower-rate taxpayers and standard-rate taxpayers receive 80p and have nothing further to pay. Higher-rate taxpayers are taxed at 32.5% of the 88.89p but are given a 10% tax credit. Consequently, they

TABLE 9.1 A selection of accounting ratios

Category/ratio	Definition	Purpose
Liquidity		
Current ratio	$$\frac{\text{Current assets}}{\text{Current liabilities}}$$	Shows extent to which short-term assets cover short-term liabilities.
Quick ratio	$$\frac{\text{Current assets} - \text{inventories}}{\text{Current liabilities}}$$	As above, but excludes inventories, which may be difficult to turn into cash in some circumstances.
Cash flow liquidity ratio	$$\frac{\text{Operating cash flow}}{\text{Average current liabilities}}$$	Shows cash flow cover for short-term liabilities.
Gearing		
Debt ratio	$$\frac{\text{Debt}}{\text{Debt} + \text{shareholders' equity}}$$	Shows debt's weight in the capital structure. Long-term lease agreements involve fixed payments and may be added to numerator and denominator.
Debt-to-capitalization	$$\frac{\text{Debt at market value (MV)}}{\text{Debt (MV)} + \text{shareholders' equity (MV)}}$$	As above, but using market values.
Debt-equity ratio	$$\frac{\text{Debt}}{\text{Shareholders' equity}}$$	Debt as a proportion of equity.
Times interest covered	$$\frac{\text{Profit before interest and tax}}{\text{Interest}}$$	Shows interest cover for debt servicing.
Sales variability	$$\frac{\text{Standard deviation of sales}}{\text{Average sales}}$$	Measures how variable sales are.
Operational gearing	$$\frac{\text{Turnover} - \text{variable costs}}{\text{Trading profits}}$$	Operational gearing shows the effect of the split between fixed costs (those that don't vary with output) and variable (those that do).
Efficiency		
Profit margin	$$\frac{\text{Trading profit}}{\text{Sales}} \times 100$$	Indicates basic cost structure of a firm.
Return on capital employed	$$\frac{\text{Trading profit}}{\text{Average capital employed}}$$	Measure of how well resources have been used.
Sales to capital employed	$$\frac{\text{Sales}}{\text{Average capital employed}}$$	High figure might indicate effective use of capital, but could show insufficient capital and possible future problems.
Market ratios		
Price-earnings ratio	$$\frac{\text{Share price}}{\text{EPS}}$$	Measure of investors' regard for a company's prospects (high is better).
Dividend yield	$$\frac{\text{Net dividend}}{\text{Share price}} \times 100$$	A high yield suggests shares have little expected growth or are very risky.
Net asset value (NAV) per share	$$\frac{\text{Ordinary shareholders' funds}}{\text{Number of ordinary shares in issue}}$$	Expresses asset value on a per-share basis.
Price to NAV (or book in US)	$$\frac{\text{Share price}}{\text{NAV}}$$	Shows premium (>1) or discount (<1) of market value to amount invested by shareholders or retained on their behalf.

have to pay an additional 22.5% of 88.89p, i.e. 20p, and still end up with 60p (isn't tax fun?). If we concentrate on the extremes, the tax-exempt investor and the 40% taxpayer, their grossed-up dividends are 80p and 100p. In other words, there is no single grossed-up figure. Because of this, yields are now shown net in the press.

Forecasting Profits

There are two types of profits forecast: statistical and judgmental. In the first, a variety of statistical techniques may be used, some simple and some complex. A discussion of appropriate statistical techniques lies outside the scope of this book. Most analysts in the UK use the judgemental approach, and since academics usually avoid such mundane stuff, we will discuss it here.

The usual starting point is an attempt to forecast not profits but the components of profit—all the revenues and all the costs—and thereby derive profits. If the work described in 'Background' (p. 150) has not been done, now is the time to do it.

In the R&A, what is reported is not units sold but turnover (i.e. units times price). An attempt will be made to forecast both price and volume. Some years ago, when inflation was high, one might have begun by assuming a 10% price increase and adjusting up or down from there. Now it would be safer to assume no price change as the base forecast. Next, we would assess the state of competition in the industry and the firm's strategy (see Chapter 8). Is rivalry intense in the industry? Will weak demand and high fixed costs lead to price cutting? Is there a threat of entry by new suppliers? Is there a cap on prices because of the threat of a substitute product? What is the firm's strategy to position itself in the industry? Is it employing penetration pricing to gain market share? Is it investing heavily to be the lowest-cost producer and letting prices move down with its costs? Is it repositioning itself to the highly differentiated end of the market and increasing its prices in the process?

Out of all of this, some sort of turnover expectation will arise, although it may be as crude as volume: +10%, price: +5%, therefore turnover: +15.5%. Where data allow, this sort of approach will be applied to every segment of the business. For those involving overseas transactions, allowance must be made for exchange-rate changes, care being taken where the company states that it hedges part of its currency exposure.

Turning to costs, we have seen that firms usually show cost of sales, distribution costs and administrative costs. How much detail will appear in the notes will vary greatly from firm to firm. Some details, such as the number of staff and their wages, must be shown, as must depreciation.

How accurately costs can be forecast will depend on the industry, the amount of detail shown in the accounts, the analyst's knowledge about the proportion of the various costs (e.g. are raw materials 20% or 80% of cost of sales?). For many industries, it may be acceptable or necessary to use forecasts of general wage increases, while in others, specific knowledge will be necessary. In some industries, general inflation rates may be assumed for raw materials, but in some the price of, say, tea or oil might hold the key. All costs need to be adjusted for likely changes in output levels and for anticipated changes in efficiency (perhaps a 10% planned reduction of the labour force has been announced). Depreciation can be estimated from the R&A notes, making allowance for any expected changes in the capital stock. As with revenues, changes in exchange rates may have to be allowed for.

The P&L will also include entries reflecting whether a company has an interest in other companies. Depending on their relative size, these can either be the subject of detailed forecasts or a crude 'up 5%' type of forecast.

The P&L will show interest items, both paid and received. These can change substantially from year to year. Some debt (and cash held) will bear a fixed rate, but some will bear a variable rate, which will cause fluctuations from year to year. However, the more important consideration may be the amount of debt. The various liquidity ratios should be examined to see if raising more cash is desirable. Also, the cash flow should be forecast and assessed. To do this, assumptions will have to be made about the cost of the dividend to be paid and the tax due. If, for example, a large expansion in capacity is made, there may be substantial outgoings with little associated revenue in the accounting period. In that case, cash may be run down (lower interest received), or borrowings increased (higher interest paid), or new shares issued (higher dividend), or any combination of the three. How likely an increase in capital expenditure is may be suggested by company statements, or ratios such as sales to capital employed becoming unusually large. The choice between debt and equity will, in part, depend on the firm's gearing ratios.

For some companies, it may be necessary to have a stab at forecasting exceptional items. For example, companies in industries in decline often have regular exceptional costs associated with plant closures.

At the end of all this, we hopefully have a profit forecast. The forecast may be for the current year or even the previous year! For example, a company with a December year end might announce its 1999 results in April 2000. As a result, in March 2000, we would be looking at a forecast for the previous calendar year. However, the markets always refer to the year to be reported next as the current year. In March 2000, we would have had half-year figures in the interim statement, so it is effectively a half-year forecast, and the market would also be looking at forecasts for the next year, which in this case would be financial year 2000. Once the results for 1999 are available, forecasts for 2001 will start appearing.

For years beyond 2001, an analyst is likely to make forecasts only in the most general terms—profits are likely to grow in line with the market, or 3% faster, or whatever.

You may feel that the scope for forecasting errors is enormous. And in reality, forecasts are often wide of the mark. However, the errors are somewhat less than ought to be expected given the subjective nature of the forecasting process. What the textbooks usually omit is that analysts from the major stockbroking firms and fund management firms get to discuss the company with company executives, in particular the finance director. Companies typically want analysts' forecasts to be in the right ballpark. Providing the analyst has put in some effort, finance directors will be helpful. They often give approximate splits of activities that do not appear in the accounts. They may explain what drives profits in their industry and give non-quantitative direction ('Yes, that is definitely improving, but we would be delighted if it did as well as you are estimating'), or point to errors in assumptions ('Well, you've certainly worked out how to estimate our tea plantation profits, based on auction tea prices, but are you aware that the two groups of our Indian plantations have different year ends, so different calendar periods get consolidated into our accounts?'). Sometimes they even tell analysts when not to bother ('We find that area hard too—we just assume it will grow in line with nominal GDP'). With this sort of help, analysts forecast better than might be expected.

A final point: the executives of a firm will often be an excellent source of information on their competitors. For example, if ABC executives won't say what their market share is, JFK executives may well be happy to give their estimate of it. And while companies often stress their good points, competitors will often happily list their bad points.

FINANCIAL COOKING OR MECHANICAL MANIPULATION?

The way we have described financial analysis makes it a creative activity. Pick the ratios *de jure*, blend with some facts, sniff the liquidity crisis, stir occasionally, and strain out the forecast. The problem is that it is not always clear exactly what it is that is being made, or what should be done with it when it is. If you find a ratio of 2, you might think that it is 'OK'. And if it is 2.2? Well, that's probably 'OK' too, as might be 1.8 or 2.4. With this sort of latitude, accounts with ratios at different ends of the acceptable range for a number of ratios might all be classified as 'OK'. Does this mean that once we rule out a liquidity crisis, our only interest in the accounts is how they help to make good earnings forecasts? And if that's the case, are the right ratios being examined? And what if the accounts fall short of 'OK'? Say the accounts show different ratios pointing in different directions? How are they weighted and evaluated? These sort of questions suggest that instead of traditional ratio analysis, we should be statistically combining a number of ratios and attempting to achieve specific goals. One goal might be to pick shares that will beat the market, another might be to avoid shares that go bust. We will look at each in turn.

Predicting Winners

One goal is to use financial statement analysis to pick shares that will outperform the market. Ou and Penman (1989) showed that by using financial statement numbers, it was possible to predict abnormal (good or bad) returns from US shares. They started with 68 accounting variables and used a purely empirical approach to try to relate some of these variables to forecast earnings increases or decreases. The investment strategy was to invest in the shares with predicted earnings increases and short those with earnings decreases. This empirical approach of choosing variables by what works best may be justified on the grounds that there is no clear theory relating accounting variables to share outperformance or underperformance.

Setiono and Strong (1998) replicated Ou and Penman's study for the UK. We will describe the UK study. Setiono and Strong were able to obtain UK data for 53 of the 68 variables used in the US study. They reduced the list of variables by looking at the relationship of each variable to future earnings. They then used a statistical technique to select the best group of variables with which to make predictions from those that individually appeared to have predictive ability. They did this for the periods 1974–79 and 1980–84. In both periods, they used eight variables, four of which were common between the two periods. The common ratios, and whether the relationship was positive or negative, are shown below:

- return on opening equity (–)
- pre-tax income to sales (+)
- net profit margin (–)
- working capital to total assets (–)

In out-of-sample predictions, Setiono and Strong correctly classified about 64% of the shares as to whether they would have positive or negative earnings changes. Had a hedge fund been formed holding long and short positions (so there is no net investment), and the fund held for two years, trading profits in excess of 11% could have been earned.

Lev and Thiagarajan (1993) took a different tack. They identified a shorter list of accounting variables possibly relevant to evaluating firms' stockmarket performance and to measuring 'quality' of earnings, earning persistence, etc. by looking at the pronouncements of US security analysts on what was important. While this approach does not use prior theory, it is a 'guided' search of relevant variables. It produced 12 variables that might be relevant. Lev and Thiagarajan reasoned that the variables might have different degrees of relevance depending on the state of the economy. They described this by the rate of inflation, the annual change in GNP, and the annual change in the level of business inventories. They found that most of the 12 fundamental variables were (in the jargon) value relevant. Also, their significance varied with macroeconomic conditions. They found that their fundamental variables contributed significantly to explaining stock excess returns beyond that explained by reported earnings. They manipulated the fundamental variables to produce a single aggregate score for each stock. They believed they were measuring 'quality' of earnings. They found that the aggregate scores were related to subsequent earnings growth.

What this type of research shows is that fundamental accounting analysis can be used to predict returns over the next year. It does this by providing information that will eventually be used by the market. Abarbanell and Bushee (1997), again for the US, show that several of Lev and Thiagarajan's variables are significantly related to future earnings and, to a lesser extent, analysts' forecast revisions of future earnings. Abarbanell and Bushee find that analysts' forecasts do not reflect all the information about future earnings that are contained in the fundamental variables. Abarbanell and Bushee (1998) also show that excess returns can be earned by using fundamental variables.

Al-Debie and Walker (1999) replicate Lev and Thiagarajan's work for the UK. However, because of data limitations they were only able to use seven of the 12 variables. They used abnormal changes in stocks of finished goods, debtors, capital expenditure, gross margins, distribution and administrative expense, and labour force. They allowed for the state of the economy and also for what industry a firm was in. To get a benchmark, they forecast stock returns using only earnings data. Their model had an adjusted R^2 of 34%. Extending the basic model to include the seven fundamental variables showed the stocks of finished goods and debtors were not statistically significant. These variables were dropped. Using the remaining five variables, plus allowing for different macroeconomic circumstances and different industries, raised the adjusted R^2 to 43%. The authors suggest that the fundamental variables are value relevant and contain information about future operating costs of firms.

Clearly, the approach to accounting data adopted by the studies we have discussed is a long way from that of the creative cook approach. The approach is new, more formal, and harder to implement. As a result, it may offer more chance of beating the market; or it may turn out that the equations are unstable over time.

Avoiding Losers

Holding the shares of a stock that becomes bankrupt kills portfolio returns. (Strictly speaking, only individuals become bankrupt in the UK; companies go into liquidation or administration.) Detailed accounting and economic analysis may identify these companies, but investors who focus on attributes, for example small size or high yield, may miss the signs. Some form of accounting screen for bankruptcy would be useful.

Some early US work on this issue was undertaken by Beaver (1968) who analysed trends of seven financial ratios for five years prior to the failure of 79 firms. He compared these firms with 79 others that were matched for industry and size. He found some clear trends, for example the mean cash flow/total debt ratio for the control firms was a little under one-half in each year, whereas for the failed firms, five years before failure it was around one-quarter and it fell to minus one-quarter one year before failure.

If financial ratios can distinguish between failing and non-failing firms, then combining the ratios into an equation might lead to useful predictions. There are a number of US models, and the best known have been developed by Altman. The original Altman (1968) model utilizes five financial ratios that are combined and analysed by a statistical procedure called discriminant analysis. An overall discriminant score, or Z score, is produced for a company from the following equation:

Z = (0.12 × working capital/total assets) + (0.14 × retained earnings/total assets) + (0.33 × earnings before interest and taxes/total assets) + (0.006 × market value of equity/book value of total debt) + (0.1 × sales/total assets).

Equations such as this have limited accuracy. Some firms that are expected to survive will fail, and some firms that are expected to fail will survive. The higher the Z score, the less the likelihood of failing. Above a certain cut-off score, firms are expected to survive; below that, they are expected to fail. If the cut-off Z score is set at a very low number, there will not be many firms expected to fail that actually survive. On the other hand, a lot of the eventual failures will be classified as survivors. If the cut-off Z score is set at a high number, the opposite type of error will occur. Where the Z score cut-off is set depends on which type of error is most important. Altman chose a cut-off Z score of 2.675—firms scoring below that were expected to fail. Naturally this score gave good results on the sample Altman used to devise his numbers. On a second sample, the numbers were poorer but still useful, as Table 9.2 shows.

TABLE 9.2   Z score classification accuracy

Actual	Predicted	
	Failed	Survived
Failed	24	14
Survived	1	52

Source: Altman (1968, pp. 601–2).

As can be seen from Table 9.2, all but one of the firms expected to fail did, whereas about one-fifth of those expected to survive in fact failed. The data shown are for a one-year prediction horizon; a two-year horizon produced more classification errors and beyond that the Z score had no real power.

Altman et al. (1977) subsequently extended Altman's work to develop a Zeta model. This combined readily available financial statement data adjusted to reflect current accounting standards. The variables used measured overall profitability, size, debt service, liquidity, cumulative profitability, capitalization and stability of earnings over a 10-year period. Looking at 73 bankruptcies that occurred after the model's development, it correctly identified 68 of the 73 using data from one statement prior to failure and 62 out of 71 using data from two statements prior to failure. It is interesting that there is a high correlation between Zeta scores and Value Line's relative financial strength measure (see Altman and Spivack, 1983).

Z score models have been developed for the UK and are sold by commercial organizations. Taffler (1984) reviews these models, and his own model is discussed in Taffler (1983). Taffler uses an approach similar to Altman; the variables he uses are profit before tax/average current liabilities, current assets/total liabilities, current liabilities/total assets, and the no-credit interval (i.e. the number of days a company can continue to trade if it generates no revenues). Taffler claims that his model has true predictive ability: the probability of a firm classified as 'at risk' by his model subsequently failing within a year was six times greater than for a firm selected at random. One problem is that his model on average classifies about one-sixth of all firms as 'at risk'. This is much lower than some other models, but still a large number.

Z scores are ordinal but nonlinear. This means that a Z score of, for example, 2 is better than a Z score of 1, but it is not necessarily twice as good. However, it has been claimed that if all companies' Z scores are ranked and then transformed into a scale of 0–100, this problem is overcome. This procedure allows a company's Z score to be tracked over the years to see both whether the company is at risk and whether it is deteriorating or improving relative to other companies. The statistical validity of this approach has been challenged.

Z score models have been criticized frequently (e.g. see Pratt, 1993, on the Bank of England's experience). There is no accounting theory behind the variables used—the whole procedure is an exercise in data mining. Also, the accounting data are made available in the annual R&A, but firms can deteriorate rapidly in less than a year. Creative accounting (see below) has sometimes rendered accounts misleading. Different industries have different relationships, and one really needs industry-specific Z scores.

However, even if Z scores have predictive value, would they be useful for investors? That depends on how information about deteriorating companies is incorporated into stock prices. There is ample US evidence (e.g. Clark and Weinstein, 1983; and Aharony et al., 1980) that firms entering bankruptcy generate abnormal losses for shareholders from around five years prior to bankruptcy. Despite the long-term decline, significant losses take place on the days surrounding the bankruptcy. The studies imply that abnormal profits can be earned if bankruptcy is predicted.

Katz et al. (1985) studied a sample of New York Stock Exchange stocks for the period 1968–76. They used the Z score cut-off of 2.675 and looked for firms that went from above 2.675 to below, and vice versa; they called their two groups a 'distress group' and a 'recovery group'. Katz and co-workers found that in the 15 months preceding the issuance of the annual report that led to the change in state as classified by the Z score, significant positive abnormal returns accrued to the recovery group, and vice versa for the distress group. Both groups produced abnormal returns in the expected direction over the following nine months. The study's results held regardless of whether the market model or CAPM was used to adjust for risk. Against this study should be set that by Zavgren et al. (1988), who have produced results that they claim support a view that it is difficult to achieve abnormal returns from bankruptcy prediction models.

In the UK, Taffler (1997) claims that a portfolio of 'solvent' firms outperforms at-risk firms, as measured by Z scores, by about 1% per quarter.

What should one conclude? Clearly one does not want to hold stocks that go bust. But many stocks in poor financial health will recover and could produce spectacular returns. Indeed, some US fund managers specialize in 'phoenix' stocks, and there are books recommending such a strategy (e.g. Grace, 1985). Ignoring all stocks that are at risk could eliminate a big part of the market, including some big winners. If an investor follows a strategy of picking low price-earnings ratio stocks or neglected stocks or any approach that will select some stocks that may be cheap for a good reason, then it makes sense to scan the selected stocks to see if they might be heading towards bankruptcy. This scan can be made based on general experience and standard accounting skills, but it could also be by a Z score model.

CAN YOU BELIEVE WHAT YOU READ?

Accounting principles are not rigid and unambiguous. They are, rightly, somewhat flexible, and honest men can disagree as to how a particular issue should be treated. But this flexibility and inevitable uncertainty give scope for creative accounting, which ranges from putting the best face on a situation to misrepresentation. So, can you believe what you read?

Creative Accounting

Naser and Pendelbury (1992) found that UK auditors thought that creative accounting was widespread. But some of the practices that upset investors and regulators in the 1980s have been made more difficult under the accounting standards set in the 1990s. In many cases, the practices are still permitted, although disclosure is required. Even seemingly reasonable actions can have important consequences. For example, a company may revalue its fixed assets upwards. In terms of the accounting identities at the start of this chapter, both sides of the equals sign will be increased, i.e. assets will increase and the revaluation reserve within shareholders' funds will increase. The depreciation charge will rise, and profits will be correspondingly reduced. Profit/asset ratios will deteriorate. However, all debt/assets ratios will improve, and the absolute value of capital employed will grow. The adverse profit consequences may be a small price to pay if the goal was to increase borrowings. If, at the same time, the economic life of fixed assets was revised upwards, then depreciation per year would fall, thereby increasing reported profits, and offsetting some or all of the previous adverse effects on profits. Again, if the goal is to strengthen the balance sheet, then an issue of preference shares can be structured so that while classified as equity, they are, in reality, loans. The effect is to improve debt/capital employed ratios, while actually having the opposite effect.

Yet, since these examples are so transparent, one may reasonably wonder whether they really mislead investment professionals. Accounts are commented on in the press, and investment analysts and investors scrutinize them. Publications such as *Company Reporting* draw attention to how companies report key items in their accounts. Those who believe in efficient markets argue that creative accounting doesn't fool the markets. We think creative accounting does often mislead. There are three reasons for our belief.

Smith's *Accounting for Growth* (1992) was a highly publicized book that examined creative accounting. It was based on Smith and Hannah (1991), a stockbroking research paper that was voted by institutional investors the best piece of institutional research in 1991. If everybody was fully aware of sharp accounting practices, is it likely that this sort of paper would be held in high regard?

Second, there is evidence that a lot of analysts are weak on accounting matters. Breton and Taffler (1995), in a laboratory experiment, asked 63 experienced stockbrokers' analysts to process real accounts. The aim was to see whether the analysts would spot creative accounting and make adjustments when calculating various ratios. They found the rate of correction to be very low.

Of course, it could be argued that while most analysts don't make the necessary adjustments, prices of securities are set by those that do. In that case, creative accounting will already be discounted, and a publication noting the creativity should not affect prices. Our third point is that this does not appear to be true. Briloff, a noted critic of US accounting standards, published a number of books and various articles in magazines, such as *Barron's*, criticizing companies' financial reports. Foster (1979) looked at 15 of Briloff's articles and calculated the abnormal return (based on a version of the CAPM) suffered by 28 companies criticized in his articles. He looked at the abnormal returns for 30 days before and after publication. On average, the companies suffered an immediate 8% fall in their share price. This fall was maintained for the 30-day period following the articles. Foster looked at a number of possible explanations for the price reaction, e.g. Briloff had access to new information, other information was released at the time, and Briloff's expose might prompt government regulation, but Foster ruled these out. One is left to wonder whether this study shows how quickly new information is incorporated into prices (although one cannot say whether the price reaction is too little or too much), or whether it shows how little skilled accounting analysis is in fact incorporated into prices. The latter would suggest scope to earn substantial returns from a modest application of accounting skills.

What are the implications of our view for a professional? The typical institutional investor would be delighted to beat the market by 1% a year. Not much, but over the years it would mount up. If an institutional portfolio holds, say, 50 shares, then if just one share has a precipitous decline in value the typical institutional investor would not expect to outperform in the year that happened: it is important to avoid the investment dogs. If one employs an attribute style of investing, say combining low price-earnings ratio and good earnings growth, it is easy for fund managers to skip over some of the tedious aspects of fund management—like getting to grips with accounts. Many creative accounting problems seem to be noted by brokers' analysts or the press. Sometimes they may be a bit slow in noting the problem, but they still often do it before a precipitous share-price decline. However, many investment managers simply lack the accounting skills to appraise the accounting problem when alerted to it and to make a sensible investment judgement. If the market does not fully discount creative accounting, then some effort in improving accounting skills will be valuable. This is not to deny that the market discounts much creative accounting, just that sufficient is not discounted for it to be worth spending some time studying accounts.

Further, even if the market does fully discount creative accounting, then it is important for analysts to understand what the market is discounting so that sensible decisions can be made. For example, Coloroll was rated lowly before its spectacular collapse partly because of its contingent liabilities. A low price-earnings ratio investor who understood this fully would be in a better position to make decisions than one who did not. A pure low price-earnings ratio investor, i.e. one who looked at nothing but the level of the relative price-earnings ratio, would have believed the shares were cheap. Investors who applied fundamental analysis to a low price-earnings ratio universe would have had varying views. Those who understood the accounting issues and believed the economy would be strong might also have thought the shares were cheap. Those who understood the accounting issues and thought consumer expenditure was going to fall might have thought the company was vulnerable, and thus selected a different share from the low price-earnings ratio universe.

True and Fair

Once one has become aware of creative accounting, all changes in company accounts may be viewed with suspicion. That would be a mistake. Aboody et al. (1999) looked at upward revaluations of fixed assets by UK companies and found the revaluations were related positively to future performance, over one, two and three years. Performance was measured by operating profit and cash from operations. Aboody et al. also found that current-year revaluations were related positively to share returns. In the previous section, we explained why high-debt firms might be keen to revalue assets upwards. Aboody found the performance and returns data weaker for high debt-to-equity firms. In general, then, upward revaluations appear to reflect management's expectations about future performance and are not, in the main, creative fabrications.

OPPORTUNITY COSTS AND ECONOMIC VALUE ADDED

For the final topic of this chapter, we pose a fundamental question: what do we mean by profit? Economists might answer this question by posing another. What is the cost of a product, an experience, or indeed anything? In a fundamental sense, it is the alternative foregone. The cost of the product you produced is the most profitable product you didn't produce as a result. The cost of a walk in the park for a student might be an hour of studying. The cost of the product you bought is your most preferred product you couldn't buy as a result. These alternatives are the opportunity you missed in each case—the opportunity cost of what you did.

This analysis can be applied to a firm. The traditional example is that of a sole proprietor who works in his business and uses his capital. He might tell the Inland Revenue (and himself) that he has made a profit of £25 000 in the past year. But if he looks at opportunity costs, he might get a different picture. Say he could earn £20 000 working for somebody else. And say he could invest the £100 000 tied up in his business at 7%. Then his opportunity costs are £20 000 plus £7000, or £27 000. His business doesn't generate as much money as his alternative use of himself and his capital. He is operating a business that does not add any economic value. In fact, it destroys value by £2000.

Of course, in published accounts for firms, management salaries and interest are charged before profits are struck. But no charge is made for equity capital. To see whether a company is adding value or destroying it, shouldn't we make a charge for equity? Many economists, accountants and businessmen argue that we should. In accounting this concept is called 'residual income'.

Residual income has historically been applied to divisions. For these, income is net income less imputed interest, where the interest is the cost of capital. Assume a division has capital of £10 million, earns £1.2 million after taxes, and has a cost of capital of 9%. Residual income is calculated as divisional net income after taxes (£1.2m) less imputed cost of capital (£10m × 9% = £0.9m), which equals £0.3m. This is a profitable division—it earns more than the opportunity cost of capital employed. The conventional return on investment (ROI) would be 12% ([£1.2m/£10m] × 100%).

Why calculate residual income instead of ROI? The answer is that the two methods give different incentives. If a new project comes along with prospects identical to the numbers shown above, a division with a current ROI of 20% might turn it down to avoid reducing its ROI. A division with an ROI of 9% might want to carry it out. Top management should want the project undertaken: it adds value to the business. With residual income as the criterion, both divisions would want to undertake the project as it produces additional residual income.

Currently, the most popular variant of residual income is the US consulting firm Stern Stewart & Co.'s Economic Value Added, trademarked as EVA™. EVA is intended to be an estimate of a firm's true economic profit. It can be applied at the divisional level, and the firm level. It differs from traditional accounting profit in three ways:

1. EVA is the residual income obtained after subtracting all capital costs.
2. Capital is charged at a rate that compensates investors for the risk they bear. This risk is priced using the CAPM.

3. EVA adjusts reported accounting figures to eliminate distortions to true economic profit. Stern Stewart claims to have identified 164 accounting distortions but usually only makes 5–10 adjustments. Adjustments are made if they are significant, the information is easily available, and non-finance professionals will understand the adjustments.

EVA may be boiled down to:

> Sales
> − Operating expenses (including tax)
> = Operating profit
> − Financing expense (cost of capital × capital)
> = EVA.

Were it not for the accounting adjustments, EVA and residual income would be the same.

When EVA profits are calculated at the firm level, many firms showing profits in the P&L are found to be destroying value. The question for investors is whether traditional accounting earnings or EVA is the more useful measure for explaining stock returns. In a detailed examination using US data, Biddle et al. (1997, 1999) found that traditional accounting earnings were more highly associated with returns than was EVA. The article is criticized by O'Byrne (1999). Given the limited evidence available, it is not clear that EVA helps pick winning shares. Note carefully that this says nothing about a firm adopting EVA as an internal control and incentive mechanism. EVA may improve a firm's operations (see Biddle et al., 1999; and Kleiman, 1999) without being a useful tool for stock pickers.

CONCLUDING COMMENTS

In this chapter we outlined the major financial statements produced by a company in its R&A—the balance sheet, P&L, cash flow statement and statement of recognized gains and losses. The information in the R&A was discussed, including the types of analysis that may be employed and ways of supplementing the information. Methods used by analysts to forecast profits were discussed. The discussion to this point was concerned with traditional methods of analysis. We then looked at some newer ways of using accounting information to pick winners or avoid losers. We then looked at whether accounting information could be trusted, and concluded by looking at the opportunity cost approach to recasting reported profits.

10

Dividend Discount and Price-Earnings Models

Just making money is not enough any more. Now we have to worry about our money making money.

Woody Allen

In a classic study, Williams (1938) argued that the value of an asset could be established by a present value calculation. For equities, this calculation is made by means of a dividend discount model (DDM). A simplification of this approach involves calculating an appropriate price-earnings ratio. Each of these approaches provides a means of developing explicit return estimates for individual shares, sectors or the market as a whole. The model builder is forced to specify those factors believed to be of relevance and to systematically forecast them.

The discounted dividend approach requires knowledge of the concepts of the time value of money, present value, and discounting. Readers familiar with these concepts should skip the next section.

THE TIME VALUE OF MONEY AND DISCOUNTING

Would you rather have £100 now or next year? Most people would take the money now. Consequently, money is said to have a time value—money is preferred sooner rather than later. There are three reasons for this: utility, risk and opportunity cost. Let's take each in turn.

Money is usually wanted for what it will buy, for its ability to provide goods that give satisfaction or utility. Most people would prefer to have that utility now rather than some time in the future. Second, having money now rather than in the future would seem to be less risky. The chances of not getting a promised sum of money seem likely to rise the further into the future is the payment date. Finally, if one has money now, it can be placed on deposit and earn interest. Thus, £100 now may be worth £110 in a year's time. The £10 difference would be the opportunity cost of getting the money in a year rather than now.

Of course, while money now is worth more than money in the future, there will be some sum of future money that, if we were offered it, would make us indifferent between that sum and some smaller sum today. For example, we might be indifferent between £100 today and £110 in one year. With this background, we can now move on to discounting.

The concepts that we will discuss here are compound interest, future value, present value and a discount rate. We begin with compound interest or compound growth, with which everyone is familiar. If we leave money in our bank account, we benefit from compound interest. If we deposit £100 and earn interest at 10% on the balance, after one year we have £110 (i.e. £100 × 1.10), after two years we have £121 (i.e. £110 × 1.10), and after three years £133.10 (i.e. £121 × 1.10). The increase is larger every year because we get interest on both the original investment and the interest added in the previous periods.

Future value is the value in the future of some quantity subject to compound interest. Present value is the value of that quantity today. Thus, the future value of £100 in three years earning 10% per annum is £133.10. More generally, if P_0 is the starting principal, or present value, i is the rate of interest earned, and t is the time period, then the future value is:

$$P_t = P_0 (1 + i)^t.$$

For our example, this is:

$$P_3 = 100 (1 + 0.1)^3$$

i.e. the future value in year three is:

$$£100 \times 1.10 \times 1.10 \times 1.10 = £133.10.$$

The formula for future value can be rearranged to give an expression for present value:

$$P_0 = \frac{P_t}{(1 + i)^t}.$$

The present value of £133.10 received in three years with a discount rate of 10% is:

$$\frac{£133.10}{1.10 \times 1.10 \times 1.10} = £100.$$

What we did above was to assume a discount rate and a future value and calculate a present value. We could assume a future value and present value and find the discount rate that makes them equal. For example, we could ask what discount rate would make £133.10 received in three years' time equal to a present value of £100. We already know the answer: it is 10%. This discount rate is the return from the investment. Depending on the context, the discount rate is described as the required return or the expected return.

With this as background, we can turn to the DDM.

AN INTRODUCTION TO DIVIDEND DISCOUNT MODELS

What is the value of a share held for one year? It is the value of the dividend and the value of the share when sold in one year's time. And what is the value of the share in one year's time? It is the value of the dividend in the second year and the value of the share at the end of that year. This argument can be extended indefinitely so that the value of a share is simply the value of all the dividends for eternity. We know that money has a time value so the present value of a share (i.e. the current price) will be the sum of all the dividends, each one discounted. This can be shown as:

$$\text{Price of share} = \frac{\text{dividend in year one}}{(1 + \text{discount rate})} + \frac{\text{dividend in year two}}{(1 + \text{discount rate})^2} + \frac{\text{dividend in year three}}{(1 + \text{discount rate})^3} + \dots + \frac{\text{dividend in year } n}{(1 + \text{discount rate})^n}$$

or, using symbols:

$$P_0 = \frac{D_t}{1 + k} + \frac{D_{t+1}}{(1 + k)^2} + \frac{D_{t+2}}{(1 + k)^3} + \dots + \frac{D_{t+n}}{(1 + k)^n}$$

where P_0 is the price of the share, D is the dividend and k is the discount rate.

The reader might wonder what has happened to earnings. Earnings are still implicitly in this model because dividends are simply earnings multiplied by a payout ratio. Thus, if a firm usually pays out 60% of earnings as a dividend, then there is a direct link between earnings and dividends. It is natural to ask why we only value part of earnings, i.e. the amount paid out as a dividend. The answer is that earnings not paid out as dividends are retained in the firm and invested in the maintenance or growth of the business and should result in higher dividends in the future.

The above equation requires us to forecast each dividend until eternity. Since this is an impossible task, some simplifying assumptions are made in practice. Three common models and their assumptions are:

- a one-stage model that takes the current dividend and assumes it grows at the same rate for ever;
- a two-stage model that either makes specific forecasts for each year of the first period or assumes that growth at the same rate occurs each year, and which then assumes in the second stage the same growth rate as the average firm;

● a three-stage model that is the same as the two-stage model with an extra middle stage, during which the two different growth rates converge. A version of such a model is shown in Figure 10.1.

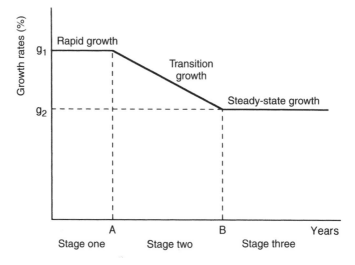

FIGURE 10.1   Three-stage dividend growth model

Most users don't go beyond a three-stage model although one UK stockbroker has used a four-stage model: stage one was forecast dividend growth for the next two years; stage two forecast normalized growth for years three to five; stage three assumed dividends moved in a hyperbolic fashion to the market rate; and stage four assumed all dividends grow at the market rate.

These various stages models greatly simplify the dividend forecasts required. Consider first the least realistic model, the one-stage constant-growth-rate model. By assuming a constant growth rate, g, it can be shown that on the assumption that k is greater than g, then the DDM can be simplified to the following (in which we have also dropped the subscripts):

$$P = \frac{D}{(k - g)}$$

i.e. price = next dividend/(discount rate – dividend growth rate).

Alternatively, if we swap the terms around:

$$k = \frac{D}{P} + g$$

i.e. expected return = dividend yield + dividend growth rate.

These last two equations are simplified DDMs for a firm growing at a constant rate, expressed in slightly different ways. Consider again the first of the two equations. Presumably the discount rate will be composed of some market rate of interest (perhaps that on a long-dated government bond) plus some extra compensation for company risk. If we change one variable at a time and hold the other variables constant, we can deduce the effect on a share price. The results are shown in Table 10.1.

TABLE 10.1   Effect of changing value of variables in a simple DDM model

Variable	Change in level	Effect on share price
Current dividend	↑	↑
Market rate of interest	↑	↓
Company riskiness	↑	↓
Growth rate of dividend	↑	↑

In the US, some investors restate the DDM by considering the retention rate, payout rate and earnings. The retention rate is the percentage of earnings retained by the firm and not paid out as dividends. If $(1 - b)$ represents the payout rate, b is the retention rate. If E represents year ahead earnings, then:

$$D = (1 - b) \, E.$$

If r represents the return on equity, the growth rate of the dividend will be a function of the return on equity and the retention rate:

$$g = br.$$

The constant growth model equation can now be restated as:

$$k = \frac{(1 - b) \, E}{P} + br.$$

This is a simplified form of the DDM that has been used by US stockbrokers Goldman Sachs.

So far we have just looked at the constant growth model. The mathematics of two- and three-stage DDMs are more complex than that of the one-stage model, but these may be readily solved by computer programmes. Fuller and Hsia (1984) have suggested a simplified approach for a three-stage model. Referring back to Figure 10.1, we assumed a rapid growth rate g_1 that lasts for A years and a steady growth rate g_2 that begins in year B. Growth in the transition period declines at a linear rate from g_1 to g_2. The Fuller–Hsia formula is:

$$P = \frac{D}{k - g_2} \left[(1 + g_2) + \left(\frac{A + B}{2} \right) (g_1 - g_2) \right].$$

This is useful for rough and ready calculations, although most dividend discount adherents do not use such shortcuts.

SELECTING SHARES

How would the DDM be used to select shares? There are two basic ways. For simplicity, we will discuss the constant growth version of the DDM. With this model, if we know the dividend of a share and the expected growth rate, we can use the market price to calculate the share's expected return. Alternatively, we can assume a rate of discount and deduce what the share price should be. Deciding what discount rate to use is a tricky process, and consequently most investors deduce a return from the share price. An example will be helpful. Table 10.2 shows data for two shares. We can take market data for the price and dividend and we must forecast the growth rate. Given these data we can calculate the expected return from each share.

TABLE 10.2   Data for two shares

Data	Share A	Share B
Current price	100p	120p
Next dividend	5p or 5%	9.6p or 8%
Forecast dividend growth	5%	3%

Recalling our earlier analysis:

Expected return = dividend yield + dividend growth rate.

The expected return for share A is 5% + 5% = 10%. For share B it is 8% + 3% = 11%. On this basis, we would prefer share B. Had we decided to use the required discount rate approach we would have had to assume a discount rate. We will assume that it is 10% for both shares. Recall the constant growth formula for the price of a share:

$$P = \frac{D}{(k - g)}.$$

For share A, the data in Table 10.2 give us a price of $5/(0.10 - 0.05) = 100p$. For share B the price is $9.6/(0.10 - 0.03) = 137p$. These are the prices the shares must trade at if we are to get our required return of 10%. Note that share A does trade at 100p: it is correctly priced. Share B, however, trades at 120p, i.e. it is selling below its correct value. Share B is more attractive than share A. Notice that both approaches have given us the same answer.

Let's assume that we have decided to implement the DDM by accepting the market price of each share and calculating the implicit return that each is offering, and we do this for all the shares in the market. We can then rank all shares by their expected return. Shares at the top of the expected return list are buys, and those at the bottom are sells. This, however, ignores risk. Individual stocks may be more or less risky than the market. In our example above, share B might have been very risky and in that case a 1% higher expected return might not be enough to compensate for the extra risk. Risk should be brought into the calculation and there are many ways of doing this. Risk can be measured using beta or other measures, such as the dispersion of analysts' forecasts (the wider the dispersion, the greater the uncertainty, or risk, associated with a share) or by some subjective measure provided by an analyst. Beta provides a readily available quantitative measure of risk that some investors have used, but we have seen that there are some doubts as to its value. An investor might prefer to use some more traditional measure of risk. For example, an analyst might score a share's risk in terms of financial strength, the uncertainty attached to earnings forecasts and political or regulatory risk. The share could then be put into one of, say, five categories of risk. This approach has been used by US stockbroker Kidder Peabody. We will adopt it here. Imagine that the expected rate of return for 15 shares has been calculated and these have been assigned a risk category. A graph of the data might look like that shown in Figure 10.2.

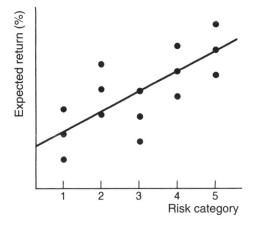

FIGURE 10.2   Expected return and risk for 15 stocks

Each dot in Figure 10.2 represents a stock and, using regression analysis, a best-fit line for the data can be calculated. This is an estimated security market line, and it shows the expected market return for each level of risk. Stocks above the line offer above-average return for a given level of risk, whereas stocks below the line offer a lower return. Stocks above the line are therefore relatively attractive.

Inevitably, the discussion here has a somewhat artificial air given the constraints of space and a desire to minimize the use of mathematics. Useful descriptions of real models are contained in Lanstein and Jahnke (1979), describing the Wells Fargo system, and Donnelly (1985). Institutional investors will be able to obtain detailed papers from US stockbrokers setting out their DDM approach to get a feel of real models in action. For readers without access to such work, the following short description of money manager and broker Sanford C. Bernstein's approach may be helpful (for details, see Goldstein et al., 1991).

Bernstein uses a three-phase DDM, applying it to S&P 500 stocks:

> An explicit five-year earnings and dividend forecast is created by an analyst for each
> stock in the model ... Earnings estimates for the next two calendar years are
> monitored versus the IBES consensus. A second phase transition growth rate is also
> specified for a subsequent period of two to six years. The default value for the second
> growth phase is 7%, with a specified range of 4.5% to 15%. In the third phase of
> growth, all companies are assumed to grow at 7%.
>
> (Goldstein et al., 1991, pp. 7 and 9)

From these data, the expected return for each stock is calculated. Forecasts for cyclical companies are made on a slightly different basis using the concept of normalized earnings, i.e. the earnings achieved at the midpoint of the economic cycle.

Of course, analysts can get any result they want for a stock by entering extreme forecasts. To make sure analysts' estimates are sensible, some data-control elements are included in the Bernstein process. Forecast returns on equity and growth rates are checked against historical experience to see that they are plausible. As well as company controls, all analysts use the same macro-economic assumptions. Errors in these assumptions are not too damaging as they affect all companies and the objective of the DDM is to produce relative rankings rather than correct absolute values. Bernstein adjusts the required return for risk, but does not use betas to do this. Instead, it uses duration, which measures the timing of investors' return on their investment, as a proxy for risk. (Duration is a concept mainly used in bond analysis; see Chapter 19.)

Bernstein's model has tended to rank most highly stocks that offer good value in the sense of having above-average yields and price-to-book and price-earnings ratios at a discount to the market. The advantage of a DDM, claims Bernstein, is its flexibility. Depending on growth prospects and how stocks are priced, high-yield stocks are not necessarily attractive, and the price-to-book discount can sometimes be quite small.

PROBLEMS WITH DIVIDEND DISCOUNT MODELS

Despite the flexibility that Bernstein notes, DDMs do tend to favour stocks with high yields and low price-earnings ratios. Many critics see this as a problem, and there has been a lively debate as to whether this is a consequence of how the market values stocks or whether there is some fatal flaw in the structure of the dividend discount model.

There are, in fact, many difficult issues that have to be faced with DDMs (e.g. see Nagorniak, 1985) but three are worth mentioning here. First, there is the question of the sensitivity of the model to changes in assumptions. Slightly different assumptions lead to dramatically different answers. To see this, assume a share has a dividend of 10, a discount rate of 10%, and a growth rate of 5%. The share price should be 200. Change the growth rate to 6% and the price changes to 250. Quite a difference. Yet it is easy to see the scope for disagreements about assumptions.

A second problem is that of the quality of the inputs. If the forecasts are poor, so too will be the model's results. We have seen above how Bernstein processes its analysts' forecasts to get consistent and plausible inputs. This forecasting problem, however, is not unique to DDMs; it applies equally to attempts to forecast the appropriate price-earnings ratio for a share. In fact, one might expect the DDM approach to lead to improved forecasts. There is a tendency for investors to categorize some stocks as growth stocks as though this was a permanent condition. In reality, periods of rapid growth seldom last for very long. The structure of the typical DDM of a major user of the approach will tend to force forecasters to be realistic. Most models in use have a third stage that pushes growth down to the average market level.

A third problem with DDMs is that they have good and bad periods. For example, Haugen (1997, pp. 602–606) provides results for a DDM for each year for the period 1979–91. Although the model outperforms over the period, in five of the 13 years the results are awful. Unfortunately, four of the years (1986, 1987, 1989 and 1990) are in a five-year span. Taking on a new client at the start of this period would certainly test a fund manager's client-relationship skills. As we will see, most types of investment style suffer poor periods and the DDM is not unique in this.

It may strike the reader that the prospects for a DDM-based approach being successful do not look promising. An approach that forecasts dividends to eternity, even if only approximately, is not easy to accept. But intellectually the approach makes sense and is only the equity equivalent of how bonds are valued, i.e. by discounting the value of a stream of interest payments and the principal. Moreover, some of the other valuation models in use have to handle the variables required by a DDM.

IS THE DIVIDEND DISCOUNT MODEL USEFUL?

The acid test is whether DDMs are used, and whether they pick out undervalued stocks. In the UK, such models are not in widespread use. In the US, the major brokers (e.g. Goldman Sachs, Salomon, and Merrill Lynch) produce data generated by some form of DDM; a number of money management firms also use this output, and some have produced their own models. A few firms manage money largely or exclusively by DDMs. Two trade press articles that give a good feel for the use of these models in the US are by Donnelly (1985) and Rohrer (1989).

Although investment textbooks usually discuss DDMs at length, scant evidence is provided that they work. Indeed, there have been surprisingly few studies published in the academic and professional journals assessing DDMs. One is by Sorenson and Williamson (1985) who tested four models; a price-earnings ratio approach, a constant growth model, a two-period growth model, and a three-period growth model. Their price-earnings ratio model simply ranked stocks from low price-earnings ratios to high. The other models were similar to those discussed in this chapter. They took a random sample of 150 firms from the S&P 400 at

January 1981. They took data necessary for model estimation at that date from IBES (which provides industry consensus estimates) and Merrill Lynch. They used each model to rank the 150 stocks by degree of undervaluation. Stocks ranked by each model were then split into quintiles, i.e. the 30 most undervalued companies, the 30 next most undervalued companies, etc. They calculated a one-year holding return for January 1981–January 1982, a two-year holding return for January 1981–January 1983, and a one-year holding return for January 1982–January 1983, which used data available in January 1982.

The results were excellent, all systems ordered the quintiles correctly in terms of returns, and the more complex the system, the better the results. Table 10.3 shows the results for the two-year holding period. The returns shown have been rounded to two figures and are not risk adjusted—risk adjustment strengthened the results.

TABLE 10.3   Rates of return (%) by quintile for four models (1981–83)

Quintile	Three period	Two period	Constant growth	PER
1 undervalued	30	29	27	27
2	28	25	23	22
3	18	14	15	14
4	6	11	9	10
5 overvalued	–5	–2	3	5

Various US brokers, e.g. Salomon and Goldman Sachs, have periodically reported on the value of DDMs and claim that they are successful at ranking shares. No real-world managers appear to produce results anywhere close to the results claimed in the Sorenson and Williamson study or by most brokers, and quite different results were reported by Michaud and Davis (1982). They examined four samples utilizing different numbers of stocks, data sources and sample periods (1973–80, 1973–76, 1977–88 and 1979–80). They concluded that the DDM had positive, but statistically insignificant, forecasting performance. The forecasting performance disappeared once the low price-earnings ratio and high dividend yield bias of their model was controlled for. Jacobs and Levy (1988b) also found positive but insignificant returns for the period mid-1982 to mid-1987.

The record of fund management firms that use DDMs can be examined, but few use solely these models. Sanford C. Bernstein claims:

> In the long term, the dividend discount model yields outperformance. The top quintile of the model has outperformed the market by about 3% a year on average since 1980. Using a longer 20-year period the premium is about 4%.
>
> (Goldstein et al., 1991, p. 14)

Nonetheless, in the paper this is taken from, the authors explain that Bernstein was going to add trends in earnings revisions (see Chapter 11) to its stock-selection model.

DISCOUNTED ABNORMAL EARNINGS

When all gains and losses pass through the profit and loss account, we have what is known as clean surplus accounting. Then, apart from capital items, such as an issue of shares, the book value at the year end is simply the book value at the start of the year plus net profit less dividends paid:

Year-end book value = starting book value + profit – dividend.

This can be rearranged so that we focus on dividends:

Dividend = profit + starting book value – year-end book value.

The dividend in the above calculation is for a particular year, say 2000. For 2001, we can make a similar calculation. In other words, we can construct a dividend stream. If we recall the dividend discount formula, we can substitute the identity for dividends into the formula and after algebraic manipulation obtain a useful expression for a share's price involving book value:

Price = book value of equity +
            present value of expected future abnormal earnings.

In Chapter 9, we explained that economists would derive profits after allowing for opportunity costs and, in particular, the cost of equity capital. Some accountants refer to profits that have been adjusted for the cost of equity capital as abnormal earnings. So in the above expression, abnormal earnings are defined as:

Abnormal earnings = net profits – (cost of capital × book values).

Equating a share's price with book value and the present value of abnormal earnings has an intuitive appeal. If firms only earn normal profits, then the equity value will simply be the book value. If firms can earn positive abnormal profits, then the equity value will be more than the book value. And if the firm earns negative abnormal profits, then the equity value will be less than the book value.

The discounted abnormal earnings approach has its origins in an article by Preinreich (1938) and a book by Edwards and Bell (1961). More recently, interest has been stimulated by articles by Ohlson (1990, 1995). The value of the theory is currently subject to a lot of research. For example, a paper by Francis et al. (2000) looks at the DDM versus a free cash-flow model, and the abnormal earnings approach. Using a sample of five-year forecasts in the US, they find that the absolute earnings value estimates are more accurate and explain more of the variation in security prices than do the free cash flow or dividend discount value estimates. They think there is little to be gained by using dividends or free cash flow over abnormal earnings as the fundamental attribute to be valued. This is especially so given that earnings are by far the most frequently forecast attribute, so there seems little basis for manipulating accounting data, for example to generate estimates of free cash flows if earnings forecasts and book values are available.

For real firms, how would we forecast abnormal earnings? One approach would be to assume that current abnormal earnings persist for ever. This seems unlikely: we expect abnormal profits to be eliminated over time. Ohlson assumes an autoregressive forecasting model: current abnormal earnings are assumed to decay each year by some fixed amount. Research suggests this decay rate is about 0.6, although it will vary from industry to industry and firm to firm. Dechow et al. (1999) give some of the factors that affect the decay rate.

As the abnormal earnings approach is not used widely in the markets, we will not develop the discussion further. For a more extended textbook treatment, readers are referred to Palepu et al. (2000, Chapter 11). The important point is that this is a theoretical approach that involves book value. We will draw on this later.

Many investors are sceptical of accounting numbers, and different firms follow different rules. How can book value be used as a valuation method? Perhaps the accounting distortions don't matter because double-entry bookkeeping means everything comes out in the wash. We can show this by means of an example.

Imagine that you buy a permit that gives you the right for two years to sell sketches of people on a beach. It costs £10 000 to buy the permit. You reckon you can achieve sales of £7000 in each year. Since you would spend your time on the beach sketching anyway, you have no selling costs. Your cost of capital, or your discount rate, is 10%.

Now let's look at Table 10.4. We begin with book value of £10 000. Revenues are £7000. You decide to spread the cost of the permit over the two years, charging £5000 in each year. Your profit in the first year is therefore £2000 (£7000 – £5000), but having done a course in economics you calculate the opportunity cost of your capital as well at £1000 (£10 000 × 10%). Your abnormal profit is therefore £1000 (£2000 – £1000). In the second year, your equity capital has been written down to £5000, so the opportunity cost is £500 (£5000 × 10%) and abnormal profits are now £1500. Profits over the two years total £2500.

TABLE 10.4 Value of a beach business

Book value (£)	Revenue (£)	Depreciation (£)	Profit (£)	Cost of capital (£)	Abnormal earnings (£)	Present value (£)	Value of business (£)
				Normal depreciation			
10 000	7000	5000	2000	1000	1000	909.09	
5000	7000	5000	2000	500	1500	1239.67	
						2148.76	12 148.76
				Fast depreciation			
10 000	7000	10 000	−3000	1000	−4000	−3636.36	
0	7000	0	7000	0	7000	5785.12	
						2148.76	12 148.76
				Dividend discount			
	7000					6363.64	
	7000					5785.12	
						12 148.76	12 148.76

You are not sure that there is a market in second-hand permits. Perhaps it would be more prudent to depreciate your permit fully in year one. In that case, abnormal earnings are now as shown in Table 10.4, quite different in pattern and total than in the previous case.

On your first day, you receive an offer for your business. What is it worth? You might use the DDM to help you. You reason that since you would pay yourself all the revenues each year, you would be receiving two dividends of £7000. According to the DDM, your business is worth the sum of the dividends discounted to their present value. Alternatively, you might use the discounted abnormal earnings approach. According to this, the firm is worth the beginning book value (£10 000) plus the sum of the discounted earnings. Of course, we used two different ways of reporting earnings, so we have two sums for abnormal earnings. If we use a 10% discount rate for both the abnormal earnings and the dividends, we can derive the present values, which are shown in the final column of Table 10.4. Two key points:

- Under clean surplus accounting, the equity value of a firm is the same whether calculated by discounted abnormal earnings or discounted dividends.
- Unbiased accounting rules affect reported profits both in size and timing, but not the value of the firm.

PRICE-EARNINGS RATIO MODELS

Although some analysts and fund managers use the DDM, more use a price-earnings ratio model for selecting stocks or analysing market levels. Here we will look at both the theory and the practice of selecting shares by assessing their 'appropriate' price-earnings ratio. A price-earnings ratio (PER) for a share is defined as:

$$PER = \frac{\text{market price per share}}{\text{earnings per share}}.$$

The theoretical background to determining the appropriate PER is straight-forward. Recall the simplest form of the DDM:

$$P = \frac{D}{(k - g)}$$

where P is the price of the share, D is the current dividend, k is the required return, and g is the rate of dividend growth. We can use this to derive some information about what affects PERs. If we divide both sides by earnings, E, we get:

$$\frac{P}{E} = \frac{D/E}{k - g}.$$

This tells us that a PER will be higher the greater the value of g, the growth rate, the larger the payout ratio D/E, and the lower the value of k, the discount rate. If we assume that a company has a 50% payout ratio, a 7% growth rate and a 12% discount rate, then we can calculate the PER as follows:

$$\frac{P}{E} = \frac{D/E}{k - g} = \frac{0.5}{0.12 - 0.07} = 10.$$

Similar calculations can be made for other discount rates and rates of growth. Such calculations are brought together in Table 10.5. Notice that the impact of a rising discount rate varies with the growth rate. As the discount rate rises from 9% to 12%, the PER for a share with a growth rate of 6% would halve, but for a share with a growth rate of 8%, it would fall to one-quarter of its previous level. Now let's read across the table. At a discount rate of 9%, extra growth has a dramatic effect on the PER, which quadruples as the growth rate increases from 5% to 8%. However, with a 12% discount rate, the effect of the same increase in growth is only a 76% increase in the PER. Some cells of the table have been left empty because the formula requires the discount rate to exceed the growth rate.

TABLE 10.5   PER as a function of growth and the discount rate

Discount rate (%)	Rate of growth			
	5%	6%	7%	8%
7	25.0	50.0		
8	16.7	25.0	50.0	
9	12.5	16.7	25.0	50.0
10	10.0	12.5	16.7	25.0
11	8.3	10.0	12.5	16.7
12	7.1	8.3	10.0	12.5

Table 10.5 is illustrative only. It assumes that the specified growth rates are maintained forever, but we know that fast-growth stocks, for example, eventually have more normal growth rates. Accordingly, the effects shown in the table will be more muted in the real world. Further, our simple calculations assume that when one variable is changed, the others remain constant. No allowance is made for interdependence amongst variables. For example, if growth prospects are good, then a firm might increase its gearing. The net effect will depend on a balance between a higher g and a possibly higher k, if increased gearing is thought to increase risk. Again, a firm that increases its payout may reduce its growth prospects.

Despite the shortcomings of Table 10.5, it does illustrate why some investors like growth stocks and some do not. A little extra growth generates a big increase in the PER, or a lot of multiple expansion in the market's jargon, and a big increase in a share's price. But when things go wrong—interest rates rise or the growth does not materialize—the scope for a share price collapse is equally obvious.

ASSESSING THE APPROPRIATE PRICE-EARNINGS RATIO

Real investors tend not to use this algebraic approach. The usual way of using a PER model to select shares is to go through the following steps:

1. Data are examined for a number of years. Although UK analysts will look at a number of previous years in their analysis, in the summary data that they present in their share evaluation conclusion they are likely to show one year's historical figure and two forecast years' figures. These will be the next financial year to be reported and the following year. The 'next' year will thus be the current year or even a year that has ended but not yet been reported.
2. For these three years, earnings-per-share data will be presented and this will necessitate forecasts for two years. Given that one of these years will be wholly or partly finished, the forecasts do not go very far into the future.
3. A PER will be calculated for each year. To do this, the current price will be used for each year.
4. A PER relative will be presented for each year, either relative to the market or the appropriate sector. For example, if the market, stock and sector are selling on PERs of 12, 10 and 8, respectively, then the stock is selling on a discount to the market (i.e. 10/12 or 83% of the market rating—usually written PERR 83, where the extra R stands for relative) and a premium to its sector (i.e. 10/8 or 125% of its sector rating).
5. An analyst may then decide the appropriate PER or PERR for the stock based on experience. The factors that are likely to be considered are growth rate of earnings, both past and present, past sales growth, profitability, stability of past earnings, financial strength, quality of management, as well as the nature and prospects of the industry, competitive position of the company, and so forth.
6. The appropriate PER or PERR derived from step 5 is compared with the current ratio. If appropriate exceeds current, then the stock is a buy; if current exceeds appropriate, the stock is a sell. Comparison will also be made based on forecast earnings.
7. As an alternative to the blending of factors and derivation of the appropriate PER of step 5, the current PER may be compared with the historical sector or market PER ranges for the past 10 years. Thus a stock that has traded in a sector relative range of 120–150 and is selling on a current relative of 125 would appear cheap. Steps 5 and 7 can be brought together. For example, if some deterioration in the company's prospects had occurred, or is expected to occur, it might seem that the future sector relative range should be somewhat lower, say 100–120, in which case a stock with a current relative of 125 would be unattractive.
8. Analysts sometimes utilize a concept of normalized earnings in their PER assessment. In cyclical sectors, a high PER may not signify growth prospects but the collapse of earnings and the market's assessment that they will

recover. Accordingly, some analysts will assess a PER based on what it would be using normalized earnings. An alternative would be to use the current rating, but when making the comparison against the market or sector relative range, to bear in mind that the stock should be assessed against not the full range but that part appropriate to the prevailing stage of the economic cycle.

The approach described above certainly seems more straightforward than the DDM discussed earlier. This is misleading, however, because the approach is driven by earnings forecasts and the determination of the appropriate PER, and the analyst should consider similar factors to those that go into the DDM. The PER approach seems simple because the factors that go into the assessment and how they are weighted and processed is skipped over in an outline such as that shown above.

The textbooks do not skip over the factors that must be considered, but they are not very helpful in explaining how the investor handles them. In determining the appropriate PER, investors are advised to analyse company accounts, review corporate strategy, appraise industry prospects, assess management, and so on. Now the problem with all of this is that it is not clear how one makes the assessment, or pulls it together. For example, if a company has the conventional levels of liquidity and gearing, what does that imply for the PER? Again, few investors will have much idea as to how to assess corporate strategy and industry prospects: one suspects they will largely extrapolate recent experience. We shall cite some evidence on this in Chapter 13.

Many investors place great store by the quality of management, but how does one assess this and reflect it in the appropriate PER? There is some evidence relating to quality of management and stock returns that is worth reviewing here, both because it is interesting in itself and because it illustrates the sort of problems that have to be faced with the appropriate PER approach.

QUALITY OF MANAGEMENT

One might expect excellently managed companies to perform well, and investment analysts often write about the quality of the management of the company they are appraising, and justify a higher rating when they perceive high-quality management. Nonetheless, it is still worth asking whether excellent management really does offer investors the prospects of abnormal returns.

There are three reasons why one might suspect that high-quality management does not lead to abnormal returns. First, good management should already be reflected in earnings, sales, etc. Second, even if good management is a separate factor (because today's earnings represent yesterday's management, whereas today's management will generate tomorrow's earnings), why is this not already reflected in a share's price? Third, what is good management, and who would recognize it? Before making some general comments, let's look at some empirical studies.

Granatelli and Martin (1984) analysed the performance of a portfolio of US stocks headed by award-winning chief executive officers (CEOs) in the period 1975–80. *Financial World* magazine published annually a list of 10 CEOs selected for gold and silver awards by panels of security analysts. One panel selected and ranked the three top CEOs in each of 53 industries. A second panel chose from these the top CEOs in broader industry groups. Granatelli and Martin constructed their portfolios by investing in the firms of the top 10 CEOs and changing the portfolio each year when the new award winners were announced. They constructed a control portfolio by selecting 10 firms in the same industries as the well-managed firms (they simply took the next firm on their database tape after the well-managed firm). They then calculated the returns and standard deviations for the well-managed portfolio, the control portfolio and the market. Their results are shown in Table 10.6.

TABLE 10.6   Risk, return and management (1975–80)

	Well-managed	Control	Market
Average return (%)	21.8	23.4	16.4
Standard deviation (%)	24.0	19.2	15.9

The well-managed firm portfolio beat the market—albeit with more risk—but randomly selected firms in the same industries as the well-managed firms offered the highest return, and with less risk than the well-managed firms.

The first detailed empirical study on management and the market was by Clayman (1987). This draws on the best-seller by Peters and Waterman (1982), *In Search of Excellence: Lessons From America's Best Run Companies*. Peters and Waterman began with a list of 62 companies considered innovative and excellent by 'informed observers'. The companies were screened for six measures of long-term financial superiority. From the list of 43 companies (36 of which were publicly traded) that passed all the criteria, Peters and Waterman deduced the behavioural attributes that contributed to excellence. There were eight, which they described as a bias towards action; close relations with customers; autonomy and entrepreneurship; productivity through people; hands-on and value-driven; stick to the knitting; simple form, lean staff; and simultaneous loose–tight properties.

Clayman (1987, p. 56) notes: 'The list of excellent companies compiled in 1981, however, makes curious reading in 1987.' Clayman gives some examples of companies that had encountered difficulties. More importantly, she studied 29 companies of the original 36 publicly traded excellent companies for which complete data was available. Data on the six financial attributes used as selection criteria for these 29 companies for the period 1976–80 are presented, as well as data for the period 1981–85. Of the 29 companies, 86% experienced declines in asset growth rates over the two periods: 93% had declines in equity growth rates;

69% had a drop in market-to-book ratios; 83% had lower average returns on capital employed; 79% had lower average returns on equity; and 83% had lower average returns on sales. These figures suggest regression to the mean, although no data are given for what was happening to the average firm over the same periods. In terms of investment results, over the period 1981–85, 11 of the 29 companies outperformed the S&P 500, and 18 underperformed. Because the companies that outperformed did especially well, an equally-weighted portfolio of all 29 companies outperformed the S&P 500 by 1.1% p.a. over the five years.

Clayman then looked at companies that were not excellent—investment dogs. Companies in the S&P 500 were ranked on the six financial variables used in the excellent companies' selection process. A portfolio was constructed that consisted of companies that ranked in the bottom third on every variable. The portfolio consisted of 39 companies. These companies showed improving ratios for two financial variables for 1981–85 compared with 1976–80, and deteriorating values for four variables. However, 25 outperformed the S&P 500 and 14 underperformed. An equally weighted portfolio of dogs outperformed the S&P 500 by 12.4% p.a. The betas and standard deviations of returns of the excellent and dog portfolios were approximately the same, but the study probably suffers from a survivorship bias (recall our comments in Chapter 7).

A later, more detailed study, by Kolodny et al. (1989), using the Peters and Waterman framework, came to the conclusion that *ex ante* knowledge of excellent firm characteristics cannot be used to produce superior returns. Bannister (1990) extended Clayman's study over a longer period and came to a similar conclusion. However, when Clayman (1994) repeated her study for 1988–92, she found that while the good companies' financial ratios deteriorated, and the bad companies' improved, the good companies outperformed on the stockmarket.

What is one to conclude from these studies? Well, one might question whether Peters and Waterman truly capture the essence of excellent management. Some writers would see excellence of management as situationally specific. Thus, excellence would always be relative to changing economic circumstances and to the type of configuration an organization has—e.g. entrepreneurial, mature, diversified, professional and innovative, to use Mintzberg's (1979) and Mintzberg and Quinn's (1992) terms. Nonetheless, Peters and Waterman's analysis is much more sophisticated than the typical broker's shallow comments on management. It is doubtful that most analysts have much idea as to how to assess management quality. They probably just interpret recent good performance as good management.

Irrespective of one's reaction to these views, the evidence suggests that regardless of whether good management is selected on the basis of analysts' votes or detailed studies, there is no guaranteed payoff to investors from good management. This should not be surprising. Not only will the market tend to discount any obvious factors, but it should always be borne in mind that economic forces tend to eliminate both good and bad margins: new firms enter attractive areas and some firms exit from unattractive areas. And, as we discuss in Chapter 11, there is a large random element in economic life. It is hard to see how one will get a more appropriate PER by adding in a quality factor. We could make similar points about many of the factors that go into judging an appropriate PER. This is not to say the judgement cannot be made; just that it is not easy.

OTHER APPROACHES TO PRICE-EARNINGS RATIOS

A rather different approach to that of looking at accounts, management quality, etc. has been to go back to theory and specify some factors that should affect PERs, and then try to find, by multiple regression analysis, the equation that best fits the real-world data. This approach was popular in the 1960s and early 1970s and one of the best known studies is for the US market by Whitbeck and Kisor (1963). They used a sample of 135 New York Stock Exchange stocks to estimate the relationship between the PER, historical growth, historical dividend payout ratio, and risk—which they measured as the volatility of past earnings around the earnings trend. The equation they estimated was:

$$PER = 8.2 + (1.5 \times \text{earnings growth}) + (6.7 \times \text{the payout ratio})$$
$$- (0.2 \times \text{the standard deviation of earnings}).$$

This equation gives us an estimate of the simultaneous impact of three factors on the level of the PER for the period studied. The signs tell us the direction of the impact. The equation tells us that the PER increased as a company's earnings growth increased and the greater was the payout ratio. The PER fell as risk increased.

The equation could be used for share selection in the following manner. For any share, calculate the values of the three variables and then use the equation to estimate the 'appropriate' PER. Compare the forecast with the current ratio, then sell if the forecast is below the current ratio, and buy if it is above. Whitbeck and Kisor claimed that their model was successful in picking shares. This led to a spate of studies for the US and some for the UK. These studies, however, have fallen out of fashion. To see why, we will examine a study by Malkiel and Cragg (1970).

Malkiel and Cragg (1970) collected data for 178 US corporations and studied the period 1961–65. In an attempt to explain PER differences, they collected data on forecasts of long-term growth rates of earnings, estimates of 'normal' earnings for the preceding year ('normal' earnings in this case assumed that the economy was operating at a normal level and were adjusted for one-off events, such as strikes), forecasts of the next year's earnings, and expectations about the future variability of earnings. The expectations data came from 17 investment firms.

For each year, Malkiel and Cragg calculated a regression equation. They used six different models and obtained high R^2 for every model. The results for one are shown in Table 10.7.

Table 10.7 shows that the four variables used in the analysis have the expected signs: PER increases with increases in long-term growth, short-term growth and the payout ratio. The PER is related negatively to risk. Long-term growth has the greatest impact on the PER. The growth variables are always statistically significant and the payout ratio and risk are usually significant. R^2 shows the

TABLE 10.7   Estimated normalized PERs using expectations data, US: 1961–65

Year	Constant	Forecast long-term growth	Forecast short-term growth	Dividend payout ratio	Instability of earnings	R^2
1961	−27.96	2.91	31.78	4.57	−0.58	0.77
1962	3.42	1.61	6.88	3.21	−2.20	0.79
1963	−11.33	2.29	15.11	8.11	−1.14	0.80
1964	−9.29	1.87	15.20	7.03	−1.13	0.78
1965	−11.15	2.42	13.78	4.22	−0.81	0.83

Source: Malkiel and Cragg (1970, p. 612).

amount of variation of PERs explained by the four variables. For example, in 1961, 77% of the variation is explained. The equations do seem to have captured variables that are important in determining a PER. But could investors have made money from the findings?

Malkiel and Cragg used their equations to pick undervalued shares and measured returns over one year. The results were poor. There were several reasons for this:

- The valuation relationship changes over time. An inspection of the table reveals that the coefficient of each variable changes from year to year. For example, growth, both long and short term, had its biggest weighting in 1961 and its smallest in the following year. Risk had its most negative effect in 1962, and its smallest effect in the previous year.
- Analysts' forecasts are not accurate. Every time a forecast changes, so too does the appropriate PER for a share.
- The model is too general and misses specific firm variables. For example, Malkiel and Cragg noted that Reynolds Tobacco always appeared mispriced and it was clear that the risk of government intervention was important but was not picked up in the equation.

Malkiel and Cragg concluded that while they could explain a large part of the variability of PERs with a few variables, their findings were not useful in selecting undervalued shares. (For a discussion of unstable coefficients in the UK, see Bomford, 1968.) Notice, however, that neither Whitbeck and Kisor nor Malkiel and Cragg are really using the price-earnings model. Neither has a discount rate in their equation and both used linear additive relationships, whereas the simple PER model we began our discussion with is not of that form.

IS THE PRICE-EARNINGS RATIO MODEL WORTHWHILE?

We have seen that whether we treat PERs informally or formally (via regression analysis), there are some difficulties. This does not mean that some investors are not able to use the method successfully, but we do seem to be looking at a craft rather than a science. However, it is hard not to believe that other approaches are more attractive. For the PER model to be useful, investors must be able to forecast profits accurately (or at worst use consensus estimates) and be able to assess the appropriate PER. If an investor can forecast profits accurately, that alone is sufficient to earn abnormal profits (see Chapter 11) and it is not necessary to go on to try to find valuation errors as well. Of course, if they can be found, they will add extra value. Faulty judgements, however, might undermine the value of accurate forecasts.

If investors wish to process information, the DDM seems a better model. It too will suffer from changes in how investors value growth and so forth (although DDM adherents tend to have longer time horizons than other investors and be willing to wait for valuations to return to 'normal'), but it is a better approach because it properly allows for the time value of returns. It also forces investors to accept that above-average growth does not continue forever. The structure of the PER approach does not encourage, but nor does it discourage, any psychological bias investors may have towards emphasizing recent experience. If this occurs, it is likely that highly-rated 'appropriately valued' stocks will, in fact, be overvalued. There is evidence that low PER stocks have often outperformed (see Chapter 13). Since most investors have, at least until recently, used an appropriate PER approach, this suggests that investors are not capable of determining 'appropriate' PERs and have a systematic bias. Rather than try to find mispriced securities on the basis of appropriate PERs, many investors might be better advised to buy lowly rated stocks. All of this suggests that for many investors, the most widely used technique may not be very useful. That is a comforting conclusion. There would probably not be much scope to beat the market if the most widely used technique had real value.

CONCLUDING COMMENTS

The evidence suggests that there is probably some merit in DDMs. The logic and evidence in favour of these models is greater than that supporting many investment approaches that have adherents, so it is perhaps a little surprising that there are relatively few fund management firms committed to the approach. Probably the discipline and commitment that is required explains this. Significant expenditure is required to set up the analytical capability, and a major cultural shift is required. Research has to be processed in a specific way, and analysts and fund managers lose their independence. Flair is played down and egotistical fund managers have to become good team players. Chief executives have to be modestly numerate. The major US brokers have invested in developing models, but smaller brokers have generally not done so, presumably because they do not have a large enough universe of stocks to make the ranking exercise worthwhile. One gets the impression that brokers' institutional salespeople are not in love with the DDM. Sexy stock stories are easy enough to peddle, but selling revisions of computer ranking lists is hard work.

DDMs have not made much headway in the UK. For example, James Capel, the leading UK research house throughout the 1980s, experimented with them and then shelved them. The UK has generally invested less in research technology than the US, and some UK fund management firms have only recently accepted disciplined investment styles. The UK financial culture has not been right for DDMs.

Good real-world results from a DDM could have two sources—superior forecasting (information) or superior processing of information (valuation). Note, however, that Sorenson and Williamson (1985) used some consensus data in their test—in that case, the DDM worked mainly as a valuation tool. Alternatively, the consensus estimate is superior to any manager's estimate. The formal structure of DDMs might, however, lead to superior information being generated.

An alternative to the DDM is the discounted abnormal earnings model. Although a hot topic amongst American academics, it is not used much in the financial markets.

Most analysts and investors prefer a price-earnings approach to that of a dividend discount approach. But price-earnings models require much the same sort of long-term forecasts as DDMs. It is possible to quantify factors that explain what is influencing PERs at any time. Unfortunately, the importance of these factors varies from year to year.

Investors with superior forecasting and analytical skills might be able to use the appropriate PER approach successfully, but it is doubtful that most investors can. Most investors who subjectively focus on growth, quality, and so forth probably rate stocks more on the basis of what the companies have achieved than what they will achieve. We saw an illustration of this in our examination of management quality.

11

Earnings-Based Share Selection

Forecasts usually tell us more of the forecaster than the future.

Warren Buffett

Expectations about earnings lie at the heart of much investment analysis. Theoretical models of share appraisal usually require earnings estimates, and investment analysts spend a great deal of time forecasting earnings. There are four main ways of utilizing earnings estimates:

- Buy shares with fast earnings growth.
- Forecast near-term earnings better than other investors.
- Respond to earnings revisions and/or forecast earnings surprises.
- Use as an input into a DDM or a PER model.

The first approach assumes that fast growth of earnings is inherently rewarding. The second assumes that shares are correctly priced, based on consensus earnings, and the investor buys or sells depending on whether he or she thinks the consensus is too low or too high. This approach relies on superior earnings forecasting skills. The third approach assumes that forecasters make predictable errors that can be exploited. The fourth approach (discussed in Chapter 10) either involves calculating the present value of a stream of dividends, or using the short-cut PER approach. The DDM ranks all shares by their prospective risk-adjusted return. In the price-earnings approach, one calculates what PER a share should stand on, compares it with the current PER, and buys or sells accordingly. A variant is to buy stocks on low PERs, which is discussed in Chapter 12.

Given the importance of earnings in investment decisions, it seems worth spending a few paragraphs discussing some aspects of earnings forecasts. As we shall show, earnings revisions are frequently discussed and monitored. We shall begin by describing a typical year for an analyst, putting stress on the times that forecasts might be revised.

Imagine a calendar year-end company. In March 2000, an analyst will have a 1999 forecast and a 2000 forecast. The company will probably announce its 1999 results during March. It will do so in the form of a release that will have the key financial statements and some comment. The analyst will talk to the company on the day of the release, and produce a revised 2000 forecast. A few weeks later, the Annual Report and Accounts will appear, containing more detail. This may lead to a forecast revision. About a month later, the annual general meeting (AGM) will be held. There may be a statement on current trading that leads to another revision. Shortly after the AGM, the analyst is likely to meet the finance director for a detailed discussion: another possible trigger for a revision. The interim statement will appear around August/September. The analyst will again speak to the company on the release day, and another revision may occur. Clearly, there are plenty of potential triggers for revisions before we consider unexpected economic events, strategic moves by other companies, and so on. Also, we have described the UK company's typical half-yearly reporting—US companies report quarterly. An analyst's work is never done!

THE BACKGROUND TO EARNINGS

Most readers will be familiar with statements like 'Our good results reflect the efforts of your executives and employees' and 'Our poor results reflect the state of the economy and tough industry conditions'. Impartial observers might be inclined to attribute some role to the economy and industry even for favourable results. In fact one US study (Brealey, 1969) found that on average 21% of the changes in a firm's earnings were accounted for by changes in the market's earnings, and a further 21% by changes in its industry's earnings. Clearly, quite a lot of a firm's results are determined by factors it can't control. And there are other forces making life unpredictable. Insurance companies, for example, may be able to predict storm damage over 20 years, but the impact in any one year is unpredictable. And many events contain the seeds of their demise. Very bad results may invite takeover or pressure from banks; very good results may invite new competition. But some firms have monopoly positions, some have strong brands, some have competencies that are hard to imitate, and so on. These factors point in the opposite direction. All this makes one wonder how predictable future results are from past results.

In a famous UK study, Little (1962) examined whether there was any correlation between above-average or below-average growth in one period and that in a second. His answer was that there wasn't. Lintner and Glauber (1967) carried out a similar study for the US. Their conclusions were broadly similar. Brealey (1969) took a slightly different approach. Using 610 US firms over a 15-year period, he split his sample every year into the 305 firms with the highest rate of growth and the 305 with the lowest. He took the firms that had begun with high growth, then counted how many firms had a second year of high growth (H) and then switched to low growth (L), i.e. HHL, how many had two subsequent high-growth years, i.e. HHHL, through to all years being high growth. He then worked out how many observations he would expect for any number of consecutive years if the outcome were determined by equal odds chance. The actual and the calculated numbers were almost identical. In short, the evidence is that there is a large random element in earnings figures.

Does this mean profits are not forecastable? It doesn't. Whether profits growth will be above average may not be forecastable from last year's profits alone, but next year's earnings will be a function of a known starting point, forecastable economic changes, other sorts of change, information from the company, and so on. What does seem likely is that the further into the future one goes, the harder it will be to forecast profits, and the greater the likelihood of high or low growth regressing to the mean. An interesting study throws light on this.

Recall our analysis of PERs in Chapter 10. We expect high-growth companies to have high PERs, and low-growth companies to have low PERs. If we divide the market into quintiles based on PER, we should have also divided the market into quintiles based on expected growth (Q5 = highest growth, Q1 = lowest). Fuller et al. (1993) formed quintiles along the lines described for US stocks in 1973–90. After forming quintiles, they observed growth rates for the next eight years. They found that high-PER stocks did grow faster than low-PER stocks. For example, after a year, Q1 stocks' earnings per share had grown nearly 10% slower than that for Q3 stocks, whereas Q5 stocks grew nearly 9% faster than Q3. But in subsequent years the growth differential fell sharply, and by year five or six there was relatively little difference. These findings suggest that relative growth is predictable. This is seemingly at odds with the earlier studies, such as Brealey (1969). However, that study used individual stocks, whereas Fuller et al. pooled stocks. And the 'random' studies relate past growth to future growth, whereas Fuller et al. use market prices and growth. But even if the market can categorize fast and slow growers, this would not necessarily lead to a decision to buy forecast high-growth stocks. Since fast growth fizzles after a few years, the question is whether there is sufficient extra growth to warrant the higher price that has to be paid.

HOW GOOD ARE EARNINGS FORECASTS?

Just how good are analysts' forecasts? This answer depends on what is meant by 'good' and what the alternative is. We shall begin by looking at the US evidence before turning to the UK. It is worth looking at the US studies not only because they are more numerous than the UK studies (which tend to follow along the lines set out in the US), but the bulk of the studies reported in this book relate to the US and it is therefore necessary to know a bit about US analysts.

One of the first questions one might have about analysts' forecasts is whether they are accurate or, more usefully, whether they are more accurate than some cheaply constructed 'naive' forecast. Such a forecast could be that there will be no change from period to period, or whatever percentage change occurred in the previous period will recur, or perhaps the absolute change will recur. In fact, most research has used rather sophisticated time-series models as a naive model. The key point about the naive approaches is that they rely solely on statistical manipulation of past data.

Some of the early studies of forecast accuracy found that the naive models did about as well as the analysts (e.g. Cragg and Malkiel, 1968; Elton and Gruber, 1972). However, these studies used small samples and short time periods. Later studies (e.g. Brown and Rozeff, 1978; Collins and Hopwood, 1980; Fried and Givoly, 1982; Brown et al., 1987; and O'Brien, 1988) used more refined techniques and longer test periods and concluded that the analysts outperformed the naive models.

One might imagine that managers would produce better forecasts than analysts. The evidence is somewhat mixed but does slightly favour managers (e.g. see Bartley and Cameron, 1991). The problem for investors is that managers do not usually, or consistently, make forecasts. Most forecasts may be unplanned and may simply be the result of the CEO wanting to share some good news with shareholders. Occasionally, however, a management will wish to correct market perceptions when these are significantly in error; in such cases it is sensible to go with the company's forecast.

Despite this, analysts appear to be the best consistently available source of earnings forecasts although they do not generate perfect forecasts. Elton et al. (1984) examined the nature of their errors using a sample of 414 firms for each of the years 1976, 1977 and 1978. Their findings were interesting:

• Analysts' forecasts improved in accuracy during the course of the year and, perhaps surprisingly, at a more or less constant rate. Analysts systematically overestimated growth for high-growth companies and underestimated growth for low-growth companies.
• By partitioning the sources of error to economy, industry and company, it was possible to look more closely at the sources of error. It appeared that analysts made relatively little error in forecasting the average growth rate of EPS for the economy, made larger errors for the industry, and the largest for the company. As the year progressed, forecast accuracy grew in general, but relatively more so for industry performance relative to company.
• Some firms are harder to forecast than others—firms for which analysts produced poor forecasts tended to be the same from year to year.
• Analysts' forecasts tended to have the greatest divergence of opinion over the first four months of the year. There tended to be greater divergence in some industries relative to other industries every year, i.e. some industries are harder to forecast than others. Finally, analysts tended to make the greatest forecast errors for the companies with the greatest divergence of analysts' forecasts. Divergence of forecasts is therefore a measure of uncertainty.

Turning now to the UK, Capstaff et al. (1996) looked at the accuracy of UK analysts' forecasts in relation to a naive benchmark of 'no change'. They looked at various forecast horizon dates, the range being three months after the year end but prior to the results being announced by the company through to 20 months before the year end. The mean forecast error was 10% for the short horizon increasing steadily through to 24% for the long horizon. The average of the errors for the six horizons studied was 17%. For the naive model, the same figure was 24%. Although the analysts beat the model over all horizons, after 16 months the difference was not statistically significant.

The forecast errors for UK analysts are much smaller than the numbers discussed in the US literature. Of course these studies use different periods, methods, etc. However Cho (1994) carried out a comparative UK/US study and found that UK analysts had smaller errors.

Capstaff et al. (1996) report that UK analysts are very poor at forecasting earnings declines. For horizons over four months, the naive model beats the analysts. Capstaff et al. also report an optimistic bias to UK forecasts. US analysts are typically found to be overoptimistic. However, Cho (1994) found that while US analysts consistently overestimated for the three years he studied, UK analysts did so in only one year. Bhaskar and Morris (1984) using data for 1970–74 found that there was a tendency for analysts to underestimate profits.

Much US evidence suggests that there are no differences between brokers in forecasting ability. Bhaskar and Morris found a difference in the UK, but explained the results away—the best forecasters were forecasting less than a year ahead, were forecasting an easily forecastable industry, and so on. Capstaff et al. (1999) examined a large number of forecasts for accounting year ends that spanned 1987–95. They found that after controlling for the size of the firm being forecast, the industry to which the firm belongs, the accounting year being forecast, and the forecast horizon, there were persistent differences in forecasting ability.

To sum up, UK analysts seem to differ in their forecasting skills more than US analysts do, UK forecast errors tend to be smaller, and UK forecasters seems less prone to overestimate profits.

THE VALUE OF ACCURATE EARNINGS ESTIMATES

This section discusses the first method of share selection based on earnings estimates that we mentioned above, i.e. attempting to produce accurate earnings forecasts.

The simplest approach to selecting shares is to assume that earnings are self-evidently 'a good thing' and that investors should buy shares with the highest consensus earnings growth. If many investors take this view, however, it is likely that shares will be priced to reflect consensus earnings estimates; therefore, there may be no relationship between returns and consensus estimates. A slightly more complex approach would be to assume that shares are correctly priced based on consensus forecasts and to try to make a more accurate forecast than the consensus. Investors with forecasting skills might assume that if their forecast is, say, 10% higher than the market's, then the share price should be 10% higher than it currently is.

Elton et al. (1981) examined the above issues. They studied US data consisting of a monthly file of one- and two-year earnings forecasts prepared in 1973, 1974 and 1975. They examined December year-end companies and looked at forecasts available in March and September. They felt that March was the first date a forecast could be made for the current year with the previous year's figures known, and September was far enough into the year for substantial evidence to be available about companies' prospects but for the full-year figure not to be known with certainty. Only firms followed by at least three analysts were studied. The total sample of firms varied between 700 and 900. Elton et al. analysed actual growth rates of earnings, consensus forecast growth rates of earnings and the forecast error. In their calculations of excess rates of return, they used the market model to adjust for risk.

Elton et al. divided stocks into deciles based on the next year's *actual* growth of earnings. In practice, this could only be done by an investor with perfect forecasting ability. They then looked at the excess returns that would have been earned if each decile had been purchased and held until actual earnings were announced. Stocks with the highest growth produced the highest returns. The returns were both statistically significant and economically significant. Over a 13-month period, the three deciles with the fastest growth returned 7.48% versus –4.93% for the three deciles with the slowest growth. Perfect forecasting ability is a desirable skill.

Can investors achieve excess returns by buying the stocks with the highest consensus *forecast* growth of earnings? Unfortunately, they cannot. Elton et al. divided stocks into deciles based on forecast growth. There was no difference in returns between deciles: it seems consensus expected earnings are reflected in stock prices. This suggests that a growth stock selection strategy will not be profitable.

Of course, there is a gap between actual earnings and forecasts: analysts make forecasting errors. What is the relationship between forecasting errors and returns? Or, in current jargon, what is the effect of an earnings surprise? Firms that produced results above expectations generated excess returns, and firms with results below expectations generated poor returns.

These results taken together show that earnings affect return, consensus earnings are discounted, and differences between consensus and actual earnings affect returns. Good forecasters would be able to generate excess returns from their skills. But exactly how good do forecasters have to be? Elton et al. provided a useful table, reproduced here as Table 11.1.

Consider the third row of the data in Table 11.1. This shows that if forecasters could have eliminated the 20% of stocks that would most disappoint by reporting earnings below consensus expectations, they would have earned 2.88% more than normal, allowing for the risk of the stocks. If, however, half of the stocks chosen were in the worst 20% but half were average stocks, then an excess return of 1.44% would have been earned. From Table 11.1, we can see that good forecasting would have earned over 10% but even quite modest forecasting ability was worth something.

TABLE 11.1 Excess annual returns (%) from avoiding firms that had the largest over-stated earnings errors

Firms eliminated (%)	Excess return if completely accurate	Excess return if 50% error	Excess return if 90% error
0	0	0	0
10	1.56	0.78	0.16
20	2.88	1.44	0.29
30	3.07	1.53	0.31
40	4.32	2.16	0.43
50	5.77	2.88	0.58
60	7.35	3.67	0.74
70	9.08	4.54	0.91
80	9.90	4.95	0.99
90	10.42	5.21	1.04

Source: Elton et al. (1981, p. 986).

Accurate forecasting of earnings can lead to superior share selection. Investors should assess their own forecasting ability, irrespective of whether this takes the form of forecasts produced *ab initio*, or from adjusting consensus forecasts for their own non-consensus views (e.g. on the economic outlook) or simply from selecting brokers who appear to have skills in specific sectors.

EARNINGS SURPRISES AND REVISIONS

Elton et al. (1981) commented on earnings surprises, and we now look at these in more detail. Benesh and Peterson (1986) took samples of 380 and 384 US firms for 1980 and 1981, respectively. They split each of their samples into three parts consisting of the 50 firms with the highest returns during the year, the 50 with the lowest returns, and finally all the rest. The January consensus earnings per share as reported by Institutional Broker Estimates Service (IBES) for the coming year and the actual earnings per share for that year were noted for all stocks. Table 11.2 shows the average projected rate of growth of earnings per share versus the actual rate for the 50 highest and lowest returns. Clearly the best-performing shares benefited from positive earnings surprises, whereas the worst suffered from negative earnings surprises.

TABLE 11.2 Projected v. actual earnings growth rates (%)

	1980		1981	
	Best	Worst	Best	Worst
Average projected rate of growth in EPS	9.1	13.5	19.5	21.3
Average actual growth in EPS	27.1	−15.3	35.4	−5.3

Source: Benesh and Peterson (1986, p. 34). Copyright © 1986. Association for Investment Management and Research. Reproduced and republished from the *Financial Analysts Journal* with permission from the Association for Investment Management and Research. All rights reserved.

If earnings surprises lead to large changes in prices, is it necessary to forecast earnings surprises, or can investors earn abnormal returns simply by responding to the surprises? Rendleman et al. (1982) studied a large sample of US stocks for most of the 1970s. They categorized earnings surprises by size into 10 groups based on standardized unexpected earnings. These were calculated by first estimating earnings on the basis of past earnings using a simple regression model and then calculating surprises in terms of the divergence of actual earnings from forecast earnings. They examined excess returns for 20 days prior to earnings announcements and 90 days after. They found perfect ranking of their 10 groups by size of surprise and excess returns, i.e. the group with the largest positive surprise earned the largest excess return, the next largest surprise group earned the next largest return, and so on. In the 20 days prior to earnings announcements, share prices correctly anticipated the surprise but continued to respond to the announcement for the next 90 days. These results were largely unaffected if an adjustment for differences in risk (measured by beta) were made for each group. This study implies that investors who respond quickly to earnings surprises will perform well. Of course, they would do even better if they could achieve some of the excess return earned before the earnings announcement. Bernard and Thomas (1989) estimated that foreknowledge of a quarter's surprise was worth twice as much as trading on a surprise once it was known. So, can 'surprises' be forecast?

The key issue here is whether earnings surprises come as a bolt out of the blue or whether analysts have some inkling that their forecasts are off the mark We have already seen from the research by Elton et al. (1984) that analysts steadily revise their forecasts, which get better the closer they are made to the end of the financial year. Benesh and Peterson, in the study cited above, looked at the course of analysts' forecasts over the year for their top and bottom 50 stocks. They found a gradual reduction in forecast errors through the course of the year as analysts revised their forecasts and became more optimistic for the top performers and less optimistic for the worst performers.

Benesh and Peterson then asked whether it was possible to make excess returns if one bought or sold stocks that had significant earnings revisions in the first half of the year. They tried two rules—buying or selling after an earnings revision from the previous month of 5% and 2%. Excess returns were achieved for seven out of the 10 holding periods for the purchases, and for all 10 periods for the sales. Unfortunately, the study does not really show what returns a real portfolio that has to hold a specific number of stocks, bear transaction costs, etc. might achieve.

Hawkins et al. (1984) also studied earnings revisions using earnings per share expectations data collected by IBES, and formed portfolios of the 20 stocks whose earnings estimates had the largest increase. They formed portfolios every quarter over the period 1975–80. The portfolios were formed at the end of the appropriate months from data available mid-month. The portfolios had holding periods of 3, 6, 9 or 12 months. Table 11.3 shows annual rates of return for the top 20 earnings revision stocks portfolio and the IBES universe.

TABLE 11.3 Earnings revision portfolios and IBES universe: annual rates of return, 1975–80

Holding period (months)	No. of linked portfolios	Top 20 earnings revision stocks (%)	IBES universe (%)
3	24	27.7	20.1
6	12	30.0	18.4
9	8	26.6	17.8
12	6	25.9	17.6

Source: Hawkins et al. (1984, p. 31). Copyright © 1984. Association for Investment Management and Research. Reproduced and republished from the *Financial Analysts Journal* with permission from the Association for Investment Management and Research. All rights reserved.

The earnings revision portfolios had higher betas than the IBES universe. Allowing for this reduced the excess return, but it was still substantial. For the three-month holding-period portfolios, the annual risk-adjusted excess return was 7.1%.

A more recent study by Dowen and Bauman (1991) asked whether the above studies (and other studies not outlined here) were picking up a smaller stock effect (see Chapter 13) or a neglected stock effect (see Chapter 14). They studied the period 1977–86. Their conclusion was that the earnings revision effect is real and has persisted despite its disclosure in earlier articles:

> Based on the results of this and earlier studies, it appears that analysts' early revisions of their EPS estimates tend to be too small, and that investors continue to be slow to respond to the useful indicators provided by analysts' consensus revisions to EPS estimates.
>
> (Dowen and Bauman, 1991, p. 90)

To return to our earlier question as to whether surprises can be forecast, the answer appears to be that they can if we watch analysts' earnings revisions.

The fact that investors react slowly to revisions and surprises might suggest that Wall Street is not interested in earnings revisions. This is not the case at all. For example, the US brokerage and fund management firm Sanford C. Bernstein has integrated earnings revision research with its DDM approach to share selection. Other brokerage houses, such as Prudential Securities and Merrill Lynch, have produced regular quantitative comments on earnings surprises. Indeed, it has been claimed that earnings revisions is now the most widely used share selection technique in the US.

In the UK, the earnings revision effect has not been researched so extensively (but see O'Hanlon et al., 1992). Bercel (1994) examined the effect in seven countries, including the UK where it appeared to work. Indeed, across all seven countries, the percentage of correct signals was about 60%, whereas for the UK it was 69%.

MORE ON SURPRISES

There are three types of research that might improve the returns to a surprise strategy: predicting surprises, improving on the consensus as a measure of market expectations, and relating returns to market conditions. We look at each in turn.

Predicting Surprises

Earnings surprises exhibit serial correlation, i.e. if there is a positive earnings surprise in one quarter, for example, there are likely to be positive surprises in the next couple of quarters (Bernard and Thomas, 1990; Peters, 1993a). Small stocks have the largest initial surprises and subsequent surprises (Peters, 1993b). Stober (1992) compared analyst forecasts with those generated by the Ou–Penman summary statistic (see pp. 158–9). When there was a difference in sign between analysts and the statistic concerning the future direction of profits, the profitable strategy was to follow the statistic.

In a series of publications, Brown has tried to predict surprises (Brown et al., 1996; Brown, 1997a; Brown and Jeong, 1998). Unfortunately, the ESP™ (Earnings Surprise Predictor) he uses is a proprietary model, and few details are provided, except that it is based on a variety of publicly available data, including past earnings surprises and size. The model is shown to be successful in generating outperformance.

Improving on the Consensus as a Measure of Market Expectations

The assumptions underlying consensus earnings figures are that individual analysts are homogeneous, so that looking at the average of their forecasts will be better than looking at any one or a subgroup, and that the consensus measures the market's expectations. These assumptions are false.

Some forecasts used in the consensus are dated, and may not be the analyst's real current forecast. Alternatively the forecast may be current, but the analyst doesn't really follow the stock. For example, an analyst following the food manufacturing industry may produce forecasts for 20 stocks, but in reality may only be seriously interested in 12 of them. Some of his forecasts may be dated. Taking all analysts' forecasts together, the more recent forecasts should be weighted more than old forecasts (O'Brien, 1988).

When a number of analysts revise their forecasts at the same time, it is likely that news has become available. It may improve the consensus forecast just to use the forecasts in the latest cluster of forecasts, for example those forecasts with issue dates no more than two days apart from other forecasts (Mozes and Williams, 1999).

As we saw earlier, some evidence claims there are differences in analysts' forecasting ability (e.g. Jacob et al., 1999; and Capstaff et al., 1999), both across a sector and for individual stocks. It has been argued that some analysts are likely to follow the crowd (led by the company), while others may take the lead in producing forecasts that diverge from the company's guidance (Kahn and Rudd,

1999). The better analysts may be a better guide to market expectations than the consensus. When companies make public announcements about their profits that are intended to correct a mistaken market expectation, clearly the company, not the consensus, should be the guide.

'Whisper forecasts' that appear in the press and on Internet bulletin boards have been found to be more accurate than consensus forecasts (Bagnoli et al., 1999), although if this becomes widely believed, the whispers may become subject to manipulation.

Using several of the factors discussed, Herzberg et al. (1999) found that they could produce forecasts that were more accurate than the consensus. They also showed that where the divergence of forecast from actual was greatest, buying or selling could make high returns, although they didn't report whether the returns were better or worse than using consensus numbers. However, better forecasts would be beneficial for many share-selection techniques.

Relating Surprise Returns to the Market Conditions

There is relatively little research on this. However, Brown and Condon (1995), using a decade of US data, suggested that quintile 1 stocks (most positive surprise quintile) produced higher abnormal returns over the six-month period following revisions in up markets than in down markets. Also, the positive effect on returns continued to increase each month over the six months during rising markets, but in down markets the effect occurred almost entirely in the first month. For quintile 5 stocks (largest negative surprises), the negative abnormal returns were greater in down markets than up markets. And while the negative effect continued to increase over the six months in down markets, in up markets the effect occurred mainly in the first two months. If these findings are confirmed, investors should be adjusting their revisions strategy as market conditions change.

Can We Continue to be Surprised by Surprises?

If analysts make predictable errors, why don't they learn? One explanation might be that behavioural biases make this impossible. US and possibly UK analysts seem to be too optimistic initially, and then underreact. Using the notions of leniency (or optimism), representativeness and anchoring (see Chapter 5), Amir and Ganzach (1998) argue that one would expect, and they find, overreaction in forecast changes and underreaction in forecast revisions, and also overreaction for positive forecast modifications and underreaction and excess optimism for negative forecasts. Nonetheless, one wonders why institutional investors don't adjust forecasts made by brokers. Further, if analysts can continue to be surprised, since reacting to surprises isn't exactly rocket science, why isn't the effect fully discounted? One reason might be the huge turnover that can be involved, another that many stocks do not perform as expected, and the surprise approach is only likely to be reliable if applied across the whole portfolio.

DIVIDEND CHANGES

Research in the US and the UK suggests that companies relate dividend changes to earnings changes, but that they try to smooth the dividend changes. Thus dividend changes tend to follow changes in sustainable earnings, and transitory changes in income do not affect dividends. It follows from this that dividends have some information content and reflect management's assessment of the earning power of a company. There is a particularly strong reluctance to cut dividends. There is a large US literature that finds that announcements of dividend increases (decreases) are related to stock price increases (decreases). This suggests dividends are seen by investors as providing information.

Marsh (1992) conducted a large UK study on the effect of dividend announcements. He analysed stock price reactions to nearly 6000 dividend announcements, including 754 dividend reductions, over the period January 1989–April 1992. During the period studied, small firms underperformed large firms by very large amounts, so Marsh controlled for firm size in calculating abnormal returns. He did not control for beta, arguing that there was considerable evidence that beta adjustments make little difference to UK findings.

Some of Marsh's key findings are shown in Table 11.4, which shows that the larger the dividend increase announced, the greater are the abnormal returns at the time of the announcement, and vice versa. Table 11.4 also shows that the market anticipated the direction of the dividend announcement in the month before the announcement, but still reacted to the actual announcement. The same picture applies for dividend cuts. Further, the same basic story is repeated for a period of one year before and after the dividend announcement. Clearly, good dividend-forecasting skills would provide abnormal returns. There was not much evidence to support the notion that it was possible to make money simply by reacting to dividend changes.

TABLE 11.4 UK dividend announcements and abnormal returns, January 1989–April 1992

Dividend announcement	Abnormal returns (%, size-adjusted) during:			
	Days −20 to −1	Days −1 to 1	Days 1 to 20	Days −20 to 20
Increases of > 25%	1.1	1.7	1.8	4.6
Increases of < 25%	0.6	0.9	1.9	3.4
Maintained	−0.3	−0.1	2.4	2.0
Cuts	−2.7	−4.3	2.2	−4.8
Omissions	−5.3	−7.4	1.4	−11.1

Source: Marsh (1992, p. 23).

Marsh's paper contains much more of interest than is shown here. For example, the anticipation of dividend cuts is shown to take place two years ahead of the cut. On this point, Marsh argues that the market was responding to information about deteriorating company prospects rather than specifically anticipating the dividend cut. Of course this leaves open the question whether dividends actually contain any new information that is not included in earnings and other information. Dividend announcements are usually made at the same time as earnings announcements. Further, while analysts forecast dividends, the bulk of their effort and attention goes into forecasting earnings.

In a US study, Aharony and Swary (1980) looked at dividend announcements that were at least 11 trading days apart from earnings announcements. Sometimes the dividend announcements led the earnings announcements and sometimes they lagged. Aharony and Swary found abnormal returns around both announcements, suggesting both conveyed information. In the UK, Balachandran et al. (1996) studied interim dividend cuts and omissions. They argued that both earnings and interim dividends conveyed information, since both had predictive power for future earnings.

Dividend Surprises

If dividends convey additional information to that contained in earnings, it might follow that abnormal returns can be earned by reacting to dividend surprises and dividend forecast revisions. Aharony and Swary's study used dividend surprises, but we shall detail a study by Cole (1984), as it is of more interest to investors. Cole used a sample drawn from New York Stock Exchange firms in the period 1970–78. He formed two extreme portfolios, one based on earnings surprises and one based on dividend surprises. He defined surprises not in terms of analysts' expectations, but in relation to forecasts from models. He forecast earnings using the most recent 20 quarters' earnings data adjusted for seasonality. He assumed dividends would be the same as in the last quarter, adjusted by any change made in the corresponding quarter a year ago. To calculate surprises, he related actual earnings and dividends to forecast earnings and dividends.

Using specified definitions of high (positive) and low (negative) surprises, he formed four surprise portfolios of high dividend, low dividend, high earnings and low earnings. The portfolios formed had different characteristics, i.e. the high-dividend surprise portfolios were not replicating the high-earnings surprise portfolios. Cole calculated the various holding period returns shown in Table 11.5.

Table 11.5 shows that stocks offering favourable earnings or favourable dividend surprises earned higher returns. The high-dividend surprise stocks outperformed the high-earnings surprise stocks. According to Cole, 'The relevance for security analysts and portfolio managers is that they may use unexpected current quarterly dividends to augment portfolios determined exclusively on the basis of earnings' (Cole, 1984, p. 49). Notice that even if an investor reacted a month after the surprise, superior returns could have been achieved.

TABLE 11.5 Averages of differences in holding period returns

Period (months)	HD–LD (%)	HE–LE (%)	HD–HE (%)
1	0.5	0.6	0.6
2	3.0	1.4	1.1
3	4.3	2.4	1.9
4	4.9	2.6	2.3
5	5.9	6.2	1.8
6	7.3	6.9	2.9

HD, high-dividend surprise; LD, low dividend surprise; HE, high-earnings surprise; LE, low-earnings surprise.

Source: Cole (1984, p. 48). This copyrighted material is reprinted with the permission of the *Journal of Portfolio Management.*

CONCLUDING COMMENTS

If you can forecast more accurately than the consensus, then you can achieve superior returns. Unfortunately, this insight does not help you to forecast better. Stocks that produce favourable earnings surprises perform well, and stocks that produce unfavourable surprises perform poorly. The abnormal returns both precede and follow the announcement. It is possible to earn abnormal returns by reacting quickly to surprises. Analysts tend to be cautious in their earnings revisions, and trends in earnings revisions can be used to earn abnormal returns.

The market is inefficient in its response to earnings surprises and revisions. It is possible to base a share-selection strategy on these findings. But since these findings have been known for many years, why does the market not seem to learn? It may be that there are difficult-to-counter behavioural reasons, and some institutional investment organizations have share-selection committees that must meet before decisions to change a stance on a stock are made, making responses to surprises somewhat drawn out. However, these are rather ad hoc explanations.

Dividend surprises have not been studied as much as earnings surprises, but they may well carry additional information.

12

Aspects of Value Versus Growth

In the internet business profitability is for wimps. It means your business plan wasn't aggressive enough.

'Doonesbury' (Gary Trudeau)

Many managers describe themselves as either growth or value investors. But the distinction is less clear than often assumed. Partly this is because the word 'value' gets in the way. Everybody wants to buy stocks that are good value, even growth managers. Value managers are essentially managers who buy cheap stocks, with 'cheap' being defined as a lot of current-year earnings, or assets, or immediate income (dividends) per penny paid. Growth investors are those looking for rapid or sustained growth in the future of earnings, assets, dividends, etc. There is a tendency for these characteristics to be associated with what appear to value managers as expensive stocks.

Value can be relative as well as absolute. In early 2000, a PER of six would be absolutely cheap. A PER of 30 would not be absolutely cheap, but a PER of 30 in the telecoms sector would be relatively cheap. In Chapter 10, we saw that high-growth shares should be expected to have high PERs. A value manager could easily justify having inline sector weightings, and buying the cheapest stocks within each sector. Some stocks would be absolutely cheap, whilst others would only be relatively cheap. Is this growth or value investing?

Instead of looking at growth versus value, we can look at various measures of one style. For example, we could construct four value indexes by looking at the performance of the 50 stocks in the S&P 500 with the highest earnings-to-price, the 50 with the lowest book-to-price, the 50 with the lowest price-to-cash flow, and the 50 with the lowest price-to-sales (we discuss these ratios in the next chapter). When Bernstein (1995, p. 53) did this for a seven-year period, there was an average of 8.7% difference between the best and worst of the four styles each year. In one year, the difference was 15.8%. When he looked at four growth styles, he found even greater divergence. The growth styles were highest projected five-year earnings growth rates, the largest upward revisions in consensus earnings, the highest probability of earnings surprises, and the fastest earnings momentum (year-to-year percentage change in actual earnings). Consensus earnings revisions and earnings surprises are not necessarily a growth manager's tools, but Bernstein argues that they tend to perform better during the market's growth-driven phases.

Again, how would a growth at a reasonable price (GARP) investor be classified? GARP investors typically relate PERs to growth rates:

$$\text{GARP ratio} = \frac{\text{PER}}{\text{growth rate}}.$$

Imagine four stocks with PERs of 10, 20, 30 and 40, and growth rates of 8%, 20%, 20% and 30%. The GARP ratios would be 1.25, 1, 1.5 and 1.33, respectively. The stock with a PER of 20 would be deemed the cheapest, although it has neither the lowest PER nor the highest growth rate. Is this growth or value?

The problem of definitions can be seen in commercial growth/value indexes. In 1997 in the US, the S&P BARRA Growth Index, an index of growth stocks, rose 36.5% while the S&P BARRA Value Index rose 30%. However, the Russell 1000 Growth Index rose 30.5% while the Russell 1000 Value Index rose 35.2%. The difference is a result of definition and coverage differences. The BARRA Growth and Value indexes divide stocks according to their price-to-book ratios (high = value), rebalancing twice a year. But growth investors focus on rapid earnings growth, so how good a measure of growth is a growth stock index that ignores growth? The Russell indexes are based on price-to-book and forecast growth. While both sets of indexes are large-cap, the BARRA indexes have the higher market cap. Is a large-cap/small-cap effect being mixed in with a growth/value effect?

Academic studies of value versus growth inevitably use statistical criteria to define a style. But just because a style does well/badly statistically doesn't mean a real manager will perform well/badly. The stocks within a particular style often have sufficient diversity of performance for managers to perform somewhat differently than the style. For example, an apparently cheap stock, such as one with a low prospective PER, will be classified by a statistical sort as a cheap stock. But a value manager may note that the stock has been receiving earnings downgrades and believe that analysts are simply slow at making forecast adjustments. The market may expect a lower earnings number than the published consensus earnings forecast. In that case, the stock has a higher prospective PER than the numbers suggest. A good-value manager might avoid such a stock, while a poor one blunders in.

Managers may deviate from a style on pragmatic grounds. A low PER criterion will probably produce a small-cap bias, which the manager may feel he or she should avoid. This may compromise adherence to a low PER style. And low PER stocks tend to be concentrated in a few sectors (the sectors change over time), so to get representation in some sectors the manager may be forced to buy some high PER stocks. While all of this is reasonable enough, and clearly is a modified value approach, the returns may be quite different from those found in academic studies that measure value as simply the bottom PER quintile. Most real investors typically wouldn't tie themselves to something as specific as the bottom quintile of PER. More likely, a value investor would be arguing that he or she wouldn't buy highly rated shares, which assume rapid growth. Some might then feel that everything else is fair game, while others might have some kind of rigid screening process.

Let's pull the discussion together. We don't dispute that there is a difference between growth and value styles. But there is an overlap between the styles, and within a style investment managers can adopt different approaches. If you read too many statistical studies, you can forget that there are real people doing their own thing within any broad style. We now turn to some real people.

VARIETIES OF VALUE

To illustrate the variation that one may find within a style category we will discuss the approaches of three famous investors, Graham, Buffett and Neff.

Benjamin Graham

Benjamin Graham, of Graham and Dodd fame, is usually thought of as the classic value investor. He simplified their *Security Analysis* in 1949 in *The Intelligent Investor* (Graham, 1973) and came up with some investment rules. In an interview published in 1976 (Graham, 1976, p. 22), he stated that he was:

> . . . no longer an advocate of elaborate techniques of security analysis in order to find superior value opportunities. This was a rewarding activity, say, 40 years ago, when our textbook 'Graham and Dodd' was first published; but . . . [with all the research now available] I doubt whether in most cases such extensive efforts will generate sufficiently superior selections to justify their cost.

He now looked to pick a good portfolio rather than individual issues. He suggested two approaches. The first 'appears severely limited in its application, but we found it almost unfailingly dependable and satisfactory . . .' The approach is to buy shares at less than their working capital value, or net current asset value, and deducting all liabilities in full from the current assets. The reason this approach is limited is that during bull markets, few stocks satisfy this criterion. The second approach is to buy stocks that are cheap on the basis of one or more simple criteria. We'll look at both approaches.

Does net current asset work as a selection criterion? Oppenheimer (1986) tested it for the period 1970–82. The stock universe was taken from a December issue of the *Security Owner's Stock Guide*, which includes all New York Stock Exchange and American Stock Exchange (AMEX) stocks, as well as a large number of over-the-counter (OTC) and regional exchange stocks. The outperformance of stocks selling below net current assets—omitting transaction costs and dividends—was impressive: $10 000 invested in the net current asset portfolio on 31 December 1970 would have grown to $254 973 by 31 December 1983. The comparable figures for the NYSE–AMEX and small-firm indexes were $37 296 and $101 992, respectively.

The biggest difficulty with this study is that the number of stocks meeting the criterion each year ranged from only 18 to 89. In fact, 1983 was eliminated from the study because only four stocks met the criterion. In only four of the 13 years, 1970–82, did the number of qualifying NYSE stocks reach double figures. Vu (1988) also tested the criterion and used the Value Line Investment Survey for his data source for the period April 1977–December 1984. He found it to be a profitable strategy but again found few stocks met the criterion. They were also very small. The reality was that an institution, investing significant sums in a diversified portfolio, could not put together a portfolio in many years. This presumably applies with even more force in the smaller UK market. Of course, the rule could be extended so that stocks are ranked by net current assets and the cheapest stocks purchased, whether or not they sell at less than net current asset value. But that is a different criterion.

In *The Intelligent Investor*, Graham gave a list of stock selection criteria. These may briefly be summarized as:

- medium to large firms
- strong financial condition
- earnings stability
- dividend continuity
- significant earnings growth
- moderate to low PER
- low price-to-book ratio.

In the last years of his life, Graham, with his colleague Rea, assembled a new list of stock selection criteria; these are discussed in Rea (1977). Seven of the criteria were Graham's, and three were Rea's. The criteria were:

1. an earnings yield (i.e. the reciprocal of the PER) of at least twice the AAA bond yield (if AAA bonds yield 5%, the PER should be less than 10);
2. a PER less than 40% of the highest average PER over the previous five years;
3. a dividend yield of at least two-thirds the AAA bond yield;
4. a stock price less than two-thirds of the tangible book value per share;
5. a stock price less than two-thirds net current asset value;
6. total debt less than tangible book value;
7. a current ratio greater than two;
8. total debt no greater than twice net current asset value;
9. compound 10-year annual growth of at least 7%;
10. two or fewer annual earnings declines of 5% or more in the last 10 years.

(These are not exactly the criteria listed by Rea, but they are what Oppenheimer tested—see below.) The first five criteria deal with 'rewards' and the second five with 'risks'. It is not necessary for a stock to meet all the criteria; Graham and Rea stressed criteria 1, 3, 5 and 6. Sell signals were if a stock:

1. appreciated by more than 50%;
2. had been held for more than two years;
3. stopped paying dividends;
4. its earnings dropped sufficiently to make it overpriced by 50% or more relative to buy criterion 1.

Oppenheimer (1984) tested the Graham and Rea rules. He tested three strategies, forming portfolios meeting buy criteria 1 and 6, 3 and 6, and 1, 3 and 6 with stocks sold after either a 50% price rise or two years. The COMPUSTAT tapes were screened for all NYSE and AMEX securities satisfying any of the three sets of criteria on 31 December of each year between 1973 and 1980. In half of the years, there were less than 30 shares meeting criteria 1, 3 and 6, and in one of the years, not a single share met the criteria. In 1980, only five shares satisfied criteria 1 and 6, and 14 satisfied criteria 3 and 6. The other years provided at least 49 stocks satisfying either pair of criteria.

The returns available from these strategies are shown in Table 12.1. The superior performance was not due to systematic risk or size. The performance was much better prior to publication of the criteria (in 1977), but still offered excess returns after publication. The decline in excess returns post-publication is not necessarily related to publication, although most commentators have assumed that it is.

TABLE 12.1 Graham and Rea criteria: mean annual returns, 1974–81

NYSE–AMEX index	14%
Criteria 1 and 6	38%
Criteria 3 and 6	26%
Criteria 1, 3 and 6	29%

Source: Oppenheimer (1984, p. 72). Copyright © 1984. Association for Investment Management and Research. Reproduced and republished from the *Financial Analysts Journal* with permission from the Association for Investment Management and Research. All rights reserved.

The greatest problem with this approach is that it generates so few stocks. A long list of criteria—such as the full Graham and Rea list of 10—is quite impractical. Even for the large US market, Oppenheimer found very few eligible stocks when he used a screen of four criteria—1, 3, 6 and 9. In his eight-year sample, the number of stocks selected ranged from 38 to none.

While these tests are interesting, the real point was to illustrate a value approach to investing. One doesn't really need to know the company as long as it's cheap and safe. Growth comes in, but at points 9 and 10, not two of the criteria thought most important. This is consistent with Graham and Dodd's scepticism of industry studies:

> Insofar as these studies relate to the past, the elements dealt with have already influenced the results . . . [and share price]. Insofar as they relate to the future, the studies generally assume that past characteristics and trends will continue. We find these forward projections of the past to be misleading at least as often as they are useful.
> (Graham et al., 1962; slightly different words appear in earlier editions)

Warren Buffet

Warren Buffett is possibly the most famous investor in the world. He is seen as a value investor and a disciple of Graham. However, his investment style is unlike Graham's, and some of the stocks he holds could be classified as growth stocks. Nonetheless, he is probably best classified as a value investor. There are many books purporting to explain Buffett's approach, but they tell different stories. In our view, a book by Mary Buffett and Clark (1997) is the only one that captures Buffett's approach. Our account is based on it and Buffett's report in the 1992 Berkshire Hathaway Annual Report.

Graham was willing to buy any type of company, providing it was cheap. Of course, a cheap but unexciting stock could remain cheap for many years. Graham got round this by buying at a big discount—the margin of safety—to intrinsic value. Even if it took some time for the market to discover the value, the returns could be good.

Buffett distinguishes between excellent and bad businesses. A bad business is a commodity-type business where only the lowest-cost producer—and perhaps not even the lowest-cost product—is likely to do well. Such industries typically have low profit margins, absence of brand-name loyalty, many producers, excess capacity, erratic profitability, and profitability dependent on efficient utilization of tangible assets.

Buffett prefers excellent businesses, bought with a long-term view, that have growing earnings. This way, the shares should move up even if the mispricing is not corrected.

An excellent business is one with some kind of consumer monopoly. This is best understood in terms of barriers to entry (discussed in Chapter 8): an excellent business is one with high entry barriers. Some additional features are desirable: growing earnings, conservative financing, high rate of return on equity, surplus operating cash flow, and an ability to adjust prices to inflation. Contrast this with Graham and Dodd: 'It is our opinion that the existence of an attractive industry outlook is not a sine qua non for the purchase of a specific common stock' (Graham et al., 1962, p. 87).

Having found an excellent company, the next step is to decide whether it is worth buying. To do that one needs to know the price, the return from other assets, and projected earnings. Predictability of earnings is crucial. Buffett is well known for not buying technology stocks because he doesn't understand the industry. Presumably, Internet stocks would be ruled out too because there is no sensible way to forecast their profits. How does one know if earnings are predictable? One way is simply to look at the historical record. If earnings appear predictable, then the annualized rate of growth should be calculated (the geometric mean return p.a.).

A crude returns comparison can be made against bonds by calculating the redemption yield on a bond and the earnings yield on the stock. Say bond yields are 5%, the stock earns 5p per share, and its price is 100p. The earnings yield is $(5/100) \times 100 = 5\%$, equal to the bond yield. If we expect growth to continue, we would expect a growing earnings yield, so we would prefer the stock to the bond. If the earnings yield is less than the bond yield, more complex sums have to be carried out.

Consider again the company's historical compound rate of growth. This can be adjusted up or down, as appropriate, and then applied to current earnings per share (EPS) to calculate what EPS will be in 10 years' time. For example, EPS of 5p compounded at 10% p.a. will grow to 12.97p after 10 years. Next, we find the historical PER multiple range: say it's 10–30. Using the average of 20 (or perhaps another number), we can estimate the price in 10 years to be £2.59 (i.e. 20×12.97p). Taking the current price of the stock, say 50p, we can calculate the per-annum rate of return the stock will have provided to reach the forecast price: about 18% in this case (an allowance for dividends should also be made). Buffett is said to require a return of at least 15%. So, this stock would be attractive. If it were currently selling at 100p, it wouldn't be attractive, as the return would be 10%.

Buffett is said to use a number of valuation techniques in addition to the two outlined above. But the key idea is clear enough. Buy great companies, but only at the right price. If a company has barriers to entry protecting it, and predictable rapid growth, but offers only an 8% return, it is not an attractive share. Bargains are likely to be available where stocks are overlooked, when the entire market falls and all stocks therefore offer higher prospective returns, when one-off problems drive an excellent company's share price down, and when the management is changed of a company that has a good industry position but in which existing management has lost its way.

Buffett does not diversify as much as the typical manager. His approach rules out some areas (technology, biotechnology, etc.), and he favours knowing about companies and industries in detail, which limits the number of sectors that can be followed.

Is Buffett a value investor? No, if we concentrate on his desire for good earnings growth. Yes, if we concentrate on his willingness to ignore some of the fastest growing areas of the market, his stress on excellent businesses rather than the fastest growth firms, and his emphasis on anticipated rates of return—growth is good only if it is cheap. At the beginning of this chapter, we argued that the value/growth distinction can be misleading. Buffett agrees. In his 1992 report to shareholders he states that '. . . the term "value investing" is redundant. What is "investing" if it is not seeking value at least sufficient to justify the amount paid?' And if you thought the dividend discount model had been sneaked in above, you were right. Buffett specifically refers to William's *The Theory of Investment Value* (1938).

John Neff

John Neff is well known in the US as the former manager of the Windsor Fund, a US mutual fund. He is less well known in the UK. His record, however, is exceptional. During his 31.5-year tenure, the fund returned 5546.4% against the S&P 500's 2229.7%: he beat the market by 3.15% p.a. after expenses, 3.5% before. Neff (1999, p. 61) explains his style:

> Windsor was never fancy, fad-driven, or resigned to market performance. We followed one durable investment style whether the market was up, down, or indifferent. These were its principal elements:
>
> - Low price-earnings (p/e) ratio.
> - Fundamental growth in excess of 7 percent.
> - Yield protection (and enhancement, in most cases).
> - Superior relationship of total return to p/e paid.
> - No cyclical exposure without compensating p/e multiples.
> - Solid companies in growing fields.
> - Strong fundamental case.

Neff states that he has been described as a value investor and as a contrarian, but he prefers the description of low price-earnings investor. He discusses each of the principal elements of his style that are listed above. We will pick out a few points.

PERs reflect the past and anticipate growth. Neff likes low-PER stocks because they give 'excellent upside participation' and 'good protection on the downside'. Little is expected of such stocks so bad results don't necessarily kill them, while good results can result in multiple expansion, for example a PER of 8 might rise to 11. On the other hand, a stock selling on a PER of 40 must grow rapidly to avoid disappointing the market. And the equivalent percentage multiple expansion would require the already high PER to climb to 55.

Low PERs can be a fair reflection of a lousy company's prospects. Neff sought to avoid such stocks by seeking at least 7% p.a. growth. Growth rates above 20% p.a. were generally seen as too risky.

While not insisting on a yield, Neff liked high-yield stocks because he thought the dividend came for free as most investors focused on earnings. Neff brought yield, growth and PERs together in his 'total return ratio'. Imagine a stock with earnings growth of 10% p.a., a yield of 4% and a PER of 7. The total return would be 14% (10% + 4%), which was then divided by the PER to give the total return ratio, which in this case is 2. Neff liked stocks with a ratio of two or better. Because of current high valuations, in early 2000 he might be looking for a ratio of 0.7 or better.

Neff didn't follow the usual sector weightings (see Chapter 16). He classified stocks into four categories:

- highly recognized growth
- less recognized growth
- moderate growth
- cyclical growth.

Obviously, he didn't chase the first category, but he usually found good total return ratios in the next two. In cyclicals, timing is all. Which category was most heavily weighted in his portfolio at any one time was simply a function of perceived value. Huge deviations from traditional sector weightings were therefore possible. For example, oil and oil services averaged around 12% of the S&P 500, but Windsor's weighting varied from about 1% to 25%.

Neff undertook relatively standard financial statement analysis and tried to understand what made an industry tick. He was interested in basic issues, such as:

- Are an industry's prices headed up or down?
- What about costs?
- Who are the market leaders?
- Do any competitors dominate the market?
- Can industry capacity meet demand?
- Are new plants under construction?
- What will be the effect on profitability?

Of course, Neff is from a different age, so does what he says have relevance today? Rightly or wrongly, he believes 'All things considered, if I started again in January 2000, I'd follow the identical course' (Neff, 1999, p. 119).

CONCLUDING COMMENTS

Investment managers often classify themselves as growth or value oriented. In this chapter, we have tried to show that these terms may disguise a lot of intrastyle diversity. We illustrated this with an outline of the approaches of three value investors. Graham's approach was driven largely by a stock's ratings rather than its prospects. Neff's approach is different, but still clearly that of a value investor and in particular a low-PER investor. Like Buffett, he prefers some growth, but rather than buy good companies and hold forever (as Buffett tends to), Neff is happy to trade cyclicals. Neff falls between Graham and Buffett. While Graham and Buffett's portfolios would probably have little in common, it is quite likely that Neff would buy some of the same stocks as both of them. In the real world, the term 'value investor' can cover quite a wide range of investment behaviour.

13

Value, Growth and Size: Evidence

The greatest of all gifts is the power to estimate things at their true worth.

La Rochefoucauld

Which is the better style, value or growth? Recently, the answer has been growth. The Wilshire Large Growth Index returned 34.7% in 1999, while the Wilshire Large Value Index returned 8.3%. The differential, 26.4%, was the biggest in the index's 22-year history. The second biggest difference was 23.8% in 1998, again in favour of growth. (The third was 13.1% in 1981, in favour of value.) In 1999, the Wilshire Small Growth Index returned 52.6% versus Small Value's −1.4%.

Yet numerous academics studies covering the period from the early 1960s to the early 1990s have found that value has been the long-term winner. And one study (Davis, 1994) that looked at the period 1940–63 has found the same thing, as has another that has gone back to 1929 (Davis et al., 2000). So, for a period of 60+ years, value has beaten growth, but recently it hasn't. This leads to a lot of 'perhaps'. Perhaps the academic studies are just sample dependent: they hold only for the sample of years studied. Or perhaps the recent preference for growth stocks is something that reflects a period of intense technological change that has changed the rules of the game. Or perhaps there will be a one-off adjustment, and then value will reassert itself. Or perhaps there has been a stockmarket bubble and a sharp underperformance by growth stocks can be expected. Certainly, Internet stocks largely fuelled the extraordinary returns to growth in the US in 1998 and 1999. The Wilshire Internet Index, which consists of 364 stocks, returned 139.8% in 1999. At $1.6 trillion, that index's capitalization was larger than all the emerging markets together, was equivalent to 10% of the Wilshire 5000, and was larger than every individual country market in the world except the US, UK and Japan.

Our view is that there is an Internet bubble and our inclination is to side with the long-term studies. Accordingly, we will review the historical evidence. Even if you think the game has changed forever, the studies are of interest because there are difficult issues worth discussing when any style appears to generate outperformance.

Buying small stocks is a separate style, but small stocks pop up in our value discussion so we will begin with a discussion of those.

The size of a firm can be measured by the market value or capitalization of its ordinary shares. For many years, it was believed that small-cap stocks were the way to earn high returns. There was evidence from many countries (including Australia, Belgium, Canada, Finland, France, Ireland, Japan, Netherlands, New Zealand, Spain, Sweden, the UK, the US and West Germany) that small companies had produced higher returns than large companies. While the textbooks proclaimed the high return from small-cap based on studies carried out some years ago, many investment professionals looked at the returns in the 1990s and declared the effect dead. However, in 1999, small stocks again outperformed in the US and the UK, so perhaps the professionals were too quick to write the effect off. So, is there a small-cap effect, and if there is, what causes it?

IS THERE A SMALL-CAP EFFECT?

There are a number of ways of deciding whether there is a small-firm effect:

- Examine return indexes for small-cap and large-cap firms.
- Divide the market into size-based deciles and examine returns.
- Look at the evidence for a number of countries.

While the first method is the most obvious approach, it may just pick up a relationship that holds at the extremes of the size distribution. If we assign the smallest 10% of stocks to decile 10, the next smallest 10% to decile 9, and so on, then the evidence of a size effect would be more compelling if size decile 10 returns more than decile 9, and 9 more than 8, and so on through to 1. If the effect is found in a number of countries, this may make it more likely that the effect is real.

We'll dispose of the last point first. As we noted, the size effect has been reported in a number of countries, but the time period for most studies is short. As we shall see, the size premium is not constant, so it is possible that it was just chance that all the studies, done at much the same time, found what they did. This seems unlikely. Why would small stocks behave in that way when the markets' levels show only modest correlation, the sectors of the various markets differ, international economic cycles have not always been synchronized, and so on?

Two of the longest records are for the US and the UK. For the US, there are returns data on small stocks versus large beginning in 1926. Small stocks have outperformed. For example, over the period 1926–98, the geometric mean annual return for the smallest decile on the New York Stock Exchange was 15.1% versus 10.5% for the largest. Some writers, notably Siegel (1994, p. 85), have disputed the significance of this. He points out that if you strip out the years 1975–83, large stocks have outperformed small stocks. The justification for selecting the years that you will consider to constitute evidence is unclear. It is easy enough to show that if you drop a few carefully chosen months, then bonds have outperformed stocks, but nobody takes that seriously. (Admittedly, the months are not all together, but scattered throughout the measurement period.)

In the UK, the Hoare Govett Smaller Companies Index (HGSCI) comprises the lowest 10% by capitalization of the main UK equity market. The HGSCI has a history since 1955 and since that date (to end-1999) it has outperformed the FTSE All-Share. Figure 13.1 shows the record of the HGSCI relative to the FTSE All-Share. There is little evidence on size before 1955, but Dimson et al. (2000) claim that there appears to have been a size effect amongst the largest 100 stocks throughout the twentieth century. During the period 1900–54 (i.e. the period preceding the HGSCI), the equally-weighted index of the 100 largest shares returned about 0.5% more than the market-weighted top 100. So, as in the US, the long-run evidence for the UK shows that small stocks have beaten large, and again the outperformance is not steady and consistent. For example, in the 10-year period 1989–98, UK large-caps beat UK small-caps. In 1999, small-cap stocks beat large-caps by 30%.

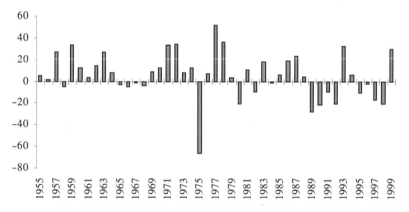

FIGURE 13.1   Return differential: HGSCI minus FTSE All-Share Index, 1955–99
Source: Drawn from data in Dimson and Marsh (2000).

The effect we are discussing is sometimes called a small-cap effect and sometimes a size effect. The latter is the better description because the finding that small firms have outperformed large firms is not restricted just to the smaller stocks doing very well or large stocks doing very badly. Rather, large stocks have returned less than medium-sized stocks, and medium less than small. In fact, some studies have found a negative monotonic relationship between size and returns when the market is divided into market cap deciles. A recent study by Heston et al. (1999) found the size decile/return (% per month) relationship over the period 1980–95 shown in Figure 13.2 for a sample of 2100 firms from 12 European countries. A believer would say that while not monotonic, the

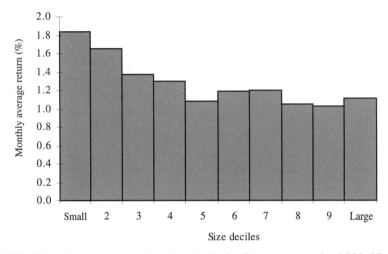

FIGURE 13.2 Average return by size decile for European stocks, 1980–95
Source: Drawn from data in Heston et al. (1999, p. 14).

tendency for a size effect to occur throughout the market is clear enough. A sceptic would argue there is no size effect for the six largest deciles, which account for nearly all of the capitalization-weighted market.

Whether or not you believe that small stocks will continue to outperform over long periods, you might wish to know when small stocks will do relatively well or badly. Most fund managers believe that small stocks are more likely to underperform during recessions. There is some evidence to support this, but it is not the whole story. During most of the years of poor performance by small-caps in the 1990s, US and UK economic growth was strong.

Support for the argument about economic conditions is suggested by the finding for the US that when small-caps beat large, both tend to produce good returns (suggestive of good economic conditions), but when large-caps beat small, average returns tend to be lower (Reinganum, 1999). Direct evidence is produced by Jensen et al. (1997). They use discount rate changes in the US as a measure of the stringency of monetary policy. They find that US small stocks only generate a statistically significant premium during periods of expansionary monetary policy.

POSSIBLE REASONS FOR THE SIZE EFFECT

If we assume that there is a small-firm effect, then how can it be explained? Many fund managers would argue that small companies are more likely to double in size than large companies, and it is superior growth prospects that explain the better performance. Smaller companies as measured by the HGSCI have generated faster earnings growth than larger companies. However, one would expect faster growth to be discounted and reflected in the share price so that smaller stocks do not keep on outperforming. After all, amongst the larger stocks it is normal for 'growth' stocks to have high PERs reflecting their anticipated growth. Nonetheless, there may be something in this fundamental approach.

Dimson and Marsh (1999) explained the small-cap return premium from 1955 to 1988, and the small-cap discount from 1989 to 1997, in the UK in terms of dividends. Recall that in a simplified DDM, returns will equal the dividend yield plus the growth rate of dividends. We can apply this to the premium/discount for small size by considering the difference in initial yields and the difference in subsequent dividend growth rates for large and small firms. In 1955, small-cap stocks had a yield premium of 3.6% over large-cap stocks, and subsequent dividend growth was 1.9% higher. Adding the two figures together gives a differential return of 5.5%, close to the actual 6% outperformance that subsequently occurred. In 1989, smaller stocks had a yield discount of 1.2% and subsequent dividend growth was 3.4% lower. This would suggest that small-cap stocks should have underperformed large by 4.6% p.a.—the actual figure was 7.7%.

This argument suggests that fundamentals drive the return on small-cap stocks. But the question then arises, why have small-cap dividends been growing at a slower rate than large-cap dividends? The sector composition of small stock indexes is quite different from that of large stocks, and of the entire market. Accordingly, if there are significant differences in the growth rates of various sectors or industries, this will have a significant effect on small stocks. Whether small stocks will outperform in future will thus depend on whether technological change, globalization, etc. have a bias for or against small stocks. But the twentieth century has seen many changes, and yet small stocks have managed to stay ahead.

A different approach is to explain the higher return as a reward for greater risk. In the CAPM framework, we might expect smaller stocks to have higher betas than larger stocks. In the US, the evidence is that small-stock portfolio betas are higher, but not sufficiently higher to explain much of the higher return. In the UK, the HGSCI has usually had a lower beta than the FTSE All-Share Index, and a lower, or similar, standard deviation of returns. In other countries, the beta of small-cap stocks is generally less than one. Small stocks, however, trade less frequently than large stocks, and because of this nonsynchronous trading, it can be shown that there is a downward bias in small firms' betas. But even allowing for this bias, small firms still do not appear to be very risky. Of course, this argument is a test of a joint hypothesis—that small firms are risky and that betas measure risk. The problem may well be beta.

Beta is not the only measure of risk, and the capital asset pricing model is not the only asset-pricing theory. Chan et al. (1985) and Chen (1988) attempt to explain the size effect in terms of arbitrage pricing theory. They claim considerable success and explain the extra return from small firms as a reward for risk. Specifically, they note that there is a relationship between small-firm returns and the difference between the returns on a low-grade bond portfolio and a government bond portfolio—the difference will widen during a recession—and with net business formation. It is argued that smaller firms suffer disproportionately during recessions and smaller stock shareholders are rewarded for this risk. Fama and French develop a similar argument, which we discuss later in the chapter.

Most investors probably believe small firms are dynamic and tomorrow's winners. Chan and Chen (1991, p. 1468), however, argue that at least for the US, the small firms studied by the academics are marginal firms:

> They have lost market value because of poor performance, they are inefficient producers, and they are likely to have financial leverage and cash flow problems. They are marginal in the sense that their prices tend to be more sensitive to changes in the economy, and they are less likely to survive adverse economic conditions . . .. Furthermore, firms that suffer from past misfortunes tend to be smaller. If they do not change their capital structure accordingly, they have higher financial leverage.

Analysis of firms listed on the NYSE supports this argument. Firms in the smallest quintile tend to have fallen from higher quintiles. Newly-listed firms tend to be successful and do not enter the bottom quintile. The financial characteristics of the bottom-quintile firms tend to support the Chan and Chen argument. If one turns to Nasdaq firms, because these are typically smaller than NYSE-listed stocks, firms the same size as the bottom quintile of NYSE firms are less likely to be fallen angels. Sure enough, they have different financial characteristics. In short, Chan and Chen speculate that the small firms that have been studied earn higher returns because they are genuinely risky.

Berk (1995, 1997) provides a more general risk argument. He argues that there is confusion between the size of a firm and its market value. The size of a firm would be measured by, say, its assets. The market value of a firm is, theoretically, the present value of its discounted dividend stream. The riskier a firm is, the higher the discount rate used to discount the dividend stream. If two companies of equal size with equal cash flows have different market values, then it must be because the lower market value firm is being discounted at a higher rate because it is riskier. When we relate returns to market value, we are not relating returns to size. Berk argues that there is no relationship between size and return, but there must be a relationship between market cap and return. He conducts various empirical tests that he claims supports his position. Accordingly, he argues that over a long time period, a well-diversified portfolio of firms with low market values must earn a higher return than a well-diversified portfolio of large-cap firms. Berk argues that market cap proxies for all unmeasured risk. If an asset-pricing model claims to explain all relevant risk factors, then inclusion of a market value variable should add no explanatory power. If it does, it suggests that there are omitted risk variables. Berk's argument is a general one, and should apply in all conditions, yet Jensen et al. found a size effect only in periods of monetary expansion, which casts doubt on Berk's argument unless economic conditions is the omitted variable.

A different explanation for the small-firm effect is the higher costs (bid/ask spread and commission) associated with dealing in small stocks (e.g. Stoll and Whaley, 1983; and Loeb, 1991). Stoll and Whaley used US data for 1960–79, and found a small-company effect. However, when transaction costs were allowed for, and portfolios rebalanced every month, the small-stock portfolio did not generate abnormal returns. Of course, as the holding period is extended, the profitability of the small-stock portfolio improves (or becomes less negative). At about a four-month holding period, the small firms start to generate abnormal returns. Institutional investors turn stocks over less frequently than every four months. Moreover, any investor willing to take a relatively or totally passive approach would achieve exceptional returns (e.g. see Sinquefield, 1991). Thus, transaction costs may diminish the small-firm effect but they do not explain it away.

Another explanation for the small-company effect might be neglect. Neglected companies—for example those neglected by analysts or institutional investors—tend to outperform (see Chapter 14). Carvell and Strebel (1987) claim that the small-firm effect is a proxy for the neglected-firm effect and there is no underlying small-firm effect. Small firms are certainly neglected. The bottom line for brokers' investment research is the value of the buy/sell orders generated by the research, and clearly the economics of investment research do not justify spending as much time and money researching a £1 million company, or even a £50 million company, as one capitalized at £1 billion. The research costs for smaller stocks are disproportionately high, and this would justify a higher apparent return from smaller stocks. The investor willing to buy stocks about which he or she has little detailed information will buy a smaller companies index fund to diversify some of the specific company risk.

One peculiarity of the size effect is that the bulk of the abnormal return in the US occurs in January (Keim, 1983). If one adds in the last day of December, most of this occurs in five days: the last day of December and the first four days of January. The January effect is discussed in Chapter 14. Dimson and Marsh (1992) report that the picture is different for the UK. January and April (the start of the fiscal year) have provided the worst relative performance for the HGSCI.

We leave it to the reader to decide whether there is a small-cap premium, and if so why.

SIX VARIETIES OF VALUE

Three issues that are critical in our discussion of value versus growth, or indeed any form of style investing, were implicit in our discussion of size. If different styles produce different returns, there are at least three possible causes:

- The return differentials between investment styles are statistical aberrations. They do not reflect differences in expected returns, and are unlikely to be repeated. This may be a result of the returns being sample dependent, or the result of data mining, or there may be errors in the data used, e.g. the COMPUSTAT data may suffer from survivorship bias, or any of the points raised on pp. 111–115.

- Return differentials between investment styles may be risk premiums. We would expect these differences to be maintained, but they are not an abnormal return, merely a return for bearing risk. Even if the return differentials represent risk, you may be willing to bear the risks for higher returns.
- The return differentials between styles may represent market inefficiencies. They are true, statistically significant findings, and offer a return above any risks that the style involves. The market is inefficient.

As we saw in the previous chapter, value investors may adopt a number of different investment strategies. For purposes of statistical studies, a value investor might be defined as one who invests in shares with one or more of the following attributes:

- low PER
- high cash flow to price ratio
- low GARP ratio
- low price-to-sales ratio
- high dividend yield
- high asset value per share.

Let's look at the reasons for believing that each of these variables might lead to abnormal returns.

Low Price-Earnings Ratio Stocks

Every investor probably accepts that a company's PER should vary with its growth prospects and perhaps with some measure of 'quality' or safety. Although PERs should be forward looking, it would not be surprising if views about the future were formed at least partly on the basis of the past. As a result, one might expect that PERs would be related to past earnings and sales growth, profitability, stability of past earnings, financial strength, and quality of management, as well as the nature and prospects of the industry, competitive position of the company, and so forth (e.g. Cottle et al., 1988). Value investors believe the market does not do a good job in judging the 'appropriate' PER for shares using this historical data plus forecasts.

An explanation for this poor judgement, associated mainly with Dreman (1982), is based on a mixture of economic facts and human psychology. A number of studies in the UK and the US have suggested that corporate earnings growth rates are essentially random, as we discussed in Chapter 11. As we noted, to say that profit increases follow a random, or near random, pattern is not to say that business life is random. Far from it. When firms make large profits, they are likely to begin to suffer increasing competition, and when firms do badly, they are likely to be under pressure to improve. Firms are also affected by the unintended consequences of other firms' actions. For example, not all UK property firms participated in the development frenzy of the late 1980s, but most will have suffered the consequences of the weak property market that followed. And firms can be affected by genuinely random factors, such as the weather. A good or bad summer can make a lot of difference to a clothes retailer; in the UK the restaurant trade is affected adversely by both very hot weather and snow. There are good reasons for believing that firms have less control over their profits than is often thought.

The market price of a share will be a function of both its earnings and the appropriate PER. We have seen that analysts have some skills in forecasting earnings, but they often make big mistakes. The essential argument for low PER stocks is that the ratings reflect the fact that investors rely too much on historical data and give insufficient weight to the large random element in profits. If a share sells on a high PER, investors expect good things of the company. If it has better-than-expected earnings, it will probably rise in price to reflect the extra earnings, but its PER may not change. If it has poor earnings, the price may well fall to reflect the lower earnings and additionally to reflect a reassessment of the appropriate PER. For low PER stocks, one would expect the same asymmetric response, but this time in a favourable direction. Notice that with this argument, analysts might generally be able to forecast which stocks will grow fastest in the next year. It is simply that given the frequent errors analysts will make, investors pay too much for growth. (Recall, however, that Elton et al., 1984 found that analysts systematically overestimated growth for high-growth companies and underestimated growth for low-growth companies.)

Some investors reject a PER strategy because it involves buying the same old stocks in the same old sectors. This is not in fact true, although there is a bias at any time to certain industries. What happens is that these sectors change over time, albeit sometimes only slowly. Some managers perceive a risk of being concentrated in a few sectors: the risk is volatile short-term performance, rather than poor long-term performance, but clients are often lost on the short-term results. Seeking greater diversification by buying shares that are cheap relative to their sector can offset this risk. Diversifying in this way will reduce a portfolio's volatility relative to the market although, if you believe the low PER argument, it will also reduce its abnormal returns.

Low Price-To-Cash Flow

Many investors are suspicious of earnings per share figures because of differences between companies in how they calculate depreciation and amortization, and differences over time in how a particular company will calculate these figures. These investors often prefer to use some measure of cash instead of earnings and calculate a cash flow ratio (CFR). There are a number of such ratios; one definition is:

$$\text{CFR} = \frac{(\text{profit after taxes} + \text{depreciation} + \text{amortization})}{\text{weighted average number of ordinary shares}}.$$

CFR is, in effect, the sceptical value investor's PER.

Low Price-To-Sales Ratio Stocks

Buying stocks with a low price-to-sales ratio is sometimes recommended in the US as a worthwhile investment strategy, but is seldom discussed in the UK. Perhaps the higher profile in the US is due to Kenneth Fisher, a columnist on the influential US magazine *Forbes*, being a proponent of the technique. He has discussed the technique in his column and elsewhere (e.g. Fisher, 1984a; and Fisher, 1984b).

Fisher claims that the reason for purchasing low price-to-sales ratio stocks is essentially contrarian. High price-to-sales ratio stocks are popular and discount too much of the future. Fisher (1984a, p. 14) argues that profit growth often comes from margin expansion and investors then form excessive expectations: 'Few companies can sustain significantly above-average profits margins for long. Even fewer analysts can tell which companies will maintain profitability.' A stock with a low price-to-sales ratio will have low sales margins and might be thought to be a candidate for recovery or improvement.

Dividing a firm's PER by its net after-tax profit margin produces its price-to-sales ratio, so there is a relation between low price-to-sales ratios and low PERs. Why would one use a price-to-sales ratio approach rather than a PER approach if they are related, especially as earnings might be thought to be more important to investors than sales? Proponents of the price-to-sales ratio approach argue that:

- sales are more stable and less subject to accounting manipulation than earnings (and assets values);
- a price-to-sales ratio is meaningful for a firm losing money, whereas a PER is not;
- a low PER strategy faces problems with cyclical and turn-around stocks. Both will have high PERs before their profits soar, and low PERs before their profits decline.

Turning to implementation of a low price-to-sales ratio strategy, Fisher does not recommend simply buying the cheapest price-to-sales ratio stocks. He notes that the technique is not applicable to every sector, not to banks for example, and that the definition of a low ratio varies with the type of sector. This makes the technique very subjective. Once an investor has screened some low price-to-sales ratio stocks, Fisher recommends traditional fundamental analysis to identify quality amongst the possible purchases.

Growth at a Reasonable Price

GARP is neither a pure value tool nor a pure growth tool, but lies somewhere in between. The basic assumption, however, is that growth prospects can be overrated, which has value overtones. There is surprisingly little research on this ratio (but see Peters, 1991).

The usual presentation implies that stocks with low GARP ratios are attractive. However, this is logically unsound. Table 13.1 is a repeat of part of Table 10.5, except that only two of the discount rates included in that table are shown and the figures after the slash are GARP ratios. Table 10.5 was drawn up on the assumption of a simple DDM, and shows how the PER should vary as a function of growth and the discount rate. As you can see from Table 13.1, as the rate of growth increases, the justified PER increases at a much faster rate. As the discount rate rises, the justified PER falls, but at a faster rate for higher growth rates than for lower.

TABLE 13.1 PERs and GARPs for various growth/discount rate combinations

Discount rate	Rate of growth			
	5%	6%	7%	8%
9%	12.5/2.5	16.7/2.8	25.0/3.6	50.0/6.3
10%	10.0/2.0	12.5/2.1	16.7/2.4	25.0/3.1

We know from the construction of the table that all the PERs shown are 'correct', given the variations in discount rates and growth rates, but the GARP ratios suggest otherwise. For example, with a 9% discount rate the GARP ratios suggest that the 8% growth rate stock is hugely overvalued compared with the 5% growth rate stock. Or if we look at the share with a 5% growth rate and a 9% discount rate, we see that it should have the same PER as a stock with a 6% growth rate and a 10% discount rate. However, the GARP ratio suggests that the latter stock is cheaper than the former. It is not obvious that GARP ratios have any value.

High Dividend Yields

There are a number of arguments why high-dividend-yield stocks might produce abnormal returns. In the context of a simple DDM, the total return on a stock will be its initial dividend yield plus its growth rate. If we expect all stocks with the same risk to offer the same total return, then low-growth stocks will have to offer higher initial yields. However, if investors are poor at assessing growth prospects—as argued in the section on low PERs—it is possible that the growth rate assumed for high-growth-rate stocks will be too high, and that for low-growth stocks will be too low. Accordingly, high-yield stocks might be expected to offer a higher total return.

A related argument might be that investors simply understate the importance of initial yield. They may focus too much on growth. For example, even with perfect growth forecasting ability, investors might not be willing to accept that a stock with a 2% initial yield advantage is worth the same as a stock with a 2% faster growth rate. This is akin to John Neff's argument that dividends come free.

A different argument, not a value argument, relates to taxation. In many countries, income is taxed at a higher rate than capital gains. Even where income and capital gains tax rates are the same, capital gains typically is not paid until the gains are realized and thus the capital gains tax can be postponed in a way that income tax cannot. If investors are interested in after-tax income, they will presumably only purchase high-yielding stocks if they offer the same after-tax return as low-yielding stocks, i.e. offer higher returns than low-yielding stocks on a pre-tax basis.

While private investors might want a higher pre-tax yield to compensate for tax, it is possible that they will not get it if enough investors require high income and they prefer holding high-yielding stocks to having continually to sell small parcels of shares to generate income from capital gains.

High Asset Value per Share

Until Fama and French's 1992 article, most modern textbooks gave asset value short shrift, although many private client managers appeared to look at it. Investors who consider asset values to be important calculate the net asset value (ordinary shareholders' funds divided by number of ordinary shares in issue) and relate it to the price per share. The US literature tends to refer to book value instead of net asset value.

Interest in net asset value seems to wax and wane, although there is always some interest. Private businesses are often purchased or sold primarily with reference to net asset value. The courts, when forced to be involved in valuing companies, will include net asset value as one of the determining factors. Corporate raiders will certainly have regard to net asset value. If a company is selling at a discount to net asset value, the acquirer will obtain assets at less than their replacement cost, plus sales and personnel. Finally, investors always have regard to asset value for some categories of company. Companies that invest in property or shares (e.g. investment trusts) are always appraised partly (often mainly) by their discount or premium to asset value. Asset values are relevant for public utilities in the US because of the regulatory structure. Banks, which hold mainly assets whose stated net worth should be close to their liquidating or sale value, are often valued in the US with regard to asset value, although this seems less common in the UK.

If the market looks at net asset value in some sectors as the main appraisal technique and raiders use it elsewhere, surely the case for valuing stocks with regard to net asset value is established? Not necessarily. If a company is worth its dividend stream (see Chapter 10), why should there be any direct connection between share price and asset value? To take an extreme example, service companies may have few assets other than their people, and these do not appear on the balance sheet or enter net asset value calculations. What merit would a net asset value calculation have in these circumstances? Clearly, prices can exceed net asset value for sensible reasons. One might be tempted to accept that the presence of corporate raiders will stop share prices from being below net asset value, but even this is uncertain. The problem is that a net asset value sum is not necessarily a very reliable guide to 'value'.

The stated net asset value will depend on a number of accounting conventions, with regard to the treatment of intangibles, depreciation policy, and the accuracy of property valuations. Further, however sensible the accounting treatment, there may be little economic rationale for the stated asset value. For general assets, such as cars, the balance sheet values may be a good guide to their sale value in the event of liquidation, but for specialized assets (e.g. the bulk of the assets of a sugar beet processor), there may be no market. Accordingly, their liquidating value may be zero.

Along with the physical assets, a raider might acquire some staff. If the raider has to lay off the staff, it may face large redundancy costs so that net asset value on a break-up basis may well be below net asset value calculated on a going-concern basis. The conclusion must be that asset values will be relevant to a corporate raider, but published asset values may be little guide to how a raider values assets and need not therefore be a prop to share prices.

The conclusion one might draw from the above discussion—which is Graham and Dodd-ish—is that in some industries, published asset value is a valuable tool, but for the stockmarket as a whole, it is an empirical issue as to whether shares selling on a low price relative to net asset value are cheap and will offer excess returns.

Whitman and Shubik (1979) provided a different view of the merits of net asset value. They felt that book value had little apparent effect on day-to-day stock prices, but they thought it was a highly useful tool for a variety of purposes, including predictions of future accounting profits:

> To us, book value, in virtually all analysis other than predictions of common-stock prices for the immediate future, is at least as significant as accounting earnings. And, in practice, one is not a substitute for the other. But . . . book value seems to us to be a better starting point . . ..
>
> (Whitman and Shubik, 1979, p. 184)

Whitman and Shubik (1979, pp. 184–5) argue that for Graham and Dodd, asset value is important in special cases only. They disagree:

We believe that a very large part of American businesses are engaged in asset-conversion activities; that is, they are not strict going concerns involved only in operations that result in recurring accounting earnings. Rather, many companies, in whole or in part, are engaged in asset-conversion activities that give rise to tax shelter, merger and acquisitions, changes in control, liquidations, investment activities and major refinancings. The analysis of businesses so engaged involves assigning a relatively increased importance to book value, or in any event a marked decrease in the significance of accounting earnings from operations.

According to Whitman and Shubik (1979, p. 186), book value is connected to earnings:

> In the bookkeeping cycle, net income not paid out to stockholders becomes a balance-sheet account, called retained earnings or earned surplus. These past profits tend to be the principal component of book value . . . Thus, as a rule of thumb, companies with large book values relative to market prices have net worths that consist in great part of retained earnings. Such companies tend also to be selling at very low prices when compared with average long-term earnings.

They argue that book value is one measure of resources. And the amount of resources a management has available is an indicator of future earning power. Analysts often stress the importance of return on investment or return on equity. But we cannot calculate these ratios without knowing the investment. So how can the former be important and the latter not? Further, book value can be a measure of potential liquidity. While short-term liquidity is best measured by relating current assets to liabilities, 'In the real world of asset conversion and the tax carry-back provisions of the US Internal Revenue Code, large quantities of brick-and-mortar assets are frequently the raw material out of which a great deal of liquidity is created' (Whitman and Shubik, 1979, p. 189).

Perhaps a way of reconciling these divergent views is via the discounted abnormal earnings approach discussed in Chapter 10. There we saw that we could derive the value of a firm as the book value of equity plus the present value of expected future abnormal earnings. This valuation approach was derived from the DDM. And we saw that unbiased accounting rules affect reported profits both in size and timing, but not the value of the firm. The gist of these arguments is that we should treat asset value more seriously than economists traditionally have. If we take this view, buying shares on a low price relative to net asset value (or a high book-to-market value) is a value strategy

EVIDENCE ON VALUE INVESTING

Evidence on value investing has come from a number of studies looking at individual value techniques or several of them in combination. Many studies sort data in some way. It is useful to begin by discussing this.

Imagine we are interested in size and low PERs, and we want to find the effect of each attribute alone and the interaction between the two. We need to find a way of stopping size varying with the PER, and to control the variation of each attribute. Here's how we could do it.

- We begin by arraying the sample by size from the largest to smallest stock, and then spitting it into quintiles, i.e. five groups ranging from large stocks through to small. (Different studies use different numbers of groups).
- Now we take the smallest quintile and array all the stocks in it by PER.
- Next, we split this smallest size quintile into PER quintiles.
- If we repeat the last two steps for every size quintile, we will have 25 groups.

So, we arrange our data by size and then sort each size quintile into PER quintiles. This will show us what happens as we vary either size or PER. (Table 13.2 gives an example.)

Some studies carry out a second sort:

- From every size quintile we can take the lowest PER group and use them to form one new group. What does it consist of? All the stocks have low PERs, but they were drawn from every size quintile so they are random with respect to size.
- Next, we can pull out the second lowest PER group from every size quintile and form our second group. And so on.
- At the end of the process, we will have five portfolios ranked by PER, but random with respect to size.

If we start with our sample arranged by PER, we can allow size to vary and randomize with respect to PER. If we think other variables move together, we have to go through the whole randomization procedure again.

Evidence on Low Price-Earnings Ratio Stocks

Since Nicholson (1960), there has been a steady stream of articles reviewing the US evidence, and this has generally pointed to low PER stocks generating abnormal returns. Amongst the most influential articles in the investment community have been those by Basu (1975, 1977, 1983). However, the academic evidence is somewhat mixed. While it is generally agreed that low PER stocks have produced abnormal returns, there have been disputes as to whether the effect vanishes when firm size is allowed for (e.g. Reinganum, 1981; and Banz and Breen, 1986), or whether it subsumes the size effect (e.g. Basu, 1983), or whether both variables have independent effects (e.g. Cook and Rozeff, 1984; Jaffe et al., 1989a; and Keim, 1990). The study by Jaffe et al. will be outlined here after first making a technical point.

Although this section is about PERs, the research literature often looks at the earnings-price ratio, the reciprocal of the PER. There are two advantages of using earnings-price ratios. First, companies with negative earnings are automatically ranked as having the lowest earnings-price ratios, whereas they are not automatically ranked as the highest PERs. (Many studies have simply ignored companies with negative earnings.) Second, PERs 'blow up' when earnings approach zero, and this can cause statistical problems; this does not happen with earnings-price ratios. While this switch is statistically convenient, it means the reader has to do some mental gymnastics. To avoid this, we will often discuss results in terms of PERs even when the study in question used earnings-price ratios.

Reverting now to the study by Jaffe et al., this used a substantially longer sample period, 1951–86, than previous studies, and examined size, PER, month-of-year effect and share price (i.e. high or low in money terms). Jaffe et al. drew their data from databases that included NYSE and AMEX firms. The number of firms for which relevant data were available ranged from 352 in 1950 to 1309 in 1974. Portfolios were constructed by the following ranking procedure. Firms were ranked by earnings-price ratio and placed into one of six groups. Group 0 included all securities with negative earnings, and groups 1–5 contained securities with positive earnings. Stocks with the lowest earnings-price ratio were placed in group 1, and the highest in group 5. Next, the stocks in each earnings-price ratio group were ranked by market value into five subgroups, with the smallest stocks in subgroup 1 and the largest in 5. This procedure resulted in 30 portfolios, each of which was updated annually.

TABLE 13.2   Average % monthly returns and size for 30 portfolios of US firms ranked by earnings-price ratio and then size, April 1951–December 1986
(a) Average monthly returns

Size	Earnings-to-price ratio					
	Negative	Lowest	2	3	4	Highest
Smallest	1.52	1.62	1.36	1.52	1.68	1.90
2	1.08	1.14	1.15	1.13	1.42	1.62
3	1.13	1.12	0.99	1.09	1.44	1.52
4	0.72	1.02	1.01	1.10	1.43	1.47
Largest	1.21	0.89	0.90	0.97	1.24	1.43

(b) Mean market value of equity*

Size	Earnings-to-price ratio					
	Negative	Lowest	2	3	4	Highest
Smallest	5	20	25	25	20	16
2	10	74	84	77	57	47
3	20	211	205	175	136	107
4	44	539	467	420	333	259
Largest	262	3095	2455	2306	1897	1464

*Millions of dollars. Data shown have been rounded.
Source: Jaffe et al. (1989, p. 139).

Jaffe et al. calculated monthly equally-weighted returns starting on 1 April and ending on the following 31 March. Table 13.2 shows some of their findings. In Table 13.2a, we can see that if we ignore the negative earnings-price ratio stocks, returns rise with higher earnings-price ratios (i.e. lower PERs). We can also see that returns rise as market capitalization decreases. In Table 13.2b, we see that the higher earnings-price ratio shares tend to be smaller stocks. We can also see that the negative earnings-price ratio shares, which seem to earn more than might be expected from the rest of the pattern shown in Table 13.2a, are especially small. These data pose the question as to whether there are two independent effects or just one.

Jaffe et al. tried to disentangle the earnings-price ratio and size effects by use of a statistical technique called seemingly unrelated regression, a particular form of regression analysis. They found that for the overall period 1951–86, there was a size and earnings-price ratio effect across all months. They also found that there was a difference between January and the rest of the year. The earnings-price ratio effect applied to January and to February–December, whereas the small-size effect only held in January. They calculated that moving from earnings-price ratio quintile 1 to quintile 5 while holding the effect of size constant led to a 3.2% increase in returns. The effect of moving from size quintile 5 to 1 while holding earnings-price ratio constant was to increase returns by 3.4%.

Fama and French (1992) find that although low PERs are related to returns, once one has controlled for size and price-to-book, picking low PER stocks offers no extra return. Roll (1995) reported different findings. Roll examined the relationship of returns to various style factors in the US over the period 1985–94. The styles considered were size, earnings-price ratios and book-to-market. He found that low PER stocks produced the highest risk-adjusted returns, whether risk was measured by the CAPM or APT. High book-to-market was also a profitable strategy, but low size was not.

Lakonishok et al. (1994) looked at various value-based strategies versus what they called glamour-based (i.e. growth) strategies. One of the variables studied was PER. The study covered the period 1968–90, and the universe was the NYSE and AMEX. The holding period was five years. They found that low PER stocks substantially outperformed high PER stocks. They actually worked with earnings-price ratios, and they found for the average of all five-year holding periods that the highest-decile high earnings-price ratio stocks returned a cumulative 139% and the lowest returned 72%. Adjusting for size, they still found that high earnings-price stocks performed best.

They then looked at the five-year average growth of earnings, cash flow, sales and operating income for each decile of the attribute being studied, i.e. earnings/price, book-to-market, etc. before portfolio formation. For most value-based strategies, there was a strong relationship between past growth and the attribute studied, e.g. high book-to-market stocks (value) had low past growth and low book-to-market stocks (glamour) had high past growth. The relationship was broadly the same for stocks ranked by earnings-price ratio, although the highest decile of earnings-price ratio stocks had fast growth, and the lowest decile had slow growth. This is probably because earnings are more variable than measures such as book value. For example, a cyclical company's earnings will collapse in a recession, and even though the price will react, the PER may soar if the market believes that earnings will recover eventually. This means that stocks at the ends of the earnings-price ratio decile distribution may have somewhat different characteristics than stocks at less extreme deciles—the extremes will include temporary winners and losers.

Based on these findings, we might argue that past performance leads to stocks being seen as glamour or value stocks, and that the value stocks have the better stockmarket performance. A refinement is to distinguish true glamour and value stocks from those that are temporarily rated as glamour or value. A true glamour stock would have both a high rating and fast past growth, whereas a true value stock would have both a low rating and slow past growth. Lakonishok et al. (1994) found such stocks by placing all stocks into one of three earnings-price ratio categories (i.e. high, medium and low) and one of three growth categories. The cumulative five-year return for true value (low PER) stocks was 172%, and for true glamour (high PER) stocks it was 67%. Picking value on this basis outperforms simply picking low PER stocks.

Switching now to evidence for the UK market, Levis (1989) studied returns over the period 1961–85. He examined returns by PERs, price, size and dividend yield. Levis used three different methods of calculating abnormal returns and he used within-groups only and within-groups plus randomization, all of which resulted in an enormous number of findings, far too many to be reported here. However, we can give the flavour of some of his findings. The excess returns we report will be simply the return from an attribute less the return from the market, as beta appeared to be irrelevant to an explanation of returns.

In Figure 13.3, we show the monthly excess returns from investing in portfolios with varying PERs and also the returns from portfolios with varying PERs but randomized with respect to each of size, yield and price. Here's how to read the chart. The PER column shows that the lowest quintile of PER stocks returned about 0.4% excess return per month. If, however, we randomize for size, so that we look at the lowest PER stocks from each size quintile, then the excess return is shown by the PER/size column, and is about 0.3%. For all four ways of

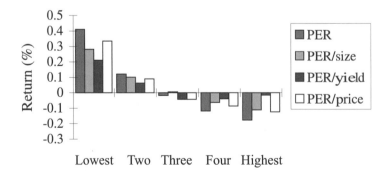

FIGURE 13.3   Monthly excess returns by PER quintiles, UK 1961–85
Source: Drawn from data in Levis (1989, p. 687).

looking at the data, low PER stocks offer excess returns. Controlling for size does not eliminate the low PER effect; in fact, controlling for yield has the greatest effect.

Is there an interaction between PERs and other attributes? If size and PERs are independent, there may be additional returns from combining low PERs with low size. Levis found that the size effect was concentrated mainly in the lowest PER quintile, and the price-earnings effect was greatest in the lowest-size quintile. Readers interested in more interrelationships should refer to Levis (1989). Suffice to say Levis thought low PERs were a source of excess returns. More recent studies, for example Miles and Timmermann (1996) and Strong and Xu (1997), have not found a statistically significant relationship between low PERs and returns.

Evidence on Low Price-To-Sales Ratio Stocks

There have been few studies of the price-to-sales ratio. Senchack and Martin (1987) examined the relative performance of low price-to-sales ratio and low PER strategies for the period 1975–84. They studied 400–450 randomly selected firms quoted on the NYSE and AMEX. They excluded financial services, such as banks and insurance companies, that do not generate sales in the usual accounting sense.

The results of this study suggested that low price-to-sales ratio stocks produced abnormal returns. They were subject to greater risk, but still produced a higher risk-adjusted return than high price-to-sales ratio stocks and an equally-weighted market portfolio of comparable risk. The price-to-sales ratio screen worked even with companies losing money. Low PER stocks in the study, however, dominated low price-to-sales ratio stocks on both an absolute and risk-adjusted return basis. The relative performance of the low PER stocks was more consistent than that of low price-to-sales ratio stocks. Low PER stocks outperformed low price-to-sales ratio stocks in more than two-thirds of the quarters studied.

Senchack and Martin ranked their universe by price-to-sales ratio quintiles and calculated for each quintile the PER, median market value, median price per share and median number of shares outstanding. For each variable, there was a monotonically increasing relationship, i.e. the lowest price-to-sales ratio stocks had the lowest PER, lowest share price and lowest shares outstanding, while the next lowest price-to-sales ratio stocks had the next lowest PER, etc. When the universe was ranked by PER quintiles, the PER/price-to-sales ratio relationship was monotonically increasing. For other variables, however, the relationship was increasing then decreasing. From these findings, one concludes that the price-to-sales ratio and PER relationships are related, but that there are differences. A price-to-sales ratio strategy is more likely to be confounded by small-size and low-price effects than is a PER strategy.

In a more recent study, Barbee et al. (1996) related returns in the US over the period 1979–91 to sales-to-price, debt-to-equity, book-to-market and market value of equity. They found that high sales-to-price was related positively to high returns. It was the only variable with a consistently significant role in explaining returns.

Evidence on High Yield

Do high yields produce high returns? A major US study by Black and Scholes (1974) found no effect, but this study has been criticized on statistical grounds. Some major studies have suggested that high yields and high returns go together (e.g. Litzenberger and Ramaswamy, 1979; and Elton et al., 1983). The latter study covered the period 1937–76, but also looked at subperiods. In two five-year subperiods, the overall finding did not hold. Keim (1985, 1986) found a similar relationship between dividend yield and abnormal return in the US as did Elton et al., but he also examined the relationship in the month of January and in the rest of the year. The return was essentially a January effect only.

A recent US study by Naranjo et al. (1998) found that actual and risk-adjusted returns for NYSE stocks increased with increasing dividend yield during the period 1963–94. Zero-dividend stocks had higher actual returns than low-yield stocks, but using a Fama–French risk adjustment they earned the lowest returns. We'll return to this point later. Naranjo et al. felt that tax effects could not account for their findings.

Turning to the UK, Levis (1989), in the study we mentioned earlier, looked at the relationship between yields and return during the period 1961–85. He found that high yield and high return were monotonically positively related. (He placed zero-yield stocks in the lowest-yield quintile.) In general, relative to size, PER and share price, the yield effect was the strongest relationship.

Morgan and Thomas (1998) found that in the UK over the period 1975–93, high yield and high returns, over the following five years, go together, although zero-yield stocks return more than the three lowest positive yield quartiles (Figure 13.4). Despite the apparent pattern, the hypothesis that returns are equal

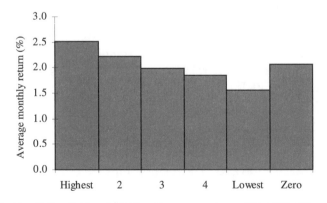

FIGURE 13.4 Portfolio dividend yield and excess return, UK 1975–93
Source: Drawn from data in Morgan and Thomas (1998, p. 410). Reprinted with permission from Elsevier Science. © 1998.

across all groups cannot be rejected. A risk adjustment pushes the zero-yield portfolio into fifth highest return rank. Morgan and Thomas argue that the UK tax structure during the period examined should have caused tax-exempt investors to have favoured zero dividends, so the pattern observed cannot be explained by tax considerations.

Two other UK studies are by Chan and Chui (1996) and Miles and Timmermann (1996). The former found for the period 1973–90 that high yields were related to higher returns, while the latter for 1979–91 found no relationship.

High Asset Value per Share

Rosenberg et al. (1985) looked at returns to a strategy of purchasing low price-to-book stocks. They constructed a retrospective test on a database of monthly stock data from January 1973 through March 1980, and a prospective study from April 1980 to September 1984. The universe of stocks consisted of 1400 of the largest stocks, mainly from the NYSE, but with a few from the American Stock Exchange, regional exchanges and Nasdaq.

The study was constructed as a hedge study, i.e. buying stocks with a low price-to-book and selling stocks with a high price-to-book. The prospective study showed an excess return of 0.32% per month with positive returns in 38 out of 54 months. Because book values do not change frequently, this is not a strategy likely to involve high transaction costs, although any transaction costs would reduce the returns.

Fama and French (1992) examined the period July 1963–December 1990. They related returns to beta, PERs, size, book-to-market equity and leverage. Relating each variable to returns they found no relationship for beta; that low PER produced higher returns; that small size produced higher returns; and that high book-to-market equity produced higher returns. For leverage, which we have not discussed so far, one would expect increased leverage to be associated with increased risk and returns. Bhandari (1988) found this relationship for US stocks for the period 1948–79, although he did not attribute the higher returns to risk. Fama and French found a higher leverage, higher return relationship for market leverage (total assets/market equity capitalization) but the opposite for book leverage (total assets/book value of ordinary shares plus balance sheet deferred taxes).

When Fama and French looked at their five variables together in a multivariate analysis, only size and book-to-market equity were related to returns, with book-to-market equity being the stronger variable. Figure 13.5 shows returns for equally-weighted portfolios arrayed by book-to-market ratios.

A number of criticisms have been made of the study, as we noted in Chapter 3. With regard to the two factors Fama and French thought explained returns, Kothari et al. (1995) found much weaker effects. Black (1993) argued that the size effect may simply be a result of data mining, and may be sample specific. With regard to the book value finding, Kothari et al. argued that this could be a

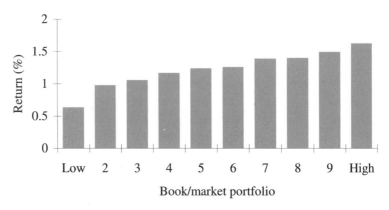

FIGURE 13.5   Average monthly returns by book-to-market equity quintiles, US July 1963–December 1990

Source: Drawn from data in Fama and French (1992, p. 446).

result of a looking backward bias. Compustat provided the data used by Fama and French. There may be a bias created by Compustat back-filling data. For example, if many firms with high book-to-price go bust they may never be included in the sample. Those that survive will be included and their historical data added. This will mean that returns to high book-to-price firms will be overstated. Using a sample free of this bias, Kothari et al. found the effect of book-to-price much reduced. Inevitably, Fama and French (1996b) dispute these findings.

Loughran (1997) notes that the academic literature makes value the winner, but in the real world, US value and growth managers have similar returns over a period of years. How can that be? He argues that it is because the book-to-price effect doesn't exist, or at least not for the largest quintile by market cap. For the period July 1963–December 1995, he finds that overall, high book-to-market quintile stocks return 6.23% more than low. But if one examines only stocks that fall in the largest quintile by size, the difference is 1.8%, which is not statistically significant. However, the largest quintile accounts for 73% of market cap, the universe most fund managers inhabit.

Loughran also finds that size and book-to-market explain none of the cross-sectional variation in returns for the three largest quintiles (representing 94% of market capitalization) once January is excluded from the sample.

Taking a different tack, Jensen et al. (1997) report that over the period 1965–94, small-firm and low price-to-book premiums are economically and statistically significant only in expansionary monetary policy periods.

In the study by Lakonishok et al. (1994), discussed on p. 232 in relation to low PERs, book-to-market was also examined. Their sample period was 1968–90, i.e. substantially the same as Fama and French's. They too found that investing in high book-to-market stocks produced significant returns. However, when they ran a regression for returns on various characteristics involving combinations of value measures, the importance of book-to-market declined relative to the other variables.

Capaul et al. (1993) examined the returns from a price-to-book strategy for France, Germany, Switzerland, the UK and Japan over the period January 1981– June 1992, and concluded that low price-to-book ratio stocks (i.e. high book-to-market) provided superior risk-adjusted performance to high price-to-book stocks.

Following Fama and French (1992), there were a number of replications of all or part of that study for the UK. Four such studies are summarized in Table 13.3.

Evidence on Cash Flow

There is less research on cash flow than on book-to-market (thankfully!). Cash flow was one of the variables included in the Lakonishok et al. (1994) study discussed above. 'True' value and glamour cash flow portfolios were formed (in the same way as described for their PER portfolios). The compounded five-year return for value was 171% versus 71% for glamour. In their regression study, cash flow and past growth of sales (the faster the growth the lower the returns) were the variables that stood out as important.

OPPORTUNITY OR RISK?

After reviewing so much evidence (but only a small sample of what is available), what are we to make of it? First, numerous studies show value 'works' or perhaps 'worked'. But value works partly because of the way it is defined. For example, both Fama and French and Roll can claim to have shown that value works. But for the former, it is book-to-market that works best, whereas for the latter it is PER. And the studies usually omit some value strategies, so we don't know what a researcher would report for a broader study. For example, price-to-sales is seldom included, but one study claims that it is more important than book-to-market. Cash flow is not included very often, yet one study stresses its significance. Some differences in findings are a result of the definitions used, the period over which returns are measured, whether stocks are market-weighted or equal-weighted, and so on.

Of course, what works at any one time may not work in the future. There are reasons to believe that value will continue its long-term record. In particular, Davis (1994) and Davis et al. (2000) found the value relationships existed in periods (1940–63 and 1929–97, respectively) before those for which readily available commercial data are available and that have been so extensively mined. Nonetheless, in Roll's study cited earlier, he made a simple test to see whether style-specific returns were nonstationary: he found they were at a 6% level of significance. Roll (1995, p. 125) noted:

> If the results are chiefly sample period-specific, they represent just another level of the investment enigma: style may matter, and style investing may produce extra-risk return,

TABLE 13.3 Four UK studies in the style of Fama and French

	Miles and Timmermann (1996)	Chan and Chui (1996)	Strong and Xu (1997)	Clare et al. (1998)
Period	1979–91	1973–90	1971–92	1970–93
Beta	No relationship in univariate or multivariate analysis.	No relationship in univariate analysis; negative in multivariate analysis.	Positive relationship in univariate analysis; none in multivariate analysis.	Economically and statistically significant role for beta.
Book-to-market	Significant positive relationship.	Significant positive relationship.	Significant positive relationship.	Positive relationship, but not statistically significant.
Size	No linear relationship, but lowest decile in size had substantially higher returns.	Not significant.	Small portfolios produce higher returns. Not significant when book-to-market or leverage variables are included.	Negative relationship, but not statistically significant.
Dividend yield	No relationship.	High yields are related to higher returns.		
PER	No relationship.		Low PER associated with higher returns, but not statistically significant.	Not statistically significant.
Leverage	Debt/market cap not statistically significant, but sign as expected—positive relationship.	Total assets/market cap: significant positive relationship. Total assets/book value: not significant.	Total assets/market cap and total assets/book value: significant positive relationship.	Book value of equity/market value of equity, positive but statistically insignificant relationship.
Share liquidity	Not statistically significant, but sign as expected—infrequent trading is associated with higher returns.			
Low price		Not significant.		Negative and statistically significant relationship; not economically significant.
General	'We conclude that book-market value, and to a lesser extent company size and liquidity, are the only company attributes that appear to contain information about variation in expected returns' (p. 379).	'In contrast to Fama and French (1992), when the book-to-market variable is broken down into market leverage and book leverage, the market leverage is significant and captures the whole effect of the book-to-market variable' (p. 1446).	No combination of variables can explain more than 8% of the variation of returns.	'. . . significant and powerful role for β in explaining expected returns . . . no role for the Fama and French variables . . .' (p. 1225).

but which particular style is most important *now*? If styles change rapidly, the practical investor may drive little benefit from knowing that styles even exist. If they change more slowly, there is hope that they can be tracked and exploited with appropriate analytics.

Whether there is likely to be persistence of the value/growth findings will depend partly on the reason that value has offered higher returns: is the extra return an opportunity because of irrational pricing, or a reward for bearing risk? If the latter, it is likely to persist. If the former, persistence is more questionable. So, is it opportunity or risk?

Value = Risk

Fama and French interpret their findings as evidence of priced risk factors. But what exactly are these factors? In our discussions on small stocks, we produced some evidence that suggests that size might reflect a distress factor. Fama and French develop the concept of distress in relation to their book-to-market factor. They argue that if rational pricing prevails, then:

- there must be common risk factors in returns associated with size and book-to-market;
- earnings must explain the pattern of returns to size and book-to-market.

Fama and French (1993) provide some evidence for common risk factors in an article that is a tough read. The gist of it is explained by Fama in an interview aimed at the general reader (Tanous, 1997, pp. 172–3).

> Fama: . . . The way we define risk, it has to be associated with something that can't be diversified away. Everybody relates to a market risk. If you hold stocks you bear stock market risk. But the stock market is more complicated than that. There are multiple sources of risk . . ..
>
> Just look at the data. It's true that growth stocks vary together, and its true that value stocks vary together. In other words, their returns tend to vary together which means that there is a common element of risk there. Now, for growth stocks that seems to be a risk that people are willing to bear at a lesser return than the return they require for the market as a whole. Whereas, if I look at the value stocks [high book-to-market], which we also call distress stocks, their returns vary together, but people aren't willing to hold those except at a premium to market returns . . ..
>
> What [investors] think is that small companies pay higher returns because they're unknown, or something like that. It's not because they're more risky. The risk, in my terms, can't be explained by the market. It means that, because they move together, there is something about these small stocks that creates an undiversifable risk. That undiversifieable risk is why you get paid for holding them.
>
> Tanous: What causes that risk?
>
> Fama: You know that's an embarrassing question because I don't know.

In Fama and French (1995), evidence is presented that size and book-to-market are related to profitability. High book-to-market signals sustained low earnings on book equity. Such stocks are less profitable than low book-to-market equity stocks for at least 11 years. Fama and French argue that a high stock price relative to book value is typical of firms with high average returns on capital (growth stocks), whereas a low stock price relative to book value is typical of firms that are relatively distressed. Size is also related to profitability. Controlling for book-to-market, small stocks tend to have lower earnings on book equity than big stocks. But in their study, the size effect in earnings is largely due to the low profits of small stocks after 1980. Before that, there is little relation between size and profitability. Then for unexplained reasons the recession of 1981 and 1982 turns into a prolonged earnings depression during the 1980s for small stocks.

Value = Opportunity

In the 1994 Lakonishok et al. study cited earlier, the authors believe that value strategies work because of extrapolation errors. The market expects glamour stocks to continue their superior growth for many years. In the first couple of years, this is borne out. But thereafter growth is much the same for value or growth stocks. This is a high returns equals opportunity explanation. But could risk really be the explanation? Well, what do we mean by risk? We have seen that beta and standard deviations of returns have been used as risk measures. But in a more fundamental sense, if value stocks are riskier, then they must sometimes underperform, and they must do so in circumstances that investors find really painful. Just underperforming sometimes isn't enough, because on average they outperform. In economic jargon, value stocks must underperform when the marginal utility of wealth or consumption is high.

Value stocks had a trivially higher beta and modestly larger standard deviation than glamour stocks in Lakonishok et al.'s sample. The differences were insufficient to account for the return differences. They looked at 'bad' states of the world—recession and stockmarket declines. There were four recessions in their sample period. Value stocks did the same or better than glamour in three of the recessions. And value did better than glamour during stockmarket declines. Risk doesn't seem to explain the findings.

Other evidence suggests an opportunity rather than risk explanation. For example, La Porta et al. (1997) argue that the market is surprised by better-than-expected growth performance from value stocks and worse-than-expected growth performance from glamour stocks. During 1971–92, looking at the three days surrounding an earnings announcement, they find earnings surprises are systematically more positive for value stocks. In a different type of study, Rozeff and Zaman (1998) looked at the purchases of corporate insiders (which are discussed in Chapter 15) and found that their transactions were not random with respect to growth and value stocks. They found that insider buying increased as stocks moved category from growth to value, and was greater after low stock returns and lower after high returns. They argue that this is consistent with stocks being misvalued.

To many people, the sort of evidence just discussed is more persuasive than the Fama and French position, which almost takes as its starting point that risk must be the explanation. As Sharpe (in Tanous, 1997, p. 96) comments:

> The Fama–French position is this kind of bizarre metaphysics that says: 'value stocks do better; but we know in an efficient market things that do better ought to, in some sense, be riskier, ergo, value stocks are riskier! Now we don't happen to have seen the manifestation of the risk . . . but it must be so, therefore the market is efficient.' End of discussion . . . This might be what we generically call a peso problem. You get something that has a very small probability of a real disaster; you can look at 20, 30, 40 years and never seen the manifestation of the disaster . . . As a result, you won't see evidence of the risk, but it's still there. A lot of people say, well, if value stocks have done better it's because when you buy value stocks, you take this gamble: there is a small probability of a total wipe out. For the last 50 years people who have taken that gamble have gotten lucky. If you say that, there is no way to test that theory.

If value offers superior returns and no extra risk, will the effect be exploited fully and cease to work? There are two reasons why investors may prefer glamour stocks. The psychological mechanisms discussed in Chapter 5 may make it hard for investors not to focus on recent vivid news about companies and ignore the inevitable randomness and eventual decline that the statistics suggest affect all companies. Second, both institutional managers and fund trustees prefer to act 'prudently' and not make mistakes. There may be less criticism when a fund holds a glamour stock that underperforms than when an unattractive stock is held and underperforms. Managers and trustees are less likely to be replaced for being wrong with the crowd than if they act alone. Moreover, many funds are instructed to buy only blue-chip stocks, i.e. yesterday's heroes.

CONCLUDING COMMENTS

Should you buy small shares or large? Value shares or growth? It depends on how you read the evidence.[1] Do you believe the evidence that small-cap and value outperform over the long run? Even if you do, can you live through the years when they don't? If you can, are you being rewarded for bearing risk, or are you exploiting an anomaly? If you are bearing risk, does the risk matter to you? If you can't answer these questions—or even if you can—you have the option of looking for other ways of picking shares.

---

[1] Postscript added in proofs, February 2001. Data for 2000 is now available. In both the UK and US small-cap stocks beat large-cap, and value beat growth. For example, the HGSCI beat the FTSE All-Share by 7% and the Russell 2000® beat the Russell 1000® by nearly 4%. The Russell 3000® Value beat the Russell 3000® Growth by over 30%.

14

A Share Picker's Miscellany

October. This is one of the peculiarly dangerous months to speculate in stocks. The others are July, January, September, April, November, May, March, June, December, August and February.

Mark Twain

In this chapter we look at a number of factors and approaches that may lead to higher returns. We begin with calendar effects. Mark Twain was wrong: all months are not the same. The evidence is that returns are related to many calendar events. Some calendar effects were noted in the previous chapter, and the discussion is extended here. We also extend the previous chapter's discussion of small stocks by looking at low-price stocks and neglected stocks. Finally, after reviewing so many studies in this and previous chapters, we consider whether you could simply ignore them all and follow published recommendations by stockbrokers and the press.

CALENDAR EFFECTS

Researchers have examined returns in relation to weekends, holidays, turn of the month, part of the month, January and December, as well as intraday. This type of research is usually described as being concerned with seasonal effects, but the term 'calendar effects' is a more accurate description.

Some commentators have found the notion of regular calendar effects slightly implausible—they imply that if you have a calendar and a watch then you can make money—and one certainly has to beware of data mining. It is all too easy to trawl through computer banks of data and discover, say, that for a 20-year period stocks have typically risen on the third Tuesday of every month or some such bizarre occurrence. However, such a finding is likely to be just a chance finding and unlikely to hold true in the next sample period. We should have more confidence in calendar effects if they are found in samples from different years, especially if they apply to various subperiods within the sample periods, and if the effects can be found in a number of different international markets. Ideally, a theory would precede the data, but there have been few academic theories about calendar effects that have preceded the empirical findings. Failing this, a plausible theory produced after the empirical discovery would be useful, especially if it could be tested independently of the data it purports to explain. With these cautionary words, we will move on to a brief review of the various calendar effects.

The January Effect

Wachtel noted in 1942 that January offered high returns. However, real interest in this January effect dates from Rozeff and Kinney (1976), who used an equally-weighted equity index (i.e. one in which a small firm has as much weight as a large one), and found that for the US for the period 1904–74, the average return per month was about 0.5%, whereas for January it was 3.5%. Subsequent research has shown that the January effect is essentially a small-firm phenomenon. Keim (1983) found that small firms earned half their abnormal returns in January. Lakonishok and Smidt (1988) using a 90-year sample (1897–1986) for the DJIA found no January effect: the DJIA is essentially a large stock index with the 30 stocks accounting for about 25% of the market capitalization of the NYSE.

A standard explanation for the January effect is that it has been tax related. The US has a calendar tax year, and it has been argued that poorly performing shares will be sold late in the year to realize capital losses and then investors will buy the shares back in the new year, pushing up prices. Does the effect exist in other countries? Gultekin and Gultekin (1983) looked for seasonality in returns in 17 countries. This means they tested whether each month offered the same return. They found that in 13 countries the months did not appear to offer equal returns, i.e. there was seasonality. In all 13 countries, there was a January effect. The effect is therefore common, but the tax-based explanation is weakened by the January effect being observed in countries that did not have capital gains tax for all or part of the period studied, e.g. Japan and Canada (on Canada, see Berges et al., 1984). On the other hand Jones et al. (1991) find no evidence of a January effect in the US before 1917, when there was no tax incentive to generate trading.

The UK and Australia also have a January effect, but the UK's tax year starts on 6 April, and Australia's on 1 July. However, the UK has also had high returns in April, and Australia in July. In the US the small-firm effect is a January phenomenon, but in the UK the small-firm effect is largest in May, not in April (e.g. see Corhay et al., 1988; and Levis, 1985). We noted earlier that Dimson and Marsh report that the HGSCI's performance relative to the FT-A All-Share Index is poorest in January and April. Interestingly, in France, which taxes capital gains, there is no January small-size premium, while in Japan, which had no capital gains tax until 1989, there is a January size premium.

One has to be careful with the UK tax year. The tax year is as noted for individuals, but for companies it is whenever they select: a 31 December year-end is common. Of course, tax-exempt institutions have no tax year. Mills and Coutts (1995) and Arsad and Coutts (1997) found a January effect in the UK. We will discuss the latter study, which used the FT 30, a large stock index, as its market measure. The period studied was 1935–94, both in its entirety and divided into 12 subsamples of five years each. Arsad and Coutts (1997) found a January, April and December effect for the entire period. For the subperiods, only April had positive returns in every one. Of these, only four were statistically significant, and all occurred before individuals were liable to capital gains tax. January also had four statistically significant positive returns, all after the introduction of capital gains tax. These results are interpreted as support for the view that the April effect is a result of individuals' behaviour and the January effect is a result of company behaviour.

We noted that small firms behave differently in January. So do high-yielding and zero-yielding stocks. The overreaction effect, the tendency for extreme performance stocks over various periods to reverse their performance in the following period, (e.g. see De Bondt and Thaler, 1985; and De Bondt and Thaler, 1989), occurs mainly in January. Finally, risk as well as return behave differently in January (Rogalski and Tinic, 1986). Jacobs and Levy (1988a) claim that after disentangling all the effects that are at work, it is the rebound for stocks with embedded tax losses and zero- and high-yielding stocks that account for most of the January effect. They claim that other January seasonals, such as small size, are merely proxies for these two effects.

Other explanations are possible. With two holiday effects (see below) close together (pre-Christmas and pre-New Year), perhaps the high spirits just carry over into January. Perhaps institutional liquidity is higher at the start of a year. Perhaps investors focus on the imminent company results season, look further ahead and become more optimistic. No matter the explanation, given the wide exposure the January effect has received, does it persist, and can it be profitably exploited?

Haugen and Jorion (1996) examined the effect from 1926 to 1993 in the US. They found no evidence that it had diminished after its rediscovery in 1976. For the market as a whole (equally-weighted basis) for 1977–93, they found an excess return for January of nearly 3%, but for the smallest decile the excess return was close to 10%. Some writers (e.g. Bhardwaj and Brooks, 1992), have argued that after allowing for dealing costs, including spreads (particularly high for small, low-priced stocks), there was no significant abnormal return to be made by playing the January effect. However, as Haugen and Jorion point out, in the US investors could effect cheap futures trades and sell a contract on a large-stock, cap-weighted index, such as the S&P 500, and buy a contract on a small-cap index, such as the Russell 2000. Unfortunately, they do not allow for the possibility of the futures market anticipating such trades (e.g. see Hensel et al., 1994).

With regard to the UK, it is worth noting that Gultekin and Gultekin's (1983) data for 1959–79 show that although January was the best single month, the period December–April consisted of months that on average produced positive returns. December through April produced more than the annual return, and the other seven months produced a negative return. More recent studies by Mills and Coutts and Arsad and Coutts found either negative or very small returns over the period May through October. They don't examine whether profitable strategies can be devised.

Draper and Paudyal (1997) find somewhat similar seasonal patterns, and calculate the returns from (i) buying at the end of December and selling at the end of January, (ii) buying at the end of March and selling at the end of April, and (iii) buying at the end of August and selling at the end of January. They argue that none of the strategies is profitable after costs. However the commission charges they assume are far too high for an institutional investor, and they don't consider a futures strategy.

Even if there is a possibility of making money by a seasonal strategy, it is unclear who would take the opportunity. First, it won't work every year even if it would over many years. Second, private investors would find any strategy difficult to implement, and most institutions would find any strategy difficult to explain to clients. Hedge funds, however, might be interested.

There is a traditional UK stock market adage of 'sell in May and go away'. It is unclear whether this was advice about returns or simply a statement that gentlemen ignored the stockmarket during the social season of Royal Ascot, Henley, Wimbledon, etc. According to Bouman and Jacobson (1999), the effect can be found in 36 of the 37 countries they examined, and has been present in the UK stockmarket since 1694.

The Weekend Effect

Fields (1931) made the earliest study of day-of-the-week effects. He found the US market tended to rise on Saturdays (the market used to open for a couple of hours on Saturday). Cross (1973) found that the market tended to rise on Fridays and fall on Mondays, and this finding has generated a flood of research, all reporting the same 'blue Monday' effect, with rates of return tending to be high at the end of the trading week. Where Friday was not the last trading day, it still has tended to produce high returns (e.g. see Lakonishok and Smidt, 1988). The fall in prices on Monday seems to take place between the close on Friday and the first 45 minutes of opening on Monday. Consequently, the Monday effect is often called the weekend effect. Whatever you call it, it is an odd effect. After all, if you think in terms of calendar time, you might expect to earn a return for Saturday, Sunday and Monday, i.e. Monday's returns should be three times the normal return. If you think returns should be related only to trading sessions, Monday's returns should be equal to other returns.

Jaffe and Westerfield (1985), Condoyanni et al. (1987), O'Hanlon and Papaspirou (1988), Chang et al. (1995) and others have examined the weekend effect for countries other than the US. It exists, but perhaps it should once again be called the day-of-the-week effect: in countries whose market's trading hours overlap with the US market's, Monday tends to be a down day (e.g. the UK and Canada), but where, because of time zone differences, the closing market value is computed before Wall Street opens for Monday trading, Tuesday is the down day (e.g. Australia, Japan, Singapore and France).

Turning specifically to the UK, Arsad and Coutts (1997) report negative mean returns for Mondays in their full sample and 12 subsamples. Choy and O'Hanlon (1989) report a strong day-of-the-week effect, and it appears to be stronger in larger, frequently traded stocks, than smaller—the opposite of the US finding. Choy and O'Hanlon rejected the effect of stocks going ex-dividend on Mondays as the explanation of the UK day-of-the-week effect. Board and Sutcliffe (1988) found evidence of a weekend effect in the UK over the period 1962–86, with the significance diminishing over time. They found that returns on Mondays that were the first day of a trading account were positive, while returns on other Mondays were significantly negative, leading to an overall negative Monday effect (see also Mills and Coutts, 1995). (The UK used to have an account settlement system for equities. An account was usually for two weeks—Monday through to Friday week—and all trades made within an account were due for settlement on the second Monday after the close of the account. A few accounts that incorporated holidays were for three weeks, and in the last two days of an account it was possible to deal for new time, which meant settlement was due as if the deal had been effected in the next account.)

Bell and Levin (1998) claim that the UK weekend effect over the period 1980–93 can be fully explained by three institutional factors. Perhaps, but the difficulty with institutional explanations is that the weekend effect is found in many countries, all with different institutional arrangements.

The Holiday Effect

If stocks rise before weekends, do they rise before other trading breaks caused by holidays? In the US, a number of studies have looked at this (e.g. Fields, 1934; Ariel, 1987; Ariel, 1990; and Lakonishok and Smidt, 1988). Lakonishok and Smidt (1988) found a pre-holiday rate of return of 0.22% for their 90-year sample compared with the regular daily rate of return of 0.0094%. This gain is 23 times the regular daily rate, and means that approximately the 10 days preceding holidays each year accounted for about 50% of the price increase of the DJIA.

Cadsby and Ratner (1992) looked at turn-of-the-month and pre-holiday effects on stock returns in various international markets. They examined returns in relation to both local and US holidays. The periods examined varied for the markets. For the UK, the period was 16 August 1983–13 June 1988. Cadsby and Ratner (1992, p. 508) concluded:

> Pre-holiday effects are significant for the United States, Canada, Japan, Hong Kong and Australia but not for any of the European countries in the sample [the UK, Italy, Switzerland, West Germany and France]. All countries exhibiting pre-holiday effects

do so with reference to their own local holidays. The only country which also exhibits a significant US pre-holiday effect is Hong Kong, though in all countries the highest returns seem to be earned on days just prior to joint local–US holidays.

Arsad and Coutts (1997) found significant holiday effects in the UK for every day of the week that preceded a holiday, except for Tuesdays, when returns were lower.

A number of explanations as to why there is a holiday effect have been suggested, but none seem compelling. Recently, Vergin and McGinnis (1999) have claimed that in the 10 years following Lakonishok and Smidt's 90-year sample period, the holiday effect in the US had disappeared for large companies and was much diminished for smaller companies.

Within-the-Month Effect

Ariel (1987) found that from 1963 to 1981, positive rates of return only occured in the first half of the month, which he defined to include the last day of the previous month. In their longer sample period, Lakonishok and Smidt (1988), defining the first half of the month in the usual way, found only mild support for Ariel's results (the results were in the right direction but not statistically significant). Jaffe and Westerfield (1989) did find a positive first-half effect in Australia, but found a second-half effect in Japan and no real effect in the UK and Canada.

Turn-of-the-Month Effect

Lakonishok and Smidt (1988) followed up Ariel's (1987) work on turn-of-the-month returns. For their 90-year period, they found that the four days at the turn of the month—the last day of one month and the first three of the next—averaged a cumulative rate of increase of 0.473% (versus 0.0612% for an average four days). The average monthly increase was 0.349%, i.e. the DJIA goes down during the non-turn-of-the-month period. This result was consistent across subperiods.

Cadsby and Ratner (1992) found a turn-of-the-month effect in the US, the UK, Canada, Australia, Switzerland and West Germany. They did not find the effect in Japan, Hong Kong, Italy or France. For the UK, the turn-of-the-month return was four and a half times the rest of the month's return.

The effect might be related to when salaries are paid, and to institutional cash flows. For example, there is a turn-of-the month-effect in Japan if counting is begun five days before the end of the month and two days into the new month: Japanese salaries are usually paid on the 25th of the month or even the 20th (Ziemba, 1991).

Hensel and Ziemba (1996) looked at returns for the S&P 500 over the period 1928–93 for various parts of the month and turn of the month. Using –1 as the last trading day of a month and +1 as the first day, they defined turn of the month to be days –1 to +4, first half of the month as –1 to +9, and rest of the month as +9 to –2. They found the average daily return per day for the 65 years to be 0.0186%, but 0.1236% per day at the turn of the month, and 0.0703% per day in the first half of the month. Returns for the second half of the month were negative.

They compare the returns from various investment strategies. They consider investing in large-cap stocks (9.5% p.a.), small-cap stocks (11.53% p.a.), investing only at the turn of the month and in cash the rest of the month (10.13% p.a.), and investing in the first half and then cash (11.06% p.a.). Although the return from the turn-of-the-month per day exceeds the per-day return from the first half of the month, because the latter period has twice as many days, the absolute return is higher from the latter. Although the return from small-cap stocks is the highest, the standard deviation of these returns is very high, and on a risk-adjusted basis the calendar strategies are superior. The strategies ignore costs. Hensel and Ziemba point to implementation by low-cost futures. But could you really come out ahead by trading in futures 24 times a year, and after bearing the risk that the futures will sometimes be mispriced?

The December Effect

Lakonishok and Smidt (1988) note that the second half of December has the highest rate of return of the 24 half-months. For their 90-year period, the average rate of return in the second half of December for the DJIA was 1.54%. This period includes two pre-holiday dates, and the return is concentrated from the pre-Christmas trading day to the New Year trading day. The DJIA is a large stock index. Lakonishok and Smidt (1988, p. 409) note: 'If the importance of an anomalous rate of return is evaluated in terms of its impact on a dollar-weighted portfolio, then the high average end-of-December rate of return is far more important than the high average rate of return for small companies in January.'

The Intraday Effect

Harris (1986) studied intraday effects by examining a time-ordered tape of every transaction in every common stock traded on the NYSE for the period 1 December 1981–31 January 1983. There were 15 million transactions. Harris found that prices fell on average on Mondays and rose by increasing amounts during the rest of the week. The negative Monday effect took place mainly in the first 45 minutes of trading. The pattern of returns for the rest of Monday was similar to other days. On other days of the week, prices rose significantly in the first 45 minutes. On all weekdays, i.e. including Monday, the market tended to rally between 12.30 p.m. and 1.30 p.m. and to fall between 2.15 p.m. and 3.30 p.m. The market rallied at the close, and prices rose on the last transaction of the day.

These results were pervasive over the period studied (i.e. one or two months did not dominate the results) and applied to all market value groups.

Harris (1986, p. 64) suggested some trading strategies based on his findings:

> Although trading strategies based only on these patterns would not be profitable because of transactions costs, portfolio managers can increase profits when they have other reasons to trade:
>
> • Purchasers of stock should avoid purchasing stock early in the morning on Monday. On the other weekdays, they should purchase as early as possible.
> • Sellers of stocks should try to sell late on Friday. If they must sell on Monday, they should do so as early as possible. On the other weekdays, if they must sell early, they should try to wait at least until 45 minutes after the open.
> • On all weekdays a 'limit sell order' at a price just above the market price and submitted shortly before the market closes may yield the best price.

The Weather Effect

The author once asked the head of institutional sales at a brokerage firm why the market was so strong that day. The answer was: 'It's a nice day and we [England] are winning at the Oval.' Since England doesn't win at cricket often enough to test the cricket win/strong market hypothesis, what about the good weather/strong market hypothesis? Saunders (1993) has presented data that support a weather/stockmarket relationship.

Saunders cites various studies that suggest that high humidity is negatively correlated with performance, that absence of sunshine correlates with negative mood, a cynical and doubting outlook, and that helping behaviour is positively correlated with hours of sunshine. He suggests a null hypothesis that NYSE prices are not related to New York weather. He collected weather data from the closest weather stations to Wall Street for the period 1927–89. Because hours of sunshine are perfectly correlated with absence of cloud cover, and humidity and cloud cover are almost perfectly correlated, Saunders focused on cloud cover. Returns from cloudy days were lower than for sunny days. These results were repeated even when variables such as January, small firm and Monday were included in the regression estimates. As Saunders notes, the effects are surprisingly large for such a minor psychological factor. So, should mood variables be included in asset-pricing models, is the market inefficient, or is this all nonsense? Whatever you conclude, chances are that someone, somewhere is writing a PhD thesis on global warming as a causal factor in the 1990s bull market.

This concludes our discussion of calendar effects; we now switch topics to consider low prices.

LOW-PRICE STOCKS

Very-low-price or 'penny' stocks seem to have attractions for many private investors. Perhaps this is because they can buy a lot of shares for a given sum of money; or perhaps it is thought that a low price has more scope to rise than a higher price. Many sophisticated investors scoff at such 'reasons', and they are probably right, yet low-price stocks have been studied for more than 50 years and most studies have concluded that low-price stocks outperform.

The first scientific study of low-priced stocks was probably by Fritzemeier (1936). He noted that low-price stocks were more volatile than high-price stocks, and 'In a "bull" market the low price stocks tend to go up relatively more than high-price stocks, and they do not lose these superior gains in the recessions which follow.' He concluded that low-price stocks offer greater prospects for speculative profit and if two shares seemed to offer equal profits, then the low-price share should be bought. More recent studies of low-price stocks include Blume and Husic (1973), Edmister and Greene (1980), Kross (1985), Tseng (1988), Jaffe et al. (1989a) (who found the low-price effect to be wholly a January effect), and Levis (1989). Let's look at the Levis study.

Levis (1989) found that in the UK, low-price stocks had outperformed in the period 1961–85. His results are shown in Figure 14.1 for price alone, and after randomization for other attributes. It is noticeable that the return pattern is significantly affected if size is controlled.

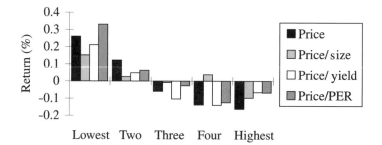

FIGURE 14.1   Monthly excess returns: price of quintiles, UK 1961–85
Source: Drawn from data in Levis (1989, p. 687).

One can surmise why low-price stocks outperformed. First, low-price stocks will be essentially small stocks (since market cap is price times number of shares) and the reasons for small stocks outperforming will apply to low-price stocks too. Second, low-price stocks are probably more illiquid than small stocks and, if investors like liquidity, this will warrant a premium return. Third, low-price stocks will have out-of-date prices. This is because the market generally moves only a small amount each day. Even a penny move for a 20p stock would be a 5% move. Low-price stocks will tend not to move for a period and then make a large percentage move to reflect past market moves. Investors may require a premium to bear this uncertainty about the value of their stock. Fourth, Elton et al. (1983, p. 142) note that many institutional investors will not hold stocks priced at less than $5 and 'stocks which sell for less than $5 are not considered as appropriate collateral for margin . . . Therefore, an investor who borrows or uses margin would find these stocks less attractive unless they offered a higher return.' Finally, one must wonder whether the estimated abnormal returns the studies report are overstated, because price spreads are greater for low-price stocks and this would make portfolio rebalancing expensive.

These arguments relate mainly to very-low-price stocks, although the relationship with return holds throughout the price range, i.e. as well as 10p stocks outperforming £10 stocks, £5 stocks outperform £10 stocks. Low price seems to be a genuine effect, but one that is hard to disentangle from size.

NEGLECTED STOCKS

For most institutional investors, stockbrokers' analysts are a major source of information. But analysts do not follow all the stocks in the market. What are the prospects for stocks followed by few analysts, or not followed at all, i.e. neglected stocks? Arbel, Strebel and Carvell have examined this in a number of papers and books (e.g. Arbel, 1985a; Arbel, 1985b; Arbel and Strebel, 1983; Carvell and Strebel, 1987; and Strebel and Carvell, 1988).

Arbel and Strebel (1983) focused on stocks in the S&P 500 in the period 1970–79. They measured analyst neglect by a ranking system based on two indicators: the number of analysts regularly following a stock, as measured by Drexel Burnham Lambert surveys, and the number of analysts reporting earnings forecasts as compiled in the Standard and Poor's Earnings Forecaster. They classified firms as highly followed, moderately followed, or neglected, depending upon whether they were followed by four or more analysts, two or three analysts, or one or no analysts, respectively. Neglected stocks outperformed highly followed stocks by 7% p.a. on average. Was this finding a result of neglected stocks being riskier or being smaller stocks? Using three measures of risk (systematic risk, unsystematic risk and total risk), neglected stocks did not appear to be significantly riskier. They were smaller, so Arbel and Strebel looked at analyst neglect by size category. They found that smaller stocks did generate higher returns than larger stocks, but within each of three size categories (as shown in Table 14.1) neglected stocks produced higher returns.

So far only one aspect of neglect has been examined. What if neglect is measured in terms of actual investment by institutions rather than analyst neglect? Arbel and Strebel (1983) studied a random sample of 510 companies

TABLE 14.1   Return by degree of analyst neglect and company size, average % 1970–79

	Small company	Medium company	Large company
Highly followed	5.0	7.4	8.4
Moderately followed	13.2	11.0	10.2
Neglected	15.8	13.9	15.3

Source: Arbel and Strebel (1983, p. 39). This copyrighted material is reprinted with the permission of the *Journal of Portfolio Management*.

drawn in equal numbers from the NYSE, AMEX and OTC over the period 1971–80. They divided firms into three categories based on the number of institutional holders according to data published by Standard and Poor's. The least owned firms produced the highest returns. Risk was examined in a number of ways, but did not seem to be the explanation of the returns.

Before we conclude that neglected stocks offer abnormal returns, we should question whether the correct notion of risk is being applied to neglected stocks. Investors' knowledge of neglected stocks is limited—estimates of returns and standard deviations and correlations of returns with other stocks must be subject to greater uncertainty than for other stocks. This means that if investors attempt to use the Markowitz approach to portfolio construction that we discussed in Chapter 2, then incorporation of neglected stocks will make the whole estimation much more uncertain. Unless investors receive higher returns for holding neglected stocks, they would rationally omit them from their portfolio construction. Individual neglected stocks may bear greater unsystematic risk than other stocks, but this can be diversified away by holding a basket of neglected stocks. However, the estimation uncertainty cannot be diversified away: it is a source of undiversifiable risk (e.g. see Klein and Bawa, 1977; and Barry and Brown, 1986).

Private investors are more important in the neglected-stock universe than in the blue-chip universe. Given the limited diversification of private investors, the extra return from neglected stocks may be a reward for both unsystematic risk and systematic estimation risk. Investors who buy a basket of neglected stocks will eliminate unsystematic risk and will get an investment free lunch. Investors must decide whether undiversifiable estimation risk is worth bearing. For many who do not approach their stock portfolio construction in the manner suggested by Markowitz, it may well be.

One distinct attraction of neglected stocks is that some stocks will always be relatively neglected, so this does not seem to be a strategy that automatically self-destructs if it becomes popular. Arbel, Carvell and Strebel go further. They claim that the size effect and the low price-earnings effect disappear once neglect is allowed for.

Although widely cited, the neglect studies are all based on the 1970s and the samples limited to the largest 500 or 1000 firms. Beard and Sias (1997) re-examined the neglected firm effect over the period 1982–95, with a sample of 7000+ firms. They found that firms that were highly neglected, i.e. not followed by an analyst, produced substantially higher returns. However, when they cross-classified by capitalization decile and by four degrees of neglect, they found that small size appeared to be more important than neglect.

FOLLOWING RECOMMENDATIONS

Many investors buy shares on the basis of other people's recommendations. In this section, three different types of recommendation—those of brokers, the press and commercial services—are examined.

Stockbrokers

Stockbrokers produce a large proportion of the research carried out on the equity and bond markets. It is bundled with execution, i.e. the largest brokers give away their research to institutional investors in return for commissions on executions. The brokers have resisted debundling, or the selling of execution and research services separately. However, there are discount brokers who charge lower commissions but produce no research.

In recent years, integrated houses have developed in the UK. These combine a brokerage firm and a market-maker in one operation. Not only can one question the amount and type of research produced—presumably that which favours dealing activity will be the most profitable for the broker—but one can wonder whether the views of the analysts and the timing of the release of their research is affected by the state of their market-makers' books.

Institutional investors vary in their attitude to brokers' research. Some use it as their major source of research; some have in-house research capabilities that largely ignore outside research; some have modest in-house research capabilities that essentially process the outside research in some way; some largely ignore the views of analysts, but use their forecasts and company analysis, and so on. In Chapter 11 we looked at analysts' forecasts; we turn now to analysts' recommendations.

There have been a large number of studies of analysts' recommendations, and we shall discuss here a few for the UK and the US. We begin with a UK study that, unfortunately, was undertaken before the development of integrated houses.

Dimson and Marsh (1984, 1985) sought the assistance of 'one of the City's largest investment institutions'. Over a two-year period, 1980–81, the institution collected 4187 specific return forecasts for 206 UK shares. These accounted for 75% of the value of the FT-A All-Share Index. Of the forecasts, 3364 were made by 35 different UK stockbrokers, and the remaining 823 were provided by the institution's internal analysts. All forecasts were of specific returns relative to the FT-A All-Share Index. (Actually, matters were more complicated than that, but the details can be ignored here.) The forecast period was typically one year.

This study is not a test of the typical output of brokers' analysts. Analysts typically grade a stock buy, sell or hold (some use a five-point scale) rather than forecast specific returns. In reality, buy and hold recommendations predominate, with few sell recommendations. The forecasts Dimson and Marsh studied were made solely for the fund and not sent to all institutional clients—this eliminated the possibility that a share price rose because of the forecast and the marketing effort of the broker.

Dimson and Marsh calculated an information coefficient between forecast returns and outcomes of 0.077, which is lower than most previous studies but may still be of some value. Interestingly, the coefficient for the brokers was 0.086 and for the fund's internal analysts 0.042. This lower number for the latter group was because they followed more small stocks—where they forecast the same stocks as the brokers, the coefficient was similar.

Dimson and Marsh claim that the forecasts had demonstrable value. In the two-year study period the fund generated 2950 transactions in the 206 stocks studied. The transaction value-weighted specific return achieved on the 2950 transactions over the year following the trade was 2.2%, or 1.7% after non-avoidable transaction expenses were deducted. The authors state that the forecasts had real commercial value. This seems a brave conclusion. Did the fund managers make decisions solely on the advice studied or on the usual flood of data from numerous brokers giving buy/sell/hold recommendations that the fund would have been receiving daily? Brokers' research, albeit not the subject of the study. Did the fund managers have any sector-weighting criteria that might have affected share selections? However, if one takes the authors' view, brokers' research has a real, but modest, value.

Are some brokers better at forecasting than others? Possibly, but Dimson and Marsh (1985, p. 33) concluded: 'For practical purposes, our best assumption is probably that all brokers have about the same degree of share price forecasting ability.'

What we have been looking at is brokers' written research. This has a bias towards buy recommendations. Over the telephone, an institutional salesperson might add something that in effect, says: 'The report carries a hold recommendation but we are brokers to the company and actually the analyst thinks the stock is a sell.' Some companies are very uncooperative with analysts who give sell recommendations, whether or not there is a corporate brokerage relationship. There appears to be no substantial research on telephone recommendations (but see Dimson and Fraletti, 1986).

We turn now to a US study. Elton et al. (1986) used data compiled by the investment group at Banker's Trust. Starting in March 1981 and continuing for 33 months, forecast data were collected from 34 brokerage firms. The data were generated by an average of 720 analysts, producing over 10 000 forecasts per month. The authors claimed that the database was three times larger than the total of the data used in all previous studies. Stocks were ranked on a five-point scale, with 1 the most attractive, 3 neutral, and 5 the least attractive. The usual broker bias to buy or hold was apparent; only 13% of the recommendations were rated as 4 or 5. About 11% of the recommendations were changed every month.

Do changes in recommendations have value? Elton et al. (1986) tackled this in an interesting way. We shall explain their methods by a specific example. For a particular month, they collected all stocks upgraded to 1 or 2, and all stocks downgraded to 4 or 5. What were the findings? Table 14.2 shows the performance of a portfolio of newly-recommended 1s and 4s compared with a portfolio of new 3s. Table 14.3 shows results for all possible changes in recommendations in less detail. Month 0 is the month of recommendation.

What do these exhibits tell us? First, following brokerage recommendations has some value. Stocks that have been upgraded do better than stocks that have been downgraded. Second, most of the excess return takes place in the first three months. Third, these effects are not enormous. Finally, notice that we have been

TABLE 14.2　Return (%) for recommendation changes

Month	Up to 1 compared with 3		Down to 4 compared with 3	
	Monthly returns	Cumulative returns	Monthly returns	Cumulative returns
0	1.91	1.91	−0.56	−0.56
1	1.24	3.15	−0.74	−1.30
2	0.28	3.43	−0.08	−1.38
3	−0.11	3.32	0.04	−1.34
4	0.37	3.69	0.17	−1.17
5	0.06	3.75	0.00	−1.17
6	0.28	4.03	−0.14	−1.31
7	0.04	4.07	−0.07	−1.38
8	−0.04	4.03	0.22	−1.16
9	−0.05	3.98	0.13	−1.03
10	−0.11	3.87	0.13	−0.90
11	−0.34	3.53	−0.33	−1.23
12	−0.34	3.19	0.53	−0.70

Source: Calculated from Elton et al. (1986, p. 705).

TABLE 14.3　Excess portfolio return comparisons

Change in class	Comparison	Month of recommendation	1 month after	2 months after	Total
Up to 1 or 2	Down to 4 or 5	2.43	1.86	0.37	4.66
Up to 1	3	1.91	1.24	0.28	3.43
Up to 2	3	1.65	0.84	0.20	2.69
Up to 4	3	0.68	0.09	−0.80	−0.03
Down to 2	3	0.29	−0.37	−0.09	−0.17
Down to 4	3	−0.56	−0.74	−0.08	−1.38
Down to 5	3	−0.38	−1.48	−0.40	−2.26

Source: Elton et al. (1986, p. 706).

examining changes in recommendations—we have not examined the value of the recommendations per se. Elton et al. (1986) looked at recommendations and concluded that there is evidence of analysts possessing some skills. However, the changes in recommendations are more valuable. Finally, the authors tried to find out whether there was a best buy amongst the brokerage firms: they thought not.

More recent US studies include Womack (1996), Stickel (1995) and Barber et al. (1998). Womack (1996) analysed brokers' recommendations that were reported on First Call, a PC-based system that collects the research output of a number of brokerage firms. He looked specifically at changes in recommendations. In the three-day period around the change, buy recommendations on average rose by 3%, while sells fell 4.7%. Over the next month, buys rose a further 2.4%, and sells declined 9.2% over the next six months. Stickel (1995) used Zach's Investment Research, which also reports numerous analysts' recommendations, to study the effect of recommendation changes. While the buys went up and the sells went down, gains and losses were all under 1% whether measured in the first 10 days after the recommendation or the next 20. Clearly, these studies come to different conclusions: in the first, analysts appear to add value, while in the second, at least after transactions costs are allowed for, they don't. One difference between the studies was the definition of buy and sell. Putting stock recommendations on a five-point scale (1 = strong buy, 5 = strong sell) Womack defined buys and sells as changes to 1 and 5, whereas Stickel defined them as changes to 1 or 2, and to 3, 4 or 5.

In a working paper, Barber et al. (1998) use Zach's database to relate consensus recommendations and returns. They report an extraordinary difference between the annualized returns of a portfolio of the most favoured stocks (18.8%) versus the least favoured (5.78%). However, they report no reliable difference when the analysis is restricted to the few hundred largest firms.

So, do brokers' recommendations have value? Possibly, with changes in recommendations perhaps having most value.

Press Recommendations

Financial journalists usually receive brokers' research and may have their own contacts with companies. Is it worth following press tips? The answer is complex.

The major UK study is by Dimson and Marsh (1986). They examined 862 recommendations from 11 national publications drawn from the period 1975–82. Half of the recommendations came from the *Investors Chronicle*. The tips outperformed the market as measured by the FT-A All-Share Index by about 3% over the year from the end of the recommendation month. The level of outperformance increased further over the next year, and eight of the publications achieved outperformance while three did not.

This seems to suggest that it is worth following press tips. However, against an equally-weighted index, the recommendations underperformed in the following year by about 6%. The problem is that there was a size effect (small firms outperformed large), and it is difficult to know which is the correct benchmark. The problem can be illustrated as follows. All UK stocks were ordered by their capitalization and then split into deciles. There was a bias in the recommendations towards large stocks, with 36% coming from the top decile. But this decile accounted for 83% of market capitalization. The tipped stocks were four times the size of the typical UK stock, but the probability of a large stock being tipped was less than proportional to its capitalization. The recommended stocks were typical of neither an equally-weighted index nor a capitalization-weighted index.

When the recommendations were measured against a set of diversified control portfolios in different capitalization classes, it turned out that the recommendations offered neutral performance over a year. The recommendations did offer outperformance of about 4% from the date of the recommendation to the end of the recommendation month. Unfortunately there was a lag between a recommendation being made and it being published. For the source of one-third of the recommendations studied, two-thirds of the performance occurred before public distribution. No information is given for the prepublication performance of the other recommendations.

US studies of press tips have produced mixed results: the safest conclusion for the US is that brokers' tips seem more likely than press tips to have value.

Newsletters

In the UK, there are only a few independent financial newsletters. They are common in the US, however, and the *Hulbert Financial Digest* tracks many of them. In 1996, it covered 93, but since inception in 1980 it has covered 153 different newsletters. Metrick (1999) used several methods of assessing these newsletters' stock-picking skills. He concluded that average abnormal returns were close to zero. And he didn't find evidence of short-term persistence of returns for individual newsletters.

Included in Metrick's sample was *Value Line*, which has been the subject of a number of academic studies and it is worth saying a little about it. The *Value Line Investment Survey* is an independent, weekly investment advisory service covering US stocks. It claims to be the largest advisory service in the world, measured in terms of revenues and numbers of subscribers. *Value Line* covers 1700 stocks, which it ranks weekly for 'timeliness' and 'safety'. It reviews all stocks every three months, and produces an information-packed page on every stock.

The emphasis here will be on *Value Line*'s timeliness rankings, although it should be noted that its safety rankings correlate highly with Altman's Zeta score (see Chapter 9) and were found in one study (Fuller and Wong, 1988) to correlate with subsequent returns better than either beta or standard deviation measures of risk.

Value Line ranks the 1700 stocks it covers on the basis of expected performance over the next 12 months. Stocks with a timeliness rank 1 are expected to perform best. The number of stocks in each category is, by design:

Timeliness rank	Number of stocks
1	100
2	300
3	900
4	300
5	100

For obvious commercial reasons, the exact details of how the timeliness ranks are determined are not published, but the key elements (Bernhard, n.d.; and Gerstein, 1986) are:

- a value position based on three factors: relative earnings rank, relative price rank and relative price momentum;

- an earnings momentum factor determined by a stock's latest quarter's earnings change, compared with a year ago, relative to that of all other stocks;
- an earnings surprise factor, where the most recent quarter's earnings are compared with the *Value Line* security analyst's forecast.

Interestingly, *Value Line* used to include its analysts' views, but it dropped them in mid-1979 because they did not add any value.

The results—pretransactions costs—are fabulous. Moreover, the timeliness ranks as a group show perfect discrimination, i.e. rank 1 beats rank 2, which beats rank 3, etc. This is true whether you look at an annual buy-and-hold strategy or a strategy of switching every time a stock's rank changes ('total conformance'). Holloway (1981) examined *Value Line*'s record and allowed for transaction costs. It turned out that a total conformance portfolio of stocks ranked 1 required so many trades that transaction costs overwhelmed the *Value Line* system and abnormal returns were not achieved. However, the buy-and-hold Value Line rank 1 portfolio did produce annual abnormal returns of 8.6%, even after transaction costs.

Copeland and Mayers (1982) also found abnormal returns pretransaction costs, but very little after. However, if investors had to trade, *Value Line* would offer scope for abnormal returns. Most of the abnormal performance appeared in rank 5 stocks. They looked at returns to both ranks and changes of ranks. For the latter they found that pretransaction cost abnormal returns were concentrated in the two weeks following a rank change. A later study by Stickel (1985) found most of the abnormal returns were concentrated in the three-day period around a rank change. Stickel (1985) found the rank change from 2 to 1 to have the biggest impact on returns, and the significant three-day period includes the Thursday preceding the official *Value Line* issue date. *Value Line* attempts to mail its weekly survey so that all subscribers receive it on the same day, Friday. In fact some subscribers are thought sometimes to receive their copy on Thursday. Hall and Tsay (1988) corrected for what they saw as deficiencies in previous studies and found that after transaction costs, neither active nor passive investors in rank 1 stocks outperformed random portfolios.

A number of academics have tried to explain how *Value Line* produces its good pretransaction cost forecasts. Affleck-Graves and Mendenhall (1992) note that *Value Line* timeliness ranks are based on, amongst other things, earnings momentum and earnings surprises. Is *Value Line*'s ranking success due solely to 'post-earnings-announcement drift'? The authors note that over half of all *Value Line* rank changes follow earnings announcements by eight days or less. They partition their sample into two roughly equal-sized groups based on the lag between earnings announcement and the rank change, and then examine the difference in abnormal returns between firms moving into rank 1 and those moving into rank 5. Abnormal returns only exist when the rank change closely follows an earnings announcement. This suggests that post-earnings-announcement drift explains *Value Line*'s results. The authors undertook further statistical tests, which supported this. It might be reasonable to assume that part of the abnormal return generated by stocks on the day before their *Value Line* rank change is a result of investors guessing rankings rather than an abnormally speedy US postal service.

Value Line is an interesting product. It seems misclassified as a newsletter. It is a formal quantitative stock-selection model. Its safety and timeliness ranks have some value. The timeliness rankings show perfect discrimination, rank 1 stocks beat rank 2, and so forth. The rankings have produced abnormal returns before transaction costs, but it is less clear if they have after costs. If an investor has to trade, for example when setting up a new portfolio, the rankings would be useful. There is evidence that over the years the abnormal returns have been earned in a shorter and shorter period; indeed it may be that returns are concentrated in three days around the weekly issue date. The major factor leading to *Value Line*'s good timeliness ranking ability may be its emphasis on earnings surprises. Finally, *Value Line* may be better at identifying losers than at identifying winners (e.g. see Copeland and Mayers, 1982; and Lacey and Phillips-Patrick, 1992).

CONCLUDING COMMENTS

Many readers will find calendar anomalies interesting and rather good fun compared with some of the topics discussed in other chapters, which call for a lot of effort if the investor is to make money. Many of the calendar anomalies seem real enough as they occur in several markets and have been discovered in times that had not examined when the effects were first found. But what causes calendar effects? There may be tax effects at work; the flow of institutional funds may be related to the calendar; private clients tend to get offered buy recommendations by their advisers and may be left to work out their own selling strategy, which they are likely to do over the weekend; good news and bad news may be released at different times, and bad news may come after the markets have closed on Friday; psychological factors may be at work, e.g. most people may prefer Friday to Monday, and so on.

Whether these explanations have merit will be debated for years, but investors should be cautious and keep matters in perspective. As Lakonishok and Smidt (1988, p. 417) note for the US:

> It is useful to relate the magnitude of the anomalies with the size of a tick (the smallest price change), which is 12.5 cents. Because the average price per share on the NYSE is about $40, a movement of one tick corresponds to a price change of 0.313 percent or more, which is much larger than most seasonal anomalies discussed [in this paper]. For example, the average Monday price decrease of –0.144 percent is well within one tick.

Exploiting some of the effects involves substantial trading. But for anyone who has to trade, it makes sense to play the odds and time the trades to take account of the calendar effects. The effects discussed in this chapter seem more the basis of trading tactics than investment strategy. The only exception to this might be the UK's seasonal pattern, which suggests being in cash from May until December and then in equities.

Low-price stocks have been found to outperform in many studies. But there is an obvious overlap with small stocks. Neglected stocks have also been found to outperform. But they too are typically small stocks. So which factor is driving which?

Should an investor follow recommendations? It would appear that brokers' recommendations are worth something, but not a lot, at least for large companies. Indeed, since analysts' recommendations will be based partly on their profit forecasts and changes, it is reasonable to ask whether their recommendations have any value over and above that contained in their profits forecasts. Since earnings surprises and revisions seem to lead to higher returns than recommendations, one might argue that analysts' views are actually a negative factor if one is already looking at their forecasts. Recall that *Value Line* dropped its analysts' views from its model. Further, investors should ask whether they are getting good value by paying enormous sums to brokers in bundled research/ execution fees. Switching some of the budget towards databases, specialist subscription services, quantitative analytical software, etc. would seem to make good sense. Press recommendations can probably be ignored. Investment newsletters probably are not useful, although *Value Line*'s timeliness recommendations contain useful information. Whether it would add much value for an investor who already monitors earnings revisions and surprises is doubtful. *Value Line*'s safety ranks contain useful information. The market seems to be reasonably—but not perfectly—efficient with regard to published advice.

15

Technical Analysis

I was a technician at Putnum, and the fund managers were giving me an unusually hard time one day. I told them, 'Yes: the boss just called me into his office, and said I had been making a lot of mistakes recently. He added that if I kept it up they'd have to give me a fund to run.'

Walter Deemer

Technical analysts are often seen, at least in the UK, as chartists, pure and simple, but most of them nowadays are more than that. Technical analysts certainly look at past prices, believing that future trends can be deduced from the past, and so may seek head and shoulders, descending triangles, flags and other exotic charts patterns. But they also look at the behaviour of various types of market participants, company directors and other insiders, sentiment and contrary opinion, liquidity levels, and so on.

Technical analysts are contrasted with fundamental analysts, who try to calculate the true underlying value of a stock by analysing dividends, growth, interest rates and other factors. The problem with this contrast is that it seems artificial. Of course, a DDM adherent and a chartist have different beliefs, but what about everybody else? Is an investor who simply buys small stocks really a fundamentalist? And what is a low-PER investor? The notion of neglected stocks sounds folksy enough to be a technician's tool—or is it fundamental because statistically oriented professors elaborated the concept? Why is insider trading a technical tool? Are calendar effects technical, fundamental or astrological? The research findings seem to be interesting, and it does not really matter how they are classified. In this chapter, we will comment briefly on some, but by no means all, of the tools a technician might use, whether to study a whole market (e.g. UK equities) or a component (e.g. the oil sector or Shell).

Technical analysis has been around a long time, predating today's fundamental analysis. Japanese candlestick analysis is thought to date from the 1600s, when it was used to analyse rice prices. And it is perhaps not surprising that people tried to deduce information from past prices early in the last century when accounting data were scarce—indeed information in general was more difficult to obtain than today—and insider trading common. But academics have tended to pour scorn on technical analysis, and for good reason:

1. The standard chartist texts provide no evidence of any kind that what they are describing has any predictive power. The best one can hope for are a few carefully chosen illustrations. And there is no carefully documented evidence of fund managers using technical analysis to beat the market.

2. One explanation as to why charts might work is essentially about reading the psychology of investors from them. Roberts (1959) used random numbers to generate a continuous series, i.e. the equivalent of the level of a stock index measured over a period of time. Since the series was random by design, it cannot be possible to use part of the data to forecast subsequent data. And there is no psychology to be unravelled in a series of random numbers. Nonetheless, patterns emerged, such as head and shoulders (Figure 15.1), that chartists claim can be used to predict. If you try hard enough, you can see a face in the clouds. But is anything really there?

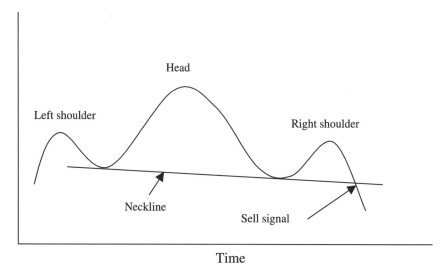

FIGURE 15.1 Head and shoulders

3. Early academic research claimed that real share prices took a random walk, i.e. the next price for a stock is not predictable from past prices and therefore a share-selection method based on past prices was bound to be flawed.

4. There are many different methods of chartist analysis, and two chartists will often come to different conclusions about whether a stock is a buy or a sell.

5. Chartist analysis is often unhelpful. For example, one might be told that if the market breaks through a certain level, it will go on rising, but if it falls below a certain level, further falls may be expected. Often the level being described is so far away that an investor could lose 10–15% of his or her assets before the chartist would conclude that the market is going down. And what does one do in the meantime? When outlining strategy to a fund's trustees, it sounds a bit lame to say, 'We are waiting for a signal.' On the other hand, if chartist analysis works, waiting for a signal would be a sound strategy.

6. Chartists sometimes point out that fundamental analysis is suspect because it is hard to tell what fundamental information is discounted in prices. This invites the question as to why chartist analysis is not also discounted in prices.

Point 4 above does not seem especially telling, for the same could be said of fundamental analysts. Points 1, 2, 5 and 6 seem reasonable, but there has been some wavering on 3, as there is recent evidence that prices do not take a completely random walk. Sad to say, these findings have not been a result of chartist research.

Before we look at the technical tools and recent evidence, it is worth noting that even when academics were most dismissive of technical analysis, investors continued to buy books of charts. Nowadays, as perusal of the advertisements at the back of any issue of the *Investors Chronicle* will demonstrate, even private investors can produce up-to-date charts by buying cheap CD-ROMs containing chart programs, and downloading data from the Internet. It is, at the very least, interesting that so many people have ignored the academic assertions. Also, it is worth stressing that we will discuss only chartist analysis in the stock and bond markets. Chart analysis is even more common in the foreign exchange markets, where it may be more successful than other techniques for predicting short-term moves (see Chapter 20).

TECHNICAL ANALYSIS TOOLS

Some of the tools that a technical analyst might use are:

- charts
  - Dow theory
  - moving averages
  - support and resistance
  - patterns
- volume
- breadth
- smart money
- contrary opinion.

Charts

It is beyond the scope of this book to outline chartist theories. The interested reader should refer to the standard work by Edwards and Magee (1984) or a long article by Shaw (1988). An old, but still worthwhile, review of the evidence is Pinches (1970). US technical analysts often look at price and volume statistics (such as number of shares traded) together. UK chartists generally seem to omit volume.

Dow Theory

Dow theory is one of the most famous methods of forecasting the market. It was never stated explicitly, but has been deduced from articles published by Charles Dow in the *Wall Street Journal* at the turn of the last century, and from the editorials of Hamilton, who assumed editorship of the *Wall Street Journal* on Dow's death in 1902, and claimed to follow Dow's analysis. Charles Dow was the originator of the 'Industrial Average', consisting of 12 blue-chip shares, and the 'Rail Average', consisting of 20 railway shares. These subsequently became the DJIA and Dow Jones Transportation Average.

Dow thought that a stock's price reflected everything that was known about the stock, and that the market average reflected everything known by investors. But he also thought the market was subject to three trends:

- The *primary trend*, which lasted for at least one year but probably several, was bullish or bearish. If the market made successive higher highs and higher lows, then the trend was up. Lower highs and lower lows indicated the trend was down.
- *Secondary trends* were corrective reactions to the primary trend. They lasted for a few months and retraced one-third to two-thirds of previous secondary trends.
- *Minor trends* were short-term movements that lasted for up to a few weeks.

A bullish primary trend is initiated by informed investors anticipating a recovery from gloomy conditions, for example a recession. The second phase of the primary trend results from improving conditions, and the final phase from much improved conditions with the general public joining the stockmarket bandwagon. At some stage in this phase, the informed investors start selling.

If the primary trend appears to have changed, this must be confirmed by both the industrial and the transportation averages. In a bear market, for example, there will have been some secondary trends that led to a local high. If the market starts to rise, then a change in trend will be confirmed when both the industrials and transports make a high above their previous secondary peak, as shown in Figure 15.2 for one index.

While primarily a theory about prices, Dow theory does consider trading volume. Moves made with heavy volume should be of particular significance. Volume should increase with moves made in the direction of the primary trend. For example, if the primary trend is down, then volume should be heavier for falls than advances.

Finally, a trend is thought to remain intact until a definite reversal signal is given. Thus if the primary trend is bearish, even if the market starts trading sideways for a long period, a change in trend only occurs when both averages rise above a previous secondary peak.

In a famous study, Cowles (1934) tested and rejected Dow theory. The test was based on the editorials of Hamilton in the *Wall Street Journal* over the

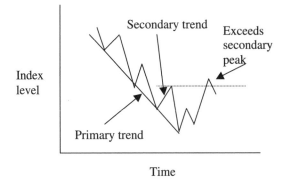

FIGURE 15.2   Change in trend

period 1902–29. However, Brown et al. (1998) re-examined Cowles' analysis and concluded that Hamilton had in fact achieved positive risk-adjusted returns. He seems to have been particularly successful at bear market calls. Of course, although Hamilton may have claimed to be using Dow theory, he may actually have been making shrewd idiosyncratic judgement. Brown et al. (1998) test this by seeing whether they can relate Hamilton's market calls to preceding movements of the DJIA. Their results confirm that Hamilton used a momentum strategy. The regression methods they use suggest that there may be a nonlinear response to past price movements. To test for this, they use a methodology that is related closely to artificial intelligence (AI) based methods, such as neural nets and evolutionary computation. This confirms that Hamilton's strategy was based on recent market trends.

Brown et al. (1998) use their AI model to market time over the period 15 September 1930–1 December 1997. The results depend on a number of assumptions, such as how quickly the strategy could be implemented and the cost of transactions. It is unlikely that the strategy would produce large excess returns. Nonetheless, the strategy does especially well in periods of sharp market decline. One problem has to be noted: there is a subjective element in Dow theory, so what was examined was a joint hypothesis: Dow theory is true, and Hamilton made the calls any other Dow theory proponent would have made.

Moving Average

Chartists often calculate moving averages for markets, stocks, sectors, etc. for a variety of periods, such as 10 days, 50 days and 200 days. A 10-day moving average for yesterday would be calculated by adding, for example, the price of a share for each of the last 10 days and dividing by 10. To calculate today's moving average, you would drop the oldest price and replace it with today's price (when known) and recalculate the average.

The simplest use of moving averages involves calculating two moving averages, a long period and a short period average. A common version uses a 200-day long period and a one-day short period. When the one-day average rises through the 200-day average, a new positive trend is confirmed. When it falls through the 200-day average, a new negative trend is confirmed. Often there are numerous signals that are quickly reversed. To avoid this, a 1% band may be imposed. Signals within the band are ignored. Sometimes three moving averages are used instead of a band. For example, using one-, five- and 200-day moving averages, a buy or sell signal would only be confirmed when both the one-day and five-day averages moved through the 200-day average. Evidence on moving averages is considered in the next section.

Support and Resistance

Some technical analysts argue that shares, markets, etc. have psychological support and resistance levels. The idea is that the market will find it hard, for example, to rise through a resistance level, but if it does, it can move ahead until a new resistance level is established. The resistance level and support level might be a previous high and low for the market. The high and low might be that attained in the last 200 days.

The best known study of moving averages and support/resistance (or trading range breakouts) is by Brock et al. (1992). They tested both rules for the DJIA for the entire period 1897–1986, and for four subperiods.

There are two problems with testing these rules. First, they are capable of being stated in a huge number of ways. Is it to be two averages, or two averages and a band, or three averages? And if it is two averages, then are they to be one and 200, five and 200, one and 150, or what? The second problem is that with breakouts, a chartist may not have a fixed timespan: each stock or market may have a particularly significant high or low—skill in deciding what these are may be what distinguishes a good chartist from a bad one. We'll ignore this second point. Obviously, Brock et al. (1992) had to use a fixed rule for purposes of their test. As to the first problem, the obvious solution is to try many moving averages and see what works best. The problem with this is that one is data mining. To avoid this, Brock et al. report all their tests, use a very long time period, and assess the results for non-overlapping subperiods.

The results were startling. Both methods worked in the sense that buy periods produced returns significantly above the average market return, and sell periods generated negative returns. For example, using 10 different specifications of the two moving averages rule, buying the market on a buy signal and holding it until a sell signal, then staying out until a new buy signal, the average buy return was about 12% p.a. and the average sell return was about –7% p.a. It would seem that the market is not even weak-form efficient.

While the return distribution may not be what the efficient market theory expects, can you actually make money from the strategy? The best strategy gave a return of 10.1%, versus 5% for the Dow (dividends were omitted in this study.) But what is your benchmark? If it is being in the market all the time, you might implement the trading strategy by holding a portfolio, then doubling it on a buy signal, and selling it on a sell signal. You would have to borrow to double up, but could lend after selling. If we ignore the complications of different borrowing and selling rates, effectively you have to trade 200% of the portfolio on every trade except the first. Since there were 3.5 signals a year on average, a 700% turnover p.a. would take a sizeable bite out of the apparent profitability of the rules. Using the same trading rules as Brock et al., but a different database and for the period 1926–91, Bessembinder and Chan (1998) get broadly similar results, although returns after sell signals were not significantly different from zero. However, after making more sophisticated adjustments for trading costs than we did above, they conclude that while the rules have statistically significant forecast power, they are not profitable.

Finally, Sullivan et al. (1999) test and extend Brock et al.'s work. Using a new statistical test devised by one of the authors, they attempt to resolve whether Brock et al.'s results are a consequence of data mining. They conclude they are not. But using 10-year out-of-sample DJIA data (1987–96), the superior performance of the best trading rule is not repeated. They also examine the S&P 500 future contract, which has traded since 1984. For the period 1984–96, they find no evidence that any trading rule outperforms over the entire sample period.

How would Brock et al.'s rules work in the UK? Hudson et al. (1996) and Mills (1997) tried the rules using the FT30 index for the period 1935–94. Mills (1997) reports that technical trading rules work (ignoring transaction costs) for the 20-year subperiods 1935–54 and 1955–74, but not for 1975–94. Hudson et al. (1996) use 15-year subperiods. They find that the rules have predictive ability—buy signals offer positive returns and sell signals offer negative returns. Sell signals have greater predictive ability than buy signals. However, the results are better for the first two subsamples. When they allow for trading costs, they find that the rules would not have been profitable.

Pulling all of the discussion together, it appears that some trading rules have had predictive ability in both the UK and the US. Unfortunately, that predictive ability has become smaller, or disappeared, in recent years. And after trading costs, it is unlikely that the rules were profitable. Notice that this discussion was about the level of the entire market; we do not know whether the rules would work for individual stocks, sectors, etc.

Patterns

Some chartists believe that a variety of patterns give good predictions. One of the best known is the head and shoulders pattern (Figure 15.1). When the right shoulder falls through the neckline, a bearish signal is given. Osler (1998) tested this pattern on the DJIA, and concluded it was not a useful predictor. We are not aware of research on most of the many patterns that are discussed in the technical literature, so we will omit them here.

Volume and Breadth

It is beyond the scope of this book to review the volume literature; interested readers should refer to Karpoff (1987), who reviews the academic literature on the relation between price changes and trading volume, although he does not tie it to specific technical rules.

Breadth is a market indicator. It relates the number of advancing issues to the number of declining. Because the major market indexes are cap-weighted, it is possible for the market to rise on the back of a few large shares. Many analysts have expressed concern in recent years in the UK that a few stocks in the bank, oil, telecoms and pharmaceutical sectors have driven the market, while many shares have fallen significantly, and small-cap stocks have performed poorly. The market is thought to be 'healthier' if most shares are participating in a rise. We are not aware of any evidence that this is so.

A variation of advancing/declining issues is the number of sectors showing relative strength. Relative strength is discussed below.

Relative Strength

Relative strength is calculated for a stock to show how it has been performing relative to its sector or to the market as a whole, or for a sector relative to the market. Relative strength is expected to persist.

An early test of relative strength was by Levy (1967), who concluded that relative strength was a useful technique. He looked at 68 different trading rules and his study is open to the charge of data mining. It was also subject to other criticisms by Jensen and Bennington (1970), who did not find relative strength useful. Subsequent studies have suggested that relative strength does have some validity (e.g. Akemann and Keller, 1977; Bohan, 1981; Brush, 1986; Pruitt and White, 1988; Jacobs and Levy, 1988a; and Reinganum, 1988). Arnott (1979) did not support relative strength.

Some of these studies used stocks, and some used sectors. The definition of relative strength also varied in terms of the period used to calculate it, and the period afterwards that the outperformance was to occur in. The periods used were also often quite short. Despite the evidence in favour of relative strength, one is left with an uneasy feeling of too many models, too much data mining, and so on.

The relative strength studies have been published mainly in the professional journals. In the last decade or so, there has been a growing academic literature on price momentum, persistence and reversals. This is relative strength revisited. Unfortunately, this literature is more interested in whether past prices can be used to predict (the answer is yes) rather than whether the predictive content is sufficient to make money.

The academic studies have typically gone through the following steps:

1. Select a universe of stocks and the years for the analysis.
2. Define the period over which price performance is to be measured, e.g. one month.
3. Rank stocks by performance over the previous month.

4. Define winner and loser portfolio cut-offs, e.g. the best performing 10% of all stocks versus the worst 10%.
5. Calculate the return for the portfolios for the next month.
6. Make any necessary adjustments for risk.

The leading studies (Lehmann, 1990; Jegadeesh, 1990; Jegadeesh and Titman, 1993; Rouwenhorst, 1998; De Bondt and Thaler, 1985; and De Bondt and Thaler, 1987) cover a variety of time periods and countries. The findings are:

- If you buy a portfolio of stocks that have done well over the past week or month, then you will do poorly over the next week or month. And vice versa. Returns reverse.
- If you buy a portfolio of stocks that have done well over the past six months or year, then you will do well over the next six months or year. And vice versa. Returns persist.
- If you buy a portfolio of stocks that have done well over the past three or five years, then you will do poorly over the next three or five years. And vice versa. Returns reverse.

Some commentators dispute these results, pointing to measurement errors, incorrect benchmarks, and so on. (For a review of the literature, see Forbes, 1996.) Even if one accepts the results at face value, are they just a result of data mining? There are two arguments against this. First, the results do have a pattern in that the shortest-period results, the medium-period results and the longer-period results are consistent within themselves. Second, most early studies are on US data, but similar results were subsequently found for European markets. However, one would be happier if there was an explanation as to why the market switches—in relative strength terms—from negative strength, to positive strength and then back to negative. Possible explanations include the following:

- Short-term reversals may be caused by price pressure. A spate of buy or sell orders may have excessive impact on prices in the short term, but this will quickly be reversed out.
- Medium-term persistence may be explained by the findings that there is an underreaction to earnings information.
- Long-term reversals may be explained by the market overreacting to a series of good or bad results. This explanation is the same as that used for arguing that the market pays too much for glamour stocks and too little for value stocks.

Most fund managers will be more interested in the medium-term relative strength than the other two periods. If medium-term relative strength is explained by the market's underreaction to earnings information, then accounting for the earnings effect should remove the profitability of relative strength. But price strength might also contain other, broader information that is not fully discounted, such as an improved long-term expected growth rate. In that case, the short-term earnings information will not fully explain relative strength. Chan et al. (1996) found for the US in the period 1977–93 that relative strength for six and 12 months can be predicted on the basis of prior price movement and earnings information, and that one does not subsume the other (see also Chan et al. (1999) for an out-of-sample test.)

Recently, Moskowitz and Grinblatt (1999) have shown that in the US, there is a strong momentum effect in industry components of stock returns that accounts for much of the individual price momentum. They argue that portfolios based on individual share price momentum are not well diversified, and that if one were going to trade on momentum, using industries would provide a more profitable and more readily implementable strategy.

We will close by mentioning a few UK studies. Liu et al.'s (1999) main analysis relates to 2434 non-financial stocks, and covers the period 1977–98. Their approach is similar to Jegadeesh and Titman (1993). They examine the profitability of going long in the highest-decile (winner) portfolio and shorting the lowest-decile (loser) portfolio. They find annualized returns ranging from 10% to 23% using a 3×3 strategy, a 6×6 strategy and a 12×3 strategy. (A 3×3 strategy is one where winners and losers are determined by the previous three months' returns and the returns on the strategy computed over the following three months). They examine a wide range of variables to try and account for their findings but find no evidence of total risk or systematic risk that explains their results.

Taffler (1999) raises a number of issues relevant to whether investors could actually make money with this strategy. His points are applicable to many studies. First, are the results time period specific? The period covered might be considered to be a continuous bull market. Other studies have shown that relative strength does not work so well in down markets. Second, many of the stocks in the winner and loser portfolios are small. Is it really possible to short small low-relative-strength stocks? The authors also assume 0.5% transactions cost, which is absurdly low for small stocks. Third, the portfolios are equally weighted and it is possible that the results would be less impressive if stocks were value weighted. Finally, how much of the effect is an industry momentum effect? If industry momentum is important, then the resulting portfolios will not be well diversified, and this may be unacceptable to many investors.

Momentum investing is currently very popular. Most managers who use it are probably not aware that they are closet chartists.

SMART MONEY

If you can't decide how to invest, then copying somebody who knows what they are doing seems a reasonable tactic. Of course, you will have to act quickly or the information may have no value. Judging by the number of books on Warren Buffett, many people want to follow the 'smart money'. In the US, there are a number of indicators that can be examined, but similar information is not available in the UK. We shall discuss just one type of smart money, company directors.

Insider Trading

Insider trading, which, loosely speaking, is the use of certain types of non-public information by company directors in connection with a share transaction, is illegal in the US and the UK. Illegal insider trading can be remarkably profitable, as Levine and Hoffer (1992) demonstrate. (Levine was convicted for such trading, so perhaps the risk-adjusted returns were not so good.) In the US finance literature, even legal trades made by 'insiders' are usually referred to as insiders' or insider trading. We will use the term 'insider trading' to mean legal trading by insiders.

US federal law requires directors, officers and shareholders owning 10% or more of a share traded on an organized exchange, i.e. insiders, to report their transactions within 10 days of the end of the month in which the transaction was made to the Securities and Exchange Commission (SEC). The SEC should publish details of trades by insiders in its *Official Summary* in the following month. Thus, information about insider trading should be available within about two months of a trade taking place.

Insiders have been described as 'America's most knowledgeable investors'. Can these investors make abnormal returns and, more importantly, can the rest of us make money by following their trades? Many books written by practitioners answer these questions affirmatively, but the evidence is less clear cut, although it is true that many of the early studies did suggest that following the insiders was a winning strategy (e.g. Pratt and DeVere, 1968; Jaffe, 1974; and Finnerty, 1976).

A more recent US study is by Seyhun (1986), who studied the period 1975–81. His sample comprised all firms listed on option exchanges plus a stratified random sample based on the size of firms' equity of all publicly held firms. He analysed 769 firms and a total of 59 148 open-market sales and purchases.

Insiders trade for many reasons. They may be using their specific knowledge, taking up stock options, selling to raise cash for family reasons, and so on. It is therefore not unusual to observe both purchases and sales being made by different insiders at the same time. If the number of insider buyers exceeded the number of insider sellers in a month, then Seyhun considered this to be an insider purchase (and vice versa); if the number of purchasers and sellers was equal, then the month was ignored. Seyhun used the market model to measure the expected return for securities. He found that during the 300 days following the insider trading day, abnormal returns were 4.3% for purchases and –2.2% for sales.

These are not enormous numbers, but if the SEC is tough about insiders acting illegally, then it would be surprising if insiders act in advance of very noticeable events affecting their company. Accordingly, one might expect modest returns. But what of the earlier studies that suggested much bigger returns? There are a number of possible explanations. First, the studies used samples of insider trades and there may simply be large sampling errors. Second, the differences in results may be a result of the methodologies employed, for example the definition of an insider trade, the dating of the event day, and the method of measuring abnormal returns. In particular, Seyhun argues that some previous studies using the CAPM may have had a smaller company bias. Seyhun's sample showed that small-firm insiders are far more likely to be buyers than large-firm insiders are. If small firms produce higher returns than large firms do, then other studies may really have been picking up a small-firm effect.

Seyhun further analysed his data in terms of looking for relationships with regard to particular types of insiders. Seyhun (1986, p. 206) reported:

> It appears that insider information arises as a result of insiders' association with the firm, since insiders who are closer to day-to-day decision-making [e.g. officer-directors] trade on more valuable information. Second . . . most profitable insider trading occurs in small firms. Third, insiders can distinguish the differences in the value of their information and trade a larger volume of stock when they have more valuable information.

The first point is demonstrated in Table 15.1.

TABLE 15.1 Abnormal returns from purchases by insider type, 1975–81

Insider	Abnormal return (%)*
Chairman	3.3
Officer–director	3.3
Director	2.3
Shareholder	1.9
Officer	1.5

*Earned in 100 days following insider trade.
Source: Seyhun (1986, p. 205).

Turning to outsiders (i.e. ordinary investors) trading on the back of insiders' reported deals, the findings were not encouraging. The *Official Summary* does not report insider trades as fast as it might. The delay between the insider trading day and the availability of the *Official Summary* exceeds 90 days for 31% of transactions and 60 days for 84%. Various commercial organizations produce insider trade information on a more timely basis by collecting the relevant data from the SEC offices rather than waiting for the *Official Summary*. Seyhun (1986, p. 208) reports:

> If an outsider trades on the basis of insiders' transactions as soon as insiders' reports are received by the SEC, he can earn 1.4% [abnormal return] after 100 days and 1.9% after

300 days. If the outsider waits until after the *Official Summary* is available, the gross abnormal return is only 1.1% during the next 300 days.

Once one allows for transaction costs, the abnormal returns disappear. This conclusion was not affected by using more selective rules based on the identity of insiders, the dollar volume of trading, and so forth.

Seyhun's study can be summarized simply: insiders can make modest abnormal profits; outsiders copying them make very little indeed. As was noted above, these findings are somewhat at odds with most studies. Apart from the points noted earlier about differences in sample and methodology, what other reasons might account for the finding of an absence of abnormal returns to outsiders? Following insiders has become a popular strategy in recent years, with a number of commercial services providing up-to-date information, the *Wall Street Journal* publishing a monthly 'Inside Track' column, and so on. One might be tempted to conclude that insider actions are now instantaneously compounded in stock prices. However, that does not seem correct: in Seyhun's study, the failure of the strategy is caused primarily by the modest returns to the insiders and by part of the abnormal return being earned in the period before the insider trades are published.

Some years ago, Finnerty (1976) had noted that insiders who bought shares were buying companies that were smaller, had larger earnings and had larger dividends compared with those companies insiders were selling. What if allowance is made for the abnormal returns likely from small size and low PER? Zaman (1988) examined this issue for 1973–82, a period that substantially overlaps Seyhun's. His key findings were as follows. On the basis of the market model, insiders earned abnormal profits over one-, three-, six- and 12-month holding periods; if 2% transaction costs were assumed, they earned abnormal profits of around 0.5% per month over the three-, six- and 12-month holding periods. Outsiders also earned abnormal returns over all holding periods if no transaction costs were allowed for, but only over six and 12 months after costs. They earned about 3.7% over 12 months. When Zaman allowed for size and PER effects, insiders still made abnormal returns after 2% costs, although returns were more than halved. Outsiders, however, made no abnormal returns.

Before drawing all this together, one other study is worth mentioning. Seyhun reported that insiders can tell the value of their information. Oppenheimer and Dielman (1988) reported a rather different finding. They looked at insiders' profits in relation to two specific information releases: the announcement of the resumption of dividend payments after at least two years of non-payment and the announcement of the omission of dividend payments after at least two years of steady payment. The results were startling:

> Insiders as a group seem to exhibit little timing ability. Some insiders (for example, insiders buying shares of firms omitting dividends) exhibit terrible timing ability. Officers, however, perform better than insiders as a whole do. It is suggested that the book on insider trading is still open; it is not clear that insiders as a group always utilize insider information to achieve profits'.

> (Oppenheimer and Dielman, 1988, p. 539)

We would appear to know the following about insider trading in the US. A number of studies have shown that insiders and the outsiders who follow them have made abnormal returns. Recent studies show lower returns than the early studies and possibly no abnormal returns, but these returns are calculated after making adjustments for small size and low-PER effects.

Regan (1991) reports that Mark Hulbert, who monitors the performance of US investment newsletters' stock recommendations, found that for the period January 1985–September 1990, *The Insiders*, a major newsletter issuing stock recommendations based on insider trades, underperformed the US market by about 9%. During this period, small stocks and low-PER stocks performed poorly. Pratt, co-author of one of the early studies, and owner of a newsletter, performed so poorly that he sold the newsletter.

UK Studies

Turning to the UK, insider trading has been much less thoroughly studied. UK directors must notify their company as soon as possible of any share transaction for their personal account, and the company must notify the Stock Exchange immediately. The Stock Exchange then releases the information through its Regulatory News Service that appears on the usual City screens. The information is also published on a weekly basis. Three UK studies of insider trading will be outlined here.

King and Roell (1988) took a sample of insider transactions reported in a weekly 'share stakes' column in the *Financial Times* from January 1986 to August 1987. They point out that this is far from a complete set of disclosed transactions: 'each week, the journalists composing the news item review all such transactions and include only those they judge particularly interesting or significant, subject to column space constraints.' Thus, King and Roell actually appear to be testing not insider trades per se but the share selection skills of *Financial Times* journalists drawing stocks from a universe consisting of stocks involved in insider trades. They found that both insider buys and sells outperformed over one, three and 12 months following publication, although the sell figures were not statistically significant. Although there was a small-firm bias, this effect would not have been sufficient to explain away the over 50% outperformance by the insider purchases.

Pope et al. (1990), who estimated returns from following directors' trades as reported in the Stock Exchange's *Weekly Official Intelligence*, reported quite different results. They studied the period April 1977–December 1984, looking at returns for a six-month holding period for three subperiods as well as the overall period. Outsider purchases generated a positive abnormal return, but this was not statistically significant for two of the subperiods and the whole period. Outsider sells produced negative abnormal returns of 6.7% before costs for the entire period. This was statistically significant and the returns for two of the subperiods were also significant.

Gregory et al. (1994) took a 150-firm sample of UK listed non-financial companies and examined insider trades and returns over the period 1984–86. Their sample was stratified so that roughly equal numbers of firms came from the largest decile of firms by market-cap, deciles two through five (medium-size firms), and six through 10 (small firms). Numerous results are presented for a variety of periods and definitions of what constitutes a trade. To give a flavour of the results, we will consider the 12-month returns when trades exclude those related to options and rights issues. Cumulative abnormal returns for buys was 9% and for sales –5%. But there was a strong size effect. Small-firm buys returned 33% while small-firm sales returned 19%. For large firms, the figures were –6% and –10%. After allowing for a size effect and beta, the whole sample generated 6% for buys and –2% for sales. The first figure was statistically significant, but the second wasn't.

It is hard to know what to conclude for the UK. Based on Pope et al. (1990), one might argue that investors should construct a portfolio by whatever strategy they wish but should guide their selling decisions by following insider sales. Based on Gregory et al. (1994), one might do the reverse.

Insiders and the Market Level

It is widely believed that insiders' trades are a useful guide to forecasting the market's level. The justification for this is a belief that insiders act partly in response to firm-specific information and partly in response to general economic factors that impact their firms. If they react to such general information before it is widely known, they might provide a good guide to the market's likely level. Such a guide is unlikely to be infallible. Insiders may just be taking a view on the market and expressing it by dealing in their own firm's shares. In that case, their knowledge may not be 'inside'. Further, the economy and market do not have an exact correspondence. Industrialists might see surprisingly weak sales figures and believe a recession is continuing, while the market may have focused on a likely change in economic policy and the prospects of growth in, say, six months. The market might be looking further ahead than the industrialists are.

The popular view of knowledgeable insiders is supported by the tendency to focus on a few supporting instances. It is well known that US insiders bought heavily after the 1987 crash, and there were substantial numbers of corporate repurchases of shares authorized (e.g. see Seyhun, 1990; and Netter and Mitchell, 1989). The ratio of insider transactions rose to record levels during the week of 19 October 1987. Top executives were especially active. The insiders were a good guide after the crash. But before the crash, they were a poor guide. Insiders were neither heavy buyers nor heavy sellers during the first nine months of 1987, but in the week of 12 October the insiders started to buy. A reasonable interpretation would be that the insiders got it wrong before the crash and right afterwards: about as useful as flipping a coin.

There have been a number of attempts to study the value of insiders' aggregate trades more formally. Lee and Solt (1986) examined the period May 1971–December 1982. They used data from Vickers Stock Research Corporation, which produces more timely disclosure of insider activity than the SEC. They related the ratio of total insider buying/total insider selling to market movements. They found that, on balance, aggregate insider trading followed market movements, but market movements did not appear to follow insider trading. Lee and Solt looked at extremes of insider activity, tested various trading rules, and so on, but found no case of statistically significant excess returns accruing from a strategy of following insiders.

Seyhun (1988) used SEC data and examined the period January 1975–October 1981, i.e. part of Lee and Solt's (1986) sample. Seyhun used a different approach and concluded that future market returns are predictable to some extent after publication of insider trading information. Nonetheless, he concluded that this information could not be used to obtain a profitable switching strategy between Treasury bills and the stock market, even ignoring transaction costs. Seyhun (1992) extends the analysis from 1975 to 1989. He again finds that the future market return is predictable using past aggregate insider trading. While such trading is related to future real activity, the trading still has some predictive value when future real activity is included as an explanatory variable. When implementation delays are allowed for because of slow reporting, the predictive content of aggregate insider trading is minimal. Chowdhury et al. (1993) also report that there is no profitable trading rule.

It would seem that the aggregate activity of corporate insiders is not a useful forecasting guide for the US stock market. There does not appear to be UK research on this topic.

CONTRARY OPINION

Going against the crowd is often described as contrary thinking or contrarian investment strategy. Going against the crowd just for the sake of it does not seem sensible, but when emotions run strongly and one can see how the crowd could be wrong, a contrarian bet may be warranted. Now there are two potential problems with this line of argument. First, is it true that the market loses touch with reality? And second, how do we know when this has happened?

There is little doubt that investors look at the fundamentals of earnings, dividends, future prospects, and so on. It also seems from the rating that groups of stocks and the market sometime sell on, that how these fundamentals are valued varies—this is discussed further in Chapter 22. The fundamentals are subjected to waves of optimism and pessimism and, occasionally, mania. The first of our two potential problems can probably be answered in favour of the contrarians. Knowing when the crowd has got out of touch with reality is, in a sense, the justification for low-PER and some other value-based share strategies, and is also the basis of value-based tactical asset allocation. Some contrarians base their view on some measure of intrinsic value, but more of them probably act on a view that price trends reverse. Most investors, however, when they talk of contrarian strategies, have something much folksier in mind than price trend reversals. So, just for a change, let's get off the research treadmill and look at some more subjective indicators.

Anyone who has read the investment columns for a period will have seen articles with titles such as 'How to tell if it's the top' or 'How to spot a company going bust'. These articles consist of lists of serious and jokey points, and usually most investors would agree that there is some sense in the lists. The lists are then forgotten. Since there are some sound observations in the lists, we'll resurrect a few here.

Let's begin by looking at the characteristics of a market top. The following points are quoted from Band (1989, p. 34), describing a market top:

- A breathtaking parabolic rise in prices.
- A widespread rejection of old standards of value [it is often said that the four most expensive words in investment are 'this time it's different'].
- A proliferation of dubious investment schemes promising high returns in an inordinately short time.
- Intense and—for a time—successful speculation by uninformed members of the public.
- Popular fascination with leveraged investments.
- Heavy selling by corporate 'insiders' and other investors with a long-term orientation.
- Extremely high trading volume that enriches brokers and snarls back offices.

We can find similar lists for specific areas. The following quotes are from Band (1989, pp. 198–200), discussing the top in the property market:

- Glowing news reports about the booming real estate market, perhaps tempered by worries about rising mortgage rates.
- A peak in housing starts followed by several declines.
- Low vacancy rates in apartments and office buildings, sparking a construction spree. When you see construction crews working on every vacant lot in town, you should think about selling.
- A multiyear low for the local unemployment rate, followed by two or three seemingly innocuous upticks.
- Rude, hard-nosed brokers [estate agents]. The universal hard sell will tip you off that the market is about to go bust.

Now nobody would claim that all these signs apply to every peak and trough, but many of them will apply to very overheated markets. Putting a scientific hat on, one would have to say this is a little vague. But maybe a little subjectivity is worth bearing if it helps avoid being the last buyer. Let's relate these ideas to the UK property market of 1987–89.

House prices had been rising rapidly, and commercial rents, especially in the City of London, were also rising rapidly. The ratio of house prices to income reached new heights. London's Docklands had a forest of construction cranes, and new office buildings were going up in the City. There were no estimates of demand that suggested the onstream supply of office buildings could possibly find tenants. Two tax-avoidance opportunities flourished: Enterprise Zone property schemes and Business Expansion Schemes, which focused on real assets, mainly property. At first, the Enterprise Zone schemes sold mainly buildings that had tenants, but soon there was a move to unlet properties and sometimes properties not yet built, backed by rent 'guarantees'. Unfortunately, tenants can go bust and so too can the property developers involved. Many of the tenants and Enterprise Zone developers did. A large number of Business Expansion Scheme property developers went into liquidation.

The Business Expansion Scheme companies often geared up for investors. The Enterprise Zone schemes encouraged the investors to gear up. For every £1000 invested, the Inland Revenue gave tax relief to higher-rate taxpayers of approximately £350, so the net cost was £650. A yield of 6% on the property produced an income of £60. If the investor borrowed £650 at 9%, the interest would equal the income; so why not borrow the £650, and have an investment for no down-payment? Indeed, if rents rose, the deal would be cash-flow positive. When the building is eventually sold, the investor can pay off his borrowings and pocket the profit. That was the story in the promotional literature. Unfortunately, interest rates soared, many tenants and developers defaulted in a falling property market, rents vaporized, and the investor had a negative income stream and an asset with declining value.

Office rents in Docklands (outside of Canary Wharf) fell from £20 per square foot in 1988 to probably £5 per square foot (after incentives) in 1993. Even at £5, 55% of Docklands commercial property was unlet. This story is a contrarian's dream! Greed, gearing and the top of the market.

Sticking with major moves, many investors believe that one can get a good clue to big market moves by looking at the covers of the news magazines. If *Business Week*, *Time* or *Newsweek* runs a cover story such as 'The death of the dollar', then that is the time to buy the dollar, according to this contrarian approach. Regan (1981) gives some examples. On 1 June 1962, *Time*'s cover story picture was of a large black bear mauling a red bull. The Dow had fallen 21% from December 1961 to May 1962. After the story, the Dow fell another 6% to 536 and then began a four-year climb to 1000 in January 1966. The market then fell to 767 by August. *Time*'s 19 August cover was 'Wall Street: The Nervous Market'. Six weeks later, the Dow bottomed at 744 and then rallied to 943.

Band (1989) reports that Montgomery reviewed *Time* covers back to 1924. He claimed that in four out of five financial cover stories, the outcome within a year was the opposite of what the editors foresaw. This suggests that while not a perfect contrary indicator, cover stories are worth bearing in mind when forming a market view. Some readers may feel uncomfortable with this type of indicator, since it seems to be based on other peoples' incompetence. But there is a more charitable and comforting explanation. As Regan (1981, p. 13) notes:

> The cover story syndrome applies to all journalists—media as well as print. The only time the television camera crews visit the stock exchange or interview leading analysts is when volume and price fluctuations are unusually large. Because the articles and interviews are fostered by extremes in market psychology, they are often ill-timed.

We are not aware of an analysis of UK cover stories. But *The Economist* Christmas 1999 issue (p. 61) carried an interesting article entitled 'We woz wrong'. Reviewing 1999, it noted:

> Our cover 'Drowning in oil', on March 6th, . . . speculated that having fallen to $10 a barrel, the price of oil might soon fall further, even as far as $5 . . . It wasn't long before this was proved wrong. About four days, in fact: the following week, OPEC ministers agreed to cut their production . . . By December, [the oil price] had hit $25 and was therefore getting close to having trebled since our forecast that the price might soon halve.

The Economist also drew attention to its cover story on 'America's bubble economy'. It ran bubble stories on the US stockmarket in April and November 1998 and September 1999. In round number terms, the stories appeared when the S&P 500 was standing at 1100, 1200 and 1300, respectively. At December 1999, it was 1400.

Turning to companies, there have been many lists published of things that make a contrarian squirm. For example, Costello (1992) has provided a list relating to companies likely to go bust. He gives 10 warning signs of candidates for bankruptcy, although his article actually covers more points. The following list combines some of his points and some others, and should be seen in terms of possibly overvalued stocks rather than bankruptcy candidates:

- Reliance on creative accounting (Polly Peck).
- Resignation of directors (Marks and Spencer).
- Changing financial advisers.
- Chairman or managing directors with bow ties, gold bracelets, toupees and sun tans (all these are signs of vain management).
- Moves to new headquarters or sumptuous headquarters buildings (e.g. Saatchi and Saatchi). Before they were common in the UK, this point was often expressed as 'company with atrium'.
- Bullies holding the position of chairman and chief executive.
- Changing the year-end (Maxwell) or company name.
- Bear squeezes and profits warnings. Bear squeezes often do have some basis in reality, and one company profit downgrade is frequently followed by another (e.g. Reed Elsevier, 3 December 1998, 7 June 1999, and 5 August 1999).
- Substantial director share sales.
- The research file on a company is full.

A tough-minded approach would be to say these lists are worthless because they apply when they apply and don't when they don't and this makes good copy for journalists but is not the stuff of professional investment. A kindlier view is that most investors will recognize some truth in these lists, and they remind one that many investment disasters could be avoided if investors showed a bit of common sense and scepticism. The market appears to get carried away by emotion from time to time. Shares that collapse wreak havoc on investment performance. There are thousands of shares in the world that one can invest in: it doesn't seem necessary to gamble in shares, sectors or markets that common sense or a bit of contrary thinking would make one cautious of. Of course, if the company or sector in question comprises a large share of the market index, then the professional money manager may prefer to be wrong with the crowd (of other money managers) rather than take a contrary view. His risks and rewards are not the same as the client's.

Sentiment and Market Levels

Contrary thinking requires going against the crowd. But how can we quantify the crowd's views? For the market as a whole, there are a number of measures. *Investors Intelligence* collects the views of a large number of US investment advisers and calculates a bearish sentiment index (BSI). This is the ratio of the number of bearish advisers to all advisers expressing an opinion, i.e. bearish advisers divided by bulls plus bears. Investment advisers are thought to be bullish at the top and bearish at the bottom. Figure 15.3 relates their views to the DJIA.

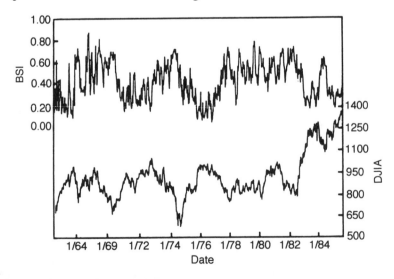

FIGURE 15.3   BSI and DJIA, 1963–85

Source: Solt and Statman (1988, p. 52). Copyright © 1988. Association for Investment Management and Research. Reproduced and republished from the *Financial Analysts Journal* with permission from the Association for Investment Management and Research. All rights reserved.

Can an investor make money from this relationship? Alas, no, according to Solt and Statman (1988). They estimated for the period January 1963–September 1985 an equation of the following form:

$$\text{Return over four weeks} = a + b \times \left(\frac{\text{bearish advisers}}{\text{bulls} + \text{bears}}\right) + \text{random errors.}$$

The sentiment ratio was calculated at the start of the four-week period. The value for b turned out to be not statistically different from zero, i.e. there was no relationship between the ratio and returns. The equation was rerun for 26- and 52-week periods with the same result.

It is sometimes argued that it is at extremes of emotion that a contrary indicator will be of most use. Ratios of above 0.55 and below 0.15 on the BSI are said to be the most important for prediction purposes. Solt and Statman (1988) examined these extremes, their results are shown in Table 15.2.

TABLE 15.2 **The relationship between the BSI and changes in the DJIA in subsequent periods**

DJIA and BSI relationship	4 weeks	26 weeks	52 weeks
Number of observations when DJIA increased following BSI ratio above 0.55	37	12	11
Number of observations when DJIA decreased following BSI ratio above 0.55	37	9	3
Number of observations when DJIA increased following BSI ratio below 0.15	9	3	1
Number of observations when DJIA decreased following BSI ratio below 0.15	7	2	2

Source: Solt and Statman (1988, p. 47). Copyright © 1988. Association for Investment Management and Research. Reproduced and republished from the *Financial Analysts Journal* with permission from the Association for Investment Management and Research. All rights reserved.

Why should the BSI work? The argument is that advisers are trend followers—they will be bullish when the market has risen and when they should be switching tack. Solt and Statman (1988) checked to see whether advisers really were trend followers. They reran the equation shown above, but this time they related return over a one-month period to the BSI at the end of the period and discovered that there was a significant relationship. Now, the important point is that if advisers tend to be trend followers, then a graph of their sentiment is bound to be related closely to a graph of the market. A chart of the relationship will look great to the eye but will not be very useful. The advisers will tend to lag the market rather than lead it. Most of us will be unable to interpret the graph sensibly and will give too much weight to the seemingly strong relationship.

Clarke and Statman (1998) extended this analysis to 1995. They found that the passage of time had not improved the forecasting ability of newsletter writers.

CONCLUDING COMMENTS

A distinction is frequently drawn between fundamental and technical analysis. The distinction is sensible in theory but more problematic in practice. A number of approaches can be viewed as either technical or fundamental.

There are a number of reasons to be suspicious of chart analysis. Little evidence has been put forward by chartists to support their work; the form of chartist statements is often not refutable, i.e. it is unscientific; and it is not clear why, if chartist analysis has merits, it is not already largely discounted in prices. That said, there is evidence that returns are not completely random.

There is interesting work relating to what can be described as momentum, relative strength or returns persistence over three to 12 months. Many investors find sector weighting especially difficult: momentum strategies are worth exploring in this area. There is also interesting work on moving averages. While it may not generate excess returns, the moving average rule is particularly interesting because it has been good at forecasting periods of negative returns. Many investors find selling harder than buying, so this is worth exploring. However, it must be remembered that this work has been on the market as a whole. Since the market is less volatile than individual stocks, the work may have no relevance to shares, where there might be too many whiplashes (quickly reversed signals). Recent evidence suggests that even Dow theory might have something going for it.

Following the investment decisions of insiders may be of limited value. But it is unclear whether adjustments should be made for size. Contrary opinion inevitably appeals to anybody who believes that markets overreact. The problem, at least for the more popular versions of contrary opinion, is getting testable hypotheses to examine. Nonetheless, combining a bit of contrary thinking with some more rigorous techniques will appeal to some investors.

16

Sector Strategy

The debate about top-down versus bottom-up investing has always seemed a little fuzzy to me. I just keep an eye on the economy and ask, where is a sector that's overdue for recognition?
John Neff

Investment organizations vary in the amount of time they devote to sector strategy and in their approach. Some take the pragmatic view that it is too difficult to add value at the sector level and simply set their sector weightings equal to those of an appropriate index or take very modest sector bets. Other managers take a more aggressive stance.

Some managers make stock and sector decisions at the same time, e.g a DDM might show that all bank shares offer exceptional value and this will automatically lead to an overweight position in the bank sector. This would be a bottom-up approach to sector strategy. Other managers form sector views based on macroeconomic views: a top-down approach. This may be criticized because the macroeconomic insights should already be reflected in earnings forecasts. Looking at the macroeconomy as a separate input is double-counting the same factors. This would be true if analysts' forecasts were always up to date or were based on the same macroeconomic view as the investment manager's, but this may not be the case. In the UK, the market has been periodically convulsed by big interest rate or currency moves, and managers must act before analysts revise and circulate their individual stock earnings estimates and views. A broad view of sector strategy related to the macroeconomy may be necessary. Again, a fund manager may rely on external analysts for company forecasts and may take the view that his forecasts for the economy may differ from the analyst's and that he must therefore adjust the analysts' forecasts in some broad-brush way and derive a sector strategy based on his top-down view.

In this chapter, we will comment briefly on these various approaches. We begin with some broad aspects of sector strategy.

WHAT IS A SECTOR?

Sectors are groups of stocks that have some features in common in terms of the industry in which they operate. In both the US and the UK the major indexes used for portfolio evaluation consist of a number of sectors, but the sectors are aggregated in different ways. In the first edition of this book, we said that in the UK investment managers would typically look at the FTSE All-Share Index sectors aggregated in terms of the type of industry involved, e.g. industrial, consumer and financial. US investment managers were more likely to aggregate sectors in a way that reflects their response to the economy and the business cycle, e.g. cyclical, growth and stable. Since those comments, the FTSE All-Share sectors have been revised to include cyclical and non-cyclical groupings. Table 16.1 shows the FTSE All-Share Index by sector at the start of 2000, and the S&P 500 by sector as it was some years ago, and the sort of aggregation that might be used by an investment manager. US fund managers in practice use a few more categories than shown in Table 16.1, but this classification is shown because it was used in an interesting study by Farrell (1974, 1983) (for a related study, see Arnott, 1980).

Farrell (1983, p. 206) explained his sector groupings as follows:

- Growth: 'Earnings of these companies are expected to show a faster rate of secular expansion than the average company.'
- Cyclical: 'These companies have an above-average exposure to the economic cycle. Earnings would be expected to be down more than the average in a recession and up more than the average during the expansion phase of the business cycle.'
- Stable: 'These companies have a below-average exposure to the economic cycle. . . . Earnings of these companies are the most adversely affected by inflation but fare relatively the best during periods of decelerating inflation, or disinflation.'
- Energy: 'The earnings of these companies are affected by the economic cycle but, most importantly, by trends in the relative price of energy.'

Farrell wondered whether the classification shown above really consisted of homogeneous stock groups. Since stocks tend to move with the market as a whole, Farrell stripped out this market effect and then examined monthly returns for 100 stocks over the period 1961–69. If the aggregate sectors had any meaning, then stock returns should be correlated within sectors, but not between sectors. That is what he found. This suggests that the approach to sector aggregation sometimes used in the US, and that puts disparate industries into the same broad group, is worthwhile. Farrell's findings suggest that there may be scope to add value by an active sector strategy, although this is not to say managers will realize the potential. UK fund managers think in terms of the sector classification of the All-Share. While this has moved in the right direction, it probably could be improved. For example, the basic industries grouping might go into a cyclical classification. UK managers might find it profitable to replicate Farrell's study for the UK.

SEXY SECTORS AND SORROWFUL SECTORS

You might expect that sectors' performances diverge. But you may be surprised by the extent. Table 16.2 shows the top five and bottom five sectors in 1999.

TABLE 16.1 Sector classifications

UK sectors classified by FTSE All-Share Index	US sectors classified by type*
Resources	Growth
Mining	Hospital management
Oil and gas	Pollution control
Basic industries	Cosmetics
Chemicals	Drugs
Construction and building materials	Hospital supplies
Forestry and paper	Electronics
Steel and other metals	Entertainment
General industrials	Hotels and restaurants
Aerospace and defence	Computers
Diversified industrials	Oil service
Electronic and electrical equipment	Newspapers and broadcasters
Engineering and machinery	Speciality chemicals
Cyclical consumer goods	Growth retailers
Automobiles	Stable
Household goods and textiles	Food processors
Non-cyclical consumer goods	Beverage
Beverages	Tobacco
Food producers and processors	Household products
Health	Retailers
Packaging	Utilities
Personal care and household products	Telephones
Pharmaceuticals	Banks
Tobacco	Insurance
Cyclical services	Finance
Distributors	Cyclical
General retailers	Aluminium
Leisure, entertainment and hotels	Copper
Media and photography	Miscellaneous metals
Restaurants, pubs and breweries	Autos
Support services	Auto parts and trucks
Transport	Building materials
Non-cyclical services	Chemicals
Food and drug retailers	Containers
Telecommunications services	Textiles
Utilities	Tyres
Electricity	Electrical equipment
Gas distribution	Machinery
Water	Forest products and paper
Information technology	Steel
Information technology hardware	Railroads
Software and computer services	Energy
Non-financials	Coal
Financials	Domestic oil
Banks	International oil
Insurance	Crude-oil products
Life assurance	
Investment companies	
Real estate	
Speciality and other finance	

*Source: Farrell (1983, p. 223).

TABLE 16.2 Best and worst performing UK sectors in 1999

Sector	% price change
Information technology hardware	+635
Software and computer services	+132
Steel and metals	+131
Mining	+126
Electronics	+104
Electricity	−25
Personal care and household	−31
Tobacco	−31
Food producers	−31
Water	−37

You may remember that 1999 was the year of technology stocks, and it is not surprising that three of the top five sectors were technology sectors. The degree of outperformance by IT hardware is very surprising. However, the other two technology sectors were matched by two rather dreary sectors, steel and metals and mining. Both are cyclical sectors and benefited from optimism about world economic conditions. Steel and metals is a somewhat artificial sector, consisting of one company, Corus (formed from the merger of British Steel and Hoogovens). The underperforming sectors were affected by a variety of concerns. For example, the water and electricity sectors suffered from regulatory fears, and some water companies cut their dividends. Tobacco stocks were overshadowed by litigation concerns in the US. Food producers suffered from continued pressure for lower prices from food retailers and fear about the effect of Wal-Mart's entry into the UK.

Clearly, there are big returns available to anyone who can spot the best sectors and avoid the worst.

SECTOR AND SHARE WEIGHTINGS

In Table 16.3, we show the weightings of the various sectors at the end of May 2000 for three indexes, the FTSE All-Share, FTSE 100 and the FTSE SmallCap. As you can see, the sector weightings (by market capitalization) vary significantly within an index and between indexes. For example, the telecommunications sector comprised about 18% of the All-Share, while packaging was about 0.1%. Or consider construction and building materials, which is around 0.2% of the Footsie but about 10% of the SmallCap index. Companies in this sector are not especially large, but there are a lot of them. They therefore are not a big percentage of a large-cap index, but are important in a smaller-cap index.

The number of companies in each sector varies substantially. In the All-Share, while steel and other metals consists of one company, the investment companies sector consists of 126 companies. Some large sectors consist of a few very large companies. In Table 16.4 we show the contribution to the All-Share and Footsie made by various companies and indexes.

TABLE 16.3   Sector weightings for various indexes, May 2000

Sector	Sector as % of index		
	All-Share	FTSE 100	SmallCap
Resources	13.2	15.6	1.4
Mining	1.7	2.0	0.0
Oil and gas	11.6	13.7	1.4
Basic industries	2.9	1.1	12.6
Chemicals	1.0	0.6	2.2
Construction and building materials	1.6	0.2	10.3
Forestry and paper	0.1	0.0	0.0
Steel and other metals	0.2	0.2	0.0
General industrials	3.3	1.9	9.0
Aerospace and defence	1.3	1.2	1.7
Diversified industrials	0.0	0.0	0.0
Electronic and electrical equipment	1.1	0.7	2.5
Engineering and machinery	0.9	0.0	4.9
Cyclical consumer goods	0.6	0.5	2.5
Automobiles	0.5	0.5	1.5
Household goods and textiles	0.1	0.0	1.1
Non-cyclical consumer goods	15.9	17.0	8.9
Beverages	1.7	1.9	0.5
Food producers and processors	1.8	1.6	3.4
Health	0.6	0.3	1.5
Packaging	0.1	0.0	0.7
Personal care and household products	0.3	0.3	0.7
Pharmaceuticals	10.6	12.3	2.2
Tobacco	0.9	0.6	0.0
Cyclical services	15.0	11.8	28.7
Distributors	0.4	0.0	2.7
General retailers	2.6	2.2	6.1
Leisure, entertainment and hotels	1.5	1.0	4.4
Media and photography	5.6	5.6	3.5
Restaurants, pubs and breweries	1.2	0.8	2.4
Support services	1.8	0.9	6.2
Transport	1.9	1.3	3.7
Non-cyclical services	18.9	21.4	1.3
Food and drug retailers	1.6	1.5	1.0
Telecommunications services	17.3	20.9	0.2
Utilities	4.0	3.8	0.9
Electricity	1.9	1.9	0.0
Gas distribution	1.4	1.7	0.0
Water	0.8	0.3	0.9
Information technology	4.2	4.1	3.8
Information technology hardware	1.8	2.1	0.1
Software and computer services	2.4	2.0	3.7
Non-financials	77.8	78.5	68.8
Financials	22.0	21.8	30.9
Banks	12.3	14.8	0.0
Insurance	2.0	2.2	2.1
Life assurance	2.4	3.4	0.0
Investment companies	2.7	0.5	18.6
Real estate	1.4	0.3	7.0
Speciality and other finance	1.1	0.6	3.2

Aggregate sectors (e.g. resources) have been calculated from the original data, not the rounded sector data.

Source: Derived from HSBC (2000, p. 12).

TABLE 16.4   Companies and indexes as a percentage of the All-Share and Footsie, May 2000

	% of All-Share/FTSE 100
Largest 5 companies	29.9/36.3
Largest 15 companies	49.7/60.3
Largest 50 companies	70.8/85.9
FTSE 100	82.4
FTSE 350	95.8
SmallCap	4.2

Dimson et al. (2000, pp. 23–7) show the UK top 100 shares' sector composition and weights at the start and end of the twentieth century. As you would expect, there has been substantial change. Railway stocks constituted 49% of the market capitalization of the top 100 shares at the start of the century. The largest three shares comprised 30% of the market capitalization of the top 100 shares in 1900, and the top 10 shares over 50%. This concentration declined, albeit erratically, over the course of the century, but increased quite sharply from the mid 1990s. With the Vodafone/Mannesmann and Glaxo Wellcome/SmithKline Beecham mergers in 2000, the degree of concentration in the top 100 will return to the levels of the start of the previous century.

Institutional investors would be happy if they could consistently beat the market by 1–2% p.a. The structure of the market is such that if you could call a couple of the big sectors correctly, and index weighted everything else, you could achieve the magic extra couple of per cent performance. Indeed, some of the stocks are so large that if you could call a few of these you would outperform.

Some commentators have pointed to the size of a few sectors and stocks and argued that this is a consequence of index funds, and that it drives the market ever higher. This seems unlikely. First, the big sectors don't always outperform. None were in the top five positions in 1999. Telecoms and oils were in the top half of sector performance, but banks only moved inline with the market, while pharmaceuticals underperformed. Big stocks often fade away. Remember Hanson, BTR, and Marks and Spencer? And going further back, the railway stocks have also largely faded away.

Imagine the UK has adopted the euro. Should the manager of a UK portfolio look at the All-Share index (it is the UK market); a European index (all European shares become UK shares because there is no currency risk); or the UK index, but include European shares if they are cheaper than UK shares (the UK index reflects the structure of the UK economy, but European shares are substitutes for UK shares)? We discuss this in Chapter 21.

SECTORS HAVE DIFFERENT FEATURES

Even if a fund manager does not attempt to make sector bets, sectors are of some interest. Different industries have different features and it is sensible when appraising accounting ratios to make comparisons within sectors. For example, sales margins vary greatly between industries, and the only sensible way to judge whether, say, Allders has a high or low margin, is to look at comparable firms within the General Retailers sector. Again, some ratios are important in some sectors and not in others. A stock/turnover ratio is important in the retail trade but less so in banking.

Fund managers and analysts often focus on a few indicators as a guide to what is happening in a sector, and these indicators vary with the sector. It is beyond the scope of this book to provide a detailed analysis of unique sector features, but we'll give a few examples:

- Retail and restaurant industries. When analysing sales and earnings data for these industries, it is usual to break them down into same-store basis and new openings. For example, a hamburger chain might be suffering falling sales at each restaurant, but by opening new restaurants it will mask this in the aggregate figures. If the restaurant openings slow or stop, sales may collapse. Same-stores/new-stores analysis will show what is really happening.
- Hotels. Two statistics that are watched in this sector are the occupancy rate—heads on beds—(number of room nights sold divided by number of room nights available) and revenue per available room.

In the above two cases, we are simply looking at rules of thumb that are helpful in forecasting earnings, or in assessing earnings figures. In the case of life insurance, earnings figures are treated in a different way.

- When a life company sells an endowment policy, it incurs administration costs and pays an insurance broker a commission. Profits will not be earned for some years. Conventional accounting will show the firm to be making a loss. Alternatively, if it stops taking on new business, it avoids the up-front losses and makes money from earlier sales. The company appears to be doing well. To get round this, the concept of embedded value may be used. This is the expected value of contracts already signed. (A related, but more complex, notion is achieved profits).

Companies that have never earned a profit are especially difficult to value. Internet stocks are a good example. A company such as Freeserve gives free access to the Internet. What is it worth?

- A website in the UK will earn money from the telephone companies paying part of the cost of the calls subscribers incur. But the real money will come from advertisers and income from transactions generated by the site. The more site visits, the better. The statistic that is watched is the unique site visits (USV) in a month. If we don't know that, but we know the number of pages visited on a site in a month, we can estimate the number of site visits (in the US, each site visit leads to 28 pages being visited). To value the company, we have to put a value on a site visit.

- Most pure Internet stocks are in the early stages of growth. They may or may not be making a profit, but even if they are, their free cash flow is likely to be negative. Free cash flow is a measure of cash flow from operations and also capital expenditures and dividend payments to shareholders. Firms with negative free cash flow must spend cash reserves, sell investments, reduce capital expenditure, improve profitability, or obtain cash from borrowing or issuing equity. A rapidly growing firm making losses will find it difficult to change its business activities, and may also find it difficult to raise new finance. Accordingly, there is interest in how long its existing cash will last. The 'burn rate' is obtained by relating the amount of cash a firm is consuming to its available cash.

Some companies have earnings, but nobody looks at them.

- Investment trusts are companies that invest in the shares of other companies. They may have a quite general orientation, such as UK equities, or be specialized, such as Japanese smaller companies. They produce standard accounts but the earnings figure doesn't really mean anything being simply dividends received less expenses. Investors are more interested in net asset value growth. The prospect for this depends on whether the market the trust is invested in is one that investors expect to do well, and whether the manager is any good, i.e. whether he or she will beat the market or underperform it. Since investment trusts normally sell at a fluctuating discount to asset value, investors judge whether the discount is abnormally large (and may be expected to narrow), or vice versa.

Every sector has its quirks.

FOR EVERY SECTOR THERE IS A SEASON

Many managers think in terms of a stylized economic cycle, with different sectors performing at different stages of the cycle. Figure 16.1 shows one version of when different US sectors show their best relative performance. Figures like this have to come with a wealth warning: no two cycles are the same and the research basis of such exhibits is unclear.

It used to seem that US managers were more inclined to think in terms of an economic cycle than UK managers. Perhaps because of the openness of the UK economy and more dramatic interest rate moves, UK managers seemed to be at least as interested in questions such as which sectors gain from a rise/fall in sterling and which sectors are interest rate sensitive. These questions seemed to be approached in a manner that divorced them from the economic cycle, presumably a consequence of the crisis nature of much UK economic policy. This difference in emphasis appears to have been changing in recent years, as the UK economy has become more stable.

Nonetheless, let's look at the effect of interest rate changes. Wadhwani (1991) examined the interest sensitivity of stocks based on a multiple regression equation for the period 1970–91. Sectors were defined in terms of the All-Share sector

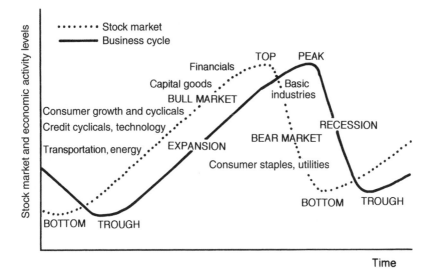

FIGURE 16.1   Business cycle and relative sector performance
Source: Markese (1986, p. 31). Reproduced and reprinted by permission of the American Association of Individual Investors.

classification at the time. The most interest-rate-sensitive sectors were (most responsive first), telephone networks (–), merchant banks (–), oil and gas (+), property (–), composite insurance (–), brewers and distillers (–) and chemicals (+). The stock market as a whole benefits from lower interest rates; responsiveness is measured here as the additional effect on a sector over and above the market impact. The sign of each sector shows the response relative to a rise in interest rates, i.e. telephone networks perform relatively poorly, oil and gas relatively well.

These findings are interesting, but how useful are they? First, can we be confident that the historical relationship will apply in the future? Sectors change their economic structure over time, and the composition of the stock market continually evolves. Second, the amount of variation explained is low, although not to be ignored, and high in comparison to many relationships in investment research. Third, to use the historical relationship, we must make interest-rate forecasts. These may be just as hard to make as sector forecasts. Alternatively, we may wait for an interest change to take place, and then react quickly. However, big changes in interest rates or sterling often lead to a sharp movement in markets the day they happen and the bulk of any relationship may be quickly discounted. This catalogue of problems may lead many managers to place more reliance on sector valuations than macroeconomic themes as a way of deciding sector weightings.

SECTOR VALUATIONS

Weighting sectors based on their valuation can be approached in several ways. A couple of possibilities are discussed by Dreman and Lufkin (1997), who ranked US stocks by price-to-earnings, price-to-cash flow, price-to-book and price-to-dividends. They then formed portfolios based on the lowest quintile of PER stocks, the next quintile, and so on, and repeated this for the other variables. The portfolios were left intact for up to five years (i.e. they didn't rebalance the portfolios periodically). The study covered the period 1970–95. During this period, they found that the value portfolios outperformed the market. For example, the lowest PER quintile portfolio outperformed the market, over one-, two-, three-, four- and five-year holding periods. The annualized return difference was a low of +2.9% and a high of +3.9%. Low price-to-cash flow and low price-to-book did equally as well, while high dividend-to-price did only modestly better than the market. The portfolios composed of the highest PER quintile, highest price-to-cash flow, etc. all underperformed the market.

Next, Dreman and Lufkin ranked stocks in each industry, as defined by the standard industrial classification (SIC), by the four valuation variables. Now, for example, the low-PER portfolio consisted not of the 20% of stocks with the lowest absolute PER, but the lowest PER quintile of stocks from each industry. These portfolios might be described as relative value portfolios, as opposed to the preceding paragraph's absolute value. All the value portfolios again outperformed, and by similar amounts to the absolute value portfolios, although the high-dividend portfolios did a little better than before.

Finally, Dreman and Lufkin ranked stocks by the PER etc. of the industry they are in, i.e. the lowest PER quintile consists of stocks from the lowest quintile PER industries, irrespective of the stocks' PERs. The value portfolios still outperformed over most periods, but by much less than before. For example, the five-year annualized return difference between the lowest quintile portfolio and the highest was 8.62% for the absolute value portfolios described two paragraphs above. For the industry-based absolute value portfolio, the figure was 2.92%.

This study would lend support to the view that instead of buying cheap sectors, you should buy cheap stocks relative to the sector they are in.

A different approach is to buy sectors that are cheap in relation to their own history on some valuation measure. For example, a sector may have sold at a PER premium to the market over the past 20 years of, say, 20%, with a range of –5% (i.e. a discount) to +45%. If the sector currently stands at a premium of say, 10%, the sector might be deemed cheap.

Jones (1989) looked at the two approaches of buying sectors that are absolutely cheap and those that are cheap relative to their own history. He used US data for the period 1969–87, and measured cheapness in terms of 12 measures (e.g. DDM, earnings yield, small capitalization, etc.) and a multifactor model combining these measures. Unfortunately, both approaches appeared to be unreliable guides to sector strategy.

Wadhwani (1992) looked at sector selection strategies for the UK based on buying (i) sectors trading at a PER discount to their historical average, and (ii) sectors with a dividend yield above their historical average. His dividend strategy results will be outlined here. His buy signal was that the relative dividend yield should exceed its average by more than one-half its standard deviation. Over the period 1974–91, this strategy led to a 4.4% p.a. outperformance of the purchased sectors over the residuals. The portfolio was rebalanced quarterly. It was not stated how diversified the portfolio was, nor the returns after costs.

Of course, many stocks sell on high historical dividend yields when the market anticipates a dividend cut. Wadhwani tested an alternative strategy of holding high-yield sectors when GNP growth was not expected to be negative (dividend cuts are most likely in recessions) and to hold the other sectors when it was. Outperformance increased to 5.5% p.a. This outperformance increased further if high-yielding sectors could only be purchased if they also had above-average earnings growth. Again, one wonders how diversified such a portfolio was.

Wadhwani claimed that both low PER and high dividend yield relative to history are useful signals. Generally, he found the dividend signal to be the more powerful, but for some sectors the PERR was more important, for example construction, electricals, electronics, food retailing, health and household, and insurance brokers.

CONCLUDING COMMENTS

We have reviewed evidence relating to how an investor might set sector strategy. We have discussed the way sectors might be aggregated into economically mean- ingful categories. We reviewed some material on approaching sector strategy in terms of economic themes, and on a valuation basis. If investors think they have information nobody else has (e.g. information that sterling will be devalued) or there are valuation errors (e.g. sectors with a high yield relative to their own history) they may wish to make a sector bet. You may not have found the evidence discussed in this chapter compelling. If you didn't, you will understand why some investors set their sector weights equal to those of an index.

There is a general point to be made here. Many investors are embarrassed to admit they do not know how to add value on some issue. Yet Warren Buffett argues that the independent investor has a great advantage: he can stand at the baseball plate and wait forever until he gets the perfect pitch (see Train, 1981, p. 15). Investment is one of the few games where you get to choose exactly how and when you will play. If you can pick stocks, then do so, and if you can't, then index. And ditto for sectors. If you can pick markets, do so, and if you can't, then just adhere to your strategic asset weights. In investment, knowing what you don't know is extremely valuable.

17

Constructing a Share Portfolio

There are three classes of people who don't think markets work: the Cubans, the North Koreans and active managers.

Rex Sinquefield

There are two ways of constructing a share portfolio: by making active bets or by passively following an index. If you believe that the market is efficient, then you should index. If you believe it isn't, but few managers can exploit the fact, then you should also index. If you believe the market is inefficient and you can exploit this, then you should make active bets. We begin with the passive approach to constructing a share portfolio.

INDEX FUNDS

Active investment management is the major theme of this book, but the passive approach must be discussed because it is important intellectually and in the real world. Active investment management attempts to outperform the return on indexes by selecting underpriced shares and asset classes. Passive management involves holding securities to match the return on an index. Because of this tie to an index, passive management is often referred to as indexation or index fund management. Both bonds and equities may be indexed, but the discussion here relates to equities.

There are two important practical reasons for discussing passive management. First, active managers have not been very successful at outperforming indexes, and some investors and trustees have concluded that simply matching an index is a reasonable strategy. Second, investment does not have to be all or nothing; it may make sense for active managers to index parts of their portfolios.

Wells Fargo in the US created the first equity index fund in 1971. Since then indexing has grown rapidly in both the US and the UK. Indexing is generally associated with institutional investment; although a number of retail unit trust products are available, in the UK these have a small market share. In a 1999 survey, to which 300 of the 1000 largest UK pension schemes responded, Phillips and Drew (see Treynor, 1999) found that about half the funds employed only active managers, about 2% had only passive managers, and about half employed a combination. Interestingly, it was the smaller funds that were most heavily represented amongst the passive only, and the largest amongst the combination. For the schemes using the combination of active and passive management, about 41% of their assets were passively managed. Greenwich Associates, a US consulting firm, based on the expectations of major UK funds expect 31% of all domestic equities (up from 23% in 1995) and 26% of domestic fixed interest to be managed passively in 2001.

Index funds give up the chance to outperform an index for the security of not underperforming. In practice, broad-market index funds in the UK and the US have often outperformed the average active fund manager. For example, one of the early providers of index funds for the retail investor in the UK was Morgan Grenfell (now part of Deutsche Bank). For the decade to December 1999, *Money Management* figures show that the Deutsche UK Equity Index Tracker unit trust ranked 49th out of 157 predominantly actively managed unit trusts investing for growth in the UK market. The Deutsche Japan index fund, however, also ranked 49th amongst Japanese funds over the same period, but the total number of funds was only 51. In Japan, then, indexing was a disaster.

Selecting an Index to Track

When setting up an index fund, the first issue that has to be tackled is which index will be the benchmark. This will depend upon the objective of the investor. For example, investors who wished to index their entire UK and US equity investments would probably choose broad indexes, such as the FTSE All-Share and the S&P 500. It might be felt that 500 shares is not a very broad coverage for an economy as large as the US, and involves too much of a big company bias. In that case, the Wilshire 5000 might be thought appropriate. If an investor thought he had skill in selecting small stocks, then he might wish to index the large stocks and actively manage small stocks. In the UK, such an investor might choose the FTSE 100 as the large stock index benchmark.

Clearly, there is no correct answer to the question of which index to track. It depends on the objective. But for any given objective, say investing in large companies, some indexes are better for tracking than others. Normally, an arithmetic capitalization weighted index will be used, for reasons explained in Chapter 6. Some indexes have a large number of non-investable stocks. A non-investable stock is one in which the index fund cannot invest. For example, some countries do not allow foreigners to buy certain types of stocks or certain classes of equity. If the non-investable stock is included in the index, an index fund run by a foreigner will inevitably find it hard to track the index, i.e. there will be unavoidable tracking error. The size of this tracking error can be calculated and allowed for, but it might be better to select a different index that does not have this problem, e.g. the FTSE All-World Index Series.

Methods of Indexation

Having chosen an index, the next step is to select a method of indexation. There are four main methods, listed below, and each will be discussed in turn:

- full replication
- stratified sampling
- optimization
- synthetic funds.

Full Replication

Full replication involves buying all the stocks in the index, and in the same proportion. So, if stock ABC is 7.2% of the index, then 7.2% of the fund is invested in ABC. And if XYZ is 0.2% of the index, then 0.2% of the fund goes into XYZ. This approach can involve tedious administrative chores. A large number of stocks may have to be bought (and some of the smaller ones may be difficult to buy), and a large number of dividends handled. These dividends have to be reinvested in the correct proportions. The fund has to be adjusted for rights issues, acquisitions, and changes in the index.

A fully replicated fund will track an index closely, but not exactly, because the index does not have the costs associated with setting up the fund, reinvesting dividends, and custody. Moreover, calculations of the index with dividends reinvested usually assume that dividends are reinvested on the ex-dividend date, although the income will not be received by a fund for some time.

Contrary to the assertions of many journalists, indexed funds do not have to buy more of a stock as its price goes up, provided the index is an arithmetic capitalization-weighted index. For example, if stock ABC above doubles, and no other stock moves, and if the index was 100 before ABC's price change, then it will rise to 107.2. ABC will be 13.4% of the index $[(14.4/107.2) \times 100\%]$. It will automatically be 13.4% of the fund too. No rebalancing is required.

Stratified Sampling

Instead of holding all the stocks in an index, the stratified sampling approach aims to track the index by holding only a sample of stocks in the index. There are a variety of sampling techniques.

If an investor aimed to track the FTSE All-Share Index, all stocks above a certain size, say 0.25% of the index, might be purchased, and in proportion to their market capitalization. Further stocks might then be purchased to bring the sector distribution of the sample into line with the index. This approach will inevitably have a large stock bias, and, if there is a small stock effect, lead to large tracking errors.

An alternative approach is to set each sector weight in the sample equal to the index sector weight. Each sector then might be split into large, medium and small stocks, and samples drawn from each of these subcategories. One could go further and try to ensure that the sector samples broadly match the index with regard to a few variables, such as PER, yield and beta. This introduces a modest degree of optimization, which is discussed below.

Generally the tracking error from stratified sampling will be low, albeit a little worse than full replication, although if some individual stocks or small stocks as a group do exceptionally well, then the tracking error can be substantially greater. If all costs are allowed for in calculations of tracking errors, a stratified sample index fund could track better than a fully replicated fund if brokerage commissions or custody costs have a sliding scale (i.e. higher proportionate fees for small deals) or include a fixed sum per transaction.

Optimization

Optimization is a sample method based on the view that the return from a stock is determined by its exposure to certain attributes such as size, PER, volatility, growth, etc. In the UK, proprietary optimization models sold by BARRA use about 40 variables in the optimization procedure, which attempts to ensure that the sample has the same characteristics as the index with regard to these variables.

This seems rather hard conceptual work compared with stratified sampling, but optimization adherents, such as Rudd (1980, pp. 60–61) argue that stratified sampling 'is unsophisticated in that the only control of tracking error is by minimizing the deviations of portfolio holdings from index holdings along the two dimensions of, usually, capitalization and industry groups. Unfortunately, the intuition that keeping the differences in holdings small will cause the tracking error also to be small is frequently erroneous.' Stratified sampling adherents criticize optimization because it involves some data interpretation so that there is a blurring of the distinction between passive and active management. Moreover, the optimization model assumes that historical risk and return relationships will hold in the future, which is not necessarily true. Also, as the characteristics of the market and stocks change, portfolio rebalancing will be required. Tracking errors can vary from year to year and from user to user.

Synthetic Index Funds

It is possible to construct synthetic index funds by using a derivative product, a stock index futures. A futures is a contract that requires investors to buy or sell a given quantity of a specified asset on a specified future date at a specific price (see Chapter 21). Futures have traditionally been important for agricultural products, but they now cover financial instruments and stock market indexes. A rapidly increasing number of indexes are now traded on futures markets, both on their local market and in the US. Because no physical commodity underlies an index, stock index futures are settled by cash when the contract expires.

It is possible to construct an index fund by buying futures. A single transaction would suffice to index the S&P 500 by stock index futures. Apart from the simplicity, futures involve much lower costs. Bid–ask spreads are lower, commissions are lower, and stock exchange taxes are often avoided. Liquidity is often better in the futures markets than the underlying markets, and execution may be easier. For funds with inflows and outflows of money, it is easier to adjust exposure in the futures market than in the equity market. (For more details of the advantages of futures, see Bruce and Eisenberg, 1992.)

Against these advantages it must be noted that futures are not available for all indexes, for example there is a future on the FTSE 100 but not on the FTSE All-Share. However, it would be possible to track reasonably well a broad index, such as the MSCI EAFE or the FT-Actuaries World Index by combining various local indexes (see Meier, 1991).

There are a number of tracking risks with synthetics. First, there is the possibility that the futures will be mispriced against stocks at the time of purchase. The FTSE 100 futures has been mispriced by as much as 2%, although the S&P 500 has seldom been more than 0.5% mispriced. Second, futures contracts are short dated and managers wanting to buy large positions will have to operate with the most liquid contracts, which are usually those expiring in three to six months. This means the manager must roll over the contracts periodically to a later date. At each roll-over, there is a pricing risk. Third, in calculating the theoretical price for a future, both dividend and interest rate assumptions have to be made. If the forecasts are incorrect, then there will be tracking error. Fourth, cash-settled stock index futures are on a daily marked-to-market basis, i.e. any gain or loss on a future must be settled daily. This means that in a falling market, the futures investor will have to pay away cash, thereby earning less interest than anticipated. This will lead to underperformance. In a rising market, the fund will outperform.

In practice, there are few synthetic index funds outside the US.

Tracking Error

It is worth saying a little about tracking error, i.e. the amount an index fund deviates from its benchmark index. Many investors become obsessed with tracking error—the smaller the better, they argue. However, with the sampling approach, increasing the sample size will always reduce the tracking error. (Examples of tracking statistics and trade-offs are included in a series of publications by Mossaheb, e.g. 1988a and 1988b). Also, there will always be a trade-off between administrative chores and tracking error, and the investor must decide the optimal blend.

Further, it is worth asking whether the size of the tracking error, within reason, really matters. Is the real objective of an index fund to exactly match the index, or to avoid the unpleasant surprises that can result from an active manager underperforming by a very large amount? If the latter, a tracking error of, say, 0.5% rather than 0.35% does not seem very important.

The tracking error is, however, important as a control measure. If the change in the index and the change in the portfolio are measured daily, one can check whether the tracking error is behaving randomly. Some days the fund should outperform the index, and some days it should underperform. Based on historical data, the standard deviation of the historical tracking error can be calculated and the size of the tracking error can be related to historical experience. If the tracking error is behaving non-randomly, or growing in size, the index fund should be rebalanced, i.e. stocks should be bought and sold to get a closer match to the index.

There is an important point here. The tracking error based on market prices and ignoring costs is the best way of seeing whether the fund is correctly structured. However, what interests the investor is the tracking error after costs and this may affect indexing tactics, especially for smaller company funds. Sinquefield (1991) shows that in practice it may be better to be as much concerned with achieving good trades as attempting to always have the exact index weights. It is important that the quantitative staff and the dealers for an index fund work closely together.

The Future

In the future, the UK will probably follow the US in developing a number of 'enhanced' index funds. Such funds are tilted to stress attributes that are thought to lead to outperformance. Funds may also engage in arbitrage by holding stocks or futures depending on which are cheap relative to the other. Passive funds are also likely to be held alongside active funds to gain exposure to areas where the manager lacks expertise, such as small stocks or emerging markets, or for practical reasons.

A good example of a practical reason for indexing concerns small overseas stocks. Many fund managers' foreign holdings have underperformed the local indexes. There may be many reasons for this, but in the 1980s one was probably the small-company effect. A manager running a UK pension fund might invest, say, 8% of the fund in continental Europe. With the prospect of investing in perhaps 10 countries, the number of holdings in each country is probably going to be limited. Even in France and Germany, perhaps no more than five or six stocks might be held, and fewer in the other, smaller countries. Where a manager holds one to six stocks in a country, it is unlikely that a top-down manager will invest in small stocks; to do so would be to take a stock rather than a country bet. Inevitably, the fund will have a rather blue-chip bias. This could kill performance. One solution would be to invest part of this European exposure in a European smaller companies index fund. This would seem to be a sensible blend of active and passive management.

ACTIVE SHARE SELECTION

If the efficient market theory is true, we might be able to explain how assets are priced. The first model that we discussed that attempts this was the CAPM. The original CAPM is a single-index or single-factor model. It states that return on an asset is linked to a single factor, the market, by the asset's beta. The theory assumes that the only reason two stocks' prices would move together is because they are both moving with the market. That is clearly not the case. It is clear that there are industry or sector effects as well. This naturally leads to the notion of multifactor models, where returns depend on both a market factor and industry factors. These models were popular for a period, although the evidence was somewhat mixed. Some researchers found the single-factor model to be superior, while others found the multifactor models to be superior.

A different type of multifactor model is the APT. This looks to fundamental economic factors as the source of risk and drivers of returns. The relevant economic factors can be deduced from the DDM. Yet another model is Fama and French's three-factor model. This explains returns in terms of risk—CAPM risk, economic distress risk (reflected in the returns of a portfolio of value stocks), and undiversifiable risk (reflected in small-firm returns).

Elton and Gruber (1997) describe these three forms of multifactor theories as pre-specified. The first two versions no doubt are, but the three-factor model, while propounded as a general model, looks to many investors to be a theory that was invented after the event to fit the empirical facts that otherwise either reject CAPM or reject the efficient market theory.

Another group of multifactor theories are unashamedly empirical. The first of these is the statistical factor analysis approach to APT. Here, the existence of factors is deduced from data manipulation. Nothing is pre-specified; indeed, the factors found are nameless unless you can guess what they may be measuring.

A different type of approach is that taken by Sharpe (1982). He tried to identify the major factors that had generated returns on the NYSE in the period 1931–79. The factors or attributes he selected for study were chosen 'more or less ex cathedra'. He examined dividend yield, size of firm, S&P 500 market beta, alpha, an historical bond beta (i.e. the equivalent of the market beta but calculated against long-term bonds) and eight sector membership variables. Sharpe found that beta alone 'explained' less than 4% of the variation of a security's return. When the other attributes were added, this rose to about 8% for all attributes excluding sectors, and over 10% including sectors. This means that not much of the variation in returns was explained by the model, although it would be sufficient to add value to a stock-selection process. Sharpe noted that commercial models like his were already in use. They were provided by US firms such as Barra, Wells Fargo Investment Advisers, and Wilshire Associates. Using the large anomalies literature, these early ad hoc models have become more complex in recent years (e.g. Haugen and Baker, 1996).

This discussion is summarized in Table 17.1. The various models may be used in different circumstances. For example, you might use 2.1.1 for sector analysis, 2.1.2 to understand effect of basic economic forces on a portfolio, 2.1.3 for performance measurement, and 2.2.2 for share selection. In what follows, we assume that the ad hoc approach is the most appropriate way of selecting shares. If you adopt this approach you should ask yourself a number of questions. Figure 17.1 provides a guide.

If you believe a variable/style has predictive value, then you should make sure that this is true and not a result of inadequate methodology. Are the findings a

TABLE 17.1   Asset-pricing models

1. Single-index models—the market model (Sharpe, 1963)
2. Multi-index models
    2.1. Pre-specified
        2.1.1. Market plus industries (Cohen and Pogue, 1967)
        2.1.2. Surprises in economic indexes (Chen et al., 1986)
        2.1.3. Portfolios of traded securities (Fama and French, 1996a) (e.g. index of small minus
              large)
    2.2. Empirical
        2.2.1. Statistical factors (Roll and Ross, 1980)
        2.2.2. Ad hoc factors/attributes (Sharpe, 1982; Haugen and Baker, 1996)

result of survival bias, data mining, inadequate allowance for bid–ask spreads, etc.? If you believe that the findings are true, are they a result of a risk premium, in which case there is no risk-adjusted abnormal return. Risk can be interpreted broadly—say as something rationally disliked. For example, if investors value liquidity, a higher return for illiquid assets can be treated as a return for risk. Or are the results evidence of a market inefficiency? If true findings are a result of risk, does the risk matter to you? If liquidity is not a concern for you, a return generated by lack of liquidity is a genuine abnormal return for you and worth obtaining. If the source of return is a risk for you, the return is not an abnormal return. What if the return is a result of market inefficiency? The variable/style may or may not be useful as a share selector. If returns are high on average but subject to long periods when returns are low, the variable/style may not make commercial sense. Again, something that has worked in the past may not work in the future because it becomes discounted in the marketplace.

In previous chapters we have examined a large number of ways an investor might try to beat the market:

- APT-type bets
- sector bets
- superior accounting skills
- superior forecasting skills, e.g. of earnings and themes
- earnings revisions and surprises
- disciplined processing of information (DDM and abnormal earnings model)
- judging the appropriate PER
- value investing
- growth investing
- small-cap investing
- neglected stocks
- calendar effects
- contrarian styles
- momentum/relative strength
- technical analysis
- stockbroker recommendations
- insider trades.

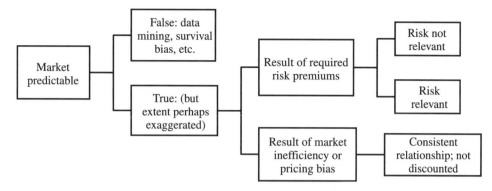

FIGURE 17.1 Making sense of predictability

This list could easily be extended. For example, on average, new issues do well initially and then underperform for the next three years. So one could build a strategy around buying all new issues, selling quickly, and then not buying them again for several years. However, we have plenty of possible approaches listed above without looking for more. So how do we select from the list? There are four possible ways:

- Use one approach.
- Use several approaches.
- Use many approaches.
- Use different approaches at different times.

In each case, you should have worked through Figure 17.1 and decided what you think you are exploiting.

You could put together a portfolio that treated all UK stocks, for example, as one group. Alternatively, you could divide the UK market into subgroups, form portfolios from each subgroup, and then make a decision as to how to weight the subgroups. This latter approach is the one usually adopted in practice, and the subgroups are typically sectors of the market (which are loosely based on industries) or groupings of sectors of the market, for example capital goods or cyclical sectors. The sector weights may be the same as those of some appropriate index, or over- or underweighted relative to the index. Constructing a portfolio in this way ensures diversification across industries. It is also usual to specify some additional constraints, such as the number of stocks to be purchased (often in the range 50–90 for the UK market, but possibly many more for a small-capitalization stock portfolio where there may be marketability problems). The maximum size of holding is often specified (typically 5–7.5% of the fund, except where the index weight of a share is greater) and sometimes a minimum size too (perhaps 0.5%). Here you have to be careful. Private client portfolio managers often equally weight their holdings, for example £10 000 into each share. If they buy 20 shares, then they are making every share 5% of the portfolio. If they buy a share that is 10% of the index, their act of purchase implies they like the share, but their weighting implies they don't.

Single Variable/Style Approach

It is possible to use just one variable/style to try to beat the market. For example, if small-cap stocks generally outperform, you could permanently hold a small-cap portfolio. Or you could always hold low PER stocks. Again, if you have superior earnings forecasting skills, you could buy stocks where your forecast is higher than the consensus, and sell stocks where your forecast is lower than the consensus.

Which variable should you choose? Obviously this depends on your skills, the variable's predictive value that you think is best supported by the evidence, and its consistency. For example, you could only use the superior forecasting ability approach if you have superior ability, whereas little skill is needed to adopt an indexed small-stocks approach. However, small-stock outperformance has not been consistent. The periods of underperformance have been long enough for it not to be a commercially viable approach for some managers. That could push you towards an approach that might give more consistent returns, even if they are lower over a long period.

Several Variables/Styles Approach

Providing variables'/styles' returns are not perfectly correlated, having more than one approach will add value. Some styles are not perfectly correlated but probably measure much the same thing. For example, if you start with a low PER, adding low price-to-book probably isn't the best choice.

How can several different share-selection approaches be brought together? There are two main ways—subjective and statistical. Subjective does not necessarily mean ill-informed; indeed, it may allow for more complex interactions than simple statistical methods. For example, Mozes (2000) links expected earnings surprises strategies to value strategies. He shows that the strategy of buying stocks for which the most positive earnings surprises are expected is more effective for low PER stocks than for high. And the strategy of selling short stocks for which the most negative earnings surprises are expected is more effective for high PER stocks than for low PER stocks. That seems easy enough, but consider value and momentum. Both seem to have been effective, but this is perhaps surprising given that value measures and momentum measures are negatively correlated. In other words, if you buy value, you tend to buy poor momentum.

Asness (1997) found value works in general, but largely fails with firms with strong momentum. And momentum works in general, but is particularly strong for expensive firms. What does this mean? First, rank stocks by momentum and form quintiles. Now rank stocks within each momentum quintile by value and form quintiles. If we take the loser quintile of momentum stocks in Asness' study, we find that the cheapest stocks earn nearly 1% per month more than the most expensive. However, if we do the same thing with the winner momentum quintile, the cheapest winner stocks produce only 0.13% more per month than the most expensive winner stocks. We can repeat the procedure beginning with value quintiles and then forming momentum quintiles. For the cheapest quintile of stocks, the return difference between winner and loser momentum quintiles is 0.62% per month. Amongst the most expensive quintile of stocks, the winner quintile earns 1.47% more per month than the loser. This is clearly a somewhat complex relationship: simply deciding that you want positive momentum and cheap stocks may not be the best way of combining these variables.

Turning to simple statistical approaches, the most widely used are forms of weighted composite or multiple cut-off. The latter approach is usually referred to in the investment literature as 'screening'. In broad terms, the composite weighting approach gives a stock points for the possession of desirable attributes; the more of an attribute possessed, the greater the number of points, and the more points the better. The screening approach is all or nothing: it's more like a hurdle race—a stock has to clear the hurdle or it's out. If low PERs are deemed to be desirable, all stocks with multiples above, say, 80% of the market's multiple will be eliminated from further consideration. The two methods will select some of the same stocks, but there will be differences. The composite method allows a poor score on one attribute to be offset by good scores on other attributes. The screening approach does not—in the case just mentioned, if a stock has a high PER, it will not be selected, irrespective of the fact that it may score highly on every other attribute. Because the screening approach imposes a series of hurdles, each one of which will eliminate stocks, setting many hurdles, or high hurdles (e.g. setting a hurdle at 50% of the market PER), soon diminishes the population of eligible stocks to a very small number. To avoid this, you have to limit the number of screens, and adjust the hurdle height, to allow enough stocks to survive to allow a diversified portfolio to be constructed.

Although there are some problems with the screening approach, most non-quantitative managers are likely to feel more at home with a screening approach. There are many articles describing this approach but for a practical discussion, Arbel (1985b, pp. 90–115) is useful. Using neglected stocks as the basic screen, Arbel tries to screen out stocks that might become bankrupt. Next he tries to screen out overpriced stocks, and then stocks that are correctly priced but cannot be expected to perform in the foreseeable future. Arbel's discussion is too long to be summarized here, but it is a useful practical guide.

Screening approaches do not systematically control for risk. Risk control tends to be informal, based on ensuring broad diversification. This usually involves sector weightings, but it can be more complex, depending on the manager's experience. Many managers will look to see if they are taking hidden and unwanted bets. For example, a fund will have exposure to property from its property sector weighting, but it will also get exposure through hotel companies, companies that own pubs, and so on. It may wish to control this exposure. Or a fund might look to see if it is selecting the more highly geared shares in each sector. A few years ago, a low price-earnings approach would have pointed to Trafalgar House, Maxwell Communications, Polly Peck, ADT and Coloroll as potential purchases. Although these companies were in different industries, each was dominated by one individual and all had interesting accounting practices. These stocks might all have been seen as involving the same sort of risk. A fund manager might be willing to hold one but not all of them. This sort of approach gives a role to the traditional fundamental research usually employed in the appropriate PER approach. However, the fundamental research is being used to discriminate amongst a universe of shares that have been selected by a less subjective, more quantitative approach.

Let's now look at the weighted composite approach. After choosing the relevant attributes, the next stage is to weight them by forecasting power. This may be done formally, or an investor may simply use several variables and give them equal weight, or weight them on the basis of prior beliefs. We can illustrate this approach with a couple of examples.

A model used by Harris Investment Management has been described by Kirscher (1990). Harris selects shares on the basis of a five-component model. The components are low PER, DDM, earnings momentum, analyst revisions and price momentum. The weights for each component are not stated, but judging from a pie chart included in the description, they are roughly 35%, 25%, 10%, 15% and 15%. The first two components are measures of value to determine whether a stock is cheap, and the remaining components are measures of momentum to discern whether the cheapness is being recognized by other investors.

Harris appears to monitor a list of only 175 stocks, and each stock is ranked on each component. The overall ranking for a stock is simply its ranking on each component times that component's weighting. The stocks are re-ranked by their overall score. The top stocks are not the buy list because they could be excessively risky and poorly diversified. A second programme is used to balance risk against return. Kirscher notes that research on enhancing the value of the model can be undertaken and, very important from a client perspective, 'the model can be gradually re-engineered without introducing drastic and unsettling change in investment style.'

Ambachtsheer and Farrell describe a model that uses forecasts on stock over- or undervaluation, and assessments of correlations of forecasts and returns to compute expected alphas (see Ambachtsheer, 1974; Ambachtsheer, 1977; Ambachtsheer and Farrell, 1979; Farrell, 1982; and Farrel, 1983). The calculation of alphas will be omitted here (see especially Farrell, 1983) but the gist of the model described by Farrell will be given.

Ambachtsheer and Farrell (1979) report work using the Wells Fargo Market Line approach (i.e. a DDM) in conjunction with the *Value Line* timeliness measure. They describe the former as long-term fundamental, and the latter as short-term fundamental. Farrell (1982, 1983) describes managing money with this approach using models identical in spirit but different in detail. In addition to the two variables noted, he includes a measure of trading fundamentals (which includes information provided by share-repurchase programmes or insider trading patterns) and a measure of analyst judgement (which monitors buy and sell recommendations of security analysts). The four variables are said to be attractive because all have demonstrated predictive content and statistical measures suggest that they are mutually independent. These share predictors are then combined to produce a composite forecast for 800 shares. Specifically, Farrell estimates an alpha for each share, the amount its return should deviate from the market's return. A portfolio is then constructed along the following lines: (i) the portfolio beta is kept between 0.95 and 1.05, i.e. risk, to the extent that beta is a measure of risk, is explicitly controlled; (ii) investments are spread over sectors in line with the S&P 500; (iii) 60–90 companies are held; and (iv) no large positions are held in individual stocks. Over the period 1974–81, this strategy outperformed the S&P 500 every year by amounts varying from 1.7% to 9.7%.

Multiple Variables/Styles

There are two distinct ways of using multiple variables/styles. One is subjective, the other statistical. The subjective approach is, in essence, what a good traditional manager would have done. It is much derided by US consultants. However, such a manager might talk you through his or her portfolio as follows: 'We are pretty much sector neutral because we have no strong sector views, except that we have a big bet on the international oil majors because we think the oil price will be strong. On the other hand, we are very overweight small stocks because they are very cheap on a yield/PER basis against the large-cap stocks. The small-cap house builders are very cheap, but their charts are horrible, so we don't have any. We have some highly rated suppliers to the Internet industry—that's a theme bet. We don't have the expertise to pick emerging markets stocks, but investment trusts investing in this area are selling on near record discounts to net asset value. Foreign investors have been active in this sector trying to get some trusts to liquidate at net asset value, so we have bought some emerging market trusts as both a market play and an asset play.'

The manager might continue in this style giving a reason for holding every stock, although possibly a different reason for each stock. The manager is using multiple styles and selection variables.

The statistical approach can use a variety of statistical techniques. We will consider only a multiple regression framework. Several studies of this nature have been reported, for example Jacobs and Levy (1988a) for the US; Haugen and Baker (1996) (see also Haugen, 1996) for the US, Germany, France, the UK and Japan; and Schwartz and Ziemba (2000) for Japan. (Jabobs and Levy are money managers. The Schwartz–Ziemba model was used by Yamaichi Securities in Tokyo for proprietary trading, and parts of the model have been used in the UK by Buchanan Partners.)

Most of the studies that have been examined in previous chapters look at returns in relation to one, or at most a few, factors at a time. We have seen that some relationships become muted or disappear if other factors are introduced. Jacobs and Levy (1988a) tried to explain returns to specific factors when a very large number of other factors were simultaneously having an effect. They carried out their analysis on a universe of 1500 of the largest US capitalization stocks on data from January 1978 through to December 1986. They estimated monthly regression equations and averaged the results. They carried out univariate (one variable or factor) and multivariate (several variables) regressions, i.e. they looked, for example, at the relationship of low PERs with abnormal returns and then at the relationship of low PERs with abnormal returns but specifically controlling for small size, neglect, low price-to-book, and so on. These variables were held at their average market value. Jacobs and Levy explain that their multivariate regressions measure all effects jointly, thereby 'purifying' each effect so that it is independent of other effects, whereas univariate regressions 'naively' measure only one anomaly at a time, with no effort to control for other related effects. Table 17.2 shows their pure and naive effects for various anomalies. Most of the anomalies listed will be clear enough, given the discussion in earlier chapters. Comments on a few are, however, necessary.

Although the capital asset pricing theory argues that only systematic risk should be rewarded, some studies have found that unsystematic risk is also rewarded, so Jacobs and Levy included unsystematic risk—or sigma—in their study. Some authors have claimed that investors may value stocks with returns that exhibit positive skewness (i.e. a higher probability of large gains than large losses). The evidence is mixed, but coskewness—a measure of this—was included. Earnings uncertainty, or unusual disagreement amongst analysts with regard to future profits for a company, was included because of the argument that such stocks produce higher returns, either as a reward for the information deficiency or as a proxy for systematic risk.

The earnings torpedo effect is the belief that stocks expected to have high future earnings growth are more susceptible to negative surprises (i.e. torpedoes). Residual reversal is more complex. Based on the regression equations, we can forecast a stock's return. Sometimes it will earn more than it should and sometimes less; there is an unexplained residual. If a stock returns too much in one month, residual reversal implies that it will subsequently return less. Finally, Jacobs and Levy try to capture the January effect by using separate proprietary measures of potential long-term and short-term tax loss selling pressure for each stock. The January effect was the only seasonal effect included in the study because the use of monthly data meant time-of-day, day-of-the-week and week-of-the-month effects had to be excluded.

If the value shown in Table 17.2 for any factor were zero, this would mean that there was no relationship between the factor and returns. It is possible for

TABLE 17.2   Monthly average returns to anomalies 1978–86

Anomaly	Naive anomaly: monthly average return (%)	Pure anomaly: monthly average return (%)
Low PER	0.59**	0.46**
Small size	0.15*	0.12*
Yield	−0.01	0.03
Zero yield	0.00	0.15
Neglect	0.14*	0.10*
Low price	−0.01	0.01
Book/price	0.17	0.09
Sales/price	0.17	0.17**
Cash/price	0.36**	0.04
Sigma	0.16	0.07
Beta	−0.01	0.04
Coskewness	0.09	0.04
Earnings uncertainty	−0.33*	−0.05
Trend in estimates (−1)#	0.48**	0.51**
Trend in estimates (−2)#	0.40**	0.28**
Trend in estimates (−3)#	0.29**	0.19**
Earnings surprise (−1)#	0.44*	0.48**
Earnings surprise (−2)#	0.47*	0.18
Earnings surprise (−3)#	−0.03	−0.21
Earnings torpedo	−0.00	−0.10*
Relative strength	0.30	0.34**
Residual reversal (−1)#	−0.54**	−1.08**
Residual reversal (−2)#	−0.13	−0.37**
Short-term tax	−0.08	−0.04
Long-term tax	−0.29	−0.00

**Significant at the 1% level. *Significant at the 10% level. #Numbers in brackets refer to months of lagged response.

factors to appear to affect returns when they do not, simply because of sampling error. It is therefore important to ask what the chances are of observing a relationship when none really exists. Some returns in Table 17.2 are labelled as significant at the 1% level and some at the 10% level. This means that there is a probability of only one in 100 or one in 10, respectively that the observed relationship occurred by chance alone.

It is worth recalling the difference between statistical and practical investment significance. A monthly average abnormal return of 0.1% may be statistically significant, but at just over 1% a year it is of less investment significance. This should be borne in mind when considering Table 17.2. Also, the transactions costs will differ between strategies. For example, small size is a relatively stable characteristic and would not require much trading, but residual reversal would require a lot of trading and the returns after costs would be much smaller than the regression estimate might appear to suggest.

The most statistically significant relationships in pure form are low PER, small size, low price-to-sales ratio, favourable trend in estimates, earnings surprise (lagged one month), relative strength and residual reversal. Neglect and the torpedo effect were significant at the 10% level. Cash flow was significant in naive form but not in pure form: it appeared to act as a surrogate for low PER in the univariate regression.

Many of the variables we found to be relevant in earlier chapters do not appear relevant in this study (i.e. yield, zero yield, low price, book/price). Is this study wrong? One might suspect it is handling too many variables that have some overlap for the data to be able to sort out true effects. Were the other studies wrong? Are the variables unstable? These problems should make investors cautious about adopting a single variable selection strategy.

Jacobs and Levy use multiple regression to identify 'pure' factor effects. However, you still have to build a model with whatever you conclude from their findings. A different approach is to use all the variables to make predictions using a multiple regression equation. Haugen and Baker (1996) adopted this approach. They used a large number of variables classified into five types. These are shown below, although some of the variables were also included in trend form:

- risk
  - market beta
  - APT betas
  - volatility of total return
  - residual variance
  - earnings per share volatility
  - debt/equity
  - interest coverage
- liquidity
  - market capitalization
  - price per share
  - average daily volume/market capitalization
- price level
  - earnings-to-price
  - book-to-price
  - dividend-to-price
  - cash flow-to-price
  - sales-to-price
- growth potential
  - profit margin
  - capital turnover
  - return on assets
  - return on equity
  - earnings growth
- technical
  - one-, two-, three-, six-, 12-, 24- and 60-month excess returns.

Haugen and Baker reason that the higher the risk, the higher should be the returns, and the higher the liquidity, the lower should be the returns. The price levels variables measure cheapness of price in relation to cash flows available to shareholders. The cheaper the stocks are, the higher the expected return. Factors related to growth potential indicate the likelihood of faster-than-average future growth and cash flows. All things being equal, the greater the growth potential, the greater the prospective returns. Technical factors reflect the history of the stock's returns and future expected returns.

Using multiple regression, we can calculate the return on a stock given its exposure to various factors. First, determine all the factors and how they will be measured. Second, calculate the exposure of each stock to each factor. Third, given each stock's exposure to the factors and its return, a multiple regression programme will calculate the payoff for each factor and the overall return.

We begin with the list of factors shown above. Consider book-to-price. We measure book-to-price at the start of the month and return over the month. For statistical reasons, we might prefer to use standard deviations rather than absolute numbers for book-to-price. Thus a stock that had a book-to-price score of +1 would be one standard deviation above the sample's average book-to-price value. We might find that returns increase as book-to-price increases. If the slope of the best-fitting line is 0.04, this gives us the payoff of book-to-price. For each standard deviation increase, return rises by 4%. So a stock with a book-to-price standard deviation of +1 would return 4% from its exposure to this factor. Now imagine size is negatively related to return, and the slope of the best-fitting line is −0.02. Then, if a stock is one standard deviation above average on size, it will receive a negative return from this factor exposure. Instead of going through more factors, assume that there are only two factors. The total expected return for this stock would then be:

Factor	Factor exposure	×	Factor payoff	=	Expected return
Book-to-price	+1 S.D.	×	+4.00%	=	+4.00%
Size	+1 S.D.	×	−2.00%	=	−2.00%
					+2.00%

Haugen and Baker (1996) used this type of analysis and the variables listed earlier. The factor payoffs were calculated on a trailing 12-month basis, i.e. the average of the last 12 monthly payoffs for a factor was used as the expected payoff for the next month. Using this approach, Haugen and Baker could account for 10% of the cross-sectional differences in US monthly stock returns. Firms were ranked by returns and then placed into deciles. The top decile (10) outperformed the bottom decile (1) by 35% p.a. over the period 1979–93. However, using monthly rankings leads to high turnover and high transactions costs. When stock turnover was restricted and trading costs allowed for, the return differential was 12%. This return exaggerates how well the system works unless you can short the lower decile; otherwise what is important is the return of the top decile versus the market average return. In 1994 and 1995 this was modest (Haugen, 1996).

What sort of stocks does this approach select as attractive?

> Collectively, they are large-cap, liquid and profitable like growth stocks. On the other hand, they sell at cheap prices and have low market risk like value stocks . . . Few, if any, individual stocks with the complete profile of Decile 10 exist. While each of the stocks in Decile 10 may be outstanding in several respects, none have the profile of the decile as a whole. Thus, if analysts try to employ commonly used screening technologies to screen for a group of stocks all with the profile [of Decile 10] . . . they would probably find an empty set.
>
> (Haugen, 1996, pp. 14 and 16)

Finally, Schwartz and Ziemba (2000) produced a similar study for Japan, but the 30 variables they used were essentially those used by Jacobs and Levy (1988a) in their US study. Shwartz and Ziemba's portfolios of the best 50, 100, 200, 300, 400 and 500 stocks had monotone increases in returns, and all outperformed the TOPIX, a capitalization-weighted Japanese index.

STYLE-VARYING PORTFOLIOS

One response to the fact that styles do not work consistently is to construct portfolios using variables that reflect a variety of styles. A different approach is to construct pure style portfolios but to vary the styles over the course of time. This raises the question as to how one knows when a particular style will work. There have been three broad types of answer in the literature:

- Select on the basis of market and economic variables.
- Select on the basis of the price of earnings growth.
- Select on the basis of risk.

We will look at each in turn.

Style and Macroeconomic Factors

An early example of this type of research is Arnott et al. (1989). More recently there have been a number of studies; according to Kao and Shumaker (1999), the most popular variables used in models relating macroeconomic factors to style are:

- yield curve spread
- real bond yield
- corporate credit spread
- high yield spread
- estimated GDP growth rate
- earnings yield gap
- historical inflation rate.

Kao and Shumaker (1999) illustrate how these variables might be used in a recursive partitioning algorithm. An illustration of the macroeconomic approach using statistical techniques that most readers will be more familiar with is Levis and Liodakis (1999) for the UK market.

Levis and Liodakis (1999) studied the UK market for the period 1968–97. They divided stocks into three market values and three book-to-market groups. They also calculated size and value spreads, i.e. the return differential between large and small stocks and between value and growth stocks. In a regression framework, they tested the size and value spreads' sensitivity to a number of economic variables. They found that small-cap returns benefit from rising interest rates and equity risk premium, widening of the yield spread between 20-year gilts and Treasury bills, and lower rates of inflation. The value-growth spread seems to be primarily determined by the one-month lagged value-growth spread, inflation (rising inflation hurts value stocks more than growth), and the pound/dollar exchange rate (a rise benefits growth stocks more than value stocks). The R^2 values for their equations don't exceed about 12%.

Levis and Liodakis attempted to build style rotation portfolios based on their logit regression model. This type of model gives a probability for a particular style outperforming in a particular month. The authors suggest three possible timing strategies, and calculated the returns these strategies would produce allowing for various levels of transactions costs. They concluded that style rotation strategies based on small and large firms could be highly rewarding, but they were only marginally successful in the case of value and growth stocks.

Valuation Versus Growth

If we think of the simple constant-growth DDM, we have:

Expected return = dividend yield + dividend growth rate.

We could replace dividends in this equation by earnings if we assume a constant payout ratio. We can write our equation for growth and value stocks as follows:

$$\text{Expected return to value} = \left(\frac{E}{P} \right)_{value} + g_{value}.$$

$$\text{Expected return to growth} = \left(\frac{E}{P} \right)_{growth} + g_{growth}.$$

If we take the difference between these two equations, we arrive at a simple style timing model:

Expected return to value—expected return to growth =

$$\left(\left(\frac{E}{P} \right)_{value} - \left(\frac{E}{P} \right)_{growth} \right) - \left(g_{growth} - g_{value} \right).$$

In words, the difference between the returns on value and growth stocks is related to the difference between their earnings yields or PERs and the difference between their growth rates. We would expect value stocks to have low PERs or high earnings yields, and growth stocks to have the opposite, so the first term on the right-hand side should be positive. If it is abnormally large, then value stocks really are cheap, other things being equal. The second term on the right-hand side of the equation has the notation reversed and would normally be positive. If it is abnormally large, then growth stocks would appear to be cheap. Asness et al. (2000) call the first term on the right-hand side the 'value spread' and the second term the 'growth spread'. If we use both spreads together, then we might be able to predict whether growth or value stocks will offer the best returns. Asness et al. tested this by examining the top 1100 most liquid large stocks. They determine whether a stock is a value or a growth stock by computing a value rank for each stock, which is based on a one-third weight of each of its earnings yield rank, book-to-price rank and sales-to-price rank. These ranks are based on industry-adjusted numbers. They measure growth for each stock by taking the IBES median long-term earnings per share growth forecast.

Although Asness et al. use a value composite, it is easier to explain their procedures by focusing on just one component—the earnings yield spread. They rank shares by their earnings yield, and divide the shares into 10 deciles. The earnings yield of the first decile (growth) is divided by the earnings yield of the tenth decile (value) to calculate the earnings yield spread. For the period 1982–99, the earnings yield spread averaged 2. The maximum it reached was 3, and the minimum 1.5. By plotting the earnings yield spread, we can see whether we are currently at the high or low end. At the end of 1999, the value was 2.9, i.e. nearly as high as it has ever been. In a similar manner, using the expected long-term earnings growth of deciles 1 and 10, the earnings growth spread can be calculated. This appears to have varied between 4% and 16%. Currently the figure is at the low end, i.e. growth stocks are expected to grow faster than value stocks by the smallest amount in the last 20 years. But they are valued at the highest level relative to value stocks. The authors find that the value strategy returns are positively related to the value spread and negatively related to the earnings growth spread. They produce a simple equation that reflects this, and has an R^2 of 39%.

Risk and Style

Macedo (1995, 1997) rates risk as measured by volatility to style selection. She does so for international markets rather than individual stocks. Her studies are discussed on pp. 387–8.

CONCLUDING COMMENTS

Shares may be selected actively or passively. In this chapter, we considered both approaches. The active approach is the most commonly used, but indexation continues to win market share.

Despite the existence of various asset-pricing models, most investors take an ad hoc approach to selecting shares. We present many styles and attributes that might aid share selection. Investors have to ask whether findings supporting any approach are true, and if so whether excess returns are risk premiums or the result of market inefficiencies. If they are risk premiums, do the risks matter to the investor? If they are the result of inefficiencies, is outperformance consistent or prone to drought periods, and will the inefficiencies get eliminated?

Investors may concentrate on one style or variable, several, or a very large number. A variety of subjective and statistical approaches may be adopted to handle multiple variables.

Because styles don't work consistently, some investors attempt to forecast which style is likely to work in a specific period and then vary their style accordingly.

Different organizations are likely to produce different share-selection models depending on their perception of the statistical relationships between attributes and returns, their own skills and interests, and the perceptions and attitudes of their existing and anticipated clients.

18

Bonds: An Introduction

One thousand dollars left to earn interest at 8 per cent a year will grow to $43 quadrillion in 400 years, but the first hundred years are the hardest.

Sydney Homer

Bonds are loans, usually with fixed regular-interest payments, and usually with repayment—or redemption—of the principal at a specific date. Bond issuers include governments and companies. Unfortunately, numerous quite dissimilar financial products geared to the private client market have been described by their promoters as bonds, for example broker bonds, single-premium bonds, guaranteed bonds, etc. These are not bonds in terms of the definition in the first sentence. In this book, the term 'bond' always refers to bonds as loans.

CLASSIFYING BONDS

There are three major ways of classifying bonds:

- where issued
- the issuer
- the type of bond.

We will look at each of these in turn.

Where Bonds are Issued

A distinction is usually made between domestic bonds, foreign bonds and Eurobonds:

- Domestic bonds are bonds issued in the country of domicile of the issuer and in that country's currency. For example, Witan Investment Trust is a UK-domiciled investment trust, and its 8.5% Debenture 2016 is a domestic sterling bond. Similarly, 9% Treasury Loan 2008 is a domestic sterling bond issued by the UK government.

- Foreign bonds are issued in a market in the local currency by a foreign entity. Foreign bonds issued in the US are called Yankee bonds, foreign bonds issued in Japan are called Samurai bonds, and foreign bonds issued in the UK are called bulldog bonds. For example, Denmark 13% 2005, issued by the Danish government in London and in sterling, is a bulldog bond.
- Eurobonds are issued by entities not domiciled in the country of issue, and not in the local currency. For example, BT is UK domiciled and its British Telecom 7.125% 2003 is a Eurobond denominated in sterling and issued outside the UK. This bond would be referred to as a Eurosterling bond. Similarly, a bond issued by a US corporation in Luxembourg in dollars would be a Eurodollar bond. The currency of the bond need not be the issuer's domestic currency. For example, a Japanese corporation might issue a sterling bond in Luxembourg: this would be a Eurosterling bond.

Eurobonds are so called because of their historical origin. Measures taken by the US authorities in the early 1960s made raising money in the US bond markets less attractive to foreign borrowers, and made financing of US corporations' foreign activities more difficult. This led to the development of the Eurobond market. In an age when most markets involved face-to-face dealing, the Eurobond market was a telephone-based market that had no physical location, although it was primarily organized by European banks.

There are a number of differences between the Eurobond and domestic markets. For example, consider the UK domestic market and the Eurobond market. A UK domestic bond issuer normally keeps a register of bondholders, whereas the Eurobond market is usually a bearer market, i.e. there is no register and ownership is proved by the possession of a security certificate. A UK domestic bond is often secured or has detailed restrictive covenants, whereas a Eurobond is normally unsecured, although it will carry a negative pledge, which means the bondholders will not consent to a lien on the firm's assets without the bondholders being treated equally. Typically, UK domestic bond payments are paid twice a year, whereas in the Eurobond market, the payment is normally once a year. UK merchant banks and stockbrokers normally issue domestic UK bonds, whereas Eurobond issues are organized by UK and overseas banks. UK domestic bonds will be listed in London, whereas in the Eurobond market Luxembourg is the usual place of listing (although Eurosterling bonds may also be listed in London). New issues of domestic UK bonds are placed at a fixed price on a specific day, whereas Eurobonds are placed over a period at varying prices. The secondary market for a UK domestic bond is the London Stock Exchange, but in the Eurobond market, trading is on an over-the-counter basis by the issuing banks. Investors in domestic UK bonds tend to be domestic investors, whereas in the Eurobond market there will be both domestic and overseas investors.

Bond Issuers

There are four main issuers of bonds:

- central governments and government agencies
- state and local governments
- companies
- supranational institutions, such as the World Bank.

One of the risks for a bondholder is that the issuer will default. Clearly, the risk of default varies between the four classes of issuer noted above, and within some of the classes. Supranational bodies are usually regarded as very-high-quality issuers. Governments, which have the ability to raise taxes or print money, are usually considered the lowest-risk issuer within their own country. However, while the US government's issues might be considered lower risk than an issue by IBM, IBM's issues may well be considered a lower risk than some African governments' issues.

The credit rating of government agencies depends on whether they are backed by the full faith and credit of the government. For example, in the US, where there are a large number of government agencies, only the Farm Credit Financial Assistance Corporation has full backing. Accordingly, the credit risk of agencies will vary with the circumstances of the agencies.

Companies issue corporate bonds, and there is a risk of default. Corporate bonds carry more risk than the government bonds of the same country. Companies such as Standard & Poor's and Moody's rate corporate bonds for their riskiness. We discuss this later.

Types of Bond

The basic idea of a bond is simple enough: it is a loan or an IOU. However, the financial markets have shown great ingenuity in inventing various forms of bond, and the following types may be distinguished:

- fixed-rate
  - straights
  - callable
  - puttable
  - convertible
- floating rate (including variable rates)
- zero-coupon
- index-linked

Fixed-Rate Bonds

A typical fixed-coupon bond is the 9% Treasury Loan 2008. Its description has three parts: a name, a yield and a date. The name usually relates to the issuer. In this case, 'Treasury' is not particularly helpful. One might guess that this is a government bond, but both the US and UK governments issue bonds with the word 'Treasury'. In fact this example is a UK government bond. The yield refers to the nominal rate of interest, or the coupon rate. For a standard bond, this represents the annual amount of interest paid per 100 units of nominal stock, for example per £100 in the UK, or per $100 in the US. Usually this is paid twice a year on fixed dates six months apart. So, in the case of our Treasury stock, if you had invested £1000 nominal, you would receive two interest payments per annum of £45. The date shown in the description of the stock is the redemption (or maturity) date, the date on which the principal is repaid. Redemption is usually at the par value. Again, in the case of our Treasury stock, one of the two coupon dates has been specified as the redemption date and on that date the investor will receive £45 interest and £1000 repayment of principal.

The price at which a bond trades in the market need not be its par or face value. Therefore in the previous example, although the investor will receive £45 every six months, if he or she had paid more than £1000 for the stock, this would produce an interest yield lower than 9% p.a. And vice versa.

The bond described is an example of a fixed-rate bond, i.e. the coupon rate is fixed. It is also an example of the first subcategory listed above, a straight bond. This refers to the fact that the bond goes straight through from issue to redemption without a change of terms. Such bonds are sometimes called plain vanilla bonds or bullet bonds. A variation of the straight fixed-rate bond is a callable bond. In this case, the issuer has the option to redeem the bond at par before the redemption date. Obviously, this will only be done in conditions favourable to the issuer, which makes the bond less attractive to the borrower unless some other features of the bond are adjusted. Puttable bonds reverse the position. Here the investor has the option to demand redemption of the bonds at par before the redemption date. These bonds are more attractive to the investor than to the issuer.

Another variation of a fixed-rate bond is a convertible bond. Convertible bonds give the investor the right to convert the bonds into another security at some time in the future. Both governments and corporations issue convertibles. Government convertibles usually convert into another government bond with different characteristics. Corporate convertible bonds usually offer the opportunity to convert into equity.

Floating-Rate Note Bonds

A floating-rate note pays a coupon that is reset at specified intervals according to a set formula. This formula usually makes reference to another variable market rate of interest. For example, the rate could be set at London Interbank Offer Rate (LIBOR) plus 1%. There are different types of 'floaters'. For example, inverse floaters have a coupon that increases as the reference rate declines. Collared floaters have caps or floors, or both, which set maximum and minimum coupon rates. There are also varieties called step-up recovery floaters (SURFs) and corridor floaters. Investors in the more unusual floaters are either highly sophisticated, or mugs. Orange County, California declared bankruptcy after extensive use of inverse floaters.

Zero-Coupon Bonds

Zero-coupon bonds do not make payments of interest. They are issued at prices well below par value so that on redemption the investor, in effect, receives all the interest payments in a lump sum along with repayment of principal.

Index-Linked Bonds

An index-linked bond's coupon and principal are linked to an index, usually a retail price index. These bonds are mainly issued by governments, and UK Government index-linked are discussed on pp. 331–3. Non-indexed bonds are often called conventional bonds.

Other Bonds

The distinction made above between the four main types of bonds is based on variations in how interest payments are determined. Another way of distinguishing bonds is according to whether they have a redemption date. Almost all bonds do have a redemption date, but there are a few bonds that are undated, or irredeemable. In the UK government bond market, 3.5% War and 2.5% Consolidated, for example, are irredeemable. Table 18.1 pulls together some of the discussion to this point.

TABLE 18.1 Characteristics of bonds classified by maturity and coupon

	Interest payments		
Type	Rate	Timing	Duration
Redeemable			
Fixed coupon			
Conventional	Fixed	Set period, e.g. every six months	Until redemption
Index-linked	Fixed in real terms; varies in money terms	Set period, e.g. every six months	Until redemption
Floating-rate	Varies according to formula	Set period, e.g. every six months	Until redemption
Zero-coupon	Implicit rate, set by purchase price	No payments	Not applicable
Irredeemable	Fixed	Set period, e.g. every six months	Forever

Another category of bond is the asset-backed bond. This is of major importance in the US market, where there are a large number of mortgage-backed
bonds. However, in the UK market this is not an important sector.

Preference shares and permanent income-bearing shares (PIBs) are, technically, shares, but offer fixed rates of income. They are usually treated as bond
investments.

THE STERLING BOND MARKET

We can bring together place of issue, type of issuer and type of bond by discussing the sterling bond market. In what follows, estimates of size are based on a
variety of sources, and should be seen as very rough and ready estimates. If we
define the sterling bond market as shown below, it probably has a value of about
£600bn:

	Issuer	% of market
(A)	Government	55%
(B)	Domestic	4%
(C)	Eurosterling	
	(Ci) UK issuer	20%
	(Cii) Non-UK issuer	20%
(D)	Bulldogs	1%

Of course, you might argue that somebody investing in sterling bonds would
expect to invest in UK entities, in which case the UK market would consist of
components A + B + Ci. Or you might argue that the UK sterling market should
consist only of sterling issues made in the UK, i.e. A + B + D.

UK government bonds are usually called gilts (or gilt-edged). Whatever definition of the sterling bond market you choose, gilts dominate the market, although in recent years, corporate issues have grown. But the numbers
exaggerate the importance of corporate bonds. Over the last decade, there has
been a marked shrinkage in the number of gilts because a strategy of having
fewer but larger issues has been followed. In early 2000, 28 gilts each had a
redemption value over £5bn. Corporate bond issues are much smaller (few
exceed £0.5bn), and so the market is much less liquid. If you want to adjust the
average maturity of your portfolio, it is easier to do this in the gilt market than in
the corporate bond market. It is worth examining the gilt market in more detail.

The value of the gilt market is about £330bn—market prices at March 2000—
or about the same size as the combined market value of two equities, Vodafone
Airtouch and BP Amoco. The gilt market is made up of a number of different
types of issues, although two predominate. At March 2000, the composition was
(rounded figures):

Conventional	76%
Index-linked	23%

Undated	1%
Floating-rate	1%

When index-linked gilts were introduced to the market, it was necessary to distinguish between them and other gilts. The non-indexed fixed-rate gilts became known as conventional gilts. Conventional gilts comprise a number of the types of bonds discussed earlier, but it is sufficient for our purposes simply to note that they make up three-quarters of the market. Index-linked raise some interesting issues and are discussed later.

Classifying gilts by their length of maturity, i.e. the number of years left to redemption, we find the following split at March 2000 (rounded figures):

Ultra short (0–3 years)	20%
Short (3–7 years)	27%
Medium (7–15 years)	26%
Long (15+ years)	26%
Undated	1%

The average maturity was 9.9 years, and the average modified duration was 7.4 years. Duration is discussed later.

It is worth stressing that the maturity structure shown is a result of both the issuing policy of the government and the passage of time. As time passes, people get older and bonds get shorter. Therefore, unless long-dated gilts are continually issued, the long sector of the market will disappear and the market will have a shorter and shorter maturity.

Eurosterling

The Eurosterling market is about two-thirds the size of the gilt market and perhaps half the issuers are UK issuers. About two-thirds of the issues are fixed rate, with the majority of these being straights. Because of the bearer nature of the market, historically clients were seen to be Europeans (and others) trying to avoid paying tax. The traditional customer was defined as the Belgian dentist. In the early days, this led to most Eurobond issues being issued with maturity of about five years. In recent years, however, the maturity has tended to lengthen. Nonetheless, the average maturity of the market is shorter than that of the gilt market. Most Eurosterling issues are credit rated, unsecured, and listed on the London or Luxembourg Stock Exchanges. Issuers have included Abbey National, British Telecom, the Kingdom of Denmark, European Investment Bank, Glaxo Wellcome, and the Kingdom of Sweden.

About one-quarter of the market consists of floating-rate bonds. UK issuers account for perhaps 80% of this market. Unlike the fixed-rate Eurosterling market, where there is a broad range of issuers, the issuers in this market are predominantly banks, building societies, and other financial institutions.

Bulldogs

The bulldog bond market is small, consisting of no more than 1% of the total sterling bond market. Most bulldogs that have been issued have been bullet bonds.

Domestic Bonds

Domestic bonds constitute perhaps 4% of the total sterling bond market. The largest component of the domestic market consists of debentures and loans. Debentures are secured on the assets of the company, whereas loan stock is not secured. The typical issuer of a debenture would be a property company or a brewery, while banks have dominated the loan stock market. Generally, debentures and loans have long maturities. The market has been stimulated by personal equity plans (PEPs) and individual savings accounts (ISAs) two forms of tax-exempt funds for private individuals.

BOND BASICS

In this section, we look at different measures of the return from a bond. In particular we will look at six different types of yield. The key points are summarized in Table 18.2. We begin, however, with a brief discussion of a money market instrument, Treasury bills. These are used in the markets, and by academics, as a proxy for a risk-free asset. We also explain accrued interest, a boring, but essential, detail.

TABLE 18.2   Six bond yields

Yield	Description
Nominal yield	The coupon rate
Interest yield (current yield, flat yield, running yield)	Current income rate
Redemption yield (yield to maturity)	Total rate of return if held to redemption (maturity)
Realized compound yield	Geometric mean return over a period
Yield to call	Total rate of return if held to first call date
Holding period return	Expected total rate of return for a given holding period or actual total rate of return for a past holding period

Treasury Bills

Treasury bills (T-bills) are issued by governments; they are short-term, marketable instruments. Treasury bills, at least in the UK and the US, do not pay interest. They are issued at a discount, i.e. they are issued at less than their nominal value, but repaid at their nominal value. In the UK, Treasury bills usually have a maturity of 91 days, but may be issued with maturity anywhere between 1 and 364 days.

UK Treasury bills are sold by tender on a competitive price basis. Tenders must be for amounts not less than £50 000 nominal, with the price specified to three decimal places. Bids are allocated in full to bidders at the highest price, until the bids exhaust the amount being tendered. Successful bidders pay the price they bid.

Accrued Interest

With equities, you are either entitled to the next dividend or you are not. With bonds, the position on interest is more complex. Bond interest is usually paid twice a year. If you bought a bond just before it paid its coupon, you would get, say, six months' interest immediately, and the seller would get nothing. To avoid this, an adjustment is required. The price quoted on the bond without taking account of interest is called the clean price. The buyer pays the clean price plus the value of the interest that is assumed to have accrued daily. The clean price plus the accrued is called the dirty price. So, the buyer receives the next coupon in its entirety, but he or she has already paid part of it to the seller. As a practical matter, if you bought a bond just before it paid its coupon, the cheque would end up going to the seller because the register would not be changed in time. To avoid this, bonds (and equities) are quoted either cum-dividend or ex-dividend. In the case of gilts, they go ex-dividend seven days before an interest payment. So, if you bought the bond six days before payment, all of the coupon would go to the seller, and you would lose six days' interest, unless an adjustment is made. This is achieved by the buyer receiving negative accrued interest, i.e. the dirty price will be below the clean price. Negative accrued interest is called rebate interest. The arithmetic of accrued interest for a semi-annual conventional gilt with standard dividend periods is:

$$\text{Accrued interest if the settlement date occurs on or before the ex-dividend date} = \frac{t}{s} \times \frac{c}{2}$$

$$\text{Accrued interest if the settlement date occurs after the ex-dividend date} = \left(\frac{t}{s} - 1\right) \times \frac{c}{2}$$

where c is the coupon per £100 nominal of the gilt, t is the number of calendar years from the last dividend date to the settlement date, and s is the number of calendar days in the full coupon period in which the settlement date occurs.

For short or long first dividend payment periods, the calculation is different (see Bank of England and HM Treasury, 1998).

Nominal Yield

The nominal yield, or coupon yield, of a bond is the percentage (say 9%) of the nominal value of the stock paid as interest each year. Only if a bond trades at its par (or nominal or face) value will this be the interest yield (see below) an investor receives.

Interest Yield

The interest yield on a bond—also called the current yield, flat yield and running yield—is simply the coupon divided by the clean price, expressed as a percentage. So, for the 9% Treasury 2008, which at the time of writing was priced at £123.25:

$$\text{Interest yield} = \frac{\text{coupon yield}}{\text{clean price}} = \frac{9\%}{123.25} = 7.3\%.$$

Redemption Yield

The yield shown above is the income you would get from buying that bond until it is redeemed. Compared with current interest rates, it seems quite high. So, what's the catch? When it redeems, you will get £100 for stock you paid £123.25 for. While you get a high income, you also get a capital loss. Your total percentage return is clearly less than 7.3%. A quick calculation for total return is:

$$\text{Approximate total return} = \text{interest yield} + \frac{\text{redemption price—current clean price}}{\text{years to redemption} \times \text{current clean price}} \times 100$$

or, for our example, assuming 8.375 years to redemption:

$$= 7.3 + \frac{100 - 123.25}{8.375 \times 123.25} \times 100 = 5.05\%.$$

Although this is a better measure of total return than the interest yield, it ignores the fact that the capital loss is some years in the future, while in the intervening years there is an income stream that could be invested to earn further interest. To allow for this we have to calculate the redemption yield or yield to maturity.

Let's step back. What determines the price of a bond? In the case of an equity, we decided that the price was the present value of the future revenue stream and we used a discounted dividend approach to calculate it. In the case of a bond, we would again expect the price to equal the present value of the revenue stream, which consists of the known interest payments and the known principal repayment. These cash flows will be discounted by an appropriate discount rate. This discount rate is the redemption yield.

Consider a simple example, ignoring accrued, and assuming one interest payment a year. Assume a bond is trading in the market at 95 and will pay a 10% coupon in one year exactly, and for the following three years, when it will be redeemed at 100. What is the redemption yield? We can set out the problem as follows, where y is the redemption yield:

$$\text{Price} = \frac{\text{coupon}}{(1 + y)} + \frac{\text{coupon}}{(1 + y)^2} + \frac{\text{coupon}}{(1 + y)^3} + \frac{\text{coupon} + \text{repayment of principal}}{(1 + y)^4}$$

substituting:

$$95 = \frac{10}{(1 + y)} + \frac{10}{(1 + y)^2} + \frac{10}{(1 + y)^3} + \frac{10 + 100}{(1 + y)^4}.$$

Outside the bond market, the discount rate that equates the present value of two sets of cash flows is called the internal rate of return. Using a standard computer package (such as Microsoft Excel™ or Lotus 1-2-3™) we can calculate that y = 11.63%.

The redemption yield takes account of the effect of reinvesting income. But what rate will be earned on the reinvested income? The calculation assumes that all income is reinvested at the redemption yield.

Although Eurobonds pay interest once a year, most government bonds in the UK and the US pay twice a year. To allow for this, we calculate the semi-annual redemption yield and double it. Converting the previous example to two payments a year we have:

$$95 = \frac{5}{(1 + \frac{y}{2})} + \frac{5}{(1 + \frac{y}{2})^2} + \frac{5}{(1 + \frac{y}{2})^3} + \frac{5}{(1 + \frac{y}{2})^4} + \frac{5}{(1 + \frac{y}{2})^5} + \frac{5}{(1 + \frac{y}{2})^6} + \frac{5}{(1 + \frac{y}{2})^7} + \frac{5 + 100}{(1 + \frac{y}{2})^8}$$

Solving for y, we find the semi-annual redemption yield = 5.8%, so the annual redemption yield = 5.8% × 2 = 11.6%.

This calculation is sometimes called the bond equivalent yield. It ignores compounding when converting from a semi-annual rate to an annual rate. In effect, it ignores that the first dividend each year earns interest in the second half of the year. To calculate the effective annual yield we use the expression:

$$\text{Effective annual yield} = \left(1 + \frac{\text{bond equivalent yield}}{2}\right)^2 - 1.$$

For our example, $(1 + 0.058)^2 -1 = 11.94\%$. To convert an effective annual yield to a bond equivalent yield we use:

$$\text{Bond equivalent yield} = 2[(1 + \text{effective annual yield})^{1/2} - 1].$$

That's the minutiae. What's the big picture? The interest yield is uninformative in an investment sense. If we want to know a bond's annualized total return, we need to calculate the redemption yield. However, the answer we get will depend on the frequency of interest payments and the assumptions made about how they compound. Different bond markets have different practices; redemption yields are only comparable if they are calculated on the same basis.

Redemption Yield for Unusual Bonds

Three bonds with unusual characteristics are:

- *Zero-coupon bonds:* these pay no interest and so there are only two entries in an internal rate of return calculation, the purchase price, say 65, and the redemption value, say 100 at the end of year four. The effective annual redemption yield is 11.37%.
- *Irredeemable bonds:* these pay the same yield forever, and have no redemption date; they therefore have no redemption yield. However, the current yield is a measure of the total rate of return if the bonds are held forever: effectively, the current yield and the redemption yield are the same thing.
- *Index-linked bonds:* these are covered in the next section.

Realized Compound Yield

The realized compound yield is the geometric mean return on an investment over a given period. It reflects the returns earned during that period. In the context of a bond, the realized compound yield will equal the redemption yield at purchase only if the bond is held to redemption and if all the coupons were reinvested at an interest rate equal to the bond's redemption yield. If the reinvestment rate for the coupons exceeds the redemption yield, the realized compound yield will be greater than the redemption yield. If the reinvestment rate for the coupons is less than the redemption yield, the realized compound yield will be less than the redemption yield.

The Yield to Call

Many bonds contain a provision that allows the issuer to call its bonds. This means that the issuer can repurchase the bonds before the redemption date at a fixed price, which is usually the par value plus a premium, perhaps 5% of par. The call provision is usually exercisable after a specified number of years, and the call premium may decline for each year past the first year the bond can be called. Clearly, if interest rates are high and then fall, the bond issuer will have an incentive to buy back the bonds and fund this by issuing new bonds at a lower interest rate. Instead of calculating a redemption yield, many investors calculate for callable bonds a yield to the first call date. In other words, interest payments are assumed through to the first call date, and on the call date the bond is redeemed on the specified terms. In reality, not all bonds are called on their first call date, or indeed ever. Consequently, the yield to call can be a misleading calculation.

Horizon Yield

When bonds are not held to redemption, the yield received will depend upon the coupon payments, the reinvestment rate, and the price at which the bond is sold. This yield is known as the horizon yield. An example of the horizon yield calculation is given in the next chapter.

INDEX-LINKED GILTS

Earlier in this chapter, we noted that bonds were normally described by a name, a nominal rate of interest, and a redemption date. The nominal rate of interest is usually a fixed percentage, for example 6%, paid on the par value, say £100. Repayment is usually at par. Index-linked stocks also have a name, coupon and redemption date, but both the coupon and the amount payable on redemption are expressed in real terms. Although there are a few index-linked stocks issued by corporations, usually only governments are willing to take the risk of issuing a bond with a potentially unlimited nominal return. Although a number of governments issued index-linked bonds before the UK government, the index-linked gilt market is currently the largest in the world. The US Treasury entered this market in 1997, and is steadily expanding it. In the spring of 2000, there were seven US issues with redemption dates ranging between 2002 and 2029.

Index-linked gilts were first issued in the UK in 1981, when £1bn of index-linked 2% stock 1996 was issued by tender. The issue was restricted to pension funds. In 1982, ownership restrictions were removed, and index-linked gilts were available to any investor, resident or non-resident. Index-linked stocks are likely to appeal to investors who have real, rather than nominal, liabilities. To governments, index-linked gilts may reduce the cost of issuing debt because it meets the needs of a particular group of investors. Also, when index-linked gilts were first issued, there was a difference between the market's and the government's perception of the likely course of inflation. The market assumed a higher rate of inflation than the government, and this meant that conventional gilts were being sold too cheaply based on the government's assumptions. By issuing a gilt that returned a known real return, this problem was overcome.

The method of indexation used for index-linked gilts is, at first sight, slightly odd. Each payment of interest and repayment of the principal is linked to the RPI. To calculate the inflation adjustment, two RPI figures are used—one applicable to when the stock was originally issued, and the other relating to the current payment. However, the RPI figures used are those of eight months preceding the two relevant dates. The reason for choosing this eight-month indexation lag was to allow the next receivable interest payment to be determined in advance of the period to which it related. When the first index-linked gilts were issued, gilts were normally quoted ex-dividend about 37 days before the due payment date, and since the RPI for any month is announced in the middle of the following month, eight months was the minimum feasible lag to calculate the dividend in nominal terms.

The formula for calculating an interest payment for an index-linked gilt is:

$$\text{Interest payment} = \frac{c}{2} \times \frac{RPI_{M-8}}{RPI_{I-8}}$$

where c = annual coupon (%); RPI_x = published RPI for month x; I = month gilt issued; and M = month in which interest payment is made.

All index-linked gilts pay two coupons a year, hence the term $c/2$ in the above equation. We will illustrate the use of this formula with an example taken from the Debt Management Office (1999), for the 4.125% index-linked Treasury 2030, which was originally issued in June 1992. The base RPI figure for this stock is the RPI figure for October 1991, which was 135.1. This gilt pays coupons in January and July, so the relevant RPI figures are those for the preceding May and November, respectively. The coupon for January 1998 was therefore calculated as:

$$\text{Interest payment} = \frac{c}{2} \times \frac{\text{RPI for May 1997}}{\text{RPI for October 1991}} = \frac{4.125}{2} \times \frac{156.9}{135.1} = 2.3953\%.$$

If you had owned £100 of stock and were eligible for that dividend, you would have received £2.395. (The market practice is to round to the nearest sixth decimal place.) When the stock is redeemed in July 2030, the value of a £100 nominal holding will be:

$$\text{Redemption payment} = 100 \times \frac{RPI_{R-8}}{RPI_{I-8}}$$

where RPI_x = published RPI for month x; I = month gilt issued; and R = month in which gilt redeems.

$$\text{Redemption payment in July 2030} = 100 \times \frac{\text{RPI for November 2029}}{\text{RPI for October 1991}}.$$

Note that the period for indexation ends in November 2029.

As we saw earlier, the redemption yield provides a measure of total return from a bond. Calculating a redemption yield for a conventional bond is easy enough, as we know all the relevant variables. However, as we see from the above equation for the redemption payment, the nominal value of the payment is unknown. Therefore, to calculate a redemption yield for an index-linked stock, it is necessary to make an assumption about the rate of inflation. You could forecast inflation in much the same way as earnings are forecast for a stock in a DDM. For example, we might have a three-stage inflation model whereby we specify actual rates of inflation for a year or two, then have some adjustment period where inflation rate moves steadily towards a constant rate that will apply for the rest of the life of the gilt. However, in practice, a constant inflation rate is normally assumed for the entire period from calculation to maturity.

Given an inflation assumption, it is possible to calculate a nominal cash flow stream for an index-linked gilt by calculating nominal dividends and a final nominal redemption sum. Given this information, the nominal yield can then be calculated by the internal rate of return formula. This nominal return will include the effect of the inflation rate assumption. The next step is to convert the nominal rate to a real rate. We saw on p. 24 how real and nominal rates are related. However, because of the two coupon payments a year, the slightly scarier looking formula shown below has to be used. Readers who dislike maths need only think in terms of the analysis on p. 24, which will give an approximate answer.

$$(1 + \frac{r}{200})^2 = (1 + \frac{n}{200})^2 / (1 + \frac{i}{100})$$

or:

$$r = 200 \times (1 + \frac{n}{200}) / \sqrt{(1 + \frac{i}{200})}$$

where r = real yield (%); n = nominal yield (%); and i = inflation assumption.

Imagine we calculate the nominal redemption yield is 5%, and we assumed 3% inflation. If we solve the above equation, the real yield turns out to be 1.99%. In newspapers such as the *Financial Times*, real yields for index-linked stock are shown based on the assumption of a 3% rate of inflation and also on the assumption of a 5% rate of inflation.

WHAT DETERMINES BOND YIELD LEVELS?

A bond's yield is determined by:

- general market interest rates
- specific features of the bond.

We look at each in turn.

General Market Interest Rates

The nominal rate of interest observed in the market on a default-free bond is assumed to consist of two parts, a real rate of interest and an additional component that offsets inflation. For bonds that might default, there will be a risk premium as well. For long-term asset allocation decisions, it is often assumed that the real rate on a long bond will be about 3%. This is discussed in more detail in Chapter 23. Day-to-day forecasts of interest rates tend to focus on nominal rates. Chapter 8 contains a brief discussion of economic forecasting, but not specifically interest rate forecasting. Here we comment briefly on some factors that the bond markets watch. A full discussion of interest rate forecasting is beyond the scope of this book.

Six factors often discussed in bond markets are:

- domestic economic conditions
- domestic monetary policy
- domestic inflation expectations
- the domestic budget deficit/surplus
- all of the above for the US
- international capital flows.

Domestic economic conditions are watched because there is some tendency for interest rates to move with changes in GDP. In periods of rapid economic growth, there will be a strong demand from business to fund increases in working capital and fixed assets. Consumers are also likely to borrow more and save less.

Inflation expectations are formed on the basis of economic conditions and monetary policy, but they are also based on whether it is likely that there will be a change in these policies. For example, a change of government may change the policy trade-off between growth and inflation. Other factors, such as what is happening to the price of commodities, especially the price of oil, are considered. Inflation expectations are also partly formed on the basis of actual or anticipated changes in the exchange rate.

In the 1970s, bond investors were surprised by the high rates of inflation, and bonds produced poor returns. Following this experience, in the 1980s bond investors were concerned that future interest rates were more uncertain than they had previously thought and bonds were therefore riskier. As a result, the real component of interest rates increased for some years.

The monetary authorities of most of the major developed economies have an objective of achieving low inflation. To do this, they may raise interest rates and sell government securities. When they sell securities, the purchaser draws cash from his or her bank, and thereby runs down the bank's cash reserves. This in turn will lead to a contraction of lending activity by the bank. When the economy is facing recession and has a modest rate of price increases, the monetary authorities will reverse these actions. Accordingly, the actions of the monetary authorities are watched carefully.

The size of the government's borrowing will affect the level of the economy and anticipated inflation, and will increase the demand for funds, unless other borrowers borrow less. In the 1970s, many governments ran deficits and the amount of government stock to be absorbed was a continuing problem. However, at the start of the twenty-first century, a number of governments, including those of the US and the UK, have budget surpluses. Many European governments have, or will have, obtained large one-off payments from the private sector as a result of bids to purchase radio spectrum.

As well as watching the domestic economy, most bond investors watch what is going on in the wider world, especially the US, even if they are only interested in their own market.

In some economies interest rates will be affected by international flows. The US budget deficits of the 1980s were partly financed by foreign investors. The effect, presumably, was to keep interest rates lower than they might otherwise have been.

Some studies have attempted to find the most important factors in determining bond rates. For example, Jankus (1997) related macroeconomic factors to the five year swap rate (which is effectively the five-year bond rate) in 15 Organization for Economic Cooperation and Development (OECD) countries. The macroeconomic factors he considered were GDP growth rate, consumer inflation rate, government budget balance as a percentage of GDP, current account balance as a percentage of GDP, and the unemployment rate. He used forecast rates for each of these variables. He also assumed that a market's liquidity was proportional to the total capitalization of the country's government bond market and included this as a variable. He found that expected inflation and expected budget balance were important variables in determining global yields.

Bond-Specific Factors

The above discussion provides background to the general level of interest rates. However, the rate on a specific bond will depend on a number of additional factors:

- term (years) to maturity
- default risk
- marketability
- tax treatment
- call provisions.

Before discussing these points in detail, let's set out the big picture. Imagine a 10-year gilt or US Treasury bond. Economic factors will have established a market yield for it. We might expect different factors to come into play for a one-year bond, so the rate may be higher or lower. In general, we would expect the term to maturity to affect a bond's yield. Now think of, say, a 10-year corporate bond. What will its yield be? Well, it won't be as safe as the government bond—the company could go bust—so we would expect it to yield more. It probably won't be as marketable as a government bond, so it will probable yield a bit more on that score too. The tax treatment of the bond may be better or worse than that for a government bond, so it may yield either a little less because of that, or a little more. Finally, there may be some special features of the bond, such as call provisions, that are disadvantageous to lenders, who will expect yield enhancement to compensate for that. That's the big picture. Let's now look at the details.

The Term Structure of Interest Rates

The term structure of interest rates refers to the yield of bonds that are identical except for their maturity dates, i.e. they have different terms to maturity or redemption. If we plot the yields of such bonds against their terms to maturity, the resulting graph is called a yield curve. Strictly speaking, the term structure of interest rates deals with pure discount bonds of different maturities. It is normal to use government bonds when constructing a yield curve, but neither the UK nor the US governments issue zero-coupon bonds. Accordingly, a theoretically correct yield curve cannot simply be observed but has to be estimated. This estimation procedure can be tackled in a number of different ways, but it is complex. We will skip the details here and simply assume that we have a yield curve.

What shape will a yield curve have? Will interest rates rise as term to maturity increases, will they fall, or will interest rates be the same irrespective of the term to maturity? There are three theories that attempt to explain the shape of the yield curve:

- expectations theory
- liquidity premium theory
- segmentation theory.

We examine each theory in turn.

Expectations Theory

Imagine that we observe in the market a one-year zero-coupon bond with a redemption yield of 5%, and that we also observe a two-year zero-coupon bond with a redemption yield of 6%. Assume also that we want to invest for two years. Should we buy the two-year bond, or should we buy the one-year bond and then when it matures buy another one-year bond? Alternatively, we want to invest for one year. Should we buy a one-year bond, or a two-year bond that we sell after one year? Expectations theory argues that it doesn't matter which we choose, because the two-year bond's yield consists of the current one-year yield plus the market's expectation of the one-year yield in 12 months' time. If investors were risk-neutral, then they would simply buy the package of bonds that gave the highest return. Therefore, if a one-year bond followed by a one-year bond gave a higher return than a two-year bond, investors would sell the two-year bond and buy the one-year bond. This would cause the price of the two bonds to change until both methods of making a two-year investment offered the same return.

Thus, if a two-year bond offers a 6% yield while a one-year bond offers a 5% yield, the market must be forecasting that one-year interest rates will rise, in one year's time, to 7.01%, as we show below. In short, we can use the yield curve to derive the market's implicit yield forecasts. The shape of the yield curve simply reflects the market's current view of the direction of interest rates. Figure 18.1 summarizes the expectations theory of term structure graphically.

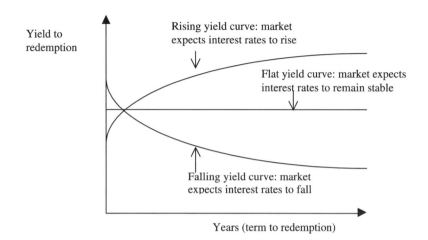

FIGURE 18.1 Expectations theory of term structure

Let's look first at the arithmetic. Imagine two zero-coupon bonds: a one-year bond costing £952.38 for £1000 nominal, and a two-year bond costing £890.00 for £1000 nominal. If we buy the one-year bond at £952.38, and receive no interest, but receive repayment of £1000 in one year, we can calculate the return (y) as:

$$952.38 \times (1 + y) = 1000$$

$$y = \frac{1000}{952.38} - 1 = 0.05 = 5\%.$$

Thus, the return on the one-year bond is 5%. What rate is being assumed as the one-year rate in one year's time? Imagine now that we buy the two-year zero. Then:

$$890 \times (1 + y_1) \times (1 + y_2) = 1000$$

where y_1 is the one-year rate now, which we know is 5%; and y_2 is the one-year rate in year 2. Substituting and rearranging:

$$y_2 = \frac{1000}{1.05 \times 890} - 1 = 0.0701 = 7.01\%.$$

There is another way of looking at the argument we made about expectations. What we have shown above is simply arithmetic. We can make an alternative argument about what it means. Since it is unusual to assume that investors are risk-neutral, an alternative explanation might be more plausible. The expectations theory assumes that investors want all bonds, whatever their maturity, to yield the same as, say, a one-year bond. In that case, forward rates forecast expected rates. But it could be that investors don't expect a shift in rates. They may wish different maturities to offer different returns. Thus, if current yields on one-year and two-year bonds are 5% and 6%, respectively, the forward rate of 7.01% is a forecast of the rate of return an investor will make from buying a two-year bond today and selling it as a one-year bond next year. In other words, we can view the yield curve in two ways. In one explanation, the expectations theory, the yield curve is forecasting interest rates; in the other explanation, the yield curve is forecasting holding period returns.

An obvious test is to see whether forward rates do forecast accurately. The evidence is that forward rates are not good short-term predictors of interest rates; on average, forward rates are too high, which suggests that bond investors expect to earn a premium for holding long-term bonds rather than short-term bonds. Indeed, in the period 1950–90, the spread between long and short rates is in the opposite direction to that predicted by the expectations theory. For example, when the yield on long-term bonds is above the yield on short-term bonds, future yields on long-term bonds are more likely to fall than to rise.

Liquidity Premium Theory

Expectations theory assumes that bond investors, or at least some, are indifferent to the maturity of the bonds they hold. Liquidity premium theory assumes that investors act much as in the expectations theory, but that they must be offered a premium for moving longer in the market. This theory, in effect, assumes that there is a shortage of buyers of long-dated bonds, and that investors who prefer the short end of the market have to be rewarded to move longer. This might be because the long end of the market bears the greatest interest rate risk, as explained in the next chapter. Borrowers, however, might prefer to borrow long to ensure a supply of funds. This would mean a potential mismatch in the market. Speculators should step in to provide the match. So, it must also be assumed that speculators are risk-averse and require a liquidity premium to induce them to hold long bonds. The effect of this theory is to give an upward bias to the yield curve: see Figure 18.2. If rates are expected to rise, then the existence of the liquidity premium will make the yield curve even steeper. If interest rates are expected to be unchanged, the yield curve will slope upwards. And if interest rates are expected to fall, then the liquidity premium will moderate this fall; indeed it would be possible, depending on the size of the premium, for the yield curve to actually rise despite expectations of falling rates.

While there is some evidence supporting this theory, at the simplest level we might expect over long periods that long bonds would offer a significant premium over Treasury bills. Dimson et al. (2000) report that over the last century, the maturity premium in the UK was 0.3%. For the 12 countries they studied, it was 0.6%. Of course, bondholders were surprised by inflation, and this means the realized and expected premiums will have diverged. If you just look at the last half-century, the risk premium is higher. For example, Campbell et al. (1997, Chapter 10), for a 40-year period in the US, find 10-year bonds earn about 1.37% more than one-month Treasury bills. However, most of the premium is earned in the first two years. The premium over one-month bills is about ⅓% at three months, at one year about ¾%, and about 1% at two years. So why don't the rewards increase significantly as you move longer? Perhaps some investors like being long, which takes us to the third theory.

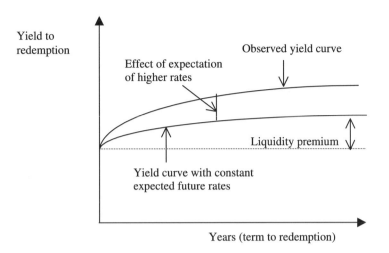

FIGURE 18.2   Liquidity premium theory of term structure

Segmentation Theory

Segmentation theory assumes that the market is divided into a number of habitats or zones that certain investors select. For example, life assurance companies often have a need for a long-dated bond to match their liabilities. Accordingly, their natural habitat would be at the long end of the market. The insurance company does have the option of buying one-year bonds and rolling them over every year, but it may see this as excessively risky. Accordingly, even if the market is not priced to reflect investors' interest rate expectations, no likely yield differential will make the investor shift out of his or her habitat. With this theory, the supply and demand conditions within the various habitats will determine the shape of the yield curve. This theory is popular with practitioners, and it is frequently assumed in many press articles, although whether the writers know that they are adopting this theory is not clear.

Taylor (1992) tested the expectations model and the market segmentation model for the UK gilt market over the period 1985–89. He rejected the expectations model, finding that long-term interest rates tended to overreact to information relevant only to short-term rates. The data supported the segmentation theory.

Summing Up

There seem to be few strict adherents to expectations theory. But investors do look at forward rates. Liquidity preference theory seems sensible, but there has historically been little reward for going long, especially if one allows for the high volatility incurred. Preferred habit theory is clearly true in some periods. But is it generally true in most periods? Forecasting the shape of the yield curve seems to be as much art as science.

Default Risk

In the discussion of bond basics, we noted that different issuers had different degrees of probability of defaulting on their payments. Since bonds offer no prospect of growth, and are bought mainly for their relatively low risk, the issue of default is an important one. The pattern of yields associated with bonds with varying default risk is called the risk structure of bond yields.

In the major bond markets, various companies assess the credit-worthiness of bond issues. This industry is particularly well developed in the US because of the large number of corporate and other issues. The US bond rating companies assign quality ratings to thousand of corporate and municipal bonds, and to preferred stock and commercial paper. The two leading rating firms are Standard & Poor's and Moody's. Each rates the bonds of more than 2000 companies. Smaller rating agencies include Fitch and Duff & Phelps.

A bond rating is the rating company's assessment of the quality of the security being rated and is a measure of its relative default risk. Bond rating services rate bond issues, not the issuer. Thus, if a company issues two bonds, one of which is secured and one of which is unsecured, there is no inconsistency if they bear different ratings. Further, the rating measures the likelihood of default, not the merits of an issue as an investment.

Standard & Poor's and Moody's ratings for corporate bonds and the meaning of some of the ratings are shown in Table 18.3. For many investors, the key issue is whether a bond is of investment grade—some investors are prohibited from investing in speculative issues.

Bond ratings appear to be quite successful. A major study by Hickman (1958) covering the period 1900–43 found that 6% of bonds (by par value) defaulted before maturity in the rating category equivalent to Standard & Poor's AAA, 13% in rating A, and 42% in the rating below BBB. More recently, Altman (1991) studied the default rates for US bonds over the period 1971–90. Altman found that the cumulative rate of default increased over time. For example, bonds rated AAA had no defaults in the first year but by year 10, 0.17% had defaulted. He also found that the rate of default increased as one moved down the bond ratings. For example, in the first year, 1.55% of bonds rated CCC defaulted, and after year 10, the cumulative default rate was 37.85%.

The ratings agencies claim to base their ratings on a mixture of information, including business analysis, financial analysis and subjective factors. However, attempts by academics to predict bond ratings by using factors such as low debt ratios, high and stable earnings levels, high return on capital, high interest cover, and high cash flow to debt have proved quite successful.

If there is a relationship between bond ratings and likelihood of default, we should expect to see that expected yields to maturity are inversely related to bond ratings. And that is what we find. One might also look directly at the underlying firm characteristics and yields. Fisher (1959) argued that the yield difference between a corporate bond and a government bond of the same maturity and coupon is due to default risk and marketability. He measured

TABLE 18.3   US corporate bond ratings

Investment rating		Description
Standard & Poor's	Moody's	
		High-grade investment bonds
AAA	Aaa	Highest quality: extremely strong capacity to repay interest and principal
AA+	Aa1	
AA	Aa2	Very strong capacity to pay interest and principal
AA–	Aa3	
		Medium-grade investment bonds
A+	A1	
A	A2	Upper-medium grade
A–	A3	
BBB+	Baa1	
BBB	Baa2	
BBB–	Baa3	Lower-medium grade
		Speculative grade bonds
BB+	Ba1	
BB	Ba2	Low grade, speculative
BB–	Ba3	
B+	B1	
B	B2	
B–	B3	
CCC+		
CCC	Caa	Issuer will probably default in adverse business conditions
CCC–		
CC	Ca	
C	C	
C–		
D		Issue is in default

marketability by the market value of the firm's outstanding debt, and default risk by three variables: earnings variability, the length of time since the firm had missed repaying its creditors, and the equity/debt ratio. The yield difference between a corporate bond and a government bond was lower the higher the marketability, the lower the earnings variability, the longer the time without default, and the higher the equity/debt ratio.

Estimating the return from a bond after making allowance for the possibility of default is quite tricky. Even if a bond eventually defaults, unless it does so immediately it will make some coupon payments, and the bond holders may receive some repayment of principal, even if not all of it. Imagine that we do such a calculation and decide that bonds with a certain rating and an expected redemption yield of 10% will, because of the pattern of defaults, only produce a realized yield of 8%. If government bonds are offering 8%, the expected returns are the same. But it would not be an equilibrium position. While we could form a portfolio of the bonds and diversify away the unsystematic risk, the risk of default would be related to the state of the economy. More companies are likely to default in a recession than in a boom period. In other words, corporate bonds also bear systematic risk. Using the arguments of the CAPM, we would expect corporate bonds to offer a risk premium as well as a default premium. The size of the risk premium is likely to vary over time, and therefore we would expect to see the spread between government bond yields and corporate bond yields to vary with the economic cycle.

An Aside: Equity Risk Revisited

Credit ratings measure an aspect of risk. There is no particular theory involved; rather it is common sense that suggests the factors used are related to risk. The publication *Value Line* assigns safety ranks to the stocks it covers. It uses two primary factors: the stock's price stability, which is a ranking of the stock's standard deviation of returns compared with that for all other stocks followed by *Value Line*, and the stock's financial strength rating, which is based on variables such as debt coverage, firm size, quick ratio, and so on. Fuller and Wong (1988) found a much better relationship between risk, as measured in this common sense way, and return than they did for beta and return. It seems odd that there has been so little interest in using common sense risk measures when assessing the relationship between risk and return for equities.

Bond Marketability

Bond marketability or liquidity refers to the ability to buy or sell a bond quickly without having to make significant price concessions. While government bonds usually are highly liquid, many corporate bonds seldom trade after issue. Although a transaction can be effected, often only with the issuing broker, the bid–ask spread will be very wide. Marketability can be assessed by the size of the issue and the quoted bid–ask spread. The smaller the issue, and the larger the bid–ask spread, the greater the redemption yield premium the bond has to offer over a comparable maturity government bond.

The importance of the size of an issue on its marketability is well illustrated by the fact that in recent years, gilt issuance has been concentrated on building up large benchmark issues. The UK authorities have maintained benchmark issues in the five-, 10- and 30-year areas by further issues of existing stocks.

Tax Effects

Different types of bonds are subject to different forms of taxation. If investors are interested in their after-tax return, different types of bond will have to pay different interest rates to produce the same after-tax return for an investor. One of the clearest examples of the tax effect involves US state and local bonds. Interest income paid by such bonds is not subject to federal tax, and usually is not subject to local tax in the state of issue. Realized capital gains are subject to tax. If we assume a local bond trading at close to par so that we can ignore capital gains, then the after-tax return on the local bond will be the same as the pre-tax return. The corporate bond after-tax return, however, will be reduced by federal taxes. If we assume these are 33.33%, then a 9% corporate bond would give the same after-tax return as a 6% local bond.

While there clearly is a tax effect in the yields offered on local and state bonds in the US, the position is less clear in other cases. In the UK, for example, UK individuals are subject to tax on interest received on gilts but are not liable to capital gains tax on the disposal of gilts. Since index-linked gilts pay more of their return in the form of untaxed gain than do conventional gilts, private investors should accept lower yields on index-linked relative to conventional. Corporate investors are liable to tax on the total return from their holdings of gilts. However, the inflation uplift on the principal for index-linked gilts is excluded from tax. Accordingly, they too should prefer index-linked gilts to conventional gilts. However, as both types of investor are small players in the gilts market, it is unclear whether these tax effects do operate.

Call Provisions

We noted earlier that many corporate bonds have call provisions. Because this is detrimental to bondholders, we expect callable bonds to sell on a higher yield than non-callable. In Figure 18.3, we show the yield curves for three types of bonds. Because of credit risk, corporate bonds offer a higher yield than government bonds, and callable corporate bonds offer a higher yield than straight corporate bonds.

We saw earlier that a yield to call can be calculated, but this is not the best way of evaluating callable bonds. A better approach is to think in terms of options analysis. (Options are discussed in Chapter 21.) The bond issuer has an option—

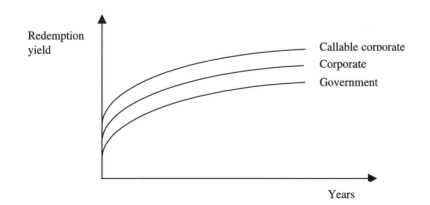

FIGURE 18.3 Yield curves for three types of bond

the right, but not the obligation—to call the bond. Therefore, we can think of a callable bond investor being:

Long a callable bond = long a straight bond + short a call option on the bond.

Readers wishing to pursue this approach should consult a specialist bond textbook.

REPOS AND STRIPS

To end this chapter we will briefly outline repos and strips. Open trading in repos and strips is relatively new in the gilt market, but since the terms are often heard in the markets, a few words seem warranted.

Repurchase Agreements

A repurchase agreement (repo) involves one party selling a security to another with an agreement to repurchase equivalent securities at an agreed price (repurchase price) on an agreed date (repurchase date). A repo could involve any sort of security, but usually repos consist of Treasury bills or government bonds. In essence, a repo is a collateralized loan, with the security being the collateral. In 1996, an open trading market in gilt repos was introduced.

How does a repo work? Investor A might sell to investor B £5 million of gilts. As part of the contract, A signs a repo with investor B to repurchase the gilt after one month for £5.05 million. In effect, investor A has paid investor B (who might be a fund manager) a rate of interest to borrow money. That rate of interest is the repo rate. There are two main types of gilt repos—general collateral (GC) repo and specific repo. With GC repos, the gilts to be received as collateral are not specified. In the case of a specific repo, a particular gilt is specified. The repo rate for a specific repo may be more or less than the GC repo rate. Readily available gilts will receive five to 10 basis points below the GC rate. A gilt that is difficult to obtain will have a repo rate five to 10 basis points above the GC rate.

Although collateral is supplied, there is credit risk in a repo. Say party A cannot repurchase the gilts. Although party B has the gilts, if interest rates have risen, then their value will have declined.

Strips

We saw earlier that zero-coupon bonds had certain unique features. Unfortunately, neither the UK nor the US governments issue zero-coupon bonds. However, if you think of a 10-year bond paying interest twice a year, you can consider this bond to have 21 components, i.e. 10×2 interest payments and one principal repayment. If each of these components were traded separately, they would constitute 21 zero-coupon bonds. In 1982, Merrill Lynch and Salomon Brothers created synthetic zero-coupon Treasury bonds. In 1985, the US Treasury announced its strips programme. Strips is an acronym for Separately Traded and Registered Interest and Principal Securities. The zero-coupon bonds created under this programme are direct obligations of the government. The programme was a huge success, and in 1997 the UK introduced a strip programme. In the UK, only a gilt-edged market maker, the Debt Management Office or the Bank of England can strip a gilt, i.e. break a gilt down into its component parts.

Despite the success of stripping Treasury bonds in the US, the UK gilt strip market has been slow to develop. The Debt Management Office attributes this to the need for pension funds to get permission from their trustees to invest in these securities, the effect of an inverted yield curve, and the adverse tax treatment suffered by private clients. On the latter point, the securities are taxed each year on their capital gain or loss, although no income payment has been made. Gilt strips can be held within an ISA, a tax-exempt savings account for private investors. However, the maximum sum that can be invested in ISAs is small, and it seems unlikely that most ISA investors will know what a gilt strip is. It seems improbable that private investors will be significant holders of these securities.

CONCLUDING COMMENTS

In this chapter we have looked at the different types of bond, the different types of issuer, and the different places of issue. We described the sterling bond market. We then looked at some bond basics, including six different types of yield. The unusual nature of index-linked bonds was outlined.

We next tackled what determines bond yields. We briefly discussed some factors affecting market rates in general before discussing bond-specific factors—the term structure of interest rates, default risk, marketability, tax treatment and call provisions. With this background we are now in a position to consider bond strategy, the topic of the next chapter.

19

Bond Strategy

Mountains of junk bonds were sold by those who didn't care to those that didn't think—and there was no shortage of either.

Warren Buffett

Bond managers, like equity managers, may adopt a passive or active style. Passive investors attempt to match the performance of an index or benchmark, while active managers attempt to outperform a benchmark or index. We will look at passive and active managers in turn. To give an indication of some of the approaches discussed, we show below some of the style definitions that managers and consultants use:

- *Index manager.*
- *Low-quality:* manager invests a high percentage of funds in bonds rated below investment grade, i.e. junk bonds or high-yield bonds.
- *High-quality:* invests only in investment-grade bonds.
- *Mechanical strategies:* management of immunized or dedicated portfolios.
- *Short-term:* manager invests mainly in bonds with a maturity of one to three years, or one to five years, the definition depending on the market. Attempts to add value by quality/coupon/sector swapping.
- *Intermediate:* manager invests mainly in bonds with a maturity of three to seven years, or five to 15 years, the definition depending on the market.
- *Long-term:* manager invests mainly in bonds with a maturity of anywhere from over seven years up to over 15 years, the definition depending on the market.
- *Interest rate anticipation:* manager moves portfolio to benefit from anticipated changes in the yield curve.
- *Specialized:* manager specializes in a narrow area, for example junk bond convertibles.

PASSIVE BOND MANAGEMENT

The argument for managing bonds passively is similar to that for managing equity funds passively: the bond market is efficient and fund managers are unable to outperform it. For example, Blake et al. (1993) measured the performance of 223 bond funds for the five-year period ending in 1991. They compared the return earned by each fund with the return on a combination of passive portfolios, each with the same risk. Most funds underperformed. The average underperformance by all funds was about 1.25% p.a., and the average expenses for these funds was a little over 1%. In other words, before expenses, these funds were a little below the market.

There are two forms of passive bond management, buy-and-hold and indexation.

Buy-and-hold

Before the 1970s, most bonds were bought with a view to being held to maturity. In effect, investors bought and held. What they bought depended on their attitude to risk, and their needs. For example, if an investor believed he would never have to sell his bonds, then it would be worth buying relatively illiquid bonds given that they would offer a higher yield. This could be implemented to various degrees. For example, on-the-run Treasury bonds, i.e. Treasury bonds recently issued and actively traded, typically trade at a slightly higher price and slightly lower redemption yield than other Treasury bonds. A buy-and-hold investor would ignore these, even if building a high-quality portfolio. Some investors might ignore government bonds altogether and buy illiquid corporate bonds. Once the portfolio is set up according to the investor's needs, action is required only under unusual circumstances, or when a bond matures.

Buy-and-hold bond management may seem rather dated, but it is probably practised more often than is thought. For example, many private client portfolio managers will manage a client's entire portfolio, both bonds and equities. Such managers often effectively adopt a buy-and-hold strategy for the bond component of the fund. It is there to generate income and reduce the volatility of the portfolio; it is not viewed as an area for active management. It probably makes sense to view institutional bond management as being undertaken at two levels. Bond specialists only invest in bonds, and, depending on their mandate, may make switches from one bond to another for very small amounts of incremental return. But some institutional equity managers who are responsible for balanced portfolios will hold a small weighting in bonds, either continuously or from time to time. They may decide that they wish to increase their weighting in bonds and, say, go to the long end of the yield curve. They may go to a bond specialist to choose particular bonds, but they will not be looking for switch opportunities. Depending on the institutional structure, a bond manager may be responsible for managing that bond component. But in other cases, the equity manager will be left to take the initiative, and may switch to a buy-and-hold strategy. At some point, the bond weighting may be changed, but again this will be viewed in the context of total portfolio strategy, and not be seen specifically as a bond issue.

Bond Index Funds

In the same way that there has been a move towards indexation of equity portfolios, there has been a move towards indexation of bond portfolios. In some areas, it is relatively easy to index. For example, the UK gilt market has only 60 or so issues. On the other hand, if you wanted to index the US bond market including Treasury, agency, investment-grade corporate and mortgage-backed, the position is much more complex. The leading three indexes are the Lehman Brothers Aggregate Index, the Salomon Brothers Broad Investment-Grade Index, and the Merrill Lynch Domestic Market Index, all of which have over 5000 issues. And constant rebalancing is necessary because, as bonds mature, they drop out of indexes (strictly speaking, they drop out one year before they mature, because issues with less than one year to maturity are not treated as bonds). Further, the income flows from bonds are larger than those from equities, and therefore reinvestment is more of an issue. As a result, full replication, which is feasible in equity markets, is less often employed in the bond markets. The tracking error for any broad index from full replication would likely be large, because of the costs of reinvesting cash and replacing maturing stocks; and also many of the prices used in the construction of the index are not prices at which deals could be effected.

While there are a number of approaches to bond indexation, the most common in practice is stratified sampling. An index could be stratified by market sectors (government, corporate, etc.), duration, maturity, coupon, credit rating, and factors that change the life of the bond, such as call features and sinking-fund features. This approach is often called the cell approach because we can think of the index as being divided up into cells. For example, if we used the market-type classification of simply Treasury and non-Treasury, and had three measures of maturity—short, medium and long—this would involve six cells, i.e. three different maturity cells for each of the two sectors of the market.

The more variables used in the stratification, and the finer the division of each variable, the greater the number of cells. If five characteristics were identified and each partitioned into two, there would be 32 cells ($2 \times 2 \times 2 \times 2 \times 2$). The idea, then, is to purchase stocks that satisfy the characteristics of each cell and have a value that reflects the weighting of the cell in the index. Clearly, the number of cells used will depend upon a trade-off of transactions costs, tracking error as a result of not matching the characteristics of the index, and the size of the portfolio to be indexed. Increasing the characteristics and their number of divisions causes an explosion in the number of cells. For example, if you used six characteristics and three divisions of each characteristic there would be $3 \times 3 \times 3 \times 3 \times 3 \times 3 = 729$ cells. Purchasing stocks for 729 cells would involve some very small positions and most of the rebalancing problems that were discussed above.

Critics of equity indexing point to the danger of being heavily invested in a few sectors because of the very high ratings of a few stocks. Without arguing the merits of the point, one can at least say that these are popular stocks. In the bond market, the problem is almost the reverse. Governments that have low or negative budget deficits don't issue many bonds. What bonds they have issued should be attractive. Governments that run deficits will need to issue bonds, but these bonds should be relatively unattractive. However, the index funds will have to buy them. Currently, Japan is continuing to issue bonds while the US and UK governments have largely withdrawn from the markets. Over the second half of the 1990s, Japan's share of the JP Morgan broad global bond index rose from about 12% to nearly 23%. Of course, trustees can establish an index benchmark that has a lower Japanese weighting if they wish.

ACTIVE BOND MANAGEMENT

Active bond management can be tackled via fundamental analysis or technical analysis. We omit from the following discussion technical analysis, which uses some of the chartist methods discussed in Chapter 15. Technical analysis is used less widely in the bond market than in the equity market.

Given a benchmark, whether to meet certain liabilities or beat a particular index, there are three main decisions to be made in active bond management:

- What is the overall market outlook, i.e. are interest rates going up or down? This will usually be tackled by some form of macroeconomic assessment and appraisal of funding requirements. An attempt to exploit interest rate expectations by switching from one stock to another is known as an interest rate anticipation switch. (What is called a switch in the UK is called a swap in the US: the UK terminology seems preferable to avoid confusion with the swaps market—see pp. 366–7.)
- What are the relative attractions of the various broad sectors of the bond market? Yield curve switches involve analysis of the level and shape of the yield curve over the course of a year or so, and choices between shorts/ mediums/longs. Intermarket yield spread switches are based on abnormal yield spreads between markets such as junk bonds versus investment grade bonds, government bonds versus corporate bonds, etc.
- Within each sector, which bonds are relatively cheap or dear? This involves comparing individual stocks with each other, either directly in pairs, or against a market average. There are two types of switch made in this category—pure yield pick-up and substitution switches.

THE PRICE VOLATILITY OF BONDS

Easily the most important factor affecting bond returns in any year is changes in interest rate levels. While all bonds are affected by a general interest rate change, some are affected more than others. Here we seek to discover what causes these differences. We begin with some basic notions.

If a bond's redemption yield changes, then the price of the bond must also change. There are five well-known bond price/yield relationships (Malkiel, 1962):

- Bond prices and bond yields move in opposite directions. If the yield on a bond rises, its price must fall; if the yield on a bond falls, the price of the bond must rise. Price and yield are like the two ends of a see-saw. Consider an irredeemable stock paying interest of 10, and that has a price of 100. The yield is 10%. If market yields fall to 5%, the price of the bond will rise to 200, since 10 divided by 200 equals 5%. If yields rise to 20%, the price of the bond will fall to 50, since 10 divided by 50 equals 20%.
- The longer the maturity of a bond, given the coupon rate, the more sensitive the price of the bond to changes in interest rates. This is illustrated in Table 19.1 in columns two to four. Three bonds of different maturities are shown, all with the same coupon rate and par value. The price of the bond is shown for a redemption yield (RY) of 10% and then for an assumed decrease to 8%. The penultimate row shows that the percentage increase in price increases with maturity. If the redemption yield instead rises by 2% from 10% to 12%, then the percentage fall in prices increases with maturity.

TABLE 19.1   Effect on price of changes in redemption yield

	1-year bond	10-year bond	20-year bond	20-year bond
Par value	1000	1000	1000	1000
Coupon rate (%)	10	10	10	0
(a) Price at 10% RY	1000	1000	1000	148.64
(b) Price at 8% RY	1018.52	1134.20	1196.36	214.55
(c) Price at 12% RY	982.14	887.00	850.61	103.67
% change in price, (a) to (b)	1.85	13.42	19.64	44.34
% change in price, (a) to (c)	−1.79	−11.30	−14.94	−30.25

RY, redemption yield.

- The responsiveness of the price of a bond to a change in required yield, given the coupon rate, increases with maturity but at a decreasing rate. This can be seen from Table 19.1, where the difference between the percentage change of a one-year bond and a 10-year bond for a given change in yield is greater than the difference between the percentage change in the price of the 10-year bond and the 20-year bond. In other words, making a switch from a short-dated stock to a medium-dated stock increases price volatility much more than moving from a medium-dated stock to a long-dated stock.
- The lower the coupon rate, given the maturity, the more volatile the price of the bond for a given change in yield. This is illustrated in Table 19.1 in the last two columns.
- A fall in the redemption yield will raise a bond's price by an amount that is greater than the corresponding fall in the bond's price that would occur if

there was an equal-sized increase in the bond's redemption yield. This is illustrated in Table 19.1 in the last two rows.

From the above points, it is clear that maturity and coupon are important in determining the price volatility of a bond. If it is thought that bond prices are going to rise (interest rates fall), then an investor will benefit most by having long-maturity and low-coupon bonds. If prices are expected to fall, then the effect can be minimized by holding short-maturity bonds and high-coupon bonds. So, from the viewpoint of a bond investor, the most attractive positions (✓) and the least attractive positions (✗) are as shown below:

		Bond prices expected to:	
		Rise	Fall
Maturity }	Short	✗	✓
	Long	✓	✗
Coupon }	High	✗	✓
	Low	✓	✗

Duration

In the above analysis, maturity and coupon are treated separately. By bringing them together, we can obtain a better indicator of price volatility. In the case of a zero-coupon bond, all the return comes on the last day of the life of the bond. With a bond paying a coupon, some payments are received throughout the life of the bond, with the largest payment on the last day of its life. And for a high-coupon bond compared with a low-coupon bond, more of the total cash flows are received during the life of the bond than at the end. Clearly, a high-coupon bond with the same maturity as a zero-coupon bond is, in some sense, shorter because part of the return is earned before maturity. A way of taking account of this is by calculating duration, which measures the weighted average maturity of a non-callable bond's cash flows on a present value basis. This measure accounts for the entire pattern, both in terms of size and timing, of the cash flows over the life of a bond.

$$\text{Duration} = \frac{\text{PV of coupon}_1 \times 1}{\text{price}} + \frac{\text{PV of coupon}_2 \times 2}{\text{price}} + ... + \frac{\text{PV of (coupon}_m + \text{repayment of principal})}{\text{price}}$$

where PV = present value; m is the number of years to maturity; and price is the bond's current price.

In Table 19.2, the data for the calculation of the duration of two bonds are displayed. The first bond is a three-year 10% coupon bond, trading at a price of 100 with a redemption yield of 10%. The second bond is a three-year zero-coupon bond, trading at 75.13 and also offering a redemption yield of 10%. Consider first the 10% coupon bond. Assuming annual interest payments, the cash flows are set out in the second column of Table 19.2. In the next column, the present value of each of the cash flows is shown. These numbers can be obtained from a computer package or calculated by dividing the first cash flow by $(1 + 0.1)$, the second cash flow by $(1 + 0.1)^2$, and the third cash flow by $(1 + 0.1)^3$. The third column shows each year's present value. The fourth column shows each present value multiplied by the time until it is received. Summing these figures and then dividing by the market price of the bond gives the duration. In this case it is 2.74 years. For the zero-coupon bond, we carry out the same steps and see that the duration is three years. This illustrates the fact that the duration of a zero-coupon bond will always be the same as the number of years to maturity, whereas the duration of a non-callable coupon bond will always be shorter than its years to maturity.

TABLE 19.2 Duration of two bonds (rounded figures)

Year	3-year 10% coupon bond			3-year zero-coupon bond		
	Cash flow	Present value	Year × present value	Cash flow	Present value	Year × present value
1	10	9.09	9.09	0	0.00	0.00
2	10	8.26	16.53	0	0.00	0.00
3	110	82.64	247.93	100	75.13	225.39
Total		100.00	273.55		75.13	225.39
	Duration = 273.55/100 = 2.74 years			Duration = 225.39/75.13= 3 years		

Duration is a measure of the price risk of a bond: the percentage change in a bond's price, given a change in interest rates, is proportional to its duration. This analysis is due to Macaulay (1938), and what has been described is known as Macaulay's duration. If Macaulay's duration is divided by (1 + redemption yield), the result is known as modified duration.

$$\text{Modified duration} = d^* = \frac{D}{1 + r}$$

where d^* is modified duration; D is Macaulay duration; and r is the bond's redemption yield. This is modified duration using annual interest; using semi-annual interest, r would be divided by 2.

Modified duration is used to calculate the percentage price change of a bond for a given change of yield. Specifically:

$$\% \text{ change in bond price} \cong \frac{-D}{(1 + r)} \times \% \text{ change in } r$$

where $\cong$ means approximately and r is the initial redemption yield. The minus sign is needed because price and yield move in opposite directions.

The approximate change in price for the three-year coupon bond discussed in Table 19.2 for a 0.5% yield increase would be:

$$\% \text{ change in price} = \frac{-2.74}{1 + 0.1} \times 0.005 = -0.0125 = -1.25\%.$$

Determinants of Duration

There are three factors that determine a bond's duration:

- *Coupon rate:* this is inversely related to duration, i.e. the larger the coupon rate, the lower the duration; the lower the coupon rate, the higher the duration. The rationale is that as the coupon is increased, more of the cash flows come during the early years of the bond's life.
- *Term to maturity:* in general, the longer the term to maturity, the longer the duration. Broadly speaking, the longer the term to maturity, the longer the period one has to wait to receive all the cash flows.
- *Redemption yield:* this is inversely related to duration. For example, an increase in interest rates increases the rate at which cash flows are discounted, which increases the importance of the near-term cash flows at the expense of the long-term.

Convexity

When the use of duration in estimating price changes for changes in yield was discussed, we used an approximation sign in the equation. This is because the expression only gives correct answers for very small changes in interest rate. The reason is that there is an assumption that the relationship between price and yield is linear. However, the relationship is not linear. If you refer back to Table 19.1, you will see that for similar percentage changes in redemption yield, the percentage change in price differs depending on whether rates are rising or falling. You can see in the bottom two rows that the fall in price is smaller in absolute terms than the rise in price. This is because there is a curvilinear relationship between bond prices and yields. This is illustrated in Figure 19.1, which shows a plot of price against redemption yield for a zero-coupon 20-year bond.

The significance of convexity varies with the type of bond. Convexity is greatest for low-coupon, long-maturity and low-redemption-yield bonds. Convexity calculations can be made in a similar manner to that made for modified duration, and the results of the two added together. However, for details of the procedure, the reader should consult a specialist bond text.

Duration: Pro and Con

Duration is a better method of assessing price sensitivity to interest rate changes than is maturity. It can be calculated for individual bonds and for portfolios.

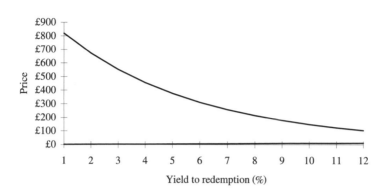

FIGURE 19.1   Bond price and yield relationship

By using market-value weighting, individual bonds' durations can be combined to produce an overall portfolio duration. This provides an easy way of assessing the price sensitivity of two portfolios. However, duration is by no means a perfect measure. The measure is accurate only for only very small changes in interest rates. For larger moves, a convexity correction needs to be made. The second problem is that duration errors are not symmetrical: they are greater when interest rates decline. Third, a portfolio duration effectively assumes that there is only one market interest rate. However, interest rates vary by sector and by maturity. Different portfolios with the same duration will be affected differently by changes in sector spreads and the term structure of interest rates. Fourth, many corporate bonds have call features. These change the relationship between price and yield at lower interest rate levels.

HORIZON RETURN

With active strategies, nothing is forever. You expect to change your portfolio. The redemption yield tells us the annualized total return from a bond if the bond is held to redemption and if the reinvestment rate is equal to the redemption rate. That the reinvestment rate can be important cannot be disputed, but it is often given too much attention in investment textbooks. If you plan to hold a 20-year bond for a year, the bond's redemption rate and reinvestment rate are not the full story. If you engage in interest rate anticipation, you don't intend to hold a bond forever. What you want to know is the return over a year, or some other investment horizon, and here price changes may be dominant.

   Consider a bond with 10 years to redemption, with a 10% coupon paid once a year, priced at 100. Its redemption yield is 10%, and if yields are unchanged it will always be priced at 100. Say market yields change to 11%. The bond is now unattractive as it offers a lower yield than a new bond would. Its price therefore falls until it too offers 11%. In Table 19.3, we show the price of a 10-year 10% coupon bond for various redemption yields. In the 11% row, we can see our bond would initially be priced at 94.1. If rates don't change, over the years the

TABLE 19.3   Horizon analysis: 10-year 10% bond prices

Redemption	Years to maturity									
yield (%)	10	9	8	7	6	5	4	3	2	1
6	129.4	127.2	124.8	122.3	119.7	116.8	113.9	110.7	107.3	103.8
7	121.1	119.5	117.9	116.2	114.3	112.3	110.2	107.9	105.4	102.8
8	113.4	112.5	111.5	110.4	109.2	108.0	106.6	105.2	103.6	101.9
9	106.4	106.0	105.5	105.0	104.5	103.9	103.2	102.5	101.8	100.9
10	100.0	100.0	100.0	100.0	100.0	100.0	100.0	100.0	100.0	100.0
11	94.1	94.5	94.9	95.3	95.8	96.3	96.9	97.6	98.3	99.1

bond's price will steadily rise to 100. On the other hand, if market rates fell, say to 9%, our bond would be attractive, and its price would be bid up to 106.4. Over the years, its price would decline to 100. How was Table 19.3 constructed? Ten annual payments of 10 were assumed, plus repayment at par of 100, and the net present value calculated for various redemption yields.

Let's assume that the bond is trading at 106.4. We believe that interest rates are going to continue falling over the next five years to 6%. We plan to buy and hold the bond for five years. What will our return be? We can break it down into four parts:

Money return = time effect + yield change effect + coupons + interest on interest.

We might have a view as to what rates will be every year. But we could assume that rates will stay where they are until the last day of the period, and then fall. In that case, we can just move five years along the 9% row, and we see that the passage of time will generate a capital loss of 103.9 − 106.4 = −2.5. However, if yields now fall to 6%, this will generate a capital gain of 12.9, i.e. 116.8 − 103.9. We will also receive five coupons of 10 each, i.e. 50, and we will get interest on that (interest on interest). But what should the reinvestment rate be? We could use rates that depend on the time path we assume for rates to drop from 9% to 6%. Or we could just use the average, 7.5%. We'll do that. The extra interest is 8.1. Pulling this together:

Money return = −2.5 + 12.9 + 50 + 8.1 = 73.5

or:

$$\text{Percentage return} = \frac{73.1}{106.4} = 0.687 = 68.7\%.$$

We now move on to some forms of active management.

INTEREST RATE ANTICIPATION

Easily the biggest effect on a bond portfolio's returns in any year is a shift in the yield curve. The yield curve can make a parallel shift whereby, say, yields are 1%

higher throughout the entire yield curve. Or there may be a change in the shape of the yield curve so that, say, short rates remain at their previous level while long rates decline sharply. Focusing here on parallel shifts of the yield curve, we know from the previous discussion that if rates rise, bonds with a long duration will suffer a greater price decline than bonds with a short duration. Accordingly, if a manager can anticipate interest rates, he or she can adjust the duration of his or her portfolio as appropriate. Managers who adopt this investment style typically invest only in high-quality, highly liquid bonds, such as government bonds and supranational bonds. Underlying this strategy is an assumption that the fund manager can forecast interest rates more accurately than others can.

Interest Rate Forecasting

To assess whether particular forecasts are useful, a comparison is usually made with a naive forecast. Naive forecasts include a no-change forecast, i.e. the next period will be the same as this period, and simple statistical models, such as using a weighting of past values of the factor being forecast. In the case of interest rates, one could also make a comparison with the forecast implicit in forward rates. Studies of predictions derived from statistical and econometric models have usually found that a simple no-change forecast outperforms the models (e.g. Elliott and Baier, 1979; and McNees, 1986).

Studies of the interest rate forecasts of money market professionals have produced mixed results. One study (Prell, 1973) found that the professionals did better than the no-change model in predicting short rates, but were worse than the no-change model at predicting long rates. Another study (Throop, 1981) compared money market professionals' forecasts of short rates against those produced by a no-change model, against the forecast produced by forward rates (adjusted for a liquidity premium), and against a model using weighted past interest rates. The professionals beat the first two models but not the third.

Since January 1982, the *Wall Street Journal* has published interest rate forecasts of prominent financial analysts. The surveys appear twice a year and present estimates of the levels of interest rates on 90-day Treasury bills and 30-year government bonds six months ahead. Kolb and Stekler (1996) analysed 17 of these surveys. They concluded that there was usually a consensus amongst analysts of the likely level of these rates, and that there was no significant difference in the ability to forecast short-term rates, although there was with respect to long-term rates, but that these forecasts were not significantly better than a forecast of no change.

In sum, there is no compelling evidence that economists can forecast interest rates better than simply assuming that interest rates will be in the next period what they are this period. And there is little evidence of star forecasters (see Stephenson, 1997). These findings should raise doubts about the value of interest rate anticipation strategies.

A Gilt Model

If the above discussion has not discouraged you, what are the sort of variables that might be included in a model that attempts to forecast gilt market yields? One approach is to have a strongly theory-based model; another is to take a more pragmatic view, and mix factors that the market seems to pay attention to with some theoretical considerations. Brookes (1995) describes Goldman Sachs' gilt model, which is based on the latter approach. He argues that there are several distinct groups of variables that might explain gilt yields. These include international factors, domestic factors, and variables that capture the risk premia in the UK market. Separate equations were estimated for five-year, 10-year and 20-year maturity par yields. The specific variables used were:

- expected changes in real short-term interest rates over the next six months;
- current real short rates;
- underlying retail price inflation;
- the annual change in the public sector borrowing requirement as a proportion of GDP;
- the growth rate of M0;
- inflation uncertainties measured by the standard deviation of inflation;
- US and German 10-year bond yields;
- the volatility to GDP growth (this applies only for 10- and 20-year gilt yields).

The equations attempt to predict fair value for gilt yields. The operational specification of the variables is not given, nor is the form of the equation. However, some interesting results are noted. For example, an expected 1% rise in underlying inflation leads to a 40 basis points rise for five-year gilt yields and a 30 basis points rise for both 10- and 20-year yields. Again, if base rates are raised by 1% point, without a corresponding increase in underlying inflation, five-year gilt yields are expected to rise 40 basis points, while 10-year gilt yields are expected to rise 20 basis points and long-dated gilts remain unchanged. A 1% point rise in both US and German 10-year yields leads to a rise of 60 basis points in five-year yields, and 30 basis points in 20-year yields.

It is unclear how useful the model is. Some of the explanatory variables require forecasts, which are taken from the firm's UK macroeconomic forecast. And forecasts are required for US and German yields. It is not obvious why all these other variables can be forecast with sufficient accuracy to be used to forecast gilt yields. The model forecasts fair value for gilt yields, not what gilt yields will actually be. The significance of this is an empirical matter.

From the information available, one cannot say whether this is a good model. But it is probably typical of the sort of model that econometrically inclined forecasters might develop.

Supply of Gilt-Edge Stock

Investors are usually interested in the anticipated supply of government stock, as this may effect the level of yields and the shape of the yield curve. Interest rate anticipators are likely to attempt to forecast net gilt sales, as will believers in market segmentation theory. Let's see how they might go about this.

If the government needs to borrow, there are a number of sources open to it. It can:

- issue further notes and coins;
- sell National Savings instruments;
- sell Treasury bills;
- sell gilts;
- borrow directly from overseas governments and institutions;
- sell gold and foreign currency from the official reserves and receive sterling.

Clearly, to obtain an estimate of the likely supply of gilts, one needs to juggle a number of factors. This might be done in the framework of a financing table, such as that shown in Table 19.4. The table shows only the Treasury's estimates, although most fund managers would make their own estimates as well.

TABLE 19.4   Central government net cash requirement, 2000–01

	£bn
CGNCR	**−4.9**
+ Gilt redemptions	18.6
+ FX intervention	3.5
+ Underfunding from previous year	−9.5
+ Debt buy-backs	3.5
= Funding requirement	**11.2**
− National Savings	−0.8
− Treasury bills and other	−0.2
= Gross gilt sales	**12.2**
Of which	
1–3 years	0.0
3–7 years	0.0
7–15 years	2.2
15+ years	6.5
Index-linked	3.5
Net gilt sales	**−6.4**

CGNCR, central government net cash requirement; FX, foreign exchange.

Table 19.4 shows the central government net cash requirement (CGNCR) as minus £4.9bn, i.e. the central government does not have a net cash requirement but has a cash surplus. However, existing bonds mature each year, and gilt redemptions show that the government will have to repay £18.6bn to investors in the financial year being considered. We'll skip over foreign exchange intervention and debt buy-backs. The underfunding is a negative item, which means that in the previous year the government overfunded. Adding together the first five rows of the body of the table produces the funding requirement of £11.2bn.

National Savings and Treasury bills are both shown as negative items, i.e. there will be a net outflow of funds from these two items. This means that gross gilt sales will be £1bn higher than the funding requirement.

It is expected that the gross gilt sales of £12.2bn will be partly index-linked and partly conventional, predominantly at the long end of the market. Subtracting gilt redemptions (£18.6bn) from gross gilt sales (£12.2bn) results in net gilt sales of minus £6.4bn. In other words, the government will be a net buyer of gilts.

Calculations of this kind are common in bond markets. How useful they are is less clear. The problem is that the government estimates of its revenues and expenditures are subject to some uncertainty, and the size of the CGNCR is therefore also uncertain. The error associated with the starting line in Table 19.4 may well be larger than the final line that we are trying to estimate. Accordingly, these numbers have to be treated with a degree of scepticism. For example, the 1999–2000 CGNCR was first estimated at £6.2bn. In April 1999, this was unchanged; in November 1999, it fell to £1.1bn; and in the budget of March 2000, it was again revised to £5.8bn. The financing requirement was originally £21.0bn, then £19.3bn, then £14.2bn, and finally £7.2bn. Despite these huge shifts, the gilt sales required changed much less, falling from £17.3bn to £13.8bn in the March 2000 forecast. This was largely the result of the expected net sale of Treasury bills changing from a positive £3.6bn in the first forecast to minus £5.7bn in the March 2000 forecast.

A diversion here is of value. Equity managers often try to estimate the likely cash available for the equity market. They do this by starting with estimates of institutional cash flows and then subtracting anticipated gilt sales, anticipated flows overseas, and so on, until finally a residual available to the equity market is obtained. Anyone who believes that number probably believes in the tooth fairy.

While we should have only limited faith in the accuracy of the estimated net gilt sales figure, the government's switch from being a net borrower to a net lender seems real enough. This would tend to keep interest rates low. More important perhaps is the effect on the shape of the yield curve. The minimum funding requirement was introduced in 1997 and takes full effect in 2002. It has an annual solvency test for pension funds. The discount rate for valuing retired member liabilities in defined benefit schemes is the yield on the long gilt. This has led some funds to increase their long gilt holdings. This increased demand for a particular sector of the gilt market is occurring at the same time as the government is redeeming gilts. This has resulted in a steeply inverted yield curve, with long yields not much more than 4% in early 2000. Most observers think that long gilts are overpriced. Clearly, fund managers will be watching for changes that could increase the supply of gilts, or change the demand.

THE REWARD FOR INTEREST RATE RISK

Forecasting interest rates is the traditional way of playing shifts in the yield curve. A slightly different way is to ask when you get rewarded for bearing interest rate risk. When we discussed the term structure of interest rates, we noted that after a year or two there had not been much reward for risk. We also noted that contrary to the expectations theory, a rising yield curve was more likely to predict falling rates than rising. This means that to some extent bond markets must be predictable. Are there periods when bearing interest rate risk is rewarded, and if there are, are they predictable? If bearing interest rate risk is never rewarded, or if it is but the periods are not predictable, then there is little case for going long.

Ilmanen (1996) found that excess stock and bond returns in the US are related to the economic cycle. If we think of a cycle as going from trough up to peak and back down to trough, and slice this up into eight periods, i.e. 1 (trough), 2, 3, 4, 5 (peak), 6, 7, 8, 1 (trough), then excess returns are highest during the periods before and after the troughs. The excess returns are greater for stocks, and the negative excess returns are also greater for stocks. For bonds, the worst excess returns were in period 4, and for stocks, period 6. Both had their best returns in period 8.

If expected risk premiums vary with time, what is the economic explanation? There are two rational possibilities: risk varies with the economic cycle, or risk aversion varies with the economic cycle. In either case, the average investor will not seek higher-risk exposure in periods of above-average excess returns, since they are a fair reward. If you want to take advantage of this, you have to be able to forecast high risk aversion and high expected return for risk.

Ilmanen assumed risk aversion would be higher when the stock market was depressed, and that a high real bond yield and large term spread would be good proxies of high expected bond risk premium. And so it proved. Relating these three variables in a multiple regression equation to excess bond returns produced a correlation of 0.38. The coefficient of determination, adjusted for degrees of freedom showed that the equation accounts for about 10% of the variation of excess return. This is low, but potentially exploitable. Sadly, only 3.1% of the variation could be explained in a model of the UK market.

Ilmanen used a trading rule of being in cash when the predicted excess return was negative and being in long-term bonds when it was positive. This outperformed being only in bonds by 4.43% in the US and, perhaps surprisingly, by 4.01% in the UK. These returns are slightly exaggerated by the omission of trading costs, and in-sample estimation will have distorted the results (but some out-of-sample data are given.) Further, the trading rule leads to huge swings in duration, which may be unacceptable. And the approach worked better for long-term forecasts than short, trader-oriented forecasts.

However, the details of this study are less important than the idea of forecasting excess returns rather than the usual economic approach of forecasting interest rates.

YIELD CURVE EFFECTS

Although it is common to talk of interest rates as having risen or fallen, often rates both rise and fall. A distinction has to be made between parallel shifts of the yield curve and non-parallel shifts. In Figure 19.2, an initial yield curve is shown as a heavy black line. This shows an upward-sloping yield curve with long-dated maturities yielding more than short-dated maturities. If there is an upward parallel shift of the yield curve, as shown by the dash-and-dot line, then interest rates have risen unambiguously across all maturities. Similarly, we could have a downward parallel shift. In the case of the dotted line, there is a flattening twist. Here, short-maturity interest rates have increased, but long-maturity rates have decreased. In the case of a steepening twist, short rates fall and long rates rise. Finally, a humped yield curve is shown. In this case, both short and long maturity rates have fallen, while medium-term rates have risen. This is known as a negative butterfly. The corresponding curve where short and long rates rise and medium rates fall is a positive butterfly. A combination of these shifts is possible. For example, there could be an upward parallel shift of the curve so that all rates rise, but at the same time a flattening twist occurs so that short rates rise more than long rates.

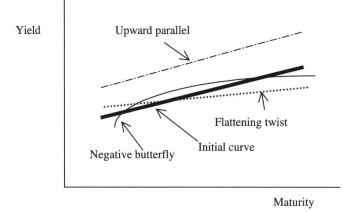

FIGURE 19.2   A variety of yield curve shifts

These changes are obviously important for fund managers. For example, in the case of the flattening twist shown, rates are generally lower, but for short bonds, yields have risen. And there are more complex issues to be faced. Consider, for example, the ways of achieving a portfolio duration of eight years. A portfolio could be invested almost entirely in, say, 10-year bonds, or split into two clusters, one at the short end of the market and one at the long, or the portfolio could be spread evenly over, say, years 1 to 20. These three possible strategies are known as bullet, barbell and ladder. Despite having the same duration, the return from these portfolios will vary depending on the size of a yield curve shift and the type of shift.

We saw earlier that duration measured how a value of a portfolio would change given a change in market yields. For portfolios with a duration of eight years and an initial yield of 10%, the value would change by 7.3% for a 1% change in yield. However, this is only true for a parallel shift in the yield curve. If

the yield curve shift is non-parallel, portfolios with the same duration will perform differently. This is because the convexity of the portfolios will differ. Duration is just the first step in the calculation of change in price resulting from a
change in the yield. For two portfolios with the same duration but different
convexities, the portfolio with the higher convexity will have a higher value
regardless of whether yield rises or falls. For example, if bond H has a higher
convexity than bond L, then if the market yield rises, the capital loss on H will be
less than on L, and if the market yield falls, H will have greater capital apprecia-
tion than L.

The bottom line on all this is whether a bullet, barbell or ladder portfolio will
perform best depends not only on duration, but also on the amount of the yield
change and the shape of the yield curve change. General rules as to which type
of portfolio will perform best are dangerous: there is no escaping crunching
estimated total return numbers for the specific assumptions a portfolio manager
makes.

THE INTERMARKET SPREAD SWITCH

The yield difference, or spread, between various sectors of the bond market
can be readily calculated. For example, the difference between industrial
bonds and government bonds, between US Treasury bonds and Eurodollar
bonds (the TED spread), between bonds with calls and bonds without calls,
and so on. Consider for example, US high-grade industrial bonds which have
typically yielded a little over a half percent more than Treasury bonds. If the
market tends to revert to this spread average, then if high-grade industrial
bonds offer the same redemption yield as Treasury bonds, the Treasuries
would appear to be cheap, whereas if high-grade industrial bonds yield 1.5%
more than Treasuries, then the corporates would appear to be cheap.
However, successful trading on this basis will depend upon the size of the
divergence from the normal spread and the speed at which the spread reverts
to normal. Of course, for any investor investing cash flow and employing a hold
to maturity strategy, the time it takes the yield spread to return to its historical
average is irrelevant.

There will usually be a reason for the spread to be at an abnormal level. For
example, in the early stages of a recession, we would expect the spread between
corporates and Treasuries to widen. We would expect more corporate defaults
in a recession. It is therefore possible that when the spread between corporate
bonds and Treasuries widens, there has been no change in the expected realized
spread. However, we would imagine that the expected realized spread would
widen. If investor risk aversion increases in a recession, the required rate of
compensation for bearing systematic bond risk will increase, and the spread
should allow for this. A wider spread may therefore just reflect the new required
reward. It is only an opportunity if your risk aversion has increased by less than
other investors' risk aversion.

CREDIT ANALYSIS

Bond yields are related to their credit rating. Can you make money by buying or selling bonds when there is a rating change? In general, the answer would appear to be that you cannot. For example, Weinstein (1977) examined 100 rating changes that took place between 1962 and 1974, and found no evidence of price reaction in the six months before or after the change. However, there was evidence that ratings changes were anticipated in the period seven to 18 months before the change. One might expect this result, given that bond ratings changes are largely predictable and use publicly available information. However, this does not rule out the possibility that investors with superior accounting skills are able to make a profit from their ability. Of course, since the bulk of the bond market is made up of government issues, credit analysis is restricted to a limited area of the market.

Altman and Kao (1992a, 1992b) produce some interesting evidence on rating drift. For the period 1970–89, they found that original issue speculative-grade bonds displayed no tendency to rise or decline in quality over time. However, for low-grade bonds that do experience an initial downgrade in their rating, the outlook was bleaker, and there was a tendency for a rating downgrade to be followed by a second downgrade. There was a weaker tendency for high-yield bonds that were upgraded to have a subsequent upgrade. In the majority of cases, AAA/AA/A original issues that were downgraded continued to be downgraded. Among the investment-grade bonds, only those initially rated BBB tended to be upgraded more than they were downgraded. It is not clear whether investors can exploit this information profitably.

MISPRICED BONDS

To decide whether individual bonds are cheap or dear, comparison may be made between individual bonds or against the market. Comparison of one bond against another may be made by price differences, price ratios, yield differences and ratios, switch profit projections, performance indices, and balance-of-term yields. Comparing one bond against a market average involves yield curve analysis or price model analysis. Yield difference is probably the most widely used approach, and will be discussed here. For the other approaches, see Phillips (1984, Chapter 7).

A pure yield pick-up switch is made when a bond held in a portfolio can be switched for another that is identical in all major characteristics yet offers a higher redemption yield. Such switches can only occur if there is some kind of market imperfection. It seems unlikely that many opportunities would arise in the gilt market or the US Treasury market. However, it is possible that such opportunities occur from time to time in the Eurobond market.

Sometimes, an investor's income requirements change, and he or she wants more immediate income at the expense of future capital gains. This is sometimes described as a yield pick-up switch, even though it is only current yield that is increasing, and this does not involve mispriced bonds.

A different type of yield difference switch is the substitution switch. Here, the yield spreads between groups of substitutable bonds are tracked. When the spread between two bonds within the same group reaches the limit of the historical spread relationship, a switch is executed. The idea is that if the spread returns to more normal levels, the switch can be reversed. Such switching opportunities undoubtedly occur, but the profitability per trade will be small and is heavily dependent on the speed of the spread relationship reverting to its normal level.

RIDING THE YIELD CURVE

A (barely) active form of bond management is known as riding the yield curve. The strategy assumes that an upward-sloping yield curve is the norm, and that the average change in bond yields of all maturities is zero. For example, we assume that three-month yields are 5% and six-month yields are 5.5%, then in three months' time the same rates will hold. In that case, if our benchmark is three-month rates, we could buy the six-month bond and hold it for three months. At that point, the bond purchased will have moved to the three-month rate, and thereby generated a capital gain. We now sell the bond and buy another six-month bond.

Whether this strategy works depends on whether there are reliable liquidity premiums. We have seen that liquidity premiums are most reliable up to a year or so. Thereafter the position is less certain. Riding the yield curve is in fact more popular among managers of short-term securities. Even here, the strategy is vulnerable to generally rising rates, a downward-sloping yield curve, and transaction costs that are twice those of a buy-and-hold strategy.

MATCHING STRATEGIES

One specialized form of active management involves portfolios that are dedicated to matching a set of liabilities. Although active management is involved, the constraints are very tight. The techniques involved are cash matching, immunization and horizon matching.

We saw earlier that the promised redemption yield will only be achieved if all interest cash flows can be reinvested at the redemption yield. The expected return from a bond is therefore subject to roll-on or reinvestment rate risk. For an investor who requires a specific sum of money on a set date, this poses a problem. Matching methods have been devised to 'immunize' funds against these risks. As this topic affects a minority of bond managers, and is of limited interest to equity managers involved in equity/bond tactical asset allocation, the treatment here will be brief.

The simplest approach to immunizing a portfolio is cash matching. Given a liability structure, one aims to match the liabilities. For example, if you require £100 in 91 days' time, you can simply buy a 91-day Treasury bill today at a price of, say, £99—Treasury bills are sold on a discount to par value basis—and you will receive £100 on the required date. Similarly, a requirement for £100 in 15 years' time might be met by purchasing a 15-year zero-coupon bond. In reality, the most common bond is a coupon-bearing bond, and it may be impossible to put together a package of assets that exactly cash match liabilities. Further, even if it is possible to put together such a package, it may be that a cheaper package could be constructed if the constraints were less tight.

If exact cash matching is not followed, the fund is opened to reinvestment rate risk as was noted above, and also to price risk if the portfolio is constructed so that bonds have to be sold to meet liabilities. However, price risk and reinvestment rate risk work in opposite directions. We can get these two effects to offset each other if we set the duration of the portfolio to equal the liability investment horizon. For example, assume a 10-year bond with a duration of eight years and an investment horizon of eight years. If interest rates fall, the reinvestment rate will be lower, and there will be a shortfall from that source. But lower rates mean higher bond prices, so the receipts at the end of the investment horizon from the sale of what is then a two-year bond will produce an approximately offsetting capital gain.

Having immunized the portfolio in this manner, can the manager now go to sleep? Unfortunately not, which is why this is an active, not passive, strategy. Duration declines more slowly than term to maturity; duration also changes with changes in market interest rates, and is affected by shifts in the yield curve. Consequently, duration has to be continually adjusted.

Sometimes cash matching and duration-based immunization are brought together. Approximate cash matching is used for a period, say five years, and thereafter duration-based immunization is used. Non-parallel movements of the yield curve create a problem for immunization, but the biggest changes in the shape of the yield curve usually occur at the short end of the market, and therefore this combination approach overcomes this problem.

A different combination approach is called contingent immunization. Here, the aim is to allow the bond manager to pursue high returns through active management, but to use immunization techniques to ensure a specified minimum return over the appropriate horizon. For details of this, and examples of the application of the other techniques discussed in this section, the reader should refer to a specialist bond text. The important thing to note about the techniques discussed in this section are that they are attempts to achieve returns over a specified period, without regard to the annual fluctuations in return.

SWAPS

Swaps can be remarkably complex, but in their simplest, plain vanilla form, swaps are contracts that involve two counterparties exchanging sets of cash flows over a predetermined period. Swaps can involve any asset, but the commonest are interest rate swaps, currency swaps and commodity swaps. We shall consider only interest rate swaps here.

Swaps have grown from a small market 20 years ago to being larger than the world bond market. They are used by banks, industrial corporations, and some fund managers. Swaps have a variety of uses, including taking on risk and hedging risk. As an example of the former, consider two fund managers with different bond portfolios. One has floating-rate notes, while the other has conventional gilts. Imagine that the floating-rate note holder expects interest rates to be generally lower over the next five years, while the conventional gilt holder believes that interest rates will be generally higher. The income from conventional gilts will be unaffected by the change in market rates, but the income from a floating-rate note will fall if interest rates fall. Fund managers could incur transaction costs and sell their holdings and reinvest accordingly. However, for less cost they could use a swap bank to swap the income flows of their assets. More formally, the counterparties agree to exchange period interest payments. The amount of payment exchanged is based on a predetermined nominal principal, which is called the notional principal amount. The interest payment that changes hands is the net amount. The swaps market is an over-the-counter market, not a regulated exchange. Swaps contracts are therefore subject to counterparty risk, but it is only on the interest rate differential because the principal doesn't change hands.

What determines the terms of a swap? This can be approached by thinking of what the seller of the fixed interest payments is getting when he or she swaps for a floating-rate note paying LIBOR. For a known sum—the fixed interest payments—the seller gets in each period of the contract delivery of the then prevailing LIBOR rate. In effect, the seller has purchased a package of LIBOR forwards contracts. Alternatively, you could consider a swap transaction to be two bond transactions. For example, you might view the fixed-rate payer as having the same position as someone who had invested in a floating-rate note and borrowed at a fixed rate to pay for the purchase, i.e. long floating and short fixed.

Given the above arguments, we might expect the terms of a swap to reflect rates in the futures market and rates in the bond market. In reality, short-dated swaps tend to be priced off short-dated futures, and longer-term swaps tend to be priced off a spread over government bonds.

CONCLUDING COMMENTS

Like equities, bonds can be managed passively or actively. Passive management strategies include buy-and-hold and bond index funds. Active management can take a large number of forms. It can involve all or part of the following: forecasting the course of interest rates (interest rate anticipation); forecasting excess returns; making switches between various sectors of the market; riding the yield curve; and finding mispriced bonds. A specialized form of active management was briefly discussed that involves matching specific liabilities.

An important issue in any strategy is the volatility of returns. While maturity and coupon are important factors in determining volatility, duration is a better measure. Duration and convexity were discussed. In any active strategy, horizon yields are important, and an illustrative calculation was made.

20

International Investing

The new electronic interdependence recreates the world in the image of a global village.

Marshall McLuhan

Investors are not restricted to investing in their domestic market: they can invest in the international markets as well. Let's begin with some background. Table 20.1 shows the Morgan Stanley Capital International (MSCI) World Index region and country weights at the start of 2000. Also shown for each region and country are their shares of world GDP.

As you can see, the US makes up nearly half of the world's equity market by capitalization. The next biggest market is Japan and then the UK. Arguably, the countries of the European Union (EU) that have adopted the euro (see p. 382) should be treated as a single entity. In that case, Euroland would be the second largest equity market. The world index excluding North America is often referred to as EAFE (Europe, Asia and the Far East). At the start of 2000, the MSCI World Index had a value of about $20 trillion. The FT/S&P Actuaries World Index, which has broader stock coverage, was valued at about $25 trillion. The new FTSE All-World Index will be slightly larger. The countries and segments included in it are shown in Table 20.2

Table 20.1 shows that there can be a wide divergence between a country's weight in the world index and its weight in world GDP. This is a consequence of countries having different percentages of their GDP supplied by the state sector, national differences in the proportion of company debt/equity financing, and differences in PERs.

Although most popular financial commentary, and indeed the content of this book, is oriented towards equities, the world bond market is in fact larger than the world equity market. At the start of 2000, the world bond market was worth approximately $30 trillion. The world bond market has three main components: dollar bonds, yen bonds and Euroland bonds. These account for about 47%, 23% and 18%, respectively, of the total market. Sterling bonds are the next biggest component, accounting for a mere 3%.

Drawing the equity and bond data together, we can derive the pie chart shown in Figure 20.1. In this chart, countries that constitute less than 2% of the total

TABLE 20.1   MSCI World Index weights

% of world GDP	Region/country	% of world equity capitalization
35.2	**North America**	**51.4**
32.5	US	49.1
2.7	Canada	2.3
39.5	**Europe**	**32.0**
0.7	Austria	0.1
0.7	Belgium	0.4
0.8	Denmark	0.4
1.0	Finland	1.5
7.2	France	5.0
11.0	Germany	5.2
0.4	Ireland	0.2
5.4	Italy	2.1
1.5	Netherlands	2.4
0.6	Norway	0.2
0.5	Portugal	0.2
2.3	Spain	1.3
1.3	Sweden	1.4
1.0	Switzerland	2.6
5.1	UK	9.0
24.9	**Pacific**	**16.6**
1.3	Australia	1.2
0.7	Hong Kong	1.1
22.9	Japan	13.7
–	Malaysia	–
0.2	New Zealand	0.1
0.4	Singapore	0.5

Source: MSCI (for further information see **http://www.msci.com**).

TABLE 20.2   FTSE All-World Index components

		Developed	
Australia	France	Netherlands	Sweden
Austria	Germany	New Zealand	Switzerland
Belgium/Luxembourg	Hong Kong	Norway	UK
Canada	Ireland	Portugal	US
Denmark	Italy	Singapore	
Finland	Japan	Spain	
		Advanced emerging	
Brazil	Israel	Mexico	Taiwan
Greece	Korea	South Africa	
		Emerging	
Argentina	Egypt	Morocco	Russia
Chile	Hungary	Pakistan	Thailand
China	India	Peru	Turkey
Columbia	Indonesia	Philippines	Venezuela
Czech Republic	Malaysia	Poland	

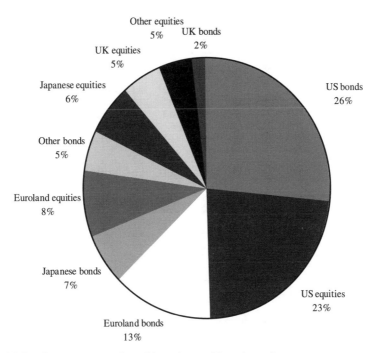

FIGURE 20.1 **Components of world equity and bond markets**
Source: author's calculations.

have been aggregated under 'other'. Although the US domestic market for bonds and equities is almost as large as the international market (as viewed by a US investor) for all other countries, the international market is much larger than the domestic market. For example, for a UK investor the international market is 15 times as large as the domestic market.

These weightings are not set in stone. For example, for a short period in the late 1980s, the Japanese equity market was larger than the US equity market. However, the Japanese market then halved in value and did very little in the 1990s, while the US market went on a great bull run.

Having looked briefly at the size and distribution of the world equity and bond markets, the next obvious point of interest is the historical returns. Data for world equities are shown in Table 20.3, and for world bonds in Table 20.4. Note that the returns are stated in sterling terms.

WHY INVEST INTERNATIONALLY?

The fundamental reason for investing internationally is the favourable effect it has on portfolio diversification. This benefit arises from the opportunity to invest in an additional range of securities, which together have a relatively low correlation to the domestic market. The result is that it is possible to construct a portfolio with a lower standard deviation than would be possible if only domestic assets where considered. We saw earlier in Figure 2.9 the effect on risk of

TABLE 20.3   Annual equity returns in sterling (%)

	1990	1991	1992	1993	1994	1995	1996	1997	1998	1999	10-year average
UK	−9.7	20.8	20.5	28.4	−5.8	23.9	16.7	23.6	13.8	24.2	17.9
US	−19.7	35.1	32.8	11.7	−4.2	37.8	11.0	38.6	28.0	24.3	−0.7
Canada	−26.3	11.3	7.8	23.1	−7.9	18.2	18.3	18.2	−5.7	48.3	14.9
Japan	−46.8	13.0	−3.6	27.7	14.8	0.2	−23.9	−22.7	5.2	77.5	10.8
Germany	−23.6	9.5	11.1	39.5	−2.5	16.3	6.4	26.6	22.0	15.7	16.9
Switzerland	−19.3	18.8	41.6	47.3	−1.0	46.1	−7.0	50.1	21.5	−3.1	13.3
France	−27.4	21.4	24.4	25.7	−9.8	13.5	11.1	18.8	37.7	35.5	18.0
Netherlands	−18.8	22.0	27.0	38.9	5.9	30.5	14.8	29.4	30.1	11.8	8.3
Italy	−31.8	2.3	−7.2	30.5	5.3	0.1	4.7	48.9	52.1	4.7	18.4
Sweden	−29.1	19.6	15.5	23.2	12.8	38.3	25.0	17.7	7.4	82.8	13.2
Spain	−25.1	19.3	−3.7	27.3	−7.3	30.6	24.2	31.3	47.8	8.1	12.0
Belgium	−25.4	17.7	19.2	28.9	1.3	29.3	2.1	19.4	66.0	−13.0	8.8
Denmark	−18.8	19.9	−12.5	37.3	−2.7	17.0	12.2	33.8	11.8	4.1	5.9
Norway	−13.4	−8.3	−3.7	35.4	13.8	11.3	18.1	14.3	−30.7	45.3	1.0
Austria	8.6	−11.3	5.9	36.8	−5.8	−2.7	0.3	5.2	−2.1	−1.0	8.8
Australia	−31.0	37.9	6.2	40.7	0.2	15.4	9.7	−3.1	1.7	25.1	8.3
Singapore	−23.4	45.2	22.1	78.8	−2.7	11.6	−5.4	−43.6	−3.1	63.9	8.4
Hong Kong	−9.0	55.1	59.9	132.2	−35.3	23.8	22.0	−24.6	−10.4	62.4	18.8

Source: Philips & Drew (2000, p. 31)

TABLE 20.4   Annual bond return in sterling (%)

	1990	1991	1992	1993	1994	1995	1996	1997	1998	1999	10-year average
US	−10.7	23.0	32.3	12.6	−8.2	18.2	−6.6	14.4	9.0	0.3	7.6
Japan	−12.8	29.6	37.8	30.1	2.6	11.3	−14.6	−0.5	14.6	19.5	10.4
UK	5.6	18.7	18.8	22.0	−7.0	16.7	7.3	14.8	19.8	−1.3	11.1
Germany	−6.7	17.9	30.9	9.8	3.2	27.5	−9.5	−5.3	18.9	−13.8	6.2
Switzerland	5.4	7.9	30.7	18.0	2.3	30.2	−18.3	2.1	12.6	−13.6	6.6
France	−0.6	20.7	29.0	16.0	−1.1	28.8	−4.9	−3.3	19.9	−14.5	8.0
Netherlands	−5.4	15.3	35.0	12.4	0.2	29.8	−9.2	−5.3	19.4	−14.2	6.6
Canada	−12.5	29.6	22.9	14.1	−14.8	23.7	1.3	9.0	1.0	7.7	7.2
Australia	−2.5	32.4	23.3	19.2	0.5	15.8	8.7	−3.6	2.7	7.4	9.8

Source: Philips & Drew (2000, p. 47)

increasing the number of domestic stocks held and also the effect of investing internationally.

If overseas securities offer a higher return than domestic securities, this is clearly a win/win situation. But security returns overseas may be lower than domestic returns, in which case there is a trade-off between the benefits of diversification on risk reduction and the adverse effects of adding securities with lower returns. Providing foreign returns are only a few percentage points below domestic returns, international investing will still be worthwhile. For example, if the equity risk premium in the UK is 5%, and US equities have a beta of 0.7 with respect to the UK market, then the required CAPM equity risk premium from the US market would be only 3.5%.

The correlation of returns between the international markets varies depending upon the period measured, the frequency of measurement, and so on. Studies using monthly data for the last 20 or 30 years show the UK having a correlation with the major markets of between about 0.35 (with Italy) and 0.66

(with the Netherlands) with the major markets and lower correlations with many smaller markets. The UK/US correlation has been about 0.5. Thus the common variability in UK and US stock returns is about 25% (i.e. $R^2 = 0.5 \times 0.5 = 0.25$).

Over the last decade or so, the correlation between international markets has increased. This may well continue, but international investment will likely remain an efficient way of diversifying compared with the alternatives. For example, a large-cap investor in the US could diversify out of the S&P 500 into the Russell 2000 (correlation about 0.85) or into the UK (correlation about 0.50).

In recent years there has been a marked increase in the correlation between international markets at times of crisis. However, with the passage of a month or two, the correlations have returned to their usual levels.

If a Markowitz efficient frontier is calculated for the world equity and bond markets, and the resulting distribution of assets compared with the average distribution of institutional funds in any country, then it is usually found that the real portfolios have far too large a weighting in the domestic market compared with that indicated by the efficient frontier. This tendency to overinvest domestically is known as the home bias problem.

There have been a number of attempts using financial and economic theory to explain home bias. The interested reader is referred to a review article by Lewis (1999). The gist of the empirical evidence is that the theories do not explain very much: common sense explanations are at least as good. One such explanation is that the home bias is not particularly an international asset allocation problem at all. Investors may well tend to prefer investing in firms, assets, countries, etc. that they are familiar with. For example, Huberman (1998) found that US individual investors when investing in the regional telephone companies (the 'baby Bells') tend to invest in their local regional Bell. Coval and Moskowitz (1999) found that US investment managers showed a strong preference for firms with headquarters close to their own location. These studies suggest that there is nothing special about the international home bias—there is a general home bias.

There is, however, probably an additional international bias as well. We saw earlier (p. 79) that Siamese twin companies, such as Shell/Royal Dutch, are often misvalued relative to each other and that arbitrage does not take place. Froot and Dabora (1999), in their study of this phenomenon, found fund managers were constrained by client mandates or their benchmarks, and were unwilling to switch between the Netherlands and the UK markets.

A second common sense explanation for home bias is simply that trustees or plan sponsors do not think in terms of a Markowitz efficient frontier. They see international investment as a mismatching of assets and liabilities and therefore high risk. Investing in international assets has two aspects. First, there is the underlying risk and return opportunities of the underlying asset, and second, there are risks and opportunities associated with the foreign currency that is involved. To buy a foreign asset, a UK investor will have to buy the appropriate foreign currency and then, when the asset is sold, convert the foreign currency back into sterling. There is a risk that the exchange rate at the time of the purchase and of the sale will differ.

The currency risk could be eliminated by hedging, but many plan sponsors would still see foreign assets as risky. However, the beneficiary of an investment fund, say a UK pensioner, will spend part of his or her income or wealth on foreign goods. Accordingly, an international weighting that reflects the ratio of imports to GDP should not be seen as risky. Since import ratios are typically under 35%, and almost every country has some imports, this would suggest that overseas exposure might run somewhere between 10% and 35% for large countries. Of course, because of the cognitive explanation given above, we would expect to find funds in many countries investing less abroad than the import ratio would suggest appropriate.

FOREIGN EXCHANGE

Currency risk is an important issue in international investing, and it is worth going through some of the basics of the foreign exchange market and the arithmetic of foreign currency returns.

The price of a currency can be expressed in two ways. For example, the relationship between the Canadian and US dollar can be expressed either as the number of Canadian dollars that one US dollar will purchase, or the number of US dollars that one Canadian dollar will purchase. At the time of writing, $1 would purchase C$1.4857, and C$1 would purchase $0.673, i.e. 67 US cents. Most countries use 'direct quotation', which expresses the number of units of the domestic currency that can be exchanged for one unit of a foreign currency. Sometimes, 'indirect quotation' is used, which expresses the number of units of a foreign currency that can be exchanged for one unit of the domestic currency. Sterling is, by convention, quoted in this way. So, somewhat confusingly, if you look in a table of sterling exchange rates against a variety of currencies, and a table of dollar exchange rates against a variety of currencies, the number shown for the US dollar in the sterling table will be the same as the number shown for the sterling rate in the dollar table. The only advice one can give is to be sure that you know how a currency you are interested in is quoted.

Currency Rate Changes and Returns

The easiest way to see the effect of currency changes on returns from investments is to work through an example. Assume a UK institution invests in the US market and buys an investment for $80 that it sells after one year for $100. It also receives $4 of income. The dollar return is easily calculated to be 30%, as shown below:

$$\text{Dollar return} = \frac{\text{purchase price} - \text{selling price} + \text{dividends}}{\text{purchase price}} = \frac{100 - 80 + 4}{80} = 0.3 = 30\%.$$

However, the UK institution is interested in the sterling return. This is calculated as follows:

$$\text{Sterling return} = \frac{1 + \text{dollar return}}{1 + \text{currency exchange}} - 1.$$

This expression includes a term 'currency change'. Let us assume that over the course of the year, sterling depreciated against the dollar falling from, say, $1.5 per £1 to $1.25 per £1. We calculate the currency change as follows:

$$\text{Currency change} = \frac{\text{closing \$ per £}}{\text{opening \$ per £}} - 1 = \frac{1.25}{1.5} - 1 = -0.1667$$

and we can now calculate:

$$\text{Sterling return} = \frac{1 + 0.3}{1 - 0.1667} - 1 = 0.56 = 56\%.$$

So, a depreciating pound has resulted in an investment that returned 30% in dollar terms, giving a sterling return of 56%. If we had assumed that sterling had appreciated, say from $1.5 per £1 to $2.0 per £1, then a 30% dollar return would have been turned into a negative sterling return of 2.2% because:

$$\text{Currency change} = \frac{2.0}{1.5} - 1 = 0.33$$

and substituting the currency change into the sterling return formula, we have:

$$\text{Sterling return} = \frac{1 + 0.3}{1 + 0.33} - 1 = -0.0227 = -2.3\%.$$

From this example, you can see that currency adds considerable uncertainty to the return an investor will receive. One approach to deal with this is to hedge the currency. To understand this we have to distinguish between spot and forward transactions.

Spot and Forward Transactions

A spot transaction is one undertaken immediately. It is the spot currency rate that is quoted on the TV news, and it is the spot rate that has been used in the above calculations. A forward transaction is one where the terms are agreed now but delivery is made at some time in the future. Forward currency rates may be quoted in the same way as spot currency rates, or as a premium or discount to the spot rate. To hedge the exchange rate risk in the above example, we could have locked in a known exchange rate by making a forward currency transaction. For example, if the forward one-year rate was $1.52 per £1, we could buy sterling and sell dollars at that rate in one year. Then, when we sell the investment and receive dollars, we know with certainty what the exchange rate will be when we convert them.

Notice that we would reduce our return by hedging in the first example and increase it in the second. Also, currency uncertainty is not completely removed. With some investments, you know the exact money value you will receive. For example, a zero-coupon bond with one year to run will pay a specified sum. Accordingly, the amount of dollars to be sold forward is known. But for an equity investment, for example, the money value in one year's time will not be known. We therefore do not know the exact amount to hedge. Further, our timing may be out. After one year, our equity investment may not have performed as well as we had hoped, but we might remain optimistic that it will. In that case, another forward contract will have to be agreed.

What determines the forward rate? According to the interest rate parity argument, the forward rate for a currency will be related to the spot rate by interest rate differentials. Assume \$1.5 = £1, US interest rates are 10%, UK rates are 5%, and the one-year forward rate is \$1.5714 = £1, a premium to the spot rate, i.e. sterling is strong. Consider now two ways of investing £1000:

1. Invest £1000 in the UK at 5% for one year. The year-end value will be £1050.
2. Convert £1000 into \$1500. Agree a one-year forward currency contract at \$1.5714. Invest \$1500 at 10%. Receive \$1650 in one year. Convert to sterling at agreed rate (\$1650/1.5714) and the year-end value is £1050.

The returns are identical. But what if the forward rate was \$1.5 = £1? It would be possible to earn a risk-free 5% interest rate differential by investing in the US and buying sterling forward (because \$1650/1.5 = £1100, versus £1050 from the UK investment). Arbitrageurs would keep buying sterling forward until the forward rate changed by sufficient to eliminate the risk-free return, i.e. until it reached \$1.5714. The difference between the spot and equilibrium forward rate is given by:

$$\frac{\text{Dollar interest rate} - \text{sterling interest rate}}{1 + \text{sterling interest rate}}.$$

For our example:

$$\frac{0.1 - 0.05}{1 + 0.05} = 0.0476 = 4.76\%$$

and the equilibrium forward rate is:

$$\$1.5 \times 1.0476 = \$1.5714.$$

In sum, arbitrage should ensure that the forward rate is related to the spot rate by interest rate differentials. The evidence is that currency forward rates are priced in this way in the real world when there are no exchange restrictions.

We have related today's spot rate with today's forward rate. Is there a relationship between today's forward rate for, say, one year and the spot rate in one year's time? Imagine we know, with complete certainty, that the $/£ spot rate will be $2 in one year, and the forward rate for delivery in one year is $1.5. If we bought £100 forward we would, in one year's time, pay $150 and receive £100. We could then go to the spot market and pay £100 to receive $200, making a risk-free $50. Accordingly, we would expect arbitrageurs to buy sterling forward until the forward rate is $2 and the risk-free profit eliminated. In short, the forward rate should be the market's expectation of the future spot rate.

Of course, we don't know the spot rate in one year's time with complete certainty. Nonetheless, we might argue that the forward rate will be driven to what is the market's best guess of the future spot rate. While the forward rate will often be a poor guide, there is no reason to believe it will be biased to under- or overpredict exchange rate movements.

If the forward rate equals the expected future spot rate, then if the forward rate is at a premium to the current spot rate, the market expects the currency to appreciate. Unfortunately, the evidence goes the other way. Currencies with forward premiums tend to depreciate. When we related forward rates to current spot rates, we found that the currency with the forward premium, and therefore the currency expected to appreciate, was the one with the lowest interest rate. The evidence suggests the opposite (Froot, 1990). It is currencies that have high interest rates that tend to appreciate.

These findings may imply that the market is inefficient. Market efficiency can be saved if we assume that market participants are risk-averse or their expectations turn out to be wrong. For example, since in reality we don't know with certainty the future spot rate, if currency investors are risk-averse, the un-covered interest parity condition may be distorted by a risk premium. Investors may demand a higher rate of return than the interest rate differential because of the risk of holding a foreign currency. The literature on this is extensive and beyond the scope of this book. Surveys include Froot and Thaler (1990) and Taylor (1995). These surveys have slightly different viewpoints, but it is hard to disagree with Froot and Thaler (1990, p. 190): 'Taken as a whole, the evidence suggests that explanations which allow for the possibility of market inefficiency should be seriously investigated.' If currency market inefficiency is a possibility, we might hope to be able to forecast currency rates.

Before we look at currency forecasting, it is worth recapping the four types of prices that have been discussed:

- *Spot prices* are those that currently prevail—they are the price we would pay if we made a cash transaction today.
- *Expected spot prices* are the spot prices that we expect to prevail at the end of an investment horizon.
- *Realized spot prices* are the spot prices that actually prevail at the end of the investment horizon.

- *Forward prices* are those that are agreed today for transactions to take place at agreed future dates.

FOREIGN CURRENCY MANAGEMENT

If an investor can forecast currencies, then it is sensible to use this as part of the process of making international asset allocation decisions. If an investor cannot forecast currencies, then a passive currency approach should be adopted. Passive can be defined as 100% hedged or 100% unhedged, or any predetermined number in between.

Active Versus Passive Currency Management

Active currency management requires an ability to forecast currency rates. There are four methods of forecasting currency rates:

- using economic models;
- using technical analysis;
- using market data, such as the spot price or the forward price;
- using a combination of the above.

Economic Models

There are a number of economic models, but the usual starting point is the law of one price. This simply asserts that in open markets the same price must prevail everywhere. This underlies the purchasing power parity theorem, which assumes that the exchange rate for two countries is determined by the relative price levels of the two countries. If prices in one country rise relative to the other's, the exchange rate will adjust so that goods will cost the same in whichever country they are bought. Of course, this invites the question: what determines the relative price of goods? This is usually answered by a monetary model, whereby prices in a country are determined by the money supply, therefore relative prices are determined by the relative money supplies of the two countries being analysed. Depending on the assumptions made, purchasing power parity is attained immediately through rational expectations, for example the moment relative money supplies change, or alternatively only when the effect of changes in the money supply shows up in prices. It is also possible to devise overshooting models in which the equilibrium exchange rate is overshot because prices are sticky, for example they do not fall when relative money supply is cut.

Other economic approaches to the determination of exchange rates focus on the balance of payments or, in a much more abstract model, portfolio balances. Most of the empirical economic studies relating to these models will not interest most practitioners. However, an out-of-sample forecasting performance study is

of interest. Meese and Rogoff (1983) examined the ability of economic fundamentals to predict the level of exchange rates for periods of up to one year. They
used various fundamental-based economic models, as well as statistical models
that did not incorporate economic assumptions. They found that a naive strategy
of using today's exchange rate as the forecast worked at least as well as any of
the economic or statistical models. In other words, in the short run, economics
doesn't offer much to the currency forecaster.

In the long run, however, the economic models do seem to have some merit.
For example, purchasing power parity does seem an important factor, and relative changes in money supply do appear to have some effect after a couple of
years. Froot and Rogoff (1995) estimate that once disturbed, purchasing power
parity takes an average of eight years to become re-established. Mark (1995) has
demonstrated some forecasting ability for economic models at forecasting horizons greater than three years. Taylor (1995, pp. 41–2), in his review of the
literature, concluded:

> The data provide support for some of the long-run relationships suggested by economic
> theory [which] suggests that progress might be made by concentrating on the long-run
> determinants of exchange rates. But it seems that further attempts to provide explana-
> tions of short-term exchange rate movements based *solely* on macroeconomic funda-
> mentals may not prove successful . . . The macroeconomic fundamentals are clearly
> important in setting the parameters within which the exchange rate moves in the short-
> term, but they do not appear to tell the whole story.

Technical Analysis

To fill in the missing parts of the currency story, economists have turned to
analyse the microstructure of currency markets, i.e. instead of looking at the
markets at an aggregate level, they have started looking at the behaviour of
traders (see, e.g. Frankel and Froot, 1990).

One feature of the international currency markets is that while prices are
readily available, the market is non-transparent, as specific transactions quantities and prices are not public information. Moreover, the participants have
significantly different amounts of information. For example, the banks that
make a market in currencies transact for both customers and themselves. Clearly
they know more than other participants because they know both their own
demand and their customers' demand. It is likely that the banks will act on any
trends they see, and less informed participants may act on the basis of significant
moves in currency rates on the grounds that the better informed agents are
trading. This might lead to extrapolative behaviours, which would be amenable
to technical analysis. Certainly technical analysis is very important in the foreign
exchange market.

Taylor and Allen (1992) sent questionnaires to those banks in London that
report their foreign exchange exposure to the Bank of England, and to various
other institutions that act as market makers in foreign exchange. For the shortest
horizons (intraday to one week), approximately 90% of respondents said they

use some form of chartist input when forming exchange rate expectations, with 60% judging charts to be at least as important as fundamentals. At forecast horizons of one year or longer, 85% of respondents judged fundamentals to be more important than charts.

If technical analysis is widely used, and if economic fundamentals fail to explain short-run movements in currencies, then the obvious implication is that technical analysis might be useful in making short-term currency forecasts. A number of studies (e.g. Neely, 1997; Levich and Thomas, 1993; and Silber, 1994) report that technical analysis can be used to generate profits in the currency markets. Most tests have used moving averages or filter rules rather than charts. Notice, however, that even if technical trading strategies generate currency profits, this is not the same thing as producing a forecast suitable for calculating a currency-adjusted expected annual return on the foreign equity or bond market.

Market-Based Variables and Combination Approaches

Another approach to forecasting currencies is to use market rates, for example the current spot rate or the current futures/forward rate. It seems that the spot rate tends to be the better predictor (e.g. Arnott and Pham, 1993; Bracker and Morran, 1999). Bracker and Morran (1999) tested the trading rule that if the current spot rate of exchange was higher than the current futures rate, then you should buy one futures contract and hold for one month, and if the current spot rate of exchange is lower than the current futures rate, then you should sell short one futures contract and hold for one month. They studied data from 1978 through to 1996 for the dollar versus five other currencies. They found that this rule, and those of buying high-interest-rate currencies and chasing trends, were generally successful, and even more so if more than one rule pointed in the same direction. They note that their study's time period is largely the same as that of Arnott and Pham (1993), except for the period 1992–96; they point out that their trading rules are generally less successful in this latter period.

Passive Currency Management

If you can't forecast currencies, then you should adopt a passive approach. But what is the correct passive approach? Should you hedge or not? The question can be answered culturally, empirically or theoretically. Anyone who tried to persuade Americans to invest overseas in the 1980s (or before) was met with great suspicion. US investors didn't care for anything foreign at all. US consultants were less xenophobic, but didn't much care for foreign currencies. Many wanted foreign currency exposure permanently hedged. European investors, on the other hand, tended to assume that if you invested abroad you invested in foreign stocks and foreign currencies. To the extent that the Europeans hedged, it was a tactical and not a strategic decision.

Much of the literature of the 1980s and even early 1990s used short periods of history to show what would have happened if certain policies had been adopted. For example, it was shown that over a specific 10-year period (using quarterly data), hedging would have reduced international portfolios' volatility substantially (see Pérold and Schulman, 1988). On the other hand, using 150 years of returns it could be shown that over longish holding periods, say eight years or more, currencies were mean-reverting and hedging did not reduce volatility (Froot, 1993).

A more theoretical approach was taken by Black (1989b) with his universal hedging rule. He argued that the optimal hedge ratio depended on three inputs: the expected return on the world market portfolio, the volatility of the world market portfolio, and the average exchange rate volatility. He concluded that you should hedge your foreign equities, you should hedge equities equally for all countries, and you shouldn't hedge 100% of your foreign equities. He argued that the formula applied to every investor who holds foreign securities, whatever his country of domicile. The universal hedging ratio was 0.7. Few people seem to have accepted Black's analysis.

Sharpe et al. (1999, p. 883) list the following as determinants of the optimal currency hedge:

- correlations between currencies;
- correlations between domestic returns and currency returns;
- the proportion of the portfolio invested in foreign securities;
- the cost of hedging;
- the premium earned for holding foreign currencies;
- the variability of foreign security returns;
- the variability of currency returns;
- the percentage of the investor's consumption that is imported;
- the investor's degree of risk aversion;
- the investor's time horizon.

Given a list like this, it is hardly surprising that Solnik (1998, p. 49) has concluded: 'There is no simple practical solution, and no theoretically unquestionable benchmark for the currency allocation, and there will never be one.'

Clearly any statement on whether one should hedge tells you more about the author than about what you should do. Bearing that in mind, for a long-term fund, such as a UK pension fund, this author would not consider strategic hedging until foreign assets exceeded 30% of the fund. This number is chosen to roughly match the foreign consumption liabilities of the beneficiaries. Moreover, being a long-term fund, a pension fund should be willing to look through short-term currency fluctuations. If, however, a decision is made to partially hedge, this should begin with bonds rather than equities. Although both equities and currencies are volatile, the risk is not additive because of the low correlation between currencies and equity returns. Weak currencies often mean strong equity markets. The total risk from investing in a foreign equity market is therefore only marginally higher than the equity return risk alone. For bonds, however, the total risk is significantly higher than the bond return risk. This is because bond prices and currency movements are often positively correlated, and because the variability on bonds is lower than the variability on equities, so the addition of currency risk matters more.

THE EURO

On 1 January 1999, 11 members of the EU adopted the euro. The euro countries were Austria, Belgium, Finland, France, Germany, Ireland, Italy, Luxembourg, the Netherlands, Portugal and Spain. The other four members of the EU— Denmark, Greece, Sweden and the UK—retained their national currencies. Denmark, Sweden and the UK had announced they did not want to join the common currency at the start. Greece has subsequently adopted the euro.

Currently, each of the euro countries has retained its own bank notes. The euro is, however, used for all official and interbank transactions, and financial assets are priced in euros. On 1 January 2002, all national coins and notes will cease to be legal tender in Euroland, and private individuals will have to use the euro. The exchange rates between the national currencies and the euro were fixed on 1 January 1999, so although Deutschmarks, French francs, etc. still exist physically, as far as investors are concerned, the national currencies have disappeared.

The European Central Bank (ECB) is the centrepiece of the European System of Central Banks, which includes the central banks of the 15 EU members. The 12 Euroland central banks will continue to exist and carry out all functions they previously did, except that they will now engage in monetary policy operations only when instructed to by the ECB. Monetary policy decisions are made by its governing council, which includes the governors of the participating national central banks plus a six-member ECB executive board appointed by the heads of state of the member nations. The ECB's monetary policy operations are independent of EU institutions and the governments of the participating nations. Its statutory objective is to maintain price stability and, without prejudice to that objective, to support the general economic policies in the community.

The potential benefits from a common currency include:

- a more efficient price-discovery process, because a single currency allows direct comparison of the price of goods throughout the community;
- removal of uncertainty about exchange rates for intra-Euroland trade;
- removal of currency conversion costs;
- reductions in the cost of maintaining transactions balances.

There are, however, significant one-time conversion costs and, longer term, potentially much greater problems. There is uncertainty as to how the ECB will act given divergent economic experiences in the member nations. In practice, the size of Germany and France mean that policy will essentially be geared towards their needs. Other countries have, however, lost the power to make adjustments by following an independent monetary policy. They do have the ability to alter their fiscal policies, but these fiscal powers are not unlimited. The Stability and Growth Pact requires that each country undertake to comply with the medium-term budgetary objective of positions close to balance or in surplus, and to correct excessive deficits as quickly as possible.

The euro raises many issues for international investors, especially UK investors. Will the euro survive? Will the UK join? If it does, at what rate of exchange will it join? If it is not the current rate, how will it get from the current rate to a new one? Should Euroland be considered one market for asset allocation purposes? Should we give different answers to this question for bonds and equities? Is Euroland more attractive than the individual components, justifying a higher weighting, or should the weighting be reduced because the common currency means that the diversification potential has declined? And does the answer depend on whether an investor hedges? These questions are easier to pose than to answer. Many commentators compare Euroland (the United States of Europe) with the US. Perhaps a better analogy is with the Canadian currency zone. After more than a century, Canada has still not integrated, and has different languages, limited labour mobility, and so on.

Some Investment Issues

Before the establishment of the common currency, bond yields varied widely throughout Europe. In anticipation of a single currency, and a common monetary policy, Sovereign bond yields converged before January 1999. However, there are still modest yield differences, reflecting differences in credit ratings and in market liquidity. For example, in 2000, Italian and Portuguese long-term government bonds yielded about 30 to 35 basis points more than German government bonds. Germany is rated AAA by Standard and Poor's, while Italy and Portugal are rated AA. The analogy with Canada applies here. Although there is a common Canadian currency, and a common monetary authority, the yields on the various provinces' bonds differ.

In the past, many European bond managers concentrated on choosing between the various European markets on the basis of interest rate anticipation and likely currency movements. This approach is now more tightly constrained, although switches between sterling, Swiss and Euroland issues are possible. Credit ratings and credit analysis are likely to take on greater importance as an active strategy. Most US corporate bonds are rated, and many US institutional investors will invest in the full range of ratings. European institutional investors have tended to purchase high-grade bonds, and a European company that has issued exclusively domestic bonds has usually not been rated, but relied upon its reputation. Foreign investors, however, tend to look at ratings. An increase in credit analysis and high-yield issues seems likely.

Over the last few years, there has been a growing shift amongst equity brokers to publish pan-European research. Historically, research has been organized by country and investors have made country allocation decisions and then gone on to choose their sector weightings within each country. Now, research is presented on a European sector basis on the assumption, presumably, that the European equity manager will determine his or her bank sector weighting, resources weighting, etc. and thereby his or her country weighting. This is probably a caricature of both positions. For example, with the traditional country approach, after making a country weighting and selecting stocks, a check would be made to ensure that within each country, oil and bank stocks, say, had not been selected in every case. And currently, sector weightings are not chosen without regard to country weightings. In fact a matrix approach, as shown in Table 20.5, is probably widely used. To avoid too many numbers, data for only one country, the UK, and only one sector, financials, are shown. You read the table as follows: The first row shows the sectors, and the first column shows the countries. We find in the first column that the UK is 33% of the European market, and we see from the last column that the financials sector comprises 23.8% of the European market. In the cells within the table there are figures for country and sector. The first figure of the shaded cell tells us that financials make up 21% of the UK market and the second figure tells us that UK financials make up 29% of the European financials sector. In other words, the UK has a smaller financials sector than the European market as a whole (21% v. 23.8%), so it only comprises 29% of the financials sector in Europe as against its 33% weighting in the entire market. An investor might think in terms of taking overweight positions in both particular countries and particular sectors.

TABLE 20.5 European asset allocation

	Resources (8.7%)	Basic industries (4.3%)	General industrials (7.7%)	Cyclical consumer (3.4%)	Non-cyclical consumer (12.8%)	Cyclical services (8.7%)	Non-cyclical services (18.1%)	Utilities (2.9%)	IT (9.5%)	Financials (23.8%)
UK 33%	13/50	3/20	2/10	1/4	16/40	13/52	25/45	4/46	2/8	21/29
France 14.7%										13/8
Germany 11.8%										33/16
Italy 7.9%										34/11
Netherlands 7.6%										27/9
Switzerland 7.5%										31/10
Sweden 5%										19/26
Spain 4.1%										34/6
Belgium 1.5%										65/4
Ireland 0.7%										34/1
Portugal 0.6%										21/1

The justification for this change in emphasis from countries to industries is presumably that the common currency will reduce differences in countries economic circumstances and therefore industries will become more important. Whether this will really be the case remains to be seen. The historical evidence is quite clear—countries are more important than industries in determining returns. Numerous studies have been made that attempt to determine returns on the basis of international, national, currency and industry effects. The studies usually show that the country effect predominates. What this means is that if you know the return on the UK market, then you will get a better estimate of the return on a UK bank share, say, than you will get by knowing the return on the European banking sector. For example, Drummen and Zimmermann (1992) looked at 11 European markets over the 1986–89 period. They found that the country factor explained 19% of the average stock return variance, the world stock market 11%, overall European trends 8% and industry trends 9%. Rouwenhorst (1999a) looked at industry and country effects for the European equity markets over the period 1982–98. He found that country effects on stock returns had been larger than industry effects, and that this continued during the 1993–98 period despite the convergence of interest rates and the harmonization of fiscal monetary policy following the Maastricht Treaty.

SHARE SELECTION IN INTERNATIONAL MARKETS

While there are undoubtedly differences between markets, if only in the sector distributions and relative importance of large-cap stocks versus small, what is perhaps surprising is how frequently findings relating to the US market can be applied elsewhere. Throughout this book we have related the UK to US findings and in a number of places mentioned other markets. It is beyond the scope of this book to attempt to look at similarities and differences between the international markets. However, a few points can be made. Much of the so called anomalies literature can be applied worldwide. The interested reader is referred to Keim and Ziemba (2000). This book covers security market imperfections around the world. The interested reader is also referred to Fama and French (1998) for international evidence on value versus growth, and Arshanapalli et al. (1998) for evidence on the Fama and French three-factor model in 18 equity markets.

APPROACHES TO ASSESSING MARKETS

A variety of approaches are used in deciding which international markets are the most attractive. Some investors:

- ignore countries and simply buy the cheapest stocks in the world, deriving their country allocation as a residual;
- compare markets as though they were simply different stocks within a market;
- treat each market separately and rate it cheap or expensive relative to its own history;
- use international business cycle anticipation;
- forecast total returns.

Buying the Cheapest Stocks

Simply selecting the cheapest stocks in the world and ignoring international asset allocation appeals to many investors who believe they have stock-selection skills. This approach could take the form of buying, say, the 40 cheapest stocks in the world, and if they are all telephone companies, so be it. Usually, however, investors construct portfolios that are diversified by sector, for example the cheapest oil company in the world, the cheapest chemical company, and so on. Whether this is a sensible approach depends on whether stocks' returns are more correlated with their global industry's return or that of their national market. While picking cheap stocks may be a viable strategy, the evidence points to country factors as being the most rewarding starting point for international asset allocation.

Selecting Markets as though they are Stocks

The argument for selecting markets as though they are stocks is that assets are assets and investors are investors. Presumably whatever the reason for low price-earnings stocks or small stocks performing well within a market should carry across to entire markets too. If investors concentrate too much on the past and reward past success, and that accounts for low price-earnings stocks tending to outperform, then that should apply to markets too. And if poor liquidity is the explanation for small stocks performing well, that should probably affect markets too. On this tack, we should look for low PERs, high yields, high book value, and so on. Of course, there are vast differences between markets in terms of accounting policies, growth prospects, political risk, etc. But growth differences exist between stocks within a market, so there is nothing special about this at an international level. And while different countries do use different accounting methods (e.g. with regard to depreciation), one can reduce the effect of this (e.g. by looking at cash flow instead of earnings).

What is the evidence? Keppler (1991a, 1991b) looked separately at cash flow and dividends as a basis for country asset allocation. In both studies, he used the same procedure, and we will discuss the studies together. He used 20 years of data ending in December 1989 drawn from the MSCI country indexes, and he sorted the countries into quartiles based on their price-to-cash flow ratios and, separately, on their dividend yields. For each variable, he looked at six investment strategies, which consisted of investing in various quartiles, or groups of quartiles. The hypothetical portfolios were constructed with equal initial investments in each market, grouped according to the selection variable being studied, and rebalanced to equal investments at the end of each quarter. Returns were examined over rolling one-, two-, three-, four- and five-year periods. By and large, the two selection criteria were successful in ranking portfolios by return, whether measured in local currency or a common currency. High-yield countries and low price-to-cash flow countries produced the highest returns.

Asness et al. (1997) noted that within the US, firms with high book-to-market ratio, small size, and high past-year returns (i.e. upward momentum) outperformed stocks with low book-to-market, large size and downward momentum. They sorted countries on the basis of these variables. The countries were those included in the MSCI World Index (except Finland, Ireland, New Zealand and Malaysia), and the period covered by their study varied depending on the variable, but was approximately 20 years, finishing at the end of 1994. Their results mirrored those found for the same variables for US stocks.

Another stock-selection technique discussed earlier (Chapter 15) was winner–loser reversals. Richards (1997) applied this approach to international markets. He used return indexes of 16 national markets for the period 1970–95. He used various ranking periods (e.g. three months, six months, 12 months, etc.) and in each period ranked the countries by return. He then divided the ranked list into quartiles and calculated the returns in a subsequent test period, which was the same length as the ranking period. He found that for the three-, six-, and 12-month periods, the winner quartile outperformed the loser quartile. After that, the loser portfolio outperformed the winner portfolio. He found this to be true for 24-, 36-, 48- and 60-month periods, but the effect was greatest for 36 and 48 months. These country findings are in line with the findings for stocks within the US market. Richards found no support for the hypothesis that the reversals reflected risk differentials.

In Chapter 10, we discussed the relationship between earnings revisions and stock returns. An earnings revision approach can also be applied to the international markets. Emanuelli and Pearson (1994) provide some evidence on this. Using IBES international data, they focused on the direction and degree of change in analysts' corporate earnings forecasts. They measured the extent of estimate revisions in terms of an estimate-revision ratio. For example, a one-month ratio for a particular country is calculated by taking the total number of current fiscal year estimates raised during the previous month and dividing it by the total number of current fiscal year estimates lowered during the month. Emanuelli and Pearson studied 24 international markets, most of which were included in the study from September 1987 for 52 months. They constructed two portfolios, a top portfolio and a bottom portfolio. The first consisted of equal investments in the indexes of the countries with the five highest revision ratios. The bottom portfolio consisted of equal investments in the five countries with the lowest revision ratios. The authors provide a battery of tests and conclude that investment in the top portfolio would have outperformed the mean return of all 24 countries included in the study by up to 6% over a one-year holding period, and outperformed the MSCI Global Index by 10%. The bottom portfolio consistently underperformed.

Macedo (1995, 1997) attempts to select international markets on the basis of style selection. She notes that value and relative strength appear to be viable international market selection tools. She argues that each tends to work when the other doesn't. But how do you know which style to use and when? She argues that if investors' risk tolerance decreases, the premium to those styles thought to be riskier must increase. Riskiness is measured by global market volatility, i.e. the standard deviation of returns. High market volatility reflects, and perhaps increases, investor uncertainty. Macedo assumes that whenever volatility is higher than its prior average, investors are assumed to be risk-adverse. She argues that the premium for uncomfortable, or contrarian, styles should be high after a period of high volatility, and a comfortable style, such as relative strength, should work when volatility is low. Macedo's empirical results support her arguments.

Based on the above evidence, it would seem that treating countries as though they were stocks and using standard share-selection screens has some value. However, this approach is essentially a ranking approach, rather than a return forecasting approach. All we can say is that we prefer country X to country Y, not the return we can expect from each country.

Selecting Markets by Local Standards

The case for assessing markets on the basis of local standards is that despite the evidence of the previous section, there is room for doubting that markets are directly comparable; moreover, within each market the local investors are the dominant force. If local investors everywhere relate their own equity market more to local bonds and local cash than to other equity markets, then the sensible approach might seem to be to go native. International valuation then becomes a process of assessing markets on the basis of relative cheapness and dearness of each market based on its domestic valuation standard. These valuation standards may be based on simple measures, such as the PER in relation to its historical range and average, or more complex standards, such as an equity risk premium comparison with local bonds.

There is surprisingly little published evidence on selection by local valuations. In an interesting article, Arnott and Henriksson (1991) give a clear statement of the local valuation approach. They note that if an equity risk premium is measured in any one country and compared with the normal risk premium for that country, an abnormal risk premium can be calculated. While normal risk premiums may differ from country to country, and are not directly comparable, the abnormal premiums are directly comparable. The evidence they produce, however, does not prove that this approach actually leads to good portfolio selection in practice. Moreover, the equity risk premium says something about potential *relative* performance within a market. It does not necessarily help an international equity investor to select just equities. For example, UK equities may seem cheap relative to UK gilts, and Australian equities may seem fairly valued against Australian bonds, but if Australian bond yields are very high and start to tumble, then Australian equities may well outperform UK equities while being only fairly valued relative to Australian bonds. Nonetheless, this does seem a sensible approach.

Some investors use different valuation measures for different markets. For example, the book-to-price ratio might be thought to be especially relevant for

Japan, or the gap between the earnings yield and long bond yield. In Hong Kong, however, there is no local long-bond market; accordingly, the earnings yield/long bond relationship is not appropriate. If there are some market idiosyncrasies so that different measures may be important in different markets, this may suggest a chalk-and-cheese problem: how can the cheapness/dearness of the UK, say, on a yield basis be related to the cheapness or dearness of Japan on a book value basis? One solution is to measure each market's value in terms of the number of standard deviations it is from the mean of the selection variable. Then, if the UK is one standard deviation above its average dividend yield, and Japan is half a standard deviation above its average book-to-price ratio, the UK would be cheaper. Some investors use this sort of approach, but there does not appear to any published evidence on its value.

International Business Cycles

Conover et al. (1999) looked at monetary conditions and international investing. They rated the monetary environment either expansive or restrictive. The period following a discount rate increase is classified as restrictive, and the period following a discount rate decrease is classified as expansive. They studied the returns from 16 countries, over the period 1956–95. They found that investing in equities only when both US and local monetary policy was expansive, and investing in Treasury bills at other times, produced better returns than a passive fully invested strategy. How useful these results are is unclear. Transaction costs do not appear to have been allowed for, an investor would have been out of the market 56% of the time, and all markets were equally weighted.

Forecasting Total Returns

The approaches discussed above rank markets rather than produce total returns. Of course, a local market equity risk premium approach involves making a total return forecast, but that is not the aspect focused upon. Total return forecasts can be made in a number of ways, for example by the constant-growth DDM approach or by using PERs. The latter approach requires a forecast of the expected change in the market PER, the expected change in profits, and the expected yield.

Attempts have been made to forecast market returns on the basis of economic variables (Dumas, 1994; Ferson and Harvey, 1994) and financial market variables that have been found to be useful in the past (e.g. Fama and French, 1993). As an illustration, Solnik (1993) tried to forecast returns for eight major bond and equity markets for the period 1971–91. He used the following variables:

- the national one-month interest rate;
- the national term spread (long-term minus short-term interest rate);

- the national dividend yield;
- the interest rate differential (national minus US short-term rate);
- the lagged asset return;
- the January seasonal.

Although the explanatory power was low, Solnik (1993) shows that the results would have been useful in tactical asset allocation.

EMERGING MARKETS

In the late 1980s, many mainstream professional managers had some exposure to emerging markets, although this was probably thought of more in terms of an odd cheap Thai stock, a cheap Hong Kong stock, or whatever, rather than an emerging markets' weighting. In the first edition of this book, it was argued that many managers paid insufficient attention to emerging markets. That part of the text was written in late 1992, but by the time the book had appeared in January 1994, almost every private client seemed to own an emerging markets unit trust or investment trust. The markets boomed, but then suffered a series of crises, including the Mexican debt crisis in 1994, the Asian crisis in 1997–98, and the Russian debt crisis in 1998. However, in 1999, the emerging markets bounced back. Clearly, the emerging markets experience great swings in sentiment and returns. Although the preceding analysis can be applied to emerging markets, a more detailed examination is worthwhile.

What is an Emerging Market?

Had you studied economics in the 1960s, you might have taken a course in development economics, and you would have studied underdeveloped countries (UDCs). In the 1970s, the UDCs became less-developed countries (LDCs). In the early 1980s, these economies were again repackaged as emerging markets. The first two terms have an unfortunate connotation of poverty and being a loser, whereas the last term has a connotation of being tomorrow's winner. Emerging-market countries are essentially poor countries with low GDP per head, although sometimes emerging markets are so classified on the basis of a low market capitalization relative to GDP.

Whether emerging markets will be tomorrow's winners is hard to say. Optimists will point to the fact that emerging markets have about 84% of the world's population, about 20% of the world's GDP, and about 7% of the world's equity market capitalization. Pessimists will point out that many emerging markets are essentially re-emerging markets. Investors who were looking for good returns in the nineteenth century invested in India, Egypt, Argentina, Peru, etc. Many of these economies have disappointed for a century. Why will it be different this time?

A difficulty in answering questions of this sort is that the 'facts' are difficult to come by. Although many emerging markets have local stock market series going back a long period, most analysis is done with composite emerging market indexes. These have a very short record, and given the volatility of the emerging markets, the period studied greatly affects the conclusions. Further, the various emerging markets indexes can produce sharply different returns over short periods because of their different methods of construction.

The three major emerging market indexes are produced by Morgan Stanley Capital International (MSCI), Baring Securities, and Standard and Poor's/ International Finance Corporation (S&P/IFC). The composition of the S&P/ IFC Composite Index is shown in Table 20.6. The S&P/IFC also produces a Frontiers Index, the components of which are Bangladesh, Botswana, Bulgaria, the Ivory Coast, Croatia, Ecuador, Estonia, Ghana, Jamaica, Kenya, Latvia, Lithuania, Mauritius, Romania, Slovenia, Trinidad and Tobago, Tunisia, and the Ukraine. Frontier markets tend to be relatively small and illiquid, even by emerging market standards, with generally less information available.

Emerging market indexes are inherently unsatisfactory. Because emerging markets often have restrictions on the number of shares in a company that foreigners can own, emerging markets can be conceived of either in terms of the total market, which reflects their size for the domestic investor, or in terms of an investible index, which represents the size of the markets for foreign investors. MSCI and S&P/IFC each offer both types of index. The MSCI Emerging Markets Global (EMG) and the S&P/IFC Global (S&P/IFCG) are weighted by total market capitalization, while the MSCI Emerging Markets Free (EMF) and the S&P/IFC Investible (S&P/IFCI) are weighted by the proportion of market capitalization accessible to foreigners. The target coverage of an S&P/IFCG Index is about 70–75% of total market capitalization, drawing on stocks in order of their liquidity. The S&P/IFCI indexes further screen stocks for foreign ownership restrictions, and factor in minimum market capitalization and liquidity parameters. Stocks are assigned weights, representing the amount foreign institutional investors may buy either as a result of national foreign investment restrictions or individual company corporate statute restrictions.

Because of the variation in the construction of indexes, especially where the index capitalization as a percentage of the entire market capitalization is modest, different indexes produce different returns. Further, once we make the investible/non-investible distinction, the difference between index returns can be marked. For example, the compound annual growth of the MSCI EMF index was 19.9% over the period 1989–96, whereas the compound annual growth rate of the S&P/IFCG Index was 9.2%.

The composition of emerging market indexes changes constantly as a result of country and stock changes. For example, in 1995, the S&P/IFC added South Africa to its investible index, and the South African weighting changed from 0% of the index to 25%. Sometimes countries exit the index through 'promotion'. For example, at the end of 1997, Portugal was promoted out of the MSCI Emerging Markets Indexes. As well as country weightings changing because of

TABLE 20.6   S&P/IFCG Composite Index, end 1999

Market	Market capitalization ($bn)	Weight in S&P/IFCG (%)	Number of listed companies
Latin America	**309.4**	**21.3**	**294**
Argentina	23.3	1.6	28
Brazil	107.8	7.4	90
Chile	42.6	2.9	48
Columbia	5.4	0.4	23
Mexico	118.4	8.2	57
Peru	7.6	0.5	32
Venezuela	4.2	0.3	16
Asia	**735.5**	**50.7**	**1047**
China	78.5	5.4	219
India	92.5	6.4	143
Indonesia	23.3	1.6	55
Korea	182.0	12.6	162
Malaysia	68.9	4.8	139
Pakistan	3.1	0.2	49
Philippines	26.0	1.8	58
Sri Lanka	1.0	0.1	52
Taiwan, China	231.0	15.9	106
Thailand	29.2	2.0	64
Europe	**203.5**	**14.0**	**221**
Czech Republic	4.2	0.3	28
Greece	90.1	6.2	59
Hungary	13.1	0.9	15
Poland	11.8	0.8	33
Russia	25.3	1.7	19
Slovakia	0.4	0.0	14
Turkey	58.7	4.1	53
Middle East/Africa	**202.2**	**13.9**	**359**
Bahrain	4.3	0.3	15
Egypt	11.4	0.8	69
Israel	26.5	1.8	49
Jordan	4.1	0.3	40
Morocco	8.1	0.6	18
Nigeria	1.8	0.1	28
Oman	2.8	0.2	34
Saudi Arabia	30.9	2.1	20
South Africa	110.7	7.6	64
Zimbabwe	1.6	0.1	22
Composite	**1450.6**	**100.0**	**1921**

Source: Standard & Poor's (2000, p. 44).

countries entering and exiting the indexes, the weighting of countries can change dramatically because of a change in the number of quoted companies in a country. For example, if a country engages in a spate of privatizations, its weighting may soar. Given these index problems, it is clear that risk-and-return data should be treated with some scepticism.

Emerging Market Risks

As with any foreign investment, investing in emerging markets involves currency risk. In addition, it involves political risk, information risk, liquidity risk, and repatriation of capital risk. We will look at each of these in turn:

- *Political risk:* given the interest with which markets follow political events in developed economies, it is clear that political risk exists everywhere. But the risks are higher in emerging markets, where complete changes in economic policy can take place, corruption scandals often occur, and there may be the odd military coup. A number of commercial services assess political risk. For example, Political Risk Services publishes the *International Country Risk Guide*, which provides a monthly measure of political risk for a variety of countries. Diamonte et al. (1996) found that changes in political risk had a bigger impact on emerging market returns than on developed market returns. They found the average difference in returns between emerging markets experiencing political risk upgrades and those experiencing political risk downgrades was approximately 11% a quarter for emerging markets against 2.5% in developed markets.
- *Information risk:* reporting standards tend to be lower in emerging markets than in developed markets and, of course, there are language and cultural barriers. Many firms are controlled by family groups, and it often appears that it is their interests, rather than all shareholders' interests, that are being pursued.
- *Liquidity risk:* many emerging markets have poor liquidity, and it is difficult to deal in size unless wide spreads are accepted.
- *Repatriation of capital:* many emerging economies suffer periodic economic crises, and regulations governing the repatriation of capital may be introduced or tightened. Although no longer classified as an emerging market, Malaysia introduced restrictions on repatriation by foreign portfolio investors a few years ago.

A common summary measure of risk is the standard deviation of market returns, which is usually much higher for an emerging market than for a developed market. For emerging markets, standard deviations can range between 25% and 90% per year in contrast to perhaps 15–25% in developed markets. Many people find these sorts of numbers difficult to grasp. Some illustrations will be useful. For example, in 1998 and 1999 the world index, depending how measured, was up somewhere over 20% in each year. These were high returns, but Thailand did even better—up 27% and 31% respectively. Meanwhile, Ghana went from boom to bust, up 62% and then down 34%. Turkey went from bust to boom, down 51% and then up 240%. Romania went from bust to bust, down 63% and then down 37%, while Jamaica did nothing—up 3% and up 2%. An interesting feature of these numbers is that while the annual changes are large, different countries are moving in different directions. This means that the standard deviation for the emerging markets taken together, while higher than that for the developed markets, is nowhere near as high as you would expect from looking at the individual country figures. However, one has to be a little careful with standard deviations as a measure of the risk of emerging markets. The distribution of returns is not a normal curve, and there is a greater chance of large adverse returns than is typical of developed markets. This would make emerging markets riskier than their standard deviations suggest.

An attraction of emerging markets has been the low correlation of emerging market returns with developed market returns. Unfortunately, the correlation has been increasing over time. For example, Barry et al. (1998) report a correlation of 0.27 between the S&P 500 and the S&P/IFCI Index for the period 1975–95. However, the correlation was 0.41 for the period 1990–95. In the latest S&P annual review, the correlation for December 1994–December 1999 is 0.56. These correlations are difficult to interpret, as the 1990s were affected by both the Mexican and the Asian crises. The correlation between the emerging markets and the developed markets increases during crises that affect the entire world and during recessions in the developed economies. It is therefore difficult to disentangle one-off spikes from trends. However, the best guess would appear to be that the correlation is increasing.

Emerging Market Returns

As noted earlier, emerging market returns have to be treated with considerable scepticism because of the short period of return data that is typically used. Longer term, there is a survivorship bias problem. Also, because of the volatility of individual country returns, studies using an arithmetic average return will show a much higher return than would be shown by a geometric return.

The usual assumption is that the return from emerging markets has been high—high risk, high return. However, the second half of the 1980s was an especially favourable period for the emerging markets, and any relatively short measurement period that includes those years will show that the emerging markets did indeed offer a higher return. However, taking the entire period December 1975–June 1995, Barry et al. (1998) found that the S&P 500 produced a compound return of 1.1% per month, whereas the emerging markets produced a return of 0.99%. The emerging markets also had a higher standard deviation.

Emerging Market Weightings

There are three broad approaches to identifying how much to invest in emerging markets:

- by selecting markets
- by diversifying broadly
- by selecting stocks.

Some investors stress country selection. There are two reasons why this might be appropriate (see Divecha et al., 1992). First, low intra-emerging markets' return correlations, which offer scope for outperforming. Second, individual stock returns in emerging markets are more homogeneous than in developed markets. This is partly because the emerging markets have a slightly higher concentration in the largest stocks and in a few sectors than is the case in the developed markets. More important is the high volatility of the emerging markets; for example, when the market goes up by a large amount in a short period, it is likely that most stocks will move up. After country selection, institutional investors might simply buy the larger stocks in each market, while the private investor might buy unit trusts, investment trusts or World Equity Benchmark shares, which are passively managed open-ended mutual funds investing in single countries and indexed to the MSCI country indexes.

A different approach would be to let the number of cheap stocks determine the emerging market weighting. A decade or so ago it was argued that many emerging markets stocks were mispriced based on simple criteria such as asset value. Some investors now argue that the easy pickings have long gone, and it is more difficult to pick stocks in emerging markets. Whether this is true is unclear, but there has been some research as to whether factors associated with abnormal stock returns in the developed markets also apply to the emerging markets, in particular studies by Fama and French (1998), Claessens et al. (1998) and Rouwenhorst (1999b). Unfortunately, while Fama and French and Rouwenhorst reach broadly similar results, Claessens et al. produce contrary results.

Rouwenhorst (1999b, p. 1441) summarizes his findings as follows:

> In a sample of 1705 firms from 20 emerging markets taken from the Emerging Markets Database (EMDB) of the International Finance Corporation (IFC) I find that the return factors in emerging markets are qualitatively similar to those documented for many developed markets. The combination of a small number of stocks in some countries and the high volatility of returns often precludes precise measurement of return premiums in individual countries, but averaged across all emerging markets, stocks exhibit momentum, small stocks outperform large stocks, and value stocks outperform growth stocks. There is no evidence that high beta stocks also outperform low beta stocks, nor do I find that average returns are related to liquidity, as measured by share turnover.

Claessens et al. (1998) reported rather different findings. However, Fama and French (1998) argue that Claessens et al.'s statistical approach was sensitive to outliers, and extreme outliers are common in the returns on individual stocks in emerging markets.

The third approach to emerging markets is simply one of broad diversification. This would involve investing in most of the markets, perhaps on an equally-weighted, rather than a value-weighted, basis, and having a closet index fund in each country.

Developed Versus Emerging Markets

This still leaves the total allocation to emerging markets undetermined. The weightings of the emerging market countries relative to each other and to the developed markets might be determined by forecast annual returns, or derived from an optimizer. (Optimizers are discussed in Chapter 24.) The optimizer could use either forecast returns or historical returns. If historical returns are used, then we come back to the problem of the indexes. As we saw, over the period 1989–96 there were vastly different returns depending on which index was used. Masters (1998) found the optimal emerging market asset allocation in a global equity portfolio varied from 13% to 5.8% depending on which index figures he used.

Masters' weightings are much lower than many early studies' suggested emerging markets weighting of 20–40% for a global equity portfolio. These studies were misleading. First, the studies typically used returns data that were highly favourable to the emerging markets. Second, the correlation of emerging and developed market returns is probably higher than assumed in the studies. Third, as we noted, the standard deviation of returns probably underestimates the risk of emerging markets. What is the correct weighting? Lower than most studies suggest, and higher than the tiny weightings most institutional managers have!

EMERGING MARKET BONDS

As the emerging equity markets became better known, so too did the bonds issued by those countries. However, the data on bonds are even worse than for equities. The broadest index is probably the Lehman Emerging Markets Index, which covers the bonds issued by governments, agencies, and companies in 38 countries. JP Morgan has a series of emerging market bond indexes; the most widely used is the Emerging Market Bond Index (EMBI), which includes only Brady bonds. Brady bonds are discussed below.

Emerging market bonds constitute less than 4% of the world bond market. The emerging market component is made up of a large number of countries, and many of the bonds are not very liquid. Given the depth of knowledge required to deal in this market and its small size, many investors will simply ignore it. However, the average sovereign spread over US Treasury bonds for the period 1991–99 averaged nearly 8%. This is a sufficiently large number to make at least some investors put in the effort to master this area of the bond market. Further, emerging market bonds should be of interest to emerging market equity managers because the two assets are much better substitutes for each other than are developed-market bonds and equities. Using the JP Morgan EMBI Index from inception in 1991 through to July 1997, Erb et al. (2000) find that emerging market bonds are most highly correlated with the S&P/IFCI Index, then the CSFB high yield index, then the S&P 500 and finally the Lehman LT Government Index. Kelly et al. (1998) find that the lower a country's perceived credit worthiness, the higher the correlation between its bond and equity markets. Essentially, because of the high default risk of emerging market bonds, they should be treated more as equities than bonds.

The largest issuer of bonds in emerging markets is usually the government. Government bonds come in two forms, direct issues to the market and restructured bank debt. Most bonds that come from restructuring are called Brady bonds, after Nicholas Brady, a former secretary of the US Treasury. Brady bonds have their origins in the 1973 oil shock, when many commercial banks received large cash deposits which they recycled to the less developed countries. When many of these countries got into difficulties in the 1980s, they were unable to service their debts. In August 1982, Mexico declared a temporary moratorium on interest payments, and a number of other countries followed suit. The Brady plan allowed for the restructuring of emerging market debt to foreign banks by converting the loans into bonds. Many of these bonds had a longer maturity than the loans and an asset backing of US Treasury securities. The emerging countries received a reduction in claims against them, while the lenders received credit enhancement through collateralization. The first Brady plan restructuring was by Mexico in March 1990. Since then a number of other countries have completed similar programmes. The terms of the individual issues differ in terms of maturity, fixed or floating coupons, and amortization schedules, and the degree to which principal and interest payments are collateralized. Mexico, Brazil, Argentina and Venezuela account for about 85% of the Brady bonds market. Brady bonds are the most liquid emerging market bond investments.

The guarantees that come with Brady bonds vary. Usually the principal is collateralized by US Treasury zero-coupon bonds. These are purchased by a combination of the emerging country, the World Bank and the International Monetary Fund (IMF). Usually only the first three semi-annual interest payments are collateralized by securities, which are deposited with the New York Federal Reserve Bank. If the country defaults on its interest payments, the securities are drawn on. If it meets its payments, the interest guarantee is rolled over.

Brady bonds carry three risk components: the risk that the US Treasury will default; the risk that the emerging country will default on the interest payments (sovereign risk); and the risk that the deposited securities will be of lower value than is required. A full analysis of Brady bonds is beyond the scope of this book.

CONCLUDING COMMENTS

Investing internationally reduces risk because international market returns are only modestly correlated. International returns are affected by both market risk and currency risk. Currencies can be treated actively or passively. There is little evidence supporting the view that currency rates can be forecast. However, technical analysis may provide profitable currency trading opportunities. Passive currency management can involve 100% hedging through to no hedging. The factors that affect the optimal degree of hedging are numerous and complex. There is no generally accepted ideal hedging ratio. The introduction of the euro requires some changes in traditional international management practices.

A variety of approaches are used in deciding which international markets are the most attractive. They include (i) ignoring countries and simply buying the cheapest stocks in the world, deriving the country allocation as a residual; (ii) comparing markets as though they are simply different stocks within a market; (iii) treating each market separately and rating it cheap or expensive relative to its own history; (iv) using international business cycle anticipation; and (v) forecasting total returns. Another approach is Markowitz optimization. This is discussed in Chapter 24.

International markets may be divided into developed and emerging. Emerging equity markets are individually very risky. However, because their returns are not highly correlated, collectively they are not so risky. It is unclear whether they also offer high returns. Emerging-market bonds are more similar to emerging market equities than developed-market bonds are to developed-market equities. Brady bonds are an interesting class of emerging market debt.

21

DERIVATIVES

There are two times in a man's life when he should not speculate: when he can't afford it, and when he can.

Mark Twain

A derivative security is one whose value depends on, or is derived from, the value of another. Derivative securities include forwards, futures, options, convertibles, warrants, swaps, and so on. This chapter covers futures and options. Swaps were outlined in Chapter 19, and forwards were discussed in Chapter 20. We begin our discussion of futures by extending our discussion of forwards.

FUTURES

In the previous chapter, we discussed forward contracts for currencies. Forwards have a long history, and traditionally have been used in commodity markets, such as grains, livestock and metals. A major problem with forward contracts is that when a contract is going your way, the other party has an incentive to default. Of course, this doesn't apply to the major world banks dealing in currencies today. But in the past, it certainly applied to small firms in different countries that made infrequent use of the forwards market. To circumvent this, about 150 years ago, organized futures markets were developed. These in effect standardized forwards contracts, provided a public marketplace, and took steps to stop default.

In the last 20 years or so, there has been an explosive growth in the use of futures. This growth has come from the development of financial futures, of which there are three types: interest rate futures, stock index futures and currency futures. There are a large number of futures exchanges, and each deals in a variety of contracts. The S&P 500 Stock Index futures contract traded on the Chicago Mercantile Exchange is used as an example in this chapter. It is by far the most heavily traded stock index futures contract in the world.

There are some important differences between forward contracts and futures. In a futures contract, you do a specific deal with another party. You have to find that party, and trust them to honour their obligation. Second, if you are a wheat speculator dealing with a farmer, for example, you may not want to take physical delivery of tons of wheat, and the farmer may not want to let you off the hook by accepting cash. To see how futures differ, we need to understand how a futures exchange functions. A futures exchange is an organization composed of members holding seats on the exchange. These seats are traded at a price set by supply and demand. Members can trade on the exchange, as can other parties, who trade through an exchange member. The exchange determines what it will trade, and the types of contracts. The contracts are standardized, calling for delivery on set dates of a carefully defined product, such as No. 2 Hard Red Winter wheat. The party who agrees to buy the underlying asset is the owner of the futures contract, and is said to have a long position. The party who contracts to deliver the asset is the seller of the futures contract, and is said to be short that contract.

When a futures deal is struck, there is a specific buyer X and a seller Y. The clearinghouse then undoes this relationship. Each exchange has a clearinghouse, which is a well-capitalized institution that interposes itself into each trade. Once a trade has been done, the sale is deemed to have been made by Y to the clearinghouse, and X is deemed to have bought from the clearinghouse. In sum, the existence of an exchange makes it easy to find a party to take the other side of a trade, and the two parties need not know each other, let alone trust each other, as their deal is with the clearinghouse.

Default risk has not disappeared; it has simply been passed to the clearinghouse. The clearinghouse protects itself by requiring traders to make a deposit with their brokers. This deposit is known as margin, and must be cash or, usually, short-term government securities. The margin is small in relation to the value of a contract, perhaps 5–10%. Since losses could be much larger, the clearinghouse protects itself by requiring daily gains or losses to be settled. This is known as daily settlement, or marking-to-market. Gains may be drawn on, and losses must be paid to the broker. There are two margin requirements. When a deal is struck, the margin that has to be paid is the initial margin. There is a second margin, the maintenance margin, that is set at a lower level. At first, a broker will not ask for losses to be paid but will simply draw on the margin deposit. When this falls below the maintenance margin, the broker will make a margin call for a sum that will take the margin deposit back to the initial margin level. If losses are not paid, the broker draws on the margin deposit. The clearinghouse is therefore exposed to default only to the extent that a day's losses exceed the maintenance margin.

When a futures contract is approaching the date for delivery, the clearinghouse will pair a buyer with a seller to fulfil their obligations. But hardly any contracts are settled in this way. The usual way of fulfilling obligations is by means of a reversing trade. If you were a buyer of a contract, you can cancel it by selling the same contract. The party in your original deal doesn't have to agree to this because the clearinghouse interposed itself in that deal. After you have carried out the reversing trade, the clearinghouse again interposes itself, and

TABLE 21.1   Differences between forwards and futures

Forwards	Futures
Over-the-counter private contract	Traded on an exchange
Contract not standardized	Standardized contract
Specified delivery date	Range of dates
Settled at end of contract	Profits and losses settled daily
Delivery usually takes place	Contracts usually closed before expiry

you now have two contracts with it that cancel each other. The main differences between forwards and futures are shown in Table 21.1.

S&P 500 Index Futures

A futures contract is an agreement between a buyer and seller to respectively take delivery and to deliver a commodity at a specified future date. In the case of the S&P 500 futures, the commodity is a portfolio of stocks represented by that index. However, delivery is not actually made in the underlying stocks but is a cash settlement of the difference between the original transaction price and the final price of the index at the termination of the contract. Because of the practice of marking-to-market, the cash settlement actually occurs in daily increments until the termination of the contract.

Say the price of an S&P 500 Index futures for June delivery is 1350, and we buy one futures. This means we have agreed to buy the S&P 500 Index on a set date in June at a price of 1350. If, for example, the index closes on that date at 1400, we will have made a profit of 50. Because we don't pay the 1350 today, just post margin, this is a highly geared transaction.

In reality, the numbers are different from this simple example. The value of an S&P 500 futures contract is calculated by multiplying the futures price by $250, the value of one unit of the index. For example, buying a contract for delivery of the index at an index level of 1350 would have a value of $250 × 1350, or $337 500. The minimum amount by which a contract price can change is 0.1. The minimum price change is known as a tick. A tick up or down has a value of $250 × 0.1, or $25 per contract. If you had bought (gone long) a futures contract and the price change over the day was plus one tick, $25 in cash would be added to your account. If you decide to close your position, you can do so by selling a contract for the same delivery date. If your long contract was marked to close yesterday at 1350 and you sell a similar contract today at 1340, your account will be debited with the difference of 10 points or $2500, and you would have no open position. If you hold a contract until it expires, settlement is by cash rather than delivery of securities. This consists of a final debit or credit to your account marking the contract position from the settlement price on the last day of trading to the opening quotation of the index the next day.

We would expect the S&P 500 futures price to move with the underlying S&P 500 Index. Since at expiry the two must have the same value, if they did not move together, it would be possible to make arbitrage profits by buying the cheaper of the two and selling the dearer. However, although there should be a relationship between the index and the futures, it will not be an exact one for one. This is because the holder of a futures does not receive dividends, and to that extent, the futures should be cheaper than the index. On the other hand, the holder of a futures has only had to put up the margin requirement, not the full value of his or her exposure to the market. The difference between the holder's exposure and the margin requirement can be invested in a risk-free asset, such as Treasury bills. This would justify the futures trading at a higher price than the index. Because the return from Treasury bills has generally exceeded the dividend yield, the net effect is that we would expect the futures to trade above the index. The income differential is worth less and less as the contract gets closer to the delivery date, and at expiration the futures price and the index level will be identical.

What has been described above is the cost of carry approach to calculating the theoretical price of a stock index futures contract. Specifically:

$$\text{Cost of carrying} = (\text{risk-free rate} - \text{annualized dividend yield}) \times \frac{\text{days to expiry}}{365}.$$

If we assume that the risk-free rate is 4%, the dividend yield is 1%, and the number of days to delivery is 100, then the cost of carry is:

$$\text{Cost of carrying} = (0.04 - 0.01) \times \frac{100}{365} = 0.0082192.$$

If the index value is 1350, then the theoretical futures price would be:

$$1350 \times (1 + 0.0082192) = 1361.10.$$

The difference between the value of the index and the futures price observed in the market is defined as the basis of a futures contract, i.e.

$$\text{Basis} = \text{cash price} - \text{futures price}.$$

The theoretical basis, based on the cost of carry argument, for the example above is –11.1, the difference between the index value of 1350 and the futures price of 1361.10. If we compare this theoretical basis with the basis observed in the market, we can determine whether the futures price is high or low relative to the index.

In reality, the maths is a lot more complex than shown above. Dividends are paid frequently and irregularly. For example, if you hold stocks for three months and the yield is 4%, you won't get 1% on the last day. You will receive dividends throughout the period, and some quarters receive more of the annual dividend payout than others. Also, we have ignored that futures are marked-to-market, so the sum deposited in Treasury bills will fluctuate. The previous discussion gets the big picture right, although the details are slightly out. In fact, if we simplify further and ignore dividends we can tackle the question of the expected spot rate and the price of a future.

Assume we are looking at the current price of a one-year futures, the current spot price, and the expected spot price in one year. How is the futures' price related to the expected spot price? The following diagram is useful:

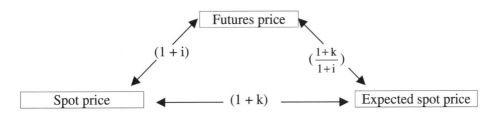

Based on our previous discussion, the futures price will be higher than the current spot price by the risk-free rate of interest (i) (or, alternatively, the net present value of the futures equals the spot price). So:

$$\text{Futures price} = \text{spot price} \times (1 + i).$$

The expected spot price will presumably exceed the current spot rate by some appropriate discount rate (k). For example, if the risk-free rate is 5%, and we think the equity risk premium is 6%, then we might expect a stock index spot in one year to be 11% higher than the current spot. So:

$$\text{Expected spot price} = \text{spot price} \times (1 + k).$$

Algebraic manipulation of the above two relationships yields:

$$\text{Expected spot price} = \text{futures price} \times \frac{1 + k}{1 + 1}.$$

Since the discount rate on a risky asset should exceed the risk-free rate for any positive beta asset, the expression in brackets above will usually exceed one, so the futures should be priced below the expected spot rate. For negative beta assets, the reverse should be true.

Futures Strategies

There are two main reasons for trading in futures contracts—hedging or speculation. Hedgers use futures to reduce the uncertainty of the price at which they will eventually buy or sell an asset, or to offset another risk. Speculators trade in futures to earn a profit. A survey in 1998 by the National Association of Pension Funds found that 26% of private pension fund schemes and 44% of public schemes invested in derivatives. A further 41% of private schemes and 26% of public schemes could invest in derivatives if they wanted to, but had not. Most fund managers were subject to some constraints, the most typical being a maximum percentage of fund value that could be affected, or only currency and other forms of hedging could be undertaken.

For a futures market to work effectively, speculators are needed to contribute to the liquidity of the market and reduce price variability over time. Speculators could operate in the underlying asset markets, but futures markets have a number of attractions. Transaction costs are low, and it is easy to undertake transactions that would be difficult in the underlying markets. For example, it would be difficult to short a bond or to invest in the entire stockmarket. In the latter case, either a huge number of transactions would have to be undertaken to get a high correlation with the market, or fewer stocks could be purchased with a consequently poorer correlation. Perhaps the major attraction for many speculators is the high gearing that futures permit. No payment is made to enter a futures agreement; the only outgoing is the initial margin payment. Accordingly, the investor can gear up and buy more exposure to an asset than would be possible in the underlying market. A small change in the value of the underlying asset will have a dramatic effect on the futures contract returns.

Trading Opportunities

The simplest use of futures is to implement a trading decision. For example, buy futures if you think the market is going to rise; sell futures if you think the market is going to fall. In effect, one is simply buying or selling the market. However, futures permit a geared exposure if desired.

A slightly more complicated strategy, but one that is less risky, involves spread trading. If you buy one contract and sell a related contract, the price difference is called the spread. If two contracts are really related, both prices will tend to move in the same direction, although the spread between them will change. An S&P 500 contract with a September delivery date will be related to an S&P 500 contract with a December delivery. Buying one of these contracts and selling the other is called a calendar spread. If you expect interest rates to rise before September, you would sell the September contract and buy the December contract. The reason is that higher interest rates will increase the basis, but because the basis declines to zero at delivery, the basis will be smaller for the September contract than the December contract. Even if rising interest rates push the market down, you should gain more on the December delivery contract than you lose on the September contract.

Another type of spread transaction is the intermarket spread. For example, towards the end of the 1990s you would have been aware that smaller stocks had underperformed for a long period. You may have felt that smaller stocks were likely to outperform larger stocks. One way of trading this view would be to buy a stock index that is biased towards smaller companies, and sell a stock index that is biased towards large companies. You could short the S&P 500 futures and purchase the Russell 2000 futures, both contracts for delivery at the same date. This strategy would protect you to some degree against market movements.

Protecting Equity Investments

If you hold an equity portfolio and believe the market is likely to fall in the short term, you may wish to reduce your exposure to the market. This can be done by selling stock or by selling a futures. The problem with selling stock is that it is expensive, and may not be possible in a short period. If you have many small-cap stocks, for example, there may be limited liquidity. Either it takes a long time to sell parts of these stocks, or in the interest of speed, you sell your larger, more liquid stocks, and unbalance your portfolio. For some investors, there may also be tax reasons for not wishing to sell.

If, for whatever reason, you wish to sell futures to protect your portfolio, you have to decide whether you wish to protect all or only part of the portfolio. Let us assume that you wish to put a full hedge in place. How do you calculate the number of contracts required? You would first calculate the value of your portfolio. Then you would calculate the value of a contract, which is obtained by multiplying the index level by the futures contract multiple ($250 in the case of the S&P 500). Your portfolio, however, may not move in line with the market. If you have a high-beta portfolio, it will move more than the market. Accordingly, you will have to buy more contracts than you would if your portfolio beta was 1. If we assume your portfolio is worth $10 million, its beta is 1.2, and the S&P 500 is standing at 1350, then the calculation is:

$$\frac{\$10\,000\,000}{\$250 \times 1350} \times 1.2 = 35.56.$$

Because you cannot deal in parts of a contract, you would sell 35 contracts.

If your expectation of a falling market changes, you should make a reversing trade. If, however, your view does not change, but the market has not fallen by the delivery date, you can roll the hedge forward into a later delivery contract. To do this you can allow the existing contract to expire and sell S&P 500 futures contracts with whatever you think the most appropriate delivery date.

A slightly different form of hedging is making purchases or sales of futures based on anticipated inflows or outflows of cash and your view of the direction of the market.

Hedges may be perfect or imperfect. A perfect hedge would be one where all price risk is eliminated. Often this will not be possible because:

- your fund's calculated beta might not be its actual beta during the hedge period;
- a futures delivery date may not exactly match the date you would like the hedge for. For example, if a futures delivery date is the 15th of every month, and you wish to hedge until 1 February, you have two choices. You could choose the futures with the delivery date of 15 January, and then be un-hedged, or you could choose the futures with a delivery date of 15 February and sell that futures at the end of January. The latter approach would seem

more sensible, but you are still exposed to the risk that the basis will not be the same at the end of January as it was when you bought the future;

- the quantity of the underlying asset that you wish to hedge may not be exactly covered by units of the futures contract;
- the asset underlying the futures contract may not be identical to the asset you wish to trade. For example, if you wanted to invest in South East Asian markets, weighted on the basis of their GDP, a capitalization-weighted South East Asian index would provide an imperfect hedge.

Creating an Index Fund

The usual way of creating an index fund is to buy all the stocks in the index or a sample of the stocks (see Chapter 17). This involves lots of transactions and bookkeeping, especially if money flows in and out of the fund. Index futures provide a simpler approach.

To create an index fund using futures involves four steps. As an example, assume the purchase of one S&P 500 futures contract when the index is at 1300, a risk-free rate of 5%, and a dividend yield of 1%, and assume that delivery is in one year to avoid having to deal with quarterly rates of return.

1. Buy Treasury bill (or equivalent) with maturity equal to the stock index futures delivery date (one year) and equal in value to the current spot price of the index, i.e. $250 × 1300 = $325 000.
2. Purchase a futures contract, which, if priced correctly, will require that you pay $338 000 [$325 000 × (1 + 0.05 − 0.01)] in one year.
3. At the delivery date three things will happen:
   (i)   You will receive $341 250 [$325 000 × (1 + 0.05)] from the Treasury bill.
   (ii) You will settle the futures contract by paying $338 000. The net effect of this and the previous transaction is that you have received the dividend on the equity market, i.e. ($325 000 × 0.01 = $3250) and ($341 250 − $338 000 = $3250).
   (iii) You will sell the futures and be paid the exact value of the index.
4. Repeat, throwing brokers' company research into the bin. Use time to meditate.

This procedure will achieve perfect indexing, providing that the futures contract is always priced correctly. Since in reality it fluctuates around the correct theoretical value, perfect indexing will not be achieved. The possibility that you will have to buy an incorrectly priced contract when your existing contracts expire and you roll over the funds into a future delivery date is called roll-over risk.

Index Arbitrage

We can calculate the theoretical value for any stock index futures. If the actual price is different from the theoretical price, an index arbitrage can be undertaken. If, for example, the actual futures price is higher than the theoretical price, then an arbitrage is possible, consisting of selling the futures and buying the underlying stocks. Because these stocks have to be paid for in a few days, this transaction needs financing; this can be done by selling Treasury bills short. At the delivery date, the short position in Treasury bills is repaid. Second, the underlying stock is sold and the same quantity of futures is purchased. Third, dividends will have been received on ownership of the underlying stocks through the period. The arithmetic on all of this is a little tedious, but in essence one is making a risk-free gain by simultaneously selling the futures and buying stock, and financing this with a risk-free security.

Transportable Alpha

Consider a fund that is constrained by its liability structure to have a 70% weighting in bonds. It has a 30% weighting in equities, where it has consistently outperformed the index. Clearly, the possibility of increasing the equity weighting would be very attractive. The manager might decide to reverse the proportions and invest 70% in equities and 30% in bonds. Because the liability structure demands 30% equity and 70% bonds, futures contracts on the stock-market index should be sold and futures contracts on bonds should be bought in sufficient amounts to restore the proportions. Imagine that the equity market returns 20% and the manager achieves 22%, and that the bond market returns 10%, which is what the manager achieves. The fund will have outperformed on 70% of the portfolio by 2%, i.e. by 1.4%. Had futures not been used, the outperformance would have been 0.6% (30% × 2%). In effect, 0.8% of the abnormal return, called alpha, has been transferred—or transported—to the bond portfolio.

Since there are no free lunches, there is obviously a downside to the strategy outlined. It is that it is based on the assumption that the equity manager will continue to outperform. If the manager underperforms, negative alpha would be transferred to the bond portion of the fund.

Overlay Strategies

An overlay strategy is one in which a futures position overlays an underlying strategic position. Some of the strategies discussed above are overlay strategies. Another type of example would be where you were happy with the US equity market but thought that the dollar might fall. You could leave the equity position in place but use a currency future to hedge your dollar exposure. If you were a UK institution, you might be looking at the dollar/sterling relationship. But if you also thought the euro would strengthen against sterling, you might go short dollars/long euro. When your bet works, or when you admit that it never will, you can remove the overlay.

Broader Issues

Before turning to options, we will look quickly at a couple of issues that affect fund managers but are of broader significance.

Limits

An unusual feature of futures markets is the existence of limits. Many financial futures markets have limits on the size of the position an investor can take, and a limit on the size of the price change that can occur during any trading day. The futures price is permitted to trade within a band centred on the settlement price at the close of business on the previous trading day. When the purchase price reaches the upper side of the band, the market is said to be limit up. If the market hits the lower band, it is limit down. Depending on the particular market, this may cause the market to close for an hour or so or for the entire trading day. When the market is closed, no trades are possible. If the limit-down price is, say, 10 below the previous settlement price, and the spot market falls 30 points, the futures market would go limit down the same day. If the market closes for the day when it has gone limit down, it will open the next day and immediately go limit down and close; the same thing will happen the following day, assuming in each case that there has been no other movement by the spot market. While price limits give a chance for a market to cool down, this is achieved at the price of illiquidity and constitutes an added risk to investing in futures. The social cost/benefit balance of limits is unclear.

Effects on Spot Markets

What are the effects of futures markets on the underlying spot markets? There is a huge amount of literature on this, which we will not attempt to summarize. Instead, we will simply quote the conclusions of Board and Sutcliffe (1992, p. 14) who looked at the volatility of the UK equity market and stock index futures. They concluded:

- Futures markets are more volatile than spot markets and this finding is consistent with those of other researchers examining non-UK markets . . .
- There is no evidence that the existence of futures markets has caused an increase in the volatility of the spot market.
- There is little evidence that the level of trade in index futures has increased the volatility of the spot market. The weak association which we do find may be explicable in terms of information being transmitted from futures to spot markets. If this is so, the effect may be regarded as economically beneficial.
- These results continue to hold when we change the definition of volatility, the period over which volatility is measured and when we adjust the analysis to allow for other factors which might affect spot volatility.

OPTIONS

Having looked at futures, we now turn to another form of derivative security, options. An option is an instrument that gives its holder the right, but not the obligation, to buy or sell something at a fixed price. Options are available on a wide range of products. For example, the London International Financial Futures and Options Exchange (LIFFE) lists options on interest rate futures, government bonds, commodities, individual equities and the FTSE 100. There are three main ways of using options:

- as a hedge;
- as a means of speculation;
- as a source of income from an existing shareholding.

In this chapter, we will discuss only options on individual stocks and indexes.

Option Basics

An option gives the right to buy or sell a particular asset at a certain price for a limited period. The asset in question is called the *underlying security*. A *call option* gives the owner the right, but not the obligation, to buy the underlying security. A *put option* gives the holder the right, but not the obligation, to sell the underlying security. The price at which a stock can be bought or sold is called the *exercise price*, or *striking price*. The right to buy or sell an option is for a limited period and therefore all options have an *expiration date*.

There are both European options and American options. With European options, the right to buy or sell can only be exercised at the expiration date. With American options, the right to buy or sell can be exercised at any time on or before the expiration date. Despite the geographical names, both types of options are traded in Europe and the US.

There are four aspects to any option contract:

- the type (put or call)
- the underlying stock
- the expiration date
- the exercise price.

These four aspects are shown in Table 21.2 in the form you might see in a newspaper or on a screen.

Table 21.2 shows option data for the underlying share XYZ. The number shown below XYZ is its current price. The table shows data for puts and calls for the next three expiration dates and for three exercise prices (in column two). This is a UK example, so the numbers are in pence. As you can see, one cell has been highlighted. This is for a January call with a striking price of 600. The

TABLE 21.2   Options price data

Option	Exercise price	Calls			Puts		
		Jan	Apr	Jul	Jan	Apr	Jul
XYZ	550	77	95	107	24	34	51
605	600	49	68	80	46	58	77
	650	29	48	60	76	88	107

number 49 is the mid-point of the price you would have to pay or would receive if you bought or sold that particular option. It is referred to as the premium. Option contracts are specified for a particular number of shares, for example for 1000. Thus, one contract at a price of 49p would cost £490. (For the FTSE 100, the unit of trading is £10 per index point.)

Details will differ by exchange, but in the UK and the US, it is usual for the expiration dates to be three months apart, some on a cycle beginning in January, some beginning in February, and some in March. There are never more than three expiration dates quoted at any one time. At the expiration date, the option 'expires' and is either worthless or has a value. If the option has a value, it is 'exercised'. This means the right to buy or sell shares is enforced. As with futures, a clearinghouse imposes itself between buyers and sellers. When an option holder exercises his or her option, the clearinghouse randomly selects a writer and notifies them that they are required to deliver or take shares.

Opening transactions create an investor's initial position, while a closing transaction reduces it in whole or part. The opening transaction may be a purchase or sale. An investor whose initial transaction is a purchase is called the option holder—he or she is long the option. An investor whose initial transaction is a sale is called the writer of the option—he or she is short the option. So:

	Buyer—long position	**Writer—short position**
Call	Right to buy stock	Obligation to sell stock
Put	Right to sell stock	Obligation to buy stock

There is a margin requirement with options, although the position is different from that for futures. Margin is the amount of collateral that option writers are required to deposit with their brokers. The collateral may take the form of cash or securities as determined by the broker. The amount is also determined by the broker, subject to it being at least an exchange set minimum. The amount is calculated on a daily basis.

The Relationship between Option and Stock Prices

A call option is described as being 'in the money' if the stock price is above the striking price of the option. A call option is said to be 'out of the money' if the stock is selling below the striking price of the option. Thus, in the example above, the XYZ January 550 call is in the money, whereas the XYZ January 650 call is out of the money. With a put option, this is reversed. Thus, the XYZ January 650 puts are in the money.

An option that is in the money is said to have intrinsic value. Imagine that on the expiration date XYZ is trading at 600. What will be the price of a 550 call? We would expect the premium on this in-the-money option to be 50, because at this price the investor would be indifferent between buying the underlying share in the equity market at 600 or buying the option for 50 and paying a further 550 on exercising the option. This difference between the price of a share and the exercise price for an in-the-money option is said to be its intrinsic value. An out-of-the-money option has no intrinsic value. Now imagine the same circumstances as above, but that the expiration date is three months away. The premium is likely to be more than 50 because there is some probability that the price of the share, and hence the option, will move higher. This extra payment is known as the time value or time premium. Thus:

Option premium (or price) = intrinsic value + time premium.

For an in-the-money option:

Intrinsic value = stock price – exercise price.

Options are wasting assets, and as the time to the expiration date draws closer, the time premium will steadily decrease. Usually an option has the largest amount of time value when the stock price is equal to the exercise price. The more in or out of the money an option is, the more the time value premium shrinks.

The amount of money you can make or lose with an option depends on the price of the underlying stock and whether you are a buyer or a seller. In the example above, assume you have bought XYZ January 600 calls and paid 49 (we'll ignore the complication of a contract being for 1000 shares). If the price at expiration is 700, you will have made 700 (what you can sell the stock for) minus 600 (what you must pay when you exercise your option) minus 49 (what it cost to buy the option), i.e. 51. If the stock is 800 at expiry, you make 151. And so on. Your gains are therefore theoretically unlimited. The seller of the calls faces a gloomy outcome. At a stock price of 700, the loss is minus 700 (the cost of buying the stock) plus 600 (the price you pay to the seller for delivery of stock) plus 49 (the premium received for undertaking the contract), i.e. a loss of 51. At a price of 800, the loss is 151. The losses are theoretically unlimited.

What happens if the stock is 400 at expiry? The option holder can demand delivery of the stock at 600. But why would he? He can buy it in the market at 400. When options are defined, there is a mantra that is always included: 'The right, but not the obligation . . .' This is where the 'not the obligation' comes in. The holder would, in the situation described, just tear up the contract. The maximum loss is therefore the option purchase price, or premium. It follows that the maximum gain for the writer is the premium. So:

	Buyer	**Writer**
Maximum gain	All the upside less premium	Premium
Maximum loss	Premium	All the downside less premium

It is worth stressing the symmetry of the position of holders and writers of options. This makes options a zero-sum game. When you win, somebody loses. In fact, the above calculations are simplified. The spread on an options price has been ignored. This is often wide, and there are dealing costs. For investors as a whole, in terms of returns, options are a negative sum game. It is also worth stressing how geared options are. For instance, in one of the examples above, the stock price rose from 700 to 800, but the option price rose from 51 to 151.

OPTION STRATEGIES

Options may be used on their own, independently of any other positions held in the portfolio, or with regard to other positions. Investment made in options without regard to other positions is described as a naked option strategy. Investments made in options with regard to an underlying stock or market so that the option will help offset investment risk in the underlying asset is described as a covered option or hedged strategy.

Naked Strategies

We examine five naked option strategies:

- buying call options (long call)
- selling call options (short call)
- buying put options (long put)
- selling put options (short put)
- buying call options and investing in risk-free bills.

The profit and loss from each strategy depends on the price of the underlying security at the expiration date. (We assume in this discussion that all stock options are held to expiry.) It is often helpful in understanding an option strategy to draw a chart of how profit and loss vary with the stock price at expiration. Such a chart is known as a payoff chart or diagram. The charts are somewhat unusual, but easily understood if we take them in two stages. Figure 21.1 shows the axes used for the payoff charts. The horizontal axis shows the stock price at expiration. The closer you are to the black arrowhead, the higher the stock price at expiration. The vertical axis measures profit or loss and is bisected by the horizontal axis at zero profit or loss. Profits increase as we move in the direction of the upper black arrowhead and losses increase as we move to the lower arrowhead. These axes will be common to all the diagrams shown. They are not

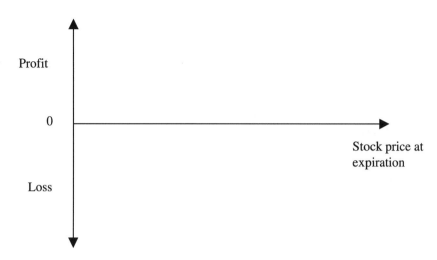

FIGURE 21.1   Elements of an option payoff diagram

drawn to scale: we are interested in the general pattern rather than the detail. With this as background, we can begin discussing the naked strategies.

Buying Call Options

Imagine that we buy a call option on stock XYZ, and pay a premium of £5 with an exercise price of £100. Whether the option will prove profitable will depend upon the price at the expiration date. We can analyse the problem by assuming five different expiration prices for the underlying stock of £80, £100, £103, £105 and £120. As a call buyer, we have the right, but not the obligation, to demand the stock of XYZ for a price of £100. What would we do in each of the five possible outcomes listed? At a price of £80, it would clearly make no sense to exercise the option. Why would we want to pay £100 for XYZ when we can buy it in the market for £80? Clearly, for any expiration price under £100, we would not exercise the option. Accordingly, the purchase price of the option represents a loss: a loss that does not vary with any expiration price below £100. If the stock was trading at £100 at the expiration date, and we wish to own the stock, it would be a matter of indifference as to whether we exercised the option and took stock from the option writer at £100, or we went to the market place and bought XYZ at £100. So, at the expiration price of £100, we would make the same loss as before, i.e. the premium paid. At an expiration price of £103, we would want to exercise the option, not because it is profitable but because this would reduce our losses. By exercising the option, we receive delivery of XYZ at a cost of £100, which we can now sell in the market at £103. This transaction makes a profit of £3, although this is more than offset by the £5 we paid as a premium. At an expiration price of £105, we receive delivery at £100, sell the stock at £105, and make a profit of £5, which offsets the cost of the premium. So, at £105 we break even. Finally, at a price of £120, we would exercise the option, pay £100, and sell in the market at £120, with the profit of £20 on this transaction partially offset by the £5 cost of the premium.

In Figure 21.2, we have taken Figure 21.1 and added to it a bent line, which shows the shape of the payoff for any long-call options strategy, with some of the specific numbers of the previous example added. The horizontal section of the line we have added shows that as we move to the right of the page with the stock price at expiration continuously increasing, up to a price of £100 the loss is a constant £5. For expiration prices between the exercise price (£100) and the exercise price plus the premium (£100 + £5), the losses will steadily fall. When the stock price at expiration is the exercise price plus the premium, the payoff is zero profit or loss. Beyond that point, profit continuously increases; indeed the profit is theoretically unlimited.

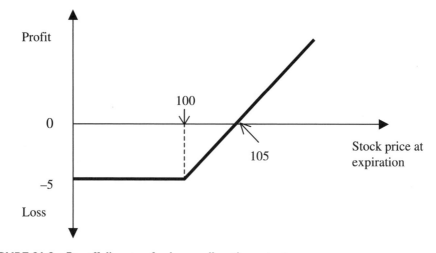

FIGURE 21.2 Payoff diagram for long-call options strategy

You would buy a call when you thought the underlying stock or index was going to rise a reasonable amount (i.e. by more than the premium).

In this discussion, two simplifications have been made. First, the time value of money has been ignored. The investor who pays premium either has to incur cost by borrowing the money or suffers an opportunity cost by not being able to deposit the sum in a risk-free asset. The investor receiving premium can earn interest on it. Therefore, the break-even price for a buyer is somewhat higher than suggested in the payoff diagrams and somewhat lower for the seller. Second, we have made no allowance for any dividends earned. We will make these two simplifications throughout our discussion of payoff diagrams.

Is the payoff profile in Figure 21.2 an attractive proposition? One way of answering this is to look at the alternative of buying the stock. Assume that when the option was purchased, the market price of XYZ was £100. If we invest in the stock, every £1 increase in price will result in a £1 increase in profit. And vice versa for falls. We can graph the profit-and-loss line for the stock and add it to the option payoff chart. This is shown in Figure 21.3. At any price above £95, the purchase of the stock rather than the option will produce a higher profit or smaller loss. This is a consequence of not having to pay the premium. The maximum loss the option buyer can suffer is £5. The stock purchaser would also suffer a loss of £5 if the price at expiration dropped to £95. Below that price, however, the stock purchaser continues to make losses. Indeed, if the price falls to zero the stock purchaser will make a loss of £100. This is shown in Figure 21.3 (remember this is not drawn to scale).

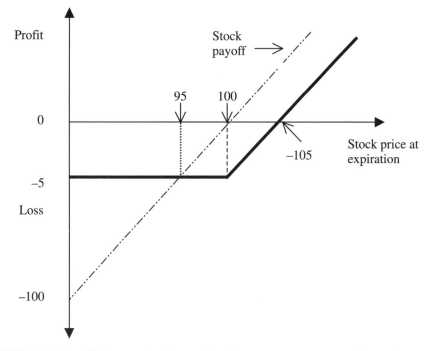

FIGURE 21.3   Payoff diagram for long-call option strategy versus stock purchase

Figure 21.3 compares the purchase of one option with the purchase of one share. But if the shares cost £100 and the option premium is £5, then 20 options could be purchased instead of one share. If the price of XYZ at expiration is £110, the purchase of one share will yield a profit of £10 or 10%. The options, however, will give a return of 100% [(£110 – £100 – £5) × 20 = £100]. This is the favourable side of option gearing. The unfavourable side is that if the expiration price is less than £105, but greater than £100, the stock investor makes a profit while the option trader suffers a loss. At a price of £100 or below, the option purchaser loses his or her entire investment.

Selling Call Options

This is the reverse of the previous strategy. The maximum profit is earned when the stock price at expiration is equal to or below the exercise price. As the stock price at expiration moves from the exercise price up to the exercise price plus premium, the amount of profit earned falls. Prices at expiration higher than the exercise price plus premium lead to increasing losses. Theoretically, these losses may be unlimited. The payoff profile for selling a call is shown in Figure 21.4. Selling calls is a strategy that would be used by an investor who believes that the price of XYZ will not move much or will fall.

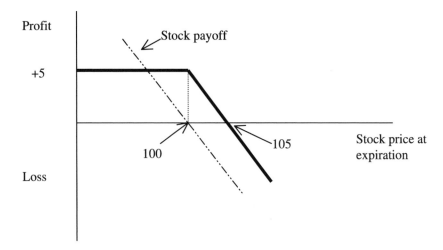

FIGURE 21.4   Payoff diagram for naked written call versus short stock position

In Figure 21.4 we also show the payoff from selling stock short on the assumption that it is sold at £100. While the call writer can make at most £5, if the stock fell to zero, shorting the stock would produce a profit of £100. But if the stock rises, the option writer suffers a little less than does the seller of stock.

Buying Put Options

If a more negative view of the prospects for XYZ's price is taken than that assumed in the previous example, an investor might buy puts. The purchaser of a put has the right, but not the obligation, to sell stock to the put writer at the exercise price. For example, if the exercise price is £100, and the stock is selling at £80 at the expiration date, the put holder can buy stock in the market at £80 and require the put writer to purchase it from him or her at £100. If we considered five prices, in the manner that we did for buying calls, we would see that the payoff profile for buying puts is as shown in Figure 21.5. The put purchaser makes a profit if the price falls below the exercise price less the premium paid. The maximum profit is the exercise price less the premium. At prices above the exercise price, the put holder simply loses his entire premium, as he will not exercise his option. Looking at the alternatives of buying a put and selling stock, we see that the option sets a limit to losses, and participates in gains, albeit reduced by the cost of the premium.

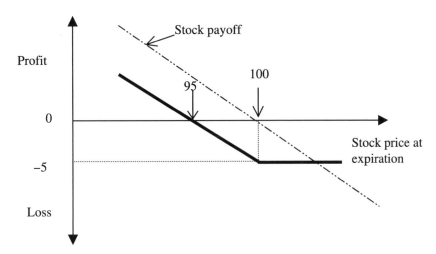

FIGURE 21.5 Payoff diagram for long-put option strategy versus short stock position

Selling Put Options

The payoff profile for this strategy is the mirror image of the previous strategy and is shown in Figure 21.6. It would be used if an investor thought that the price of XYZ would rise. The maximum profit is the premium received, and the maximum loss is the exercise price less the option premium.

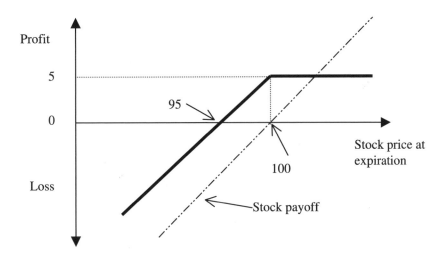

FIGURE 21.6 Payoff diagram for written put versus long stock position

Buying Calls and Investing in Bills

Any of the above strategies can involve the whole or only part of a portfolio. For example, your portfolio could be all calls or some calls and some stock. One strategy worth mentioning where the options are just part of the portfolio involves putting only a small part of the portfolio into buying equity calls and the rest into Treasury bills or other safe investments. This is a very safe strategy with limited risk but some chance of sharing in equity gains. The usual recommendation is to put 90% of the fund into bills and 10% into call options, but the exact ratio depends on interest rates and the importance of avoiding losses. For example, with 10% interest rates, the downside on a 90/10 ratio would be 1% (i.e. for a portfolio of 100, with the call expiring worthless, $90 \times 1.1 = 99$). A 95/5 ratio would mean a guaranteed increase ($95 \times 1.1 = 104.5$) but at the expense of less equity exposure.

Five Naked Strategies

We can summarize when the five naked strategies might be used:

Strategy	Circumstances
Buy calls	When bullish
Sell puts	When positive but not bullish
Sell calls	When negative but not bearish
Buy puts	When bearish
Buy call/hold bills	Protection is key, but want some upside potential

Covered Option Strategies

While there are a large number of exotic option strategies, institutional investors tend to focus on two covered, or hedged, options strategies—covered call writing and protective put buying.

Covered Call Writing

Covered call writing is often marketed as a way of getting something for nothing. The sales pitch goes like this: 'Are there any stocks in your portfolio that you think are fairly valued? If there are, you must be indifferent between holding them or selling them. Imagine a strategy that, if the price of a stock remains much the same or falls, gives you an extra income by way of premium—it's effectively another dividend. If the stock rises and you are forced to sell the stock to meet a call, and you said you were indifferent whether you held it or not, the premium effectively gets you a higher selling price.' The strategy sounds too good to be true. The payoff profile from writing a covered call, and the payoff profile from the underlying stock, are shown in Figure 21.7.

In previous diagrams, we compared the option payoff with the stock payoff. In Figure 21.7 we show the effect of doing two things at once. We show the buying stock payoff as a light broken line, the written call payoff as a heavy broken line, and the payoff of the two combined as a solid line.

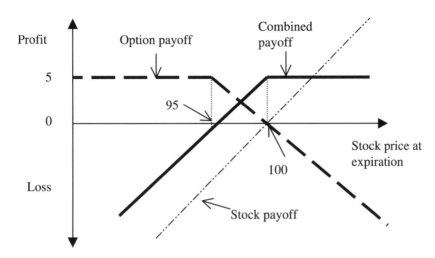

FIGURE 21.7   Payoff diagram for covered call writing

Writing fully covered call options is sold as reducing the risk of holding stock, while giving either a higher income or a higher selling price. And yet since we expect risk and return to be related, any strategy that reduces risk should reduce return. The problem is that the return from stocks depends partly on infrequent, but large, price movements. The writer of a covered call always misses these large movements. Risk will be reduced, but so too will return. In fact, if a large number of calls are written, an investor's portfolio will gradually convert into a portfolio of loser stocks, the winners all having been sold. If you believe the relative strength/momentum literature, this would be a remarkably bad strategy.

Buying Protective Puts

Puts may be purchased as a means of protecting the value of a portfolio. Imagine you have a portfolio consisting of one share, XYZ, which is currently trading at £100, and a put can be purchased for £5 with a strike price of £100. If the price of the stock at expiry is greater than £105, you will realize a profit. For example, an expiry price of £110 will result in the portfolio in being worth £110 less the cost of the put £5, i.e. an increase of £5. If the share value falls to, say, £90 at expiry, you will require the put writer to purchase the stock from you at £100. Because you paid £5 for the premium, your portfolio will be worth £95. The loss of £5 will be the maximum loss you can suffer. The payoff profile is shown in Figure 21.8. The strategy limits the downside loss while maintaining the upside potential, albeit reduced by the size of the premium. As an exercise, you might like to derive Figure 21.8 by drawing a long stock payoff line and a long put payoff line, and then combining the two.

You might ask in this case, why not simply use a stop-loss order? (A stop-loss order instructs a broker to automatically sell your holding when its price falls to a level you have specified.) Such an order incurs no costs beyond the normal

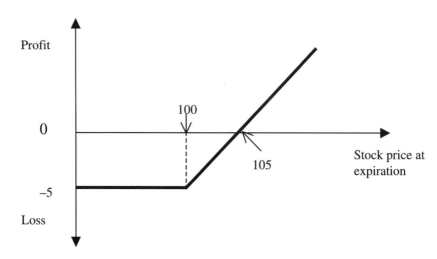

FIGURE 21.8   **Payoff diagram for protective put strategy**

commission charges, so if you instructed a broker to sell your stock at 95, you would appear to be no worse off. The usual answer is that if the stock fell to 95, you would have your stock sold with a stop-loss, but with an option you need do nothing until expiry, so if the stock bounces back to 110, you will benefit with the unexercised option but not the automatically exercised stop-loss. However, if you believe in efficient markets, you might ask whether the implicit assumption that the bounce performance will exceed that from a new stock purchase is plausible.

Other Option Strategies

We have only scratched the surface of the number of possible option strategies. There are spread strategies (which often have great names and include bull spreads, calendar spread, butterfly spreads, ratio call spreads, combined calendar/ratio spreads, reverse spreads), straddles, and so on. McMillan (1980) provides a detailed discussion of these strategies.

FACTORS DETERMINING AN OPTION'S PRICE

In the preceding discussion of option strategies, we assumed the current price of the stock was the expiration price. We assumed an arbitrary option price. We also judged strategies in terms of their value at expiration. In reality, the situation is much more complex. So, how are option prices really determined?

In Figure 21.9, we show the bounds on the price of a call. The two parallel lines are drawn at 45%, one from the intersection of the axes, and one from the exercise price. If each axis begins at zero and is drawn with the same scale, the heavy sloping line to the left shows equal call and share prices. A call option cannot be priced above that line. Why? If an option expires worthless, i.e. the stock is below the exercise price, the option holder has nothing, whereas the stockholder has the stock. Therefore, the option must be worth less than the stock. If the stock is above the exercise price at expiration, the option is worth the stock price less the option price. Clearly, the option cannot be priced above the stock, and must therefore lie to the right of the heavy line.

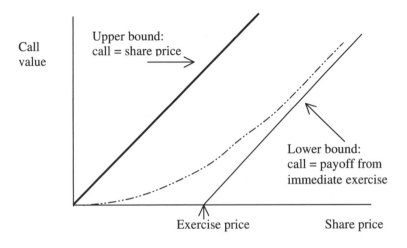

FIGURE 21.9   Call option boundaries

The second parallel line shows the lower bound. It has been constructed so that the call price is always equal to the amount the stock price is above the exercise price. So, if the exercise price is 100 and the share price is 105, the call price would be 5. Imagine in this case that the call is actually priced at 4, while the stock is 105, i.e. a position to the right of the line. Now you could buy a call, pay 4, exercise the call, pay 100, and sell the stock for 105. Arbitrage would eliminate this opportunity by pushing the call price up. Therefore, call prices cannot be to the right of the second parallel line.

We conclude that a call option price must be somewhere between the parallel lines. In fact, the relationship between the share price and call price will probably be like the broken line. The next question is what determines the shape and location of the curve? Seven factors might determine an option's value:

- *The current price of the underlying stock.* The option price will change as the price of the underlying stock changes. For a call option, as the price of the stock increases, the option price increases, all other factors being held constant. And vice versa for a put option.
- *Exercise price.* The lower the exercise price, the higher will be the price for a call option. For a put option, the higher the exercise price, the higher the price.

- *Time remaining to the expiration of the option.* Because an option is a wasting asset, i.e. it has no value after the expiration date, the longer the time to expiration of the option, the higher the option price.
- *Anticipated volatility of the underlying stock.* The greater the expected volatility (standard deviation) of the stock price, the greater the chance that the stock price will move in favour of the option buyer before expiration. Accordingly, the greater the stock volatility, the higher the option price.
- *Level of the risk-free rate.* Buying a call option is an alternative to buying the underlying stock. The higher the interest rate, the greater the opportunity cost of buying the stock. Therefore, the higher the interest rate, the more attractive would be the purchase of a call option relative to the purchase of the stock, and the higher the option price. For a put option, the higher the interest rate, the lower the price.
- *Dividend payments.* Options contracts exclude dividends, therefore the higher the expected dividend before the expiration date, the lower the value of a call option. For a put option, the higher the anticipated dividend before the expiration rate, the higher the option price.
- *Future price of the stock.* This may seem an odd factor to leave to last. But that's because it probably doesn't matter. Obviously, we don't know the future price, but if we are bullish on the stock, then we will be bullish on the option, other things being equal. If we expect a high return from the stock, then we will expect a high return from the option. The option's value for a given stock price is unaffected.

Table 21.3 summarizes how the first six factors above affect the price of an option.

TABLE 21.3 Impact of six factors on the price of an option

Factor	The effect of an increase of a factor on:	
	Call price	Put price
Current stock price	Increase	Decrease
Exercise price	Decrease	Increase
Time to expiration	Increase	Increase
Anticipated stock price volatility	Increase	Increase
Short-term interest rate	Increase	Decrease
Expected dividends	Decrease	Increase

Pulling all this together is difficult without a model. Two option models that are widely used by professionals are the Black–Scholes model (Black and Scholes, 1973), and the binomial option pricing model (Sharpe, 1978; Cox et al., 1979; Rendleman and Bartter, 1979). We will briefly cover the Black–Scholes model.

The Black–Scholes Model

The Black–Scholes model prices European call options. It is a scary piece of mathematics, and the formula is displayed in the box below. Fortunately, the mathematical details can be ignored because professionals use computer programs that simply require insertion of a few values, letting the machine do the hard work. The Black–Scholes model uses five of the six variables shown in Table 21.3. It doesn't take account of dividends—you can consider the formula as the appropriate formula for a non-dividend-paying stock. The model also assumes that it is a European option that is being priced, i.e. the option cannot be exercised until the expiration date. If you look at the five factors in Table 21.3 that the Black–Scholes model includes, four of them will be determined from the option's contract details. However, anticipated stock price volatility has to be estimated. Two methods are used to estimate this factor, an historical method and an implied volatility method.

The Black–Scholes formula is shown below. Readers of a nervous disposition should look away now.

$$w(x,t) = xN(d_1) - ce^{-r(t^* - t)} N(d_2)$$

where

$$d_1 = \frac{\ln(x/c) + (r + 1/2v^2)(t^* - t)}{v\sqrt{t^* - t}}$$

and

$$d_2 = \frac{\ln(x/c) + (r - 1/2v^2)(t^* - t)}{v\sqrt{t^* - t}}$$

w is the value of a call option or warrant on a stock; t is today's date; x is the stock's price; c is the strike price; r is the interest rate; t^* is the maturity date; v is the standard deviation of the stock's return; N is the cumulative normal density function; and ln is the natural logarithm function.

The historical method of calculating anticipated volatility requires a time series of continuously compounded returns from the underlying stock. The period used can be days, weeks, months, quarters, etc. From these data, the standard deviation can be calculated. This has to be in the form of annualized volatility. To calculate annualized volatility, multiply the standard deviation calculated by the square root of however many increment periods there are in a year. For example, if you have used weekly returns, you calculate the square root of 52; for quarterly returns, you calculate the square root of 4. The answer obtained using the historical approach will depend upon the measurement period adopted, the number of observations and, if you use daily data, the number of days you think there are in a year (365 or 240, the number of days the option market is likely to be open). Clearly, using historical data to estimate volatility can produce a range of estimates.

A different approach is to take an options price and solve the Black–Scholes formula for volatility. Volatility calculated in this way is known as the implied volatility. The implied volatility can be used to determine the price of another option. Alternatively, if you have faith in your estimate of the historical volatility, you could compare the two volatilities. If the volatility as estimated by using historical data is higher than the implied volatility, then the option is cheap; if it is less than the implied volatility, then the option is dear. Implied volatility can also be calculated for options of the same maturity, but having different strike prices. If the implied volatility differ, then arbitrage is possible. The arbitrage is effected by purchasing the low implied volatility option and selling the higher implied volatility option.

Using the Black–Scholes Model

Black–Scholes is a model for non-dividend-paying European call options. That sounds restrictive, since most traded options are American. However, it can be shown that for any dividend-paying stock, it is not worthwhile exercising an American option before expiry. We can therefore treat many American options as if they were European. Also, for a European option it can be shown that there is a relationship between call options and put options. Accordingly, we can adapt the Black–Scholes model to value puts. Finally, there are a number of ways of making ad hoc adjustments for dividends.

In short, the model gives a workable way of pricing options. This allows you to judge whether you should use options, and if so, which. For example, say we are bullish on XYZ. Should we buy stock or options? First, we would determine by a payoff diagram what the implications of each course of action are. If call options are acceptable, then we would then check whether they are correctly priced or not. If they are cheap, then the decision is easy. If they are dear, then you might prefer to buy stock. And it may be that you cannot say 'options are dear': you may find that cheap/dear varies with the expiry date, and the expiration price.

The Holes in the Black–Scholes Model

The Black–Scholes formula makes several assumptions. Black (1989a) has listed 10 that are unrealistic:

- The stock's volatility is known, and doesn't change over the life of the option.
- The stock price changes smoothly: it never jumps up or down a large amount in a short time.
- The short-term interest rate never changes.
- Anyone can borrow or lend as much as he wants at a single rate.

- An investor who sells the stock or the option short will have the use of all the proceeds of the sale and receive any returns from investing these proceeds.
- There are no trading costs for either the stock or the option.
- An investor's trades do not affect the taxes he pays.
- The stock pays no dividends.
- An investor can exercise the option only at expiration.
- There are no takeovers or other events that can end the option's life early.

Black notes that these assumptions are mostly false, so we know the formula must be wrong. But as he points out, you may not be able to find any other formula that gives better results in a wide range of circumstances. Black suggests that there may be strategies that make sense if other investors continue to make unrealistic assumptions. We will give a couple of examples.

Changes of the volatility of a stock may have a significant impact on the value of some options, especially far-out-of-the-money options. Black gives an example using a volatility estimate of 0.2 for the annual standard deviation of a stock. Assuming the interest rate to be zero, you obtain a value of $0.00884 for a six-month call option with a $40 strike price written on a $28 stock. If we double the volatility, the value of the option increases to $0.465. Doubling the volatility estimate has increased the value by a factor of 53. Since volatility can change, this should be allowed for in options strategies. You should 'buy volatility' if you think the volatility will rise, and 'sell volatility' if you think it will fall. To buy volatility, you buy options instead of stock.

The model assumes continuous price moves. What if there are jumps? Both in-the-money and out-of-the money options will have higher justified prices, and at-the-money options lower prices, than the Black–Scholes model will compute. This difference will be largest for short-term options. Say you think the market is likely to rise sharply, and you think this more likely than do other investors. If the market is priced in line with the Black–Scholes model, you should buy short-term out-of-the money calls.

Is the Black–Scholes Model Useful?

While there are limitations to the Black–Scholes model, how does it work in practice? The obvious test is to compare market prices with estimated prices. This is a joint test: that the Black–Scholes model is the true option-pricing model and that the market is efficient. In general, the market is priced according to the model, although there are some biases. The interested reader will find relevant empirical articles listed in Hull (2000).

The Greeks

Having seen the factors that go into the Black–Scholes model, and how they can be combined to estimate the fair price for an option, the next question we might ask is how sensitive the option premium is to a change in one of those factors. The sensitivities are usually expressed as ratios and each one is described by a Greek letter—delta, gamma, theta and vega (sometimes called kappa or zeta). These concepts are better known amongst traders than fund managers, but as they get mentioned in markets, it is worth briefly explaining them.

Delta

If the price of the underlying stock changes by 1p, how much will a call option price change by? We would expect different options to change by different amounts. This will depend on the amount of time value and intrinsic value. For an option that is deep out of the money, there will be very little response in the option price to a change in the underlying security's price. An option deep in the money will move more or less penny for penny with the underlying. An option at the money will move by about half as much as the underlying. This responsiveness of the price of a call option to the change in the price of the underlying stock is usually referred to as delta, i.e.

$$\text{Delta} = \frac{\text{change in option's price}}{\text{change in underlying's price}}.$$

Delta for a call option varies from zero for call options deep out of the money, to 1 for call options deep in the money. For call options at the money, delta is roughly 0.5.

Imagine you have shorted a stock, and you now wish to hedge the position. You can do this by buying calls. If delta is 0.75, a change of £1 in the stock price results in a change in the option price of 75p, so you will need 1.33 options per share to form a full hedge. Thus if you have shorted 100 shares and the price rises by £1 per share, you will lose £100. But if you have 133 call options, they will rise by 75p each, or £100 in total. This is known as delta hedging.

Gamma

Delta changes as the underlying stock price changes. The rate of change in delta can also be quantified; this is called gamma:

$$\text{Gamma} = \frac{\text{change in delta}}{\text{change in price of underlying}}.$$

Long calls and short puts have positive gamma, whereas short calls and long puts have negative gamma. Gamma does not change rapidly for deep-in-the-money or deep-out-of-the-money options. Portfolios with high gammas need rebalancing more frequently than low-gamma portfolios to maintain a hedge. The ideal position to maintain a hedge is a gamma-neutral portfolio.

Theta

Options are wasting assets and lose some of their time value every day. Theta measures how much an option will lose in value due to the passage of time.

$$\text{Theta} = \frac{\text{change in option's price}}{\text{change in time}}.$$

Theta is negative for long-option positions and positive for short. Theta is smaller the larger the divergence between the strike price and market price.

Vega

Vega is a measure of how much an option's value changes with changes in the volatility of the underlying security:

$$\text{Vega} = \frac{\text{change in option's price}}{\text{change in volatility}}.$$

Vega is highest when an option is at the money, and falls as the market and strike price diverge. Vega is lower for options close to expiry than for options with a long period to expiry.

FUTURES VERSUS OPTIONS

Which derivative security is the better buy, a futures or an option? At first sight, it may appear that it is the option. In Figure 21.10, the terminal values of a position in a call option and a futures are shown. At the point just before expiration, the position for a call option is shown in Figure 21.10a. If the price of the underlying stock is below the exercise price, the options contract will be worthless and the buyer will take no action. However, if the stock's price is above the exercise price, the buyer will exercise the right to buy stock, and his or her profit will be greater the higher the price of the underlying stock. The profit made by the buyer is mirrored by the loss made by the seller. In Figure 21.10b, the payoff profile for a buyer and seller of a futures contract just before it expires is shown. The buyer makes a profit if the price of the underlying stock exceeds the contract price; these profits are mirrored by losses by the seller. However, below the contract price the buyer makes losses and the seller makes profits. So in the case of the call option, the buyer can't lose; and in the case of the futures contract, the buyer can lose. Nonetheless, this does not make buying an option preferable to buying a future.

The more attractive profile for the buyer of an option is reflected in the fact that he has to pay the premium to acquire the option—and he can lose that. In the case of a futures, there is no premium. Were we to look at selling an option or a futures, similar arguments would apply. In short, futures and options have

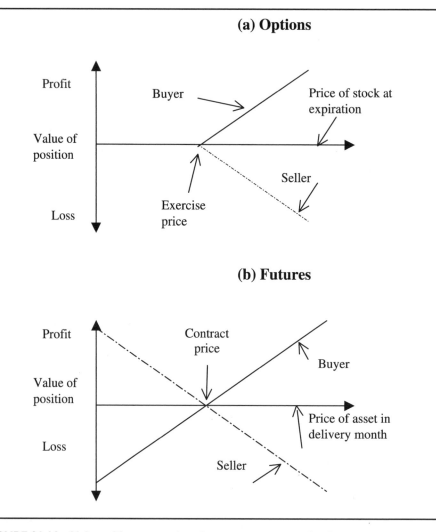

FIGURE 21.10   Value of futures and option contracts at expiration

different risks and payoffs, and the pricing structure reflects this. There is a symmetric risk/reward relationship for buyers and sellers of futures, but not for buyers and sellers of options. This means that futures should be used to protect against symmetric risks, while options should be used for asymmetric risks.

FUTURES OPTIONS

As well as options on stocks, indexes, and so on—spot options—there are also options of futures. If you buy an XYZ share spot option and exercise it, you will receive XYZ shares. If you buy an XYZ futures option and you exercise it, you will receive an XYZ futures contract. You would want to exercise a call option only if the current futures price is above the call's exercise price, and you would only exercise a put if the current futures price is below the call's exercise price. For either, you would receive a futures position effective the next day and would receive the difference between the exercise price and the current futures price. You could hold the futures contract (you would be required to post margin) or make an offsetting transaction.

The need for futures options on financial market assets is not self-evident. Perhaps it's true that even fleas have fleas. However, there are some useful properties of options on futures. Options buyers can suffer only limited losses, whereas this is not the case for futures. Holders of options on futures do not have to meet margin calls, whereas they would with the underlying futures. This means the option holder can sustain adverse price movements that a futures holder might not. But writers of options still need to post margin.

PROBLEMS WITH DERIVATIVES

While for many investors derivatives are the ultimate tool to balance risk and reward, many other investors see derivatives as dangerous. Academics tend to scorn the latter view: derivatives are fine, it's just the people who use them that are the problem. This view has a somewhat unsettling similarity to the view that people, not guns, kill. Most of the discussion that follows relates to problems with the use of derivatives. That seems more interesting than saying that derivatives can be a straightforward tool. However, it is perhaps worth saying that most managers who use derivatives do so in an essentially uncontroversial manner. For example, Koski and Pontiff (1999) analysed the use of derivatives by US equity mutual funds. They found that most equity mutual funds did not use derivatives. In their sample of 679 general domestic equity mutual funds, only 21% used derivative securities, although that is a large number in absolute terms. They found the most significant determinant of derivative use was being a member of a family of funds. Funds that used derivatives were not particularly different in terms of investment outcome from those that didn't. They had similar standard deviations of return, similar idiosyncratic risk, similar exposure to market risk, and so on. Derivative use was also found to be unrelated to performance. It would seem that most investment managers who use derivatives combine them in such a way with non-derivative investments that the net portfolio returns are comparable with those of managers who do not use derivatives.

One management problem with derivatives worth noting is the issue of whether to use in-house specialist managers. For many money management firms, derivatives are something that may be used from time to time. In other words, a specialist derivatives manager could often be sitting around doing nothing or, more likely, will spend his or her time dreaming up whizzy trades. There is a danger that the derivatives' tail will wag the dog. On the other hand, if the mainstream managers are responsible for derivatives, then there is a danger that in a fast-moving market they spend all their time watching their derivatives positions. They can end up neglecting the bulk of their portfolio.

Let's move on from management difficulties to disasters. A full list of derivative disasters would fill many pages. Here is a sample from a number of countries. In the US, Proctor & Gamble is reported to have lost $157m when it used derivatives to bet on movements on German and US interest rates. Paine Webber used fixed-interest derivatives in its mutual funds and lost $268m. Kidder Peabody bought back particularly risky derivatives and compensated the funds it managed. Askin Capital Management, a Wall Street hedge fund operator, went bust because its deals went wrong. Eastman Kodak closed positions and took a loss of $220m. Orange County, California lost $1.7bn and declared bankruptcy: the treasurer had used immense gearing to make a bet that interest rates would not rise. In Canada, Confederation Life, the fifth largest insurer, was driven into bankruptcy following massive investments in derivatives. In Singapore, Leeson lost £860m and broke a bank when he bet on the direction of the Japanese market. In the UK, Allied Lyons lost £150m dealing in currency options, and Union Discount also lost millions. The US subsidiary of the German firm Metallgesellschaft lost $1.3bn using derivatives in the oil market.

Some of the people involved in these disasters may not have known what they were doing; for example, it is doubtful whether Leeson understood option-pricing models. Nonetheless, even intelligent people can go astray in the derivatives market. The biggest disaster appears to have been the collapse of Long-Term Capital Management (LTCM), which required a $3.6bn bail out. The 16 general partners of LTCM included Scholes and Merton, who both won Nobel prizes for their work in the pricing of financial instruments.

LTCM's biggest bet appears to have been that the spread between high-yielding, less-liquid bonds and low-yielding, more-liquid bonds was too large. Basically, junk was undervalued. Part of LTCM's problems were of its own making. Its dealings were so large that it became a substantial holder of illiquid assets. During the spring of 1998, continuing concerns about the Asian financial collapse led many investors to unload their risky, illiquid bond positions. Consequently, there was very little market in these stocks, and yields increased. In August 1998, Russia devalued the rouble and defaulted on its debt. Russian institutions exercised *force majeure* clauses, and refused to honour derivatives contracts they had sold to customers wishing to hedge the currency risk in their positions in Russian bonds. This caused a flight to quality, and the spread between low-quality and high-quality bonds widened further. This signalled the end of the game for the highly-geared LTCM. (This account is based on Edwards, 1999).

A few general points emerge from the above examples:

- In some cases, it would appear that the people involved found it hard to admit that they had made a mistake. They may have started out with good intentions, but once things went wrong, they started lying and covering things up. Therefore, no derivatives fund manager—indeed no fund manager—should be responsible for his or her own settlement. Leeson did his own and could hide his true position.

- Even when a fund manager is separated from the administration of his or her funds, he or she may become involved via the back door. Some derivatives, say Korean convertibles, are difficult to price because there is a limited market. If the administration staff ask the fund manager the price of a particular asset, the scope for concealing losses exists. A fund manager should not be involved in the valuation of his or her own portfolio.
- All managers should have a supervisor who understands what they are engaged in. Leeson was unsupervised, as was the treasurer of Orange County.
- The supervisor should not have a conflict of interest. For example, if the performance of the fund manager affects the bonus of the supervisor, then the supervisor may tend to exercise lax controls when there is seemingly good performance. The fund managers who perform much better than their peers, whether by making more money or making smaller losses, probably should be supervised more carefully rather than less.
- Where hedges are involved, care must be take that the hedge is a perfect hedge, or that the extent of the mis-hedging is clearly known and controllable. Metallgesellschaft had a number of very imperfect hedges.
- Irrespective of the rocket science involved, many derivatives disasters boil down to high gearing on a single bet. The bet may be on the direction of interest rates, or that a yield spread will narrow or widen, or whatever. Such bets are only sensible if the fund has sufficient cash to see a position through to the end. Mean reversion may occur, but not quickly. The unexpected should be expected—fat tails to the distribution of returns are the norm in financial markets. Leeson was affected adversely by increased volatility caused by the Kobe earthquake. LTCM was affected adversely by the default of Russia.

The derivatives disasters are frequently treated as unusual events. And they are. But they are probably unusual only in their size. Mini disasters are almost certainly much more common occurrences. They get covered up and you don't hear about them, for the same reason you don't hear fund managers admitting to poor performance. Trustees or plan sponsors who allow the use of derivatives, or are thinking of doing so, should at least ask themselves, and answer, the following questions (which are taken mainly from Morse, 1993, p. 50):

- Is the use of derivatives permitted for this fund?
- Is the use of derivatives to be related to the total fund in a way that you can explain and justify?
- Will derivatives increase or decrease diversification?
- Will derivatives increase or decrease fund liquidity?
- Will derivatives affect risk in a manner consistent with the fund's objectives?
- Can the objectives of a derivatives programme be achieved in another way?
- How will the use of zero-sum instruments (negative after costs) be beneficial?

- What evidence is there that the managers are competent in this area?
- What internal controls do the managers have?
- What controls over the manager, and what monitoring procedures, does the plan sponsor have?
- What is the basis of the plan sponsor's belief it is competent to monitor derivatives managers?

It goes without saying that a fund manager should be able to provide satisfactory answers to these questions.

CONCLUDING COMMENTS

In this chapter we have discussed two types of derivative securities, futures and options. A futures contract calls for the delivery of a specified asset, at a specified place, at a specified time and at a specified price. An option gives the holder the right, but not the obligation, to buy (call option) or sell (put option) a specific asset at a specific price within a specific period. Options have an intrinsic value (which may be zero) and a time value. The fair value of an option can be calculated in a number of ways—one commonly used method, the Black–Scholes valuation model, was described. Both futures and options are highly geared and can be used for hedging or speculative purposes.

Although there are enormous markets in derivatives, the majority of institutional investors do not use options and futures on a regular basis. But use is growing. All fund managers bungle things from time to time, but the effect is usually modest. The gearing permitted by derivatives has resulted in spectacular losses: banks and companies have gone bust, and the Federal Reserve has been forced to act to protect the world financial system. When fund managers use derivatives, both the fund management company and the client need good control systems.

22

Strategic and Tactical Asset Allocation

For big money, stock picking is irrelevant. Asset allocation is the whole game.
Barton Biggs

In Chapter 1, we outlined the six broad issues that must be addressed in managing a portfolio. In this chapter, the third and fourth items, strategic and tactical asset allocation, will be examined. Tactical asset allocation is discussed further in the next two chapters.

SETTING STRATEGIC WEIGHTS

There are four ways of setting strategic weights:

- Use the proportions of assets in the world portfolio as the benchmark.
- Do what other funds are doing.
- Use risk/return optimization.
- Relate asset distribution to liabilities.

Of course, the applicability of these approaches will vary with the type of fund.

Capitalization-Based Strategic Weights

The first approach of basing strategic weights on a capitalization-weighted world portfolio of assets can be justified in terms of some of the asset-pricing models discussed earlier. Recall the argument that all investors should hold the same risky portfolio—the market portfolio—and should vary their holding of a risk-free asset to obtain the risk/return trade-off that they desire. Although most investors think of risky assets in terms of a broad domestic index, strictly speaking the argument applies to all assets, including all international markets, so the world market portfolio might seem a useful starting point. Yet most investors would find this approach a little bizarre as both Japanese and British investors, for example, would hold identical portfolios that would be dominated by US dollar assets. Portfolios are not normally managed with regard to a world portfolio of assets benchmark, but it may be appropriate for some funds, and appropriate in part for all.

For countries such as Kuwait and Saudi Arabia, with few domestic financial assets available for investment and with a US dollar-based economy (because oil is priced in dollars), a world index may well be an appropriate starting point. Further, to the extent that any institutional fund invests in, for example, overseas equity markets, the weights of the world equity index ex- the domestic market may be considered to provide a benchmark for strategic policy weights for the international portion of the fund. Thus, UK pension funds might consider the distribution of a world equity index ex-UK as providing the appropriate strategic weights for their international equities. In fact, most of them do not appear to have taken this approach (or the permitted range of deviation from the strategic weight has been exceptionally broad). In recent years, most funds have been massively overweight in continental Europe. Funds with a global equity brief run by the same managers have usually had a quite different continental European weight. This suggests that UK investment houses either lack discipline or follow a strategy of having weights close to their competitors in each distinct fund management market.

Following the Median Manager

A second possible strategic asset-allocation method is doing what other funds are doing or, as it is usually described in the pension fund management market, following the median manager. This seems an unjustifiable approach. Fund trustees and their actuaries should set the strategic asset allocation (plus a permitted range of deviations for tactical asset allocation), and fund managers should operate within those parameters. Only the fund trustees and their advisers are in a position to assess the fund's liabilities and the trustees' attitude to risk. Currently in the UK, fund managers tend to set a fund's strategic asset allocation based on the median institutional asset distribution, plus some notion of their own competitive interests. Strategic asset allocation in the UK seems more designed to maximize the fund manager's utility than that of the funds they manage. Part of the problem is that too often it would seem that trustees and their advisers shirk their duties: most trustees are not chosen for their ability to tackle strategic asset allocation. While the correct approach is complex, it is surely more sensible to make even rough and ready calculations relevant to the fund than to follow the crowd.

Mean-Variance Optimization

A third approach to setting strategic asset weights is to use a mean-variance optimization model, i.e. to calculate an efficient frontier, as was discussed in

Chapter 2, and then choose an efficient portfolio. The difficulties with this approach for setting strategic weights are that mean-variance optimization is essentially a one-period model and no explicit attention is paid to the liabilities of the investor. These problems can be overcome, but the approach feels strange and is cumbersome. Essentially, one would replace the mean return on a portfolio at the end of a period with the excess of assets over liabilities, or the surplus. Mean-variance analysis would then be used to produce an efficient frontier of expected surplus/standard deviation of surplus. Liabilities would be treated as negative assets and knowledge of the value of liabilities along with their variance and covariance with assets would be needed. Mulvey (1994) gives an application of this approach to a real institution.

Asset-Liability Modelling

The basic idea of asset-liability modelling is to project the assets and liabilities of an institution, which may be a bank, insurance company, pension fund, or whatever, to see how they might develop in relation to each other under a number of different conditions. We are interested in the cash flows and the values of assets and liabilities and we need models to produce projections for the assets and liabilities separately. (For a general discussion, see Wise, 1988.)

In some cases, the liabilities may always equal the assets. Recall that there are two major types of pension fund—defined contributions and defined benefits. In the case of defined contributions, your pension is worth whatever the investments provide. Usually the beneficiary will have some say in how the investments are managed to the extent that the manager offers a choice of funds. For example, there may be funds investing in UK equities, international equities, bonds, cash, etc., and the beneficiary can select a fund, or some combination of funds, or allow the manager to make a selection via a 'managed fund'. But after that, the manager takes over and will compare his or her performance against some appropriate index. Unit trust and investment trusts are much the same—you make a choice, hand over your money, and get back what you get back.

For defined benefit pensions and many types of insurance products, there are liabilities that are defined in terms other than the assets of the fund. For example, a defined benefit pension fund may make the promise to pay you two-thirds of your final salary at retirement plus a 5% p.a. increase or the increase in the RPI, whichever is lower, every year thereafter. Here there is a clear liability that is expressed in money terms and based on a figure (your final salary) that is not known when the deal is struck. No reference is made to the value of any assets that the pension fund may acquire to be able to meet its liabilities. Some insurance contracts will have similar features, but others may be for a fixed sum of money to be paid in certain circumstances, for example £10 000 on death before age 30.

Many fund managers are therefore in the position that they manage assets that are intended to meet specific liabilities. In an uncertain world, having assets and liabilities that are not in some sense 'matched' introduces the risk that the liabilities will not be honoured, or that the assets have to be topped up.

If a fund's investments are arranged so that inflows of income and capital exactly match in both amount and timing all outgoings of the fund, then changing economic circumstances will not affect the fund. The fund would have achieved 'absolute matching'. In reality this is impossible to achieve because there are insufficient guaranteed assets (such as gilts) to match every possible income payment date, and because of the unknown value and timing of many liabilities.

One of the simpler types of problem involves providing a known nominal sum at some known date. All one has to do is purchase a zero-coupon bond that provides the required sum on the required date. If such a bond is not available, a conventional interest-paying bond maturing on the required date can be purchased. The bond will produce a series of interest payments and repayment of the par value. However, the calculation of the return will depend on the assumption that interest payments can be reinvested at the redemption yield of the bond. If interest rates fall (rise), this will not be the case and there will be a shortfall (surplus). To avoid the shortfall risk, the portfolio will be immunized, i.e. invested in such a way as to produce the same end value irrespective of the course of interest rates. This can be achieved by buying a bond with a duration equal to the investment horizon. This was discussed in Chapter 19.

Deterministic Versus Stochastic Modelling

Turning to defined benefit pension funds, the asset-liability problem is much more complex. It is easier to think about matching if we do so in the context of a closed fund. This is a fund that has no new entrants. Accordingly, the fund will have a finite life and by making a series of assumptions about contributions, payments, inflation, returns, mortality, and so on, one can calculate whether the fund will end in surplus or deficit.

We have two sets of calculations:

Net cash flow over year = contributions + income from assets – benefits paid.

Year-end asset value = [initial asset value × (1 + total return)] + contributions – benefits.

Of course, the assumptions made may be incorrect, but further calculations may be made using different assumptions. What we are doing here is producing a series of deterministic solutions to assess the match of assets and liabilities.

The problem with what has been suggested is that we are using our view of just the average expected outcome for certain variables. But the key feature of, say, equity returns is their variability. In fact, with the exception of the initial asset value, all of the variables in our calculation of the likely surplus or deficit are stochastic, i.e. they have a random component. And most funds are open, not closed. We need a stochastic model of inflation and returns. With such a model, the surplus will be a random variable with a probability distribution. The nature of this distribution can be affected by a number of factors, including the investment asset allocation.

It is usually impossible to solve complex stochastic models using numerical methods. In practice, all such models are subjected to simulation to produce numerical values. The idea is to run a number of simulations (say 1000) to find the distribution of the possible outcomes for different assumptions about the variables that can be controlled/affected by the fund. For example, the asset allocation can be controlled by the fund, but the outcome will depend on both the asset allocation and the capital market outcomes. Again, the fund can control the contribution rate, although the money value will depend on the rate of salary inflation. Although the fund controls certain variables, it only affects—it does not determine—the outcomes.

What is a simulation? We will give an illustration drawing on some calculations made in an article by Fielitz and Muller (1983). They assume that for a particular period, stocks are expected to have a return of 17% with a standard deviation of 15%, and bonds have an expected return of 13% with a standard deviation of 3%. They assume that stocks and bond returns have a correlation of 0.1, i.e. there is a very weak tendency for returns from stocks and bonds to move in the same direction.

We can estimate the distribution of returns if we vary the equity/bond mix by simulating returns. Imagine a huge bag of billiard balls, each with a return value written on it representing the annual return on the equity market. The values would be set to be consistent with a distribution of returns with a mean of 17% and a standard deviation of 15%. A lot of billiard balls will have a value of 17%, rather less will have a value of 16%, and so on, down to a few extreme values. Now if we dip into the bag and pull out a ball, we can read off a simulated return for the equity market. If we do this twice more, we have simulated a three-year return for the equity market. We can repeat this hundreds of times, and we will produce a distribution of possible three-year equity market returns. At the same time, we can also simulate returns for the bond market. Things are a little trickier here because the returns have to be slightly related to the equity returns (recall the small positive correlation) but a computer can cope with this. Two sets of computer calculations are shown in Tables 22.1 and 22.2.

In Table 22.1, the distribution of terminal wealth for three years is shown for various asset mixes. The mixes range from 0% in stocks through to 100% in stocks. Let us focus on the bottom row, the 100% in stocks row. Remember that we made many simulations so that we have a whole range of possible outcomes. If we order these outcomes, we can observe the return at various percentiles. In Table 22.1 we see that a terminal value of 90 (i.e. over three years the investor has lost 10) was observed at the 1 percentile level. At the other end of the spectrum, we see at the 99 percentile a terminal value of 264. For the all-bond portfolio we see that the corresponding terminal values are 129 and 160.

TABLE 22.1 Distribution of terminal wealth in three years (per £100 initial investment for various bond/stock combinations)

Bond/stock mix (% stocks)	Distribution percentiles										
	1	10	20	30	40	50	60	70	80	90	99
0	129	135	138	140	142	143	145	147	149	152	160
10	129	136	139	141	143	145	147	149	151	154	163
20	127	135	139	142	144	146	148	151	154	158	169
30	123	133	138	141	145	147	150	154	158	163	177
40	118	131	137	141	145	149	152	156	161	169	187
50	113	128	135	141	145	150	154	159	166	175	198
60	108	126	134	140	145	151	156	162	170	181	209
70	104	123	132	139	146	152	158	165	174	187	222
80	99	120	130	138	146	153	160	168	178	194	235
90	94	117	129	137	145	153	162	171	183	200	249
100	90	114	127	136	145	154	163	174	187	207	264

TABLE 22.2 Average annual compound return (summary statistics and probabilities of achieving given returns or greater for various bond/stock distributions)

Bond/stock mix (% stocks)	Mean	Standard deviation	Probability level (%)				
			95	75	50	25	5
0	12.9	1.6	10.0	11.7	12.9	14.1	15.9
10	13.3	1.7	10.3	12.0	13.3	14.5	16.4
20	13.6	2.1	9.9	12.1	13.6	15.2	17.5
30	13.9	2.7	9.1	11.9	13.9	16.0	18.9
40	14.2	3.3	8.2	11.7	14.2	16.8	20.6
50	14.5	4.1	7.3	11.5	14.5	17.6	22.3
60	14.8	4.8	6.2	11.2	14.8	18.5	24.0
70	15.0	5.6	5.2	10.9	15.0	19.3	25.8
80	15.2	6.4	4.1	10.5	15.2	20.2	27.6
90	15.4	7.2	3.0	10.2	15.4	21.0	29.4
100	15.6	8.0	1.8	9.8	15.6	21.8	31.3

In Table 22.2, the data are presented in a slightly different way. The annualized mean and standard deviation for the three-year period are shown for every stock/bond mix, and the probability of achieving a given or greater annual compound return for each mix is shown. If we focus on the all-bond portfolio, we see that there is a 95% chance that the portfolio will return at least 10%, and a 5% chance that it will return at least 15.9%.

At this point, the fund's trustees or sponsors must decide what their liabilities are and their attitude to risk. Imagine that the liabilities require a 10% annual compound return. How does one make the risk return trade-off? Fielitz and

Muller (1983) provide an expected utility analysis based on power functions. Normally some form of quantitative analysis would be made, but we will approach the matter in a more intuitive manner. Note that an all-equity portfolio gives the best expected return. The possible rewards from an aggressive equity stance are high. On the other hand, there is a 25% chance that the all-equity portfolio will fail to produce a 10% return. There is a 5% chance that an all-equity portfolio will fail to produce even a 2% return. If 10% is the minimum required, then an all-equity approach seems too risky. As we introduce bonds (i.e. moving up Table 22.2 from the bottom) matters improve, but only at the 20% equity/80% bond mix do we get within a whisker of achieving 10% with a 95% probability. If we look at Table 22.1, we see the 1 percentile returns from the 20/80, 10/90 and 0/100 mixes are similar. Given the higher expected returns from the 20/80 mix, that would seem to be preferable. But while this analysis is plausible if we are analysing a medical charity paying, say, research academics' wages, what if we are analysing a pension fund? Here the company might reason a little differently.

If the required 10% is not achieved by the investments, that may not be the end of the world. The company may simply top up the scheme out of current profits. A 100% equity strategy might involve a lot of topping up if a return of 1.8% is achieved, but look at the 50/50 split. At the 75% probability level, the returns from this strategy are not very different from strategies with more bonds. At the 50%, 25% and 5% probability levels, the returns are distinctly better. At the 95% level, the return is smaller than for more bond-oriented strategies, but perhaps this risk is bearable for the expectation that the returns will be superior. Would all firms reason in this way? Probably not. A highly cyclical, poorly financed company should be more risk-averse. A well-financed, well-diversified company might be willing to take larger risks.

A UK Model

Although we have allowed for uncertainty in the asset values in the previous example, we have not allowed for uncertainty in the liabilities. A major uncertainty will be the rate of inflation. This will affect the money value of contributions and the money value of benefits. But the rate of inflation will also affect the investment returns. One needs a way of bringing together assets and liabilities and making them subject to the same stochastic influences. A well-known investment model has been developed by Wilkie (1986, 1987). It has been frequently debated in the actuarial journals.

Wilkie explained that his model was based on an analysis of data over a long period, and he used time series techniques. His goal was to develop a model that is economically realistic and had a reasonable long-term structure, but he was not concerned with short-term forecasting. The resulting model has four variables: the RPI, the dividend yield on the FTSE All-Share, an index of ordinary share dividends, and the yield on consols. While one might expect a full multivariate model, it turned out that a cascade model sufficed:

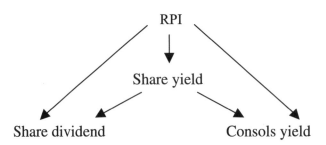

Before looking at each variable, we should explain a couple of technical terms. An autoregressive process is one in which the level of the process is a linear function of past values. Your income next year might be a linear function of your income this year. If only this year matters, then the model is autoregressive of order one (or first-order autoregressive). If three years matter, it's third-order autoregressive. A time series consists of white noise if the underlying variable has a zero mean, constant variance and no correlation between successive variables. All the variables in the Wilkie model have a white noise component.

Wilkie found that prices from 1661 to 1914 appeared to have no upwards or downward drift, and successive changes were independent. But from 1919 to 1982, the data were best explained by a first-order autoregressive model where expected inflation consisted of two components—a fixed mean plus a proportion of last year's deviation from the mean. The share dividend yield depended on the current rate of inflation (high inflation is associated with high yields) and a first-order autoregressive process similar to that for inflation. The index of share dividends depends on inflation, the residual from the yield model, and white noise. The yield on Consols depends on expected inflation, which is given by a weighted moving average of past inflation, and the real yield, which has a mean of 3.5%.

Wilkie (1987, p. 69) notes that the model is self-contained. Only the four variables matter. He argues:

> In my view, whatever may be the case for short-term forecasting, such a self-contained model is better for long-term simulations. The rate of inflation, the amount of company dividends, the level of interest rates, and the prices at which shares trade may well depend on such extraneous factors as government policy, business conditions and the political, military, economic and climatic conditions of the world. But they are not forecastable in the long run and their influence is subsumed in the white noise series.

To engage in simulations, some starting values have to be assumed. And it is useful to calculate three derived series, a share price value (i.e. dividends divided by yield), and a share index and Consols index that include reinvested dividends and interest.

You may reasonably object that Wilkie stops short of recent years during which time there may have been a change in the prospects for inflation, that it is wage changes and not inflation that matters for liabilities, and that other assets besides bonds and equities are important too. There is good and bad news. The good news is that Wilkie (1995b) updates the model by including data to 1994, and extends it to include models for wages, short-term interest rates, property rentals and yields, yields on index-linked gilts, and extension of aspects of the model to other countries. The bad news is that this article runs to 187 pages. However, the model is available in the form of an asset-liability software package. Other models are also available.

In running any simulation, detailed specification of a particular fund's situation will be required. The contribution rate for employees and the company must be specified, any planned contribution holidays allowed for, the benefit structure must be detailed, demographic assumptions imposed, and so on. Various constraints may be set, whether imposed by the fund trustees or by statute. A time period for the simulation must be selected, for example 30 years. The simulation must be repeated numerous times. From these simulations, one can see the expected surplus, the probability of insolvency, and so on. Simulations can be re-run with different assumptions, asset distributions, etc. From all this information, trustees and consultants can determine the appropriate investment strategy given the trustee's objectives and attitude to risk.

TACTICAL ASSET ALLOCATION

> To buy when others are despondently selling and to sell when others are greedily buying requires the greatest fortitude and pays the greatest reward.
>
> Sir John Templeton

The tactical asset allocation decision determines what deviation, based on current market valuations, should be made from the strategic asset allocation. It is the fourth of our six tasks discussed in Chapter 1. Although investors have always tried to time markets, tactical asset allocation was something of a fad in the US fund management industry in the late 1980s/early 1990s, However, as an expensive-looking US equity market kept rising through the 1990s, tactical asset allocation lost its fad status.

We shall discuss whether tactical asset allocation is worthwhile, and how an investor might go about it, but we first need to make a link between tactical asset allocation and strategic asset allocation. Tactical asset allocation will take place within ranges around the strategic weights. How are these ranges set? There is, unfortunately, no good answer. The range should be narrower, the greater the size of transaction costs and the more modest the timing skills possessed. This will often suggest quite narrow ranges. However, many clients expect their managers to possess timing skills. They often accept that short-term timing may be difficult but add a plea to the effect, 'But you will get us out if everything looks awful, won't you?' The clients then permit quite wide ranges to allow for their disaster scenario. This then gives managers a range that they either implicitly ignore and act well within, or they get bullied to act more aggressively than their skills warrant. A better solution might be to have relatively narrow ranges, with a clear understanding that in exceptional circumstances the clients will be contacted and asked if they will allow the manager to breach the range for specified reasons.

Is Tactical Asset Allocation Important?

Asset allocation is generally accepted as *the* investment decision (see especially Brinson et al., 1991). This is only partly valid. The usual argument is based on the fact that the typical manager will have an equity return not too far adrift from the appropriate index, and there are big differences in returns between asset classes and the international markets. Some investors go further and assert that the efficient market theory applies to security prices within markets and so the only way to win the performance game is to make bets between rather than within markets. It may be that classes of assets are more often mispriced relative to each other than securities within an asset class. Additionally, there may be less information and smaller flows of money between countries so that international asset class inefficiencies may be even greater. But, even if the inefficiencies exist, it has to be shown that they can be exploited. We'll come back to this.

The practical argument about the differences in return between asset classes is, however, misplaced. It is true that there are often large differences in return, but there are even bigger differences in return within each equity market. Every year, some shares will go bust and others will soar. This will generate greater differences than are usually observed between asset classes. This might suggest share selection is the most important decision. Of course, institutional investors have diversified portfolios and do not make the sort of stock bets necessary to achieve the potential returns. But if we shift the argument to checking actual returns from stock picking rather than possible returns, we ought to do the same for actual returns from actual asset shifts. Most funds do not make huge swings in asset allocation, and so the realized return from tactical asset allocation is likely to be modest. If a fund switched from an 80/20 equity/gilt split to a 90/10 split, and equities outperformed gilts by 10%, then the allocation change would result in a 1% gain in performance—before transaction costs. Now that is the sort of difference that is attainable by stock selection. Consultants Mercer Fraser (1988) examined the performance of UK institutional funds for the period 1983–87, and found that there was indeed little difference in the returns from asset allocation versus stock selection (see also Hensel et al., 1991.)

Although UK managers like to point to statistics that purport to show that asset class strategy dominates investment returns, and they spend a great deal of time talking about strategy, in reality they make few tactical asset allocation changes. If one looks at portfolio composition over 30 or 40 years, one sees substantial change. But a lot of this is a consequence of new assets becoming available (e.g. index-linked gilts and overseas assets after the removal of exchange control), assets becoming unavailable (corporate bonds in the 1970s and, currently, long-dated conventional gilts), or changes in relative prices of asset classes. Little change is seen quarter by quarter, i.e. we would not expect changes in strategy weighting to much affect performance.

Blake et al. (1999) examined nine years (1986–94) of monthly data on the holdings of eight asset classes for 306 UK pension funds. They point out that UK pension fund managers probably operated with fewer constraints than any group of institutional managers anywhere in the world during the period they studied. Most pension funds had large surpluses, trustees tended not to interfere, and there were few regulatory constraints. Blake et al. did find that strategic asset allocation accounts for the bulk of the time-series variation in returns. But the cross-sectional variation in average total return across the funds in their sample was remarkably low. Just over 1% separated the 25th and 75th percentile fund, and less than 3% p.a. separated the fifth percentile fund from the 95th. Blake et al. found little cross-sectional variation in returns to strategic asset allocation, market timing, and security selection. What cross-sectional variation they did find was dominated by the security-selection component.

The reason for the similarity in results was probably a consequence of managers offering a similar product—balanced management instead of specialist funds—and the compensation/risk structure. Managers' financial interests were related to relative rather than absolute performance. If they performed poorly relative to their peer group, then they were more likely to lose funds than by performing poorly in absolute terms but on a par with their peer group. The tendency for managers to try and second-guess each other was reinforced by the highly concentrated nature of the industry: five firms managed the bulk of funds placed with external managers. (In terms of Chapter 8, one might expect new entry and competition from substitute products. And that is what has happened with the entry of US firms, the growth of specialist managers, and index funds.)

Note carefully what is *not* being said. It is not being denied that an all-equity fund is likely to outperform an all-bond fund over a long period. The strategic asset weights are very important in determining return. The tactical deviation from those weights, however, is likely to be modest in practice, and so the additional returns achieved will be more modest than is often implied.

Before focusing on what measures we might use to predict the level of an equity market and make tactical asset allocation decisions, it is worth looking at some of the academic research on what moves markets and whether they move too much, i.e. whether they are efficient with regard to level.

The Efficient Market Theory Revisited

Some economists believe that markets tend to overdo things. Keynes, writing in 1931 for the Board of National Mutual, an insurance company, thought:

> There is a great deal of fear psychology about just now. Prices bear very little relationship to ultimate values or even to reasonable forecasts of ultimate values. They are determined by indefinite anxieties, chance market conditions, and whether some urgent

selling comes on a market bare of buyers. Just as many people were quite willing in the boom, not only to value shares on the basis of a single year's earnings, but to assume that increases in earnings would increase geometrically, so now they are ready to estimate capital values on today's earnings and to assume that decreases will continue geometrically . . . In the midst of one of the greatest slumps in history, it would be absurd to say that fears and anxieties are baseless . . . I consider the prospects of 1931 to be extremely bad . . . [But] the situation is quite capable of turning round at any time with extreme suddenness. Our fundamental position remains extraordinarily strong. The introduction of a tariff, a change of Government, and all sorts of things quite unpredictable in advance will suddenly cause people to turn right round, and to appreciate how very cheap almost everything is . . .

(Reprinted in Moggridge, 1983, pp. 17–18)

Of course, the efficient market adherents don't believe the markets allow easy gains to be made. Probably because, sadly, it is about as good a joke as one gets in economics, most investment texts carry the story of two professors walking along the street; one says he sees a $20 bill lying on the pavement. The other, an efficient market type, replies, 'Don't be silly: if there were, somebody would already have picked it up.'

Keynes didn't believe it was easy to beat the market. He had, after the First World War, persuaded King's College to invest in ordinary shares: 'At that time I believed that profit could be made by what has been called a credit cycle policy, namely by holding such shares in slumps and disposing of them in booms . . .' (reprinted in Moggridge, 1983, p. 106). While, subsequently, King's managed to buy particular shares at depressed prices, they were less successful with broad market swings despite Keynes broadly being able to see what was ahead. Twenty years on he was wary of market timing, arguing that 'most of those who attempt it sell too late and buy too late, and do both too often, incurring heavy expenses and developing too unsettled and speculative a state of mind . . .' (reprinted in Moggridge, 1983, p. 106). Nonetheless, Keynes would have picked up the $20, for after giving three investment principles to guide King's, he added:

On the other hand, it is a mistake to sell a £1 note for 15s. [75p] in the hope of buying it back for 12s 6d. [62.5p], and a mistake to refuse to buy a £1 note for 15s. on the ground that it cannot really be a £1 note (for there is abundant experience that £1 notes *can* be bought for 15s. at a time when they are expected by many people to fall to 12s.6d).

(Reprinted in Moggridge, 1983, p. 107)

There are two types of efficient market response to this. The first relies on risk-free arbitrage. However, as we saw in Chapter 5, there is little reason to believe that it will be very effective at the asset class level. The second response is that the market price is likely to be the best estimate because no one person is smarter than the entire market. The argument is akin to Hayek's (1945) classic justification for the superiority of markets over state planning. Sinquefield, in Tanous (1997, pp. 269–270), argues:

. . . are there some people who can systematically see the future? That's what it comes down to. The problem here is understanding how the market mechanism works. The central point is that no one person has very much information. In fact, regardless of how smart they are, they have a tiny fraction of the information that is available to the entire market at any point in time. The markets are completely inter-related. Do you think it is credible that there is one person who systematically has more information than a dispersed market of six billion people? That's not remotely credible. But that's the condition that somebody has to prove. That there is such a person who has all this information—and the information changes second by second—who is so good that he or she is going to come to better conclusions than the worldwide market that is setting hundreds of millions of prices every moment? That's not plausible.

This argument suggests that nobody is likely to make gains from timing the markets, but it doesn't rule out that markets may be mispriced. When prices deviate from fundamental value, there is said to be a speculative bubble. Various types of bubble have been suggested, including rational, irrational and endogenous. Rational bubbles are interesting theoretically, but implausible in reality, so we shall ignore them.

Irrational bubble theories assume two classes of investor, informed and uninformed. Uninformed investors may follow feedback strategies—the easiest being to follow trends. What goes up will continue to go up. Informed investors see that assets are mispriced but follow the trend too. After a while they jump ship, and the market drops back. There is scant evidence to support the existence of these two groups, or that they act in this way. The American literature simply asserts that private investors are uninformed.

Endogenous theories assume that bubbles are inherent in the system. As the latest crash, scandal or whatever becomes a distant memory, the risk-aversion of speculators declines. As a market rises, the speculators become more optimistic and may take on debt to finance their activities. But as prices rise, while the perceived risk is low, the actual risk is rising. Some surprising event may then trigger a crisis. The nature of the event is not especially important as long as it requires a re-evaluation of the situation.

Some Evidence on Macromarket Efficiency

Let's move on to some evidence on macromarket efficiency. The markets will be efficient if they react only to relevant information, don't overreact, and returns are not predictable (except in certain circumstances). We will look at the evidence on the first two points in this chapter, and on the third in the next two chapters.

News or Noise?

While markets react to relevant news, they also seem to react to irrelevant news or no news at all. In a famous study, Roll (1984) examined US orange juice futures prices. These should reflect the spot prices investors expect when the future expires. Roll argued that the only thing that could give information about spot prices in the short run was the weather. A frost in Florida would be bad news for the orange crop. Other factors could not vary much in the short run—new trees cannot be planted and produce a crop in a year, it is unlikely that consumers suddenly get an urge for apple juice rather than orange juice, and so on. Roll found that low temperatures did push up orange juice futures prices; however, temperature could explain only a few per cent of futures' price variation, and Roll could find no other important variables. In short, prices varied too much. Other studies paint a similar picture.

New information will cause prices to move. If public information drives the markets and information arrives all the time, prices should be as volatile when the markets are shut as when they are open. How do we know the price change when a market is shut? By comparing the closing price with the next opening price. Prices are more volatile when markets are open: the volatility during the hours of a typical market day is six times that of a typical weekend, which is 11 times longer. Since company and economic information tends to be released when the markets are open, there will be more information when the markets are open, so the evidence may not seem very interesting. Yet the differences in volatilities seems excessive: political news may be released when the markets are shut, earthquakes and storms are not scheduled for trading hours, major economic news is often released when the markets are shut—devaluations tend to take place on weekends—and many companies release bad news after market hours.

All this suggests that more than public information drives the markets. A study by French and Roll (1986) supports this. The US stock market was closed on Wednesdays for a period in 1968 as back offices tried to catch up with their paperwork. French and Roll found more price volatility on Wednesdays when the market was open than when it was closed, yet the flow of public information should not have varied. In short, much trading seems to take place based on private information—the market generates its own news.

In a different approach, Cutler et al. (1989) tried to explain market movements by news. They tried to explain monthly US stock returns for the period 1926–85 by using seven measures of monthly macroeconomic activity. They tried a number of approaches but concluded that a substantial portion of return variation—more than half, and perhaps as much as 80%—could not be explained by macroeconomic news. What about non-economic news? Cutler et al. (1989) took important events from the *World Almanac* and selected those most likely to have an impact on the market and then those described in the *New York Times* as actually having had an impact on the market. The impact of events on prices was disappointingly small. They then tried to approach the issue from the other direction. They selected days with large price movements and looked for the news that caused the movement. Generally, they were unable to find significant news.

If it is hard to establish what news moves the market, then this would seem to support the view that the market moves too much: the market seems to feed on itself. Investors make decisions based on other investor's decisions. This does not necessarily mean that bubbles exist: a market that moves too much could move too much around fair value, but not depart very far from it. But that doesn't seem to be the case. Consider the crash of 1987. In October 1987, most world markets crashed. The most studied market has been the US.

US stocks had performed strongly in the first three-quarters of 1987. Many people thought the market was overvalued. The market was weak in the two weeks before 19 October, but on that day the DJIA fell by 23%. Although the market was highly volatile for the rest of October, it ended November at about the same level as at the close of 19 October. Reasons put forward for the crash include trade and budget deficits, tax legislation, overvaluation, volatility and programme trading. Schwert (1992) reviews these explanations and finds them wanting. We will not cover this here, except for the overvaluation issue. While the market was highly rated, not all highly rated markets crash. And the market had been highly rated for much of 1987. Moreover, the prices of puts and calls on the S&P 500 implied a fear of a crash from October 1986 to February 1987, and from June 1987 to August 1987, but not in October.

Schwert finds the cause of the crash uncertain, and notes there was no accompanying economic or political news that could account for a worldwide crash. And there is no evidence that investors had suddenly become gloomier about interest rates or profitability: Shiller has reported surveys of institutional investors' views on these matters. What seems to have happened is that, conditioned by a view that the market was overvalued, when prices started to fall, other investors (including those in foreign markets) reacted to the falls. The market itself seems to have provided the news that prices should fall.

Volatility Tests

A direct test of bubbles is to compare actual prices with fundamental prices. The approach often adopted in tests is to compare the variability of the actual price with the variability of the fundamental price. Then the question is whether the two series are consistent. The economic jargon for such tests is variance-bounds tests. But how does one determine the fundamental price? Shiller (1981; reprinted in Shiller, 1989, which contains many relevant articles) used the DDM. The DDM assumes that the price of an asset will be the value of the discounted stream of dividends. We can apply this to the equity market as a whole. If we assume a constant discount rate, and also that investors can forecast dividends perfectly, then it is possible to use actual dividends to calculate the level the market should have been priced at in particular years and then compare it with the actual level.

LeRoy (1990) transforms the argument slightly, and calculates simulated rates of return that would have been achieved if the market was priced by discounting dividends. He then compares these returns with the actual returns the market delivered. Of course, investors did not know what future dividends would be, but LeRoy assumed investors could forecast dividends perfectly for five years and that they then extrapolated dividends using a constant growth rate. His results are shown in Figure 22.1. The simulated rate of return is less volatile than the dividend growth rate. This is what should be expected if the market discounts future dividends, for this means stock prices should behave like a weighted average of dividends over time, and any average will always be less volatile than its components. Turning to the actual rate of return and dividend growth rate, we see that the rates of return are more volatile than the dividend growth rate: they are too volatile.

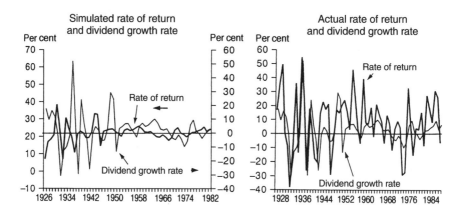

FIGURE 22.1   Simulated and actual rates of return and dividend growth rates
Source: LeRoy (1990, p. 35). Reprinted with permission from the Federal Reserve Bank of San Francisco, *Economic Review*, Spring 1990.

The types of test proposed by Shiller and LeRoy to decide whether the market moves 'too much' have been challenged by a number of writers (notably Kleidon, 1986; and Marsh and Merton, 1986). The arguments are too complex for a full discussion in this book. However, we can note a couple of points. First, we would expect the discount rate to vary over time. It will depend on the risk-free rate and the riskiness of equities. Both will fluctuate. This will lead to fluctuations in the market greater than that justified by dividend fluctuations alone. Second, managers smooth dividends, which upsets the notion that stock prices and returns must be more stable than dividends. Imagine managers smooth dividends to the extent of not paying dividends at all, intending to do so only far into the future. The expected value of that future payout will surely fluctuate, so while dividends will follow a smooth path (of zero), stock prices and returns, which will reflect the present value of that future payment, will fluctuate.

These are important criticisms, and yet when all is said and done, the outcome still appears to many observers to be that the market moves too much. The conclusion most academics reach seems to be more an indication of what they first believed rather than a consequence of the arguments. The majority US view is probably that the market moves too much. For the UK, Bulkley and Tonks (1989) have provided similar evidence that UK prices fluctuate too much. This type of evidence is consistent with bubbles but, as we shall see, it is not necessarily inconsistent with efficiency.

Let's look at excess volatility in a more subjective manner. In a recession, for example, we might expect earnings and dividend forecasts to be reduced, and risk aversion to increase. Clearly, there must be some set of assumptions about discount rates and growth of earnings that justify any market level. We can ask if investors were being 'reasonable' in the assumptions they must have been making, or the returns they were demanding, for particular extremes of market movement.

This is inherently subjective, and complicated by hindsight bias. Because we know what subsequently happened, we have to be very careful not to say that the assumptions investors must have made were implausible. Nonetheless, some attempts have been made to see if investors were being reasonable in bull and bear markets (for example, Barsky and De Long, 1990). We will illustrate these issues with the collapse of the UK market during 1973–74.

In Table 22.3, we list some economic statistics for the period 1972–75. At the beginning of the period, the equity and gilt markets were not on particularly unusual ratings. The FT30 ended 1972 at 505.4 with a yield of 3.22% and a PER of 19.23. The Government Securities Index stood at 71.11 and undated stock yielded 9.84%. In Table 22.4, we list some of the political and economic events outlined by Blakey (1994). For readers who don't remember this period, a constant theme was whether government or unions were running the country.

TABLE 22.3 Economic statistics 1972–75

	Inflation (%)	Change (%) in GDP	PSBR (£bn)	Balance of payments current account (£bn)	Change (%) in sterling exchange rate index
1972	7.1	2.8	2.0	0.2	–3.6
1973	9.2	7.6	4.1	–1.0	–9.3
1974	16.0	–1.5	6.5	–3.2	–3.1
1975	24.2	–0.7	10.2	–1.5	–7.8

PSBR, public sector borrowing requirement.
Source: ONS.

Did the market move too much, or were investors being reasonable? Given the turnaround in 1975 (1975 is the year with the returns bar that sticks out like a sore thumb in Figure 2.2), investors got it wrong. But were they being unreasonable? Table 22.4 is, after all, a catalogue of economic and political mishandling. The corporate sector was in poor shape and the unions appeared to run the country. The oil price problem was outside the government's control. The way out was not obvious. Given the then current inflation rate, returns on cash were high in nominal terms. This, plus the expected inflation rate, made gilt yields not unreasonable. Given the yield on gilts, it is not surprising that the equity yield was

TABLE 22.4   Some events in 1973–74

18 January 1973	FT30 began the year over 500, but fell below it when Prime Minister Heath (Conservative) revealed details of powers for the government to regulate prices, rents and dividends for the next three years. Trades Union Congress (TUC) refused to do a deal on wage restraint.
6 March 1973	Despite a dwindling trade surplus, rising interest rates, and a large public sector deficit, the policy of expansion was maintained. Public sector borrowing requirement (PSBR) was forecast to rise from the previous year's £2.8bn to £4.4bn. The Government Securities Index fell to 69.71.
July 1973	After some better news in the previous months, there was some sterling depreciation, and the minimum lending rate (MLR—'bank rate') was raised to 11.5%. Equities and gilts fell. Heath and Chancellor Barber maintained the 'go for growth' policy. Financial markets wanted public expenditure cuts and control of the money supply.
October 1973	After the Yom Kippur War, various oil producers started raising prices. $3 per barrel price raised to $5, then to $7. Threat of output cut of 20% by Arab producers. UK power workers took industrial action.
November 1973	Miners introduced overtime ban in support of pay claim. Record trade deficit for October was announced. Heath declared a state of emergency. The MLR was set at 13%, and credit squeeze intensified. There was a threat of rail strike. First signs of secondary banks being in trouble. Wall Street sliding. FT30 fell to 365; Government Securities Index fell to 62.39.
14 December 1973	Heath announced introduction of three-day working week to conserve fuel supplies. London and County Bank collapsed. Poor trade figures. Public spending cuts announced. Gulf states raised price of oil to $11.50.
January 1974	Some bits of good news, such as prospects of moving to four-day week. But there were fears over the effect of oil prices on the trade balance, and it became clear that the miners would go on strike. FT30 fell to 301.7, and Government Securities Index fell to 57.45.
28 February 1974	General election—surprise Labour win. Wilson became Prime Minister and Healey became Chancellor.
March 1974	Miners won a large pay increase and ended the strike. Two days after settlement, Yorkshire miners asked for another £20. Budget raised tax rates (top rate 83% for earned income and 98% for investment income). National Insurance rates were raised. Corporation tax was raised. Record trade gap. FT30: 267.4, Government Securities Index: 54.2. Yields on long gilts closed at 15%.
April/May 1974	Various bits of good news led to gilts and equities rallying. Then concern at vitality of industry when industrial costs rising, world trade declining, wage inflation soaring, and price controls. Wave of collapses in finance and property sectors.
June/July 1974	Slater, of Slater Walker, announced at their AGM: 'Cash is the best investment now.' Herstatt Bank in Germany and Franklin National Bank in the US collapsed. 'Lifeboat' arranged by Bank of England for secondary banks thought to be inadequate. Banks were reluctant to lend to companies facing difficulties; low share prices made share issues unattractive; high bond yields and heavy government borrowing squeezed companies out of corporate debt market.
August 1974	Several prominent companies collapsed or bailed out. Resignation of Nixon failed to stop US markets' continued decline. FT30 hit 199.8 on 19 August—1972/1974 was worst ever bear market. Record low for gilts of 53.13. Undated gilts yield over 16%.
October/November 1974	Labour won the general election. November budget forecast PSBR at £6.3bn, up from March forecast of £2.73bn. Pay increases covering 10 million workers pushed the rise in wage rates to 26.4%: the miners were thought to be planning a huge claim. Fears over stability of various companies, including National Westminster Bank.
December 1974	*Financial Times* survey found that industry expected the trend in costs and prices to worsen. British Leyland sought financial assistance. National Institute forecast 25% inflation in 1975. Stock Exchange demanded monthly returns from member firms to ensure they were financially viable. Record trade gap reported. Colonel Stirling formed a group of former professional soldiers ready to infiltrate picket lines in the event of trade union disruption. FT30 fell to 161.4, yielding an historical 12.5% and a PER of 3.8. The Government Securities Index stood at 49.8, and undated stock yielded 17%.
January 1975	The markets turned round and enter a bull phase.

Source: Based on Blakey (1994, pp. 135–69).

high and the PER low. Moreover, the figures were historical. With companies collapsing, who could tell what the prospective yield and PER would be?

The market appears to have been approaching matters in a rational manner. Note it was anticipating events: the truly awful figures in Table 22.3 are in 1975, not the two years of the bear market. And Blakey (1994, p. 175) tells us that in the middle of 1974: 'A few commentators wondered whether staying on the sidelines after such an unprecedented fall in equities would in due course be seen as a classic case of lost opportunity.' Or again, before the October 1974 election, Blakey tells us that there was a belief that whichever party won would be forced by circumstances to restore profitability and keep wages and consumption under strict control.

Clearly, given the actual course of dividends, the market moved too much in 1973–75. But it is more difficult to conclude that the market was being irrational. At least in part, it was just making a genuine mistake, and partly it was demanding a higher return. The situation was unusually risky. Equity investors needed the prospect of exceptional returns to justify holding equities: their risk-aversion had probably increased.

Mean-Reversion

A slightly different way of looking at whether the market is too volatile is to see whether returns follow a pattern of reversals. If the market overreacts, we might expect good periods to be followed by bad periods and vice versa. Fama and French (1988b) examined monthly return data from 1926 to 1985 for NYSE firms. They regressed returns for various time periods on the previous time period of the same length (e.g. an 18-month period was related to the previous 18 months). The correlations were close to zero for short periods, but generally negative for periods of 18 months or more and around –0.25 to –0.4 for three- to five-year returns. This implies that returns tend to reverse, that good periods are followed by bad. The results are weaker than they appear, however, because (i) the return reversal weakened over time (and the results disappear if the period 1926–40 is deleted); and (ii) 60 years, using five-year subperiods, is not a large sample.

Poterba and Summers (1988) examined the same issue, but used US data for the period 1871–1985 and a different statistical technique. Their results were consistent with finding negative autocorrelation of returns for periods of from two to eight years. For periods of less than a year, they found positive autocorrelation. They also looked at foreign countries, including the UK, for which they found evidence in the period 1939–86 of short-horizon positive serial correlation and long-horizon negative serial correlation.

The problem with these studies is that there is too little evidence to reach reliable conclusions. One way round this is to go back even further. Goetzmann (1993) used three centuries of data. He found patterns in the data for the UK and for the US, but for the latter these patterns were not statistically significant. Another approach is to use data for many countries. Balvers et al. (2000) adopted this approach for 18 countries. They claim strong evidence of mean-reversion.

What these findings mean is unclear. They could indicate speculative bubbles, but they could also be consistent with rational variations in risk aversion. However, if mean-reversion occurs, equities held for long periods are less risky than they would appear from annual returns data. Mean-reversion can be forced on a simulation model used for strategic asset-allocation decisions. This is not done in the Wilkie model, but mean-reversion might still appear. Because the model for equities is autoregressive, changes in equity prices in successive years are negatively correlated (i.e. mean-reversion). But the rates of inflation are positively correlated, and so therefore are rates of dividend increases. As Wilkie has noted (1995a, p. 283), 'It is not obvious, without further investigation and experimentation, what the net result is over different time periods.'

Assume Bubbles Exist

A different approach might be just to assume bubbles exist because there is often broad agreement in markets that there is a bubble during a particular period. Why not just study a number of such periods and see whether there are common features? In particular, what conditions favour a bubble forming? King (1999) looked at a number of bubbles for a variety of assets and countries. He thought bubbles are likely to be found in optimistic economic conditions where there is no pressure on the authorities to take action. He suggests that a bubble is more likely to occur when there is above-trend growth in the economy, below-trend inflation, global commodity prices have fallen, the exchange rate of the economy in question has either stopped declining or is rising, there is fast real money supply growth, financial innovation is occurring, foreign exchange reserves are rising, private sector savings are falling, and there is talk of a paradigm shift. Of course, this approach doesn't really prove bubbles exist. But the fact that there are common features of markets that move up a lot and then fall is of some interest to investors.

Can Tactical Asset Allocation Add Value?

It would seem from the above that market moves often cannot be explained by news. There appears to be too much trading and prices appear to be too volatile. Some of the market swings possibly can be explained by reasonable, if erroneous, views about likely dividend prospects. Some by a non-constant discount rate. Some of the movement is probably the result of bubbles or fads. Arbitrage is unlikely to force markets back to their 'fair value'. Does this mean that successful tactical asset allocation is possible?

Some commentators have argued that in principle it is unlikely that managers will perform well. They make two important points. First, it can usually be shown that return differentials are earned in short bursts. For example, Chandy and Reichenstein (1991) report that for the period 1926–87, the excess return from the S&P 500 over Treasury bills was achieved in 3.5% of the months.

Because the market often moves quickly out of bear markets, a very high success rate has to be achieved in calling bull markets (e.g. Jeffrey, 1984; Chua et al., 1987; and Droms, 1989). A fully invested position is always wrong in bear markets, but it is 100% correct in bull markets, and that is the important call—you have to be in it to win it. The second point relates to the variability of most measures used in making tactical asset-allocation decisions. Methods that involve value assessed by yields, PERs, risk premiums and so on use measures that have varied widely over time. (For some sample calculations, see Carman, 1981.) Given the wide historical range, do investors have the skills to foretell which is the correct value for markets at any moment? And how quickly will a bubble burst? Finally, rewording Sinquefield: 'Why do you think you know more than the rest of us put together?'

Despite these comments, some studies have claimed some success for tactical asset allocation both in the US and the UK either in terms of enhanced return or reduced risk (e.g. Vandell and Stevens, 1989; Weigel, 1991; Mercer Fraser, 1991; and Wagner et al., 1992, who omit transaction costs). Moreover, many studies of tactical asset-allocation decision tools suggest the tools can be used to make profitable decisions. However, Philips et al. (1996) found that while tactical asset allocation managers performed well up to the end of 1987, the results were more mixed in the following seven years. Chen et al. (1993, p. 52) examined the performance of 15 asset allocation mutual funds: 'The results indicate counterproductive market-timing performance.'

The evidence is clearly mixed. It seems sensible to discuss tactical asset methods and leave the reader to decide whether they might be valuable.

Tactical Asset Allocation Methods

There are a number of tactical asset allocation methods; they are shown in Figure 22.2, which also relates tactical to strategic asset allocation. There are two basic approaches, top-down and bottom-up. Top-down can be further subdivided:

- business cycle anticipation;
- comparative valuation, e.g. aggregate DDM, bond yield versus equity earnings yield, foreign versus domestic markets;
- liquidity and flow of funds, e.g. money supply, cash reserves;
- technical analysis.

The top-down approaches attempt to choose between asset classes, but share selection is an intraclass decision. How can it give a guide to the value of asset classes? There are two answers. One relates to intracountry decisions and the other intercountry. Fund managers often say they cannot find anything to buy. This feeling can be used as an asset class decision rule. For example, the number of stocks that are cheap on a net asset basis might be a guide to the cheapness or dearness of the market. However, not many share-selection techniques can be

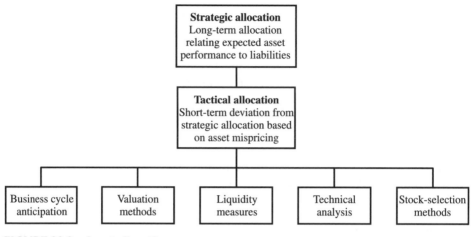

FIGURE 22.2   Asset allocation

used in this way. The bottom-up approach is more often used in selecting international equities. A manager may look for cheap shares on a worldwide basis and ignore the share's national origin. Thus, if German chemical stocks look very cheap, German chemical stocks are purchased, either to add to other chemical stocks or as the portfolio's sole chemical sector exposure. This results in country and currency exposure being determined by stock selection (although constraints in terms of maximum exposure to one country or maximum deviation from a country's index weighting may limit the impact of the bottom-up approach).

We discussed some technical approaches in Chapter 15. In the next two chapters, we discuss economic and valuation approaches to tactical asset allocation.

CONCLUDING COMMENTS

There are four major ways of setting strategic asset weights: matching a world index, doing what other funds are doing, mean-variance optimization, and asset-liability modelling.

The most widely used method is probably doing what other funds are doing, which maximizes the manager's utility, rather than the client's. Matching a world index to tactical asset allocation seems wholly appropriate for only a few funds, but appropriate in part for many. Asset-liability modelling is a sensible way of setting strategic weights, but there is no ducking the fact that it is complex. And, the investment models used may well be inadequate. Nonetheless, asset-liability modelling will probably attract increasing attention. The discussion of this approach given in this chapter is but a bare outline of what is necessary to determine the appropriate strategic weights. It is essentially a task that trustees and their actuarial advisers should undertake.

Tactical asset allocation determines what departures should be made from long-term strategic weights. We reviewed the evidence as to whether asset class pricing is efficient. There were reasons to believe that it is probably less efficient than intra-asset efficiency. The evidence on the success of tactical asset allocation is somewhat mixed, but it is worth examining the various approaches. However, given the modest size of tactical bets that most managers make, any manager with share-selection skills who sticks to his or her strategic asset weights would probably not come to grief in the performance stakes. Chapters 23 and 24 outline various methods of tactical asset allocation. Given the wide range of market valuations over time, it is probably sensible not to make asset switches in response to small price changes. Cheap markets can become cheaper. Extremes of valuation probably should be acted on. Extremes of valuation can be recognized by investment decisions being relatively insensitive to significant changes in assumptions.

23

Tactical Asset Allocation: The Economy and Market Ratios

Every bull has a bear behind.

Wall Street saying

In this chapter and the next, we discuss how tactical asset allocation (TAA) might be undertaken. We examine ways of forecasting the level of the equity market, and ways of deciding whether equities are cheap or dear against bonds or cash.

BUSINESS CYCLES AND THE STOCKMARKET

The course of the economy is not smooth: there are periodic fluctuations in economic activity, usually referred to as the business cycle. As the economy moves through a cycle, from recession to boom, profits rise and fall, as do interest rates, the rate of inflation, and so on. These factors are important in valuing securities, so it is not surprising that the financial markets move in response to the business cycle. But the economy and markets do not move in perfect unison; in fact the markets tend to anticipate the course of the economic cycle. If there is some regular pattern to the business cycle, and if the markets respond in some regular way to the business cycle, business cycle anticipation becomes a method on which TAA can be based. For example, Siegel (1991) reviewed US data and claimed that switching from stocks to bonds before business cycle peaks and back into stocks before business cycle troughs significantly improved returns. So let's look at business cycles and the stockmarket.

Business cycles and their relation to the financial markets are much more intensively studied in the US than the UK. The average sequence of business cycle and financial market leads and lags in the US for the period 1920–82 is shown in Table 23.1. The same broad pattern may be expected in the UK.

TABLE 23.1   Business cycle and financial market leads and lags, US 1920–82

Event	Months
Stock price trough to business cycle trough	5
Business cycle trough to bond yield trough	8
Bond yield trough to stock price peak	13
Stock price peak to business cycle peak	7
Business cycle peak to bond yield peak	1
Bond yield peak to stock price trough	6

Source: Moore and Cullity (1988, p. 62).

We can explain the general pattern shown in Table 23.1 as follows:

● The story begins with the stockmarket anticipating, on average by five months, the end of recession. At this time, interest rates are likely to be low, reflecting low demand for credit, falling inflation and monetary easing.
● Once the economy starts to pick up, bond yields will begin to rise, on average eight months after the trough of the recession. Credit demands increase and bond purchasers will anticipate future inflation and expect higher nominal returns. The authorities will stop easing monetary policy, and there will be a expectation that the next move in short interest rates will be up.
● Rising interest rates at first do not hurt the stock market. Investors will be focusing on large corporate profit gains, and equities will look attractive, especially against rising bond yields (i.e. falling bond prices). As time passes, rising credit demands, increasing inflation and tighter monetary policy will force interest rates up further, and this will start to slow the economy. The equity market will begin to focus on the competition from higher yields on bonds and cash. Prospects for profits will deteriorate as costs rise and margins can no longer be pushed up. Investment in plant and machinery may slow as a result of inadequate prospective returns caused by poorer profit prospects and a higher investment discount rate, resulting from higher interest rates. The stockmarket will peak.
● The pressure from the authorities to slow the economy, and the natural slow-down resulting from reduced business investment, will cause the economic cycle to turn down. The stockmarket will fall.
● The pressures pushing bond yields up when the economy was growing now operate in reverse, and bond yields will start to fall.
● The move into recession will continue, the authorities will start easing policy, inflationary pressures will begin to dissipate and, after a period, the stock-market will trough.

Now this story is illustrative only, and the exact same pattern will not be followed on every occasion. Indeed, the growth phases were longer in the 1980s and 1990s. Also, the story focuses on monetary policy, but fiscal policy will be adjusted too. Sometimes recessions may be triggered by external factors, such as a world oil price hike. Booms, inflation, etc. can also be triggered by external factors. The general thrust of the story, however, seems sensible enough.

One question often asked is whether the stockmarket forecasts the economic cycle or simply responds to concurrent events. The answer is probably a bit of both. Certainly, investors do try to act in advance of the economic cycle. But they also respond to some concurrent events, for example market peaks and troughs are within a few months of profit peaks and troughs.

A problem with business cycle anticipation as a timing strategy is that what has been described are averages within wide ranges. For example, while on average US bond yield toughs have led stock price peaks by 13 months, the range is 1–31 months. Further, the turning point in bond yields, the stockmarket and the economy do not always match up, so a sequence cannot always be recorded. Do these problems mean business cycle anticipation has no value for TAA? Not necessarily.

First, some notion of a business cycle provides a useful framework around which an investor can organize his or her views of the economy. Most investors probably use some version of the cycle to help them with their timing decisions. Second, although each business cycle is unique, this is not a problem if there are different causal factors that can be identified and that are simply combined in different amounts for each cycle. Of course, because stock prices lead the economy, what we need are factors that lead both the economy and stock prices. In Chapter 8, we discussed using leading indicators for forecasting the economy. In this section, we are discussing using economic variables to form a leading indicator of markets. An example will be useful.

DuBois (1988) argues that measures of liquidity, interest rates, Federal Reserve policy, and so on are important lead factors of the US stockmarket. He claims high predictive ability for a cyclical equity index he created combining four variables. The information coefficients claimed (e.g. 0.29 on a one-month horizon and 0.46 on a 12-month horizon) are far higher than is typical in investment analysis and higher than DuBois found for valuation-based approaches. (An information coefficient is the correlation between predicted and actual stock or asset returns.) DuBois also has a bond cyclical index based on measures of economic, financial and inflation pressures, and again claims high information coefficients. It is worth noting that the values for the variables used in DuBois' model are current values and not forecasts. The variables used, and the way of combining them, are proprietary.

Zweig (1986) offers a simple system for forecasting whether to be in or out of the equity market by combining monetary indicators and momentum indicators. One model uses three monetary indicators: changes in the prime rate, a measure of the Federal Reserve Bank's policy, and an installment debt indicator. Each indicator is measured on a simple scoring system and the points are then added up. This aggregate score gives bullish, bearish or neutral signals. Another model uses a momentum indicator. A 'super model' combines the three monetary measures with the momentum measure. These are perfectly straightforward approaches involving business cycle anticipation, and Zweig claims good results. Vergin (1996) reworks Zweig's calculations and suggests the strategies gave an annual return of 14.2% versus a buy-and-hold return of 8.6%. (The periods studied varied, but run from 1951 to 1984.) Vergin found, using an out-of-sample period, 1984–95, that the strategies returned 9% versus buy-and-hold's 14.4%. One wonders how well DuBois' model held up.

A study by Boehm and Moore (1991) attempts to allocate between stocks, bills and bonds in five countries by use of leading indexes. For Australia, Japan, the UK, the US and West Germany, longer leading stock indexes have been developed. These are made up of four leading indicators—new housing permits or approvals, real M1 or M2, a price-cost ratio, and the yield on long-term bonds. Each index gives buy and sell signals based on the movements of the smoothed growth rate of the index. How well does this method work? Table 23.2 summarizes the investment experience in stocks and short-term securities during bull

TABLE 23.2 Summary of investment experience in stocks and short-term securities during periods signalled by long-leading indexes in five countries

	Australia, 1970–89	Japan, 1971–89	UK, 1968–89	US, 1969–89	West Germany, 1970–90
(1) Stocks					
(i) Total average annual rates of return					
Bull market periods	17.8	20.1	16.7	14.0	11.2
Bear market periods	3.7	8.3	10.9	5.9	3.8
All periods	13.2	18.3	15.0	11.3	8.7
(ii) Standard deviation of rates of return					
Bull market periods	10.4	37.3	27.7	5.5	8.6
Bear market periods	18.1	21.9	13.7	21.3	15.0
All periods	15.6	31.4	21.9	16.3	12.2
(2) Short-term securities					
(i) Total average annual rates of return					
Bull market periods	11.5	6.1	10.1	6.9	5.2
Bear market periods	12.2	10.5	9.8	8.8	8.3
All periods	11.7	6.8	10.0	7.6	6.1
(ii) Standard deviation of rates of return					
Bull market periods	3.2	1.0	3.0	3.9	0.9
Bear market periods	3.5	2.1	3.5	2.3	1.8
All periods	3.4	1.9	3.3	3.3	1.5
(3) Holding stocks during bull markets and short-term securities during bear markets					
(i) Total average annual rates of return					
All periods	16.3	18.7	14.6	12.2	10.3
(ii) Standard deviation					
All periods	8.1	30.7	19.9	4.2	6.5

Source: Boehm and Moore (1991, p. 367).

and bear periods signalled by the long leading indexes for five countries. Note that these are not true bull and bear market returns but returns achieved during periods designated as bull or bear by the indicators.

The first and second rows of section (1) suggest the model can distinguish between periods of high and low returns. The third row shows the return from holding stocks for the entire period. Section (2) shows the return from short-term bills. Section (3) shows the return from investing in equities in bull periods and bills in bear periods. Notice that in the UK a higher return would have been achieved by always being invested in equities, and the difference between the buy-and-hold strategy and the bull/stocks and bear/bills strategy is modest for two other countries. Moreover, Boehm and Moore (1991) do not appear to allow for any costs. The standard deviation of returns is lower for the mixed strategy than the buy-and-hold strategy, so on a risk-adjusted basis the strategy appears slightly better. However, Boehm and Moore note that in the cheap-money 1950s and 1960s, the buy-and-hold strategy outperformed in both Japan and the US.

What happens to the analysis if investment in bonds is permitted? Leading inflation indexes have been constructed for Australia and the US, which use measures of the proportion of the labour force in employment, commodity price movements, the growth of debt, and survey data on business price expectations (for details, see Cullity, 1987). The indexes give about a six-month lead in forecasting inflation. Boehm and Moore (1991) use the smoothed growth rate of the index as a signal for rising or falling interest rates. They argue that if a bear signal is given for the equity market and the inflation index gives a signal that interest rates and inflation will fall, then bonds should be bought. But if interest rates and inflation are likely to rise, then cash should be held. Unfortunately, the results for the US and Australia show no substantial difference between switching between stocks and bills, and between stocks, bills and bonds.

All in all, the business cycle approach to forecasting gets a mixed scorecard.

SCENARIO FORECASTING

Instead of looking at every blip in the economic numbers, one might try to characterize a period. For example, for the next three to five years do we expect a depression, high inflation, or what? Most people would assume that during a depression, for example, equities would produce poor returns. Because equities are real rather than monetary assets, economists would assume that equities will be unaffected by inflation, i.e. they will be an inflation hedge. The price of stocks should rise enough to offset inflation and provide the same real return as one might have expected at a lower rate of inflation. In fact, in the short run, inflation is bad for equities: real returns are lower in periods of high inflation than in periods of low. For example, Ibbotson and Brinson (1993, p. 261) examine US data for the period 1790–1990. They classify each year's inflation rate into one of six categories: –4% and below; –3.99% to –1%; –0.99 to 0.99%; 1% to 3.99%;

4% to 7.99%; and 8% and above. For the first four categories, the arithmetic mean real total return varies between 10.35% and 12.9%, but the next two categories have returns of 4.15% and –5.65%. (For a more formal econometric study for the US and the UK, see Boudoukh and Richardson, 1993). Clearly, knowing the inflationary environment is important for equity investors. It hardly needs saying that it is important for conventional bonds.

But why do equities do relatively poorly in periods of high inflation? We can value the market by a constant-growth DDM, i.e.

$$P = \frac{D}{k - g}$$

where P is the index value; D is the next dividend; k is the discount rate, required rate or expected return; and g is the growth rate of dividends. Clearly, P will be lower if D falls, k rises or g falls. In essence, P will fall if economic prospects worsen or risk increases. Inflation may adversely affect D, k and g.

Inflation may just redistribute resources within an economy. But inflation caused by a rise in the oil price will lead to a fall in expected real earnings because of the transfer of resources to oil producers. With any inflation, some firms will suffer adverse cost and price impacts. Some firms may not be able to achieve price increases as quickly as they suffer cost increases. Many firms may face government pressure to restrain prices and be subject to increased international competition. Capital investments and stocks will be more expensive, and this will affect cash flow. Historical cost company accounts will become more inaccurate. All of this increases uncertainty and risk. Finally, real dividends may be affected because of the tax system—depreciation based on historical cost rather than replacement cost will result in profits being overstated, but these fictitious profits will be taxed.

A very different type of argument is that investors simply make valuation errors when inflation is high. First, they don't properly adjust profits—they are too gloomy. They are aware that reported company profits are overstated because of historical cost depreciation and historical cost inventories. But they do not make an adjustment for the fact that the value of monetary obligations, such as loan stock, is declining in real terms. This requires an upward adjustment to profits.

The second valuation error is more complex. We can rearrange the terms of our DDM so that:

$$k = \frac{D}{P} + g$$

i.e.

Expected return = dividend yield + dividend growth rate.

In equilibrium, we would expect the returns from equities to equal the return from bonds (i.e. the redemption yield) plus an equity risk premium to compensate for the greater risk of equities:

> Dividend yield + dividend growth rate =
>   bond redemption yield + equity risk premium.

If we assume that bond investors are interested in real returns, we can rewrite the above as:

> Dividend yield + dividend growth rate =
>   bond real redemption yield + expected inflation + equity risk premium.

We would expect bond investors to focus on real returns, i.e. the redemption yield less the rate of inflation. (The calculation of real rates is a little more complicated than this—see p. 24—but this is a reasonable approximation for our purposes.) If inflation were to rise by 1%, then we would expect nominal bond prices to fall so that nominal bond returns rise by 1% to offer the same real return. If inflation has no real effect on the economy, then firms should be able to raise their earnings by 1% and their rate of dividend growth by 1%. This keeps both sides of the identity equal, and equities are properly priced in relation to bonds. But if investors focus on the nominal dividend yield and the nominal bond yield, then they may demand an increase in the dividend yield when bond yields rise. Others things being equal, a higher dividend yield requires equity prices to fall. Equity investors would be making a valuation error, because they will automatically be compensated for higher inflation through faster dividend growth. Thus equity prices are forced down unnecessarily, and the equity risk premium rises automatically. This valuation error argument has been propounded by Modigliani and Cohn (1979, 1982), who argue that investors have underpriced equities during periods of inflation.

Whatever your view on these explanations, the fact is that inflation is watched by investors. More generally, it may be worth thinking in broad terms, such as a disinflation scenario, a goldilocks scenario (not too hot, not too cold), and so on. What we have discussed isn't a valuation tool as such, but it does say something about expected returns. We now turn to traditional valuation measures.

ABSOLUTE VALUATION MEASURES

Two of the most widely used market valuation measures are the market dividend yield and the PER. These may be considered on their own as absolute measures or in relation to other variables as relative measures. We will look at each ratio in turn.

Market Yield

Figures 23.1 and 23.2 show the UK and the US market yields for the twentieth century. In both charts, the horizontal line is the average yield for the entire period. The average for the UK is 4.94%, and for the US 4.56%.

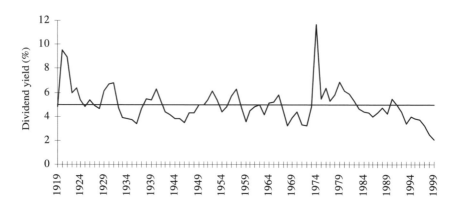

FIGURE 23.1   UK equity market yield, 1919–99
Source: Drawn from data in CSFB (2000, pp. 97–98).

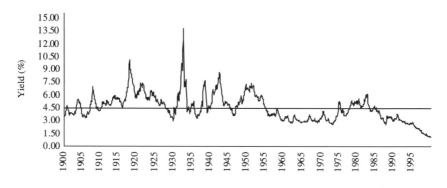

FIGURE 23.2   US equity market dividend yield, 1900–99
Source: Drawn from data on Robert Shiller's website (**http://www.econ.yale.edu/~shiller**).

If we believe that valuation ratios will stay within their historical ranges and will not stay fixed close to an extreme value, then when an extreme value is approached, we can forecast a change in the valuation measure. For a ratio such as the dividend yield (or the PER), either the numerator or the denominator must change. In other words, the ratio must forecast either the market level or dividends (or earnings for the PER valuation measure). Campbell and Shiller (1998) examine this issue using US data that go back to 1872. They find that over a one-year period, there is a negative relationship between yield and dividend growth (i.e. high yield, low growth) and no relationship between yield and price movements. But if we take a 10-year horizon, there is only a small relationship between yield and dividend growth, which is now positive (i.e. high yield, high growth), but a stronger relationship between yield and price movements. Thus, this evidence tells us that yield can be used to forecast market movements over long, if not short, horizons. A number of other studies support the finding that dividend yield predicts returns, and that forecast power increases as the investment horizon is lengthened (e.g. Rozeff, 1984; Fama and French, 1988a; Campbell and Shiller, 1988; and Fuller and Kling, 1990).

Campbell and Shiller (1998) look at the yield relationship in 11 other countries. The database they use provides less than 30 years of observations, so they shorten their horizon from 10 years to four. For seven of the countries—including the UK—the same relationship is found as for the US.

If we examine the last decade in Figures 23.1 and 23.2, we see that the dividend yield in the UK and the US has been below its historical average value and has tended to move further and further from its average. This can be explained in three ways:

- the markets are very overvalued—a crash is inevitable;
- the markets are highly valued for good reasons;
- the dividend yield is now a poor valuation tool.

We will comment on the third possibility here: as the argument is mainly applicable to the US, we shall discuss only the US. There are two ways shareholders can benefit from a share—dividends and capital growth. Shareholders can receive cash flow from the firm or, where prospective returns are high, the firm may retain all its cash flow and all the return will come as capital gains. Dividends are the usual method by which cash flow is paid out. But a firm could use cash flow to buy back shares. This may confer tax advantages to some investors. Many firms have, in recent years, engaged in share repurchases, and it has been argued that their value should be added to the value of dividends to produce a 'dividend-equivalent' series. This seems somewhat generous. Share repurchases took off in 1984, but there is no obvious change in the aggregate dividend payout ratio after that date as one might expect if share repurchases were replacing dividends. And while firms are reluctant to cut dividends, there seems to be no problem in halting a share-repurchase programme. If it is right to add share repurchases to dividends, then a dollar of repurchase would not seem to be worth a dollar of dividend. In practice, most analysts have ignored this. Moreover, if share repurchases are positive dividends, then share issues should be counted as negative dividends.

Cole et al. (1996) recalculate the US dividend yield by adding the value of repurchases and subtracting the value of new issues. They cover the period 1975–95. The yield for the most recent years is raised after their adjustments. For example, the actual yield for 1995 was 2.2%, and the adjusted yield was 3%. However, the early years of the sample have lower adjusted dividends, for example in 1975, 4.1% actual becomes 2.8% adjusted. This rewriting of history gives cause for concern. A better approach might be to leave the dividend yield as it is. Share repurchases should increase earnings per share, subsequent growth of earnings and dividends per share. In other words, rather than change the reported yield, investors should change their forecast growth rate. This reluctance to tamper with history is reinforced by the argument that many new share issues have gone to executives at prices below market value, making them very negative dividends. After allowing for this, actual dividends could be overstated rather than understated.

A different, but related, point is that many of the largest companies do not pay dividends. At the time of writing, the largest two US firms (by market capitalization) were Microsoft and Cisco Systems. Neither paid dividends. In fact, eight of the largest 30 companies didn't. No doubt it has always been the case that some major US companies have chosen not to pay dividends. However, it is unusual that so many have opted not to, and that they have become so large so quickly. (They are mainly technology and Internet stocks.) Over the last 15 years, there has been a significant effect on the market yield as a result.[1] The yield could be adjusted for this, although again we think it should be reflected in growth estimates.

Perhaps the simplest way to handle these problems is to view comparisons of the dividend yield with its history, at least in the US, with some scepticism.

Market Price-Earnings Ratio

Figure 23.3 shows the UK PER from 1965 to 2000. Figure 23.4 shows the market PER for the US for the twentieth century. In both charts, the horizontal line is the average PER for the entire period. For the UK, it is 13.3 and for the US, it is 14.1.

Campbell and Shiller (1998) note that there are various spikes in the PER because earnings get temporarily depressed in recessions. To overcome this, they do not calculate the usual market PER (current price divided by most recent 12 months' earnings), but calculate one that uses a 10-year moving

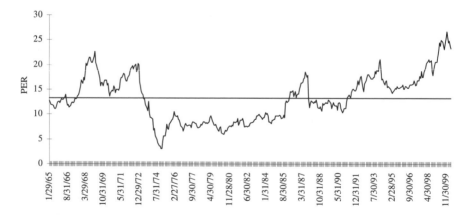

FIGURE 23.3   UK equity market PER, 1965–2000
Source: Thomson Financial-Datastream.

---

[1] This is a different point from that made by Fama and French (1999). They note that there has been a huge drop in the number of US companies paying dividends. However, as mainly small firms are affected, this would not impact a large capitalization index, such as the S&P 500.

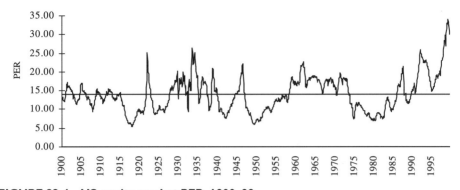

FIGURE 23.4   US equity market PER, 1900–99

Source: Drawn from data on Robert Shiller's website (**http://www.econ.yale.edu/~shiller**).

average of real earnings. They find that there is little relationship between market price movements and their ratio over one year, but strong forecasting power ($R^2 = 37\%$) over a 10-year horizon. Of course, this means that two-thirds of the price variation is still unexplained.

Are the Ratios Useful?

While the evidence that long horizon returns are predictable using PERs or dividend yield, this is not very helpful for a fund manager's time horizon. From the mid-1980s, the US dividend yield was suggesting the market was on the expensive side (see Figure 23.2). But the Dow has gone from around 2000 to around 11 000 (in early 2000). We will look at a study that perhaps gives a better guide to the usefulness of the valuation measures than do regression equations.

Bleiberg (1989) sorted quarterly US market PERs from 1938–87 into quintiles. He then examined market performance by quintile. His data are shown in Table 23.3.

TABLE 23.3   US market index performance by PER quintiles, 1938–87

PER quintile	PER values		S&P 500 average % change over subsequent:		
	Low	High	6 months	12 months	24 months
1 High	17.81	22.43	−0.99	0.24	−0.68
2	14.29	17.77	5.82	6.96	8.86
3	11.23	14.28	3.34	8.09	16.57
4	9.04	11.19	4.20	8.99	25.57
5 Low	5.90	9.01	7.99	16.21	29.79
Overall average			4.07	8.18	16.39

Source: Bleiberg (1989, p. 27). This copyrighted material is reprinted with the permission of the *Journal of Portfolio Management.*

The final column of Table 23.3 shows that over a two-year period, there was a clear relationship between quintiles and performance. Over shorter periods, the relationship holds for the extreme quintiles, but either weakly or not at all for the intermediate quintiles. It must be stressed that the relationship shown is what happens on average—there is, nonetheless, plenty of scope for it not to hold true for any particular period. For example, the frequency of the market rising in a six-month period was 63%. While there was a 73% frequency of the lowest PER rising in a six-month period, there was a 60% frequency of the highest rising. Or, to take another example, there is a one-in-four chance that the market will decline in the next six months even when the PER is low, and a three-in-five chance that it will rise even when the PER is high. Over a two-year horizon, the odds of a low multiple market falling are reduced and vice versa for a high multiple market.

It is likely that low market PERs go hand in hand with high bond yields. If falling bond yields are part of the reason for a rising market, perhaps low multiple markets perform well, but bonds perform better because they start with a high yield, and then achieve capital gains as well. Bleiberg (1989) examined this possibility by relating the relative return of stocks over bonds to PER quintiles. The results were very similar to those just discussed. Low PER markets performed better.

So far, so good, but what decision rules should we use for real-world asset allocation? Bleiberg (1989) used all the available data in the above analysis. For his decision rules, he determined the cut-off values for his quintiles by looking at the first 25 years of his data. He decided the portfolio would be invested in 50% stocks and 50% bonds if the market PER fell in the middle quintile, would shift more to equities if the market ratio was in the second lowest price-earnings quintile, and would shift even more if it was in the lowest—and vice versa for high multiple quintiles. The amount of the portfolio that was switched varied by 5% increments from 5% through to 25% in a test of five different allocation strategies.

The future wasn't the same as the past. First, the multiples differed in the two periods: 40% of the observations of the market multiple in the period 1963–87 fell into the top quintile as defined by the 1938–62 observations. Second, the return relationships were a bit erratic. The lowest PER stocks did perform best over six, 12 and 24 months, both in absolute terms and relative to bonds. But the other quintiles had an erratic relationship with returns over six and 12 months, and also for the returns relative to bonds for the 24-month period. The result was that none of the five active asset-allocation strategies produced a higher return than a static 50/50 stock/bond mix, and only one beat the 50/50 mix if both return and volatility of returns were considered. Note too that Bleiberg (1989) stopped in 1987. If you refer to Figure 23.4, you will see that once again the future wasn't the same as the past.

Bleiberg's (1989, p. 31) final comments provide a sensible conclusion:

> Is P/E useless as a valuation measure? No, not that. What I'm saying is that yes, the
> future will be like the past but only in broad outline . . . On average, the return on

stocks (both absolute and relative) will be higher in the periods following low P/E values than in periods following high P/E values . . . But that's as far as we can go . . . An 'overvalued' market can do well for quite a while. Historical P/Es are not graven in stone as valuation indicators. They tell us something about probabilities and expected returns, but it remains far from clear how portfolio managers can use that information profitably.

Why do Valuation Measures Predict?

Whether or not the valuation measures can be profitably exploited, they predict in the sense that they are correlated with returns. Why do they predict? To answer this, recall the constant-growth DDM:

$$P = \frac{D}{k - g} .$$

We can simplify this further. Assume the economy not only has constant growth, but that it is constant zero growth ($g = 0$). And let's assume that all earnings are paid out as dividends ($D = E$). Finally, we assume that k equals the risk-free rate (r) plus the equity risk premium (ERP). Then:

$$P = \frac{D}{k} \text{ and } P = \frac{E}{k} .$$

Rearranging:

$$k = \frac{D}{P} = \frac{E}{P}$$

or:

$$r + ERP = \frac{D}{P} = \frac{E}{P} .$$

This tells us that, under the assumptions made, the risk-free rate and the equity risk premium equal the dividend yield and the reciprocal of the PER. Let's assume some numbers. Say $r = 3\%$, ERP = 3%, D = 6 and P = 100. This satisfies the identity as 6% = 6%. And we'll also assume that the equity risk premium is 3% on average over long periods. Now imagine that for some reason the equity risk premium rises to 6% (r + ERP = 9%). The market level will adjust so that D/P = 9%, i.e. P will fall to 67. If we assume that the equity risk premium reverts over time to its average value, the high dividend yield will predict the rise in the market that will occur as P moves back to 100. Yield and the PER are acting as proxies for the equity risk premium.

What triggers a move in the risk premium, irrational factors or rational? Fama and French (1989) think the answer hinges on whether the expected returns can be tied to the economic cycle.

Business Cycles Revisited

Fama and French (1989) examine the periods 1927–87 and 1941–87 for the US. They try to predict bond returns and stock returns by the equity market dividend yield, the default spread and the term spread. The first variable is known to predict stock returns and the other two to predict bond returns. The default spread is the difference between the corporate bond market yield and the yield on government bonds. This measures the difference between high- and low-grade bonds. We would expect the default spread to widen in recessions. The term spread is the difference between the Aaa yield and the one-month bill rate, and measures the return difference between long- and short-term bonds. They find all three variables are related to returns for both stocks and bonds. Presumably the variables are forecasting components of expected returns that are common across assets.

The default spread and dividend yield are highly correlated, 0.61 during 1927–87 and 0.75 during 1941–87. These variables appear to track components of expected returns that are high in periods like the Great Depression, and low during generally good periods. The impact of the default spread and dividend yield increases from high-grade to low-grade bonds, from bonds to stocks, and from an equal-weighted stock portfolio to a value-weighted portfolio. This corresponds with how we might expect assets to be affected by business conditions risk.

The term spread is more related to short-term business cycles. Its effect is similar in size for all stock portfolios and long-term bond portfolios. The term spread appears to be picking up discount rate risk. Long-term assets are more affected by changes in the discount rate than short-term assets. The component of expected returns captured by the term spread is low around business cycle peaks and high around troughs.

What does all this tell us? When, in particular, the default spread and the equity dividend yield are high, investors are requiring a high return from their assets. This occurs when the environment is poor in terms of economic growth. Investors perceive a higher risk from investing in such periods. Also, when income is low in relation to wealth, investors may wish to save less. To encourage investment and the postponement of consumption requires higher returns.

There are many other related studies. All reach slightly different conclusions because of differences in time periods, data, variables used and so forth. Chen (1991), for example, uses a larger number of variables; Jensen et al. (1996) and Booth and Booth (1997) emphasize monetary conditions. These studies tend to suggest a rational time-varying risk explanation for market swings. But for an investor these studies are not so helpful. While some broad story can be constructed to tie the evidence together, unless one can produce a predictive quantitative model, it is not clear that we are any better off than we were with the rather vague economics that we began the chapter with, or the subjective discussion of the 1973–74 UK market in the previous chapter. So which variables should we use, and how should we combine them? Pesaran and Timmermann (1995) have given an interesting answer.

Pesaran and Timmermann claim that the literature suggests that the following variables might be useful in predicting the market's return: dividend yield, earnings-price ratio, one-month Treasury bill rate, 12-month Treasury bill rate, the year-on-year inflation rate, year-on-year rate of change in industrial output, and year-on-year growth rate in narrow money supply. This gives a total of nine variables: the seven listed plus an additional lagged version of each of the two interest rate variables. Using monthly historical data, Pesaran and Timmermann use multiple regression to forecast the excess return on the S&P 500 using the nine variables. They use every possible combination of the variables, which results in 512 models. They specify a number of model-selection criteria. One that most readers will be familiar with is adjusted R^2—the higher this number, the better the model. The best model under each criterion is then used to forecast the next period's returns. The next month, they add in the latest month's data and recalculate their 512 models, select the best, and make their forecast. In other words, they use a process that allows the model to change every month.

Over the period 1960–92, Pesaran and Timmermann (1995) correctly predicted whether excess returns would be positive or negative 57% of the time. The best period was the 1970s, when they were right 61% of the time. Pesaran and Timmermann calculated the returns from a strategy of being in equities when excess returns were forecast to be positive, and in bonds when they were negative. The strategy was very successful, in the sense of a higher mean and lower standard deviation if zero transaction costs were assumed, but more mixed if each equity transaction cost 1% and each bond transaction cost 0.1%.

In a study of the UK equity market, Pesaran and Timmermann (2000) allow for the possibility that new variables may be added after the modelling exercise begins. They distinguish between three levels of variables. Set A contains their core variables that are always included in their forecasting equations; set B consists of variables that are always considered for inclusion; and set C variables are included only when the forecasting equation behaves badly (in a sense they specify). The three sets are shown below. (A dummy variable is a variable that has a value of one or zero. In this case, January is distinguished from all other months.)

Set A: a constant; dividend yield; three-month Treasury bill rate; rate of inflation.

Set B: change in consols; change in three-month Treasury bill rate; January dummy.

Set C: change in industrial production; change in narrow money supply; change in oil prices.

Pesaran and Timmermann (2000) analyse the period 1965–93. They proceed to forecast and select models much as described for the US. They claim that it was possible to use their procedures to improve on the risk-return trade-off of the market portfolio. This seems too strong a claim. It is not clear why changes in industrial production and changes in narrow money supply have been relegated to set C, when in their US study these variables were included on the basis of their literature search. Nor is it clear why set A variables have to be included in every forecast given that the spirit of their approach is to include only what works. Further, their investment strategy is to invest in stocks or bills based on which has the highest forecast return. This is a very aggressive strategy, and the criterion for success would presumably require the portfolio to achieve a higher return than the stock index. But Pesaran and Timmermann's portfolio has a lower return than the market, although it has a much lower standard deviation. Is this really an improved risk-return trade-off for someone making aggressive switching decisions? Pesaran and Timmermann seem to have found the UK stockmarket harder to forecast than the US stockmarket.

We asked at the end of the previous section whether rational or irrational factors triggered moves in the equity risk premium. What we have discussed suggests rational factors. However, the correlations are so weak that there is plenty of room for fads and bubbles to play a part too.

Book Value

A popular measure in the US, but not in the UK, for assessing the level of the market is to compare the value of shares with the value of corporate assets. The book value of quoted American companies is the value of their assets less their liabilities, or net worth. The ratio of the value of the stockmarket to corporate net worth is often referred to as q:

$$q = \frac{\text{value of stockmarket}}{\text{corporate net worth}}.$$

Why should q predict the level of the stockmarket? The argument is that when q is low, it will be cheaper for companies to invest by buying assets in the form of existing firms than by investing in new assets. When q is high, companies will be able to raise capital by equity issues relatively cheaply, and will invest in physical assets. In other words, corporate takeover activity and issuance of new equity will tend to push q back to some typical average level. Of course, if q reverts to some average value, either the value of the stockmarket or the value of corporate net worth could be changing. In reality, corporate net worth changes slowly and it is the level of the stockmarket that drives q.

Despite the popularity of this measure, there is surprisingly little evidence to support its usefulness. Smithers and Wright (2000) suggest a number of trading rules for the US market. The simplest rule is to hold stocks when q is below average and hold cash when it is above. Over the period they studied (which appears to be 1900–98), the returns from the trading rule are 0.2% p.a. better than from buy-and-hold. Whether the rule was tested on daily data, quarterly date, annual data, or whatever is not made clear, and there is no mention of transactions costs. The second rule they suggest is that instead of getting out when q is above average, investors should wait until it is 50% above average. They claim that this would lead to an average return of 1.5% p.a. better than buy-and-hold. The third trading rule requires investors to sell stocks when q rises 50% above its average, and repurchase stocks when q falls below its average. They claim that this leads to an average return of 1.7% p.a. better than buy-and-hold. Apart from the points made earlier, Smithers and Wright appear to have used all the data in deriving their rules. However, q has risen more or less consistently over the last 20 years. Clearly, the average value of q calculated for 1900–80 would be different from that calculated for the entire century. As Smithers and Wright point out, a q investor could face many years where apparent overvaluation simply gets worse.

At the end of the 1990s, q for the US equity market was at its highest level in the twentieth century.

RELATIVE VALUATION MEASURES

Academics tend to relate equities to cash, no doubt as a result of their schooling in CAPM and the risk-free rate. Although investors sometimes do this, they usually relate equities to bonds, which is more likely to be the alternative investment. Moreover, although we accepted a Treasury bill as a risk-free asset to get our discussion going in Chapter 2, Treasury bills are not risk free. Very rapid inflation will destroy the value of bills, as will default—which was the experience of German investors in the 1920s. Of course, in the circumstances that Treasury bills are not safe, nothing else is likely to be. However, cash equivalents are risky to anyone with a nominal liability, such as an insurance company might have for certain kinds of business, since the return after three months is unknown. A bond with the appropriate duration would be a better risk-free proxy in these circumstances. In this section we look at relative valuation measures for equities versus bonds.

Equity Yields Relative to Bond Yields

It is useful to begin with a short history of inflation. (This is based on Wilkie, 1995.)

Inflation History

Many UK investors, especially those who experienced the events of the 1970s discussed in Table 22.4, are very wary of the dangers of inflation. But when we look back to the start of the twentieth century, to understand what investors were doing we have to understand the world as they would have seen it. During the entire period 1600–1914, prices rose by about 20%. During the nineteenth century, despite some inflation during wars, prices were on a generally down-ward trend. Wilkie (1995a, p. 253) asserts that 'The thoughtful investor in 1914 would have taken expected future inflation as zero.' During and immediately after the First World War, prices rose dramatically, peaking in 1920 with an index value of 99.9 (base 1000 in January 1987). But prices fell about 20% in 1921 and then, for a number years, prices drifted down, and the index was under 50 in both 1933 and 1934. Prices rose in the late 1930s, but at the start of the Second World War, the index was 56.1. Prices rose 32% during the course of the war. There were a couple of years after the Second World War when inflation was 6–7%, and a couple of years after the Korean War in which prices rose by around 7–8%, but, Wilkie argues, these might be seen as war related. However, during 1950–58, the compound rise was 4.5% p.a.

Wilkie argues that until 1958, it was reasonable to believe that the expected rate of inflation was zero. This may seem an implausible view. After 1934, there was no year in which prices didn't rise. But this is with the benefit of hindsight. In 1934, investors didn't know that prices would keep rising. Periods of inflation didn't make zero inflation on average impossible, because in the past there were periods in which prices fell. And after the falls at the start of the 1930s, there were only a few years of rising prices before the war, so one can easily see that there may have been grounds for believing in zero inflation at least to the end of the 1940s. Scott (1993, p. 57) argues that '. . . it seems likely that right up to the 1950s the long-term expected inflation rate was approximately zero. For the UK, apart from wars, that had been the experience of the previous 250 years or more.'

During the first part of the twentieth century, it is not surprising that bonds were seen as safe. Equities were seen as risky (as they are today), and with zero expected inflation, it was not obvious that equity prices or dividends would rise faster than real growth. As a result, if equities were to offer a higher return than bonds to reflect their riskiness, it was thought they had to offer a higher yield than Consols.

A US study by Smith (1925) attracted considerable attention. He showed that whether stocks were bought in rising or falling markets, in the long run they gave superior returns. Keynes (1925) reviewed the book and argued:

> This actual experience in the United States over the past fifty years affords *prima facie* evidence that the prejudice of investors and investing institutions in favour of bonds as being 'safe' and against common stocks as having, even the best of them, a 'speculative' flavour, has led to a relative over-valuation of bonds and under-valuation of common stocks.

Withers (1938), a prolific investment writer of the 1920s and 1930s, reports Smith's study, and notes that Raynes had conducted a similar study for the UK and presented a paper to the Institute of Actuaries in 1927. Withers reports that Raynes, who had selected a sample of shares from many sectors as his measure of equity performance, also found that equities outperformed fixed income securities. These studies came as great surprises, but did not persuade most investors to become pro-equity.

The Yield Gap

We now return to yield valuation measures of equities versus bonds. In the past, a popular measure was the yield gap. This is defined as:

$$\text{Yield gap} = \text{dividend yield} - \text{gilt yield}.$$

In the academic literature, it is sometimes argued that this is a measure that relates the income of the two investment classes. This is incorrect. If we accept the zero-inflation hypothesis, the market gilt and equity yields are both real returns. Although nowadays redemption yields of long-dated gilts usually serve as the proxy for gilt yields, in the past, Consols were used. An irredeemable stock does not have a redemption yield (it has no redemption date). Its flat yield is a measure of total return. The equity yield is not the total return from equities because we have to allow for growth. We might assume this to be 1–2%. Recall our equity risk premium identity:

Dividend yield + dividend growth rate = bond redemption yield + equity risk premium.

Rearranging the terms:

Dividend yield – bond redemption yield = equity risk premium – dividend growth rate.

The left-hand side of the identity is the yield gap. Thus the yield gap measures the equity risk premium understated by the growth rate, say 1.5%. In Figure 23.5, we show the yield gap for the period that Wilkie (1995a) claims an assumption of zero expected inflation is applicable to. The horizontal line is the average value of the yield gap, 1.38%. Adding in growth of 1.5% suggests an equity risk premium of under 3%.

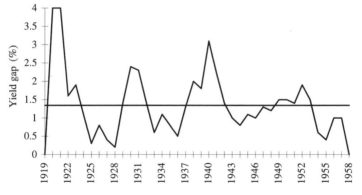

FIGURE 23.5   UK yield gap 1919–58
Source: Drawn from data in CSFB (2000, pp. 97–99).

After 1958, investors appear to have accepted inflation as a permanent feature of the economic landscape. Given that the return from a conventional bond is fixed in money terms, but dividends from an equity may be expected to grow in money terms, the initial yield of an equity can be below that of a bond, and still offer a higher expected return. After 1958, bond redemption yields exceeded equity yields. On this switch, the yield gap—equity dividend yield minus gilt redemption yield—became the reverse yield gap as the numbers became negative. Nowadays the gilt redemption yield minus the dividend yield is described by some writers as the yield gap, and by others as the reverse yield gap. Whatever the name, it is expressed as a positive number. It is used to decide whether gilts or equities are likely to give the better return.

The old yield gap measure had a certain logic to it. It pointed towards the equity risk premium and the investor could judge whether this was too high or low. But once inflation enters the picture the yield gap has no simple meaning. Imagine zero inflation, 5% dividend yield, 1.5% real dividend growth, and a 3% required real return from bonds. Given:

Dividend yield + (real dividend growth + expected inflation) =
(bond real return + expected inflation) + equity risk premium

we can calculate that the equity risk premium is 3.5% (i.e. 5% + 1.5% + 0% = 3% + 0% + equity risk premium). The yield gap is 2% (i.e. 5% − 3%), or −2% measured the modern way.

Imagine now that 5% inflation is expected. This has no effect on the equity risk premium because we simply add 5% to each side of our equation:

$$5\% + (1.5\% + 5\%) = (3\% + 5\%) + 3.5\%.$$

The yield gap is 8% − 5% = 3%.

For 10% inflation:

$$5\% + (1.5\% + 10\%) = (3\% + 10\%) + 3.5\%$$

and the yield gap is 13% − 5% = 8%.

Presumably, because the yield gap has widened in favour of gilts, we should be more pro-gilts. But note the real total return differential in favour of equities hasn't changed, i.e.

	5% inflation	10% inflation
Equity nominal return	5% + 1.5% + 5% = 11.5%	5% + 1.5% + 10% = 16.5%
Equity real return	11.5% − 5% = 6.5%	16.5% − 10% = 6.5%
Gilt nominal return	3% + 5% = 8%	3% + 10% = 13%
Gilt real return	8% − 5% = 3%	13% − 10% = 3%
Differential real return	6.5% − 3% = 3.5%	6.5% − 3% = 3.5%

In short, the yield gap now appears to be telling us more about the change in the rate of inflation than the relative attraction of equities and gilts. The indicator becomes worthless. Figure 23.6 shows the history of the gap from 1959. This broadly traces the smoothed inflation rate.

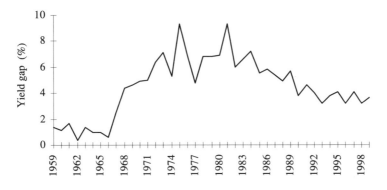

FIGURE 23.6   The UK yield gap, 1959–99
Source: Drawn from data in CSFB (2000, pp. 97–99).

The Yield Ratio

An alternative approach is to relate the two yields by the ratio of the redemption yield on gilts divided by the equity dividend yield. The higher the yield ratio, the more attractive are gilts thought to be. If you refer to the above examples for 5% and 10% inflation, the ratio will be 1.6 (i.e. 8%/5%) and 2.6 (i.e. 13%/5%), respectively. Clearly, gilts should be favoured in the 10% inflation scenario under this rule. But we have just seen that both cases give the same real return differential. So again this rule makes little sense.

The yield ratio seems inherently flawed, and over the years its typical value has changed, seemingly related in a broad way to inflation. Nonetheless, from the 1960s it has been widely used as a valuation tool. Figure 23.7 shows the long-run history of the ratio, and Figure 23.8 shows the period 1969–99. During this period, it was frequently argued that gilts should be more heavily weighted when the ratio exceeded 2.6 and equities should be more heavily weighted when the ratio was below 2. This has generally been a successful strategy, but it has only worked for extreme values, for example a ratio of, say, 2.2 does not necessarily suggest higher equity returns than a ratio of 2.3.

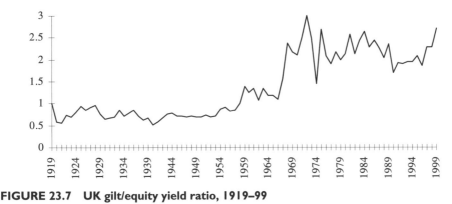

FIGURE 23.7   UK gilt/equity yield ratio, 1919–99
Source: Drawn from data in CSFB (2000, pp. 97–99).

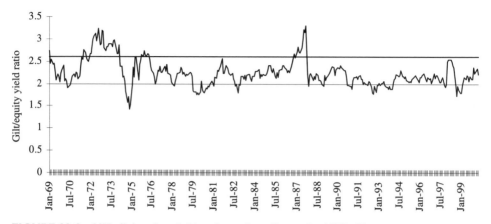

FIGURE 23.8   UK gilt/equity yield ratio and trading rule, 1970–99
Source: Thomson Financial-Datastream.

One broker reported an R^2 of 0.37 between excess equity returns and the gilt/equity ratio for the period 1973–93 (Wadhwani and Shah, 1993). Although not the best single valuation indicator, it was by far the most important component of a composite valuation indicator. A number of academic authors (e.g. Clare et al., 1994; and Levin and Wright, 1998) have suggested the ratio has some empirical value. Wilkie (1995a, p. 266) has taken a more sceptical view:

> I believe that it is fortuitous that long-term gilt-edged yields have been roughly twice share yields during this period. Dividend yields have typically been around 4% to 5%, and this is similar to the allowance for expected future inflation included in long-term fixed-interest yields; but the equality is by accident rather than necessity.

Despite the widespread use of the yield ratio, it is worth remembering that it relates the total return from bonds to only a component of equity returns. Let's now compare like with like.

The Price-Earnings Ratio Relative to Gilts

We looked earlier at the PER as a valuation measure. Although some investors look at the absolute PER alone, most relate it to cash or bonds. A common way of making these relative valuations is to look at graphs of the earnings yield (the reciprocal of the PER) and the redemption yield on long gilts or the interest yield on an irredeemable stock. Figure 23.9 shows the earnings yield for the UK equity market and the yield on Consols 2.5%.

We can discuss the width of the gap between the bond yield and the earnings yield or, alternatively, calculate a bond yield/earnings yield ratio. Either approach can use current or prospective data (i.e. using interest rate forecasts and earnings growth forecasts to project the lines forward 12 months). Using current data, the bond yield will be the redemption yield, and the earnings yield will be

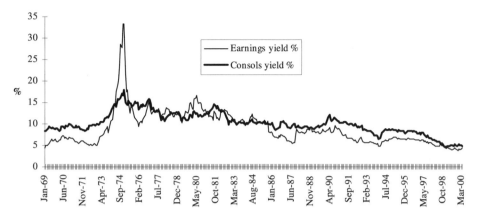

FIGURE 23.9   UK earnings yield and bond yield, 1969–2000
Source: Thomson Financial-Datastream.

the current earnings yield. The simplest approach is just to relate these variables to their average value. If one uses forecast variables, and allows for time varying risk, the steps would be:

1. Forecast bond yields and calculate the one-year total return.
2. Forecast profit growth over the next year and calculate the prospective earnings yield.
3. Decide whether the bond yield less earnings yield gap should widen or narrow based on factors such as inflation, stage in the economic cycle, political uncertainty, and so on.
4. Decide the change in the equity market required to make steps 2 and 3 consistent.
5. Calculate the prospective total return on equities (i.e. capital change plus income) and compare this with the total return from bonds.

The bond yield/earnings yield ratio is not a particularly powerful predictor in the UK, but Wadhwani and Shah (1993) found that it was for Italy, Germany, Norway and Switzerland. Their tests, however, do not incorporate time varying equity risk premiums. There is little evidence on the latter approach.

When bonds are used to determine the price for equities, usually an assumption is being made that bonds are correctly priced. Few equity investors really believe their bond colleagues are smarter than they are. (Market joke: 'What's the difference between a bond and a bond trader?' 'The bonds mature.') Whether a bond is correctly priced will depend on an evaluation of:

- real yields
- expected inflation
- risk premia.

Risk premia will include a premium for uncertainty about inflation, and additionally for corporate bonds, a default premium. We'll ignore the latter and just deal with government bonds.

In step 1 above, we forecast bond returns. A difficulty in doing this is that we do not know what the market is assuming in the current bond price. For example, Wilkie (1995a) claims that the long-run real return on gilts, deduced from returns during a zero inflation environment, was 3.7% (arithmetic average). Scott (1993) claims the rate was 3%. But the real return achieved over the last century was lower, and the return over a 10-year period at the end of the last century was much higher. So, what real rate should we assume the market is assuming? And the relevant inflation rate is not the current rate, a recent historical rate, or even that of a long historical period, but the rate of inflation expected over the life of the bond. What will that be, and how should we price a premium for uncertainty about that rate?

Fortunately, the advent of index-linked gilts allows us to answer these questions. We can divide the return from a conventional gilt into three parts:

Real redemption yield + expected inflation + inflation risk premium.

The yield quoted on an index-linked gilt is a real yield. We therefore know the first term above. A common assumption is that the inflation risk premium is small, say 0.5%. Wilkie (1995a, p. 273) offers a different view:

> One could argue that a risk premium should also be included in this difference, but it is not obvious what sign such a premium should have. There are some investors who wish to hold index-linked stocks as a gilt-edged hedge against inflation; there are also some who wish to hold conventional fixed-interest stocks, possibly to match the liabilities they have incurred. It is understood that the Government is willing to issue stocks of either type where there is a demand for them, so it is reasonable to assume that neither type of stock now commands a scarcity premium. I see no reason to include a premium here other than zero.

We'll assume that this view is correct. It then follows that we know the expected inflation rate. For example, if conventional gilts of a specified duration offer a 10% redemption yield, and index-linked of the same duration offer 3%, then expected inflation must be 7%.

Now that we know what the market is assuming, we can plug in our assumptions of what the real yield and inflation should be, and then decide whether gilts are cheap or dear. At this point we can go back and compare gilts with equities.

The Modern Yield Gap

Indexed-linked gilts allow us to resurrect the yield gap. We can rewrite the equity-gilt identity as:

Dividend yield + (real dividend growth +inflation) =
  (index-linked gilts real redemption yield + inflation) + equity risk premium.

We can cancel out inflation from both sides, and then rearrange the terms:

Dividend yield + real dividend growth
　　　　　 – index-linked gilts real redemption yield = equity risk premium.

If we assume a rate of real dividend growth, say, 1.5%, then we can simply add 1.5% to the dividend yield, subtract the index-linked real yield, and we have an estimate of the equity risk premium. In Figure 23.10, we show the history of this estimate, beginning in 1986. We have chosen that date because the market— launched in 1981—was initially distorted by the scarcity of index-linked gilts, and by restrictions on which investors were permitted to purchase them. The decision rule is to sell equities when the equity risk premium is low if you think the discount rate is constant or, if you think it varies, when you think it low relative to what you think it should be given the investment environment.

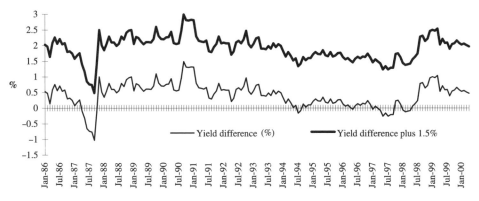

FIGURE 23.10　UK equity dividend yield and index-linked yield difference
Source: Thomson Financial-Datastream.

Most investors simply relate the yield curve difference between equities and index-linked gilts to the historical average. On this basis, the equity market was very expensive just before the 1987 crash, but isn't expensive currently.

Index-linked bonds have been issued in about a dozen countries, including Israel, Canada, Australia, New Zealand, Sweden and, since 1997, the US. While this modern yield gap can be calculated for these countries, there may be problems in interpretation. In most countries, real yields have been generally higher than in the UK. The UK index-linked market is currently the largest in the world, and much more liquid than other markets, and this might suggest that other markets would offer higher rates to compensate for poor liquidity. But while pre-tax returns are higher, post-tax returns may not be so different. UK private investors are only taxed on income from any type of gilt and not on capital gains: many institutional investors are not taxed at all. In most other countries, the uplift on principal repayment for index-linked gilts is subject to domestic taxation, at least for private investors. In the US, interest is taxable in the year it is received, as is the increase in principal in the year that it is credited, although the investor won't receive the income until the bond matures, maybe in 10 or 20 years. If inflation is high, then high-rate taxpayers may face negative cash flows because of this taxing of 'phantom' income.

INDEX-LINKED VERSUS CONVENTIONAL BONDS

Although index-linked are technically bonds, their characteristics—such as a low running yield, and probable growth (in money terms) of income—are more like those of equities. Nonetheless they should be compared with all other asset classes, including conventional bonds. The usual approach is to consider the break-even inflation rate, which is the rate of inflation that would produce identical money returns from an indexed bond and a conventional bond with the same redemption date. For example, if the break-even rate is 3.65% and you expect inflation to be greater than this for the life of the bonds you are analysing, then you should buy index-linked, but if you expect it to be lower, you should buy conventional bonds. Why? Since the nominal cash flow from a conventional bond will not change, an inflation rate higher than the break-even rate can only benefit the indexed bond whose nominal cash return will increase. And vice versa for lower inflation.

The break-even inflation rate will vary with the investor's tax position. For individuals, gilt income is taxed, but capital gains are not. Conventional gilts have more of their return in the form of income than capital compared with a low-coupon index-linked. Accordingly, they are taxed more heavily. This means the break-even inflation rate is lower for a taxpayer than for a tax-exempt investor. In effect, the indexed stock needs less uplift from inflation because the conventional bond's return is being dragged down by tax.

TO BE CONTINUED . . .

The material in the next chapter is a continuation of the material in this. We are breaking it into two parts to reduce chapter fatigue.

24

Tactical Asset Allocation:
Risk and Return

In investing money, the amount of interest you want should depend on whether you want to eat well or sleep well.

J. Kenfield Morley

The previous chapter made substantial use of the constant-growth DDM. The equity risk premium was involved in our discussion at a number of points, but we did not specifically examine it. We remedy that in this chapter. We will look at three issues: (i) how to use the equity risk premium as a market-timing tool; (ii) why the historical equity risk premium has been so high; and (iii) making sense of market levels in 2000.

The equity risk premium—the extra return for bearing equity risk—is one way of looking at risk and return. Another is the efficient frontier approach of Chapter 2. In this chapter we apply that analysis to asset allocation.

USING THE PREMIUM TO TIME THE MARKET

If the equity risk premium tends to revert to some average value, it follows that there should be a market-timing tool based on selling shares when the premium is low and buying when the premium is high.

We can calculate the equity risk premium by using either the constant DDM or a version that allows growth rates to vary. The latter approach can be attempted in either of two ways—bottom-up or top-down. With the bottom-up approach, returns calculated by a DDM for individual companies are aggregated on a market capitalization-weighted basis. This approach has been used by firms such as Kidder, Peabody. The most common approach, however, is top-down, and the DDM framework is applied to the market as a whole.

The easiest top-down approach is to use a constant-growth model. But some investors wish to give current economic circumstances more weight. This suggests a two-stage model, for example making estimates over the next five years and then applying a constant-growth model from that point. If we adopt this approach, we can make specific estimates for every dividend, or we can take the starting dividend and apply what we think is the appropriate growth rate for the next five years. This permits us to value the market in five years, using assumptions affected by current optimism or pessimism. We can value the market from year six onwards by using a constant-growth model based on long-term trends. Adding the two calculations together gives us the value of the market today, i.e.

$$P_0 = \frac{D}{1+k} + \frac{D(1+g_1)}{(1+k)^2} + \frac{D(1+g_1)^2}{(1+k)^3} + \frac{D(1+g_1)^3}{(1+k)^4} + \frac{D(1+g_1)^4}{(1+k)^5} + \frac{D_6}{k-g_2}$$

where P_0 is the market level, D is the dividend, g_1 and g_2 are growth rates, and k is the discount rate that is made up of the sum of the redemption yield on long bonds and the equity risk premium. Of course, we know the value of the market today, the long bond yield and D, and we have assumed g_1 and g_2, so we can solve this equation for the equity risk premium.

Whether this additional effort leads to estimates superior to the constant growth model is unclear. Some authors have claimed good results with the simpler approach. DuBois (1988) describes a model somewhere between the two. He uses the current yield on the S&P 500 plus the expected nominal growth of dividends. DuBois derives the latter from inflation expectations and real growth expectations. Inflation expectations are based on an annualized 20-quarter exponentially-weighted moving average of inflation rates, measured by the GNP deflator. This is adjusted by the recent trend in wholesale prices, which picks up changes in inflation faster than the GNP deflator. Real growth is an assumed average of 2.8%, adjusted up or down when inflation is expected to be low or high. DuBois uses historical data for inflation, but exponential weighting is a way of giving most weight to recent observations. His growth assumption is a long-term average, but is modified by relatively recent historical inflation experience. From these measures, DuBois derives an expected return, which he compares with the expected returns on bills and bonds. The expected return on bonds is assumed to be the redemption yield on long-dated bonds. (One could forecast a one-year holding period return for bonds that could produce a very different benchmark return from that obtained from the redemption yield.) The return on cash is taken to be the yield on a Treasury bill.

In Table 24.1, we show DuBois' data for equities and bills. The expected equity return less the three-month Treasury bill yield—the premium—is related to the excess return from stocks over bills. Table 24.1 shows that when the expected return from stocks relative to bills is high, stocks have returned more than bills over the following months with a high probability. The greater the premium, the greater should be the allocation to stocks.

DuBois calculated information coefficients for the excess return approach for stocks/bills, bonds/bills and stocks/bonds. The average information coefficients

TABLE 24.1   Stocks/bills premium and subsequent performance, US 1951–85

Premium range	No. of observations	Average subsequent excess return (%)			Probability of positive excess return (%)		
		1 month	3 months	12 months	1 month	3 months	12 months
>10	10	2.5	6.8	26.1	80	80	100
8–9.9	64	1.9	4.8	16.7	66	78	89
6–7.9	102	0.5	2.0	6.1	57	63	63
5–5.9	62	0.7	1.3	4.6	61	69	66
4–4.9	91	0.1	1.0	2.8	57	59	64
2–3.9	74	(0.2)	(1.1)	0.9	42	36	55
<2	16	(1.9)	(3.6)	(8.6)	31	19	38
	420	0.5	1.4	5.7	56	60	66

Source: DuBois (1988, p. 294).

for one month, three months and 12 months for the period 1951–85 were 0.18, 0.27 and 0.42, respectively. These all provide useful amounts of information.

DuBois' results are encouraging, but Carman (1988) sounds a cautionary note. Carman produced figures showing that asset allocation between US bonds and equities using the equity risk premium approach would have produced higher returns in the period 1951–87 than an all-equity portfolio. These results, however, depended on good performance in the 1970s and 1980s. The results were neutral in the 1950s and negative in the 1960s. Presumably most investors would have quit the method before they got to the good years. Carman's simulation assumed that the average risk premium for the entire period (3.5%) was used as the guideline. But in the 1950s, the premium was in the range 4–11%: how would investors have anticipated the roughly four-decade average premium of 3.5%? Investors might instead have used a rolling five-year average for the premium. When Carman tried this, tactical asset allocation relative to being fully invested in equities produced lower returns in the 1950s and 1960s, and higher returns in the 1970s and 1980s. There was no return advantage over the entire period. Tactical asset allocation is like many other valuation tools—it will produce poor results if there is a sea change in valuation standards.

HOW MUCH IS RISK REWARDED?

Tactical asset allocation models using the equity risk premium approach have to assume an average value. The obvious starting point is the historical average. As we shall see, pinning down the historical average is not a simple task.

Historical Averages

For many years, the accepted long-term return figures for the UK were those calculated by stockbrokers Barclays de Zoete Wedd (BZW), and continued in the last few years by both Barclays Capital and Credit Suisse First Boston (CSFB). BZW's starting point was 1919. For the period since 1919, BZW's figures suggest an equity risk premium of a bit below or a bit above 6% p.a., depending on whether we use cash or bonds to calculate it. Wilkie (1995a) using different indexes for the period 1923–93, and using nominal returns, finds a cash-based equity risk premium of 6.24% and a gilt-based equity risk premium of 5.47%. Blending these numbers together suggests 6% as the historical UK equity risk premium.

In the US, one of the most frequently cited sources of returns data is Ibbotson Associates. Using the same source data, but with some modifications, Wilson and Jones cover a slightly longer period, so we will report their results (presented in Jones, 2000, p. 141). They find the geometric mean real return from US equities over the period 1919–98 has been 8.15%, and the returns from bonds and cash have been 2.59% and 1.37%. This gives equity risk premiums of 5.6% and 6.8%.

In a famous paper, Mehra and Prescott (1985) calculated the geometric real return on US equities over the period 1889–1978 to be 6.98%. The return on bills was 0.8%. The equity risk premium was therefore 6.18%. They deemed this a puzzle—we explain why shortly.

Siegel (1994) provides returns data back to 1802. He splits his period into three major subperiods: 1802–70, 1871–1925, and 1926–92. He calculates real returns for equities of 7%, 6.6% and 6.6%, respectively. Using bond returns, the equity risk premiums for each of the periods in turn are 2.2%, 2.9% and 4.9%. Using cash, the numbers are 1.9%, 3.4% and 6.1%. Obviously, the equity return would increase for the most recent period if the period were extended to the end of the century. And the equity risk premium for the period would rise, taking us back towards our ballpark equity risk premium of 6%. But the equity risk premiums for the other periods are quite different. For the entire period, the equity risk premium is 4.3% (bonds) or 3.8% (bills).

Recently, Dimson et al. (2000) have recalculated returns for a number of countries. They extended the UK returns data to 1900, based partly on indexes they constructed. They argue that one of the equity indexes used by BZW suffers from being unrepresentative and having survivorship bias. This leads to inflated returns. They calculate the UK real geometric return equity risk premium for the twentieth century based on cash was 4.9%, and based on bonds 4.6%. Splicing together various US indexes and series, they calculate the US real geometric return equity risk premium for the twentieth century based on cash was 5.8% and based on bonds 5.3%.

The Puzzle

Mehra and Prescott (1985), you will recall, calculated an equity risk premium of over 6%, and they wondered why equity holders were so well rewarded. The usual explanation is risk. Mehra and Prescott measured risk by the consumption capital asset pricing model (CCAPM), which we will outline.

If we assume all investors are risk-neutral, i.e. they don't care about risk, then under any measure of risk all assets will end up offering the same return. But we expect investors to be risk-averse. The CAPM, as described in Chapter 3, measures risk in a particular way. It considers the variability of asset returns in relation to the 'market portfolio' (whatever that is). More variable, or riskier, securities have higher expected returns. These returns depend on the security beta, and the market portfolio's return. But what determines the market's return? The CAPM is silent on this: it just takes it as given. To explain the equity risk premium, we need to go back to first principles.

The ultimate goal of economic activity is consumption. When we invest, we postpone consumption, and we expect to be rewarded for this. We expect consumption to be subject to diminishing marginal utility. That is to say, if we have a lot of wealth, we will be able to consume a lot and presumably will put a low value on extra consumption. But if our wealth is low, additional consumption will be more valuable. If low returns from an asset occur when our wealth is low, we will view that asset as riskier than one with equal returns but that has its low returns when our wealth is high. Indeed, we may prefer an asset with lower returns if its good returns come when our wealth is low. When we are assessing classes of assets, riskiness is measured by the riskiness of the associated consumption patterns.

The CCAPM implies that if we think bills and bonds are less risky than stocks in the sense just explained, they will receive lower returns. But how much lower? This will depend on: (i) the variability of asset returns; (ii) the covariance of stock, bill and bond returns with consumption; and (iii) how risk-averse investors are, i.e. how much they value additional funds when consumption is low. If we know (i) and (ii), then we can estimate (iii). Mehra and Prescott (1985) estimated a coefficient of relative risk aversion. But the number they obtained they deemed implausible—it implied that investors are so risk-averse that faced with a situation where they could either lose half their wealth or increase it by 50%, with each outcome a 50/50 possibility, they would be willing to pay 49% of their wealth as insurance to avoid the bet. Using what Mehra and Prescott consider a plausible coefficient, the equity risk premium should be about 0.35%. Hence the 'puzzle'.

Since theory and facts don't match, we can reject the theory, query the facts, or do both. We'll do both, beginning with the facts.

History Rewritten

If we accept that equity risk premium numbers for the twentieth century broadly agree, then the only way we can get a lower equity risk premium is by going back further. As we noted above, Siegel (1994) found, as a rough approximation, that the equity risk premium was nearer 2.5% during the nineteenth century and the first quarter of the twentieth century. This might make us look again at the meaning of the twentieth century numbers. What the record shows is the returns that were obtained, not what investors expected to obtain. In fact, there are good reasons to believe investors in bills and bonds received negative surprises.

Consider the UK. The yield on Consols over the period 1756–1958 varied between 2.5% (1896–98) to 5.9% (1797–98). The arithmetic average is 3.7%. Wilkie (1995a, p. 225) argues: 'It is reasonable to assume that this was a "real" rate of interest, since it was not necessary to make any allowance for future inflation, expected future inflation being taken as zero.' Scott (1993, p. 54) takes the same line, although he produces a different number:

> The average yield on long-term UK government bonds (Consols) in the 40-odd years before the first world war was close to 3 per cent per annum. This was both the nominal yield . . . and the real yield . . . Furthermore, it was probably also the real expected yield, since the period was one of great monetary stability.

If we assume that these numbers represent the sort of return bond holders expect, and that bondholders have been surprised by the level of inflation, then the 1.3% real return on bonds reported by Dimson et al. (2000) as the realized return in the twentieth century understates the expected return by about 2%. This suggests that the expected equity risk premium over bonds may have been about 2.5%. This corresponds to Siegel's equity risk premiums for 1802–70 and 1871–1925 when inflation was near zero (0.1% and 0.6% respectively). Wilkie argues that UK investors in 1923 were expecting an equity risk premium of 2%, the difference between equity and gilt yields. He argues that looking forward, one should expect an equity risk premium of 2% over index-linked gilts—a 1% yield gap and 1% real dividend growth.

Wilkie has used his stochastic model (discussed on pp. 439–41) to run 1000 simulations of returns for 70 years using five sets of assumptions. When he assumes expected inflation of zero, and actual inflation also zero, the equity risk premium turns out to be about 2%. When he assumes expected inflation of zero and actual inflation of 5%, the equity risk premium turns out to be about 5%. This accords with expected and actual returns generated by our 'surprise theory'.

It is worth stressing that the analysis here, while reducing the equity risk premium, does not reduce the expected real return from equities; instead, it argues for higher expected future gilt and cash real returns.

Reverting to the equity risk premium puzzle, the above arguments would substantially reduce the puzzle, although even a 2% equity risk premium is well above Mehra and Prescott's suggested 0.35%. We will have to try a different tack to solve the puzzle.

Survivorship Bias

One argument that is hard to deal with is that investors are rationally afraid of disasters that may have a low probability of occurring but are possible nonetheless. In other words, when we model the CCAPM using observed consumption variation, we understate the variation in consumption that may concern investors. If we assume that consumption might fall 25% in a recession, then we can explain away the observed premium. But even in the Great Depression, in no year did US consumption fall by more than 9%. Thus it's unlikely that just an anticipated recession or depression that never materialized is a sufficient explanation. The circumstances that involve a market not surviving presumably would be.

Looking at UK and US returns involves looking at economies that have survived. World equity returns would be lower than for these economies if the markets that didn't survive were included. Jorion and Goetzmann (1999) collected data on 39 equity markets, going back to the 1920s. They found nearly all markets had been subject to dramatic change with a number being closed or suspended due to financial crises, wars, expropriations, or political upheaval. The US market was one of the few that wasn't seriously affected, and its returns were exceptional. However, this doesn't square with Dimson et al.'s more detailed analysis of 12 countries (Australia, Canada, Denmark, France, Germany, Italy, Japan, the Netherlands, Sweden, Switzerland, the UK and the US). For this group, the geometric mean return from US equities over the twentieth century was only 0.3% above the average.

Further, one has to be careful in going from equity returns to statements about equity risk premiums. For example, German equity investors were not wiped out in the hyperinflation of the 1920s, but bill and bond investors were. In circumstances that cause equity markets to be suspended or closed, other asset holders may fare worse than equity investors. Of course, Dimson et al.'s data do have a survivorship bias, and world equity returns would probably be lower than that of their dozen markets.[1] But that doesn't necessarily tell us anything about the equity risk premium.

---

[1] We think there is survivorship bias because the markets shown are all from currently successful countries. But markets that are unimportant today were popular at the start of the twentieth century. For example, in 1904, a British company, the Investment Registry, which claimed to be the world's largest private client organization, asserted that for British investors, experience had shown that international investing may best be divided into the following nine subdivisions: England, the English Colonies, Europe (North), Europe (South), Asia, Africa, the US, South America, and general international investments (companies that derive their revenues from international trade, such as steamship, telegraph and insurance companies).

The company recommended that because most English investors prefer investing at home, the English proportion of the portfolio should receive a double weighting. It claimed that the best investments in Asia were in India, and those in Africa were in Egypt, Cape Colony, the Transvaal and Orange River Colonies.

The first British investment trust, Foreign and Colonial, launched in 1868, was initially invested in Peru, Italy, Egypt, Spain, Turkey, Chile, Brazil, Russia, Austria, Danube, Portugal, Argentina, Canada/Nova Scotia, the US and Australia/New South Wales.

We do not know the returns from these markets, but neither company's list sounds like history's winners.

Some Theoretical Modifications

The CCAPM assumes that investors care about the level of their consumption. But perhaps investors care about their level of consumption relative to other people. You often hear sentiments such as 'Times were hard, but they were hard for everyone,' given as an explanation why some objectively bad circumstances were not really that bad. Not keeping up with the Joneses is more painful. Since we expect consumption per capita to grow steadily over time, equities that can plunge in any year are very unattractive in this situation. Again, if our satisfaction with our lot depends on our consumption being at least as high as last year's, then the possibility of negative returns from equities makes them unattractive except with a high premium. Drawing on this line of reasoning, one model reasons that when consumption is low relative to past history, investors will be more risk-averse, and vice versa. Accordingly, although consumption doesn't fluctuate much in reality, variable risk aversion magnifies the effect.

We have explained that the coefficient of relative risk aversion required to solve the puzzle was too high to be plausible. However, Kandel and Stambaugh (1991) have pointed out that for risks that affect only a small portion of total wealth, high coefficients are not implausible. For example, if the gamble described on p. 487 applied to only 1% of wealth, the implication is not that the investor would be willing to spend 49% of his or her wealth on insurance, but 15% of the amount at stake. This is more plausible.

A quite different theoretical approach is to abandon the CCAPM and use behavioural theory, in particular prospect theory (see Chapter 5). In prospect theory, what matters for investors is more a change in wealth rather than the absolute level of wealth. Investors are assumed to be loss-averse: losses hurt more than gains. In fact, a loss of x seems to hurt more than twice as much as the pleasure of a gain of x.

Gains and losses are usually determined in the context of an investment horizon. If we evaluate equities on a daily basis, then they will be very risky. Measured daily, stocks go down about as often as they go up. If we evaluate daily, we will lose as often as we gain, but each loss will be twice as painful as each gain. If we evaluate every 30 years, equities won't appear as risky because the historical evidence suggests that it is very likely that we will see a gain. Daily evaluation requires a high equity risk premium, while 30-year evaluation permits a small premium. This is true irrespective of any effect that wealth changes may have on consumption. Benartzi and Thaler (1995) calculate what evaluation period is consistent with a 6.5% equity risk premium. The answer is 13 months, which is close to the usual annual performance reviews that institutional investors are subjected to, and the tax cycle for taxpayers. Managers usually report quarterly, which suggests the equity risk premium should be higher. On the other hand, most institutional clients report that they will stick with a manager for three to five years, which suggests a lower equity risk premium. On balance, 13 months sounds about right. An implication of this approach is that investors who evaluate their portfolios less than the norm will see equities as less risky than the typical investor, and will therefore see equities as more attractive.

Some Implications

What are the implications of our discussion? If you want to use the average equity risk premium for tactical asset allocation, you will have a difficult job in deciding what it is. Is it 6%, because that's the figure most people know? Is it 4% because the previous number suffers from measurement errors? Is it 2% because that's what investors expected for about 150 years? And when you have selected an average, is it time varying?

More generally:

- If you think the equity risk premium is not as high as believed, then there is not so much of a puzzle. Siegel's estimate of the equity risk premium for 1802–1925 is the expected equity risk premium; the post-1925 equity risk premium is the unanticipated equity risk premium resulting from negative surprises for bondholders. This view implies equities will still return more than bonds and cash, but not as much as most people believe.
- If you believe the equity risk premium really is around 6% because investors are very risk-averse, then you should determine whether you are more or less risk-averse than other investors. If you are less risk-averse, then you may prefer more equities. You should figure out who the 'you' is—if you are a fund manager, are you measuring your risk of underperforming your peer group or your client's risk?
- If you believe investors make mistakes, whether from using too short a valuation period or giving too high a probability to a disaster for equities, and especially one that would affect bonds more, then equities will be very attractive.

SHIFTS IN THE EQUITY RISK PREMIUM

Many investors don't understand the implications of a shift in the equity risk premium (ERP). It is useful to work through an example. Given that:

$$\text{Market value} = \frac{\text{next dividend}}{\text{ERP} + \text{gilt redemption yield} - \text{dividend growth rate}}$$

if we assume some values for the right-hand side of the equation, we can value the market. Assume that dividend = 5, ERP = 5%, redemption yield = 5%, and dividend growth = 4%. Then:

$$\frac{5}{5\% + 5\% - 4\%} = 83.$$

In Table 24.2, we enter the above as year 0. In all subsequent years we assume dividends grow by 4%. In years 2–4, we make an additional assumption— that the equity risk premium falls by an absolute 1% p.a. In year 5, we assume dividends keep growing but the equity risk premium doesn't change. In year 6, we assume dividends grow but the equity risk premium reverts to 5%. The market value can be calculated for each year and also the percentage change in the market value.

TABLE 24.2   Effect of a varying equity risk premium (rounded figures)

Year	Valuation components	Market level	% change year-on-year	Yield (%)	PER
0	5.00/(5% + 5% – 4%)	83.33		6.00	10.0
1	5.20/(5% + 5% – 4%)	86.67	4.00	6.00	10.0
2	5.41/(4% + 5% – 4%)	108.16	24.80	5.00	12.0
3	5.62/(3% + 5% – 4%)	140.61	30.00	4.00	15.0
4	5.85/(2% + 5% – 4%)	194.98	38.67	3.00	20.0
5	6.08/(2% + 5% – 4%)	202.78	4.00	3.00	20.0
6	6.33/(5% + 5% – 4%)	105.44	–48.00	6.00	10.0

In year 1, the market rises modestly in line with the assumptions. In the next three years, the continually declining equity risk premium generates spectacular returns. When the equity risk premium stops falling, the market returns to its modest advance. If the equity risk premium returns to its starting level, the market roughly halves in value. Note, however, that the market level is higher in year 6 than in year 0: this is because of the steady growth in dividends.

Given the market level and dividend, we can calculate the yield for the market. On the assumption that 60% of earnings are paid out as dividends each year, we can deduce from the dividends what earnings must be and therefore we can calculate a market PER. We'll assume that for this market the historical yield has averaged 5% and the PER has averaged 12. This invites the question as to whether the market is overvalued in years 4 and 5. In one sense, the market cannot be overvalued—we derived all the numbers using the standard theory. But we did it based on a declining equity risk premium. So the question moves back a step and becomes one of whether this decline was driven by rational or irrational factors.

An investor might be considered to be acting irrationally if he or she looked at the market's gain in years 2 and 3, assumed that was the norm for stocks and heeded his or her broker's advice to 'fill your boots [with stocks]'. If enough investors act this way, then the market will be forced higher, and the *ex post* equity risk premium must fall. (We assume here no change in growth or interest rate expectations.) A rational approach might be to reason that changes in the structure of the economy have lowered equity risk. One can invent other rational stories, but this is enough for our purpose. The point is that the rational investor is knowingly driving down the equity risk premium because he or she believes it to be excessively generous.

The rational investor will reason that once the equity risk premium gets to the desired level, the market will offer modest returns, albeit better than bonds. So a 4% rise in year 5 needn't be a surprise. An irrational investor will expect the good times to keep rolling, and year 5 will be a nasty shock. The significant feature of a declining equity risk premium is that while it is happening, returns will be boosted, but when the decline stops, expected returns are lower than in the past. And vice versa for a rising equity risk premium.

If we ask investors their expectations for future returns after a sustained fall in the equity risk premium, and they do not suggest substantially lower returns than they have achieved in the recent past, then they must expect the equity risk premium to fall further, or there to be a transformation of economic prospects, or they are being irrational. Let's move on from doing sums to looking at the UK and US markets.

THE 1990S' BULL MARKET

During the 1990s, many markets rose to levels that made them look expensive relative to traditional valuation measures, such as the dividend yield or PER. Using the constant-growth DDM, we can calculate the UK equity risk premium at the start of the twenty-first century as 2.1%:

Dividend yield + dividend growth − long gilt redemption yield = ERP.

$$2.4\% + (1.5\% + 2.9\%) - 4.6\% = 2.1\%.$$

The numbers were derived in the following manner. The dividend yield is simply the yield on the All-Share Index at the start of 2000, increased by 10% (to estimate the year's dividend). The long-run real growth rate of dividends has been below the growth rate of the economy and somewhere between 1.5% to 2% p.a., depending on the measurement period. We have assumed 1.5%. We have estimated future inflation by subtracting the real yield on the longest dated index-linked stock from the flat yield on 2.5% consols. We have taken the redemption yield on the longest dated conventional gilt as a measure of redemption yield. Because of a shortage of stock at the long end of the gilt market relative to investing institutions' appetite, it can be argued that the rate used is too low. If we raise it by 1%, then the equity risk premium falls to 1.1%.

A similar exercise carried out for the US provides similar results. However, long-run inflation has to be estimated in a different manner, as we do not believe that Treasury Inflation Protected Securities provide a true indication of expected real yield. For the US, we estimate the equity risk premium as follows: we have taken the S&P 500 dividend yield at the start of 2000 and increased it by 5%. The redemption yield of 30-year Treasury bonds was 6.2% at the start of 2000. We assume a real rate of interest of 3%, and then deduct this from the redemption yield to derive our inflation estimate. Dividend growth is forecast to be 2%, approximately the historical real rate of growth, plus our inflation estimate. The equity risk premium is therefore 0%:

Dividend yield + dividend growth – long bond redemption yield = ERP.

$$1\% + (2\% + 3.2\%) - 6.2\% = 0\%.$$

The expected equity risk premiums for the UK and the US at the start of 2000 were low by the standards of the twentieth century. We must assume that either investors were willing to accept a lower equity risk premium, or that they had different forecasts for the prospects for the markets than assumed above, or they were acting irrationally. We will work our way through these possibilities, beginning with the rational decline in the equity risk premium based on short-run factors.

The Good News Years

Many market commentators focus on long-term averages of valuation measures, but what is noticeable is how little time such series usually spend at their average values. Two aspects of any investment should be noted. The first relates to the economic environment in which the investment is made, while the second relates to whether too much is being paid given the economic prospects. It appears that most investors focus more on the business conditions risk than the price risk. The market appears overvalued by the usual indicators during periods of good business conditions, and undervalued in bad conditions. Alternatively, if you believe the market is always correctly priced, you can argue that risk aversion is low during a period of good economic conditions and vice versa.

The conditions for much of the 1990s were extraordinarily favourable. In terms of global politics, there was only one super power, the US Democrat President Clinton took no actions that threatened, or seemed likely to threaten, US business, and the financial markets respected Federal Reserve Chairman Greenspan. In the UK, the Labour Party transformed itself, and the markets lost their fear of Labour governments. At the end of the 1990s, the US's growth phase of the economic cycle was one of the longest on record. Moreover, for most of the 1990s, economic forecasts typically were for continued growth. Inflation did not appear to be a significant problem in the US or the UK, and the Labour chancellor appeared tougher on inflation than his predecessors. His first action was to transfer the power to set interest rates to the Bank of England.

Since the economic background we have described is so favourable to equity investors, it would be surprising if the equity risk premium was not at the low end of its range. However, to justify the actual number probably requires more than just short-term factors. Accordingly, we turn to examine long-term factors.

Good News Forever?

Investors may have assumed a much higher earnings/dividend growth rate than we have, thereby generating a higher equity risk premium. This might have been based on three arguments: (i) economic management has greatly improved; (ii) the nature of the business cycle has changed; and (iii) new paradigm economics. All these arguments can be overstated. In what follows we will discuss the US as the arguments have been made most forcefully there, the valuations are higher in the US than in the UK, and whatever happens in the US affects the rest of us.

It is very hard to know how to assess a claim of improved management of the economy. There has been a shift towards anti-inflation policies in all the major economies. This change in policy objective has encouraged the markets. But whether new problems—domestic or international—would be well handled is unclear. The Japanese, for example, didn't have much success in restarting their economy after it went into recession, and the East Asian crisis of 1997 does not appear to have been handled well. Stiglitz (2000, p. 58), former Chief Economist and Vice President of the World Bank, has recently written about the IMF's mishandling of the crisis. He argued that the IMF's policies undermined the region's social fabric, and with regard to its economic achievements: 'All the IMF did was make East Asia's recession deeper, longer, and harder.' He is similarly critical of the support Russia received on its transition to a market economy.

Some of the good news discussed earlier might eventually be reappraised. For example, whether the Fed has done a good job will depend partly on whether you view the US market as hopelessly overvalued. If it is, you might expect a crash at some stage, and stockmarket crashes have usually been followed by recessions. If this outcome occurs, the Fed will almost certainly be blamed for mismanaging the economy, in particular mismanaging asset price inflation.

Many investors have claimed that the economic cycle has become more stable. One of the arguments for this is better management of the economy. Based on the points above, this is far from compelling. Let's look at some other claims and some counter arguments (this list is based on Zarnowitz, 1999, pp. 70–1).

- *The US economy is more stable because of downsizing.* This seems unlikely because there is nothing unusual about layoffs and reorganization during economic cycles. Also, if the downsizers started to grow, would they become upsizers and destablize the economy?
- *Technological breakthroughs in computer hardware and software will lead to greater economic stability.* It is unclear why this technological change should have effects that previous technological change hasn't.
- *Inventory control has greatly improved, which will lessen the impact of inventory changes on the economy.* Swings in inventory levels have been one of the major causes of economic cycles. Just-in-time manufacturing has reduced inventory levels relative to sales, so this argument seems correct. However, inventories are still large enough to cause problems.
- *Services are a more important component of the economy than in the past, and are more stable than the manufacturing sector.* But in the recessions at the start of the 1980s and the start of the 1990s, business and consumer services declined, whereas previously only their growth rate had slowed.

- *Deregulation has helped stabilize the economy.* Some has, especially that relating to the savings and loans industry (building societies). Deregulation in airlines, trucking, banking, etc. has probably increased efficiency and made prices more flexible, which should make their output less unstable. But it is unlikely that these changes are sufficient to stabilize the entire economy.
- *Globalization is a force for stabilization.* Perhaps, but it can also be a force for destabilization, as the Asian crisis demonstrated.

There may have been some modest improvement in the cyclical prospects of the US and thence world prospects, but the case for a transformation seems weak. And long expansions may involve risks (Zarnowitz, 1999, p. 88):

> Long business expansions benefit society by raising employment, consumption, productivity, and profitability, but they generate imbalances and are difficult to sustain. The interaction of profits, investment, credit and financial markets is an enduring feature of market economies, which plays a central role in business cycles. The US upswing of the past three years [1996–1998] provides a vivid example of how profits and investments can reinforce each other, especially when combined with an exuberant stock market. Recent events in Asia demonstrate how investment-dominated booms can give way to a protracted stagnation with tendencies toward deflation and underconsumption [Japan] or to severe recessions harking back to the worst depressions of the past [East Asia] . . .

The most aggressive case for a better economic outlook is the 'new paradigm' view. Traditionally, economists have seen a limit to the rate at which the economy can grow set by the availability of resources. With lots of unemployed resources, the economy can grow quickly. Once labour becomes scarce, inflation will become a problem. There is some level of unemployment that marks the boundary between growth with low inflation and growth with high inflation. Once the economy has reached that point, further non-inflationary growth can only come from growth of the labour force (immigrants, more women working) or productivity growth (more output from the same resources). The new paradigm claims that the US economy can now grow at a faster rate than in the past because globalization will keep a lid on inflation, and because information technology has, and will, result in rapid productivity growth. The evidence for this view is the experience of the US in the high-growth/low-inflation 1990s.

Unfortunately, the facts don't really support these claims. Growth at the beginning of the recovery from the trough in 1991 was slower than in recoveries in the 1960s and 1980s (the 1970s were marked by policy blunders). Although growth was fast at the end of the decade, over the eight plus years, the increase in real GDP was lower than typical.

The rate of inflation at the end of the 1990s was, however, much lower than in previous cycles at a similar stage. A number of reasons have been put forward to explain this. Globalization doesn't seem to be an explanation. The UK has been more open to foreign competition than the US is ever likely to be. Yet, over long periods, the UK has had much higher inflation than the US. Global competition doesn't put a lid on prices. (For a fuller analysis, see Krugman, 1997.) Old paradigm economics can account for a large part of the lower than expected inflation. For example, one part of the explanation for lower inflation is oil prices (see Carruth et al., 1998). In 1998, the real price of oil fell at one point to one-half the real oil price in the 1950s, or one-fifth the real oil price at the start of the 1980s. On past form, the rise in oil prices in 1999 should be pushing up prices in 2000.

Rapid productivity growth, generated by computers and the Internet, is the second leg of the new paradigm. The problem is that it is not obvious why computers and the Internet should have such a dramatic effect. Until the end of 1995, the sceptics had the better of the argument, summed up in Solow's paradox: 'We can see the computer age everywhere except in the productivity statistics.' But since the last quarter of 1995, the productivity figures have been coming in somewhat higher than for the preceding 20+ years. So, is there a golden age in the making? Probably not.

Gordon (2000) estimates the growth in non-farm private business output to have been 2.82% p.a. over the period 1995:4–1999:4 (i.e. fourth quarter to fourth quarter) but only 1.47% p.a. over the period 1972:2–1995:4. Strong cyclical factors were at work in the late 1990s, and Gordon attributes 0.54% of the 1.35% excess over the previous trend to these cyclical factors (which are transitory). That leaves 0.81% increase in trend. This is a significant increase. Unfortunately, Gordon finds that the entire increase comes from the durables sector. There is no trend increase in the other 88% of the economy.

In other words, the US is getting better at making computers and other durables, but it is not clear that the rest of the economy is gaining. That isn't necessarily surprising. Computers have been around for half a century. Many of the easy applications of computers have been made, and computers face diminishing returns in many areas. For example, the great advantage of word-processing over typing is that mistakes can easily be corrected and reformatting of a document will automatically occur even if 30 lines are replaced by half a line. The computer you use now may be 100 times more powerful than the one you used 10 years ago, but you probably don't type a letter any faster.

Of course, the full effect of the Internet has yet to be felt. But is the Internet a great invention? Gordon bravely, or foolishly, takes a stab at what the great inventions of the last 140 years have been. He suggests five clusters:

- electricity, including both electric light and electric motors;
- the internal combustion engine, which made possible personal cars, motor transport and airlines;
- petroleum, natural gas and related chemical processes;
- communication technologies—the telegraph, telephone, radio, television, etc;
- running water, indoor plumbing and urban sanitation infrastructure.

The Internet doesn't seem as revolutionary as those clusters. Much of the information available on the Net is as easily available elsewhere, a lot of material simply duplicates existing material without displacing it, and a lot of business on the Net is personal business done by employees during office hours. While the Internet will have some productivity-enhancing effects, it seems unlikely that it is as revolutionary as the great inventions of the past, which led to fast productivity growth.

Rationality, Irrationality and Pretty Girls

We have now reviewed some arguments for assuming that the economy is less risky than before, or has better growth prospects. We are on the sceptical side, but there are some very bright people who wouldn't agree with any of what we have argued. They would argue that the rules of economics have been rewritten, while we think they may have been recalibrated to a limited degree. Who is right matters in the real world, but not for the purposes of this book. Here, our intention is solely to illustrate the complex issues that have to be tackled. In fact, they are so complex, and one can have so little confidence that one is right, that efficient market arguments for the pricing of asset classes that rely on arbitrage seem simply absurd. Who truly knows the fair market value?

If you now refer back to the final paragraph of the section 'The 1990s' Bull Market' (p. 494), you may feel that the possibility that investors were acting irrationally must be given some weight. The gist of this and the last chapter is that the US and UK markets appear overvalued on the basis of many traditional measures. However, the required equity risk premium varies over time. With good economic circumstances, we should expect the market to look expensive compared with its average valuation, because investors will require a lower return. However, some investors have such optimistic economic views, and the equity risk premium is so low, that we find it hard not to believe that the markets are not somewhat overvalued. If there is a recession or higher inflation, the equity markets will be very overvalued. That's the easy part; here's the problem: whose view should the institutional investor bet on? Keynes ([1936] 1961, p. 156) stated the problem many years ago:

> . . . professional investment may be likened to those newspaper competitions in which the competitors have to pick out the six prettiest faces from a hundred photographs, the prize being awarded to the competitor whose choice most nearly corresponds to the average preferences of the competitors as a whole: so that each competitor has to pick, not those faces which he himself finds prettiest, but those which he thinks likeliest to catch the fancy of the other competitors, all of whom are looking at the problem from the same point of view. It is not a case of choosing those which, to the best of one's judgment, are really the prettiest, nor even those which average opinion genuinely thinks the prettiest. We have reached the third degree where we devote our intelligences to anticipating what average opinion expects the average opinion to be. And there are some, I believe, who practise the fourth, fifth and higher degrees.

ESTIMATING THE EFFICIENT FRONTIER

In this and the previous chapter, we have looked at various tools of tactical asset allocation. Some of the tools produce total return forecasts, while others offer some indication of relative attraction. To bring everything together, and choose our overall tactical asset allocation, we can use quantitative or qualitative approaches. Decisions can be made for all asset classes simultaneously or for groups of assets. The first approach would determine the complete bond, equity, cash, property, etc. allocation decision for both international and domestic assets. Alternatively, the problem can be treated in stages, for example by allocating domestic assets (e.g. gilts v. equities) as one decision, international assets (e.g. US equities v. Japanese) as another, and finally deciding the weights for domestic versus international assets.

We will discuss first a quantitative approach that can consider all assets simultaneously, and then a two-stage approach mixing quantitative and qualitative factors.

The Efficient Frontier Calculation

If investors have a set of total return forecasts, they can simply pick the markets with the highest returns. If, however, we recall the analysis of Chapter 2, we realize that this would be an inefficient approach. It would not achieve the best blend of risk and return because it ignores the correlation of returns between markets. The efficient frontier traces out portfolios that offer the best return for a given level of risk and the least risk for a given return. In Chapter 2, we developed a graphical analysis of the efficient frontier. In this chapter, we discuss this approach in practice. The process is usually called optimization, and the computer software that does the calculations is called an optimizer.

In our earlier discussion of Markowitz optimization we noted the large number of estimates required to construct a share portfolio. However, in asset allocation work, the numbers involved are much smaller, and many investors undertake full Markowitz optimization.

To calculate a Markowitz efficient frontier, an investor needs to know the expected returns for all assets being considered, their variances and the correlation between their returns. The efficient frontier is then generated by a programming routine called quadratic programming, although there are approximate ratio methods as well, for example that developed by Elton et al. (1978). Fortunately, numerous commercial software products will do the calculations.

An example of a commercial optimizer is Sharpe's asset allocation tools (AATs) (Sharpe, 1985). This requires six inputs—upper and lower bounds for each asset's proportion in the portfolio, expected return forecasts, standard deviation of returns, correlation of the returns of each asset with every other asset, the risk tolerance of the investor, and transaction costs. Investors can take historical values from databases provided with the AAT for the expected returns, standard deviations and correlations, or insert their own estimates. It is common for investors to provide forecasts of returns but to accept historical standard deviations and correlations. Investors who believe that historical volatilities and correlations will not hold in the future should insert their own estimates. An investor's risk tolerance is expressed as a number from 0 to 100 that indicates the added risk an investor will accept to increase expected return by 1%. The risk tolerance can be roughly interpreted as the percentage of a portfolio that an investor would choose to have in equities if the only choice was equities versus Treasury bills, i.e. a score of 70 indicates a 70/30 split.

Given all the required information, the program will crunch out either a single optimization, i.e. the portfolio that offers the highest utility for a particular risk tolerance, or multiple optimizations, i.e. portfolios for a range of risk tolerances. The latter is an especially useful feature. The estimation of risk tolerance is difficult, and investors may find that quite large changes in their risk tolerance will not greatly affect the composition of the optimal portfolio. Most investors would find this reassuring. If modest changes in risk tolerance lead to large changes in portfolio composition, then investors know that long and hard thought about risk tolerance is required. Investors can also easily check to see how changes in forecast values lead to changes in the optimal portfolio.

The AAT handles risk by calculating positive and negative utilities. Positive expected returns generate positive utility, and this is reduced by the negative utility of transaction costs and the negative utility of risk. This negative utility is measured by dividing the variance of the expected return by the risk tolerance. For example, for an investor with a risk tolerance of 80, a portfolio with an expected return of 20%, a variance of 240 and transaction costs of 1%:

Contribution to utility:	
Expected return	+20%
Decrements from utility:	
Risk penalty (240/80)	–3%
Transaction costs	–1%
Portfolio net utility	+16%

This description of the AAT is rather dated, and the product may well have changed since Sharpe described it, but it gives an idea of what is available. Professional investors will almost certainly have some form of optimizer software available, and hands-on experience is recommended. Students and interested non-professionals should consider the software and manual by Elton et al. (1998). This costs about £25, and contains an optimizer as well as programs for CAPM, options and futures valuation, bond valuation, etc.

PROBLEMS WITH OPTIMIZERS

In Chapter 2, we examined the basis of the efficient frontier; in this chapter, we have seen that optimizers are readily available and provide a convenient means of seeing the effect of changing return and variance assumptions, changing attitudes to risk, and so on. Optimizers apparently efficiently utilize a lot of relevant information, and can recalculate rapidly as conditions change. And yet many fund managers do not calculate efficient frontiers. Why? Optimizers present both practical and conceptual problems.

Many fund managers resist any quantitative product because they fear they lack the necessary skills and, possibly, because they think quantitative products will eventually make them redundant. In the past, the senior people who sat on investment committees tended to lose power to the new process and to new people. This is probably less of a problem nowadays, as knowledge of quantitative techniques has grown.

An optimizer requires information that a fund manager may not normally produce. For example, many managers resist producing expected returns. They often reason in a series of paired comparisons. They might decide that UK equities are cheap relative to gilts based on a yield ratio or other valuation measure. What will equities return? Well, more than gilts. But what exact return? 'Don't know' is likely to be the answer. Or recall the Japanese market when the index was at its peak a decade ago. Many managers felt happy to substantially underweight Japan because it seemed overvalued. How many would have forecast an expected return of minus 50%? They might have believed that was the extent of the overvaluation, but many, if forced to give a quantitative forecast, would probably have indicated a return of zero to –10%. Fund managers simply don't say they expect a market to halve in value. Yet, when not forced to be specific on returns, many probably found it easier to underweight Japan to a degree that came close to reflecting their view on valuation. Again, if you look at UK managers' US equity market weights over the past few years, you will see that they must have been assuming something terrible for the US market. But if you read their comments on markets, you will get a less extreme view. In this case, actions speak louder than words.

Of course, fund managers can always be forced to produce return forecasts, so lack of data is seldom a critical problem; but if managers reason and act in the way described, then an optimizer's output may not truly reflect their views. Bringing together the data required by the optimizer and the thought process of a manager can be a difficult, although not impossible, task.

A much more serious problem is what an optimizer does with the data it is given. Optimizers are often derided for producing obvious or silly results. For example, you don't need an optimizer to tell you to invest in cash for a low-risk portfolio. On the other hand, the optimizer might tell you to invest 25% of your high-risk portfolio in Sweden. Would that be a sensible allocation? The usual reason that an optimizer produces strange results is that it will significantly overweight assets with large expected returns, negative correlation of returns with other assets and small variances. Yet, these assets are likely to be the ones that have the largest errors in their estimates. If an asset looks too good to be true, it probably is. Optimizers are, in effect, estimation error maximizers (Michaud, 1989). The error-estimation properties of optimizers mean that an 'optimal' portfolio's risk is likely to be understated. The problem may seem to be one of poor forecasts, but it is more general than that. Simple random errors in estimation will always pose a problem because the program, in effect, goes looking for certain types of errors.

Some attempts have been made to determine which errors in estimates are the most damaging. The typical finding is that mean-variance portfolios are most sensitive to errors in means, then errors in variances, and finally errors in covariances. For example, Chopra and Ziemba (1993) found that at moderate risk levels, errors in means were 11 times as damaging as errors in variances, and 23 times as damaging as errors in covariances. At high-risk levels, the corresponding figures were 21 and 57.

Another problem with optimizers is that the optimizations are often highly unstable in the sense that small changes in assumptions lead to quite different solutions. Again, because of errors in inputs, the unique solution produced by the optimizer is better seen as highlighting an area on the efficient frontier within which the optimal portfolio may lie. Unfortunately, even quite close points on the efficient frontier can imply quite different combinations of assets. This is a problem because it reduces users' faith in the process, and it will mean that small changes in estimates may involve substantial portfolio changes. In such cases, it may make more sense to have a 'near' optimal portfolio rather than blindly follow the black box.

Some of the disadvantages of optimizers can be reduced by setting constraints on the size of deviation from index or other benchmark positions (e.g. see Frost and Savarino, 1988; and Chopra, 1993). But with many constraints, one may wonder what exactly the optimizer is left to do, and whether an experienced fund manager would not do as well by eyeballing the problem. One option is to run the optimizer and then add constraints if you don't like the results. The downside of this is that there is a danger that you are just changing the rules to get the answer you want. The upside is that you are responding to the forecast inputs you have least confidence in.

Another approach is to tackle the input estimation problem. Sharpe (1990) claims that for predicting future values, historical data appear to be quite useful for standard deviations and correlations but virtually useless for expected returns. Also, there is a well-known tendency for future risks and correlations to be more like those of the recent past than like those of the distant past. Along with the findings that errors in returns are the most important input error, this suggests that we might accept historical numbers as our forecasts for standard deviations and correlations, but for the last 20 years, say, rather than since records began. However, although we have focused on returns here, there has been work on improving correlation estimates. For example, Erb et al. (1994) find the correlations of returns between countries are higher during recessions that during growth periods, and lower when countries' business cycles are out of phase.

An interesting approach to the problem of forecasting returns has been to set all forecast returns to zero, or some other uniform return, or to 'shrink' returns. The latter approach uses Stein estimators. The idea is that similar objects should behave in a similar way. Thus, over the years, European equity markets might be expected to produce similar returns. One way of reflecting this would be to average your forecast return for a country with your forecast for all European countries, and use this number in the optimizer. Full shrinkage would be just to use the European average for each European country. Chopra et al. (1993) tested this approach on 16 international indexes, and found that relative to an unadjusted portfolio, the Stein portfolio had higher returns, lower risk and less turnover.

If we forecast returns in a common currency, this implies a currency forecast. But what if you have adopted a passive currency approach because you can't forecast currencies? One approach might be to simply assume current exchange rates will remain unchanged. Another might be to use consensus forecasts. Or you might average these two approaches. Although this sounds crude, the argument and evidence of the previous paragraph might be thought to be supportive.

Blending Quantitative and Subjective Analysis

More investment managers use an optimizer for tactical asset allocation than for constructing a share portfolio. But most don't use an optimizer even for asset allocation. A non-optimizer approach can be quantitative or largely subjective. We will discuss a non-optimizer approach taking a two-stage approach. An investor might look at his or her intradomestic tactical asset allocation and separately at the intra-international, and then as another decision look at the domestic/international weight.

We have reviewed a number of tactical asset allocation tools that might be used to help determine the domestic allocation. The same considerations as were discussed in share portfolio construction apply—to the extent that tactical asset allocation tools have some predictive value, and are not perfectly correlated, it is worth using several tools. Most investors use a combination of business cycle analysis and valuation measures. Some managers use the same measures consistently, whereas others look at a variety of indicators and subjectively combine them, giving different measures prominence at different times. Some tools involve estimating a total return (e.g. the equity risk premium) whereas others provide only a relative qualitative valuation (e.g. the yield ratio). Managers who use the same measures consistently, especially a measure such as the equity risk premium, are more likely to follow a quantitative rule for relating the degree of over- or underweighting of an asset class to its degree of mispricing.

Devising a sensible international equity mix is harder than devising a sensible domestic equity/bonds/cash mix. There is more of an ad hoc juggling of rules of thumb feel about the process. As with domestic assets, most investors use a variety of inputs. These include elements of national business cycle anticipation, such as the level and direction of inflation and interest rates, profits momentum and expected economic policy. Valuation measures may consist of domestic comparisons—local equities versus local bonds—or intermarket comparisons, which may be based on absolute measures, such as high-dividend yields, low

PERs or relative measures, such as country X's dividend yield relative to its own history compared with country Y's dividend yield relative to its own history. Less frequently used are technical measures and liquidity factors.

The above factors may be pulled together in a formal or informal manner. An in-between approach is to produce some form of checklist such as that shown in Table 24.3 (not all of the factors shown would be included, because many measure much the same thing). Each factor may be given a cheap or dear response or a rating on a five-point scale for each country. Countries can then be rated by either the number of cheap responses or the number of points awarded. A slightly more complex approach is to give each valuation measure a different weight.

TABLE 24.3   Factors involved in rating international markets

Factor	Favourable relationship
Earnings per share growth	Fast
Earnings surprises	Positive
PER	Low
PER relative to own history	Low
Yield	High
Yield relative to own history	High
Bond yield/dividend yield ratio	Low relative to own history
Bond yield relative to earnings yield	Low relative to own history
Trend in interest and bond yields	Down
Yield relative to world yield	High relative to history
PER relative to world PER	Low relative to history
Equity risk premium	High
Stage in economic cycle	Near end of recession; early growth
Long-term growth potential	High
Scenario forecasting	Growth and low inflation
Politics	Lack of uncertainty; promarket government

The tools used by a manager for making intradomestic allocation and intra-international allocation may differ. For example, total returns may be calculated for the domestic market and measures of relative value used in the international markets. One way of linking the two sets of analyses is to evaluate the UK equity market in the same way as the international equity markets have been. Then, after deciding whether UK equities are relatively cheap or dear, and after allowance for currency changes, a decision can be made on the weighting of domestic and international assets.

CONCLUDING COMMENTS

In this and the previous chapter, we have examined various methods of making tactical asset allocation decisions. We examined business cycle and scenario approaches, absolute valuation methods (dividend yield, PER, book value), relative valuation methods (yield gap, gilt/equity yield ratio, earnings/yield relative to gilt yield, equity yield and index-linked yield difference). We then looked at various ways of using the equity risk premium, and some of the associated problems.

We concluded by looking at the benefits and costs of using Markowitz optimization, as well as more subjective ways of constructing a portfolio.

This book is not a financial tip sheet, but a few words on the market level in mid-2000, drawing on a number of chapters, seem appropriate. At the start of 2000, strategists were mildly bullish, with some exceptions—one forecaster expected the FTSE 100 to end the year at around 8800. A forecast of 8800 required the equity risk premium to continue shrinking from already low levels.

In 1999 and 2000, many analysts were quoted to the effect that many of the new economy stocks could not be valued by the old methods. What they meant was that if you valued these stocks by a dividend discount model, the net present value of a string of losses doesn't come to much. For example, Lastminute.com is not a substantial business—it makes losses. Since old-fashioned mail order is not a particularly attractive business, and neither is being a travel agent, it is not obvious why an electronic version will be. What is the value of a deeply out-of-the-money option on the travel/entertainment booking industry worth? One should probably start at zero and try to argue up.

Vodaphone, on the other hand, is clearly a substantial business. But should it be valued at one-seventh of the entire UK stockmarket? It is an international business and therefore not constrained by the size of the UK economy. But many UK firms are international businesses, and Vodaphone is not the only UK telecommunications firm. Foreign firms can compete in the UK too. So, in crude terms, do you think this one firm will produce one-seventh of UK output, or even stockmarket quoted output? It is not obvious why it should be bigger than, say, an oil giant. On this basis, you might start thinking of Vodaphone at around half its current value. Notice that this alone implies a fall in the total market of 7%. Of course, if you believe the market is too high and will fall, Vodaphone would fall further. This would suggest that in the next year or two, Vodaphone might trade at 35–50% of its peak share price of about £4, i.e., £2 to £1.40. Even at £1.40 it would be on a PER about 40 for 2001.

In terms of the contrarian analysis of Chapter 15, we might argue that mid-2000 is a market peak. Traditional valuation standards have been ditched for both individual stocks and the market as a whole. That valuations should be higher than average is not disputed. Times have been good, and risk aversion will be low. Moreover, one can argue that the world economy will grow faster than it has in the past and that the required equity risk premium is lower than most investors believe. But one can easily argue that there has been very little long-term change in economic prospects and, even if there has been, a cyclical slowdown is overdue in the US. If such a slowdown occurs, investor risk aversion will rise. The question that must be answered is: will the news get better or worse? If you think the latter, you should be aware of how much above past valuation averages the market is. The equity risk premium is so low in the US and UK, that even a move back to the 2%+ of the nineteenth century would imply a substantial fall. We calculated earlier that the UK equity risk premium at the start of 2000 was between 1–2%. If it were to rise by 1%, this would require the market to fall by sufficient to push the dividend yield up by 1% (from 2.4% to 3.4%). At the start of 2000, the FTSE All-Share was about 6900, so the market would fall to 4870. Will this happen? Who knows?

If there isn't a recession, and providing the market doesn't rise, rising profits and dividends will eventually work off the overvaluation. So the market doesn't have to fall. But the market would have to move sideways. Whether the market moves sideways or falls will matter to a derivatives investor. But a long-term investor might be less bothered—either way, cash would outperform shares over the two-year period beginning in 2000. Yet, even if institutional investors reason in this way, most are unlikely to build up cash, because they will play Keynes' pretty girl contest: they will choose not what they think is the best asset allocation, but the asset allocation they think other managers will have. We discuss this further in the next chapter.

25

Fund Managers: Buy, Sell or Hold?

The only big loss for the investment management profession over these years has been the disappearance of the balanced manager. The stylish cafeteria of specialised managers that we see today leads to a mishmash of risks and co-variances that most clients fail to understand.

Peter Bernstein

In this final chapter, we look at some of the factors that go into the hiring and firing of fund managers. We look at investment performance measurement (but only for equities), the ability of fund managers to outperform, and some practical aspects of selecting fund managers.

EVALUATING INVESTMENT PERFORMANCE

To evaluate a manager's investment performance, we have to know the return achieved on the portfolios he or she manages. The total return from a portfolio is calculated (see p. 22) as the capital value of a portfolio at the end of a period less the value of the portfolio at the start of the period plus income received during the period divided by market value at the start of the period. Multiply this by 100 and we have the percentage return. It is important to know how the manager has calculated the income received, and the closing value. In particular, have management fees, administrative fees, custody fees, etc. been deducted? Calculations that exclude such fees tell us something about the manager's ability as an investor. The return after deduction of costs tells us how much the investor will receive.

Calculating a return is easy if there are no cash flows. Most portfolios do have inflows and outflows of money, and there are two ways of calculating a return in this case. Imagine that we are measuring the return of a portfolio over one year; at the start of the year the portfolio is worth £1000 and halfway through the year another £1000 is added. Clearly, the end value of the portfolio should not be compared with the starting value. One way to calculate the return is to use a discounted cash flow approach, in which the average return over the period is obtained by finding the rate that equates the present values of the terminal value and cash inflows and outflows to the initial value. This return is sometimes described as the *money-weighted rate of return*. This method accurately computes the return an investor actually receives. However, the fund manager does not control the timing of the cash flows and clearly the return the manager earns will differ if given additional funds to manage just before or just after a bull market run. A way round this problem is to calculate the *time-weighted rate of return*. To do this, we calculate the return to the portfolio up to a cash flow, then the return from that cash flow to the next, or to the end of the period. We then use these numbers to calculate the geometric mean return for the entire period.

Fund managers keep a record of the performance of the funds they manage. The performance figures may be calculated by the manager or by a firm specializing in performance measurement. However calculated, the manager will aggregate the performance of the funds managed to provide a performance composite figure. A distinction is usually made between discretionary clients, advisory clients, and non-discretionary clients. In the case of a discretionary client, the fund manager manages the fund as he or she sees fit, although the trustees ultimately can control what the manager does. Most institutional funds are managed on a discretionary basis. Although some are on an advisory basis, this is more typical of private client funds. For example, a private client may have an account with a stockbroking firm, and may talk to a private client fund manager from time to time. The manager will provide ideas, but it is up to the client as to whether any action is taken, and the client may initiate transactions. Obviously, the performance of such accounts does not reflect the performance of the fund manager. Some accounts fall into neither category, and are often described as non-discretionary. Here, all transaction ideas come from the manager, but the client must be consulted on each idea. These types of accounts should be excluded from a manager's performance composite.

In the US, the Association for Investment Management and Research (AIMR) has established a set of performance presentation standards. Some of the practices it has tried to stamp out include performance composites that exclude some discretionary accounts; performance composites that intermingle simulated with real portfolio results; and performance composites that eliminate records of terminated accounts. Somewhat similar industry standards apply in the UK.

These types of performance standards make it difficult for new firms to become established. They have no performance record. There are three ways round this. One is to take the results a manager has achieved at another firm. Obviously these will be treated with considerable scepticism, as it will be difficult to establish which accounts the manager actually ran, and the manager's results will be a mixture of his or her own ability, the firm's ability, and the interaction of the manager and the firm. A second way of producing a performance history is to present simulated returns. For example, a new firm may claim that it will select its equities on the basis of momentum. It then produces data that show how well this approach would have worked over the past few years. The results will again be treated with considerable scepticism. What transaction costs are assumed? What allowance was made for some orders not being executable? Why was the particular starting date chosen? And so on. A third way of entering the market without a record is to target the least sophisticated investors. Many unit and investment trusts are launched by managers with no record in the area of the product being launched. After a period, a record for these products can be used in the institutional market.

Theory-Based Performance Measurement

So far, we have discussed returns, but in order to properly judge performance, we also need to consider the risks involved in achieving the returns. Two measures of risk that we have discussed in other chapters are the standard deviation of returns and beta, which is an estimate of systematic risk. Three well-known risk-adjusted measures of performance are the Sharpe (1966) ratio, the Treynor (1965) ratio, and the Jensen (1969) alpha. We discuss each in turn.

The Sharpe ratio is a reward-to-variability ratio equal to a portfolio's arithmetic mean return in excess of the risk-free interest rate divided by its standard deviation. So, if a manager has an annual arithmetic average return of 15%, the risk-free rate is 5% and the manager's annualized standard deviation is 10%, then the Sharpe ratio is $(15\%-5\%)/(10\%) = 1$. The Sharpe ratio measures return as the excess return over the risk-free rate, and measures risk as total risk. It therefore measures the excess return per unit of total risk. Consequently, the higher the ratio, the better the portfolio performance. Different portfolios can be ranked on the basis of their Sharpe ratios. We can therefore rank funds not only against each other but also to tell whether they have outperformed or underperformed the market on a risk-adjusted basis. A variation of the Sharpe ratio has been introduced by Modigliani and Modigliani (1997). It is usually referred to as M squared (for Modigliani squared). It produces the same results as the Sharpe ratio, but some investors argue that its form is more client-friendly.

Treynor's ratio is a reward-to-volatility ratio. Treynor's measure is similar to Sharpe's, but it distinguishes between total risk and systematic risk. Treynor considered only systematic risk to be relevant, so he divides by the portfolio beta instead of the portfolio standard deviation. The use of systematic risk implies that portfolios are perfectly diversified and that there is no non-systematic risk. Treynor's ratio can be used to rank portfolios.

Jensen's alpha is a differential return measure. If the market returns an excess return over the risk-free rate of 10%, and a fund has a beta of 1.5, then the expected excess return would be 15%. If the fund actually produces 16%, the Jensen alpha is +1%, which indicates superior performance. Jensen's alpha is calculated from a linear regression of a time series of portfolio returns in excess of the risk-free rate against the benchmark's returns in excess of the risk-free rate.

The slope of the regression line is beta and the intercept is alpha. In any regression equation, it is normal to check the statistical significance of estimated parameters. In other words, although alpha may be positive, it may not be statistically significantly different from zero. Because of the high variability of returns data, it will often be the case that positive or negative alphas cannot be said to be statistically significant, even if the manager really does add value or subtract it.

The three measures just discussed are only useful if the CAPM is valid and the true market portfolio is being used. They are subject to Roll's critique (see p. 56) on the appropriateness of the benchmark index. It is possible to construct APT-based risk/return measures, but we will not go into the details because APT doesn't specify the fundamental factors, so any particular APT benchmark is just one of many that could be constructed by varying the factors. Asset pricing theories are so lacking in credibility that using them to evaluate performance seems misguided.

Theory-Free Performance Measurement

Rather than rate managers relative to a theory's view of how they should have performed, most fund managers and clients are interested in performance relative to other ways of managing the fund. There are two ways to make this judgement: by comparison with performance universes (i.e. against other fund managers' records) and by comparison with performance benchmarks (i.e. against an index).

Performance universes are constructed by aggregating the market valuations and the inflows and outflows for a large number of individual portfolios. From this, quarterly time-weighted returns are calculated for the universe as a whole. Averages can be calculated for a number of subdivisions of the universe, for example pension funds and charities, or pension fund managers with more than £xbn under management. Many institutional managers do not invest in property, and the universe of returns can be calculated with or without property. The best known performance universes in the UK are those constructed by the WM Company and by Combined Actuarial Performance Services (CAPS). In the US, Wilshire, Frank Russell, and SEI maintain large performance universes. US performance measurement services have been much keener to subdivide their universes by managers' investment style than have the UK services. Funds that have had their performance measured can be ranked relative to their universe or universe subdivision. The ranking usually takes the form of a percentile ranking, although in the UK, managers normally think in terms of which quartile of performance they are in. The liturgy is that if you can be in the second quartile every year, then your long-term record will be in the first quartile.

It is important that performance-universe data are based on all managers who started and not managers who finished. What does this mean? If a manager loses an account because of bad performance, and this is the most likely reason for losing an account, then the manager no longer puts that account in the performance universe. The past data should be retained in the universe (managers who started basis) and not deleted (managers who finished basis). If they are deleted, then there is an upward bias to the returns. For example, imagine three managers, A, B and C, with returns for the last decade of 0%, 10% and 20%, respectively. If you are B, you are the median manager with the average return. If A gets fired and his or her performance data are removed, you now appear to be a poor manager because you are 5% below the new average of 15%.

Instead of, or in addition to, performance universes, some investors and clients look at performance benchmarks. The usual approach is to define a passive benchmark for the fund being evaluated. The return of the fund and the benchmark are calculated, and the difference between the two returns is attributed to manager decisions on stock selection, market timing and currency and country selection. For a UK equity fund, the normal benchmark would be the FTSE All-Share Index. However, if the manager's investment style is to invest in large-cap growth stocks, the fund might be measured against a benchmark for this investment style.

There are some problems here. Is the style benchmark constructed properly? Does the manager change his or her style? For example, the manager may decide to invest in stocks that are not consistent with his or her investment style. If a growth manager anticipates growth stocks underperforming value stocks, and starts investing in value stocks, then against his or her benchmark, the manager will appear to be a good stock-picker. However, the manager has actually shown style timing abilities. Tightly specified benchmarks may encourage the manager to index relative to the benchmark. Finally, passive benchmarks incur no transaction costs and are always fully invested. A manager suffers commission costs, bid–ask spread, and price impact caused by dealing, and usually will hold some cash to facilitate transactions or meet outflows.

In addition, there is a conceptual problem. Assume small-cap and earnings surprises are both successful styles and that is the basis of your share selection. Imagine that each style beats the FTSE All-Share by 2% p.a. in alternate years (odd-numbered years for small-cap and even-numbered years for surprises) and matches the index in the other. It is common to have a small-cap benchmark but not an earnings surprise benchmark. So, the benchmark comparison would imply that in even-numbered years, you outperformed by 2%, and in odd-numbered years you performed in line. Why does one style's excess return get deducted, and not the other's? Clearly, this type of performance measurement is arbitrary and should be treated with some scepticism.

There are a number of other approaches to performance measurement, but as they all have problems of one kind and another, and the most widely used approaches have been covered, we will move on to attribution analysis.

Attribution Analysis

Attribution analysis attempts to show why a manager has either under- or outperformed a benchmark. There are a number of ways of tackling this, but a common one is to determine how much of any difference was the result of asset allocation, and how much security selection. The easiest way to discuss attribution analysis is by means of an example.

Consider the data in Table 25.1. Assume that the investor can only invest in equities, bonds or cash, and that a benchmark has been established that involves 75% of the portfolio being invested in equities, 20% in bonds and 5% in cash. For a particular period, the returns on the appropriate benchmark indexes were 9%, 11% and 6%, respectively. In the rest of Table 25.1, we see how the manager has invested the fund, and the excess allocations to each market and the excess returns achieved within each market. To calculate the return achieved by the portfolio and the return achieved by the benchmark, we simply have to multiply the appropriate weights and returns. Thus the portfolio return is:

$$\text{Portfolio return} = (0.8 \times 10\%) + (0.15 \times 10\%) + (0.05 \times 6\%) = 9.8\%$$

and the benchmark return is:

$$\text{Benchmark return} = (0.75 \times 9\%) + (0.20 \times 11\%) + (0.05 \times 6\%) = 9.25\%.$$

TABLE 25.1   Attribution analysis

Asset class	Investment weights			Returns		
	Actual	Benchmark	Excess	Actual (%)	Benchmark (%)	Excess (%)
Equities	0.80	0.75	0.05	10	9	1
Bonds	0.15	0.20	−0.05	10	11	−1
Cash	0.05	0.05	0.00	6	6	0

In this example, the manager has outperformed the benchmark. But how? To calculate the effect of asset allocation, we have to look at each asset category and relate the manager's degree of over- or underweighting of that class to the relative performance of that class. So, for example, the benchmark return is 9.25%, but benchmark return on equities was only 9%. The relative performance of this category was poor and the manager overweighted it by 5%. The manager's allocation decision therefore lost 0.25% on 5% of the fund. Reasoning in a similar manner for each asset class, we can work out the overall contribution of asset allocation, i.e.

$$[0.05 \times (9\% - 9.25\%)] + [-0.05 \times (11\% - 9.25\%)] + [0 \times (6\% - 9.25\%)] = -0.1\%$$

so in this case, the manager lost 0.1% in performance due to his or her asset allocation decisions. The amount is so modest because there is only a small deviation from the benchmark asset classes, and the difference in returns of the two classes where there was a deviation was small.

The effect of individual security selection is the difference between the actual returns and the benchmark return on a particular asset class times the weight of that asset class in the portfolio. Thus for Table 25.1:

$$[0.80 \times (10\% - 9\%)] + [0.15 \times (10\% - 11\%)] + [0.05 \times (6\% - 6\%)] = 0.65\%.$$

In this example, superior security selection has added 0.65% to the portfolio. If we now bring together the effect of share selection and asset allocation, we can calculate the total value added (or subtracted) by the manager, i.e.

$$\text{Value added} = (0.65) + (-0.1\%) = 0.55\%.$$

As a quick check, we add 0.55% to the benchmark return of 9.25% and this is indeed the 9.8% return we calculated for the portfolio.

This sort of calculation can be extended to incorporate more assets or applied to slightly different problems, such as the effect of sector strategy within the equity market. There are, however, limitations with this type of analysis. For example, no allowance for risk has been made—maybe the equities chosen were simply riskier. Also, although we calculated that the manager had superior security selection skill, notice that the manager underperformed the benchmark on bonds and outperformed on equities. The overall return to security selection came not from uniform security selection skills but skill in the biggest asset class in the portfolio.

DO SUPERIOR MANAGERS EXIST?

If the market consists mainly of professionals competing against each other, then they cannot all beat the index. Indeed, after allowing for costs, they must on average do a little worse than the index. The way to tell if some managers are winning is to look for consistency of performance—or persistence as it is called in the professional literature. However, given the difficulties in achieving meaningful performance measurement, how much weight you should place on the following material is debatable.

Casual inspection of CAPS's data of the number of pension fund managers who have been in the top half of the performance league over a five-year period suggests there isn't persistence. A manager could appear in the top half every year for four years, three years, and so on, down to no years. If there are no superior managers, then the distribution of managers in each of the six categories will be the same as the number of heads observed if a coin is flipped five times. The distributions are very similar.

Brown et al. (1997) studied UK pension fund managers' performance, and provided a more formal analysis. They used risk-adjusted returns, ranked the funds by performance, and then split them into quartiles. For each two-year period, the number of funds that remained in the same quartile both in the first and second years of the period, or moved from one quartile in year one to a different quartile in year two, were recorded. They felt the study provided limited evidence of persistence. For example, pension funds that display top-quartile performance in one period have a higher probability then we would expect by chance of sustaining top-quartile performance in the next period.

Blake et al. (1999), in the study discussed on p. 443, found some evidence of trivial persistence amongst UK pension funds. They found the top quartile of funds in one year generated an average superior return of 0.4% in the following year compared with the bottom quartile. But there was no persistence over three years.

In the US, the evidence is mixed. For example, Lakonishok et al. (1992) found that relative performance from year to year was not consistent, but over two-year and especially three-year periods, there did appear to be some consistency of performance. However, the data used could have a bias towards finding consistency, and the expected returns even for the good managers, net of fees, were below the S&P 500.

Malkiel (1995) studied pooled funds in the US market over the period 1971–91. He looked at all US general equity mutual funds. He found no evidence that mutual funds could, on average, beat the market. He did find, however, that there was some consistency of good and bad performance in the 1970s. If you bought a past winner, the odds were in your favour that you would do well in the next period. During the 1980s, there was no evidence of consistency in performance—indeed, in the late 1980s, winners did especially poorly. Malkiel felt that other studies suffered from statistical flaws (in particular, survivorship bias) and those that had found persistence had sampled from the short period when he had found evidence of persistence of performance, but not from the period when he hadn't found it.

In his study, Malkiel ignored front-end fees (i.e. the initial sales charge). But if retail investors adopted a strategy of buying recent winners, and switching when-ever a winner went 'cold', these costs would be incurred, which would offset performance gains. These costs could be avoided by taking a long-term view, for example by buying the 20 funds that were best over the period 1970–80, and holding them over the period 1980–90. In the first period, the best funds beat the average fund by over 9%, but in the second period—the period of investment—they underperformed the average fund by 0.69%. The average fund, in turn, underperformed the market by 2%.

Financial advisers claim to pick the best of the best, the most consistent of the winners. Malkiel tested this by examining a publicly available version of this—*Forbes* magazine's 'Honor Roll Funds'. They didn't outperform over the long run. Malkiel's advice was that most investors would be better off looking for a low-cost index fund rather than trying to find 'hot' managers.

In another study of US mutual funds, Kahn and Rudd (1995) found persis-tence of returns only for fixed-income funds. Unfortunately, this persistence did not overcome the average underperformance of fixed-income funds resulting from fees and expenses. Kahn and Rudd used style analysis to separate fund total returns into style and selection components. They warn that studies that don't allow for styles can find persistence where none exists.

Other studies reach different conclusions. Elton et al. (1996) used style ana-lysis when looking for performance persistence in US mutual funds. They used a four-index model, which is composed of the S&P index, a size index, a bond index, and a growth versus value stocks index. They found that there was persistence of performance. Using modern portfolio theory techniques to allocate capital among funds, they constructed a portfolio of funds based on prior data that significantly outperformed a rule based on past rank alone and that produced a positive risk-adjusted excess return. But was their four-index model a good benchmark?

In a comprehensive study of US mutual fund managers, Carhart (1997) found evidence of persistence. Good and bad performance, at least for the extreme deciles, persisted for four years after being ranked. If true, this is good news for some managers, but not necessarily for potential clients. If it takes a couple of years to decide that a fund manager is good, then that leaves only a couple of years of modestly superior performance.

So are there good fund managers? Possibly, but not many. The current state of performance measurement makes it difficult to reach a conclusion.

SELECTING AN INVESTMENT MANAGER

A distinction is often made between multi-asset management and specialist management. Multi-asset management means that one manager manages several asset classes, whereas specialist management means that a manager manages only one asset class. An example of specialist management would be a fund that has a manager managing solely Japanese equities. The standard form of multi-asset management in the UK has been balanced management. This means a manager manages the full range of assets held in a fund. Multi-asset management incorporates balanced management, but would cover the case, for example, where a manager manages all bonds, cash and UK equities, while another specialist manager manages international equities. These terms should be viewed as descriptions of roles a fund requires the managers to adopt, rather than descriptions of the managers themselves. A manager may well be a balanced manager for some accounts, and a specialist manager on other accounts. However a fund arranges the management of its assets, it may employ several managers in the same role. For example, a small fund might have two balanced managers and a large fund perhaps four. Each would manage a separate slice of the fund.

In a 1999 survey, to which 300 of the 1000 largest UK pension schemes responded, Phillips and Drew found that 80% of schemes used multi-asset management although there was a strong trend towards using a combination of multi-asset managers and specialists with higher performance targets (Treynor, 1999). Given that a multi-asset manager makes both intra- and intermarket decisions, it is perhaps not surprising that most have their performance evaluated on the universe basis. Three-quarters of multi-asset management funds set CAPS/WM Company benchmarks, whereas a quarter set customized benchmarks. An unfortunate consequence of this is that fund managers pay more attention to the median asset allocation of the CAPS/WM Company universe than they do to the liability structure of the fund. However, this is a problem caused by the trustees, rather than the fund managers. Phillips and Drew found that 81% of specialist mandates were measured against the relevant market index.

If trustees make exclusive use of specialists managers, then they have to determine the strategic and tactical asset allocation. They can, of course, hire a specialist tactical asset allocation manager. Of the 20% of respondents in the Phillips and Drew survey that used specialist management exclusively, only 13% hired separate tactical asset-allocation managers. Two-thirds of the funds seem to ignore tactical asset-allocation decisions altogether.

Since few consistently superior fund managers appear to exist, how are investment managers, whether balanced, specialist or whatever, selected in practice? The typical process will involve the trustees of a fund seeking the assistance of an investment consultancy division of a consulting actuary (in the UK) or an investment consultancy firm (in the US). Such firms have details of fund management firms, and will help trustees to draw up a shortlist of potential managers. The trustees and their consultants will then interview these managers, and a manager will be selected.

Although consultants deny it, they are largely guided by past performance numbers, albeit negatively. That is to say, they don't necessarily automatically include the best performing fund manager of the last year or two, but will exclude managers with average or poor short- or medium-term records. The consultants have substantial organizational information about the manager. Some of this information is descriptive, and some is the basis of qualitative analysis by the consultant. Most consultants say their selection analysis is driven largely by the qualitative analysis, but this is not reassuring. After all, if superior managers do not exist, the figures will show this, so what point is there in making a qualitative assessment? If they do exist, shouldn't you begin with the performance data? Qualitative analysis is perhaps best seen as a negative screen. It is used to reject some managers with superior performance records because they are not superior!

Fund managers usually complete consultants' questionnaires that seek information on:

- the history of the firm;
- the ownership of the firm;
- the firm's investment philosophy and investment style;
- the structure of the firm's decision-making process;
- the source of its research (i.e. how much is generated internally and how much is generated externally);
- the number of personnel and their experience in the areas of portfolio management, research, marketing, trading, and back-office administration;
- biographical details of the key staff, and in particular of the fund manager or managers who would work on a particular account;
- the maximum and minimum account sizes accepted and fees charged;
- total assets under management and the number of clients;

- performance data relevant to the account;
- staff turnover;
- compensation structure for key personnel.

As well as this information, for a particular account, information will be sought on how the manager would meet the trustees' objectives in terms of asset allocation, service level, etc. From this, an attempt will be made to understand the financial stability of the manager and whether the reward structure motivates individual portfolio managers. An attempt will be made to identify the individual or group that runs the show. Have these people worked together for a long time, and is there sufficient depth of staff to cope with illness, resignation, etc.? How many accounts does each portfolio manager look after? Is this a reasonable number, and has it been rising or falling? Does the firm have a clear investment philosophy that is actually put into practice? How is this monitored? Do individual portfolio managers have considerable discretion, for example in the selection of UK equities, or must all portfolios hold more or less the same stocks? If the latter, do the performance statistics show a narrow dispersion of returns?

The consultant and client will sift through the questionnaires and come up with a shortlist of potential managers. These will usually be interviewed in a 'beauty parade'. Trustees have to be careful with interviews. The psychological literature generally finds that interviews are a poor selection technique. While the objective of the investment beauty parade is to help the client choose the manager with the best investment skills, there is a danger that the manager with the best communication skills will be selected. As Weiss (1999, p. 68) notes:

> There is a mini-industry devoted to training people how to make presentations. The main point trainers stress is that content does not matter; what matters is what the audience thinks of you as a person. Yet when you are choosing a money manager, content is critical . . . In general, the traits you look for when trying to fill most managerial positions are either irrelevant or harmful for a money manager. A manager's aggressiveness, self-confidence, and leadership ability have no effect on markets. For most jobs outside portfolio management, you want managers who believe they can overcome odds through effort. This is a disastrous mind set for a money manager. People who think they can move markets are going to end up bankrupting their clients. You don't want anyone who is trying to overcome odds managing your money—you want someone who is making favorable odds bets.

With that cautionary note, what special characteristics will a good fund management firm have? Urwin (1991, p. 29) has argued that three important factors in identifying a winning organization are:

> First, the quality of the individuals will be paramount. Secondly, first class investment processes are vital and involve a clear philosophy, and strong disciplines. Thirdly, investment management houses also require sound management just like any other business.

The investment processes, apparently, should be quantitative. Few would disagree with these three points (although many would dispute the necessity for a quantitative process), but the problem with this sort of list is that one wonders if it says more than 'get good people: do good things'. Good things, of course, are identified retrospectively. A firm investing in smaller stocks would have looked good in the 1980s and bad in the 1990s.

It is perhaps easier to identify the characteristics of a losing organization. One of the problems in managing fund management companies is that they bruise easily. Firms can be reasonably well organized and then fall apart quickly. Clearly, a losing organization might simply be one that failed to satisfy the factors listed above. However, Urwin (1990, p. 28) produced some interesting general observations of a different nature. He noted:

> There appears to be a slight link between the number of individuals in the team and the results produced which supports the idea that strength in depth is helpful . . . There is a stronger link between changes in the team and performance. The negative impact of staff leaving an organization is statistically significant. On the other hand, growth in staff is positively associated with performance . . . [but] there was a clear inverse link between *fast* new business growth and future performance.

More generally, consultants are usually concerned when they see one or more of the following (e.g. see Owen, 1990, p. 117):

- one or more key investment personnel leave the firm;
- several major clients have terminated their accounts with the manager or reduced their allocations;
- assets under management have increased dramatically;
- performance has deteriorated;
- ownership of the firm changes;
- one or two accounts make up a disproportionately large percentage of the manager's assets under management;
- there is high turnover of marketing personnel.

Some of these don't need explanation, whereas some may be surprising. While rapid growth of assets under management is attractive for the manager, few firms seem able to cope with the organizational changes that this inevitably brings. The back office will be put under strain, as will the investment staff. Either new managers are recruited, or the workload of existing managers increases. These managers may also spend a growing percentage of their time making presentations to potential clients. Fund management firms are often poor at managing their business because superior investment managers often end up in the key executive positions and retain some investment role. With steady growth, this can work, but rapid growth forces these executives to neglect their investment role to cope with the business growth.

When the ownership of a firm changes, there are usually winners and losers amongst the staff. This is often very disruptive, and turnover may increase. Also, the investment style of the acquiring organization may be different from that of the acquired. It is then difficult to know which performance figures should be examined.

The best staff tend to want to be part of a winning team, enjoying good performance, good internal relationships and winning funds. When things start to go wrong, investment firms can decline rapidly. Some accounts may be lost, and consultants will not offer the opportunity to present for new business. Some firms will begin a stream of retail product launches in a probably futile attempt to offset the declining institutional business. This entire process is assessed quickly and accurately by the better fund managers, who will shift their focus from fund performance to getting another job. Marketing personnel also start looking for new jobs. Morale declines, and the firm moves swiftly from winner to loser status.

Despite the scepticism expressed above of the value of 'do good things' lists, here is one: an organization that will have a chance of winning and continuing to win is probably one that has good people, has a clear investment discipline, is well managed in a general business sense, grows at a steady and manageable rate, probably does not get involved in mergers, and keeps its staff together (but gets an injection of new blood by the requirements to recruit for growth). Although it is not essential that investment firms be partnerships, it is probably ideal if they are, or can act as though they are, with a profit share for the managers and with the sole focus on investment management. It hardly needs adding that the scope for problems is enormous when a bank or insurance company acquires a performance-oriented manager but tries to manage it in the same way as it manages its traditional commodity-like products.

CONCLUDING COMMENTS

In this chapter, we looked at some aspects of performance measurement. We noted the difference between time-weighted and money-weighted returns. We looked at some theory-based performance measurement and some theory-free measurement. We also looked at attribution analysis. Given the somewhat unhappy state of performance measurement, it is not surprising that studies of whether there are superior fund managers produce mixed results. However, the rapid growth of passive management suggests that the clients have reached a conclusion. Finally, we discussed some aspects of the process of hiring a new investment manager.

Appendix: Statistical Methods

This appendix will introduce to you some of the statistical methods used in investment reporting and research. It won't make you a statistician, but it will acquaint you with some of the methods and terms statisticians use.

ORGANIZING DATA

In many subjects, finding relevant data is a problem. With investments, there is almost too much. Often one needs to organize the data to get a feel for them. Say we are interested in the percentage annual change of the equity index for country XYZ. We might begin with a table showing the return for every year, or since a picture is said to be worth a thousand words, it might be useful to graph the data.

Graphs

In Figure A.1, we show a simple line graph of the annual capital gain or loss for the index for 100 years. We can tell quite a bit from the graph, including:

- there have been some years that produced huge gains, and some that produced big losses;
- the market has produced a positive return more often than a negative return;
- recent years have produced positive returns.

Frequency Distribution

These observations are useful, but by calculating a frequency distribution we can see a bit more. A frequency distribution shows how often each possible

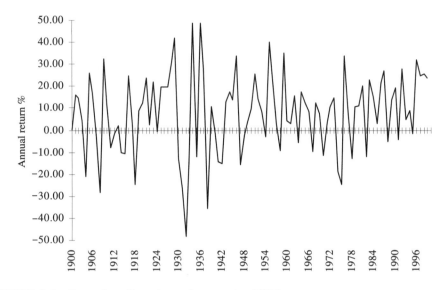

FIGURE A.1   Annual equity returns for country XYZ

return, or group of returns, actually occurred. So, for the data from which Figure A.1 was drawn, we could ask how many times the return was below –40%, how many times it was below –30% but above –40%, and so on. The answer is shown in Table A.1.

TABLE A.1   Frequency distribution of XYZ equity returns

Return (%)	Frequency
–50 – –40.1	1
–40 – –30.1	1
–30 – –20.1	5
–20 – –10.1	12
–10 – –0.1	13
0 – 9.9	19
10 – 19.9	25
20 – 29.9	14
30 – 39.9	7
40 – 49.9	3

Histograms and Frequency Polygons

These data can in turn be graphed by putting the returns on the horizontal (or x) axis, and the frequency of each return on the vertical (or y) axis. Figure A.2 shows the result. Graphs constructed from frequency distributions using bars above each return, or range of returns, are called histograms. We could also have plotted the data as a conventional line graph, in which case the result would be called a frequency polygon.

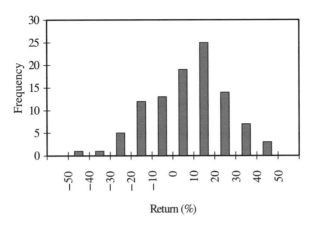

FIGURE A.2   Histogram of XYZ equity returns

Table A.1 and Figure A.2 show that the most frequent return has been in the 10–20% range, and as we move to returns above or below that, the frequency of their occurrence steadily falls.

Percentiles

Another method of organizing the data would be to array them from lowest to highest. This enables us to find the percentage of readings that are equal to or less than a given value. For example, 90% of the observations in Table A.1 are equal to or less than 29.9%. This may be referred to as the 90th percentile. The entire data set ranges between the 0th and 100th percentile. Data that are shown at values separating every 10% of the readings are said to be divided into deciles. Some investment studies show data by deciles; others use quintiles (a value separating off 20% of the data). The performance record of fund managers is usually shown by quartiles.

DESCRIBING DATA

Having organized the data and got a feel for the general picture, we can be more precise if we calculate some statistics that describe and summarize the data.

Arithmetic and Geometric Mean

If we had to summarize the information we have with a single number, we would want to try and find some representative measure or, as statisticians say, some measure of central tendency. The most popular measure is the arithmetic mean, sometimes called simply the mean or the average. We are all familiar with this concept. We are often told the average temperature for this time of year is, say, 15 degrees, or the average man is 67 inches tall. To calculate an average, we add up all the relevant scores (returns in our case) and divide by the number of observations, i.e.

$$\text{Arithmetic mean} = \frac{\text{sum of all scores}}{\text{number of observations}}.$$

Thus the arithmetic mean of XYZ's equity returns in the last 100 years is simply every annual return added together and divided by 100, the number of years. It turns out to be 7.7%. We can, of course, calculate a mean for a subperiod. For example, for the last 30 years the mean is 9.9%.

The arithmetic mean is frequently used in investment analysis, but it does have one drawback. Consider the data in Table A.2. At the end of year 1, an equity index is standing at 100. During the next year, it falls to 50, and the following year it rises back up to 100. Ignoring dividends, an investor will have a zero return. But if we calculate the arithmetic average return, it is $(-50 + 100)/2$, or 25% p.a. In this extreme example, the arithmetic average return is not a good guide to an investor's terminal wealth.

TABLE A.2   Annual returns

Year	Index	Return (%)
1	100	
2	50	−50
3	100	100

To find the average annual return that would produce the terminal portfolio value given the starting value, the geometric mean must be calculated. To do this, we express the returns in decimal form and then add 1 to each of them, i.e. −50% is converted to −0.5, then 1 is added, which gives 0.5. Similarly, 100% becomes 2. Once returns have been expressed in this manner, they are multiplied together and the nth root is calculated, where n is the number of observations, finally we subtract 1.

We can calculate the geometric mean for our XYZ data. If we take the last 30 years, we have to multiply all the annual returns together and take the 30th root and then subtract 1 (a statistical software package will do the number crunching). The geometric mean for XYZ equity returns over the last 30 years is 8.5%, lower than the arithmetic mean of 9.9% (we've used 30 years simply because Excel™ can only handle 30 observations.)

Median

Sometimes, where you might expect an arithmetic mean to be calculated, you find reference to the median. This is the middle score in a list of scores that have been arranged in increasing order. Consider the case of personal wealth in the US. If we calculate the mean, we will have to include everybody, including Bill Gates. If he is worth $30 billion, and there are 300 million Americans, then his wealth alone would add $100 dollars to the mean. Given a few more very rich people, you can see that the mean is not going to be a good description of central tendency. It will be too high. Arranging wealth from poorest to richest and then picking the middle number is likely to be a better guide. This will be the case whenever scores are not symmetrical around the mean but are skewed to one side.

Range

While the mean (of whatever type) and median are useful statistics, they only attempt to measure central tendency. They don't tell you how variable the data are. For example, are all data points close to the mean or scattered widely? One way of answering this is to calculate the range, which is the difference between the highest and lowest observation. For the returns data used for XYZ above, the lowest return over the 100 years was –48% and the highest was 48%. The range is therefore nearly 100%. This implies that the mean of around 7.7% doesn't tell us very much. But if we look at the histogram in Figure A.2, we see that most observations cluster round the mean. Just looking at two extreme numbers is not a good way to judge variability; we should use all the information available.

Standard Deviation and Variance

A measure of variability that uses all the information is the standard deviation. It tells us how much, on average, the observations differ from the mean. To calculate a standard deviation for the returns data, we subtract the mean from each return. Deviations above the mean will be positive, and those below will be negative. The positive scores will exactly offset the negative. To avoid this, we square all the deviations, which will eliminate the negative numbers. To calculate the average of the squared deviations, we divide by the number of observations (100 years in our case). The result is called the variance. If we now take the square root of the variance we have calculated the standard deviation. The formula is:

$$\text{Standard deviation} = \sqrt{\frac{\text{sum of (each return} - \text{arithmetic mean)}^2}{\text{number of observations}}}.$$

For our data, the standard deviation for the last 30 years is 15.3%. The larger the standard deviation, the more variable are the data. Standard deviations are of particular interest in the context of a normal distribution.

Normal Curve

In many studies in the physical and social sciences, when a very large number of observations are available, they are found to have an approximately normal distribution. When a normal distribution is plotted as a frequency polygon, it has a symmetrical bell-shaped appearance, as shown in Figure A.3.

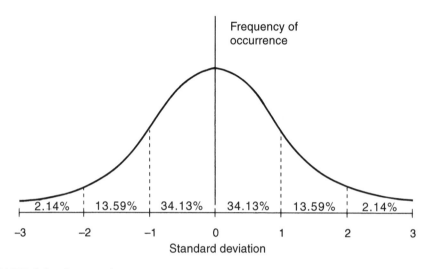

FIGURE A.3   A normal curve

The curve is referred to as a normal curve. Normal curves do not all look alike. Some are a bit squashed compared with others. Their shapes and location are determined entirely by their mean and standard deviation. However, regardless of a normal curve's mean and standard deviation, the percentage of the observations falling between the mean and a given point on the horizontal axis is always the same. Specifically, 34.13% of the distribution falls between the mean and +1 standard deviation, 13.59% falls between +1 and +2 standard deviations, and 2.14% falls between +2 and +3 standard deviations. Because the normal curve is symmetrical, the same percentages apply to minus standard deviations. A bit of arithmetic will show that 68.26% of the distribution (i.e. about two-thirds) lies between +1 and –1 standard deviations, 95.44% falls between +2 and –2 standard deviations, and 99.74% falls between +3 and –3 standard deviations. Since most distributions only approximate a normal curve, you might as well round these down to whole numbers and forget the two decimal places.

Although the histogram in Figure A.2 isn't a normal curve, we might find it useful to assume that it's a reasonable approximation. If that is the case, with knowledge only of the mean and standard deviation we can now describe the returns data for the last 30 years in a succinct but useful manner. The arithmetic average is 9.9% and about two-thirds of the returns will have been between

25.2% (9.9% + 15.3%) and –5.4% (9.9% – 15.3%). Further, about 95% of the returns will have been between 40.5% (9.9% + 15.3% + 15.3%) and –20.7% (9.9% – 15.3% – 15.3%). You can check the plausibility of these sums in a rough and ready way by drawing horizontal lines at these numbers on the last 30 years of data in Figure A.1.

Sometimes data clearly don't follow a normal distribution. There are techniques for dealing with this, but they lie outside the scope of this brief review of concepts.

STATISTICAL INFERENCE

Using data to describe a situation is useful, but often we want to use data to test a prior hypothesis. Usually the data are drawn from a sample. If the data disagree with the hypothesis, is this a result of the hypothesis being wrong or a result of sampling error? One way of answering this would be to take a bigger sample. Another way would be to use statistical inference. This will involve a test of significance.

Statistical Significance

How would we test a belief that small-capitalization stocks have different returns from large-capitalization stocks? The starting point is to specify a null hypothesis. This takes the form that there is no difference in the returns of big and small stocks. Any observed relationship is just a chance fluctuation. The alternative hypothesis is that there is a difference. We test the null hypothesis, the one we don't think is true, rather than the one we do. The reason is that we can specify exactly the null hypothesis—no difference—whereas the alternative is that there is some unspecified difference, i.e. something that cannot be tested directly. The statistical techniques for testing hypotheses vary (e.g. you may find references to a t-test, or an F-test) but the reasoning is always the same. If the test shows the difference to be very unlikely, then the sample value is said to be statistically significant, i.e. the difference is probably real. The null hypothesis is therefore rejected.

Let us assume that we find for the year we study that small-capitalization stocks produce a higher return than large stocks. How different from zero must the return difference be for us to reject the null hypothesis? Imagine we could collect data for every year, past and future, and that the relationship doesn't change. It can be shown that if the data were simply being muddied by random influences, then the sampling distribution of the difference between the mean returns of large and small stocks would be normally distributed. If the null hypothesis is true, then the mean of the distribution will be zero. While we don't know the standard deviation of the sampling distribution, we can estimate it using our sample data. Consequently, we can tell how many standard deviations the observed difference is from zero. For example, if our return difference is plus two standard deviations above the mean of the sampling distribution, we can check back with Figure A.3 and see that we would expect to find a number that is this high or higher only about 2% of the time. In other words, if there really is no difference in the returns, then there is only about a 2% chance of finding the return we did.

Usually in the social sciences if there is only a 5% chance of finding the result being studied, then the null hypothesis will be rejected and the alternative hypothesis accepted. The result is said to be statistically significant. If there is only a 1% chance of finding the result, then it is sometimes described as highly significant.

Statistical significance should not be confused with practical significance (or 'so what?'). A relationship might be true but unimportant. For example, first-born children are brighter than their siblings, and this relationship is statistically significant. But the difference is about one point of IQ. So what? Statistically, but not practically, significant.

Also, finding statistical significance is related to the sample size. If the sample is small, then statistical significance is less likely to be found. If the sample size is large, then statistical significance is more likely to be found, but the chances of the finding being of no practical significance increase.

Correlation

Correlation measures the relationship between two variables. Two variables may be related positively (positive correlation) or negatively (negative correlation), or may be unrelated (not correlated). There is a positive correlation when a high score on one variable is associated with a high score on another, for example height and weight. Tall people tend to weigh more than short people. There is a negative correlation when high scores on one variable go with low scores on another, for example the more you smoke, the shorter your life expectancy. There is no correlation if scores on one variable are completely unrelated to scores on another; for example, as far as we are aware, preferences for sleeping on the left or right side of the bed are unrelated to political beliefs.

The degree of correlation is measured by the correlation coefficient, which is on a scale ranging from +1 to –1, which ranges from perfect positive correlation through to perfect negative correlation. A score of zero would show no correlation. In Figure A.4, we show a scatter plot graph of price and sales for a product (economists usually plot price on the vertical axis). The data show a negative correlation of –0.68. A perfect negative correlation would require all the data points to lie on a straight line. In general, correlations in real life tend to be modest.

Most measures of correlation assume a linear (i.e. straight line) relationship. One has to be careful not to miss nonlinear relationships. For example, consider anxiety and job performance. Somebody with zero anxiety might be so laid back

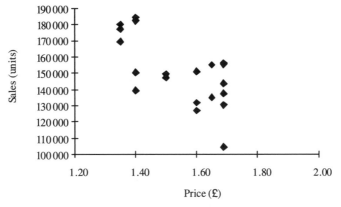

FIGURE A.4 Negative correlation of price and sales

that they don't bother to work. As we look at workers with increasing levels of anxiety, we may find that job performance improves. After a while, increasing anxiety may interfere with job performance, and extreme anxiety may mean the worker can't work at all. A linear correlation for anxiety/performance would be weak, but there is a strong inverted U-shaped relationship.

Finally, it must be stressed that correlation shows that two variables are related: it doesn't necessarily show they are causally related. For example, there is probably a correlation between number of hours spent lying on a beach and skin cancer, but lying on a beach does not cause skin cancer. Exposure to the sun causes skin cancer, and lying on a beach is related to exposure to the sun.

Regression[1]

If you refer back to Figure A.4, we might expect the relationship shown to be a causal relationship. If we cut prices, then sales will increase. But if we set a specific price, what is our best guess of the sales that we will achieve? One way of answering this is to use regression analysis to draw a line that best fits the data. The equation of a straight line is:

$$y = a + bx.$$

For our example:

$$Sales = a - b \ (price)$$

where y is the dependent variable (sales in this case), x is the independent variable (price in this case) and a and b are parameters (numbers) that have to be estimated. For the data shown, the best-fitting line calculated by a standard computer package is:

$$Sales = 308\,046 - 102\,017 \ (price).$$

So, for a price of, say, £1.69, we would expect sales to be:

$$Sales = 308\,046 - (102\,017 \times 1.69) = £135\,637.$$

---

[1] This discussion ignores a technical issue known as the 'identification problem'.

The computer also calculates some statistics useful in judging our equation. These include a t-statistic, so that we can see whether the parameter b is statistically significant, a correlation coefficient (which we already know), and a coefficient of determination. The latter is simply the correlation coefficient squared, and can range from 0 to 1; for this equation it is 0.46. This tells us that 46% of the variation of sales can be explained by the equation. The coefficient of determination is usually referred to as R^2.

In Figure A.5, we have added the regression line to the scatter plot of Figure A.4. As you can see, the data do not lie exactly on the line. In fact, the observation at the bottom right (price £1.69 and sales of £104 650) is some way off. Using the regression equation, we forecast sales of £135 637 for a price of £1.69, an error of £30 897. Earlier, we said regression could find the best-fitting line for a group of data, but we didn't say what the criterion was for 'best fitting'. Now we can. A widely used criterion is least squares, i.e. the best-fitting line is the one that minimizes the sum of all the squared errors. So, for this first observation, the error would be $30\,897^2$. A similar calculation would be made for every other observation. Why do we square the errors? If we didn't, positive and negative errors would cancel out.

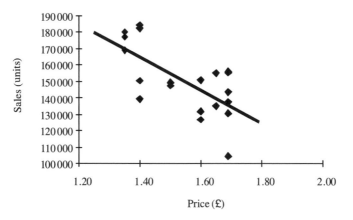

FIGURE A.5 Regression line

Multiple Regression

Is it likely that sales are determined just by price? Advertising might be relevant. If the data are annual, then we can be sure that GDP will have changed over the 20-year period, and that may be significant too. If there are competitors, their prices may be relevant too. For the sake of simplicity, we will assume that the firm's price, advertising and GDP are the only relevant variables, i.e.

$$\text{Sales} = a - b \text{ (price)} + c \text{ (advertising)} + d \text{ (GDP)}.$$

More advertising and higher GDP should lead to more sales, hence the plus signs in front of them in the equation. In this equation, a, b, c and d have to be estimated. The procedure is as before, although when we have one independent variable the analysis is usually called simple regression, whereas when we have several it is called multiple regression.

A computer will happily crunch the numbers for the multiple regression equation, just as it did for the simple regression equation. But the coefficient for price in the simple regression will be different to that in the multiple regression. The value of the number in the simple regression is questionable because the equation is mis-specified. Relevant variables were omitted. We should have more confidence in the numbers for the properly specified equation. This is an important point for investment studies. You probably readily accepted that the multiple variable equation (multivariate analysis) was better than the single variable study (univariate analysis) in the example, either on the grounds of economic theory or common sense. Unfortunately, there is often no clear theoretical guidance in investment studies as to what variables are relevant. So, if a researcher reports that a variable is related to returns, but has not allowed for another variable that another researcher claims is related to returns, what should we conclude? There is no easy answer.

As more independent variables are added to a regression equation, the coefficient of determination can never decrease. As a result there can be a temptation to add more and more variables, whatever their theoretical merits, as this may increase R^2 and will never decrease it. But this runs the risk of picking up spurious findings—findings that are true only for the period studied. It is possible to calculate an adjusted coefficient of determination that reflects the sample size and the number of independent variables and that can decrease as more variables are added. This is reported in studies as $\overline{R}^2$.

Sometimes in a multiple regression study, two or more independent variables are highly correlated. In the sales example, we assumed that the independent variables were unrelated to each other. But perhaps every time there is a recession, the advertising budget gets cut, or every time the price is increased, the advertising budget is also increased. In these cases, it will be impossible to work out which variable is affecting sales as they are both changing at the same time. Independent variables should be checked to see whether they are correlated. If they are, this will probably not affect how well the regression equation predicts, but the coefficients of the correlated variables will be unreliable.

There probably aren't 57 varieties of regression, but there are quite a few, including maximum likelihood and seemingly unrelated regression (SUR). These are beyond the scope of these notes. The important thing to remember is that while the statistical assumptions vary, and the estimation techniques differ, all aim to seek to establish the effect of independent variables on a dependent variable.

Glossary

Abnormal rate of return. Return earned on an asset in excess of the return required to compensate for the risk borne. Should be distinguished from excess return, but often isn't.

Accounting Standards Board. Main accounting standard-setting board in the UK. Replaced the Accounting Standards Committee. The Board is developing a set of Financial Reporting Standards (FRS). These are established after consultations and after circulation of a Financial Reporting Exposure Draft (FRED). An associated body, the Financial Reporting Review Panel, can ensure compliance with the standards, ultimately by going to court.

Accrued interest. Interest earned on a bond since the last interest payment date. Bonds are quoted at clean prices, which exclude any accrued interest. The buyer of a bond will pay the clean price plus accrued interest.

Active investment management. Investment management process that aims to purchase mispriced securities and assets and thereby earn a positive abnormal rate of return.

Advisory client. A client who receives advice from a stockbroker or fund manager, but takes his or her own decisions.

Air pocket. Slang. When a stock drops rapidly and without warning, it is said to have hit an air pocket.

Alpha. Used in a number of different senses, including the *y*-intercept of the characteristic line, and the difference between a security's expected return and the equilibrium return predicted by the capital asset pricing model.

Alternative investment market (AIM). UK market for smaller stocks, traded on the London Stock Exchange, with less onerous listing requirements than the main market.

American option. An option that can be exercised at any time during its life.

American Stock Exchange (AMEX). Second-largest US stock exchange. Its listed firms tend to be smaller than New York Stock Exchange firms and larger than Nasdaq firms. Sometimes abbreviated to ASE.

Anomalies. An empirical regularity not predicted by an asset-pricing model, e.g. calendar effects, low price-earnings effect, small-capitalization effect.

Arbitrage. Simultaneous purchase and sale of identical or similar assets in different markets for favourably different prices. The aim is to earn a risk-free return.

Arbitrage pricing theory (APT). An equilibrium asset-pricing model that states that the expected return of a security is a linear function of the security's sensitivity to various common factors.

Arithmetic mean return. A measure of central tendency calculated by summing period returns and dividing by the number of periods.

Ask price. The price at which a dealer is offering to sell an asset.

Asset allocation. The process of selecting the best allocation of an investor's portfolio amongst various asset classes.

Asset-liability modelling. An approach to asset allocation based on relating expected returns and risks from investments to the expected liabilities of a fund.

Attribute screening. Process of searching through stocks seeking those possessing attributes that are thought to be associated with positive abnormal returns.

Attribution analysis. Analysis of investment returns to determine how much of the return was generated by stock selection, asset allocation, etc.

Autocorrelation. See *Serial correlation*.

Balance of payments. A record of all financial flows into and out of a country during a given time period.

Balance sheet. Statement of assets, liabilities and shareholders' funds at a specific date.

Balanced manager. A fund manager who has discretion to diversify a fund's investments across a range of asset classes.

Barbell strategy. A bond strategy in which positions are concentrated at the extreme ends of the yield curve.

Basis. The difference between the spot price and the futures price of a commodity.

Basis point. One-hundredth of 1%.

Basis risk. The risk arising from uncertainty about the basis at a future time.

Bearer security. A security whose ownership is not recorded on a register. Ownership is indicated by possession of a certificate. Interest or dividend payments are obtained by clipping a coupon and presenting it to a paying agent.

Benchmark. A specified measurement used to evaluate the performance of a portfolio.

Benchmark bonds. Liquid bonds, usually with large outstanding amount, and a coupon in line with the general level of interest rates, used to price other instruments of similar maturity, for example corporate bonds.

Benchmark portfolio. A portfolio against which investment performance can be evaluated.

Beta. A measure of the sensitivity or responsiveness of an asset's return to an underlying factor or index. The most common beta is a market beta where the underlying factor is the market. See also *Arbitrage pricing theory*.

Bid price. The price that a dealer will pay for an asset.

Bid–ask spread. The difference between the bid and ask prices.

Bid–offer spread. The difference between the bid and offer prices.

Black–Scholes model. A model for pricing European options that calculates the value of an option based on the price of the underlying stock, the strike price, the period until expiration, the stock's price volatility, and the current risk-free interest rate.

Blue-chip stock. Shares of a large company with a record of steady growth of earnings and dividends over a long period.

Bond. An IOU issued by a company, government or agency. Bondholders are creditors and receive interest payments.

Book value. Aggregate value of ordinary shareholders' equity, i.e. ordinary share capital plus reserves.

Book value per share. Book value divided by issued ordinary shares.

Bottom-up. An investment approach based on share selection that generates sector or country weightings by default.

Brady bonds. Bonds issued by emerging countries under a debt-reduction plan named after Nicholas Brady, former US Secretary of the Treasury.

Bulldog bond. A sterling-denominated security issued by a non-UK entity, listed on the London market.

Bullet strategy. A bond strategy in which positions are concentrated at one point on the yield curve.

Buy-and-hold strategy. A strategy whereby assets are purchased and held without any trading or asset rebalancing to the original mix.

Calendar effects. The effect of the time of the year, week, day, etc. on security returns.

Call option. An option that gives the buyer the right, but not the obligation, to buy a specified quantity of the underlying security at a stated price on or before a specified date.

Call provision. A provision giving a bond issuer the right to buy back all or part of an issue before maturity at a specified price.

Capital account. A balance-of-payments component covering short-term and long-term capital transactions.

Capital asset pricing model (CAPM). An equilibrium asset-pricing model that states that the expected return of a security is a linear function of the security's sensitivity to changes in the market's return.

Capital market line. The set of portfolios obtained by combining the market portfolio with risk-free borrowing and lending. It is a tangent from the risk-free rate to the efficient frontier of risky assets.

Capitalization-weighted (or value-weighted) index. A market index in which each security is weighted according to its market capitalization.

CAPS. Combined Actuarial Performance Services, one of the two leading UK performance-measurement companies.

Cash flow matching. See *Dedicated portfolio*.

Cash flow statement. Statement of a company's cash inflows and outflows during one accounting period.

Cash settlement. Procedure for settling a futures contract in cash rather than by delivering the underlying asset.

Central tendency. The typical value in a set of data, usually represented by the mean, mode or median.

Certificate of deposit (CD). Issued by banks and building societies with specific maturity dates. They can be traded in the secondary market.

CGBR. Central government borrowing requirement.

CGNCR. Central government net cash requirement.

Characteristic line. The linear relationship between the expected return on a security and the expected return on the market portfolio.

Chartered financial analyst (CFA). US professional qualification awarded by the Association for Investment Management and Research.

Clean price. The price of a bond excluding accrued interest.

Clearinghouse. A firm that guarantees the performance of the parties in an exchange-traded derivatives transaction.

Closed-end investment company. US name for an investment trust; an investment company that is traded on the stock market at the market clearing price, which may be above or below the company's net asset value.

Closet indexing. The process by which an active investment manager seeks to avoid poor performance by constructing a portfolio that broadly mimics an index.

Coincident indicators. Economic indicators that move at the same time as the business cycle.

Composite leading indicator series. Economic indicators that move in advance of the business cycle.

COMPUSTAT Data Tape. Data source providing profit and loss, balance sheet and other data on a large number of US stocks.

Contingent immunization. A hybrid strategy whereby a bond manager can use active management until the value of a portfolio falls to a specified level, and then is obligated to use an immunization strategy to lock in the safety net return.

Contrary opinion. Investment strategy based on trading against the crowd.

Conventional gilt. Gilt on which interest payments and the principal repayment are fixed in nominal terms.

Convertible bond. A bond that can be converted into another bond or into an equity at a specified price at the option of the holder.

Convexity. A measure of the curvature in the relationship between bond prices and bond yields.

Core/satellite portfolios. Investment management approach in which the core portfolio is a major component of a fund's assets and which usually aims to achieve close to market returns while the remainder of the fund's assets are managed more aggressively in satellite portfolios.

Correlation coefficient (R). A measure of the degree to which two variables move together. Correlation coefficients range from -1.0 to $+1.0$. A coefficient of $+1.0$ means the variables move in perfect lockstep, -1.0 means they move in perfect negative lockstep, and 0.0 implies that they are completely unrelated. Correlation coefficients measure the strength of a relationship but do not imply causality. The correlation coefficient squared (R^2) is called the coefficient of determination and measures the percentage of variance of one variable explained by its relationship with the other.

Cost of carry. The cost of financing an asset less the income earned on the asset.

Coupon. The interest payment due on a bond, expressed as a percentage of the nominal value of the bond.

Covariance. A measure of the degree to which a pair of variables move together. Covariance is related to, but not the same as, the correlation coefficient.

Covenant. A protective clause in a loan agreement to protect the lender's claim.

Credit analysis. The process of analysing information on companies and bond issues in order to assess the probability of a default.

CRSP Data Tape. A standard source for investment research. The Center for Research in Security Prices (CRSP) at the University of Chicago provides stock price, dividend and return data for all stocks on the New York Stock Exchange from 1926.

Current account. Balance of payments component covering payments and income for goods and services.

Day-of-the-week effect. See *Weekend effect.*

Dead-cat bounce. Slang. Some stocks or markets will start rising after a sharp fall—but even a dead cat, if dropped from a window, will bounce without this implying any life.

Debenture. A bond having a prior claim on the assets of the issuer, or specific assets of the issuer. A debenture holder may appoint a receiver.

Dedicated portfolio. A bond portfolio that has been designed to insulate the portfolio from the effect of interest rate changes by matching the asset's cash flows to the liabilities' cash flows.

Default risk. The risk that an issuer of a bond may be unable to make principal and interest payments.

Delta. The rate of change of the price of a derivative with the price of the underlying asset.

Delta-neutral. A portfolio with a delta of zero. The portfolio is not sensitive to small changes in the price of the underlying asset.

Derivative security. Security, such as an option or futures, whose value derives from the underlying asset.

Diminishing marginal utility. Utility is the satisfaction we get from a good or money. If additional satisfaction diminishes with additional increments of a good, then there is diminishing marginal utility. If wealth is subject to diminishing marginal utility, then this will imply risk-aversion because additional wealth produces less utility than a loss of the same quantity of wealth.

Dirty price. The total price of a bond, including accrued interest.

Discount rate. The rate of interest used to discount a stream of cash flows to a present value. The discount rate reflects both the time value of money and the riskiness of the cash flows.

Discount rate on Treasury bills. The annualized difference between the redemption value and the purchase price of £100 nominal value of the bills, expressed as a percentage.

Discretionary client. A client who gives a manager discretion to manage the client's assets without reference to the client.

Dispersion. Extent to which observations of a sample deviate from the sample's measure of central tendency (e.g. its mean). The standard deviation is the most common measure of dispersion.

Diversification. The adding of assets to a portfolio to reduce its specific risk and thereby its total risk.

Dividend. Payment made from a company's after-tax earnings, which is distributed to shareholders. Dividends are not guaranteed for ordinary shareholders.

Dividend discount model (DDM). A valuation model for equities that assumes that the intrinsic value of a stock is equal to the discounted value of its future stream of dividends.

Dividend payout ratio. Percentage of earnings paid out as dividends (= one minus the retention rate).

Dividend yield. Annual dividend per share divided by the current market price.

DMO. The UK Debt Management Office.

Domestic bond. A bond issued in the country and currency in which the borrower is domiciled.

Double-dated bonds. Bonds that the issuer may redeem on any date between two fixed redemption dates.

Dow Jones Industrial Average (DJIA). Best known US index. A price-weighted index of 30 leading industrial shares with a divisor that is adjusted for stock splits; its construction makes it of limited relevance for portfolio analysis or for judging the trend of the market.

Duration. A measure of the timing of a bond's cash flow taking into account its coupon, redemption payment, and period to redemption.

EAFE Index. A share index for Europe, Australia and the Far East.

Early exercise. An exercise before the maturity date.

Earnings multiplier model. Model for estimating the value of a stock or a market as a multiple of its earnings.

Earnings per share (EPS). A company's earnings divided by its number of issued shares. The earnings used in the calculation may be the last reported earnings (sometimes called historical or trailing) or forecast earnings (sometimes called prospective).

Earnings surprise. Difference between reported earnings and analysts' prior expectations.

Earnings yield. Earnings per share divided by the price per share: reciprocal of the price-earnings ratio. Also called earnings-price ratio.

Efficient frontier. The locus of all efficient portfolios, i.e. portfolios that have varying combinations of risk and return such that no other portfolio can offer the same return for less risk or the same risk for more return.

Efficient market theory. States that security prices fully reflect all available information. The theory is sometimes stated in three versions. The weak form of the theory states that prices reflect all past price information. The semi-strong version states that prices reflect all publicly available information. The strong form states that prices reflect all information, both public and private.

Efficient portfolio. A portfolio with the highest expected return for a given level of risk or the lowest level of risk for a given return.

Emerging markets. The financial markets of developing economies.

Equally-weighted index. A market index that weights each share equally. This means a small company will have as much impact on the index as a large company. See also *Capitalization-weighted index.*

Equity risk premium. The difference between the return on equities and a riskless asset. Academics usually use Treasury bill returns for the latter, whereas UK practitioners often use long gilt redemption yields.

Eurobond. A bond that is offered to investors in a number of countries and issued outside the jurisdiction of any single country.

Eurocurrency market. Interbank market for short-term borrowing and lending in a currency outside of its home country.

Euro-issuance. The issue of securities denominated in euros.

European option. An option that can be exercised only at the end of its life.

Event study. Analysis of the reaction of stock price movements to new information.

Excess return. The difference between the return on a security and the return on a risk-free asset. Should be distinguished from *abnormal return.*

Exchange rate risk. Also known as currency risk; the risk of an investment's value changing because of a change in the exchange rate.

Ex-dividend date. A date given when a dividend is declared. Holders of the shares up to the ex-dividend date receive the dividend.

Exercise price. The price at which an option holder has the right to buy or sell the underlying asset. Also known as the strike or striking price.

Expectations theory. A theory that the shape of the yield curve is determined by investors' expectations of movements in short-term interest rates.

Expected return. The return anticipated by an investor over a particular holding period.

Expiry. The expiration date of a derivative security.

Factor. Aspect of the investment environment that affects the returns of assets. Some factors affect only a few assets while others affect many—these are referred to as common, pervasive or systematic.

Factor analysis. Group of statistical techniques used to analyse intercorrelations within a set of variables. Often used to uncover underlying factors determining security returns.

Factor beta. A measure of the variation of a factor with the return on the market portfolio.

Factor loading or sensitivity. A measure of the sensitivity of an asset to a particular factor.

Factor model. Model that relates the return on a security to its sensitivity to movements in various common factors.

Factor risk. That part of a security's total risk that derives from common factors and cannot be diversified away.

Fallen angel. Slang. A former high-flying growth stock that has since crashed to earth.

FASB. Financial Accounting Standards Board (in the US).

Federal Reserve (Fed). The US government agency that controls monetary policy.

Financial analyst. Usual US name for a person who analyses the risk and return characteristics of financial assets in order to identify mispriced assets. Usually called an investment analyst in the UK.

Financial Reporting Exposure Draft (FRED). See *Accounting Standards Board.*

Financial Reporting Standards (FRS). See *Accounting Standards Board.*

Fixed interest (or income). Income stream that is constant during the life of the asset, such as from bonds or preference shares.

Flat yield. Coupon rate times 100 divided by current price. Also known as interest yield or running yield.

Flattening of the yield curve. A change in the shape of the yield curve whereby the spread between the yield on long-term and short-term bonds decreases.

Floating-rate bond. A bond where the coupon rate is tied to some variable interest rate benchmark such as LIBOR or base rate.

Foreign bond. A bond issued by a foreign issuer on a local market and in the local currency.

Forex. Foreign exchange.

Forward contract. A contract between two parties that specifies the exchange of an asset at a fixed time in the future and at a fixed price. Forward contracts are not traded on exchanges.

Forward interest rate. The interest rate for a future period implied by the rates prevailing in the market today.

FRN. Floating rate note. See *Floating-rate bond.*

FTSE 100 Index. Capitalization-weighted index of the 100 largest London-listed stocks.

FTSE All-Share Index. The major UK capitalization-weighted index, consisting of over 800 shares and broadly representative of the UK market.

FTSE SmallCap Index. Capitalization-weighted index consisting of all companies in the FTSE All-Share Index not large enough to be in the largest 350 shares. It comes in two versions, one including and the other excluding investment trusts.

FTSE World Indexes. Group of capitalization-weighted indexes for individual countries and groups of countries. Includes only investable stocks.

Fundamental analysis. Evaluation of firms and markets and possible security mispricing based on analysis of economic and financial factors.

Futures contract. An agreement to make or take delivery of a specified quantity of an asset at a particular time and price in the future. Futures contracts are traded on exchanges.

Futures option. An option on a futures contract.

Futures price. The delivery price currently prevailing on a futures contract.

Gamma. The rate of change of delta with respect to the asset price.

GDP (gross domestic product). The value of a country's output produced by residents within the country's borders.

Generally accepted accounting principles (GAAP). The accounting practices authorized in the US by the Financial Accounting Standards Board.

Geometric mean return. The compounded per-period average rate of return over a particular period. The rate of return that makes the initial value of an investment equal to its end-period value.

Gilt repos. A sale of gilts with an agreement to repurchase them at a fixed time and price. Buying gilts with a resale agreement is called a reverse repo.

Gilts, gilt-edged securities. Fixed-interest securities issued by the UK government with initial maturity over one year. Interest payments are usually made semiannually. Some issues have no redemption date.

Graham, Benjamin. Pioneered fundamental security analysis in the US and, with Dodd, wrote the major textbook of the 1930s–50s.

Greeks. The name given to a group of variables used in hedging with derivatives, for example delta, gamma, vega/kappa and theta.

Growth manager. A fund manager who selects stocks that are expected to achieve above-average profits growth.

Growth stock. The shares of a company expected to achieve above-average profits growth.

Hedge. A trade designed to reduce risk.

Hedge ratio. The ratio of the size of a position in a hedging instrument to the size of the position being hedged.

High-yield bonds. See *Junk bonds*.

Historic volatility. Volatility estimated from historical data.

Hoare Govett Smaller Companies Index (HGSCI). Index comprising the lowest 10% by capitalization of the main UK equity market.

Holding period return (HPR). The total return from an investment over a specified holding period expressed as a percentage.

Idiosyncratic risk. See *Unsystematic risk*.

Immunization. A bond portfolio strategy that aims to minimize the impact of interest rate changes and lock in a known redemption yield.

Implied volatility. Volatility implied by an option price.

In-the-money. Term used in options. A call option is in-the-money when the exercise price is below the current price of the underlying security. A put option is in-the-money when the exercise price is above the current price of the underlying security.

Index arbitrage. Simultaneous purchase (sale) and sale (purchase) of stock index futures and the stocks in the index to earn a risk-free return resulting from pricing differences.

Index fund. A passive investment fund that aims to achieve the performance of a particular index.

Index futures. A futures contract on a stock index or other index.

Index option. An option based on a market index.

Index-linked gilts. A special class of UK gilt that has both coupon payments and principal indexed to the retail price index.

Information coefficient. Correlation coefficient derived from relating *ex ante* predictions with *ex post* results.

Initial margin. The cash a futures trader has to deposit at the time of a trade.

Initial public offer (IPO). The initial offer of a company's shares to the public.

Insider, inside information. Insider and inside information have specific legal meanings in the UK and the US, and trading on the basis of inside information is illegal. However, the research studies use the terms in a more general sense to assess the activity of investors (such as company directors) with access to information not generally available to the public.

Internal rate of return. The discount rate that equates the present value of future cash flows from an asset to the cost of the asset.

Intrinsic value. Term used in options market. For a call option, it is the excess of the asset price over the exercise price. For a put option, it is the excess of the exercise price over the asset price.

Investment analyst. See *Financial analyst*.

Investment grade. A bond that is assigned a rating of at least BBB (Standard and Poor's) or Baa (Moody's).

Investment horizon. The period over which an investor makes investment plans.

Irredemable bonds. Bonds without a stated maturity. Also called undated bonds or perpetual bonds.

January effect. Empirical regularity observed in the US and other countries that stock returns appear to be higher in January compared with other months.

Jensen's index. A portfolio performance measurement that is the difference between the actual return on a share or portfolio and the expected return given its beta and the market return.

Junk bonds. Debt securities that have high yields because they carry below-investment-grade credit ratings.

Laddered portfolio. A strategy of spreading a bond portfolio evenly over a range of maturities.

Lagging indicators. Economic indicators that follow movements in the business cycle.

Leading indicators. Economic indicators that lead movements in the business cycle.

LIBID (London interbank bid rate). The rate at which international banks borrow from each other.

LIBOR (London interbank offer rate). The rate at which international banks lend to each other.

LIFFE. London International Financial Futures and Options Exchange.

Limit move. The maximum price movement permitted by an exchange in a trading session.

Liquidity preference theory. Theory that bondholders require a higher yield on long maturities than on short.

Long position. Position involving the purchase of an asset.

LSE. London Stock Exchange.

Maintenance margin. If a trader's margin account falls below the maintenance margin level, then the trader is required to top up the account to the initial margin level.

Margin. The cash or security deposit required from a futures or options trader.

Margin call. A request for extra margin when the balance in a margin account falls below the maintenance margin level.

Marked-to-market. The process of valuing securities against the current market price to determine profit or loss to date.

Market model. Describes the relationship between the rates of return on securities and portfolios and the rate of return on the market.

Market portfolio. Contains all risky assets in proportion to their market value.

Market risk premium. The additional return above the risk-free rate that investors expect from the market to compensate for systematic risk.

Market segmentation theory. A theory that bonds of different maturities are not perfect substitutes for each other. The shape of the yield curve depends on demand and supply in each maturity segment of the market.

Marketability. The degree to which stocks can be traded without significantly affecting the price.

Market-cap. Abbreviation for market capitalization. Also large-cap, mid-cap and small-cap, which refer to the groups of companies that fall in the large-, medium- and small-capitalization groups.

Market-maker. A company or individual that facilitates trades by acting as a principal and holding an inventory of stocks. The market-maker attempts to make a profit by the difference in the bid and ask prices and by being long or short of stocks when the market rises or falls.

Married to a stock. Holding a stock long after its relative attractiveness has diminished.

Mature scheme. A pension scheme with a high proportion of pensioners relative to current members.

Maturity. The period to the redemption of a bond.

Mean reversion. The tendency of a variable to revert back to some long-run average.

Modern portfolio theory. Widely used term, but without precise definition. Usually implies a belief in the efficient market theory and the capital asset pricing model or some other asset-pricing model that quantifies the relationship between risk and return.

Modified duration. Modification of the standard duration measure that improves the measurement of the relationship between proportional changes in a bond's price and absolute changes in its yield.

Momentum indicator. Indicator that provides information about past price movements.

Momentum investing. Investment strategy based on the assumption that trends continue.

Morgan Stanley Capital International (MSCI) Indexes. Group of capitalization-weighted indexes for individual countries and groups of countries.

Multi-asset management. An arrangement by which a manager invests in a range of asset classes specified by the client.

Multicollinearity. The tendency for the independent variables in a multiple regression to be correlated with each other. This may lead to poor regression estimates.

Multifactor capital asset pricing model. Extended version of the capital asset pricing model that includes factors such as size and liquidity as well as systematic risk.

Multiple regression analysis. Regression analysis that estimates the linear relationship between a dependent variable and more than one independent variable. See also *Regression analysis*.

Naked position. An options position that does not involve an offsetting options or stock position. For example, a short position in a call option that is not combined with a long position in the underlying security.

Nasdaq (National Association of Securities Dealers Automated Quotations). US electronic stockmarket providing bid–ask quotes from at least two market makers on over-the-counter securities.

Neglected firm effect. Empirical regularity that stocks neglected by analysts or investment institutions provide positive abnormal returns.

Net asset value. Ordinary share capital plus retained reserves divided by the number of ordinary shares in issue.

New issue. Initial stock sale by underlying firm.

New York Stock Exchange (NYSE). The largest US stock exchange.

Nominal rate of return. Rate of return expressed in monetary terms. Not adjusted for inflation.

Nominal value. The value that appears on a security's certificate. Also known as par value. The market value is usually different from the nominal value.

Non-synchronous trading. Not all securities trade at the end of every return interval, e.g. every day. Return data for different securities thus may relate to different periods, and this is refered to as non-synchronous trading. This leads to various statistical problems, in particular securities that trade infrequently will have underestimated betas unless a correction is made.

Normal probability distribution. Bell-shaped probability distribution whose properties are completely described by its mean and standard deviation. The normal distribution is frequently used in making statistical inferences from measures derived from samples.

Normalized earnings. The earnings one would expect in a 'normal' year or a mid-cycle year.

Odd-lot theory. US investors who trade in less than 100 shares are said to trade in odd lots. Odd-lot theory presumes that these small investors are ill informed and provide a contrary investment indicator.

Offer price. The price at which a dealer is offering to sell an asset.

On-the-run issues. The most recently issued Treasury bond for each maturity that is used as a benchmark.

Open-end investment company. A mutual fund (in the US) or a unit trust (in the UK) that stands ready to issue or redeem new shares at net asset value (possibly subject to a sales load).

Optimal portfolio. The portfolio lying on the efficient frontier that offers the most value to an investor given his or her attitude to risk.

Options. A derivatives security that gives the right to buy or sell a security at a specified price on or before a specified time.

Ordinary shares. Securities that give an ownership interest in a company.

OTC (over-the-counter) market. The market in stocks not listed on the recognized exchanges. Some listed stocks are also traded on the OTC market. The security dealers act as market-makers.

Out-of-sample data. Data that have not been used in the estimation of a statistical relationship. Also called a holdout sample.

Out-of-the-money. A call option whose exercise price is above the current underlying share price or a put option whose exercise price is below the current underlying share price.

Overpriced security. A security whose expected return is less than its required return.

Overreaction hypothesis. Hypothesis that investors tend to overreact to news causing asset prices to deviate from their intrinsic value.

Overweight. A fund is said to be overweight in an asset when it holds more than the appropriate index or benchmark weight.

Parallel shift. A movement in the yield curve whereby each point on the curve changes by the same absolute amount.

Passive investment management. An investment strategy that does not involve trying to find mispriced assets. Usually will involve some use of an index fund.

Percentiles. Measures of the distribution of data given by ranking data from lowest to highest. The percentile of a given number is the percentage of other numbers that are less than that number.

Plain vanilla. Slang. Used to describe a securities issue without 'bells and whistles' such as calls, puts or warrants.

Plan sponsor. The organization that is the employer of a pension scheme's members.

Pooled fund. A fund in which the assets of several investors are pooled together. An investor's ownership is determined by the number of units of the pool that are held.

Portfolio. The collection of assets held by an investor.

Preference share. An equity investment with a fixed dividend. Preference shares do not have voting rights but rank before ordinary shares in respect of dividend payments and capital repayment.

Premium. The price of an option.

Present value. The equivalent value today of future income streams. It is calculated by discounting future income by an appropriate discount rate.

Price-earnings ratio (PER). Share price divided by earnings per share.

Price-to-book-value ratio. Share price divided by the book value of assets.

Price-to-cash flow ratio. Share price divided by cash flow, usually calculated as earnings plus non-cash expenses, the largest of which is depreciation.

Price-to-sales ratio. Share price divided by company's sales per share.

Privatization. The opposite of nationalization. Selling state industries to the private sector.

Profit and loss account (P&L). Statement of revenue, expenses and profit of a company for an accounting period.

Programme trading. The purchase or sale of a basket of securities as though the trade were a single security, for example a trader may agree to supply a basket of shares at the closing mid-market London price plus a 1% fee. The trader may effect the trade either as a principal trade or as an agency trade.

Protective put. A put option combined with a long position in the underlying asset.

Put option. An option that gives the buyer the right, but not the obligation, to sell a specified quantity of the underlying security at a fixed price on or before a specified date.

Quality spread. Also called credit spread. The difference between yields on bonds of different credit ratings.

Quantitative management. A statistical/mathematical approach to fund management.

Random walk theory. When applied to share prices, this asserts that the next percentage price change of a stock cannot be deduced on the basis of past changes.

Rate of return. The percentage return from an investment, over a specified holding period, which includes both income and capital gains or losses, whether realized or unrealized.

Real exchange rate. The exchange rate adjusted by the inflation differential between two countries.

Real return. The inflation-adjusted return on an investment.

Redemption date. The date on which the principal of a bond will be repaid.

Redemption yield. The discount rate that equates the present value of all future cash flows from a bond to the current price. In the US, this is called yield-to-maturity.

Regression coefficient. Indicates the responsiveness of one variable to changes in another. The regression coefficient between a security's rate of return and the return on the market is called beta.

Regression equation. An equation that is fitted by statistical methods and that attempts to explain the level or changes of a variable of interest, the dependent variable, as a function of one or more independent variables.

Regression to the mean. Tendency of extreme observations to become more like the average over a period of time.

Reinvestment risk. The risk that proceeds received in the future will have to be reinvested at a lower interest rate.

Relative strength. Measure of the price performance of shares or sectors relative to an appropriate index. Technical analysts believe that past high relative strength predicts good future performance.

Repo (repurchase agreement). A means of borrowing money by selling securities to a counterparty and agreeing to buy them back later at a specified price.

Repo rate. The rate of interest in a repo transaction.

Required rate of return. The minimum expected return necessary to induce an investor to invest.

Retention ratio. The percentage of a firm's earnings not paid out as dividends but retained by the firm (= one minus the payout rate).

Return. The value received from an investment in terms of income and capital appreciation/depreciation.

Reward-to-variability measure. See *Sharpe's index.*

Reward-to-volatility measure. See *Treynor's index.*

Risk. The uncertainty that an asset will earn its expected return. Usually measured by the variability of past returns.

Risk premium. Rate of return above the risk-free rate required as compensation for bearing risk.

Risk-adjusted return. The return on an asset adjusted for the risk it bears.

Risk-averse. Investors are said to be risk-averse if they dislike risk and will choose from two investments with equal returns the one with least risk. They will incur additional risk only if they expect additional return. Consequence of diminishing marginal utility.

Risk-free asset. An asset whose holding period return is known with certainty. Treasury bills are usually used as a proxy for this rate.

Risk-free rate. The return on a risk-free asset.

Risk-neutral investor. Investor who is indifferent between investments that have the same expected return but varying levels of risk.

Runs test. A test that looks for series or runs of positive or negative price changes for a security greater than would be expected in a random series.

S&P 500. US capitalization-weighted share index published by Standard and Poor's consisting of 500 shares. The 400 industrial shares included also form a separate index, the S&P 400.

Samurai bond. A yen-denominated bond issued in Japan by a non-Japanese organization.

Securities and Exchange Commission. US federal agency that regulates security issuing and trading.

Security market line. A linear relationship between the risk of a security as measured by its beta and the expected return.

Segregated fund management. A process in which each client's fund is managed separately from all other funds controlled by a manager.

Semistrong-form efficient market theory. See *Efficient market theory.*

Separation theorem. Theorem that states that the selection of the optimal portfolio of risky assets is separate from an investor's attitude to risk and return.

Serial correlation. The relationship between one period's observation and a subsequent period's observation. A positive relationship, i.e. positive serial correlation, indicates the presence of trends, while a negative relationship, i.e. negative serial correlation, indicates the presence of reversals.

Sharpe's index. Portfolio performance measure over an evaluation period of the excess return of the portfolio divided by the portfolio's standard deviation of returns.

Single factor (or index) model. Model that relates the returns on a stock to the return on the market.

Sinking fund. A condition that requires a bond issuer to retire a specified portion of debt at periodic intervals rather than all at maturity.

Size effect. Empirical regularity that over long periods small-capitalization stocks have outperformed large stocks on a risk-adjusted basis.

Small stock effect. See *Size effect.*

Sovereign risk. The risk that a government will default on its debt.

Specialist fund management. A process whereby a number of managers manage a fund. Each specialist manager manages a subfund for a specific asset class. Asset allocation decisions are taken by the trustees or their advisers.

Specific risk. Another name for unsystematic risk.

Spot price. Current market price of an asset.

Spread. The difference between a market-maker's buying and selling prices.

Standard deviation. A measure of dispersion calculated as the square root of the difference between each score and the mean of the data, divided by the number of observations.

Statements of standard accounting practice (SSAPs). Statements of recommended accounting practice issued by the UK's Accounting Standards Committee. Companies that depart from the standards have had to justify the departure. See *Accounting Standards Board.*

Statistically significant. Term used to describe a research finding when the outcome of a statistical test indicates that the probability of the result occurring by chance is small, usually less than 5%.

Steepening of the yield curve. A change in the shape of a yield curve whereby the spread between the yield on long-term and short-term bonds increases.

Stochastic variable. A variable whose future value is uncertain.

Stock dividend. A dividend paid in the form of additional shares.

Stock index futures. Futures on a stock index.

Stock index option. An option on a stock index.

Story stock. A security that rises in value because of a 'sexy story' rather than on the basis of value.

Straddle. A long position in a call and a put with the same strike price.

Straight bond. A bond with fixed-coupon payments and no special features. Also called plain vanilla bond.

Strangle. A long position in a call and a put with different strike prices.

Strategic asset allocation. Asset allocation that is appropriate given an investor's liabilities and objectives. The benchmark portfolio from which tactical asset allocation may be made.

Stripping. Process of dividing a fixed-interest security into its component coupons and principal repayment.

Strips. Acronym for separately trading registered interest and principal securities.

Strong-form efficient market theory. See *Efficient market theory*.

Structural macroeconomic econometric model. A statistical model of the economy based on economic theory, used to test economic theory and make forecasts.

Style. Classification of approach to asset selection.

Swap. An agreement to exchange cash flows according to prearranged formula.

Systematic risk. The part of a security's total risk that cannot be diversified away.

Tactical asset allocation. Determines what departure, based on current market valuations, should be made from the strategic asset allocation.

Technical analysis. Form of security and market analysis that uses past price movements and volume levels plus other indicators to forecast future price movements.

Term spread. The difference in yield between bonds with different maturities, e.g. three-month and ten-year bond yields.

Term structure. See *Yield curve*.

Theme investing. Investment style that attempts to exploit investment themes, such as disinflation, 'new economy', etc.

Theta. The rate of change of the price of a derivative with the passage of time.

Third market. US term for the trading of exchange-listed securities on the over-the-counter market.

Time value. The value of an option arising from the time left to expiry.

TIPS. Treasury Inflation Protected Securities. The US equivalent of index-linked gilts.

Top-down. An investment management approach that begins with country allocation, sector allocation, and finally individual security selection.

Total return. Return calculated using both income and capital appreciation/depreciation.

Total risk. Usually measured as the standard deviation of the return on an asset or portfolio.

Trade balance. The balance of a country's imports and exports.

Transactions costs. Cost of carrying out a trade, i.e. commissions, plus the bid/ask spread, plus applicable taxes (e.g. stamp duty in the UK).

Treasury bill. A security issued by the UK or US government that has a maximum maturity of one year. The bills are issued at a discount and redeemed at par.

Treasury bond. A US government fixed-income security with a term to maturity of over 10 years. Income is paid semi-annually, and the principal is returned at maturity.

Treasury note. A US government fixed-income security with a term to maturity of between one and 10 years. Income is paid semi-annually, and the principal is returned at maturity.

Treynor's index. Portfolio performance measured over an evaluation period of the excess return of the portfolio divided by the portfolio's beta.

Triple witching hour. The last trading hour on the third Friday of March, June, September and December when stock index futures, stock index options, and options on stock index futures all expire together.

***t*-test.** A tool of inferential statistics that allows the probability to be determined that a difference between the means of sets of data occurred by chance.

Underlying security. The security on which a derivative instrument is based.

Underweight. A fund is said to be underweight in an asset when it holds less than the appropriate index or benchmark.

Unsystematic risk. That portion of total risk unrelated to a specific factor and which can therefore be diversified away.

Value Line. A firm that publishes various financial analysis, including the *Value Line Investment Survey*, a weekly service that rates 1700 US stocks.

Value manager. A manager who selects stocks on the basis of their valuation as measured by ratios such as yield, price-earnings, book-to-market, etc.

Value-weighted market index. An index whose components are weighted on the basis of their market capitalization.

Variance. A measure of the volatility or dispersion of a variable. The squared value of the standard deviation.

Vector autoregressive models. Economic forecasting models that use variables selected on the basis of economic theory but allow the data to determine the interrelationships between the variables.

Volatility. The variability of an asset's return over time, usually measured by the standard deviation of returns.

Warrant. An option issued by a company or a financial institution. Most investors encounter warrants that are issued by companies on their own stock.

Weak-form efficient market theory. See *Efficient market theory*.

Weekend effect. Empirical regularity that stock returns appear to be lower on Mondays in the US and some other countries.

Weighted average number of shares in issue. If a company issues new shares part way through a financial year, all 'per share' calculations are made on the weighted average number of shares in issue during the year.

Wilshire 5000 Index. Value-weighted equity index consisting of all New York Stock Exchange and American Stock Exchange common stocks, plus the most active over-the-counter stocks.

WM. The WM Company. One of the two leading performance measurement firms in the UK.

Writing an option. Selling an option.

Yankie bond. A dollar-denominated bond sold in the US by a foreign organization.

Yield. Income from an investment times 100 divided by the value of the investment. In some cases, for example the redemption yield, yield refers to a measure of both income and capital return.

Yield curve. The mathematical relationship between yield and maturity calculated for a class of bonds (e.g. gilts). Also known as the term structure of interest rates.

Yield gap. Difference between the redemption yield of long-dated government bonds and the yield on equities.

Yield spread. The difference in the redemption yields of two fixed-income securities with different attributes such as maturity or issuer (e.g. five- and 10-year securities, and corporate and government securities).

Yield to call. For a callable bond, the yield to the first call date.

Yield to maturity. See *Redemption yield*.

Zero-coupon bond. A bond without coupon payments. The bond trades at a discount to its redemption value.

References

Frequently cited journals have been abbreviated as follows:

ABR	*Accounting and Business Research*
AER	*American Economic Review*
AFE	*Applied Financial Economics*
EJ	*Economic Journal*
FAJ	*Financial Analysts Journal*
HBR	*Harvard Business Review*
JACF	*Journal of Applied Corporate Finance*
JAE	*Journal of Accounting and Economics*
JAR	*Journal of Accounting Research*
JB	*Journal of Business*
JBF	*Journal of Banking and Finance*
JBFA	*Journal of Business Finance and Accounting*
JEP	*Journal of Economic Perspectives*
JF	*Journal of Finance*
JFE	*Journal of Financial Economics*
JFQA	*Journal of Financial and Quantitative Analysis*
JI	*Journal of Investing*
JPE	*Journal of Political Economy*
JPM	*Journal of Portfolio Management*
QJE	*Quarterly Journal of Economics*

Abarbanell, J.S. and Bushee, B.J. (1997) 'Fundamental analysis, future earnings, and stock prices', *JAR*, 6, Autumn, 159–78.

Abarbanell, J.S. and Bushee, B.J. (1998) 'Abnormal returns to a fundamental analysis strategy', *Accountancy Review*, 73, 19–45.

Abeysekera, S.P. and Mahajan, A. (1987) 'A test of the APT in pricing UK stocks', *JBFA*, 14, 377–91.

Aboody, D., Barth, M.F. and Kasznik, R. (1999) 'Revaluations of fixed assets and future firm performance: evidence from the UK', *JAE*, 26, 149–78.

Affleck-Graves, J. and Mendenhall, R.R. (1992) 'The relation between the Value Line enigma and post-earnings-announcement drift', *JFE*, 31, 75–91.

Aharony, J. and Swary, I. (1980) 'Quarterly dividend and earnings announcement and stockholders' returns: an empirical analysis', *JF*, 35, 1–12.

Aharony, J., Jones, C.P. and Swary, I. (1980) 'An analysis of the risk and return characteristics of corporate bankruptcy using capital market data', *JF*, 35, 100–16.

Akemann, C.A. and Keller, W.E. (1977) 'Relative strength does persist!', *JPM*, 4, Fall, 38–45.

Al-Debie, M. and Walker, M. (1999) 'Fundamental information analysis: an extension and UK evidence', *British Accounting Review*, 31, 261–80.

Altman, E.I. (1968) 'Financial ratios, discrimination analysis and the prediction of corporate bankruptcy', *JF*, 23, 589–609.

Altman, E. (1991) 'Defaults and returns on high yield bonds through the first half of 1991', *FAJ*, 47, November–December, 67–77.

Altman, E.I. and Kao, D.L. (1992a) 'The implications of corporate ratings drift', *FAJ*, 48, May–June, 64–75.

Altman, E.I. and Kao, D.L. (1992b) 'Rating drift in high-yield bonds', *Journal of Fixed Income*, 1, March, 15–20.

Altman, E.I. and Spivack, J. (1983) 'Predicting bankruptcy: the Value Line relative financial strength system vs. the Zeta bankruptcy classification approach', *FAJ*, 39, November–December, 60–67.

Altman, E.I., Haldeman, R. and Narayanan, P. (1977) 'ZETA analysis: a new model to identify bankruptcy risk of corporations', *JBF*, 1, 29–54.

Ambachtsheer, K.P. (1974) 'Profit potential in an "almost efficient" market', *JPM*, 1, Fall, 84–7.

Ambachtsheer, K.P. (1977) 'Where are the customer's alphas?', *JPM*, 4, Fall, 52–6.

Ambachtsheer, K.P. and Farrell, J.L. (1979) 'Can active management add value?', *FAJ*, 35, November–December, 39–47.

Amir, E. and Ganzach, Y. (1998) 'Overreaction and underreaction in analysts' forecasts', *Journal of Economic Behavior and Organization*, 37, 333–47.

Antoniou, A., Garrett, I. and Priestley, R. (1998) 'Macroeconomic variables as common pervasive risk factors and the empirical content of the arbitrage pricing theory', *Journal of Empirical Finance*, 5, 221–40.

Arbel, A. (1985a) 'Generic stocks: an old product in a new package', *JPM*, 11, Summer, 4–13.

Arbel, A. (1985b) *How to Beat the Market with High-Performance Generic Stocks*. New York: Morrow.

Arbel, A. and Strebel, P. (1983) 'Pay attention to neglected firms!', *JPM*, 9, Winter, 37–42.

Arbel, A., Carvell, S. and Strebel, P. (1983) 'Giraffes, institutions and neglected firms', *FAJ*, 39, May–June, 57–63.

Ariel, R.A. (1987) 'A monthly effect in stock returns', *JFE*, 17, 161–74.

Ariel, R.A. (1990) 'High stock returns before holidays: existence and evidence on possible causes', *JF*, 45, 1611–26.

Arnott, R.D. (1979) 'Relative strength revisited', *JPM*, 5, Spring, 19–23.

Arnott, R.D. (1980) 'Cluster analysis and stock price comovement', *FAJ*, 36, November–December, 56–62.

Arnott, R.D. (1985) 'The use and misuse of consensus earnings', *JPM*, 11, Spring, 18–27.

Arnott, R.D. and Henriksson, R.D. (1991) 'A disciplined approach to global asset allocation' in Aliber, R.Z. and Bruce, B.R. (eds) *Global Portfolios: Quantitative Strategies for Maximum Performance*. Homewood: Business One Irwin.

Arnott, R.D. and Pham, T.K. (1993) 'Tactical currency allocation', *FAJ*, 49, September–October, 47–52.

Arnott, R.D., Kelso, C.M., Kiscadden, S. and Macedo, R. (1989) 'Forecasting factor returns: an intriguing possibility', *JPM*, 16, Fall, 28–35.

Arsad, Z. and Coutts, J.A. (1997) 'Security price anomalies in the London International Stock Exchange: a 60 year perspective', *AFE*, 7, 455–64.

Arshanapalli, B., Coggin, T.D. and Doukas, J. (1998) 'Multi-factor asset pricing analysis of international value investment strategies', *JPM*, 24, Summer, 10–23.

Asch, S. (1951) 'Effects of group pressure upon the modification and distortion of judgements' in Guetzkow, H. (ed.) *Groups, Leadership and Men*. Pittsburgh: Carnegie Press.

Asness, C.S. (1997) 'The interaction of value and momentum strategies', *FAJ*, 53, March–April, 29–36.

Asness, C.S., Friedman, J.A., Krail, R.J. and Liew, J.M. (2000) 'Style timing: value versus growth', *JPM*, 26, Spring, 50–60.

Asness, C.S., Liew, J.M. and Stevens, R.L. (1997) 'Parallels between the cross-sectional predictability of stock and country returns', *JPM*, 23, Spring, 79–87.

Bachelier, L. (1900) 'Theorie de la Speculation', PhD dissertation, l'Ecole Normale Superieure. English translation in Cootner, P. (ed.) (1964) *The Random Character of Stock Market Prices*. Cambridge: Massachusetts Institute of Technology Press.

Bagnoli, M., Beneish, M.D. and Watts, S.G. (1999) 'Whisper forecasts of quarterly earnings per share', *JAE*, 28, 27–50.

Balachandran, B., Cadle, J. and Theobald, M. (1996) 'Interim dividend cuts and omissions in the UK', *European Financial Management*, 2, 23–38.

Ball, R. (1989) 'What do we know about stock market "efficiency"?' in Guimaraes, R.M.C. et al. (eds) *A Reappraisal of the Efficiency of Financial Markets*. Berlin: Springer-Verlag.

Balvers, R., Wu, Y. and Gilliland, E. (2000) 'Mean reversion across national stock markets and parametric contrarian investment strategies', *JF*, 55, 745–72.

Band, R.E. (1989) *Contrary Investing for the '90s*. New York: St Martin's Press.

Bank of England and HM Treasury (1998) *Changes to Gilt Market Trading Conventions*. London: Bank of England and HM Treasury.

Bannister, B.B. (1990) 'In search of excellence: a portfolio management perspective', *FAJ*, 46, March–April, 68–71.

Banz, R. (1981) 'The relation between return and market value of common stocks', *JFE*, 9, 3–18.

Banz, R.W. and Breen, W.K. (1986) 'Sample-dependent results using accounting and market data: some evidence', *JF*, 41, 779–93.

Barbee, W.C., Mukherji, S. and Raines, G.A. (1996) 'Do sales-price and debt-equity explain stock returns better than book-market and firm size?', *FAJ*, 52, March–April, 56–60.

Barber, B. and Odean, T. (1999) 'The courage of misguided convictions', *FAJ*, 55, November–December, 41–55.

Barber, B., Lehavy, R., McNichols, M. and Trueman, B. (1998) 'Can investors profit from the prophets? Consensus analyst recommendations and stock returns', at http://www.ssrn.com.

Baron, M., Clare, A.D. and Thomas, S.H. (1995) 'APM technology in fund management', *Professional Investor*, 5, June, 15–16.

Barry, C.B. and Brown, S.J. (1986) 'Limited information as a source of risk', *JPM*, 12, Winter, 66–72.

Barry, C.B., Peavy, J.W. and Rodriguez, M. (1998) 'Performance characteristics of emerging capital markets', *FAJ*, 54, January–February, 72–81.

Barsky, R.E. and De Long, J.B. (1990) 'Bull and bear markets in the twentieth century', *Journal of Economic History*, 50, 265–81.

Bartley, J.W. and Cameron, A.B. (1991) 'Long-run earnings forecasts by managers and financial analysts', *JBFA*, 18, 21–41.

Basu, S. (1975) 'The information content of price-earnings ratios', *Financial Management*, 4, Summer, 53–64.

Basu, S. (1977) 'The relationship between earnings' yield, market value and return for NYSE common stocks—further evidence', *JF*, 32, 663–81.

Basu, S. (1983) 'The relationship between earnings' yield, market value and return for NYSE common stocks', *JFE*, 12, 129–56.

Beard, C.G. and Sias, R.W. (1997) 'Is there a neglected-firm effect?', *FAJ*, 53, September–October, 19–23.

Beaver, W.H. (1968) 'Market prices, financial ratios and the prediction of failure', *JAR*, 6, 179–92.

Beaver, W., Kettler, P. and Scholes, M. (1970) 'The association between market determined and accounting determined risk measures', *Accounting Review*, 45, 654–82.

Beenstock, M. and Chan, K. (1986) 'Testing the arbitrage pricing theory in the United Kingdom', *Oxford Bulletin of Economics and Statistics*, 48, 121–41.

Beenstock, M. and Chan, K. (1988) 'Economic forces in the London Stock Market', *Oxford Bulletin of Economics and Statistics*, 50, 27–39.

Bell, D. and Levin, E. (1998) 'What causes intra-week regularities in stock returns? Some evidence from the UK', *AFE*, 8, 353–7.

Benartzi, S. and Thaler, R.H. (1995) 'Myopic loss aversion and the equity premium puzzle', *QJE*, 110, 73–92.

Benesh, G.A. and Peterson P.P. (1986) 'On the relation between earnings changes, analysts' forecasts and stock price fluctuations', *FAJ*, 42, November–December, 29–39, 55.

Bercel, A. (1994) 'Consensus expectations and international equity returns', *FAJ*, 50, July–August, 76–80.

Berges, A., McConnell, J. and Schlarbaum, G. (1984) 'The turn of the year in Canada', *JF*, 39, 185–92.

Berk, J.B. (1995) 'A critique of size-related anomalies', *Review of Financial Studies*, 8, 275–86.

Berk, J.B. (1997) 'Does size really matter?', *FAJ*, 53, September–October, 12–18.

Bernard, V. and Thomas, J. (1989) 'Post-earnings-announcement drift: delayed price response or risk premium?', *JAR*, 27 (supplement) 1–36.

Bernard, V.L. and Thomas J.K. (1990) 'Evidence that stock prices do not fully reflect the implications of current warnings for future earnings', *JAE*, 13, 305–40.

Bernhard, A. (n.d.) *How to Use The Value Line Investment Survey: A Subscriber's Guide.* New York: The Value Line Investment Survey.

Bernstein, R. (1995) *Style Investing: Unique Insight Into Equity Management.* New York: John Wiley & Sons.

Bessembinder, H. and Chan, K. (1998) 'Market efficiency and the returns to technical analysis', *Financial Management*, 27, 2, 5–17.

Bhandari, L.C. (1988) 'Debt/equity ratios and expected common stock returns: empirical evidence', *JF*, 43, 507–28.

Bhardwaj, R.K. and Brooks, L.D. (1992) 'The January anomaly: the effects of low share prices, transaction costs, and bid–ask bias', *JF*, 47, 553–76.

Bhaskar, K.N. and Morris, R.C. (1984) 'The accuracy of brokers' profit forecasts in the UK', *ABR*, 14, Spring, 113–24.

Biddle, G.C., Bowen, R.M. and Wallace, J.S. (1997) 'Does EVA® beat earnings? Evidence on associations with stock returns and firm values', *JAE*, 24, 301–36.

Biddle, G.C., Bowen, R.M. and Wallace, J.S. (1999) 'Evidence on EVA', *JACF*, 12, Summer, 69–79.

Black, F. (1989a) 'How to use the holes in Black–Scholes', *The Continental Bank JACF*, 1, Winter, 67–73. [Reprinted in Lofthouse, 1994.]

Black, F. (1989b) 'Universal hedging: optimizing currency risk and reward in international equity portfolios', *FAJ*, 45, July–August, 16–22.

Black, F. (1993) 'Beta and return', *JPM*, 20, Fall, 5–18.

Black, F. and Scholes, M.S. (1973) 'The pricing of options and corporate liabilities', *JPE*, 81, 637–54.

Black, F. and Scholes, M.S. (1974) 'The effects of dividend yield and dividend policy on common stock prices and returns', *JFE*, 1, 1–22.

Black, F., Jensen, M.C. and Scholes, M.S. (1972) 'The capital asset pricing model: some empirical tests' in Jensen, M.C. (ed.) *Studies in the Theory of Capital.* New York: Praeger.

Blake, C., Elton, E. and Gruber, M. (1993) 'The performance of bond mutual funds', *JB*, 66, 371–403.

Blake, D., Lehmann, B.N. and Timmermann, A. (1999) 'Asset allocation dynamics and pension fund performance', *JB*, 72, 429–61.

Blakey, G.G. (1994) *The Post-War History of the London Stock Market.* Didcot: Management Books 2000.

Bleiberg, S. (1989) 'How little we know – about P/Es, but also perhaps more than we think', *JPM*, 15, Summer, 26–31. [Reprinted in Lofthouse, 1994.]

Blume, M. (1971) 'On the assessment of risk', *JF*, 26, 1–10.

Blume, M. (1975) 'Betas and their regression tendencies', *JF*, 30, 785–95.

Blume, M.E. and Husic, F. (1973) 'Price, beta, and exchange listing', *JF*, 28, 283–99.

Board, J.L.G. and Sutcliffe, C.M.S. (1988) 'The weekend effect in UK stock prices', *JBFA*, 15, 199–213.

Board, J. and Sutcliffe, C. (1992) 'Stock market volatility and stock index futures', *Stock Exchange Quarterly with Quality of Markets Review*, Summer, 11–14. [Reprinted in Lofthouse, 1994.]

Boehm, E.A. and Moore, G.H. (1991) 'Financial market forecasts and rates of return based on leading index signals', *International Journal of Forecasting*, 7, 357–74.

Bohan, J. (1981) 'Relative strength: further positive evidence', *JPM*, 8, Fall, 36–9.

Bomford, M.D. (1968) 'Changes in the evaluation of equities', *Investment Analyst*, 22, 3–12.

Booth, J.R. and Booth, L.C. (1997) 'Economic factors, monetary policy, and expected returns on stocks and bonds', *Federal Reserve Bank of San Francisco Economic Review*, 2, 32–42.

Boudoukh, J. and Richardson, M. (1993) 'Stock returns and inflation: a long-horizon effect', *AER*, 83, 1346–55.

Bouman, S. and Jacobson, B. (1999) 'The halloween indicator', working paper at http://www.ssrn.com.

Bower, D.H., Bower, R.S. and Logue, D.E. (1984) 'A primer on arbitrage pricing theory', *Midland Corporate Finance Journal*, 2, Fall, 31–40.

Bowman, C. and Daniels, K. (1995) 'The influence of functional experince on perceptions of strategic priorities', *British Journal of Management*, 6, 157–67.

Bracker, K. and Morran, C. (1999) 'Tactical currency allocation revisited: four simple currency trading rules', *JI*, 8, Fall, 65–73.

Brealey, R. (1969) *An Introduction to Risk and Return from Common Stocks*. Cambridge: Massachusetts Institute of Technology Press.

Breton, G. and Taffler, R.J. (1995) 'Creative accounting and investment analyst response', *ABR*, 25, 81–92.

Brinson, G.P., Singer, B.D. and Beebower, G.L. (1991) 'Determinants of portfolio performance II: an update', *FAJ*, 47, May–June, 40–8.

Brock, W., Lakonishok, J. and LeBaron, B. (1992) 'Simple technical trading rules and the stochastic properties of stock returns', *JF*, 47, 1731–64.

Brookes, M. (1995) *Modelling Gilt Yields*. London: Goldman Sachs.

Brown, L.D. (1997a) 'Can ESP yield abnormal returns?', *JPM*, 23, Summer, 36–43.

Brown, L.D. (1997b) 'Earnings surprise research: synthesis and perspectives', *FAJ*, 53, March–April, 13–19.

Brown, M.R. and Condon, K.C. (1995) 'Estimate revisions: a quantitative study', *JI*, 4, Winter, 56–62.

Brown, L.D. and Jeong, S.K. (1998) 'Profiting from predicting earnings surprise', *Journal of Financial Statement Analysis*, 3, Winter, 57–66.

Brown, B. and Rozeff, M.S. (1978) 'The superiority of analyst forecasts as measures of expectations: evidence from earnings', *JF*, 34, 1–16.

Brown, G., Draper, P. and McKenzie, E. (1997) 'Consistency of UK pension fund investment performance', *JBFA*, 24, 155–78.

Brown, S.J., Goetzmann, W.N. and Kumar, A. (1998) 'The Dow theory: William Peter Hamilton's track record reconsidered', *JF*, 53, 1311–33.

Brown, L.D., Han, J.C.Y., Keon, E.F. and Quinn, W.H. (1996) 'Predicting analysts' earnings surprise', *JI*, 5, Spring, 17–23.

Brown, L.D., Richardson, G.D. and Schwager, S.J. (1987) 'An information interpretation of financial analyst superiority in forecasting earnings', *JAR*, 25, Spring, 49–67.

Bruce, B. and Eisenberg, A. (1992) 'Global synthetic index funds', *JI*, 1, Fall, 45–7.

Brush, J.S. (1986) 'Eight relative strength models compared', *JPM*, 13, Fall, 21–8.

Buchele, R.B. (1962) 'How to evaluate a firm', *California Management Review*, 5, Fall, 5–17.

Buffett, M. and Clark, D. (1997) *Buffettology*. New York: Rawson Associates.

Bulkley, G. and Tonks, I. (1989) 'Are UK stock prices excessively volatile? Trading rules and variance bounds tests', *EJ*, 99, 1083–98.

Burmeister, E., Roll, R. and Ross, S.A. (1997) *Using Macroeconomic Factors to Control Portfolio Risk*. BIRR Portfolio Analysis, Inc., http://www.birr.com.

Burton, J. (1998) 'Revisiting the capital asset pricing model', *Dow Jones Asset Manager*, May–June, 20–28. [Available at http://www.stanford.edu/~wfsharpe.]

Cadsby, C.B. and Ratner, M. (1992) 'Turn-of-month and pre-holiday effects on stock returns: some international evidence', *JBF*, 16, 497–509.

Campbell, K. and Limmack, R.J. (1997) 'Long-term over-reaction in the UK stock market and size adjustments', *AFE*, 7, 537–48.

Campbell, J.Y. and Shiller, R.J. (1988) 'Stock prices, earnings, and expected dividends', *JF*, 43, 661–76.

Campbell, J.Y. and Shiller, R.J. (1998) 'Valuation ratios and the long-run stock market outlook', *JPM*, 24, Winter, 11–26.

Campbell, J.Y., Lettau, M., Malkiel, B.G. and Xu, Y. (2000) 'Have individual stocks become more volatile? An empirical exploration of idiosyncratic risk', NBER working paper no. 7590.

Campbell, J.Y., Lo, A.W. and MacKinlay, A.C. (1997) *The Econometrics of Financial Markets*. Princeton: Princeton University Press.

Capaul, C., Rowley, I. and Sharpe, W.F. (1993) 'International value and growth stock returns', *FAJ*, 49, January–February, 27–36.

Capstaff, J., Paudyal, K. and Rees, W. (1996) 'Looking at the bright side of life', *Professional Investor*, 6, April, 25–7.

Capstaff, J., Paudyal, K. and Rees, W. (1999) 'The relative forecast accuracy of UK brokers', *ABR*, 30, 3–16.

Carhart, M. (1997) 'On persistence in mutual fund performance', *JF*, 52, 57–82.

Carman, P. (1981) 'The trouble with asset allocation', *JPM*, 8, Fall, 17–21.

Carman, P. (1988) *Tactical Asset Allocation: Have We Finally Found an Acceptable Name for Market Timing?* New York: Sanford C. Bernstein. [Reprinted in Lofthouse, 1994.]

Carruth, A.A., Hooker, M.A. and Oswald, A.J. (1998) 'Unemployment equilibria and input prices: theory and evidence from the United States', *Review of Economics and Statistics*, 80, 621–8.

Carvell, S.A. and Strebel, P.J. (1987) 'Is there a neglected firm effect?', *JBFA*, 14, 279–90.

Chan, K.C. and Chen, N. (1991) 'Structural and return characteristics of small and large firms', *JF*, 46, 1467–84.

Chan, A. and Chui, A.P.L. (1996) 'An empirical re-examination of the cross-section of expected returns: UK evidence', *JBFA*, 23, 1435–52.

Chan, L.K.C. and Lakonishok, J. (1993) 'Are the reports of beta's death premature?', *JPM*, 19, Summer, 51–62. [Reprinted in Lofthouse, 1994.]

Chan, K.C., Chen, N. and Hsieh, D.A. (1985) 'An exploratory investigation of the firm size effect', *JFE*, 14, 451–71.

Chan, L.K.C., Jegadeesh, N. and Lakonishok, J. (1996) 'Momentum strategies', *JF*, 51, 1681–1713.

Chan, L.K.C., Jegadeesh, N. and Lakonishok, J. (1999) 'The profitability of momentum strategies', *FAJ*, 55, November–December, 80–90.

Chandy, P.R. and Reichenstein, W. (1991) 'Timing strategies and the risk of missing bull markets', *AAII Journal*, 13, August, 17–19.

Chang, E.C., Pinegar, J.M. and Ravichandram, R. (1995) 'European day-of-the-week effects, beta asymmetries and international herding', *European Financial Management*, 1, March, 173–200.

Chen, N. (1988) 'Equilibrium asset pricing models and the firm size effect' in Dimson, E. (ed.) *Stock Market Anomalies*. Cambridge: Cambridge University Press.

Chen, N. (1991) 'Financial investment opportunities and the macroeconomy', *JF*, 46, 529–54.

Chen, C.R., Chan, A. and Mohan, N.J. (1993) 'Asset allocation managers' investment performance', *Journal of Fixed Income*, 2, December, 46–53.

Chen, N., Roll, R. and Ross, S.A. (1986) 'Economic forces and the stock market', *JB*, 59, 383–403.

Cho, J.Y. (1994) 'Properties of market expectations of accounting earnings by financial analysts: UK versus US', *ABR*, 24, 230–40.

Chopra, V.K. (1993) 'Improving optimization', *JI*, 2, Fall, 51–9.

Chopra, V.K. and Ziemba, W.T. (1993) 'The effect of errors in means, variances, and covariances on optimal portfolio choice', *JPM*, 19, Winter, 6–11.

Chopra, V.K. Hensel, C.R. and Turner, A.L. (1993) 'Massaging mean-variance inputs: returns from alternative global investment strategies in the 1980s', *Management Science*, 39, 845–55.

Chowdhury, M., Howe, J.S. and Lin, J. (1993) 'The relationship between aggregate insider transactions and stock market returns', *JFQA*, 28, 431–7.

Choy, A.Y.F. and O'Hanlon, J. (1989) 'Day of the week effects in the UK equity market: a cross-sectional analysis', *JBFA*, 16, 89–104.

Chua, J.H., Woodward, R.S. and To, E.C. (1987) 'Potential gains from stock market timing in Canada', *FAJ*, 43, September–October, 50–6.

Claessens, S., Dasgupta, S. and Glen, J. (1998) 'The cross section of stock returns: evidence from emerging markets', *Emerging Markets Quarterly*, 2, 4–13.

Clare, A., Priestley, R. and Thomas, S. (1997) 'The robustness of the APT to alternative estimators', *JBFA*, 24, 645–55.

Clare, A.D., Priestley, R. and Thomas, S.H. (1998) 'Reports of beta's death are premature: evidence from the UK', *JBF*, 22, 1207–29.

Clare, A.D., Thomas, S.H. and Wickens, M.R. (1994) 'Is the gilt-equity yield ratio useful for predicting UK stock returns?', *EJ*, 104, 303–15.

Clark, T.A. and Weinstein, M.I. (1983) 'The behavior of the common stock of bankrupt firms', *JF*, 38, 489–504.

Clarke, R.G. and Statman, M. (1998) 'Bullish or bearish?', *FAJ*, 54, May–June, 63–72.

Clayman, M. (1987) 'In search of excellence: the investor's viewpoint', *FAJ*, 43, May–June, 54–63.

Clayman, M. (1994) 'Excellence revisited', *FAJ*, 50, May–June, 61–5.

Clemen, R.T. (1989) 'Combining forecasts: a review and annotated bibliography', *International Journal of Forecasting*, 5, 559–83.

Cohen, K. and Pogue, J. (1967) 'An empirical evaluation of alternative portfolio selection models', *JB*, 40, 166–93.

Cole, J.A. (1984) 'Are dividend surprises independently important?', *JPM*, 10, Summer, 45–50.

Cole, K. Helwege, J. and Laster, D. (1996) 'Stock market valuation indicators: is this time different?', *FAJ*, 52, May–June, 56–64.

Collins, W.A. and Hopwood, W.S. (1980) 'A multivariate analysis of annual earnings forecasts generated from quarterly forecasts of financial analysts and univariate time series models', *JAR*, 18, 340–406.

Condoyanni, K., O'Hanlon, J. and Ward, C.W.R. (1987) 'Day of the week effects on stock returns: international evidence', *JBFA*, 14, 159–74.

Conover, C.M., Jensen, G.R. and Johnstone, R.R. (1999) 'Monetary conditions and international investing', *FAJ*, 55, July–August, 38–48.

Cook, T. and Rozeff, M.S. (1984) 'Size and earnings/price ratio anomalies: one effect or two?', *JQFA*, 19, 449–66.

Copeland, T.E. and Mayers, D. (1982) 'The Value Line enigma 1965–1978: a case study of performance evaluation issues', *JFE*, 10, 289–321.

Corhay, A., Hawawini, G. and Michel, P. (1987) 'Seasonality in the risk-return relationship: some international evidence', *JF*, 42, 49–68.

Corhay, A., Hawawini, G. and Michel, P. (1988) 'The pricing of equity on the London Stock Exchange: seasonality and size premium' in Dimson, E. (ed.) *Stock Market Anomalies*. Cambridge: Cambridge University Press.

Costello, E. (1992) 'How to spot a company going bust', *Investors Chronicle* (supplement) 26, 12–13.

Cottle, S., Murray, R.F. and Block, F.E. (1988) *Graham and Dodd's Security Analysis*, 5th edn. New York: McGraw-Hill.

Coval, J.D. and Moskowitz, T.J. (1999) 'Home bias at home: local equity preference in domestic portfolios', *JF*, 54, 2045–73.

Cowles, A. (1934) 'Can stockmarket forecasters forecast?', *Econometrica*, 1, 309–24.

Cox, J.C., Ross, S.A. and Rubinstein, M. (1979) 'Option pricing: a simplified approach', *JFE*, 7, 229–63.

Cragg, L. and Malkiel, B. (1968) 'The consensus and accuracy of some predictions of the growth of corporate earnings', *JF*, 23, 67–84.

Cross, F. (1973) 'The behavior of stock prices on Fridays and Mondays', *FAJ*, 29, November–December, 67–9.

CSFB (2000) *The CSFB Equity-Gilt Study*. London: Credit Suisse First Boston (Europe) Ltd.

Cullity, J.P. (1987) 'Signals of cyclical movements in inflation and interest rates', *FAJ*, 43, September–October, 40–9.

Cutler, D.M., Poterba, J.M. and Summers, L.H. (1989) 'What moves stock prices?', *JPM*, 15, Spring, 4–11.

Davies, G. and Shah, M. (1992) 'New methods of forecasting GDP growth in the UK', *The UK Economics Analyst*, June.

Davis, J.L. (1994) 'The cross-section of realized stock returns: the pre-COMPUSTAT evidence', *JF*, 49, 1579–93.

Davis, J.L., Fama, E.F. and French, K.R. (2000) 'Characteristics, covariances, and average returns: 1929 to 1997', *JF*, 55, 389–406.

De Bondt, W.F.M. and Thaler, R. (1985) 'Does the stock market overreact?', *JF*, 40, 793–808.

De Bondt, W.F.M. and Thaler, R. (1987) 'Further evidence on investor overreaction and stock market seasonality', *JF*, 42, 557–81.

De Bondt, W.F.M. and Thaler, R. (1989) 'A mean reverting walk down Wall Street', *JEP*, 3, Winter, 189–202.

Debt Management Office (1999) *Gilts: An Investor's Guide*. London: Debt Management Office.

Dechow, P.M., Hutton, A.P. and Sloan, R.G. (1999) 'An empirical assessment of the residual income valuation model', *JAE*, 26, 1–34.

Detzler, M.L. (1999) 'The performance of global bond mutual funds', *JBF*, 23, 1195–217.

Deutsch, M. and Gerard, H. (1955) 'A study of normative and informational influence upon individual judgment', *Journal of Abnormal and Social Psychology*, 51, 629–36.

Devenow, A. and Welch, I. (1996) 'Rational herding in financial economics', *European Economic Review*, 40, 603–15.

Dhrymes, P.J., Friend, I., Gultekin, M.N. and Gultekin, N.B. (1985) 'New tests of the APT and their implications', *JF*, 40, 659–74.

Diacogiannis, G.P. (1986) 'Arbitrage pricing model: a critical examination of its empirical applicability for the London Stock Exchange', *JBFA*, 13, 489–504.

Diamonte, R.L., Liew, J.M. and Stevens, R.L. (1996) 'Political risk in emerging and developed markets', *FAJ*, 52, May–June, 71–6.

Dimson, E. (ed.) (1988) *Stock Market Anomalies*. Cambridge: Cambridge University Press.

Dimson, E. and Fraletti, P. (1986) 'Brokers' recommendations: the value of a telephone tip', *EJ*, 96, 139–59.

Dimson, E. and Marsh, P. (1984) 'An analysis of brokers' and analysts' unpublished forecasts of UK stock returns', *JF*, 39, 1257–92.

Dimson, E. and Marsh, P. (1985) 'Stock pickers, chumps, chimps or champs?', *Investment Analyst*, 75, 26–35.

Dimson, E. and Marsh, P. (1986) 'Event study methodologies and the size effect: the case of UK press recommendations', *JFE*, 17, 113–42.

Dimson, E. and Marsh, P. (1992) *The Hoare Govett Smaller Companies Index*. London: Hoare Govett.

Dimson, E. and Marsh, P. (1999) 'Murphy's law and market anomalies', *JPM*, 25, Winter, 53–69.

Dimson, E. and Marsh, P. (2000) *The Hoare Govett Smaller Companies Index 1999*. London: ABN Amro Hoare Govett.

Dimson, E., Marsh, P. and Staunton, M. (2000) *The Millennium Book: A Century of Investment Returns*. London: ABN Amro/LBS.

Divecha, A.B., Drach, J. and Stefek, D. (1992) 'Emerging markets: a quantitative perspective', *JPM*, 19, Fall, 41–50. [Reprinted in Lofthouse, 1994.]

Donnelly, B. (1985) 'The dividend discount model comes into its own', *Institutional Investor*, March, 157–9, 162.

Dowen, R.J. and Bauman, W.S. (1991) 'Revisions in corporate earnings forecasts and common stock returns', *FAJ*, 47, March–April, 86–90.

Draper, P. and Paudyal, K. (1997) 'Microstructure and seasonality in the UK equity market', *JBFA*, 24, 1177–204.

Dreman, D. (1982) *The New Contrarian Investment Strategy*. New York: Random House.

Dreman, D.N. and Lufkin, E.A. (1997) 'Do contrarian strategies work within industries?', *JI*, 6, Fall, 7–29.

Droms, W.G. (1989) 'Market timing as an investment policy', *FAJ*, 45, January–February, 73–7.

Drummen, M. and Zimmermann, H. (1992) 'The structure of European stock returns', *FAJ*, 48, July–August, 15–26.

DuBois, C.H. (1988) 'Tactical asset allocation: a review of current techniques' in Arnott, R.D. and Fabozzi, F.J. (eds) *Asset Allocation: A Handbook of Portfolio Policies, Strategies and Tactics*. Chicago: Probus.

Dumas, B. (1994) 'A test of the international CAPM using business cycle indicators as instrumental variables' in Frankel, J.A. (ed.) *The Internationalization of Equity Markets*. Chicago: University of Chicago Press.

The Economist (1999) 'We woz wrong', *The Economist*, 353, 18 December, 61–2.

Edmister, R.O. and Greene, J.B. (1980) 'Performance of super-low price stocks, *JPM*, 7, Fall, 36–41.

Edwards, F.R. (1999) 'Hedge funds and the collapse of Long-Term Capital Management', *JEP*, 13, Spring, 189–210.

Edwards, E. and Bell, P. (1961) *The Theory and Measurement of Business Income*. Berkeley: University of California Press.

Edwards, R.D. and Magee, J. (1984) *Technical Analysis of Stock Trends*, 5th edn. Springfield: John Magee.

Elliott, J.W. and Baier, J.R. (1979) 'Econometric models and current interest rates: how well do they predict future rates?', *JF*, 34, 975–86.

Elton, E.J. and Gruber, M.J. (1972) 'Earnings estimation and the accuracy of expectational data', *Management Science*, 18, 409–24.

Elton, E.J. and Gruber, M.J. (1997) 'Modern portfolio theory, 1950 to date', *JBF*, 21, 1743–59.

Elton, E.J., Gruber, M.J. and Blake, C.R. (1996) 'The persistence of risk-adjusted mutual fund performance', *JB*, 69, 133–57.

Elton, E., Gruber, M. and Blake, C. (1998) *The Investment Portfolio*. New York: John Wiley & Sons.

Elton, E.J., Gruber, M.J. and Grossman, S. (1986) 'Discrete expectational data and portfolio performance', *JF*, 41, 699–714.

Elton, E.J., Gruber, M.J. and Gultekin, M. (1981) 'Expectations and share prices', *Management Science*, 27, 975–87.

Elton, E.J., Gruber, M.J. and Gultekin, M.N. (1984) 'Professional expectations: accuracy and diagnosis of errors', *JQFA*, 19, 351–63.

Elton, E.J., Gruber, M.J. and Padberg, M.W. (1978) 'Optimal portfolios from simple ranking devices', *JPM*, 4, Spring, 15–19.

Elton, E.J., Gruber, M.J. and Rentzler, J. (1983) 'A simple examination of the empirical relationship between dividend yields and deviations from the CAPM', *JBF*, 7, 135–46.

Emanuelli, J.F. and Pearson, R.G. (1994) 'Using earnings estimates for global asset allocation', *FAJ*, 50, March–April, 60–72.

Erb, C.B., Harvey, C.R. and Viskanta, T.E. (1994) 'Forecasting international equity correlations', *FAJ*, 50, November–December, 32–45.

Erb, C.B., Harvey, C.R. and Viskanta, T.E. (2000) 'Understanding emerging market bonds', *Emerging Markets Quarterly*, 4, Spring, 7–23.

Estrella, A. and Hardouvelis, G.A. (1991) 'The term structure as a predictor of real economic activity', *JF*, 46, 555–76.

Fama, E.F. (1970) 'Efficient capital markets: a review of theory and empirical work', *JF*, 25, 383–417.

Fama, E.F. (1991) 'Efficient capital markets: II', *JF*, 46, 1575–1617.

Fama, E.F. (1998) 'Market efficiency, long-term returns, and behavioral finance', *JFE*, 49, 283–306.

Fama, E.F. and French, K.R. (1988a) 'Dividend yields and expected stock returns', *JFE*, 22, 3–26.

Fama, E.F. and French, K.R. (1988b) 'Permanent and temporary components of stock prices', *JPE*, 96, 246–73.

Fama, E.F. and French, K.R. (1989) 'Business conditions and expected returns of stocks and bonds', *JFE*, 25, 23–49.

Fama, E.F. and French, K.R. (1992) 'The cross-section of expected stock returns', *JF*, 47, 427–65.

Fama, E.F. and French, K.R. (1993) 'Common risk factors in the returns on stocks and bonds', *JFE*, 35, 3–56.

Fama, E.F. and French, K.R. (1995) 'Size and book-to-market factors in earnings and returns', *JF*, 50, 131–55.

Fama, E.F. and French, K.R. (1996a) 'Multifactor explanations of asset pricing anomalies', *JF*, 51, 55–84.

Fama, E.E. and French, K.R. (1996b) 'The CAPM is wanted, dead or alive', *JF*, 51, 1947–58.

Fama, E.F. and French, K.R. (1998) 'Value versus growth: the international evidence', *JF*, 53, 1975–99.

Fama, E.E. and French, K.R. (1999) 'Disappearing dividends: changing firm characteristics or lower propensity to pay?', Centre for Research in Security Prices, working paper no. 509, University of Chicago.

Fama, E.F. and MacBeth, J.D. (1973) 'Risk, return and equilibrium: empirical tests', *JPE*, 81, 607–36.

Fama, E.F., Fisher, L. and Roll, R. (1969) 'Adjustment of stock prices to new information', *International Economic Review*, 10, 1–21.

Farrell, J.L. (1974) 'Analyzing covariation of returns to determine homogeneous stock groupings', *JB*, 47, 186–207.

Farrell, J.L. (1982) 'A disciplined stock selection strategy', *Interfaces*, 12, October, 19–30.

Farrell, J.L. (1983) *Guide to Portfolio Management*. New York: McGraw-Hill.

Ferson, W.E. and Harvey, C.R. (1991) 'Sources of predictability in portfolio returns', *FAJ*, 47, May–June, 49–56.

Ferson, W.E. and Harvey, C.R. (1994) An exploratory investigtion of the fundamental determinates of national equity returns' in Frankel, J.A. (ed.) *The Internationalization of Equity Markets*. Chicago: Chicago University Press.

Fields, M.J. (1931) 'Stock prices: a problem in verification', *JB*, 4, 415–18.

Fields, M.J. (1934) 'Security prices and stock exchange holidays in relation to short selling', *JB*, 7, 328–38.

Fielitz, B.D. and Muller, F.L. (1983) 'The asset allocation decision', *FAJ*, 39, July–August, 44–50.

Finnerty, J.E. (1976) 'Insiders and market efficiency', *JF*, 31, 1141–8.

Fischhoff, B. (1975) 'Hindsight ≠ foresight: the effect of outcome knowledge on judgment under uncertainty', *Journal of Experimental Psychology: Human Perception and Performance*, 1, 288–99.

Fischhoff, B. and Beyth, R. (1975) ' "I knew it would happen": remembered probabilities of once-future things', *Organizational Behavior and Human Performance*, 13, 1–16.

Fisher, K.L. (1984a) 'Price-sales ratios: a new tool for measuring stock popularity', *AAII Journal*, 6, June, 13–17.

Fisher, K.L. (1984b) *Super Stocks*. Homewood: Business One Irwin.

Fisher, L. (1959) 'Determinants of risk premiums on corporate bonds', *JPE*, 67, 217–37.

Forbes, W.P. (1996) 'Picking winners? A survey of the mean reversion and overreaction of stock prices literature', *Journal of Economic Surveys*, 10, 123–58.

Foster, G. (1979) 'Briloff and the capital markets', *JAR*, 17, 262–74. [Reprinted in Lofthouse, 1994.]

Fouse, W.L. (1976) 'Risk and liquidity: the keys to stock price behaviour', *FAJ*, 32, May–June, 35–45.

Francis, J., Olsson, P. and Oswold, D.R. (2000) 'Comparing the accuracy and explainability of dividend, free cash flow, and abnormal earnings equity value estimates', *JAR*, 38, Spring, 45–70.

Frankel, J.A. (ed.) (1994) *The Internationalization of Equity Markets*. Chicago: University of Chicago Press.

Frankel, J.A. and Froot, K.A. (1990) 'Chartists, fundamentalists, and trading in the foreign exchange market', *AER Papers and Proceedings*, 80, 181–5.

Fraser, P. (1995) 'UK stock and government bond markets: predictability and the term structure', *AFE*, 5, 61–7.

French, K.R. and Roll, R. (1986) 'Stock return variances: the arrival of information and the reaction of traders', *JFE*, 17, 5–26.

Fried, D. and Givoly, D. (1982) 'Financial analysts' forecasts of earnings', *JAE*, 4, 85–107.

Friend, I., Westerfield, R. and Granito, M. (1978) 'New evidence on the capital asset pricing model', *JF*, 33, 903–20.

Fritzemeier, L.H. (1936) 'Relative price fluctuation of industrial stocks in different price groups', *JB*, 9, 133–54.

Froot, K.A. (1990) 'Short rates and expected asset returns', National Bureau of Economic Research working paper no. 3247.

Froot, K.A. (1993) 'Currency hedging over long horizons', National Bureau of Economic Research working paper no. 4355.

Froot, K.A. and Dabora, E.M. (1999) 'How are stock prices affected by the location of trade?', *JFE*, 53, 189–216.

Froot, K.A. and Rogoff, K. (1995) 'Perspectives on PPP and long-run real exchange rates' in Grossman, G.M. and Rogoff, K. (eds) *Handbook of International Economics*, Vol. 3. Amsterdam: North-Holland.

Froot, K.A. and Thaler, R.H. (1990) 'Anomalies: foreign exchange', *JEP*, 4, Summer, 179–92.

Frost, P.A. and Savarino, J.E. (1988) 'For better performance: constrain portfolio weights', *JPM*, 15, Fall, 29–34.

Fuller, R.J. and Hsia, C. (1984) 'A simplified common stock valuation model', *FAJ*, 40, September–October, 49–56.

Fuller, R.J. and Kling, J.L. (1990) 'Is the stock market predictable?', *JPM*, 16, Summer, 28–36.

Fuller, R.J. and Wong, G.W. (1988) 'Traditional versus theoretical risk measures', *FAJ*, 44, March–April, 52–7. [Reprinted in Lofthouse, 1994.]

Fuller, R.J., Huberts, L.C. and Levinson, M.J. (1993) 'Returns to E/P strategies, higgledy-piggledy growth, analysts' forecast errors, and omitted risk factors', *JPM*, 19, Winter, 13–24.

Garrett, I. and Priestly, R. (1997) 'Do assumptions about factor structure matter in empirical tests of the APT?', *JBFA*, 24, 249–60.

Geroski, P.A. (1998) 'An applied econometrician's view of large company performance', *Review of Industrial Organization*, 13, 271–93.

Gerstein, M.H. (1986) 'Timeliness ranks: how they're computed and why they change', *Value Line: Selection and Opinion*, 41, 19 September, 871–75.

Goetzmann, W.N. (1993) 'Patterns in three centuries of stock market prices', *JB*, 66, 249–70.

Goldstein, M.L., Sommer, M. and Pari, R.A. (1991) *The Bernstein Multifactor Optimization Model*. New York: Sanford C. Bernstein. [Reprinted in Lofthouse, 1994.]

Gooding, A.E. (1978) 'Perceived risk and capital asset pricing', *JF*, 33, 1401–21.

Gordon, R.J. (2000) 'Does the "New Economy" measure up to the great inventions of the past?', *JEP*, 14, 49–74.

Grace, W.J. Jr (1985) *The Phoenix Approach*. New York: Bantam.

Graham, B. (1973) *The Intelligent Investor*, 4th rev. edn. New York: Harper and Row.

Graham, B. (1976) 'A conversation with Benjamin Graham'. *FAJ*, 32, September–October, 20–3.

Graham, B., Dodd, D.L. and Cottle, S. (1962) *Security Analysis*, 4th edn. New York: McGraw-Hill.

Granatelli, A. and Martin, J.D. (1984) 'Management quality and investment performance', *FAJ*, 40, November–December, 72–4.

Gregory, A., Matatko. J., Tonks, I. and Purkis, R. (1994) 'UK directors' trading: the impact of dealings in smaller firms', *EJ*, 100, 37–53.

Grossman, S. and Stiglitz, J. (1980) 'On the impossibility of informationally efficient markets', *AER*, 70, 393–408.

Grundy, K. and Malkiel, B.G. (1996) 'Reports of beta's death have been greatly exaggerated', *JPM*, 22, Spring, 36–44.

Gultekin M.N. and Gultekin, N.B. (1983) 'Stock market seasonaility: international evidence', *JFE*, 12 469–81.

Hall, T.W. and Tsay, J.J. (1988) 'An evaluation of the performance of portfolios selected from Value Line rank one stocks: 1976–82', *Journal of Financial Research*, 11, Fall, 227–40.

Harris, L. (1986) 'How to profit from intradaily stock returns', *JPM*, 12, Winter, 61–4.

Haugen, R.A. (1996) The effects of intrigue, liquidity, imprecision, and bias on the cross-section of expected returns', *JPM*, 22, Summer, 8–17.

Haugen, R.A. (1997) *Modern Investment Theory*, 4th edn. Upper Saddle River: Prentice Hall.

Haugen, R.A. and Baker, N.L. (1996) 'Commonality in the determinants of expected stock returns', *JFE*, 41, 401–39.

Haugen, R.A. and Jorion, P. (1996) 'The January effect: still there after all these years', *FAJ*, 52, January–February, 27–31.

Hawkins, E.H., Chamberlin, S.C. and Daniel, W.E. (1984) 'Earnings expectations and security prices', *FAJ*, 40, September–October, 24–38, 74.

Hayek, F.A. (1945) 'The use of knowledge in society', *AER*, 35, 519–30.

Healy, P.M., Palepu, K.G. and Ruback, R.S. (1997) 'Which takeovers are profitable? Strategic or financial?', *Sloan Management Review*, 38, Summer, 45–57.

Henry, S.G.B. and Pesaran, B. (1993) 'VAR models of inflation', *Bank of England Quarterly Bulletin*, 33, May, 231–9.

Hensel, C.R. and Ziemba, W.T. (1996) 'Investment results from exploiting turn-of-the-month effects', *JPM*, 22, Spring, 17–23.

Hensel, C.R., Ezra, D.D. and Ilkiw, J.H. (1991) 'The importance of the asset allocation decision', *FAJ*, 47, July–August, 65–72.

Hensel, C.R., Sick, G.A. and Ziemba, W.T. (1994) 'The turn-of-the-month effect in the US stock index futures markets, 1982–1992', *Review of Futures Markets*, 13, 827–56.

Herzberg, M.M., Guo, J. and Brown, L.D. (1999) 'Enhancing earnings predictability using individual analyst forecasts', *JI*, 8, Summer, 15–24.

Heston, S.L., Rouwenhorst, K.G. and Wessels, R.E. (1999) 'The role of beta and size in the cross-section of European stock returns', *European Financial Management*, 5, 9–27.

Hickman, W.B. (1958) *Corporate Bond Quality and Investor Experience*. Princeton: Princeton University Press.

Hill, I. and Duffield, S. (2000) 'Ownership of United Kingdom quoted companies at the end of 1998', *Economic Trends*, 557, April, 85–7.

Hirshleifer, D. (1995). 'The blind leading the blind: social influences, fads, and informational cascades' in Tommasi, M. and Lerullixx, K. (eds) *The New Economics of Human Behavior*. New York: Cambridge University Press.

Holloway, C. (1981) 'A note on testing an aggressive investment strategy using Value Line ranks', *JF*, 36, 711–19.

Holmes, G. and Sugden, A. (1999) *Interpreting Company Reports and Accounts*, 7th edn. Harlow: Financial Times/Prentice Hall.

HSBC Investment Bank (2000) *The Red Book*. June. London: HSBC Investment Bank.

Huberman, G. (1998) 'Familiarity breeds investment', working paper, Columbia Business School.

Hudson, R., Dempsey, M. and Keasey, K. (1996) 'A note on the weak form efficiency of capital markets: the application of simple technical trading rules to UK stock prices – 1935 to 1994', *JBF*, 20, 1121–32.

Hull, J.C. (2000) *Options, Futures and Other Derivatives*, 4th edn. Upper Saddle River: Prentice Hall.

Ibbotson, R.G. (1989) 'On the cheap', *FAJ*, 45, September–October, 8–11.

Ibbotson, R.G. and Brinson, G.P. (1993) *Global Investing*. New York: McGraw-Hill.

Ilmanen, A. (1996) 'When do bond markets reward investors for interest rate risk?', *JPM*, 22, Winter, 52–63.

Insurance Trends (2000) 'Research update: how much in funded pensions, 1986 to 1998', *Insurance Trends*, 26, July, 24–26.

Investment Registry and Stock Exchange Limited (1904) *How to Protect Capital Invested in Stocks and Shares*. London: Investment Registry and Stock Exchange.

Jacob, J., Lys, T.Z. and Neale, M.A. (1999) 'Expertise in forecasting performance of security analysts', *JAE*, 28, 51–82.

Jacobs, B.I. and Levy, K.H. (1988a) 'Disentangling equity return regularities: new insights and investment opportunities', *FAJ*, 44, May–June, 47–62.

Jacobs, B.I. and Levy, K.N. (1988b) 'On the value of "value" ', *FAJ*, 44, July–August, 47–62.

Jaffe, J.F. (1974) 'Special information and insider trading', *JB*, 47, 410–28.

Jaffe, J. and Westerfield, R. (1985) 'The week-end effect in common stock returns: the international evidence', *JF*, 40, 432–54.

Jaffe, J. and Westerfield, R. (1989) 'Is there a monthly effect in stock market returns? Evidence from foreign countries', *JBF*, 13, 237–44.

Jaffe, J., Keim, D.B. and Westerfield, R. (1989) 'Earnings yields, market values, and stock returns', *JF*, 44, 135–48.

Jankus, J.C. (1997) 'Relating global bond yields to macroeconomic forecasts', *JPM*, 23, Spring, 96–101.

Jeffrey, R.H. (1984) 'The folly of stock market timing', *HBR*, 62, July-August, 102–10.

Jegadeesh, N. (1990) 'Evidence of predictable behavior of stock returns', *JF*, 54, 1249–90.

Jegadeesh, N. and Titman, S. (1993) 'Returns to buying winners and selling losers: implications for stock market efficiency', *JF*, 48, 65–91.

Jensen, M.C. (1969) 'Risk, the pricing of capital assets, and the evaluation of investment portfolios', *JB*, 42, 167–247.

Jensen, M.C. and Bennington, G.A. (1970) 'Random walks and technical theories: some additional evidence', *JF*, 25, 469–82.

Jensen, G.R., Johnson, R.R. and Mercer, J.M. (1997) 'New evidence on size and price-to-book effects in stock returns', *FAJ*, 53, November–December, 34–42.

Jensen, G.R., Mercer, J.M. and Johnson, R.R. (1996) 'Business conditions, monetary policy, and expected security returns', *JFE*, 40, 213–37.

Jones, C.P. (2000) *Investments*, 7th edn. New York: John Wiley & Sons.

Jones, R.C. (1989) 'Group rotation from the bottom up', *JPM*, 15, Summer, 32–8.

Jones, S.L., Lee, W. and Apenbrink, R. (1991) 'New evidence on the January effect before personal income taxes', *JF*, 46, 1909–14.

Jorion, P. and Goetzmann, W. (1999) 'Global stock markets in the twentieth century', *JF*, 55, 953–80.

Joy, O.M. and Jones, C.P. (1986) 'Should we believe the tests of market efficiency?', *JPM*, 12, Summer, 49–54.

Kahn, R.N. and Rudd, A. (1995) 'Does historical performance predict future performance?', *FAJ*, 51, November–December, 43–52.

Kahn, R.N. and Rudd, A. (1999) 'Modelling analyst behavior', *JI*, 8, Summer, 7–14.

Kahneman, D. and Riepe, M.W. (1998) 'Aspects of investor psychology', *JPM*, 24, Summer, 52–65.

Kahneman, D. and Tversky, A. (1984) 'Choices, values and frames', *American Psychologist*, 39, 341–50.

Kandel, S. and Stambaugh, R. (1987) 'On correlations and the sensitivity of inferences about mean-variance efficiency', *JFE*, 18, 61–80.

Kandel, S. and Stambaugh, R. (1991) 'Asset returns and intertemporal preferences', *Journal of Monetary Economics*, 27, 39–71.

Kandel, S and Stambaugh, R. (1995) 'Portfolio inefficiency and the cross-section of expected returns', *JF*, 50, 157–84.

Kao, D. and Shumaker, R.D. (1999) 'Equity style timing', *FAJ*, 55, January–February, 37–48.

Karpoff, J.M. (1987) 'The relationship between price changes and trading volume: a survey', *JQFA*, 22, 109–26.

Katz, S., Lilien, S. and Nelson, B. (1985) 'Stock market behaviour around bankruptcy model distress and recovery predictions', *FAJ*, 41, January–February, 70–4.

Keim, D.B. (1983) 'Size-related anomalies and stock return seasonality', *JFE*, 12, 13–22.

Keim, D.B. (1985) 'Dividend yields and stock returns: implications of abnormal January returns', *JFE*, 14, 473–89.

Keim, D.B. (1986) 'Dividend yields and the January effect', *JPM*, 12, Winter, 54–60.

Keim, D.B. (1990) 'A new look at the effects of firm size and E/P ratio on stock returns', *FAJ*, 46, March–April, 56–67.

Keim, D.B. and Ziemba, W.T. (eds) (2000) *Security Market Imperfections in World-wide Equity Markets*. Cambridge: Cambridge University Press.

Kelly, J.M., Martins, L.F. and Carlson, J.H. (1998) 'The relationship between bonds and stocks in emerging countries, *JPM*, Spring.

Kemp, A.G. and Reid, G.C. (1971) 'The random walk hypothesis and the recent behaviour of equity prices in Britain', *Economica*, 38, 28–51.

Kendall, M.G. (1953) 'The analysis of economic time-series. Part I: prices', *Journal of the Royal Statistical Society*, 116, 11–25.

Keppler, A.M. (1991a) 'The importance of dividend yields in country selection', *JPM*, 17, Winter, 24–9.

Keppler, A.M. (1991b) 'Further evidence on the predictability of international equity returns', *JPM*, 18, Fall, 48–53.

Keynes, J.M. (1925) 'An American study of shares versus bonds as permanent investments', *Nation and Athenaeum*, 2 May. [Reprinted in Moggridge, 1983.]

Keynes, J.M. [1936] (1961) *The General Theory of Employment Interest and Money*. London: Macmillan.

King, B. (1966) 'Market and industry factors in stock price behavior', *JB*, 39, 139–90.

King, S. (1999) *Bubble Trouble*. London: HSBC Investment Bank.

King, M. and Roell, A. (1988) 'Insider Trading', LSE Financial Markets Group special paper series, no. 4.

Kirscher, J.C. (1990) 'Machine "seer" handicaps stocks for customer portfolios', *Bank Management*, 66, 54–56.

Kleidon, A. (1986) 'Variance bounds tests and stock price valuation models', *JPE*, 94, 953–1001.

Kleiman, R.T. (1999) 'Some new evidence on EVA companies', *JACF*, 12, Summer, 80–91.

Klein, R.W. and Bawa, V.S. (1977) 'The effect of limited information and estimation risk on optimal portfolio diversification', *JFE*, 5, 89–111.

Kolb, R.A. and Stekler, H.O. (1996) 'How well do analysts forecast interest rates?', *Journal of Forecasting*, 15, 385–94.

Kolodny, R., Laurence, M. and Ghosh A. (1989) 'In search of excellence: for whom?', *JPM*, 15, Spring, 56–60.

Koski, J.L. and Pontiff, J. (1999) 'How are derivatives used? Evidence from the mutual fund industry', *JF*, 54, 791–816.

Kothari, S.P., Shanken, J. and Sloan, R.G. (1995) 'Another look at the cross-section of expected returns', *JF*, 50, 185–224.

Kritzman, M. (1993) 'What practitions need to know . . . about factor methods', *FAJ*, 49, January–February, 12–15.

Kross, W. (1985) 'The size effect is primarily a price effect', *Journal of Financial Research*, 8, 169–79.

Krugman, P. (1997) 'How fast can the US economy grow?', *HBR*, 75, July–August, 123–9.

La Porta, R., Lakonishok, J., Shleifer, A. and Vishny, R.W. (1997) 'Good news for value stocks: further evidence on market efficiency', *JF*, 52, 859–74.

Lacey, N.J. and Phillips-Patrick, F.J. (1992) 'Source of the Value Line enigma', *AFE*, 2, 173–8.

Lakonishok, J. and Shapiro, A.C. (1984) 'Stock returns, beta, variance and size: an empirical analysis', *FAJ*, 40, July–August, 36–41.

Lakonishok, J. and Smidt, S. (1988) 'Are seasonal anomalies real? A ninety-year perspective', *Review of Financial Studies*, 1, 403–25.

Lakonishok, J., Shleifer, A. and Vishny, R.W. (1992) 'The structure and performance of the money management industry', *Brookings Papers on Economic Activity: Microeconomics*, 339–79.

Lakonishok, J., Shleifer, A. and Vishny, R.W. (1994) 'Contrarian investment, extrapolation, and risk', *JF*, 49, 1541–93.

Langer, E.J. (1975) 'The illusion of control', *Journal of Personality and Social Psychology*, 32, 311–28.

Lanstein, R.J. and Jahnke, W.W. (1979) 'Applying capital market theory to investing', *Interfaces*, 9, 23–38.

Lee, W.Y. and Solt, M.E. (1986) 'Insider trading: a poor guide to market timing', *JPM*, 12, Summer, 65–71.

Lehmann, B.N. (1990) 'Fads, martingales and market efficiency', *QJE*, 105, 1–28.

LeRoy, S.E. (1990) 'Capital market efficiency: an update', *Federal Reserve Bank of San Francisco Economic Review*, Spring, 29–40.

Lev, B. and Thiagarajan, S.R. (1993) 'Fundamental information analysis', *JAR*, 31, Autumn, 190–215.

Levich, R. and Thomas, L. (1993) 'The significance of technical trading-rule profits in the foreign exchange market: a bootstrap approach', *Journal of International Money and Finance*, 12, 451–74.

Levin, E.J. and Wright, R.E. (1998) 'The information content of the gilt-equity yield ratio', *Manchester School*, 66 (Supplement), 89–101.

Levine, D. with Hoffer, W. (1992) *Insider Out*. London: Arrow.

Levis, M. (1985) 'Are small firms big performers?', *Investment Analyst*, 76, 21–7.

Levis, M. (1989) 'Stock market anomalies: a re-assessment based on UK evidence', *JBF*, 13, 675–96.

Levis, M. and Liodakis, M. (1999) 'The profitability of style rotation strategies in the United Kingdom', *JPM*, 26, Fall, 73–86.

Levy, R.A. (1967) 'Relative strength as a criterion for investment selection', *JF*, 22, 595–610.

Lewis, K.K. (1999) 'Trying to explain home bias in equities and consumption', *Journal of Economic Literature*, 37, 571–608.

Lintner, J. (1965) 'The valuation of risk assets and the selection of risky investments in stock portfolios and capital budgets', *Review of Economics and Statistics*, 47, 13–37.

Lintner, J. and Glauber, R. (1967) 'Higgledy piggledy growth in America', seminar paper reprinted in Lorie, L. and Brealey, R. (eds) (1972) *Modern Developments in Investment Management*. New York: Praeger.

Little, I.M.D. (1962) 'Higgledy piggledy growth', *Bulletin of the Oxford University Institute of Statistics*, 24, 387–412.

Litzenberger, R.H. and Ramaswamy, K. (1979) 'The effect of personal taxes and dividends on capital asset prices: theory and empirical evidence', *JFE*, 7, 163–95.

Liu, W., Strong, N. and Xu, X. (1999) 'The profitability of momentum investing', *JBFA*, 26, 1043–91.

Loeb, T.F. (1991) 'Is there a gift from small-stock investing?', *FAJ*, 47, January–February, 39–44.

Lofthouse, S. (ed.) (1994) *Readings in Investments*. Chichester: John Wiley & Sons.

Lofthouse, S. (1997) 'Duties of unit trust trustees', *Journal of Financial Regulation and Compliance*, 5 (3), 260–4.

Lofthouse, S. (1999) 'When agents appoint principals', *The Company Lawyer*, 20, August–September, 254–63.

Lofthouse, S. (2001) *Executive Economics*, forthcoming.

Lord, C.G., Ross, L. and Lepper, M.R. (1979) 'Biased assimilation and attitude polarization: the effects of prior theories on subsequently considered evidence; *Journal of Personality and Social Psychology*, 37, 2098–109.

Loughran, T. (1997) 'Book-to-market across firm size, exchange, and seasonality', *JFQA*, 32, 249–68.

Macaulay, F.M. (1938) *Some Theoretical Problems Suggested by the Movement of Interest Rates, Bond Yields, and Stock Prices in the United States Since 1856*. New York: National Bureau of Economic Research.

Macedo, R. (1995) 'Value, relative strength, and volatility in global equity country selection', *FAJ*, 51, March–April, 70–8.

Macedo, R. (1997) 'Style-based country-selection strategies' in Carmen, P. (ed.) *Quantitative Investing for the Global Markets*. Chicago: Glenlake.

Malkiel, B.G. (1962) 'Expectations, bond prices, and the term structure of interest rates', *QJE*, 76, 197–218.

Malkiel, B.G. (1995) 'Returns from investing in equity mutual funds', *JF*, 50, 549–72.

Malkiel, B.G. and Cragg, J.G. (1970) 'Expectations and the structure of share prices', *AER*, 60, 601–17.

Malkiel, B.G. and Xu, Y. (1997) 'Risk and return revisited', *JPM*, 23, Spring, 9–14.

Mark, N.C. (1995) 'Exchange rates and fundamentals: evidence on long-horizon predictability', *AER*, 85, 201–18.

Markese, J. (1986) 'The stock market and business cycles', *AAII Journal*, 8, November, 30–2.

Markides, C.C. (1997) 'To diversify or not to diversify', *HBR*, 75, November–December, 93–9.

Markowitz, H.M. (1952) 'Portfolio selection', *JF*, 7, 77–91.

Markowitz, H.M. (1959) *Portfolio Selection*. New York: John Wiley & Sons.

Marsh, P. (1992) 'Dividend announcements and stock price performance', working paper, London Business School, 5/8/92.

Marsh, T.A. and Merton, R.C. (1986) 'Dividend variability and variance bounds tests for the rationality of stock market prices', *AER*, 76, 483–98.

Masters, S.J. (1998) 'The problem with emerging markets indexes', *JPM*, 24, Winter, 93–100.

McMillan, L.G. (1980) *Options as a Strategic Investment: A Comprehensive Analysis of Listed Stock Options Strategies*. New York: New York Institute of Finance.

McNees, S.K. (1986) 'Forecasting accuracy of alternative techniques: a comparison of US macroeconomic forecasts', *Journal of Business and Economic Statistics*, 4, 5–15.

Meese, R. and Rogoff, K. (1983) 'Empirical exchange rate models of the 1970s: do they fit out of sample?', *Journal of International Economics*, 14, 3–24.

Mehra, R. and Prescott, E.C. (1985) 'The equity premium: a puzzle', *Journal of Monetary Economics*, 15, 145–62.

Meier, J.P. (1991) 'Tracking global equities with stock index futures', *Futures*, 20, January, 36.

Mercer Fraser, W.M. (1988) *Where Does Performance Come From?* London: Mercer Fraser.

Mercer Fraser, W.M. (1991) *The UK Equity Dividend Yield.* London: Mercer Fraser.

Metrick, A. (1999) 'Performance evaluation with transactions data: the stock selection of investment newsletters', *JF*, 54, 1743–74.

Michaud, R.O. (1989) 'The Markowitz optimization enigma: is "optimized" optimal?', *FAJ*, 45, January–February, 31–42. [Reprinted in Lofthouse, 1994.]

Michaud, R.O. and Davis, P.L. (1982) 'Valuation model bias and the scale structure of dividend discount returns', *JF*, 37, 563–73.

Miles, D. and Timmermann, A. (1996) 'Variations in expected stock returns: evidence on the pricing of equities from a cross-section of UK companies', *Economica*, 63, 369–82.

Mills, T.C. (1997) 'Technical analysis and the London Stock Exchange: testing trading rules using the FT30', *International Journal of Finance and Economics*, 2, 319–31.

Mills, T.C. and Coutts, J.A. (1995) 'Calendar effects in the London Stock Exchange FT-SE indices', *European Journal of Finance*, 1, 79–93.

Mintzberg, H. (1979) *The Structure of Organizations.* Englewood Cliffs: Prentice Hall.

Mintzberg, H. and Quinn, J.B. (1992) *The Strategy Process: Concepts and Contexts*, 2nd edn. Englewood Cliffs: Prentice Hall.

Modigliani, F. and Cohn, R. (1979) 'Inflation, rational valuation and the market', *FAJ*, 35, March–April, 24–44.

Modigliani, F. and Cohn, R. (1982) 'Inflation and the stock market' in Boeckh, J.A. and Coghlan, R.T. (eds) *The Stock Market and Inflation.* Homewood: Dow Jones-Irwin.

Modigliani, F. and Modigliani, L. (1997). 'Risk-adjusted performance', *JPM*, 23, Winter, 45–54.

Moggridge, D. (ed.) (1983) *Collected Writings of John Maynard Keynes.* London: MacMillan.

Moore, G.H. and Cullity, J.P. (1988) 'Security markets and business cycles' in Levine, S.N. (ed.) *The Financial Analyst's Handbook*, 2nd edn. Homewood: Dow Jones-Irwin.

Morgan, G. and Thomas, S. (1998). 'Taxes, dividend yields and returns in the UK equity market', *JBF*, 22, 405–423.

Morse, J.N. (1993) 'Fiduciary responsibility and the use of listed options', *JI*, 2, Fall, 47–50.

Moses, O.D. (1990) 'On analysts' earnings forecasts for failing firms', *JBFA*, 17, 101–18.

Moskowitz, T.J. and Grinblatt, M. (1999) 'Do industries explain momentum?', *JF*, 54, 1249–90.

Mossaheb, N. (1988a) *Index Portfolios for FT-SE 100.* Edinburgh: James Capel and Co.

Mossaheb, N. (1988b) *Index Portfolios for EAFE.* Edinburgh: James Capel and Co.

Mossin, J. (1966) 'Equilibrium in a capital asset market', *Econometrica*, 34, 768–83.

Mozes, H.A. (2000) 'The role of value in strategies based on anticipated earnings surprises', *JPM*, 26, Winter, 54–62.

Mozes, H.A. and Williams, P.A. (1999) 'Modelling earnings expectations based on clusters of analyst forecasts', *JI*, 8, Summer, 25–38.

Mueller, D.C. (1997). 'First-mover advantages and path dependence', *International Journal of Industrial Organization*, 15, 827–50.

Mulvey, J.M. (1994) 'An asset-liability investment system', *Interfaces*, 24, May–June, 22–33.

Nagorniak, J.J. (1985) 'Thoughts on using dividend discount models', *FAJ*, 41, November–December, 13–15.

Naranjo, A., Nimalendran, M. and Ryngaert, M. (1998) 'Stock returns, dividend yields, and taxes', *JF*, 53, 2029–57.

Naser, K. and Pendelbury, M. (1992) 'A note on the use of creative accounting', *British Accounting Review*, 24, 111–18.

Neely, C.J. (1997) 'Technical analysis in the foreign exchange market: a layman's guide', *Federal Reserve Bank of St Louis Review*, 79, September–October, 23–38.

Neff, J. with Mintz, S.L. (1999) *John Neff on Investing.* New York: John Wiley & Sons.

Netter, J.M. and Mitchell, M.L. (1989) 'Stock-repurchase announcements and insider transactions after the October 1987 stock market crash', *Financial Management*, 18, 84–96.

Nicholson, S.F. (1960) 'Price-earnings ratios', *FAJ*, 16, July–August, 43–5.

O'Brien, (1988) 'Analysts' forecasts as earnings expectations', *JAE*, 10, 53–83.

O'Byrne, S.F. (1999) 'EVA and its critics', *JACF*, 12, Summer, 92–6.

O'Hanlon, J. and Papaspirou, P. (1988) 'The daily behaviour of national equity markets: seasonal patterns and inter-relationships', *Investment Analyst*, 89, 26–35.

O'Hanlon, J., Poon, S. and Yaansah, R.A. (1992) 'Market recognition of differences in earnings persistence: UK evidence', *JBFA*, 19, 625–39.

Ohlson, J.A. (1990) 'A synthesis of security valuation theory and the role of dividends, cash flows, and earnings', *Contemporary Accounting Research*, 6, 648–76.

Ohlson, J.A. (1995) 'Earnings, book values, and dividends in security valuation', *Contemporary Accounting Research*, 11, 661–7.

Oppenheimer, H.J. (1984) 'A test of Ben Graham's stock selection criteria', *FAJ*, 40, September–October, 68–74.

Oppenheimer, H.J. (1986) 'Ben Graham's net current asset values: a performance update', *FAJ*, 42, November–December, 40–7.

Oppenheimer, H.J. and Dielman, T.E. (1988) 'Firm dividend policy and insider activity: some empirical results', *JBFA*, 15, 525–41.

Oskamp, S. (1965) 'Overconfidence in case-study judgments', *Journal of Consulting Psychology*, 29, 261–65.

Oster, C.L. (1998) 'Identifying noise traders: the head-and-shoulders pattern in U.S. equities', *Federal Reserve Bank of New York Staff Reports*, 42.

Ou, J.A. and Penman, S.H. (1989) 'Financial statement analysis and the prediction of stock returns', *JAE*, 11, 295–329.

Owen, J.P. (1990) *The Prudent Investor: The Definitive Guide to Professional Management*. Chicago, Probus.

Pérold, A. and Schulman, E. (1988) 'The free lunch in currency hedging: implications for investment policies and performance standards', *FAJ*, 44, May–June, 45–50.

Palepu, K.G., Healy, P.M. and Bernard, V.L. (2000) *Business Analysis and Evaluation*, 2nd edn. Cincinatti: South-Western.

Pennington, R.R. (1990) *The Law of the Investment Markets*. Oxford: Blackwell.

Pesaran, M.H. and Timmermann, A. (1995) 'Predictability of stock returns: robustness and economic significance', *JF*, 50, 1201–28.

Pesaran, M.H. and Timmermann, A. (2000) 'A recursive modelling approach to predicting UK stock returns', *EJ*, 110, 159–91.

Peters, D.J. (1991) 'Valuing a growth stock', *JPM*, 17, Spring, 49–51

Peters, D.J. (1993a) 'Are earnings surprises predictable?', *JI*, 2, Summer, 47–51.

Peters, D.J. (1993b) 'The influences of size on earnings surprise predictability', *JI*, 2, Winter, 54–9.

Peters, T.J. and Waterman, R.H. (1982) *In Search of Excellence: Lessons from America's Best Run Companies*. New York: Harper and Row.

Philips, T.K., Rogers, G.T. and Capaldi, R.E. (1996) 'Tactical asset allocation: 1977–1994', *JPM*, 23, Fall, 57–64.

Phillips, P. (1984) *Inside the Gilt-Edged Market*. Cambridge: Woodhead-Faulkner.

Phillips & Drew (2000) *Pension Fund Indicators*. London: Phillips & Drew.

Pinches, G.E. (1970) 'The random walk hypothesis and technical analysis', *FAJ*, 26, March–April, 104–10.

Poon, S. (1996) 'Persistence and mean reversion in U.K. stock returns', *European Financial Management*, 2, 169–96.

Poon, S. and Taylor, S.J. (1991) 'Macroeconomic factors and the UK stock market', *JBFA*, 18, 619–35.

Pope, P.F., Morris, R.C. and Peel, D.A. (1990) 'Insider trading: some evidence on market efficiency and directors' share dealings in Great Britain', *JBFA*, 17, 359–80.

Porter, M. (1979) 'How competitive forces shape strategy', *HBR*, 57, March–April, 137–45.

Porter, M. (1980) *Competitive Strategy: Techniques for Analyzing Industries and Competitors*. New York: Free Press.

Poterba, J.M. and Summers, L.H. (1988) 'Mean reversion in stock prices: evidence and implications', *JFE*, 22, 27–59.

Power, D.M., Lonnie, A.A. and Lonnie, R. (1991) 'The over-reaction effect – some UK evidence. *British Accounting Review*, 23, 149–70.

Pratt, M.J. (1993) 'Using a Z score: the Bank of England's experience', *Economia Aziendale*, 12, 277–87.

Pratt, S.P. and DeVere, C.W. (1968) 'Relationship between insider trading and rates of return for NYSE common stocks, 1960–66' in Lorie, L. and Brealey, R. (eds) (1972) *Modern Developments in Investment Management*. New York: Praeger.

Preinreich, G. (1938) 'Annual survey of economic theory: the theory of depreciation', *Econometrica*, 6, 219–41.

Prell, M.J., (1973) 'How well do the experts forecast interest rates?', *Federal Reserve Bank of Kansas City Monthly Review*, September–October, 3–13.

Preston, C.E. and Harris, S. (1965) 'Psychology of drivers in traffic accidents', *Journal of Applied Psychology*, 49, 284–8.

Pruitt, S.W. and White, R.E. (1988) 'The CRISMA trading system: who says technical analysis can't beat the market?', *JPM*, 14, Spring, 55–8.

Rea, J.B. (1977) 'Remembering Benjamin Graham – teacher and friend', *JPM*, 3, Summer, 66–72.

Regan, P.J. (1981) 'The cover story syndrome', *FAJ*, 37, January–February, 12–13.

Regan, P.J. (1991) 'Insider transactions: watch what they do', *FAJ*, 47, January–February, 13–15.

Reinganum, M.R. (1981) 'Misspecification of capital asset pricing: empirical anomalies based on earnings' yields and market values', *JFE*, 9, 19–46.

Reinganum, M.R. (1988) 'The anatomy of a stock market winner', *FAJ*, 44, March–April, 16–28.

Reinganum, M.R. (1992) 'A revival of the small firm effect', *JPM*, 18, Spring, 55–62.

Reinganum, M.R. (1999) 'The significance of market capitalization in portfolio management over time', *JPM*, 25, Summer, 29–50.

Rendleman, R.J. and Bartter B.J. (1979) 'Two-state option pricing', *JF*, 34, 1093–100.

Rendleman, R.J., Jones, C.P. and Latané, H.A. (1982) 'Empirical anomalies based on unexpected earnings and the importance of risk adjustments', *JFE*, 10, 269–87.

Richards, A.J. (1997) 'Winner–loser reversals in national stock market indices: can they be explained?', *JF*, 52, 2129–44.

Roberts, H. (1959) 'Stock market "patterns" and financial analysis: methodological suggestions', *JF*, 14, 1–10.

Robinson, W.T., Kalyanaram, G. and Urban, G.L. (1994). 'First-mover advantages from pioneering new markets: a survey of empirical evidence', *Review of Industrial Organization*, 9, 1–23.

Rogalski, R.J. and Tinic, S.M. (1986) 'The January size effect: anomaly or risk measurement', *FAJ*, 42, November–December, 63–70.

Rohrer, J. (1989) 'The Bernstein formula', *Institutional Investor*, November, 143, 144, 147, 149, 151, 152.

Roll, R. (1977) 'A critique of the asset pricing theory's tests. Part I: on past and potential testability of the theory', *JFE*, 4,129–76.

Roll, R. (1978) 'Ambiguity when performance is measured by the securities market line', *JF*, 33, 1051–69.

Roll, R. (1984) 'Orange juice and weather', *AER*, 74, 861–80.

Roll, R. (1995) 'Style return differentials: illusions, risk premiums, or investment opportunities' in Coggin, T.D. and Fabozzi, F.J. (eds) *The Handbook of Equity Style Investment*. New Hope: Frank J. Fabozzi Associates.

Roll, R. and Ross, S.A. (1980) 'An empirical investigation of the arbitrage pricing theory', *JF*, 35, 1073–103.

Roll, R. and Ross, S.A. (1984) 'A critical re-examination of the empirical evidence on the arbitrage pricing theory: a reply', *JF*, 39, 347–50.

Roll, R. and Ross, S.A. (1994) 'On the cross-sectional relation between expected returns and betas', *JF*, 49, 101–21.

Rosenberg, B. and McKibben, W. (1973) 'The prediction of systematic and specific risk in common stocks', *JFQA*, 8, 317–33.

Rosenberg, B., Reid, K. and Lanstein, R. (1985) 'Persuasive evidence of market inefficiency', *JPM*, 11, Spring, 9–16.

Ross, S. (1976) 'The arbitrage theory of capital asset pricing', *Journal of Economic Theory*, 13, 341–60.

Ross, L. (1977) 'The intuitive psychologist and his shortcomings: distortions in the attribution process' in Berkowitz, L. (ed.) *Advances in Experimental Social Psychology*, vol. 10. New York: Academic Press.

Ross, S.A. (1985) 'On the empirical relevance of APT: reply', *JPM*, 11, Summer, 72–3.

Rouwenhorst, K.G. (1998) 'International momentum studies', *JF*, 53, 267–84.

Rouwenhorst, K.G. (1999a) 'European equity markets and EMU', *FAJ*, 55, May–June, 57–64.

Rouwenhorst, K.G. (1999b) 'Local return factors and turnover in emerging stockmarkets', *JF*, 54, 1439–64.

Rozeff, M.S. (1984) 'Dividend yields are equity risk premiums', *JPM*, 11, Fall, 68–75.

Rozeff, M.S. and Kinney, W.R. (1976) 'Capital market seasonality: the case of stock returns', *JFE*, 3, 379–402.

Rozeff, M.S. and Zaman, M.A. (1998) 'Overreaction and insider trading: evidence from growth and value portfolios', *JF*, 53, 701–16.

Rudd, A. (1980) 'Optimal selection of passive portfolios', *Financial Management*, 9, 57–66.

Russell, D. and Jones, W.E. (1980) 'When superstition fails: reactions to disconfirmation of paranormal beliefs', *Personality and Social Psychology Bulletin*, 6, 83–8.

Saunders, E.M. (1993) 'Stock prices and Wall Street weather', *AER*, 83, 1337–45.

Schumpeter, J.A. (1943) *Capitalism, Socialism and Democracy*. New York: Harper and Row.

Schwartz, S.L. and Ziemba, W.T. (2000) 'Predicting returns on the Tokyo Stock Exchange' in Keim, D.B. and Ziemba, W.T. (eds) *Security Market Imperfections in World-wide Equity Markets*. Cambridge: Cambridge University Press.

Schwert, G.W. (1992) 'Stock market crash of October 1987' in Newman, P., Milgate, M. and Eatwell, J. (eds) *The New Palgrave Dictionary on Money and Finance*, vol. 3. London: Macmillan. [Reprinted in Lofthouse, 1994.]

Scott, M. (1993) 'Real interest rates: past and future', *National Institute Economic Review*, February, 54–71.

Senchack, A.J. and Martin, J.D. (1987) 'The relative performance of the PSR and PER investment strategies', *FAJ*, 43, March–April, 46–55.

Setiono, B. and Strong, N. (1998) 'Predicting stock returns using financial statement information', *JBFA*, 25, 631–57.

Seyhun, H.N. (1986) 'Insiders' profits, costs of trading, and market efficiency', *JFE*, 16, 189–212.

Seyhun, H.N. (1988) 'The information content of aggregate insider trading', *JB*, 61, 1–24.

Seyhun, H.N. (1990) 'Overreaction of fundamentals: some lessons from insiders' response to the market crash of 1987', *JF*, 45, 1363–88.

Seyhun, H.N. (1992) 'Why does aggregate insider trading predict future stock returns?', *QJE*, 107, 1303–31.

Shanken, J. (1987) 'Multivariate proxies and asset pricing relations', *JFE*, 18, 91–110.

Sharpe, W.F. (1963) 'A simplified model for portfolio analysis', *Management Science*, 9, 277–93.

Sharpe, W.F. (1964) 'Capital asset prices: a theory of market equilibrium under conditions of risk', *JF*, 19, 425–42.

Sharpe, W.F. (1966) 'Mutual fund performance', *JB*, 39, 119–38.

Sharpe, W.F. (1978) *Investments*. Englewood Cliffs: Prentice Hall.

Sharpe, W.F. (1982) 'Factors in New York Stock Exchange security returns, 1931–1979', *JPM*, 8, Summer, 5–19.

Sharpe, W.F. (1985) *AAT – Asset Allocation Tools*. Palo Alto: Scientific Press.

Sharpe, W.F. (1990) 'Asset allocation' in Maginn, J.L. and Tuttle, D.L. (eds) *Managing Investment Portfolios: A Dynamic Process*, 2nd edn. Boston: Warren, Gorham & Lamont.

Sharpe, W.F. and Cooper, G.M. (1972) 'Risk-return classes of New York Stock Exchange common stocks 1931–1967', *FAJ*, 28, March–April, 46–52.

Sharpe, W.F., Alexander, G.J. and Bailey, J.V. (1999) *Investments*, 6th edn. Upper Saddle River: Prentice Hall.

Shaw, A.R. (1988) 'Market timing and technical analysis' in Levine, S.N. (ed.) *The Financial Analyst's Handbook*, 2nd edn. Homewood: Dow Jones-Irwin.

Shefrin, H. (1999) 'Irrational exuberance and option smiles', *FAJ*, 55, November–December, 91–103.

Sherif, M. (1937) 'An experimental approach to the study of attitudes', *Sociometry*, 1, 90–8.

Shiller, R.J. (1981) 'Do stock prices move too much to be justified by subsequent changes in dividends?', *AER*, 71, 421–36.

Shiller, R.J. (1989) *Market Volatility*. Cambridge: Massachusetts Institute of Technology Press.

Shiller, R.J. (1999) 'Human behavior and the efficiency of the financial system' in Taylor, J.B. and Woodford, M. (eds) *Handbook of Macroeconomics*, vol. 1C. Amsterdam: Elsevier.

Shleifer, A. and Vishny, R.W. (1977) 'The limits of arbitrage', *JF*, 52, 35–55.

Siegel, J.J. (1991) 'Does it pay stock investors to forecast the business cycle?', *JPM*, 18, Fall, 27–34.

Siegel, J.J. (1994) *Stocks for the Long Run*. Chicago: Irwin.

Silber, W.L. (1994) 'Technical trading: when it works and when it doesn't, *Journal of Derivatives*, Spring, 39–44.

Sims, C.A. (1980) 'Macroeconomics and reality', *Econometrica*, 48, 1–48.

Sinquefield, R.A. (1991) 'Are small-stock returns achievable?', *FAJ*, 47, January–February, 45–50.

Smedslund, J. (1963) 'The concept of correlation in adults', *Scandinavian Journal of Psychology*, 4, 165–73.

Smith, E.L. (1925) *Common Stocks as Long-Term Investments*. New York: Macmillan.

Smith, A. [1776] (1976) *An Inquiry into the Nature and Causes of the Wealth of Nations*. Campbell, R.H., Skinner, A.S. and Todd, W.B. (eds) Oxford: Clarendon Press.

Smith, T. (1992) *Accounting for Growth*. London: Century.

Smith, T. and Hannah, R. (1991) *Accounting for Growth*. London: UBS Phillips and Drew.

Smithers, A. and Wright, S. (2000) *Valuing Wall Street*. New York: McGraw-Hill.

Solnik, B. (1974) 'Why not diversify internationally rather than domestically?', *FAJ*, 30, July–August, 48–54.

Solnik, B. (1993) 'The performance of international asset allocation strategies using conditioning information', *Journal of Empirical Finance*, 1, 33–55.

Solnik, B. (1998) 'Global asset management', *JPM*, 24, Summer, 43–51.

Solt, M.E. and Statman, M. (1988) 'How useful is the sentiment index?', *FAJ*, 44, September–October, 45–55.

Sorensen, E.H. and Williamson, D.A. (1985) 'Some evidence on the value of dividend discount models', *FAJ*, 41, November–December, 60–9.

Stambaugh, R.F. (1982) 'On the exclusion of assets from tests of the two-parameter model', *JFE*, 10, 237–68.

Standard & Poor's (2000) *Emerging Stock Markets Fact Book 2000*. New York: Standard & Poor's.

Stephenson, K. (1997) 'Just how bad are economists at predicting interest rates?', *JI*, 6, Summer, 8–10.

Stevenson, H.H. (1976) 'Defining corporate strengths and weaknesses', *Sloan Management Review*, 17, Spring, 51–68.

Stickel, S.E. (1985) 'The effect of Value Line Investment Survey rank changes on common stock prices', *JFE*, 14, 121–43.

Stickel, S.E. (1995) 'The anatomy of the performance of buy and sell recommendations', *FAJ*, 51, September-October, 25–39.

Stiglitz, J. (2000) 'The insider', *New Republic*, 17, April, 56–60.

Stober, T.L. (1992) 'Summary financial statement measures and analysts' forecasts as earnings expectations', *JAE*, 15, 347–72.

Stoll, H.R. and Whaley, R.E. (1983) 'Transaction costs and the small firm effect', *JFE*, 12, 57–79.

Strebel, P. and Carvell, S. (1988) *In the Shadows of Wall Street: A Guide to Investing in Neglected Stocks*. Englewood Cliffs: Prentice-Hall.

Strong, N. and Xu, X.G. (1997) 'Explaining the cross-section of UK expected stock returns', *British Accounting Review*, 29, 1–23.

Sullivan, R., Timmerman, A. and White, H. (1999) 'Data-snooping, technical trading rule performance, and the bootstrap', *JF*, 54, 1647–91.

Sutton, T. (2000) *Corporate Financial Accounting and Reporting*. Harlow: Financial Times/ Prentice Hall.

Svenson, O. (1981) 'Are we all less risky and more skilful than our fellow drivers?', *Acta Psychologica*, 47, 143–8.

Taffler, R.J. (1983) 'The assessment of company solvency and performance using a statistical model', *ABR*, 15, Autumn, 295–307.

Taffler, R.J. (1984) 'Empirical models for the monitoring of UK corporations', *JBF*, 8, 199–227.

Taffler, R.J. (1997) 'Enhancing equity returns with Z-scores', *Professional Investor*, 7, July–August, 22–6.

Taffler, R.J. (1999) 'Discussion of the profitability of momentum investing', *JBFA*, 26, 1093–102.

Tanous, P.J. (1997) *Investment Gurus*. New York: New York Institute of Finance.

Taylor, M.P. (1992) 'Modelling the yield curve', *EJ*, 102, 524–37.

Taylor, M.P. (1995). 'The economics of exchange rates', *Journal of Economic Literature*, 33, 13–47.

Taylor, M.P. and Allen, H. (1992) 'The use of technical analysis in the foreign exchange market', *Journal of International Money and Finance*, 11, 304–14.

Taylor, S.E. and Brown, J.D. (1988) 'Illusion and well-being: a social psychological perspective on mental health', *Psychological Bulletin*, 103, 193–210.

Tellis, G.J. and Golder, P.N. (1996). 'First to market, first to fail? Real causes of enduring market leadership', *Sloan Management Review*, 37, Winter, 65–75.

Thaler, R.H. (1999) 'The end of behavioral finance', *FAJ*, 55, November–December, 12–17.

Throop, A.W. (1981) 'Interest rate forecasts and market efficiency', *Federal Reserve Bank of San Francisco Economic Review*, Spring, 20–43.

Train, J. (1981). *The Money Masters*. Harmondsworth: Penguin.

Treynor, J.L. (1965) 'How to rate management of investment funds', *HBR*, 43, January–February, 63–75.

Treynor, N. (ed.) (1999) *Investment Directions: Survey of Investment Management Arrangements 1999*. London: Phillips & Drew.

Tseng, K.C. (1988) 'Low price, price-earnings ratio, market value, and abnormal stock returns', *Financial Review*, 23, 333–43.

Tversky, A. and Kahneman, D. (1974) 'Judgement under uncertainty: heuristics and biases', *Science*, 185, 1124–31.

Tversky, A. and Kahneman, D. (1981) 'The framing of decisions and the psychology of choice', *Science*, 211, 453–58.

Urwin, R. (1990) 'Identifying tomorrow's successful manager today', paper presented to the Institute of Actuaries Staple Inn Society, 20 November.

Urwin, R. (1991) 'Managers' in *Notes to Accompany: Investment Success in the 1990s Seminar*. Reigate: Watsons Investment Consultancy.

Value Line Publishing, Inc. (1993) *Value Line Investment Survey: Part 2, Selection and Opinion*, 22 January.

Vandell, R.F. and Stevens, J.L. (1989) 'Evidence of superior performance from timing', *JPM*, 15, Spring, 38–42.

VanderWerf, P.A. and Mahon, J.F. (1997) 'Meta-analysis of the impact of research methods on findings of first-mover advantage', *Management Science*, 43, 1510–19.

Vergin, R.C. (1996) 'Market-timing strategies: can you get rich?', *JI*, 5, Winter, 79–85.

Vergin, R.C. and McGinnis, J.M. (1999) 'Revisiting the holiday effect: is it on holiday?', *AFE*, 9, 477–82.

Vu, J.D. (1988) 'An empirical analysis of Ben Graham's net current asset value rule', *Financial Review*, 23, 215–25.

Wachtel, S. (1942) 'Certain observations on seasonal movements in stock prices', *JB*, 15, 184–193.

Wadhwani, S. (1991) *The Interest Rate Sensitivity of Stocks*. London: Goldman Sachs.

Wadhwani, S. (1992) *A Sector Selection Strategy for the UK*. London: Goldman Sachs.

Wadhwani, S. and Shah, M. (1993) *Valuation Indicators and Stock Market Prediction: 1*. London: Goldman Sachs.

Wagner, J., Shellans, S. and Paul, R. (1992) 'Market timing works where it matters most . . . in the real world', *JPM*, 18, Summer, 86–9.

Weigel, E.J. (1991) 'The performance of tactical asset allocation', *FAJ*, 47, September–October, 63–70.

Weinstein, M.I. (1977) 'The effect of a rating change announcement on bond price', *JFE*, 5, 329–50.

Weiss, A.M. (1999) 'Why institutions systematically underperform broadly based market indexes', *JI*, 8, Spring, 65–74.

Whitbeck, V.S. and Kisor, M. (1963) 'A new tool in investment decision-making', *FAJ*, 19, May–June, 55–62.

Whitman, M.J. and Shubik, M. (1979) *The Aggressive Conservative Investor*. New York: Random House.

Wilkie, A.D. (1986) 'A stochastic investment model for actuarial use', *Transactions of the Faculty of Actuaries*, 40, 341–73.

Wilkie, A.D. (1987) 'Stochastic investment models – theory and applications', *Insurance Mathematics and Economics*, 6, 65–83.

Wilkie, A.D. (1995a) 'The risk premium on ordinary shares', *British Actuarial Journal*, 1, 251–93.

Wilkie, A.D. (1995b) 'More on a stochastic asset model for actuarial use', *British Actuarial Journal*, 1, 777–964.

Williams, J.B. (1938) *The Theory of Investment Value*. Cambridge: Harvard University Press.

Wise, A.J. (1988) 'The matching of assets to liabilities', *Transactions of the Faculty of Actuaries*, 40, 18–63.

Withers, H. (1938) *Stocks and Shares*, 3rd edn. London: Murray.

Womack, K. (1996) 'Do brokerage analysts' recommendations have investment value?', *JF*, 51, 137–67.

Zaman, M.A. (1988) 'Market inefficiency and insider trading: new evidence', *JB*, 61, 25–44.

Zarnowitz, V. (1999) 'Theory and history behind business cycles: are the 1990s the onset of a golden age?', *JEP*, 13, Spring, 69–90.

Zavgren, C.V., Dugan, M.T. and Reeve, J.M. (1988) 'The association between probabilities of bankruptcy and market responses – a test of market anticipation', *JBFA*, 15, 27–45.

Ziemba, W.T. (1991) 'Japanese security market regularities: monthly, turn-of-the-month and year, holiday and golden week effects', *Japan and the World Economy*, 3, 119–46.

Zweig, M.E. (1986) *Martin Zweig's Winning on Wall Street*. New York: Warner.

Index